The Tank Corps in the Great War

Volume 1
Conception, Birth and Baptism of Fire
November 1914 – November 1916

Stephen Pope

 Helion & Company Limited

Helion & Company Limited
Unit 8 Amherst Business Centre
Budbrooke Road
Warwick
CV34 5WE
England
Tel. 01926 499 619
Email: info@helion.co.uk
Website: www.helion.co.uk
Twitter: @helionbooks
Visit our blog at blog.helion.co.uk

Published by Helion & Company 2022
Designed and typeset by Mary Woolley (www.battlefield-design.co.uk)
Cover designed by Paul Hewitt, Battlefield Design (www.battlefield-design.co.uk)

Text © Stephen Pope 2022
Images © as individually credited
Maps drawn by Barbara Taylor © Helion & Company Limited 2022

Cover Image: "Daredevil 1 at Dawn - 15 September 1916" by Peter Dennis (Image © Helion
& Company Limited 2022)

ISBN 978-1-912390-81-6

British Library Cataloguing-in-Publication Data.
A catalogue record for this book is available from the British Library.

For details of other military history titles published by Helion & Company Limited contact the
above address or visit our website: http://www.helion.co.uk.

We always welcome receiving book proposals from prospective authors.

Tank Corps in the Great War
Volume 1
Mapping

Map No	Title
1	England and North East France
2	British Expeditionary Force Area of Operations 1916
3	Initial Tank Deployment Locations 1916
4	Tank Area of Operations Autumn 1916
5	Tank Actions Battle of Flers-Courcelette 15 – 16 September 1916
6	Tank Actions Eastern Flank September – October 1916
7	Tank Actions Centre September - October 1916
8	Tank Actions Western Flank September 1916
9	Tank Actions Courcelette and Thiepval 25 – 26 September 1916
10	Tank Actions Northern Flank November 1916

General Key (Maps 4 – 10)

Blue	Allied	**XXXX** ☐	Army	
Red	German	**XXX** ☐	Corps	
Bav	Bavarian	**XX** ☐	Division	
BR	British	**III** ☐	Regiment (German)	
CAN	Canadian	**II** ☐	Regiment/Battalion (BR only)	
FR	French	⊠	Infantry	
Gds	Guards			
NZ	New Zealand		Tank Coy HQ	
Res	Reserve			

—— **XXXXX** ——	Army Group to Brigade boundaries (number of crosses denotes which. All armies)
··························	Railway
- - - - - - - - - - - -	Light railway/tramway
——————	Roads
░░░░	Marsh/inundation

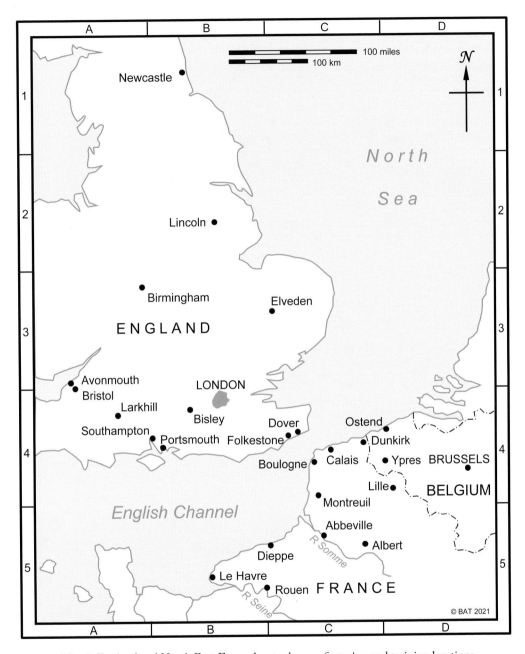

Map 1: England and North East France key tank manufacturing and training locations

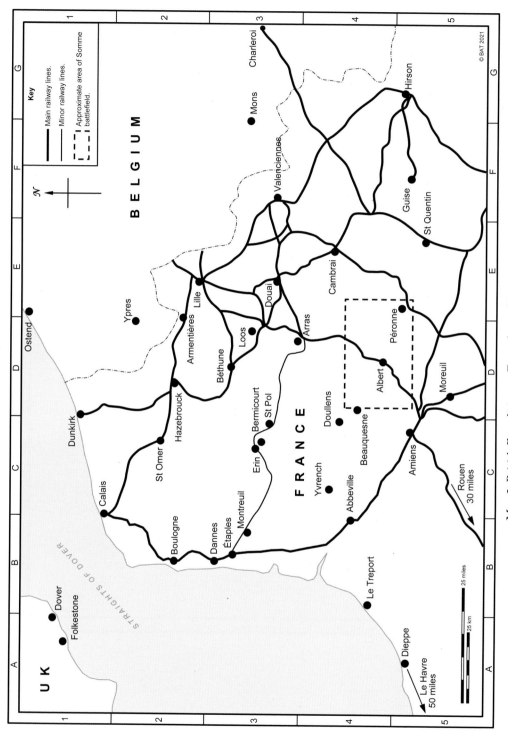

Map 2: British Expeditionary Force Area of Operations 1916

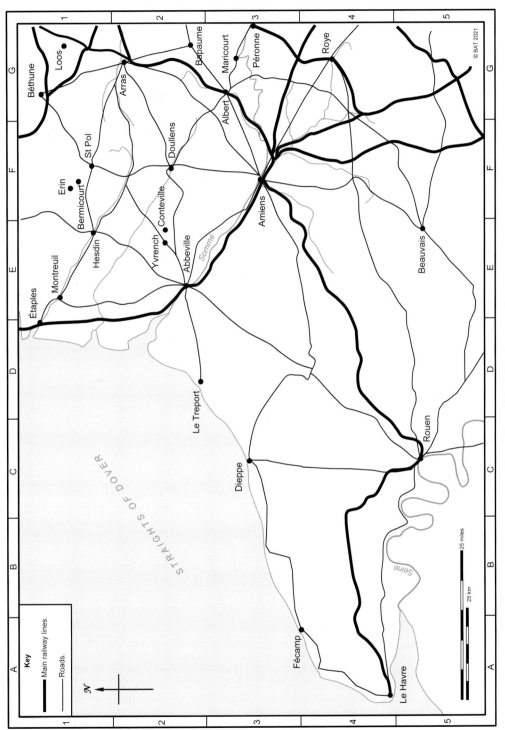

Map 3: Initial Tank Deployment Areas 1916

Map 4: Tank Area of Operations 1916

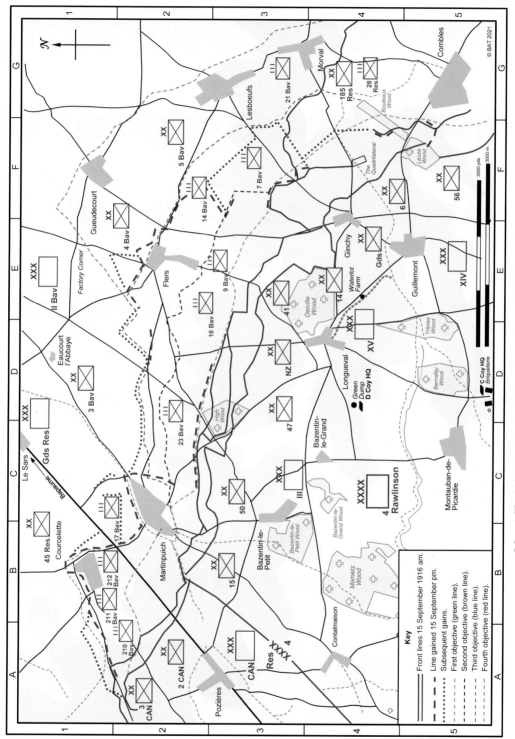

Map 5: Tank Actions Battle of Flers-Courcelette, 15-16 September 1916

Key

Front lines 15 September 1916 am.
Line gained 15 September 1916 pm.
Subsequent gains.
First objective (green line).
Second objective (brown line).
Third objective (blue line).
Fourth objective (red line).

© BAT 2021

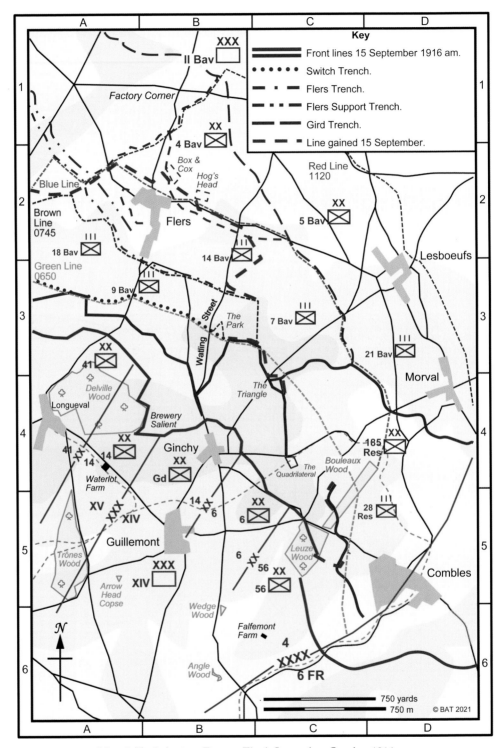

Map 6: Tank Actions Eastern Flank September-October 1916

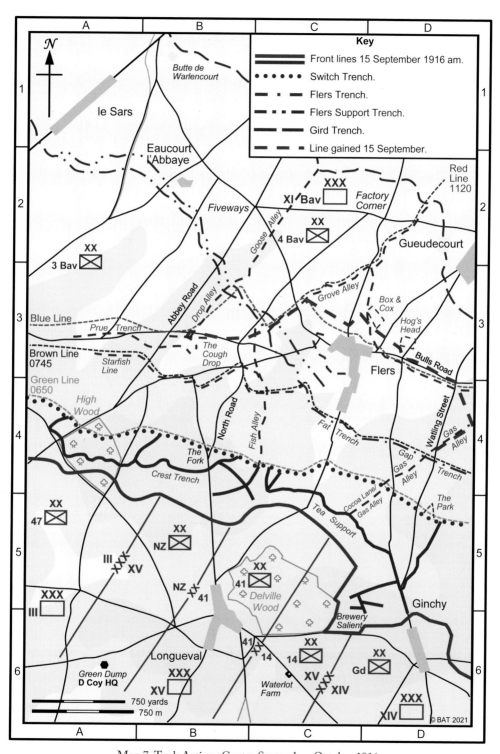

Map 7: Tank Actions Centre September-October 1916

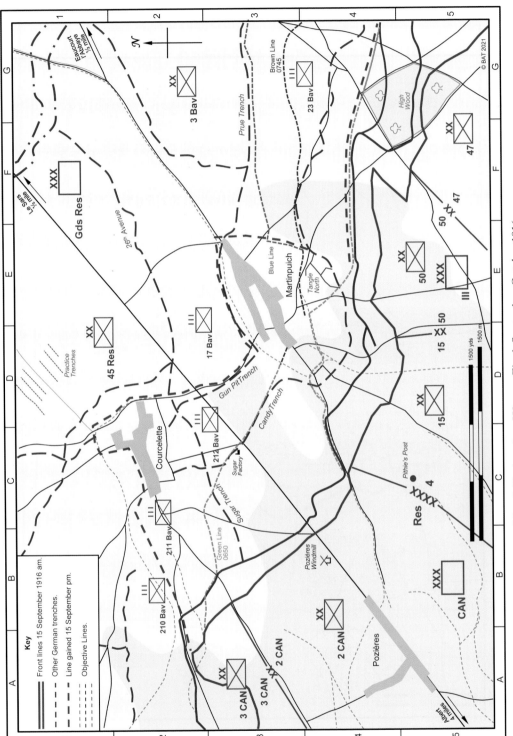

Map 8: Tank actions Western Flank September–October 1916

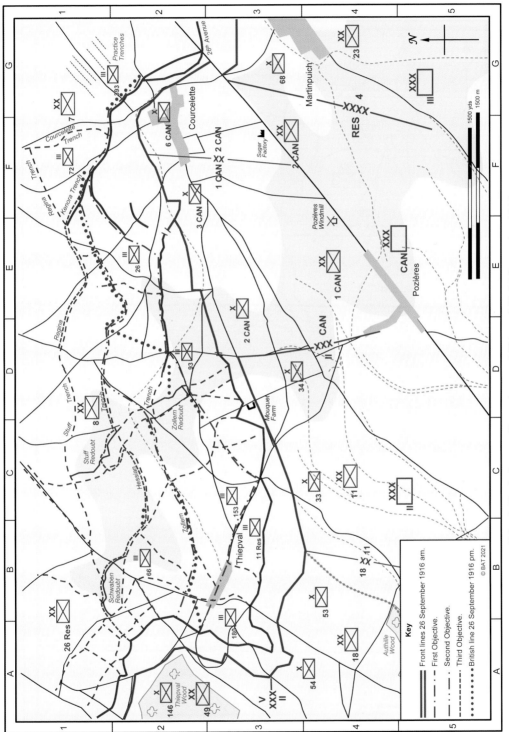

Map 9: Tank Actions Courcelette and Thiepval 25-26 September 1916

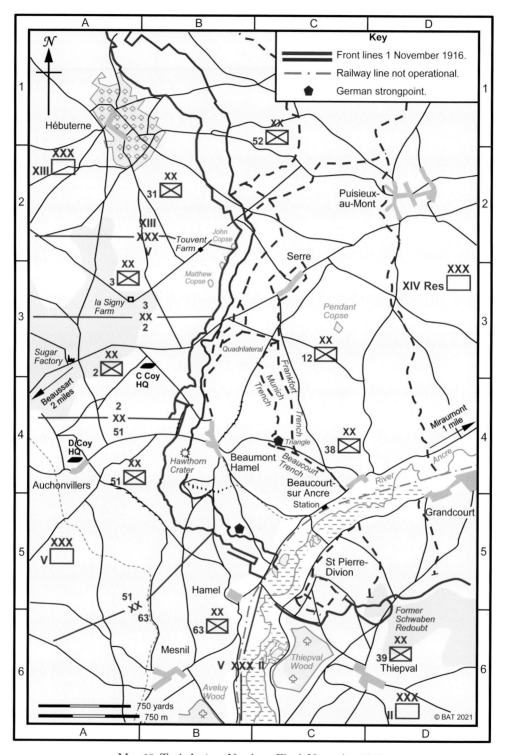

Map 10: Tank Actions Northern Flank November 1916

'The night before last, our Company went into action, and what a Baptism of Fire it was!'

2648 Gunner Victor Archard's letter to
his parents dated 16 September 1916. [1]

Dedicated to the memory of Ernest Swinton
and the men of the
Heavy Section Machine Gun Corps

---

1   A typewritten copy of Victor's diary and letters are held at the Tank Museum Archives (TMA) at
Bovington.

Contents

List of Illustrations

Monochrome photographs

Colour plates

List of Maps

Monochrome maps

Colour maps in map book

Maps drawn by and © Barbara Taylor

Abbreviations

Abbreviation	Meaning or Context
ACD	Armoured Car Division – a formation of the Royal Naval Air Service
ADT	Assistant Director of Transport
AFV	Armoured Fighting Vehicle
AG	Adjutant General
AOC	Army Ordnance Corps
ASC	Army Service Corps
A&SH	Argyll & Sutherland Highlanders
BCRs	Battle Casualty Replacements
BEF	British Expeditionary Force – in this volume it refers to the British Army and Empire formations fighting in France and Flanders.
BG GS	Brigadier General - General Staff
bhp	brake horsepower
Brig Gen	Brigadier General
Capt	Captain
Cdn	Canadian
C-in-C	Commander in Chief
CID	Committee for Imperial Defence
CIGS	Chief of the (British) Imperial General Staff
COS	Chief of Staff
Cpl	Corporal
cwt	Hundredweight – Unit of weight equal to 112 pounds or about 50.8 kg
DASD	Director of Army Staff Duties
DCM	Distinguished Conduct Medal
DD	Deputy director
DRA	Director Royal Artillery
DSC	Distinguished Service Cross

DSO	Distinguished Service Order
EEF	Egyptian Expeditionary Force
E-in-C	Engineer in Chief
FTC	*First Tank Crews*: Those who served in Mark I tanks in France in 1916
Gen	General
GER	Great Eastern Railway Company
GHQ	General Headquarters - the HQ of CinC BEF
Gnr	Gunner
GOC	General Officer Commanding a formation (brigade and above)
Glosters	Gloucestershire Regiment
GS	General Service or General Staff
GSO	General Staff Officer
HE	High Explosive
HMLS	His Majesty's Landship
HS MGC	Heavy Section Machine Gun Corps (1 May to 18 November 1916
KLR	King's Liverpool Regiment
KOYLI	Kings Own Yorkshire Light Infantry
KRRC	King's Royal Rifle Corps
lbs	Pounds (imperial weight)
LCpl	Lance Corporal
LG	*London Gazette*
LI	Light Infantry
Lt and 2Lt	Lieutenant and Second Lieutenant
Lt Col	Lieutenant Colonel
Lt Gen	Lieutenant General
Maj Gen	Major General
Metropolitan	Metropolitan Carriage Wagon and Finance Company Limited
MC	Military Cross
MG	Machine Gun
MGC	Machine Gun Corps
MGO	Master General of the Ordnance
mm	millimetres
MM	Military Medal

MMG	Motor Machine Gun
MMGS	Motor Machine Gun Service
mph	Miles Per Hour
MT	Mechanical Transport
N&MP	Naval & Military Press
NRA	National Rifle Association
NZ	New Zealand
OHGW	*Official History of the Great War, Military Operations, France and Belgium, 1916, Vol. 2*
OR	Other ranks i.e. non-commissioned military personnel
Pte	Private
QF	Quick Firing (artillery piece)
QM	Quartermaster
QMG	Quartermaster General
RA	Royal Artillery
RAMC	Royal Army Medical Corps
RE	Royal Engineers
recce	Reconnaissance or reconnoitre
RMA	Royal Military Academy (Woolwich)
RMC	Royal Military College (Sandhurst)
RMLI	Royal Marine Light Infantry
RN	Royal Navy
RNAS	Royal Naval Air Service
rpm	Revolutions per minute
RTC	Royal Tank Corps (post 1923)
RTR	Royal Tank Regiment
SAA	small arms ammunition
Sgt	Sergeant
SWB	South Wales Borderers
TCBH	*Tank Corps Book of Honour*
TF	Territorial Force – Volunteer (part-time) formations/units of the British Army
TMA	Tank Museum Archives at Bovington
TNA	The National Archives at Kew
TPA	Trevor Pidgeon archives

TSC	Tank Supply Committee
Vol.	Volume
WO	War Office – British Army HQ, Whitehall, London
Y&L	York & Lancaster Regiment

Preface

In Highland Park Cemetery, 1,200 yards south of Le Cateau, is the grave[1] of one of the first tank pioneers, Major Frederick Andrew 'Eric' Robinson, Military Cross (MC) and Bar.[2] He was accidentally killed, aged 26,[3] on 4 November 1918, only seven days before the end of the war as he returned from a successful attack. The attack was the last of 10th Tank Battalion in the Great War, by five of the nine available tanks in support of the crossing of the Sambre – Oise canal, four miles east of Le Cateau (see *Volume 5* of *The Tank Corps in the Great War* for details). He was buried by his friend, fellow First Tank Crewman and 10th Tank Battalion company commander, Harry Drader MC.[4] It was also probably the last Mark V tank action of the Tank Corps in the First World War. His death, caused by an accident, just before the end of the war, was all the more tragic because he was one of the first pioneers of tanks. He had joined the Royal Naval Air Service (RNAS), aged 22, in November 1914 and served with the Armoured Car Division RNAS from March to August 1915. The Armoured Car Division was one of the sources of the manpower for the first tank crews as was the Machine Gun Corps into which he was commissioned.[5] He arrived in France on 3 September 1916 and was in action twelve days later commanding Tank D22 in D Company at High Wood during the Battle of Flers-Courcelette on 15 September, the first tank battle in history (see *Volume 1* of *The Tank Corps in the Great War* for further details). He won an MC as a result of conspicuous bravery including spending 14 hours with his crew successfully digging out their ditched tank. His tank went into action two further times in 1916 and was hit by artillery on both occasions. The future chief of staff[6] of the Tank Corps[7], JFC Fuller, wrote later that from the point of view of the general observer it might have appeared with some small exceptions 'the tank during the battle of the Somme had not proved its

---

1   Tomb VI. E. 2.
2   The section on Robinson and 10th Tank Battalion is based on Stephen Pope's excellent, *The First Tank Crews (FTC) - The Lives of the Tankmen who Fought at the Battle of Flers-Courcelette, 15 September 1916*, (Solihull, Helion, 2016) and The National Archive (TNA): WO 95/103, 10th Tank Battalion War Diary and History except if otherwise stated.
3   Relatively old – the youngest tank company commander, and certainly one of the bravest, was Raikes (see volumes 4 and 5)
4   Pope, *FTC* p. 204. Drader had commanded a tank, *Daphne*, in D Company at the Battle of Flers-Courcelette see pp. 203 - 204. Drader and his crew were famous because of their cat, Percy, who 'pure black, small and totally fearless', was with Drader from Flers and survived the war. pp. 202 and 208.
5   Volume 1 of *The Tank Corps in the Great War* covers the tank actions in 1916.
6   Modern terminology he was the GSO1 of the Tank Corps.
7   Although the Tank Corps did not become the official name of the British tank force until 1917 the term is used to avoid confusion and for simplicity.

value'. In fact, 15 September 1916 would be noted 'as the birthplace of a new epoch in the history of war'[8] or as Liddell Hart described it 'the baptism of the Tank Corps'. [9]

Robinson's D Company was the cadre for D Battalion which was formed in late 1916 as the Tank Corps expanded and what was to become HQ Tank Corps was formed. This phase (see *Volume 2* for details) of expansion, consolidation and learning by experience, which lasted from late 1916 to just before the Battle of Cambrai, was a difficult but critical one. Robinson, now a section commander, returned home to get married over Christmas leave. He would have felt on his return the effects of the arrival of (then) Major Fuller as the Corps' chief of staff: the first instruction on training had been issued during his leave and in January and February 1917 all officers took part in a large indoor exercise which Fuller used to produce the first manual of tank tactics 'Training Note No 16'. The process of learning from experience which would lead to Cambrai and Amiens had begun.

It would be a hard one. Robinson's D Battalion's took part in the first brigade level tank action, the Battle of Arras in April 1917 (*Volume 2*). Robinson now commanded a section in 12 Company and was promoted to Captain on 12 April. Due to the poor ground condition, and the lack of obstacle crossing equipment such as the future unditching beam and fascines, 12 Company's tanks ditched whilst trying to support the successful Canadian attack on Vimy Ridge on 9 April 1917. The tanks were painstakingly recovered and moved south to support 62nd Division at the Second Battle of Bullecourt. The Battles of Bullecourt were a terrible demonstration of the power of the defence. Bullecourt is a small village and an outpost on the Hindenburg Line. The British and Australians lost 17,200 casualties to gain only small footholds in the Hindenburg Line [10] and one of the actions alienated the Australians to the tanks until the Battle of Hamel on 4 July 1918 (*Volume 4*). Robinson's 9 Section took part in the Second Battle of Bullecourt on 3 May. Eight tanks broke into the Hindenburg Line and two were put out of action.[11] The bravery of the crews was reflected in the four MCs, one DCM and 10 MMs awarded. Their bravery was all the more remarkable since they were in un-armoured Mark II training tanks. This was because the new and improved Mark IV was delivered late – their first action was the successful Battle of Messines (*Volume 2*) in June 1917.[12] This problem of late delivery was to plague the Tank Corps throughout the First World War.

The next and first large (216 Mark IV tanks) battle of the Tank Corps, and Robinson's D Battalion, was the Third Battle of Ypres, better known as the Battle of Passchendaele, (*Volume 2*). The three tank brigades and all nine tank battalions took part in this battle and would fight a few months later at the Battle of Cambrai. As such it was an important stepping stone for the Tank Corps but the ground was ill suited to any offensive let alone the use of tanks. There was a high water table, the drainage ditches had been destroyed by shell fire and there had been heavy rain. As a result, many tanks were lost in the mud. Robinson returned to UK to join J (later

8   Brevet-Colonel JFC Fuller DSO, *Tanks in the Great War 1914-1918*, (London: John Murray, 1920), p. 58. Quotes from same page.
9   Captain BH Liddell Hart, *The Tanks Volume One 1914 – 1939* (London: Cassell, 1959), Chapter IV, pp. 71 to 79.
10   Liddell Hart, *The Tanks Volume One 1914-1939*, p. 102.
11   One of those tanks, a Mark II numbered 785 of 10 Company, is now at the Tank Museum.
12   Liddell Hart, *The Tanks Volume One 1914-1939*, pp. 94 and 95. 240 Mark IV tanks were planned to be delivered for the Battle of Arras; this later cut to a planned 96 by the end of February and in fact none were delivered until late April.

10th) Tank Battalion which had started to form on 3 July 1917. One of its company commanders was the future Prime Minister, Clement Atlee. J Battalion was the first of the next wave of nine tank battalions [13] which would deploy to France after Cambrai and Robinson, an experienced and brave officer, was an obvious candidate to join this new battalion as was Captain Harry Drader MC who had also commanded a D Company tank on 15 September 1916. They received their decorations from King George V on 31 October and were later to command A and B Company of 10th Battalion respectively.

Drader and Robinson were training in England during the Battle of Cambrai – 20 November to early December 1917 (see *Volume 3* of *The Tank Corps in the Great War* for details). The Battle of Cambrai was described by Cyril Falls, a veteran of First World War, as 'the Great Experiment' and he wrote that 'the Battle of Cambrai was the type of battle of the future and its influence on the Second World War was as great as that on the remainder of the First'.[14] Its influence on the remainder of the First World War is clear. The two key turning point battles of 1918: the French counter offensive on 18 July at the Second Battle of the Marne[15] and the Battle of Amiens (see Volume 4 of *The Tank Corps in the Great War* for details) in August used lessons learnt from Cambrai. In order to ensure surprise, there was no preparatory bombardment or registration by firing; the tanks were to crush the wire and lead the infantry. A properly integrated battle force including aircraft with some improvements such as the use of a more powerful second echelon and of a rolling barrage with the tanks following very close behind. The lessons learnt were transferred to the French: officers of the *Artillerie d'Assaut*, the equivalent of the Tank Corps, 'visited HQ Tank Corps 'to discuss our organization and tactics during the Battle of Cambrai'.[16] On 20 May, Marshal Ferdinand Foch, the Allied commander in chief on the Western Front, outlined the requirements for the Battle of Amiens. These included a surprise attack with 'the use of tanks needs planned from the start for the attack of the first positions.'[17]

Robinson and Drader had moved to France on 20 December 1917 on completion of J Battalion's collective training at Bovington. The now renamed 10th Tank Battalion arrived in the midst of a changed strategic situation. The German Army had defeated the Russians in 1917 and were moving troops released from the Eastern front to launch a very large offensive against the British Army: Operation Michael or, as the British know it, the March retreat. 10th Battalion joined 2nd Tank Brigade and received Mark IV tanks which were probably in poor condition. In the very cold weather further training took place. On 25 January, the 25 year old Robinson became a major and A Company commander. In early March, the Battalion deployed near the front line between Bapaume and Cambrai. Despite its lack of experience, 10th Tank Battalion performed well during the March retreat (see Volume 4 for particulars) and had more

---

13   17th Battalion deployed as an armoured car battalion and 18th Battalion deployed at the end of the war. See Volumes 4 and 5 for details.

14   Cyril Falls, *The First World War*, (London: Longmans, 1960), p. 303.

15   See Tim Gale's excellent *The French Army's Tank Force and Armoured Warfare in the Great War*, (Farnham: Ashgate Studies in Military History, 2013) for further details

16   TNA WO 95/93, HQ Tank Corps War Diary January to May 1918, 1 January 1918. Fuller and Hotblack visited the *Artillerie d'Assaut* on 16 and 17 January 1918.

17   Service Historique, Etat Major de l'Armée, Ministère de la Guerre, *Les Armées Françaises Dans La Grande Guerre, Tome VI*, Vol. 2, L'offensive Allemande contre les Armées Françaises (1»Mai-18 Juillet 1918), *Annexes Vol. 2*, (Paris: Imprimerie Nationale, 1934) pp, 401 to 403 and Bean, *The Official History of Australia in the War of 1914-1918*, Vol. VI, pp. 151-55.

tanks left at the end of it than the five other more experienced tank battalions that also took part in that battle.

10th Tank Battalion's next battle was the decisive Battle of Amiens on 8 August 1918 (see *Volume 4*). 10th Battalion had been given probably the most difficult task of any tank battalion which was to support the British III Corps north of the Somme. The III Corps consisted of 'convalescent' divisions which had all suffered severely in the March retreat; as a result, they were short of experienced officers and NCOs and had been made to strength with young recruits. Their preparations had been disrupted by a German counter attack. The ground was difficult and there had been little infantry tank training, 10th Tank Battalion was kept in the line until 1 July when it started its conversion to the Mark V tank. It did not start to receive its new and more capable Mark V tanks until mid-July and, since the Battalion moved by rail to north of Amiens on 3 August, this would have left little time for driver training and may explain why only 30 out of 42 Mark Vs went into action on 8 August.

The Germans had shelled the back areas from 0400 and their MGs were also firing when the advance started at 0420. Fifteen minutes before Zero hour[18] a thick ground mist came down and lasted until 0800. The infantry and tanks lost each other in the mist and sometimes themselves. Robinson's A Company was advancing just south of the Bray – Corbie road in support of 36th Brigade. Due to the uncertain situation and dense mist, Robinson went forward with his reserve section, reinforced by the remaining six tanks from other sections. Led by him on foot and under shell fire, these tanks pushed onto the final objective although the infantry could not advance at the same pace. Robinson received a bar to his MC for 'his great coolness and courage'.[19] Two tanks were hit and burnt out and their second lieutenant commanders killed. III Corps failed get to its final objective that day leaving the Australians and their tanks exposed to fire from the north bank. The next two days only saw limited gains and, by 11 August 10th Tank Battalion only had 17 tanks available for action.

There was little time for congratulations[20] or recovery. Foch had realized that one of the reasons for the failure of the German 1918 offensives was that they were too far apart. As the Battle of Amiens began to peter out, he insisted on another British offensive as soon as possible. Due to the relatively small number of tank units, most including 10th Tank Battalion, were back in action at the next Allied offensive on 21 August, the Battle of Albert (see Volume 5 of *The Tank Corps in the Great War*). Due to a failure to produce enough of Mark V tanks these tank battalions were under strength. For example, 10th Battalion only had 23 tanks. Robinson was wounded on the left knee on 21 August 1918, whilst supporting 5th Division during the attack on Achiet Le Petit (seven miles WNW of Bapaume) over ground that he and 10th Battalion had fought in March 1918. He recovered quickly and returned to duty on 4 September. The exhausted and depleted tank battalions were withdrawn to reorganize and refit. For example,

---

18   H Hour in modern parlance.
19   Maj RFG Maurice, *Tank Corps Book of Honour*, (London: Anthony Rowe, 1919), p. 156.
20   TNA: WO 95/103, 10th Tank Battalion War History, p.14, The following letter from the G.O.C. 12th Div. was sent to the Battalion: "O.C. 10th Tank Battalion. Will you kindly convey to all the officers and men of your Battalion the thanks and high appreciation of all ranks of the 12th Div. for the splendid work they did in conjunction with our attacks of the 8th, 9th, & 10th August. It was very largely owing to their gallant co-operation that those attacks were most successful, Yours sincerely, (Signed) AW Higginson, Major General. 13.8.18."

between 31 July, i.e., before the Battle of Amiens, and 31 August 1918, 10th Tank Battalion strength fell from 90 officers to 46, from 568 to 425 other ranks and from 42 to 13 Mark V tanks. Probably as a result of these losses, and the overall shortage of Mark V tanks, 10th Tank Battalion handed over all its remaining tanks to 301st US Tank Battalion, the only British trained and equipped US Tank Battalion to fight with the British Army (see Volume 5). While most of the Tank Corps was supporting First, Third and Fourth Armies as they breached the Hindenburg Lines in late September and early October between Cambrai and Saint Quentin (*Volume 5*), Robinson and a composite company took part in tank demonstration at the Inter-Allied Tank School, Recloses (45 miles south of Paris).

The 10th Tank Battalion's next action, with 301st US, 11th and 12th Battalions, was not until 23 October. It was a successful and rare night attack near Le Cateau (15 miles ESE of Cambrai). The last action of 10th Tank Battalion, which resulted in Robinson's death, was on 4 November; and the last tank action of the Tank Corps was by Whippet tanks of 6th Light Battalion the next day. The final action of the Tank Corps in the Great War was by the vehicles of 17th Armoured Car Battalion. After 1030 on 11 November, while reconnoitring near the Belgian border about 45 miles east of Cambrai, the armoured car crews were told by a despatch rider that hostilities were to cease at 1100. Firing continued until 1057.

As the tragic story of Robinson illustrates, the story of the Tank Corps and its predecessors in the Great War is a remarkable one. The aim of the *Tank Corps in the Great War* series is to examine the actions of British tanks units and formations in the First World War within an overall examination of the development of armoured warfare in the First World War making use, in particular, of the detailed records available including the unique Tank Battalion War Histories and individual tank Battle Histories. While the actions of British tank units and formations on the Western Front are the cornerstone, the series also looks at their performance in the Middle East and Russia, as well as that of Tank Corps armoured cars. It also covers the pioneers such as Robinson, the commanders and staff that commanded and supported them and the equipment that they used. The series consists of six volumes[21], as follows:

- Volume 1 – *Conception, Birth and Baptism of Fire 1914 – 1916*, including armoured cars in 1914, the initial development of the tank, the Battle of Flers – Courcelette and subsequent tank actions in 1916.
- Volume 2 – *The Road to Cambrai 1917*, including the Battles of Gaza, Arras, Bullecourt, Messines and Third Ypres.
- Volume 3 – *The Battle of Cambrai 1917* including the German counter-attack.
- Volume 4 – *The Road to Victory 1918 Part 1 - Crisis, Recovery and Initial Victory* – The Mark V tank and Whippet, the March retreat and the Battle of Villers Bretonneux, the Battles of Hamel, Moreuil and Amiens.
- Volume 5 – *The Road to Victory 1918 Part 2* – The Hundred Days advance after Amiens
- *Volume 6* – Key reference material and deployments in Germany and Russia in 1918 and 1919.

---

21   The subject matters of each of these volumes was inspired by the chapter headings and content of Part 1 of Liddell Hart, *The Tanks Volume One 1914-1939* (London: Cassell, 1959). See p. xv.

The authors bring a wide spread of experience and expertise:

- Stephen Pope (Volume 1) is a retired Royal Logistic Corps officer whose predecessors provided the tank drivers and artificers in 1916. He was the author of *The First Tank Crews - The Lives of the Tankmen who Fought at the Battle of Flers-Courcelette, 15 September 1916*, (Solihull, Helion, 2016) and led the Centenary Commemorations on the Somme.
- Gareth Davies (Volume 2) and Geoffrey Vesey Holt (*Volumes 4 and 5*) are retired Lieutenant Colonels of the Royal Tank Regiment, the Tank Corps under its present name. They both run battlefield tours and have lectured and written extensively about the Tank Corps.
- Dr Tim Gale (Volume 3) brings academic rigor and is the author of the authoritative *The French Army's Tank Force and Armoured Warfare in the Great War* (Farnham, Ashgate Studies in Military History, 2013)

This series would not have been possible without the help and support of many people and organisations. First and foremost is Helion and in particular the patient and consistently helpful Duncan Rogers and Dr Michael LoCicero. This series would not exist without Duncan's initiative. I gave an after dinner talk to members of the Oriental Club about the Battle of Waterloo which managed to include 1918 and the Tank Corps and Duncan attended the talk. He kindly invited me to lunch and I mentioned the quality of the records and secondary sources including in particular Liddell Hart's *The Tanks Volume One 1914-1939* and Fuller's *Tanks in the Great War 1914-1918*. Fuller was responsible for initiating the unique just post First World War brigade and battalion histories. Some months later, Duncan asked for a six volume history of *The Tank Corps in the Great War*. I told him that I could not possibly do this on my own and he said he was sure that I knew other potential authors. He also insisted on good quality maps, a key requirement for military history and Barbara Taylor has produced superb maps with her usual patience, determination and skill.

These volumes would also not have been possible without the assistance of the Tank Museum, a true friend of the Royal Tank Regiment and the Tank Corps, and its excellent archives, led by Stuart Wheeler, whose staff never fail to be helpful and knowledgeable. The National Archives at Kew and the Liddell Hart Centre for Military Archives at King's College, London, and their staffs, have also provided patient and indispensable support. However, these books would not exist without the bravery and determination of the pioneers of the Tank Corps and its predecessors.

Geoffrey Vesey Holt
Horsted Keynes

Acknowledgements

I echo Geoffrey Vesey Holt's thanks to Helion & Company, our publishers, typesetter Mary Woolley and the archival staff at the Tank Museum for their ongoing support. Barbara Taylor produced the colour and monochrome maps of the key tank locations inserted in the text; I have never seen anything better. I would like to acknowledge Sophie Fisher of the Imperial War Museum in London and Dolores Ho of the New Zealand National Army Museum at Waiouru for their assistance in obtaining images from their collections. I would also like to thank Geoffrey for asking me to write this Volume and for his support and encouragement as I have done so,

Like all writers, my work has been influenced by those who have published earlier accounts. Surprisingly, the first Tank Corps historians, JFC Fuller and Clough and Amabel Williams-Ellis, do not appear to have access to the original records for 1916 and, as a result, their information is limited. Fortunately, the Official History, which was collated by Wilfred Miles from war dairies and official reports, is highly detailed and has been a superb resource. Although the first Volume of Liddell Hart's history also has relatively little information, its publication in 1958 set in train correspondence and meetings between surviving crewmen which promoted a series of first-hand accounts to be published or sent to the Tank Museum; I have used these throughout this book

My prime source for Chapter 2-5 is Swinton's book *Eyewitness*. I have quoted this at length as he had an unequalled view of the tank's conception, development and deployment between 1914 and 1916. I have also used Albert Stern's recollections of the tank's design and manufacture as published in his book *Tanks 1914-1918: Logbook of a Pioneer*. The War History of 3rd Light Tank Battalion includes a detailed description of the deployment of C Company; the primary input probably being Sir John Dashwood who was the only one of the original members of the unit still serving with them when it was written at Christmas 1918.

My prime source for the battle are chapters 6-9 in the excellent second volume of the *Official History of the Battle of the Somme* by Captain Wilfred Miles, which has been republished with colour maps by the Naval & Military Press. Miles' overarching view of the individual battles in September to November and the descriptions based on war diaries, unit and formation level reports are first rate. Using his work has taught me always to read footnotes where little nuggets often reveal important details which would otherwise be missed. I have also referred to the War Diaries maintained by C and D Companies and those of the formations they were supporting, I have also read various unit histories which, like Miles' work, often reveal matters of detail missing from more general histories. Allen Holford-Walker letter to Sir John Edmonds, written in 1935, also reveals the difficulties faced by C Company although many of these did not appear in Miles' work.

Graham Woods not only kept first class records in the D Company War Diary but also a notebook and diary; which he later presented to the Tank Museum. These were the prime resource for Trevor's Pidgeon meticulous research which resulted in two books: *The Tanks at Flers*, published in 1996 and *the Tanks on the Somme* (2010), which was published posthumously by Graham Keech. I met Trevor at Bovington in 2004 when I showed him my initial research into the First Tank Crews. He encouraged my efforts and, after his death, his widow Marion kindly gifted me his archives which have provided other material not in published form. Wood's correspondence book, for the period 16 September to 5 October, travelled to the USA in the care of D Company Sergeant Major Thomas "Paddy" Walsh. This book contains letters, detailed lists and post action reports which were not available to Trevor. I was fortunate to be contacted by Paddy's grandson Geoff Donaldson in the summer of 2016 and was therefore able to share accounts of the first actions with relatives of the FTC as we walked the Somme battlefield on 15 September 2016. I have drawn extensively on this book.

I have also drawn on the contemporary reports, dairies and letters of crewmen of A, C and D Companies, many of the sources being reproduced in the Appendices, as well as reminiscences written after Victor Huffam and Victor Smith appeared on a BBC panel game called 'Find the link' in 1956.[1] Since I started researching the FTC in 2003, I have located a number of relatives of the original crews who have generously shared family papers and photographs. I would particularly like to thank three other researchers – Sue Chifney, Karl-Heinz Pfarr and Dr Gerald Moore. Sue, who lives in New Zealand, has trawled the NZ National Archives, the NZ National Army Museum as well as locally published histories and newspaper archives across Australia and New Zealand. It was Sue who discovered the image of *Daredevil 1* in Chapter 1; her grand uncle Harry Leat being a member of her crew. Karl-Heinz Pfarr in Argentina has enabled us to identify several previously unidentified tanks through his analysis of contemporary photographs. He also translated the diary of the unidentified crewman of the Female tank 510 *Challenger* reprinted in the *Tanks at Flers*. Gerald Moore from British Columbia, who has been researching the first tank actions for many more years than me, has not only shared his extensive knowledge but also kindly acted as my editor. Any errors in this Volume are however mine, not his.

I would also like to thank members of the *Friends of the Lincoln Tank* Facebook research group for their assistance in answering my queries about tank manufacture. I have been guided by John Glanfield's superb study, *The Devil's Chariots*, and I would also like to acknowledge the help of David Brown, Doug Edsall, Gwyn Evans, Mike Gray, Chris Gresham, Alwyn Killingsworth and Richard Pullen in answering my detailed questions about other aspects of tank production and testing. Clem Maginness, my closest friend from Sandhurst, provided me with detailed information about railways on the Western Front and Charles Fair shared his research into officer training battalions during the Great War. Joyce Hurford and Dr Miles Kerr-Peterson assisted my research into Charles Bond, identifying a second report on *Duchess'* attack on 15 September. Will Endley, from South Africa who is writing a biography of Teddy Winder, provided me with his descriptions of his first sighting of the tanks near Dernancourt and also of the attack by 12th East Surreys in Flers.

---

1   Where first-hand accounts conflict, I have generally assumed that contemporary records are more accurate.

The photographs come from two main sources: colour images of the battlefields were mainly taken by Geoffrey Vesey Holt on 15 September 2015 whilst the majority of black and white photographs are from the TMA. Simon Jones provided two previously unknown images of *Dinkum* and Mike Haspey took two of the colour images of the battlefield near Martinpuich. Other photographs have been provided by FTC relatives and friends: Graham Archard (Victor Archard), Justin Blowers (Arthur Blowers), Steve Butcher (Mick Wheeler), Louise Brough (Eric Robinson), Nel Gilbert (Arthur Arnold), Sue Handley (Lionel McAdam), Paddi Lilley who sadly died in April 2020 (Eric Purdy), Tilly Mortimore (Harold Mortimore), Mike Nixon (Harry Nixon), John Phillips (Ernest Phillips), Alan Holford-Walker (Allen Holford-Walker) and Pam Wilkins (100th Anniversary Commemoration of the death of Gnr Cyril Coles).

I have done my best to acknowledge holders of copyright material used in this Volume and also to minimise errors within the text. Sadly, some of the sources contradict others and I have tried to deconflict them, not always to my total satisfaction. If the reader should find anything that is a cause for concern, please do not hesitate to contact me. Also, if you can identify any of the crewmen whose names are not listed in the photographs, please contact me at firsttankcrews@outlook.com. There are now more than 2,000 members of the *FTC* Facebook Group and they and I would be delighted to learn their names.

Stephen Pope
Anna Valley, Hampshire
September 2021

1

The First Tank Action

At 0530 hours on Friday 15 September 1916, in the half-light preceding dawn, the crew of the British tank *Daredevil 1* made history. Under the command of Captain (Capt) Harold Mortimore, this Male tank went into action against a German-held trench system, known as the Brewery Salient, at the eastern edge of Delville Wood on the Somme battlefield. The crew's orders were to 'clear up', that is to say destroy, a set of German machine-gun emplacements which dominated the route of British infantry battalions who would attack the main German frontline 50 minutes later. *Daredevil 1* was the first tank in the world to see combat and the first to be knocked out by indirect artillery fire.

Daredevil 1 near Delville Wood, September 1916. (NZ NAM)

Since September 1914, the British Army had no effective means of neutralising the joint perils of German barbed wire and machine-guns, which had killed thousands of Australians, British, Canadians, French, Indians, New Zealanders and South Africans attacking on the Western Front. The eight-man crew of *Daredevil 1* and the other tanks, which went into action on 15 September at the Battle of Flers–Courcelette, provided a solution. Two years later, in concert with the infantry, artillery and aircraft from Allied Armies, tank crews would defeat the German Army on the Western Front, forcing it inexorably from fiercely defended positions eastwards, across the occupied lands of France and Belgium to the borders of Germany and forcing their government to sue for peace.

This volume of the first history of the Tank Corps to be written in 60 years, tells the story of the Conception, Birth and Bloody Baptism of Fire of a wholly new weapon system – the tank. It describes the design and development of the first self-propelled, armoured fighting vehicles (AFV), the recruitment and training of the men who manned them, their deployment to France, the tactics they used, and the tank actions in the autumn of 1916.

In September 1916, there were just three effective tank companies, less than 85 operational tanks and some 750 men trained to use them. On 8 August 1918, the opening day of the Battle of Amiens, 15 tank battalions, one armoured car (AC) battalion and supporting units launched 560 AFVs of all types.[1] The majority of those crewmen who fought with the tanks, on 15 September 1916, were still serving in the army two years later. The others had given their lives or had suffered such injuries or illnesses as to cause them to be discharged. You will meet some of them again in subsequent volumes as the Tank Corps expanded and took its rightful place alongside the other arms of the British Army.

They Feared Nought
We Remember Them Still!

---

1   Fuller, *Tanks in the Great War*, pp. 203-204.

2

Conception and Birth

On 1 August 1914, the German Government declared war on the Russian Empire. The next day, German troops entered Luxembourg and their government demanded the Belgian government give their armies passage through the neutral country in order to invade the northern parts of France. On 3 August, German troops entered Belgium and, as a result, the British Government declared war on Germany that evening. The Germans mobilised seven armies and more than three million men for their attack on France,[1] whilst the French committed five armies totalling 1,286,092 men. In the north, *First Army* under von Kluck and *Second Army* commanded by von Bulow advanced through southern Belgium in order to attack the northeast of France. These two were the northernmost of the German armies on the Western Front and their initial objectives were the river crossings along the Rivers Sambre and Meuse between Maubeuge and Namur.

The British Expeditionary Force

The British Expeditionary Force (BEF), under the command of Field Marshal Sir John French,[2] was committed to fight on the left flank of the Fifth French Army which was commanded by Lanzarac.[3] The War Office (WO) deployed the majority of their home-based Regular troops, which comprised just six regular divisions, to support the French. The BEF were allocated four divisions under two army corps headquarters; HQ I Corps commanded by Lieutenant-General (Lt Gen) Douglas Haig and HQ II Corps under Lt Gen James Grierson. These were supported by the Cavalry Division, under Maj Gen Edmund Allenby and the independent 5th Cavalry

---

1   The German force allocated to the Western Front was 78 divisions (3,180,832 men); the attack against the Russians was a single army of 14 divisions (209,837 men). Robert T. Foley, 'Baptism of Fire: The German Armies' Lost Victory', presentation at the Western Front Association conference in Birmingham on 5 July 2014.
2   French, who had been Chief of the Imperial General Staff (CIGS) from March 1912 to April 1914, had actively prepared the British Army for war on the continent. He had resigned following the Curragh incident but having retained the trust of the Prime Minister H.H. Asquith, was appointed C-in-C BEF in early August 1914.
3   Fifth French Army comprised five corps and a total of 299,350 men; it was the second largest of all five French armies.

Brigade, plus their integral artillery, engineer, medical and logistic support units.[4] 1st and 2nd Divisions were allocated to HQ I Corps,[5] and 3rd and 5th Divisions to II Corps whilst the 4th and 6th Divisions were initially retained in Britain for home defence.[6]

At 1600 hours on 4 August, the WO issued the order to mobilise the British Regular Army and the Territorial Force (TF).[7] Barracks and quarters were emptied, tented camps were erected, buildings were hired and men in towns billeted on the local population. The British peacetime garrisons were recalled from Egypt, Gibraltar, Malta and South Africa.[8] The previous day had been a bank holiday and most TF units were on route to their annual camp locations. Mobilisation went smoothly and 120,000 horses were collected.[9] However, many British units were at their peacetime establishment for men and equipment and the WO had to call-up their Regular reserves to fully man the BEF to its wartime establishment. For supporting services, such as the Army Service Corps (ASC), it was also necessary to requisition civilian vehicles to provide the full establishment of cars and lorries.[10]

The Government's declaration of war was welcomed by many of the British population and recruiting offices were inundated with volunteers. One of these was an 18-year-old motor salesman, Herbert Thacker, who enlisted as a Mechanical Specialist; he deployed as a driver with 2nd Division's Ammunition Park to France nine days later.[11] To fulfil the requirements to provide communications between headquarters and units, the WO also advertised for motorcyclists to serve as despatch riders; a prerequisite being that each volunteer provided his own machine. A Balliol College undergraduate named Willie Watson, who spoke excellent French and German, went to the Scotland Yard recruiting office on 4 August and was immediately attested. The next day he bought a motorcycle and that evening reported to the Royal Engineers (RE) Depot at Chatham with two friends. On 6 August, Watson was promoted to corporal and, one week later, joined 5th Division's Signal Company in Ireland. The unit deployed directly from Dublin to Le Havre, and then reached Landrecies by train on 20 August. Watson took his first despatch at midnight and, on 21 August 1914, he arrived at Bavay, the day that HQ II Corps established itself in the town.[12]

4   Renamed 1st Cavalry Division on 16 September 1914 when a second cavalry division was formed in Great Britain.
5   In this volume, a division or a brigade refers to an infantry formation unless specified otherwise.
6   Both divisions would be deployed to France by early September 1914.
7   War was not formally declared until 2300 on 4 August. The TF had been established in 1908 for home defence and, whilst its members would be encouraged to volunteer 'for Imperial Service', overseas service was not obligatory.
8   British Regular Army battalions based in India and China were recalled in the autumn.
9   Michael Young, *Army Service Corps (ASC) 1902-1918* (Barnsley: Leo Cooper, 2000), p. 46.
10   Young, *ASC 1902-1918*, p. 48. The initial requirement to support formation headquarters and units of the six regular infantry divisions and the cavalry division which were to deploy overseas was 900 vehicles. Drivers were also encouraged to enlist; the rate of pay being six shillings a day, six times more than an infantry soldier.
11   Thacker would serve for 21 months in France before returning to England. He joined 711 MT Company ASC in June 1916 and drove the Male tank No. 747 into action on 15 September 1916. Pope, *FTC*, p.103.
12   WHL Watson, *Adventures of a Despatch Rider* (London: Blackwood & Sons, 1915) Ch. 1 and 2. Watson was awarded the DCM in February 1915 and commissioned the following month. In December 1916, he was appointed OC No. 11 Company of D Battalion Heavy Branch MGC. He commanded them

Deployment to France

HQ Royal Flying Corps (RFC) left Farnborough on 11 August, travelling via Southampton and reaching Amiens on 13 August. Squadron advance parties assembled at Newhaven on 11 August and crossed to Boulogne on 12 August. Their aircraft, which assembled at Dover, flew across the English Channel on 13 August, to Cap Gris-Nez (the most direct route) then flew down the coast to the mouth of the River Somme and then followed the river to Amiens arriving the same day.[13]

HQ I (British) Corps departed Southampton for Le Havre on 14 August with II Corps deploying the following day. On 16 August, the First Lord of the Admiralty, Winston Churchill, gave instruction that some of the 30,000 naval reservists, who were not required for immediate employment with the fleet, be formed into eight infantry battalions. Their role was to defend ports deemed essential for naval operations. Like the Royal Marines (RM) Brigade, these new battalions had no supporting arms or services and were formed into two Light Infantry (LI) Brigades. Khaki uniforms were not issued and 80 percent of the reservists went to war without such basic equipment as packs, mess tins or water bottles.[14] Like TF units, the RN Brigades were armed with Mark I Lee Enfield charger loading rifles; in the latter's case just three days before embarking.[15]

The RFC squadrons left Amiens on 16 August, flying to their forward base at Maubeuge. As II Corps was moving by rail from Le Havre to its deployment location, its General Officer Commanding (GOC) James Grierson was taken ill and died on 17 August at Amiens. Horace Smith-Dorrien was sent out immediately to replace him as GOC II Corps.[16] The BEF was to fight on the western flank of French armies, near the French border fortress complex at Maubeuge on the River Sambre.[17] I Corps was to take position to the right of the Fifth French Army with II Corps to their left (northwest). On 17 August, HQ I Corps reached Wassingey (five miles south of Le Cateau) whilst HQ II Corps reached Landrecies (northeast of Le Cateau). During its deployment, the WO decided to reinforce the BEF with 4th Division, commanded by Maj Gen Henry Rawlinson, which was planned to arrive by 25 August.

in action at Bullecourt, Ypres, Flesquières and Bourlon Wood. From January 1918, he trained and then commanded 4 Tank Supply Company in France.

13 The pilots were issued with inner tubes, worn round the waist, as life preservers; the pilots having to inflate them if their aeroplanes landed in the Channel.

14 *The Long Long Trail: 63rd (RN) Division* <https://www.longlongtrail.co.uk/army/order-of-battle-of-divisions/63rd-royal-naval-division/> (accessed on 23 February 2021).

15 Whilst these rifles were of .303-inch calibre, they could not achieve the same rate of fire as those issued to regular army units. They also suffered from stoppage problems following sustained firing.

16 Smith-Dorrien had been GOC Southern Command at Aldershot since March 1912.

17 This had been agreed at a War Council meeting on 5 August. C-in-C BEF who made the proposal, suggested that, as British mobilisation was lagging behind that of the French, it might be safer to send the BEF to Amiens which was also the view of Kitchener and Haig. C-in-C BEF also believed that the BEF might operate from Antwerp against the German right flank but this was dropped when Churchill said the Royal Navy could not guarantee safe passage.

War of the Frontiers

The French Armies in the south had already attacked across the German border. The first French offensive of the war, known as the Battle of Mulhouse, began on 7 August and was successful. German counter-attacks initially succeeded but, by 21 August, the First French Army had secured the Rhine bridges and were briefly in possession of upper Alsace. Elements of the First and Second French Armies attacked into Lorraine on 14 August. They were also initially successful but, as the elements diverged, the *Sixth* and *Seventh Armies* counter-attacked on 20 August, forcing the French to withdraw.

Meanwhile the BEF and French Armies were using aircraft and cavalry units to locate the approaching German formations; RFC aircraft carrying out their first reconnaissance (recce) patrols near Mons on 19 August.[18] The French CGS, Joseph Joffre, was aware that German cavalry were close to Dinant on 15 August.[19] There were no German armies opposite the Third and Fourth French Armies in the Ardennes, so he initially held them back behind the French border. However, on 21 August, following the German counter-attack in Lorraine, the Third and Fourth Armies began their offensive. Lanzerac's Fifth Army, which was holding a line from Sedan north to Maubeuge, was aware that the *German Third Army* (Hausen) was on the eastern bank of the Meuse and that the *First* and *Second Armies* were approaching from the northeast. On 19 August the Fifth French Army began to move into the angle of the Meuse and Sambre rivers close to Namur. This required a march of up to 60 miles and took the army far beyond the left flank of the Fourth Army, opening a dangerous gap. On 20 August, the French and German cavalry clashed in a series of skirmishes and, the next day, Joffre ordered the Fifth French Army and the BEF to advance and locate German forces west of the Meuse.

On 21 August, German aircraft spotted elements of the BEF moving from Le Cateau to Maubeuge where HQ I Corps had been established. HQ II Corps were located at Bavay, just south of the Belgian border, and Advanced GHQ BEF was at Sars-la-Bruyère, just over the Belgian border between Bavay and Mons with HQ RFC close by. The first contact between the BEF and the Germans took place that day, when a bicycle patrol from 4th Middlesex,[20] sent to the village of Obourg northeast of Mons, exchanged fire with a detachment of German cavalry. Private John Parr was killed, the first British soldier killed on the Western Front.[21]

On 22 August the Cavalry Division, which had established a screen north of the canal, clashed with German cavalry north of Mons.[22] Twelve RFC recce sorties were flown which identified German troops closing in on the BEF. One British aircraft was shot down and the observer became the first British aircrew to be wounded while flying.

18   Two sorties were undertaken and a further two the next day, but they could not locate the German forces. Fog delayed flights on 21 August but in the afternoon German troops were seen near Kortrijk.
19   These would have been elements of the Third Army under General von Hausen.
20   The 4th Middlesex were part of *8th Infantry Brigade* in 3rd Division (II Corps).
21   His body was buried in a battlefield grave, possibly by the Germans. It was subsequently recovered and reinterred at St Symphorien Military Cemetery, just southeast of Mons.
22   C Squadron, 4th Irish Dragoon Guards charged a German cavalry column just east of Mons on 22 August 1914. 2nd Dragoons (Scots Greys) were also in action in the dismounted role, protecting the rear of I Corps as part of the 5th Cavalry Brigade. They drove off the attack using machine-guns.

Meanwhile the British infantry had established a defensive line along the Mons–Condé Canal. 19th Brigade was on the left,[23] II Corps in the centre protecting four bridges over the canal, while I Corps was dug in to their right, including along the Mons–Beaumont road. This provided a flank guard should the Germans break through the French Fifth Army. Sir John French decided that, if pressure grew on the outposts along the canal, then II Corps would evacuate Mons and take up a defensive position among the pit villages and slag heaps a little way to the south.

The Great Retreat

The first battle between the Germans and the BEF took place on 23 August.[24] At 0530 hours, Sir John French met Haig, Smith-Dorrien and Allenby at his Advanced GHQ and ordered the canal outpost line be strengthened and the bridges prepared for demolition. At first light, RFC aircrews flew north of the battlefield looking for German battery positions and troop movements. The *First Army* had started their bombardment at dawn and, at 0900 hours, attacked four bridges across the canal held by II Corps. The defences held, initially because the German infantry were attacking, in close order, against the superbly trained British infantry.[25]

Despite sustaining severe casualties, the German attacks continued, albeit in less packed ranks, and by noon, the *First Army* was attacking along a seven-mile front trying to outflank the BEF. At 1500 hours, reports arrived stating that French cavalry on the British right flank were under attack and falling back and 3rd Division was ordered to retire to new, and unprepared, defensive positions south of Mons. In the evening, 5th Division was ordered to conform and by nightfall, the new defensive line was established. Oddly, the Germans did not attempt to exploit their success, their bugles sounding cease fire. Later that evening, GHQ BEF received a message stating the French Fifth Army would start to withdraw at 0300 hours. This was confirmed by Joffre at 0100 hours, so Sir John French made the decision to withdraw the BEF towards Cambrai. The retreat of the BEF started and it would continue until they reached the River Marne on 7 September.

The BEF became divided shortly soon after they started to withdraw. I Corps, on the right, tried to keep in contact with the French Fifth Army, whilst II Corps, the Cavalry Division, 4th Division and 19th Infantry Brigade were forced to move to the left (west) by the Forest of Mormal. By nightfall on 25 September the *First Army* were in close pursuit of the British left flank so Smith-Dorrien decided to halt his exhausted men at Le Cateau and give battle. It was contrary to the direction given by Sir John French but II Corps' action was successful in stopping the *First Army*, albeit with a loss of almost 8,000 men and 38 field guns. The BEF was never overrun and, indeed, withdrew effectively. As they continued to retreat, the British

---

23 19th Infantry Brigade, which was not originally part of the BEF, was formed in France between 19–22 August from line of communication defence battalions as an independent formation.

24 *The Long Long Trail* <https://www.longlongtrail.co.uk/battles/battles-of-the-western-front-in-france-and-flanders/the-battle-of-mons/> (accessed on 23 February 2021).

25 Following the Second Anglo-Boer War, which exposed the lack of skill amongst the British infantry, 'musketry' standards were dramatically improved. The British infantry soldier's pay was linked to his accuracy with the rifle. Trained to fire 15 aimed shots in a minute, and annually required to achieve it, the British Regular battalions were vastly superior in their shooting to the conscripts of the French and German armies.

fought several rear-guard actions and successfully slowed the German advance. By this time, the German soldiers were equally, if not more, exhausted as the Allies, as the *First* and *Second Armies* had initially marched halfway across Belgium during their deployment. By 5 September, the BEF were clear of their pursuers and crossed the Marne. Here they reorganised, a new III Corps being formed under Lt Gen William Pulteney.

Joffre ordered a counter-attack which stopped the Germans in their tracks. The Germans withdrew and pulled back to the line of the River Aisne. The river was 100 feet wide in places and was between 9 to 15 feet deep; either side, the valley was over a mile wide. North of the river the ground rose to become cliffs 300 to 400 feet high. The *First* and *Second Armies* made their main position two miles further north on a plateau which offered no cover to the attacking French and British units.

On the night of 13 September, under cover of thick fog, the Fourth, Fifth and Ninth French Armies, with the BEF on their western flank, made their way across the river. Reaching the plateau, the BEF came under fire as soon as the sun burnt off the morning mist. The French Armies also made negligible progress but the Germans could not expel them. Between 12 and 15 September, whilst attacking against German positions protected by artillery and machine-guns, the French suffered 250,000 casualties whilst the BEF suffered more than 13,000 dead and wounded. On 14 September, Sir John French gave orders that the BEF was to entrench, which was difficult as the troops were not carrying digging tools. Shell-scrapes then small pits were dug but these provided little protection from German artillery fire. With neither side willing to withdraw, the British trenches soon became seven feet deep; the War of Manoeuvre had effectively ended for four years.

The First Armoured Car Unit

As the First and Second Armies had pushed south in August 1914, the Belgian Army became cut off from their French and British allies. The majority of Belgian troops withdrew towards the strategically important port city of Antwerp. However, other Belgian units were being withdrawn from other ports, which created significant concern at the Admiralty. Ostend was seen as critical as its capture would enable the *Kaiserliche Marine* to base submarines forward of their home port at Kiel and attack British shipping and the BEF's supply lines across the English Channel. It was decided to deploy the RM Brigade, which started to arrive on 27 August. It was supported by a Royal Naval Air Service (RNAS) squadron which patrolled the French and German borders in order to locate advancing German formations.

The squadron's CO, Charles Samson, used motor cars to provide local protection and rescue downed aircrew. Two of the cars, one Rolls Royce and a Mercedes, were locally fitted with armoured plate and a single rear-firing machine-gun – they were the first British manned armoured vehicles to see action in the Great War. The force was quickly expanded using both locally modified cars and others armoured in Britain by RM workshops. They were the origins of the RNAS Armoured Car Division (ACD), some of whose officers would play a key role in the development of tanks.

Official War Correspondent

As a result of the Battle of the Marne (7 to 10 September), the French Armies and BEF stabilised the front north and east of Paris. The Germans therefore started to advance northwest, capturing the coalfields north of Arras, and seeking to cut the BEF's access to the Channel ports. Around this time, Earl Kitchener, the Secretary of State for War appointed on the outbreak of war, decided that the British public should 'be provided with more information about the Allies' progress.'[26] He decided that an official War Correspondent should work from HQ BEF to produce press releases which, whilst accurate, would not provide the Germans with any information of strategic importance. Churchill recommended Ernest Swinton to Kitchener for the role.[27] Swinton was a published author and an experienced staff officer who, from 1910 to 1913, compiled the final two volumes of the *Official Naval and Military History of the Russo-Japanese War*. As the former Military Secretary to the Committee for Imperial Defence (CID), Swinton also had a good understanding of

Ernest Swinton. (TMA)

how Whitehall worked and knew many of the senior naval and military officers, as well as Cabinet ministers, senior politicians and key civil servants.

On 8 September, Swinton was briefed by Kitchener about his new role and, one hour later, left London for Paris travelling with the WO's liaison officer to HQ BEF. On arriving at Paris, the next day, and having confirmed the GHQ's location,[28] Swinton was driven east to Coulommiers where GHQ was located south of the Marne. He was interviewed the next day by Sir John French, who believed that Kitchener had sent Swinton to keep watch on him.[29] Swinton then met Maj Gen Henry Wilson, the sub-chief at HQ BEF, who had a similar view to the C-in-C.[30]

26   Ernest Swinton, *Eyewitness* (London: Hodder & Stoughton 1932), p. 39.
27   Kitchener, who had also been commissioned in the RE, first met Swinton when they served in South Africa during the Second Anglo-Boer War.
28   At this point in the retreat from Mons, GHQ was moving on an almost daily basis.
29   Sir John had wished to withdraw the BEF, after the Retreat from Mons, rather than take part in the Battle of the Marne in order to reorganise his formations and only participated after an interview with Kitchener.
30   Chief of Staff in modern parlance.

On 11 September, Swinton wrote his first article, which was quickly cleared by the BEF's Head of Intelligence and then by Wilson, before being submitted to the WO. Swinton visited the frontlines regularly to gain a true picture of what was happening but wrote in such a way as to conceal any weaknesses from the Germans or the public.[31] On 21 September, he observed:

> The present battle may well last for some days more before a decision is reached since, in truth, it now approximates somewhat to siege warfare. The Germans are making use of searchlights and, this fact, coupled with their great strength in heavy artillery, leads to the supposition that they are employing material which may have been collected for the siege of Paris.

Four days later he wrote:

> The growing resemblance of this battle to siege warfare has already been pointed out. The fact that the later actions of the Russo-Japanese War assumed a similar character was thought by many to have been due to exceptional causes, such as the narrowness of the theatre of operations between the Chinese frontier on the West and the mountainous country of Northern Korea on the East, and the lack of roads which limited the extent of ground over which it was possible for the rival armies to manoeuvre, and the fact that both forces were tied to one line of railway.
>
> No such factors are exerting any influence on the present battle. Nevertheless, a similar situation has been produced owing, first, to the immense power of resistance possessed by an army which is amply equipped with heavy artillery and has sufficient time to fortify itself, and, secondly, to the vast size of the forces engaged, which at present stretch more than half way across France. The extent of country covered is so great as to render slow any efforts to manoeuvre and march round to a flank in order to escape the costly expedient of a frontal attack against heavily fortified positions. To state that methods of attack must approximate more closely to those of siege warfare, the greater the resemblance of the defences to those of a fortress, is a platitude but it is one which will bear repetition if it in any way assists to make the present situation clear.

Whilst Swinton may not have been the first person to identify that the War of Manoeuvre had ceased on the Western Front, his article was the first to be published.[32] This was confirmed during what has since become known as the 'Race to the Sea'. The BEFs II, III and Cavalry Corps moved to Flanders on the northeast flank of the French forces and fought a series of encounter battles at Le Bassée (10 October – 2 November), Armentiéres and Messines (12 October – 2 November) and three battles at Ypres (19 October – 22 November). The German advance was halted but British regular infantry battalions were destroyed in the process. The Western Front became fortified from the Swiss border to the English Channel and manoeuvre warfare ceased until August 1918.

---

31   He was assisted for a while by Colonel (Col) John Edmonds, later the supervising editor of the *Official History of the Great War (OHGW)*, and by Capt Ian Percy who would become Duke of Northumberland.
32   Swinton states that the same had been noted early in 1914 by J.F.C. Fuller. See *Eyewitness*, p. 62.

Conception

On 19 October, whilst en route to the WO from GHQ at St Omer, Swinton observed:

> Returned to the subject which had absorbed them for the past five weeks. Since I had
> been at the front, all the information I had gathered – whether from official reports,
> from the hospitals or from any other source – had consistently to bear out the fact that,
> apart from his artillery the main strength of the enemy resistance lay in his skilful
> combination of machine-guns and wire. Throughout this time, I had been racking
> my brains to discover an antidote; and within the last two weeks my vague idea of an
> armoured vehicle had definitely crystallized in the form of a power-driven, bullet-
> proof, armed engine, capable of destroying machine-guns, of crossing country and
> trenches, of breaking through entanglements, and of climbing earthworks.
>
> But the difficulty was to find or evolve something which would fulfil these
> conditions – especially the last three. It was upon this that my mind was concentrated
> when, straight ahead in the clear morning air above the ground mist, came into
> view the Pharos of Calais. Like a beam from that same lighthouse the idea flashed
> across my brain – the American Caterpillar Tractor at Antwerp! I recalled its reputed
> performance. If this agricultural machine could really do all that report credited it
> with, why should it not be modified and adapted to suit our present requirements for
> war? The key to the problem lay in the caterpillar track![33]

Swinton decided to use the opportunity of visiting London to present his idea to Kitchener and
to Maurice Hankey,[34] Secretary of the CID, for whom Swinton had worked before the war:

> On the 20th of October, I saw Hankey. I described the state of stalemate, approximating
> to a species of siege warfare, which had developed on the Western Front and seemed
> likely to become permanent. I expounded my view that the chief difficulty we should
> encounter in our attempts to thrust the Germans out of France and Belgium would be
> their employment of machine-guns and wire. I reminded him of the Holt Caterpillar
> Tractor – the existence of which I had reported to him in July.
>
> Coming down to "brass tacks", and the immediate practical aspect of the question,
> I propounded my solution and suggested that some of these tractors, if there were none
> then in England, should be obtained and modified, or redesigned, and converted into
> fighting machines, such as I contemplated. I found him a sympathetic listener. He was
> quick to appreciate the implications of a stalemate and my suggestion for dealing with
> it. We arranged that I should make a report to Lord Kitchener, if I saw him, and take

---

33 Swinton, *Eyewitness*, p 79.
34 Hankey had formerly served as a captain in the Royal Marine Artillery. In 1908, he was appointed
    Naval Assistant Secretary to the CID and, on retiring from the Royal Marines, became a civil servant.
    In 1912, he was appointed Secretary to the CID, a position that he would hold for 26 years. When
    David Lloyd George became Prime Minister, Hankey was appointed Secretary to the Imperial War
    Cabinet. He proved so effective that, when the full Cabinet was restored in 1919, the secretariat was
    retained and Hankey served as its Secretary for 19 years.

up the idea at GHQ when I returned to France, and that he [Hankey] also should put the idea before the Secretary of State for War.

The following day, Swinton met the Prime Minister, H.H. Asquith, whom he had seen regularly as Assistant Military Secretary to the CID. Swinton was one of the first officers known to Asquith to have returned from the Front, and Asquith expressed a wish to see him. Swinton explained the difficulties under which the Allies were fighting but decided not to broach the concept of AFVs until he had briefed Kitchener.[35] Swinton was due to see the Secretary of State for War the next day but this meeting was cancelled as Kitchener had a pressing appointment. Swinton was, however, able to meet Hankey over lunch and explained his proposal in outline. Also present at the lunchtime meeting on 21 October was Capt Tom Tulloch who, a few years previously, had an idea to use a steam-driven machine of a very much larger type based on the Hornsby chain track tractor.[36] Hankey, who made further investigations in concert with Tulloch, approached Kitchener without success.[37]

However, Hankey was not deterred and decided to put the matter to the War Council. This was a newly-formed organisation, which was assuming the functions of the CID and,

Hornsby steam chain track tractor. (TMA)

35   Author's note: To have done otherwise would have been unprofessional and could have wrecked Swinton's career.
36   Swinton, *Eyewitness*, pp. 91–92.
37   Tulloch would continue to play a key advisory role during the development of tanks and was Mentioned in Despatches in January 1917.

as secretary of both, Hankey believed it was his duty was to bring to the notice of the Prime Minister any matter which he considered of sufficient importance for his attention.

Understanding the ways in which the War was developing was one of the things Hankey thought all-important. In late December, he wrote a paper entitled 'Memorandum on Methods of Attack' for consideration by the War Council. He noted the deadlock on the Western Front and suggested that there were two ways of circumventing this situation; either attack elsewhere or to devise some special means for overcoming it.[38] Regarding the latter, Hankey suggested that 'numbers of large heavy rollers, themselves bullet-proof, propelled from behind by motor-engines, geared very low, the driving wheel fitted with "caterpillar" driving gear to grip the ground, the driver's seat armoured, and with a Maxim gun fitted.[39] The object of this device would be to roll down barbed wire by sheer weight, to give some cover to men creeping up behind, and to support the advance with machine-gun fire.' Hankey also suggested that a small expert committee be formed to deal with the existing state of affairs. He sent the memorandum to Asquith on 1 January, who sent it on to Kitchener and Churchill for comment.

Winston Churchill. (TMA)

Hankey's paper did not attract immediate support from the WO but Swinton, who was on leave that month, managed to speak to Maj Gen George Scott-Moncrieff, the Director of Fortifications and Works and a brother RE Officer.[40] Scott-Moncrieff was sympathetic and wrote the next day to the Master General of the Ordnance (MGO), Maj Gen Stanley von Donop.[41] A WO committee, which included the

---

38 Churchill, who read the paper, was possibly thinking along these lines when he suggested the British should intervene on the Eastern Front, a suggestion which ultimately led to the Royal Navy trying to force the narrows at Gallipoli and the subsequent ill-fated land campaign which achieved nothing but death and misery.

39 A design of a medium machine-gun; it was also used to describe the Vickers which used the same design.

40 Scott-Moncrieff was the senior RE officer by appointment at the WO, and also the appropriate person to explore any proposal dealing with a mechanical fighting device for trench warfare.

41 von Donop, who was commissioned in the RA, held this post from 1913–16. He was responsible for all British artillery, engineers, fortifications, military supplies, transport, field hospitals and allied matters,

Director of Artillery,[42] and the Assistant Director of Transport,[43] was formed to investigate options.[44]

Churchill immediately endorsed Hankey's paper on 5 January:

> The present war has revolutionised all military theories about the field of fire. The power of the rifle is so great that 100 yards is held sufficient to stop any rush, and in order to avoid the severity of the artillery, trenches are often dug on the reverse slope of positions or a short distance in the rear of villages, woods and other obstacles. The consequence is that war has become a short-range instead of a long-range war as was expected and opposing trenches get ever closer together for mutual safety from each other's artillery fire.
>
> The question to be solved is not, therefore, the long attack over a prepared glacis of former times, but the actual getting across 100 or 200 yards of open space and wire entanglements. All this was apparent more than two months ago but no steps have been taken and no preparations made.
>
> It would be quite easy in a short time to fit up a number of steam tractors with small, armoured shelters in which men and machine-guns could be placed, which would be bullet proof. Used at night, they would not be affected by artillery to any extent. The caterpillar system would enable trench to be crossed quite easily, and the weight of the machine would destroy all wire entanglements. Forty or fifty of these engines, prepared secretly and brought into position at nightfall, could advance quite certainly into the enemy's trenches, smashing away all the obstructions, sweeping the obstructions with machine-gun fire, and with grenades thrown out of the top. They would then make so many *points d'appuis* for the British supporting infantry to rush forward and rally on them. They can then move forward to attack the second line of trenches.[45]

Walter Wilson. (TMA)

but not subordinate to the CIGS.

42   Gen Herbert Guthrie-Smith.

43   Col Henry Holden, a retired RA officer, who had designed the first motorcycle with a four cylinder 1,000cc engine, the race track at Brooklands and was a fellow of the Royal Society.

44   Liddell Hart, *Tank Corps in the Great War*, Vol. I, p. 26.

45   AG Stern, *Tanks 1914–1918 – The Logbook of a Pioneer* (Uckfield: Naval and Military Press (N&MP) facsimile 2009), pp. 11–12.

Churchill started to use serving officers to undertake investigations of available equipment, which might be modified to achieve the requirement. Amongst those were Capt Murray Sueter RN,[46] Flight Commander Thomas Hetherington RN,[47] and Lieutenant (Lt) Walter Wilson RN,[48] who would have vital a role in the development of the new AFVs.

Tritton Trench Crosser. (TMA)

46 In 1909, Sueter had supervised the construction of the first RN airship *Mayfly*. He was appointed director of the Aircraft Department at the Admiralty on its formation in 1912 and had overseen the formation of the RNAS. In 1914, had been a strong supporter of the use of armoured cars within the RNAS.

47 Hetherington had been commissioned in 18th Hussars, representing the army in equestrian championships. After an accident made it difficult for him to compete, Hetherington learned to fly and then served with No 1 Squadron RFC. In July 1914, he was seconded to the RNAS and served with Samson in Belgium. In October 1914, he was placed in command of five armoured cars and, when the cars returned to the UK, Hetherington became the divisional transport officer for an armoured car battalion being formed at Wormwood Scrubs.

48 Wilson was a naval cadet on HMS *Britannia* then gained a first class degree in mechanical sciences at King's College Cambridge. An engineer and inventor, he founded the Wilson Pilcher company in 1901 which manufactured motor cars which featured an epicyclic gearbox designed by Wilson, the first of its type. He was commissioned into the RNAS on the outbreak of war and served with the Armoured Car Division (ACD).

On 12 January, Hetherington examined the Diplock caterpillar system for suitability and the next day, he inspected two Holt tractors at Aldershot.[49] On 18 January, building on Hankey's proposals, Churchill wrote to Sueter, giving direction for trials of a design of rollers to drive along a line of trenches, flattening them and burying defenders. The Admiralty previously had engaged in obtaining land-based equipment for its perceived needs, without reference to the WO. For example, in 1914, they had purchased some 15-inch howitzers, manufactured by the Coventry Ordnance Works, which were to be used by RM Artillery (RMA) batteries in the ground role.[50] These were to be towed by heavy wheeled tractors, of an existing design using the 105 bhp Daimler Knight engine, built at the Wellington Foundry by Fosters and Co. of Lincoln.

On 13 February, Churchill approved the concept of building an experimental bridge-laying tractor, which was to be based on the Fosters heavy tractor. The same day, at Shoeburyness, there was an army trial of a Holt tractor drawing a trailer carrying 5,000 pounds of sandbags to represent the weight of armour and armament, etcetera. Whilst the tractor was able to drag the trailer over a course on trenches, barbed wire and other obstacles such as entanglements, Holden reported to Scott-Moncrieff that the result was unsatisfactory.[51]

The Landships Committee

On 16 February 1916, a Pedrail 1-ton machine was demonstrated to Churchill on Horse Guards Parade. Four days later, Churchill directed the establishment of a committee within the Admiralty. The Director of Naval Construction, Tennyson D'Eyncourt, was appointed as its chairman and, at its first meeting on 24 February, its first task was to consider a proposal by Hetherington to build an armoured Landship. This enormous tricycle would weigh 300 tons and mount three turrets, each containing a pair of 4-inch guns. The crew would be protected by 3-inch armour whilst the wheels would be 40 feet in diameter and have a tread 13 feet wide. The

Tennyson d'Eyncourt. (TMA)

---

49   Bramah Diplock was an English inventor who invented the pedrail wheel in 1903. Fitted to an agricultural tractor, the pedrail used feet fitted to the driving wheels to reduce the ground pressure and improve cross country mobility. He also designed the pedrail chain-track, a type of caterpillar track, in 1910.
50   The howitzers were later transferred to RA batteries and the tractors to the ASC.
51   W. Miles, *Official History of the Great War Military Operations France and Belgium 1916*, Vol. 2 (referred to hereafter *OHGW*), p. 246.

Landship would have an overall length of 100 feet, be 80 feet wide and have an overall height of 46 feet. Hetherington was serious when he stated that the machine should have been more heavily armoured and armed but considerations of weight and the time of building 'have resulted in the proposal being reduced to the comparatively moderate one described above.'[52] Two days later, the MGO sent a minute to the Admiralty Landships Committee stating that the project was not to be taken forward unless a design produced by a competent person was submitted![53]

The committee next considered a proposal by the Pedrail Transport Company of Fulham that they supply twelve machines utilising the design seen by Churchill at Horse Guards on 16 February. It was agreed that a design should be undertaken by Col Evelyn Crompton and built by the Metropolitan Carriage Wagon and Finance Company Limited (known hereafter as Metropolitan) at their works in Birmingham.[54] This was endorsed by Churchill on 28 March who also directed that twelve Big Wheel Landships (with 16 feet diameter wheels) be built by Fosters; an initial contract for the design by their managing director William Tritton having been let on 15 March.[55]

William Tritton. (TMA)

Neuve Chapelle Offensive

Churchill's drive to produce such AFVs was probably reinforced by the failure of the British attack at Neuve Chapelle on 10–13 March. This was the first deliberately planned offensive by the BEF in 1915, the aim of which was to break through a German salient at the village, capture Aubers Ridge and ultimately capture the major German railhead at Lille. The attack was undertaken by the First Army, under Haig, using troops from I (Indian) Corps and IV Corps commanded by Rawlinson. The frontline German positions at Neuve Chapelle were constructed of four-feet-high breastworks, with three-feet-deep trenches to the rear – this being necessary due to the high water table. The RFC had achieved local dominance

---

52 Stern, *Tanks 1914–1918*, pp. 10 and 11.
53 Scott-Moncrieff had already requested advice from the WO Directorate of Transport about the availability of such a designer but none was known.
54 Crompton was an electrical engineer, inventor and high successful industrialist. Whilst still at school, he designed and built a road-going steam tractor. He then served with the Rifle Brigade from 1865 to 1875 and, during the Boer War, commanded a detachment of Electrical Engineers which operated searchlights designed to deter attacks on towns by the Boers. He was subsequently Mentioned in Despatches, appointed a Companion of the Bath, and awarded the honorary rank of colonel.
55 Stern, *Tanks 1914-1918*, pp. 17–18.

and started attacks on key railway positions and German reserve units. A 30-minute hurricane bombardment succeeded in destroying the protective barbed wire whilst twelve batteries of 4.5-inch and 6-inch howitzers targeted the German defences.

The assault was initially successful with Garhwal Brigade breaking into the German frontline positions and the village of Neuve Chapelle being captured. However, this success could not be exploited. Sir John French later told Kitchener that fatigue and shortage of artillery ammunition caused the attack to be halted. The initial attack used up 30 percent of the available ammunition in 1st Army, which was an unsustainable rate, and whilst a subsequent German counter-attack on 12 March was foiled, it was at the expense of most of the 1st Army's remaining artillery ammunition. British and Indian losses were over 12,200 of the 40,000 men committed to the attack; the Germans suffered about 8,000 casualties. On 20 March, Crompton, Hetherington, and Lt Albert Stern were deployed to France in order to measure the German defences in order to support their ongoing design work.[56] According to Swinton:

And so, it came about that when in the Spring of 1915, three officers, two in naval uniforms, were discovered nosing about behind the British front on some vague mission. Their presence was not welcomed, and they were ordered out of the zone of operations. It needed only their arrest as spies – which was in fact threatened – to have completed the farce.[57]

Their actions were, however, commendable as only the Landships Committee was actively working on AFV development. Whilst Swinton was privately working on a similar concept, there was no active examination at HQ BEF to provide an army response to the fatally successful German system of defence in depth, barbed wire, and mass use of machine-guns.

Albert Stern. (TMA)

56   Bertie Stern, who was a 36-year-old banker, was commissioned into the RNAS in December 1914. He had applied to join the army on the outbreak of the war but was rejected due to a weak ankle resulting from an earlier accident. He had written to Churchill, offering to buy, equip and crew an armoured car for use by one of the RNAS squadrons. As these were being withdrawn from the continent, it was suggested that Stern join the new ACD being formed at Wormwood Scrubs. On arrival, he was tasked to work for Hetherington. He would become the focus for tank production. *Tanks 1914-1918*, pp. 4–5.

57   Swinton, *Eyewitness*, pp. 143 was, in the longer term, more forgiving. 'So far comedy. But behind it was tragedy in which we see again the malicious fate which dogged the inception of the Tanks. At that time, within easy reach of GHQ [where Swinton was located], were three patriotic men thirsting for certain vital information in order to help their country.'

In April, Stern was appointed secretary to the Landships Committee, d'Eyncourt requiring someone to drive the work of the committee forward. The key project was the development of a Landship, capable of carrying a storming party of 50 infantrymen carrying machine-guns and ammunition, the men being protected from small arms fire by armour-plated sides.[58] The vehicle, which was to be 40 feet long, was constructed of two back-to-back machines, powered by Rolls Royce engines, with the tracks being of the Creeping Grip design made in Chicago by the Bullock company. It was to be built by the Metropolitan company, capable being steered from either end and fitted with a means of cutting barbed wire.

Killen Strait tractor fitted with a Delaunay-Belleville armoured body. (TMA)

The team were also trialling the Killen Strait agricultural tractor, which was built in the USA. It was a much lighter vehicle but was fitted, for a while, with a French armoured car body which had been fitted to an RNAS armoured car. Whilst this particular body was open, most had been fitted with a turret mounting a machine-gun. The Committee were also awaiting the completion of the prototype Heavy Tractor Bridge Layer, which was being built by Fosters at Lincoln.[59]

58   Stern, *Tanks 1914–1918*, pp 20–21. The initial plan was the infantry should stand but this was later changed to allow them to sit which had advantage of reducing the height of the vehicle. The thickness of the armour plate was also increased from 8 mm to 12 mm.
59   Also known as Tritton's Trench Crosser. See above photograph.

The Need for 'Armoured Machine-gun Destroyers'

The failure of two British attacks in May, at Aubers Ridge and Festubert, the latter being undertaken in concert with the French as part of the Second Battle of Artois, reinforced in Swinton's mind the need for action by the GHQ staff.[60] He had observed the attack at Aubers Ridge and, visiting a dressing station after the attack failed:

> Heard the same story from all those who were able to speak. As soon as our short bombardment of the German position – almost entirely with field-gun shrapnel – ceased, our infantry went over the top. As they clambered up, the Germans in their dug-outs, unhurt and hardly shaken by our shrapnel, swarmed up and manned their parapets, at some points standing entirely exposed; and not being under fire themselves, poured a steady hail of bullets into our advancing infantry, their machine-guns firing from emplacements fitted with loop-holes just clear of the ground.
>
> Some of our men got as far as the German wire but, in most cases, our assault was stopped dead on the top of our own parapets or a few yards in front, where the ground was strewn with bodies. A feature of the defence was again the slaughter dealt out by the machine-guns, firing directly and obliquely across no man's land. At a few points, notwithstanding this terrible fire, our infantry did succeed in penetrating into the German first or even second line. But in every instance, they found themselves in worse case than before, being bombed or shot at from every side, and were either driven back or surrounded and cut off. In spite of the most desperate valour, the whole operation was a bloody fiasco.[61]

Swinton was aware that his time to influence staff at GHQ was short; reporters were being invited to France, as part of the formation of a Press Bureau, and his own role as the Official Correspondent would likely soon be over. He therefore drafted a service paper, for submission to the BEF Experimental Committee, which proposed the use of self-propelled, armoured, Machine-gun Destroyers mounted on tracks. On 1 June 1915, Swinton submitted this paper to HQ BEF.[62] The full paper is at Appendix I but Swinton's proposals are so important to the development of AFVs and the formation of the Tank Corps, that the key elements are extracted below:

---

60 The lack of sufficient HE artillery ammunition, first identified by Sir John French after the Battle of Neuve Chapelle in March 1915, became public knowledge as a result of reports in the London *Times*. This, together with the resignation of the First Sea Lord, Admiral Jackie Fisher and Churchill over the failure of the Dardanelles campaign, caused the Asquith government to fall. A coalition government was formed on 25 May which included the former prime minister Arthur Balfour, replacing Churchill as First Lord of the Admiralty, and David Lloyd George being appointed as the first Minister of Munitions. After Kitchener drowned on 5 June 1916, Lloyd George was also appointed Secretary of State for War.

61 Swinton, *Eyewitness*, pp. 112-113.

62 He initially staffed it to Maj Gen George Fowke, then Engineer in Chief (E-in-C) BEF, as he was responsible for Military Works and Defences. In February 1916, Fowke was appointed Adjutant General GHQ BEF, a post he held until the end of the war.

Situation facing the Allied Forces

The Germans, possibly in order to release troops for offensive action on a grand scale elsewhere, have for some time been maintaining their front in France and Belgium with the minimum of men. They have been able to do this because they have fully recognised and exploited the principle that, on the defensive, numbers of men can be replaced to a very large extent by skilfully and scientifically arranged defences and armaments, and by machinery. They possess the knowledge, energy and skills to organise such defences thoroughly and have by now had the time to do it.

By this time, their positions consist of a strong front firing line, of trench or breastworks, backed up by a zone which includes, besides communications, a network of subsidiary supporting trenches and points, such as works and houses, which are held by few men and yet provide a great volume of fire in different directions. Some of these works give fire to the front, others run fore and aft and give lateral fire to left and right against an enemy who may have broken through the front line and seeks to penetrate further. Most are so arranged that, if lost, they can be enfiladed or bombed.

In this maze behind the front, the defenders unless absolutely paralysed and shattered by artillery fire, have all the advantages. For there the attackers, if they should succeed in penetrating find themselves without much artillery support, on strange ground, at close quarters fighting with the defenders who know every inch of the position and have marked every exposed spot, upon which they trained their machine-guns and rifles and shower bombs.

The chief feature in the novelty of the German tactics does not lie either in the preparation of a strip of ground for fighting at a disadvantage, nor in the use of machine-guns, hand-bombs or grenades. It lies in the number of machine-guns employed. And not only this the chief feature of novelty, it is the factor that has done most to make the economy of men practised by the Germans. It is also the chief factor which had rendered abortive our attempts to penetrate their positions.

So far, we have in all offensive effort, been unable with our guns to shatter the German's defensive zone to its full depth, over any considerable length and so blast a path for our advance. The machine-guns have not been neutralised and it is our infantry, either caught in the wire, in the open, or collected in the enemy's trenches, that have had to suffer from the undivided attentions of weapons shooting from protected and concealed positions. We have, so far, been unable to oppose anything on them except the bodies of our assaulting infantrymen.

Machine-guns have caused most of our casualties in the attack and have stopped our offensive efforts. And machine-guns will do the same in future unless we have sufficient artillery and high explosive ammunition to blast a way through the German positions (trenches, wire, trench mortars bombs, gas cylinders, land mines, vitriol throwers and machine-guns inclusive) preparatory to our assault OR we can have recourse to some other means of destroying these weapons or at least on meeting them on equal terms and diverting or neutralising their action so that it is not directed at our infantry.

The first alternative is not at present within our power, though it may be in the future. The second is believed to be possible through the employment of 'Armoured

Machine-gun Destroyers' which will enable us to engage with machine-guns on an equality.

Swinton's answer was to develop such a machine:

These would be petrol tractors on the caterpillar principle, of a type which can travel up to four miles per hour on the flat, can cross a ditch of four feet in width without climbing, can climb in and out of a broader cavity, and can scramble over a breastwork. They should be armoured with hardened steel, proof against the German steel-cored armoured-piercing and reversed bullets and armed with – say – two Maxims and a 2-pounder gun. It is suggested that they be employed as a surprise in an assault on the German position to be carried out on a large scale. To enable the element of surprise to come in these machines should be built at home secretly and *their existence should not be disclosed until all are ready.*[63] There should be no preliminary efforts made with a few machines, the result of which would give the game away.

Preparation for employment. The machines should be brought up to railheads by train or road, and then distributed at night along the front of action. They should be placed in deep pits with ramps leading from the rear and out to the front over our parapet, dug as required behind our front line.

Suggested employment in attack. Say fifty destroyers are available. If they are spaced, say at one hundred yards apart on the average, it will enable a front of about 5,000 yards or about three miles, to be covered. The machines being in position ready, the wire entanglements in front of the hostile trenches will be bombarded and cut early in the night before the assault is intended to take place. After this during the night, nothing should be attempted except occasional outbursts of rifle fire to prevent the Germans from repairing their entanglements. At dawn of the morning fixed for the assault, at a given signal, the destroyers will start. Climbing out of their pits and over the parapet, they will travel across the intervening space straight for the German lines. If this is 200 yards away, they will travel the distance in 2 ½ minutes travelling at a rate of 3 miles per hour. They can tear their way through any entanglement.

Wherever it has been possible beforehand to locate and mark down machine-gun emplacements in the German front line, the destroyers will be steered straight at them, will climb over them and will crush them. At other points they climb the enemy's parapet or trench and halting there will fire at any machine-gun located, with the 2-pounder gun and will enfilade portions of the trenches with their Maxims.

It is thought that the destroyers, even if they do not have by this time actually accounted for the bulk of the defending infantry, will have succeeded in attracting to themselves the attention of the enemy and most of his fire, so that our infantry, who will leave their own trenches and assault, just as the destroyers reach the hostile parapet, will be able to cross the fire-swept zone between the lines practically unscathed. After the destroyers have started out into the open and all surprise is over, our guns should

63   Author's italics.

at once start shelling the enemy's artillery in order to keep down its fire. There will be no need for them to bombard the German trenches.

While our infantry is racing for the enemy's front line, the caterpillars will move on through the German defensive zone shooting left and right as they go, those on the flanks of the section selected for the first assault will turn left and right and proceed along and behind the German defence zone to enable our infantry on either side of the selected section to advance also. The action of their 2-pounder guns will be reserved for the German machine-guns which cannot be rolled over, especially those in houses.

Once through the zone of trenches, the destroyers will proceed forwards, backed up by and supporting the first waves of the assaulting infantry which will be moving forward with them, and followed by the mass of troops forming the main body of the attack.

<u>Employment in defence.</u> In defence the destroyers stationed behind the lines, will move up if the Germans break though at any spot and will act as mobile strong points, which can be driven forward right amongst hostile infantry who have penetrated.

When no general offensive or defensive is going on, their 2-pounder gun can be used as mobile anti-aircraft artillery.

The attack, carried out as suggested, will probably result in the loss of a certain number of destroyers but not many, because the machines will be amongst the defending infantry before the German guns can be warned of their advance.

Many details of design such as contrivances to allow the destroyers to signal back to our infantry, to attract the enemy attention, to repel boarders, etc can be suggested.

Fowke asked Swinton for clarification on the feasibility of building the AFV and to define its key attributes. Five days later, Swinton replied:

It was not strictly accurate to state that is possible to build a machine exactly of the type suggested for the matter has not yet been definitely ascertained by trial. It would be more correct to say that, since tractors are now in existence which so nearly comply with the required conditions, that it is believed it would be possible to construct a locomotive that will do all that is necessary sufficiently well to effect the purpose. On the other hand, the impossibility of producing destroyers of the type requisite will not be established until trials have been made and have all failed. Strictly speaking also, the proposed machine is not a tractor for it will not be designed to draw anything. It will be self-propelling, climbing blockhouse or rifle bullet-proof cupola.

<u>Speed.</u> There is a machine now on the market (the Holt Caterpillar Tractor of which 75 are on order by the WO) which has two speeds and can travel on the top speed of something approaching 4 miles an hour.

The exact maximum rate is not known here, and to be on the safe side, 3 miles an hour was assumed in the calculation for the time required to cross 200 yards. But speed is a question of gearing and there is no reason why a Caterpillar locomotive should not be designed and constructed to travel even faster than 4 miles per hour.

It is believed that the Caterpillar trial at Aldershot (Hornsby-Ackroyd type) some years ago moved at least at 4 miles per hour.

Steering. On dry ground, the Hornsby-Ackroyd type (which is an old one) having a long propelling base or wheel belt, can turn practically on the ground on which they stand through any angle. Such sensitiveness and flexibility of steering is far beyond what would be required of a destroyer. If it is found after experiment that all power of steering is lost in wet weather (which is unlikely), the fact will merely reduce the proportion of days on which the destroyer attack could be attempted. This would vitiate the principle no more than the principle of aviation is vitiated by the fact that there are some days on which aeroplanes cannot fly.

Weight. The destroyer could correspond in size to a large traction engine, boxed in with steel and might resemble in appearance a heavy motor lorry with a caterpillar attachment carrying a large metal tank. The weight of the plate (half inch steel) to enclose a rectangular box 14 feet long, eight feet high, seven feet broad including floor and roof, would be under five tons. If the engine, gear and wheels could be built to weigh not more than ten tons, which would seem probable if steel be used, instead of the inferior metal used in the Holt tractor, which is intended for agricultural purposes and has to be cheap – the total weight of the destroyer without machine-guns, crew, ammunitions, petrol and water would be 15 tons. Fully manned and laden it would be under 16 tons.

The weight would be distributed over two driving belts and would bring far less strain on bridges that some of the weight brought up from the bases to the front by road.

Fowke submitted the initial paper, and Swinton's supplementary answers, to the BEF Experimental Committee; 'a body which by a happy coincidence had just been formed at GHQ for the investigation of the numerous suggestions being put forward from different quarters for new devices which, it was hoped, might help to win the war.'[64] Whilst it was being staffed, Swinton decided to gain as much information on in-service armoured vehicles as he could and visited the RNAS ACD based in Dunkirk. The unit was about to be disbanded but the OC gave Swinton a full demonstration of their capabilities.

The following day, 8 June, Swinton came across a battery of newly developed 8-inch howitzers being towed by Holt Caterpillar tractors:

Proud as was the artillery officer in command of his guns, no less proud was the ASC officer of the transport which, he informed me, consisted of Holt Tractors – the very machines upon which I had for eight months been building castles in the air. It was just time for the midday halt. One tractor was quickly unhooked and made to give an exhibition performance on and off the road, up and down a sloping bank about four feet high, and across a small ditch. I then disclosed the purpose of my questions and invited the transport officer to dine with me that evening. When I went further into the subject, I found that he shared my enthusiasm as to the possibilities of the machines.[65]

---

64   Swinton, *Eyewitness*, p. 138. Swinton knew the chairman of the committee and two of its members with whom he had already discussed his proposals.
65   Swinton, p. 139.

The following day, Swinton took two members of the Experimental Committee to see the tractors and they were most impressed. Swinton also decided to seek the views of an experienced formation commander as to whether a Machine-gun Destroyer would be welcomed and went to see Lord Cavan who was commanding 4th Guards Brigade.[66] As Cavan was away from his headquarters undertaking a recce when Swinton visited, he briefed one of his staff officers and the following day, he received a positive reply from Cavan:

> I welcome any suggestion in this extraordinary war that will help to take an enemy's trench without a cost of 50 per cent of the leading company and 75 per cent of that company's officers, for this is what the present-day assault amounts to, even with every precaution.
>
> To my mind, the complete destruction of wire is the key to success in an attack from trench to trench. I am positive that if any brigade is in trenches at any distance from the enemy, it will take the enemy's trench, given two things:
> (1)   Time to sap or dig near enough to make the assault less than 150 yards.
> (2)   All wire removed. The great and serious trouble is that one cannot tell, especially now in high crops, whether the enemy's wire is cut or not.
> Here comes in your 'Juggernaut'. We know that if five Juggernauts have passed through that the wire is no more. This is a certain saving of hundreds of lives, and a fat legacy to morale. I think it should be possible to pass platoons up actually hanging on to the back of the Juggernaut itself, without waiting for its enfilade fire up and down the hostile trenches, as this is easily overcome by good traverses. What one wants is the path cleared to the enemy's first trench and fire kept down from the second trench and machine-guns in strong points behind.

Cavan was clearly not the only officer to see the potential of Machine-gun Destroyers and Swinton was asked by the Experimental Committee to produce design criteria. His submission on 15 June was, he stated, tentative and subject to modification:

> Speed. Top speed on flat not less than 4 miles per hour. Bottom speed for climbing (Blank) miles per hour.
> Steering. To be capable of turning 90 degrees at top speed on the flat on a radius of twice the length of the machine.
> Reversing. To travel backwards or forwards (equally fast?).
> Climbing. To be capable of crossing backward or forward an earth parapet of 5 feet thick and 5 feet high, having an exterior slope of 1 in 1 and a vertical interior slope.
> Bridging. All gaps of up to 5 feet in length to be bridged directly without dipping into them. All Gaps above 5 feet to be climbed up to a height of 5 feet with vertical sides.
> Radius of action. To carry petrol and water for 20 miles.
> Capacity. Crew and armament to carry 10 men, two machine-guns and one quick firing gun.

---

66   Swinton, *Eyewitness*, pp. 144 and 145. Cavan commanded the brigade at the Battle of Festubert. In January 1916, he was appointed GOC XIV Corps which was heavily engaged on the Somme in 1916 and which was allocated 18 tanks for the Battle of Courcelette on 15 September – see Chapter 6.

<u>Weight.</u> Total weight of the destroyer loaded with armour, petrol, oil, ammunition and crew to be such and distributed on tracks, as not to bring a great strain than on bridges that that produced by 14 tons on a single axle with a pair of wheels. The weight of armour, armament, ammunition and crew may be taken at 8 tons.

Swinton's proposal was approved by the GHQ Experimental Committee, and on 22 June, Sir John French wrote a letter to the WO, enclosing the three papers (see Appendix I) concluding the letter thus:

> There appears to be considerable tactical value in this proposal, which adapts the peculiar qualifications of the caterpillar mode of traction to the transport of a species of armoured turrets across cultivated and uneven ground, especially in connexion with the trench warfare which is the feature of the present operations; and particularly if the production of these machines would be a surprise to the enemy.
>   As will be seen from the papers, the governing factors are:
>   (1) Whether such machines are available and can be adapted?
>   (2) If not available, can they be made?
>   (3) What would be the weight and over-all dimensions?
> It is felt that these points can only be decided by reference to manufacturers of such machines. It is therefore requested that this proposal may be placed in secret before some experienced firm for report on these points.

Sir John offered to send Swinton back to London to provide advice to the WO staff on the proposal should it prove useful. On the evening of 18 July, having returned from another battlefield visit and whilst drafting his 103rd *Eyewitness* press article, Swinton was summoned by French. The C-in-C had been requested by Asquith to release Swinton and asked for the reason – Swinton answered that it could only be to explain the details of the proposed Machine-gun Destroyer.

The next morning Swinton returned to London to find Hankey had requested that he be appointed Secretary of the Dardanelles Committee of the Cabinet, whilst Hankey was visiting that Theatre of Operations. Swinton was able to use Hankey's absence to read himself into the post and also to contact key politicians, especially following the changes which resulted from Churchill's removal from his appointment at the Admiralty.[67] He also contacted d'Eyncourt whom he met on 29 July and briefed him on Machine-gun Destroyers. The next day, at d'Eyncourt's suggestion, Stern visited Swinton and briefed him on the work of the Landship committee and its recent progress.

Landship Development

On 30 June, the *Killen Strait* machine had been demonstrated to Lloyd George, Churchill, D'Eyncourt, the Director-General of Munitions Supply Sir Frederick Black, Scott-Moncrieff and the Director of Army Staff Duties (DASD) Colonel Wilkinson Bird. Although the machine

---

67   Balfour had replaced Churchill as First Lord of the Admiralty in May 1915. Churchill remained in the Cabinet as Chancellor for the Duchy of Lancaster until November 1915 when he resigned.

was shown to be unsuitable, Lloyd George agreed to take over the responsibility for the supply of Landships once a satisfactory machine had been produced. It was also on this date that the Landships Committee first received definite instructions as to the direction in which it should work. Until then, 'it had been groping about in the dark, concentrating its efforts chiefly on the production of a vehicle to carry a large number of infantrymen in an armoured cabin rather than on an engine manned by a minimum fighting crew to destroy machine-guns.'[68]

Killen Strait tractor under trial on 30 June 1915. (TMA)

On 24 July, Tritton was tasked to build a vehicle consisting of an armoured body with a turret, powered by the Daimler Knight 105 bhp engine as fitted to the Fosters heavy-wheeled tractors, and driven by Creeping Grip tracks. This was the Tritton or Lincoln No. 1 machine – now referred to as *Little Willie*. On 4 August, Tritton and Wilson were briefed further. The original Bullock tracks were to be extended to nine feet long and Fosters were requested to produce the prototype in three weeks. The next day, Tritton attended a trial of the Bullock tracks, accepted that their use was feasible, and design work started.

On 26 August, having received an update on progress, Stern requested Tritton and Wilson also develop an AFV capable of crossing a trench eight feet wide with a parapet four feet six inches high.[69] This design work for this machine, now known as *Mother*, started although work continued on *Little Willie* with construction beginning on 28 August.

68   Swinton, *Eyewitness*, p. 166.
69   The increased specification came as a result of input from Swinton.

Little Willie, fitted with a turret, under construction at Lincoln. (TMA)

That same day, Swinton wrote a memorandum to Asquith concerning the development of the new AFVs which was being undertaken by three government departments without any agreed allocation of responsibilities. Swinton proposed that an inter-department conference be held to consider future action and the Prime Minster immediately agreed. This conference occurred two days later. Since the subject was one which most concerned the army, the chair was offered to Scott-Moncrieff. The meeting constituted an important step, for it was the first occasion on which the question was discussed round a table, as it were on neutral ground, by all the departments interested. Those attending agreed that the Admiralty should continue to experiment and design, taking its instructions as to the requirements from the WO, and when this work had been carried sufficiently far, it was to be handed over to the Ministry of Munitions. As a result, the efforts of all three departments would be on a clearly defined and agreed basis and continued without misunderstanding.[70]

On 3 September, having seen Tritton and Wilson's proposal for *Mother's* design, Stern wrote to Fosters asking that these be developed. On 8 September, *Little Willie* travelled under her

70   Swinton, *Eyewitness*, pp. 169–70.

Little Willie, fitted with Bullock tracks, at trials. (TMA)

own power for the first time and the next day, moved into the Fosters Yard. On 10 September, *Little Willie* undertook a field trial at Cross O'Cliff on Lincoln South Common. That same day, Swinton, who was at Lincoln, wrote to Major Guest, the secretary of the GHQ Experimental Committee, stating 'the naval people are pressing on the first example caterpillar [and] have succeeded in making an animal which will cross [a gap of] 4 feet 6 inches and turn on its own axis.'

In what is likely to have been in response, GHQ confirmed the operating requirement to the CID the next day, in part stemming from Swinton's proposals from June 1915 but requiring an increased the gap crossing capability. GHQ also confirmed that:

1.   The object of the caterpillar cruiser or armoured fort is required for employment in considerable numbers in conjunction with or as an incident in a large and general attack by infantry against an extended front.

2.   As a general principle, it is desirable to have a large number of small cruisers rather than a smaller number of large ones.

3.   The armour must be proof against concentrated rifle and machine-gun fire but not proof against artillery fire. The whole cruiser should be enclosed in armour.

4.   The tactical object of the cruiser is to attack; its armament should include a gun with reasonable accuracy up to a range of 1,000 yards and at least two Lewis guns which can be fired from loopholes to flank and rear.[71]

71   Author's note: This is the first reference to Lewis guns being fitted to tanks which I have discovered.

5.   The crew is to consist of six men: two for the gun, one for each Lewis gun and two drivers.

6.   The caterpillar must be capable of crossing craters produced by the explosion of high explosive shells, such craters being of 12 feet in diameter [and] six feet deep with sloping side; of crossing an extended width of barbed wire entanglements; and of spanning hostile trenches with perpendicular side width of 4 feet in breadth,

7.   The cruisers should be capable of moving at a rate of at least 2 ½ miles per hour over broken ground and have a range of action of not less than six hours consecutive movement.

8.   The wheels of the cruiser should either be of the 'Pedrail' or the Caterpillar system, whichever is most suitable for crossing marshy or slippery ground.

On Sunday 19 September, *Little Willie* was driven to Burton Park, five miles north of Wellington Foundry, for a trial which was observed by d'Eyncourt, Swinton, members of the Landships Committee as well as large numbers of Fosters' employees and their wives.[72] The machine worked well but failed to cross the trench obstacle. Weaknesses were identified in the Bullock tracks while trying to move a vehicle of 16 tons.

Swinton and the Admiralty staff were then taken back to the Fosters factory and were shown a full size wooden mock-up of *Mother*. Swinton later described his reaction:

> Although an engineer, it took me some minutes to size the thing up at such close range. Its most striking features were its curious rhomboidal, or lozenge, shape, its upturned nose, and the fact that its caterpillar tracks were led right round the hull instead of being entirely below it. These were the *clou* of the design and the essential and original characteristics of the machine and had been introduced to enable it to surmount or climb the stipulated vertical height of five feet. Its great length would also permit it to cross any gap up to nine feet in width. Various other details into which I need not here enter were pointed out by the designers, whom I congratulated heartily on a stupendous achievement.
>
> Unwieldy as this contrivance appeared in the confined space in which it was housed, it promised to solve the most difficult problems involved – the power to climb and the ability to span broad trenches; and I felt that I saw in front of me – though only in wood – the actual embodiment of my ideas and the fulfilment of my specification. Other questions, such as those of armament and armouring, were comparatively simple matters, which could be settled once the main design had been achieved.[73]

On 22 September, having tried to use a track made of balata which failed, Tritton developed a track constructed made of riveted pressed-steel plates, fitted to a newly designed frame, which was successful.[74] Three days later, the need for a Machine-gun Destroyer was, sadly, once

---

72   Swinton, who attended the trial, was astonished by the lax security at the trial. He had the same difficulty at the initial trial of *Mother* at Hatfield. See Chapter 3.

73   Swinton, *Eyewitness*, p. 172.

74   *Balata* is a rubberised belt which was extensively used in cotton and other factories for powering machinery. It was not however suitable for use in AFV tracks. The invention of the pressed steel plate

again demonstrated on the opening day of the Loos offensive. The Germans had significantly improved their defensive lines and, although there was some success on the first day, there was a dreadful loss of life amongst the six divisions involved.

On 29 September, the inter-departmental committee met again in London, this time with representatives from GHQ, the MGO and the QMG staff from the WO and from Fosters; Swinton, as the representative of the CID, was secretary. That afternoon, the committee reviewed the wooden mock-up of *Mother* which had been sent by Fosters to Wembley Park.

The design caused some discussion, the principal issue being the main and secondary armaments. It was agreed that *Mother* would be equipped with a 6-pounder Quick Firing gun (QF) in a sponson on each side, one machine-gun and four automatic rifles. The Naval 6-pounder was suggested, against the originally proposed 2½-inch mountain gun, not just because this also fired also a sufficiently heavy shell to destroy machine-gun emplacements, but more importantly, there was a shortage of mountain guns. The Admiralty representatives indicated they could provide one hundred 6-pounders by June 1916. The following day, Tritton was tasked by Stern to construct *Mother*, using steel armour plate, whilst continuing work on *Little Willie* with its new improved tracks. The building of *Mother* started on 28 October, and on 22 November, the first half of the tracks for *Little Willie* were complete.

All change

Sir John French's command of the BEF had been the subject of criticism by Kitchener and others, since the summer. After the C-in-C's failure to release the reserve corps and reinforce the initial successes of the Battle of Loos, Asquith demanded and received Sir John's resignation with the recommendation that he be replaced by his COS, General 'Wully' Robertson. Asquith however decided that Haig should succeed Sir John and wrote to him on 10 December appointing him C-in-C BEF. In Whitehall, as a follow-up to the failure of the Dardanelles, Churchill resigned from the cabinet the following day and sought command of an infantry battalion in France. Churchill had just updated his paper written in January 1915, now called 'Variations of the Offensive' which he submitted to Sir John French on 3 December. The outgoing C-in-C BEF did not however take any action as he had been appointed C-in-C Home Forces in the New Year. General Archibald Murray, who had been appointed CIGS in September 1915, was also on the move. He also left his post in December, to take command of the Egyptian Expeditionary Force (EEF) in January 1916, Murray being replaced as CIGS by Robertson on 23 December.

'How the tank got its name'

On 3 December, *Little Willie* was fitted with the steel tracks and improved frame and, five days later, she was trialled at Burton Park. This was successful although, due to the design, the machine could not meet the GHQ operational requirements. By the middle of December, knowing that *Mother* was also approaching completion, Swinton set up another meeting of the inter-departmental committee to be held on 24 December.

---

track design, which would be used on all British tanks in the Great War was announced in a telegram to the Admiralty: 'New arrival by Tritton out of pressed plate STOP Light in weight but very strong STOP All doing well thank you STOP Proud parents.'

Little Willie fitted with Tritton tracks at Burton Park. (TMA)

The Christmas Eve meeting was held in the CID's offices and its business was 'the present and future situation on the provision of Caterpillar Machine-gun Destroyers or Landships.'[75] During the discussions, the Admiralty confirmed they would supply one hundred 6-pounder guns when and if demanded by the WO. However, d'Eyncourt stated that the Admiralty would relinquish responsibility for developmental work once *Mother* had been handed over by Fosters and it was unwilling to be responsible for the delivery of other machines. The Ministry of Munitions also refused to be responsible for supply.

It was therefore agreed that, should the Army wish to introduce AFVs, a new executive supply committee should be established with the finance and authority to place an initial order for 50 machines.[76] It was also agreed that the WO would take steps to establish a force of 75 officers and 750 other ranks (OR) when they demanded the machines.

Finally, as secretary of the inter-departmental committee, Swinton was instructed to find a suitable name to replace 'Landship' or 'Land cruiser' which gave away the whole secret of AFV development. That evening, whilst drafting the record of the meeting, Swinton discussed with his colleague, Lieutenant-Colonel Dally Jones, words which might be substituted:

> The structure of the machine in its early stages being boxlike, some term conveying the idea of a box or container seemed appropriate. We rejected in turn 'container', 'receptacle', 'reservoir' and 'cistern'. The monosyllable 'Tank' appealed as being likely to catch on and be memorable.

75   Swinton issued a position paper on the issue dated 17 December. See *Eyewitness*, pp. 314–318.
76   Author's note: The number of machines appear to be directly related to the number of available 6-pounder guns.

That night, in the draft report of the conference, Tank was employed in its new sense for the first time. And thus, on Christmas Eve 1915, was given a new significance to a simple little English word, which, nine months later was to echo round the world and eventually to become incorporated in the language of every nation possessing a military vocabulary.[77]

77 Swinton, *Eyewitness*, pp. 186–187.

3

First Steps

Christmas Day 1915 at BEF GHQ in Montreuil was, in part, a working day. Having received a letter from Asquith on 10 December, appointing him as C-in-C, Haig took over command nine days later.[1] As part of this process, Haig read himself into the post and, after lunch on 25 December, considered Churchill's 'Memorandum on Variations of the Offensive'. Churchill was now in France undertaking a period of trench warfare indoctrination with the Grenadier Guards prior to assuming command of 6th Royal Scots Fusiliers. He had written the memorandum on 3 December, sending a copy to the WO and GHQ.

One section entitled 'Caterpillars' caught Haig's eye.[2]

> The cutting of the enemy's wire and the general domination of his firing line can be effected by engines of this character. About seventy of these are now nearing completion in England and should be inspected. None should be used until all can be used at once. They should be disposed secretly along the whole attacking front two or three handed yards apart. Ten or fifteen minutes before the assault, these engines should move forward over the best line of the advance open, passing through or across our trenches at prepared points. They are capable of traversing any ordinary obstacles, ditch, breastwork or trench. They carry two or three Maxim [machine-guns] each and can be fitted with flame apparatus. Nothing but a direct hit from a field gun will stop them. On reaching the enemy's [barbed] wire, they turn either right or left and run down parallel to the enemy's trench, sweeping his parapet with their fire, and crushing and cutting the barbed wire in lanes and in a slight serpentine course. Whilst doing this the Caterpillars will be so close to the enemy's line that they will be immune from his artillery. Through the gaps thus made, the shield bearing infantry will advance. If artillery is used to cut wire, the direction and imminence of the attack is proclaimed several days beforehand. But by this method, the assault follows the wire-cutting

---

1   Gary Sheffield provides an excellent description of Haig's takeover at GHQ, and his method of command, in *The Chief* (London: Aurum, 2011) pp. 131–141.
2   A second version was circulated on 7 January. See Pidgeon. *Tanks at Flers* (Chobham: Fairmile, 1996) p. 21.

almost immediately before any reinforcements can be brought up by the enemy or any special defensive measures taken.[3]

Pidgeon notes that, as Churchill was serving in France, he was unaware of the most recent progress in England. Certainly, the description of its weapons is different from those of the Mark I prototypes and the total of 75 seems more related to the numbers of the American Holt Caterpillar tractors purchased for the movement of artillery and combat supplies.[4] However, Haig was sufficiently struck by the concept to annotate the paper 'What are caterpillars?' His question was passed to the GHQ Operations Branch and one of its staff officers was tasked to investigate: his name was Hugh Elles.

Elles was, like Swinton, an RE officer. The younger son of Lt Gen Edmond Elles, Hugh Elles was born in India on 27 April 1880. Like Haig, Elles was educated at Clifton College before entering the Royal Military Academy (RMA) at Woolwich for initial officer training. He was gazetted second lieutenant in June 1899 and saw service in South Africa during the later stages of the Second Anglo-Boer War. After twelve years' service of regimental duty, Elles was trained at the Army Staff College in Camberley and then appointed DAQMG [SO3 G4] at HQ 4th Division. Deploying to France with the BEF, Elles was present at the Battle of Le Cateau, then took part in the Retreat to the Marne and the Advance to the Aisne. In March 1915, he was appointed Brigade-Major (COS) of 10th Infantry Brigade, which was part of 4th Division. Elles took part in the Second Battle of Ypres and was wounded during the division's highly effective counter-attack on 25 April. In August 1915, Elles had been selected by Robertson, then Sub-Chief [COS] HQ BEF, as one of three original General Staff Officers (GSO) II in the Operations Section. Known as the 'creche', which probably indicates they were being groomed for advancement, the officers' role was to maintain direct liaison with the frontline.[5]

Hugh Elles. (TMA)

---

3   The full extract is reproduced at Appendix 6 to the *Tanks at Flers*.
4   The inter-departmental committee recommendation that an initial order of 50 tanks had only been made the day before and it had not yet been approved.
5   Obituary, *The Times*, July 1945.

Having been tasked to investigate the Caterpillars, Elles met Churchill at St Omer. After he learned more of the background behind the paper, Elles then went to London where he visited the WO and learnt the state of play. No doubt assisted by Swinton, he then visited the Fosters factory at Lincoln, seeing *Little Willie* and *Mother*. The latter was in the final stages of being built in the erecting shed at the Wellington Foundry. Elles then returned to Montreuil and provided Haig with a concise report, a photograph of *Little Willie*, a sketch of *Mother*, and news that the latter was to shortly be trialled at Hatfield House.[6]

Mother at Burton Park near Lincoln. (TMA)

Mother first moved under her own power into the Fosters yard on Friday 7 January.[7] In the process, several track plates broke but these were quickly replaced. On 12 January, *Mother* successfully climbed several heaps of pig iron and metal scraps in the yard. Two days later, she was driven to the nearby Poppleton's Field and undertook a series of manoeuvres including crossing a simulated trench – she returned without incident.[8] Tritton informed d'Eyncourt of the success so a further trial was arranged. For this, the Directorate of Naval Construction obtained some 6-pounder, armour-piercing, solid short ammunition for *Mother*'s main armament, which was

6   Christy Campbell, *Band of Brigands* (London: Harper, 2007), p. 98.
7   John Glanfield, *Devil's Chariots* (Stroud: Sutton, 2001), p. 125. Hetherington, Stern, Wilson and Lt Kenneth Symes, who was the RNAS armour plate expert, all drove *Mother* at Burton Park that day.
8   Location details provided by Chris Gresham of the Friends of the Lincoln Tank research group.

taken to Lincoln by Stern and Hetherington on Wednesday 19 January.[9] That night, the Mark I prototype drove five miles, under the cover of darkness and a tarpaulin, to Burton Park.[10] Here, *Mother* undertook a series of manoeuvres, including climbing, traversing and descending slopes, as well as undertaking a satisfactory live firing practice with her main armament.

Mother with her parents (right to left) Tritton, Hetherington, Wilson and Swinton. (TMA)

Kitchener had demanded a field trial of the prototype tank once it had been manufactured. Having read Swinton's report on the CID meeting held on 24 December, he wrote, 'As soon as a machine can be produced, the first thing the Secretary of State for War considers necessary would be to test its practical utility under field conditions: without such a test we may be wasting material and men uselessly.'[11] The Naval Construction staff arranged access to the grounds of Hatfield House for the demonstration.[12] Hatfield had the advantage of being only 25 miles up the Great North Road from Westminster and therefore easily accessible to ministers and key staff based in London. The trial location was also within a mile of Hatfield Railway Station where the two prototype AFVs could be offloaded at night and driven quietly to the trial location.

9   Stern, *Tanks 1914-1918*, p. 47.
10   Distance calculated by Chris Gresham.
11   Swinton, *Eyewitness*, p. 187.
12   Hatfield House is the ancestral home of the Cecil family. It was occupied by James Gascoyne-Cecil, 4th Marquess of Salisbury, a former MP, Cabinet Minister and member of the House of Lords, who had previously served under Balfour.

Mother proves herself at Hatfield Park

The trial called for *Mother* to cross a simulated section of British frontline trench, then negotiate no man's land complete with shell craters, and the latest design of German trench system which was protected by a barbed wire entanglement. The dimensions were obtained by examining captured German trenches near Loos. One of the problems in building the trial course was the construction of shell craters as these required the use of explosives to produce the associated loose spoil; the sound of the explosion being difficult to pass off with the town of Hatfield being within a mile of the test site. The middle of no man's land also contained a swamp produced by damming a small stream which ran across the Cecils' golf course. The course was built by members of the Mid Herts Volunteer Infantry to specifications agreed by Hetherington and Swinton.[13] The deception plan, also developed by Swinton and Hetherington, was that the two prototypes, which were covered but otherwise left in plain sight, were new mobile water pumps which were to be used to drain water from the artificial swamp.

The initial trial, which took place on 29 January 1916, was observed by d'Eyncourt, key members of his staff, Hankey, Scott-Moncrieff, as well as the representatives from Fosters and officers of Squadron 20 of the RNAS ACD.[14] *Mother* successfully completed all of the required obstacles with ease including climbing a parapet 66 inches high, the start being in deep mud.[15] All attending were satisfied with demonstration and Sueter, who had first deployed armoured cars in 1914, told Swinton that 3,000 tanks should be ordered at once. The following day, d'Eyncourt wrote to Kitchener confirming the success of the trial and inviting him to inspect the Mark I prototype at Hatfield.

On 2 February, the trial was repeated; this time with an additional trench nine feet wide as required by Kitchener. It was observed by McKenna the Chancellor of the Exchequer, Balfour, Lloyd George, Kitchener, Robertson and key members of the WO and BEF staff.[16] The politicians were enthusiastic and, whilst Kitchener appeared sceptical, the GHQ staff stated they would recommend that Haig should ask for some of the machines.[17] On 8 February, King George V, accompanied by Swinton, also drove to Hatfield and viewed a similar demonstration. Having ridden in the machine, the King expressed his satisfaction.[18]

Formation of the Tank Detachment

Three days later, the WO received a request for 80 tanks from GHQ and Swinton recommended increasing the number to 100, presumably to ensure there was a training fleet. On 12 February

---

13   Details of the trial are shown at Appendix VII of Stern's *Tanks 1914-1918*, pp. 294–298.
14   The full list is shown in Stern, *Tanks 1914-1918*, pp. 49–50.
15   This obstacle was designed to simulate a breastwork or similar construction erected where it was impossible to dig deep trenches due to either a high water table or extremely rocky soil.
16   Stern, *Tanks 1914–1918*, pp. 54-56 provides a list of the majority of those attending. Elles, though not listed, was also present.
17   Swinton, *Eyewitness*, p. 196.
18   King George V became engaged in the tanks' development and patronised the Heavy Section and its successors.

Lloyd George approved the formation of the Tank Supply Committee (TSC)[19] and orders for first 100 tanks, of which 25 were to be built by Fosters and the remainder by Metropolitan.[20] The TSC held its inaugural meeting on Saturday 14 February at the Metropole Building chaired by Brig Gen Frederick Carleton, then Director of Ordnance.[21] Those present included Swinton, Stern and Lt Col Robert Bradley who commanded the Motor Machine-gun (MMG) Training Centre at Bisley.[22]

The TSC recommended that a Tank Detachment be formed and that:

1   The 'Tank Detachment' should form part of the MMGS of the MGC under command of Swinton.[23]
2   Personnel were to be found from men of the MMGS then at Bisley and surplus to requirement.
3   Rates of pay were to be at Field Artillery rates, as for MMGS.
4.   Existing personnel of 20 Squadron RNAS to be given opportunity to leave the Navy and join MMGS at Army pay rates [which were lower than Naval rates]. If they prefer to stay put, the Admiralty will discharge them anyway.

The TSC also proposed that a further tank design be developed which was to be capable of surviving direct fire hits from field guns. Having received an outline requirement from the WO, initial studies commenced.[24]

19   This was the body recommended by the inter-departmental committee meeting on 24 December. Full details of the formation of the TSC and the initial contracts are given in Stern, *Tanks 1914–18*, pp. 63–73.
20   The Metropolitan was the dominant manufacturer in the railway carriage and wagon industry. The split in the order reflects the capacity of the two firms to deliver the machines; the Fosters factory being much smaller than the two factories, owned by Metropolitan, at Oldbury (Sandwell) and Saltley (Birmingham). Metropolitan would become the primary producer of British tanks during the Great War. John Glanfield, *The Devil's Chariots* (Stroud, Sutton Publishing, 2001), p. 132.
21   The building was a former hotel located in Trafalgar Square at the junction of Whitehall and Northumberland Avenue.
22   Bradley had been appointed CO of the MMGS in the autumn of 1914. Initially commissioned into the South Wales Borderers (SWB), Bradley was a pre-war musketry instructor, who attended the 56th Machine-gun Instructors' course at Hythe between 31 October and 20 November prior to assuming his new role. Amongst the students on this instructors' course were four NCOs who would later serve as officers in the HS MGC: George Mann of the Royal Scots (D Company), John Reardon of the Cheshires (B Company), Henry Sayer of the RNAS (A Company) and Charles Weaver Price of the SWB (QM to C and D Companies).
23   Swinton, who was a temporary lieutenant-colonel, was appointed colonel with effect from 19 March 1916 for this role. LG dated 6 September 1916.
24   The WO required that the new tank should be capable of achieving a top speed of 6 mph, able to cross an obstacle 10 to 12 feet wide, with a 6 feet high parapet and a trench 4 feet 6 inches wide on the other side. The tank was to be fitted with the same armament as the Mark I and should be able to resist field-gun fire.

Tank Tactics

On 16 February 1916, Swinton started work in the Metropole Building, with a clerk and an orderly room sergeant; he also obtained an officer and half a stenographer from Stern. Swinton chose to be based in London, rather than at Bisley, to be close to the Admiralty, the WO, the Ministry of Munitions (all members of the TSC) and other bodies with whom he was dealing. Swinton delegated the initial training of the crews to Bradley but no-one either at the WO or at GHQ appears to have determined how the tanks were to be employed. Building on his original paper produced in June 1915, Swinton wrote the first definitive paper on tank tactics, 'Notes on the Employment of Tanks' (see Appendix III).

In his opening remarks, Swinton confirmed that his paper was to stimulate thought at the WO and GHQ as to how the tanks should be employed:

> The measures of preparations, and suitable tactics for Tanks, are not intended to imply that the whole of our offensive operations are to be subordinate to their action. They are put forward as a basis for early discussion of the possibilities and requirements of an entirely new weapon, so that by the time it is ready for employment, everything possible may have been done to ensure its success.

Swinton reaffirmed that:

> '...the Tanks were primarily machine-gun destroyers, employed as an auxiliary to an infantry assault. The weapons of each Tank against personnel will be fire from Hotchkiss machine-gun, experiments being made with special short, barrelled Hotchkiss machine-guns which will give accurate shooting out to a range of 400 yards, and possibly case shot from two 6-pounder quick firing [QF] guns, one on each flank.'

The tank's weapons against hostile machine-guns were:

> '...its own weight [which] in favourable conditions where the enemy machine-guns are situated in the trenches, be brought into play by rolling over the emplacements and crushing them as well as fire from two Hotchkiss 6-pounder QF guns, having arcs of fire from straight ahead to 30 degree abaft the beam or 120 degrees on each side. The shell[s] are common, pointed, base fused, bursting on percussion or graze and filled with black powder or some other low explosive. With the reduced propellent charge used in the guns carried, the projectile will penetrate 2 inches of plate before bursting and will therefore pierce the ordinary German loophole plate and the machine-gun and field gun shield.[25]
>
> Hostile machine-guns, which are impossible or inconvenient to crush, will be attacked by gun fire. It is specially for the purpose of dealing with these weapons ensconced in houses, cellars, amongst ruins, in haystacks, or in other concealed

---

25   Swinton's footnote: 'The Hotchkiss 6-pounder QF is a naval gun which has been adapted as being the only suitable weapon available. A reduced charge is employed because half of the guns being supplied will be of single tube construction and cannot fire full charges.'

positions behind the enemy's front line, where they may not be knocked out by our artillery, and whence they can stop our infantry advance, that Tanks carry guns. Being covered with bullet proof protection, and therefore to a great extent immune from machine-gun fire, they [tanks] can approach sufficiently close to locate the latter and pour in shell at point blank range.

Swinton then stated that:

Although the assumption is that long range fire will not be required for the above purpose, it may happen, owing to the speed of advance hoped to be rendered possible by the neutralisation of the holding power of the enemy's machine-gun fire (which has hitherto been the most important factor in checking the momentum of our assaults) that the tanks, along with our infantry will be able, soon after the start of the offensive, to get within range of the German artillery positions. The 6-pounder guns firing with reduced charges will give accurate shelling up to a range of 2,000 yards and are being fitted with telescopic sights so that full advantage may be taken of a chance of this nature should it appear.

This latter element had not previously been mentioned in his earlier papers or by members of the BEF staff. Swinton also indicated that tanks could be used in the task of exploitation, which hitherto had been a key role of the cavalry.

With regard to the use of tanks, in a defensive role, 'the hardened steel plates (up to 12 millimetres in thickness) with which the tanks are enclosed give complete protection against shrapnel balls and almost complete protection against rifle and machine-gun fire of any nature that is likely to be encountered, and considerable protection against the splinters of high explosive shells that may detonate close by.' Whilst this was true, Swinton was alive to the fact that tanks and the crews were vulnerable to German trench mortars and 77-mm field guns used in the defensive role and armour-piercing bullets, all of which were encountered on their debut during the Battle of Flers–Courcelette on 15 September 1916.

Swinton then addressed the issue of communications with their various headquarters to the rear. He states that:

Experiments are being carried out, therefore, in the following methods of communications which will be alternative in their application:

Equipping a certain proportion of Tanks (say one in every ten) with small wireless telegraphy sets capable of action up to five miles.

Equipping a certain proportion of Tanks (say one of every ten) with apparatus for laying a field telephone cable either on the surface of the ground or possibly buried 12 inches deep. These could be used for communication in clear and would also serve for artillery observation purposes.

Installing a system of visual signalling to the Tanks from the starting point by means of miniature kite balloons. This would be limited in range and would work one way (forwards) only and would serve to transmit a few pre-arranged orders.

Installing a system of signalling from the Tanks by smoke rocket. This would be more limited in scope and would also only work one way (backwards) and would serve to transmit a pre-arranged signal.

Swinton did not, however, consider the methods by which the tanks could communicate with one another across the battlefield, nor with the infantry who they were to support. It is possible that he believed this would be resolved through experimentation during tactical training but it was not and remained an issue throughout 1916–17. Swinton was, however, fully alive to the tanks' limitations regarding terrain during deployment:

The sector of front where these machines can best operate should be carefully chosen to comply with their limitations i.e., their inability to cross canals, rivers, deep railway crossings with steep sides or woods and orchards. And this should be done, as long as possible before the moment of attack, so that the time may be allowed for the execution of the work on the lines of communications and in the shelled area behind the front line necessary to allow the machines coming up to a position without delay when required.

He also stressed the impossibility of repeated employment:

Since the chance of success of an attack by Tanks lies almost entirely in its novelty and in the element of surprise, it is obvious that no repetition of it will have the same opportunity of succeeding as the first unexpected effort. It follows therefore that these machines *should not be used in driblets*[26] (for instance as they are produced) but the fact of their existence should be kept as secret as possible until the whole are ready to be launched together with an infantry assault, in one great combined operation.

As far as the frontage which could be attacked, Swinton indicated that:

The exact distance apart at which the Tanks should move forward in the assault is a matter for experiment but, it is thought that in order to enable them to thoroughly search the ground for concealed machine-guns, to support each other mutually by their own fire and to sweep the German parapets sufficiently to permit of our own infantry advancing more or less unscathed, they should not be more than 150 yards apart. It will serve to simply present calculations at present if the interval be taken at a round figure of 100 yards.

As regards the total frontage, the number of Tanks under construction is less than 100 but since it is not safe to assume that more than 90 percent of the whole number available will be in line (to allow for machines to be told off to work outwards and to move laterally for destroying wire), the front of attack of that number will be 9,000 yards or 5 miles. For the sake of discussion, this distance will be assumed in considering

---

26   Swinton's italics.

an operation undertaken by the whole of the machines available, the reduction of front where a lesser number used is pro rata.[27]

Swinton stated that tanks would have to be deployed by rail to a suitable offloading point, close to the area where they would be employed, and then moved forward to a Position of Assembly. This was to be:

…a line parallel to our front line, and say, some two miles behind it. Here the machines should remain sufficiently long for the crews to reconnoitre, ease and mark out the routes up to the [Starting] points, and to learn all that can be discovered of the German front line trenches and the defence zone behind it over which they will have to advance.

Along the Positions of Assembly, the tanks will not be distributed at equal intervals so as to attract the notice of hostile aviators but will be placed amongst trees, in villages etc so as to obtain concealment. Special tarpaulin covers coloured as to represent tile or thatch roofs can be made ready. From it they can move up early on the night preceding the attack to their final positions or starting points, just behind where they will actually cross our trenches, and wait there until the moment (assumed to be just before dawn – see later) or, if this procedure is considered impossible, owing to the intensity of the hostile bombardment directed in the vicinity of our front line, they can move straight from the Position of Assembly during the night so as to reach their Starting Points just before the time for the advance. The routes to the front line will have to be marked for night work with special lanterns to show light towards the rear of our position.

Swinton stated that the distance between the Position of Assembly to the Starting Points would be not more than two miles and should not take more than two hours. Sadly, this speed proved to be hopelessly optimistic, mainly due to tanks being directed along the roads congested with other traffic and the difficulty the tanks' drivers experienced in trying to turn the vehicles through right angles at road junctions:

If it is considered advisable for any reason that the machine should go up to their final positions still earlier, and remain there during daylight, suitable pits will have to be excavated for them beforehand so that they are not visible to the enemy over our parapets. To confuse the enemy's air scouts, several more pits than necessary will have to be dug some considerable time before the attack.

Swinton considered that the individual tanks' Starting Points 'will be 100 yards apart only, approximately, and should be carefully chosen as to be opposite some special enemy's points, such as a located field gun or machine-gun emplacements and the forward end of communication

27 Swinton's footnote states, 'This calculation as to the extent of frontage will hold good whether the tanks move forward in one continuous line or in groups with intervals between the groups so that certain areas may be "bitten off" by lateral movement as soon as sufficient forward progress has been made. The selection of either method of attack is a matter of general tactics and not one specifically connected with the employment of tanks.'

trenches etc.' This latter remark foreshadowed the way in which tanks would actually be employed during their first action. Swinton also gave thought to the tactics to be used by the tanks:

Time of the Advance. The most favourable time for the Tanks to advance, so as to avoid the chief danger to which they will be exposed i.e., hostile artillery fire, would be at night. But there are disadvantages in such a course which makes its adoption inadvisable. Firstly, no infantry could accompany the machines for the crews of the tanks would not be able to distinguish between the flashes of our rifles from those of the enemy. Secondly it would not be possible for the drivers to see the obstacles in front of them, and they could not manipulate their clutches for climbing or steer the machines so as to avoid uncrossable spots. It seems that the best moment for the start will be just before dawn, as soon as there is sufficient light in the sky to distinguish objects to some extent. A start of such a time would also give the greatest number of hours of daylight for pressing on with the offensive.

Synchronization of the Advance of the Tanks with the Infantry Assault. The Tanks, it is thought, should move forward together, say by rocket signal, sweeping the enemy's front line parapet with machine-gun fire, and after they have proceeded some three-quarters of the way across no-man's land and have succeeded in attracting to themselves the fire of the German infantry and machine-guns in the front line, the assaulting infantry should charge forward so as to reach the German defences soon after the tanks have climbed the parapet and begun to enfilade the trenches.[28] Since not much difficulty is usually experienced in rushing the German front line after a thorough bombardment,[29] it may be thought it is unnecessary for the Tanks to precede the infantry assault, or even accompany it, and they should be kept behind our front line and only sent forward to help the infantry where and when they are held up by uncut wire and machine-gun fire. There appears however to be drawback to such a course. It would result in unnecessary loss to the infantry who will only be able to discover the presence of uncut wire or of hostile machine-guns only by finding themselves checked, shot down and unable to proceed. (It is to obviate such loss that the tanks are being produced.) It would result, also, in delay, as a check would have to be experienced by the infantry, a message sent back for the assistance of the Tanks, and the latter sent forward to clear away the obstruction. This would entail the otherwise avoidable expenditure of a considerable amount of time and a consequent reduction of the speed of progress through the enemy's defensive zone (which may be some 3 or 4 miles in depth). It would therefore lessen the chance of the attack breaking through the defence whilst any beneficial effort which might be produced by its novelty was still in operation. This retardation of the advance might give the enemy time to reinforce the threatened section of the line with men, machine-guns and, what is more important from the point of view of this special form of attack, with field artillery.

Lastly, it would result, it is thought, with greatly decreasing the chance of success of the tanks themselves, owing to the fire of the German artillery which, it must be

---

28   Author's note: This paper was written before the advent of the creeping barrage.
29   Author's note: This paper was written before the losses inflicted on the attacking infantry on 1 July 1916.

repeated, is their greatest danger. The reason for this view is as follows: in whatever way the attack is made, whether it be infantry preceded by tanks or infantry alone, as soon as it is launched and seen by the Germans to cross our parapets, the message will be sent back to the hostile artillery to put down a curtain of fire. This curtain of fire, it is believed, covers no man's lands as well as our own front line so as to catch the assaulting troops and also cover the area between our front and supporting lines, so as to prevent our supports going forward. It takes place very quickly but there is nevertheless an appreciable interval between the moment when our assault is launched and its occurrence.[30]

Swinton then considered the tanks' actions after crossing the German frontline:

Except for those few machines, which are detailed to travel along the wire entanglements laterally, the Tanks will only halt at the enemy's front line, keeping it under enfilade fire, only until our assaulting infantry have reached it, when they proceed straight ahead at full speed for the German second line, as far as possible following up alongside the hostile communications trenches, which they will sweep with machine-gun fire, thus dealing with any German reinforcement and bombing parties coming up. Some of the infantry, armed with hand grenades, should follow in their wake, to assist to search out dead ground with bombs. At the same time, the 'skipper' and gun crews of the Tank will keep a sharp look out for machine-guns in the second line. When discovered those will be shelled or, if possible, crushed.[31]

Finally, he looked forward to the use of tanks in the depths of the enemy's defences.

The extent to which the attack is pressed, i.e. whether it is to be a step by step operation in which, after artillery preparation, a strictly limited advance is made over the front concerned and the gain of ground consolidated and then, after the necessary pause to give time for a renewed artillery preparation of the enemy's new front line, a further advance is made, and so on, or whether a violent effort is to be made to burst right through the enemy's defensive zone in one great rush, depends on the decision of the Commander in Chief and the strategic needs of the situation. But, as far as is known, a step-by-step advance, which had the drawback of giving the enemy time to reinforce the sector threatened, is not a course recommended for any positive advantages that it possesses. It is a course which has been forced on us by the inability, with the means hitherto at our disposal, of infantry even after immense sacrifice of life, to force their way through successive lines of defence, guarded by machine-guns and wire, of which none but the first can be thoroughly battered by our artillery.

Not only, does it seem, that tanks will confer the power to force successive comparatively unbattered defensive lines but, as has been explained, the more speedy and uninterrupted the advance, the greater their chance of surviving sufficiently long

30   Author's note: Here Swinton predicts 1 July 1916 when the BEF suffered almost 60,000 casualties.
31   Author's note: This is the first written use of the term 'skipper' I have identified but it probably indicates that the term had been used previously in informal staffing.

to do this. It is possible therefore that an effort to break right through the enemy's defensive zone, in one day, may now be contemplated as a perfectly feasible objective.

Apart from the topographical limit, placed on an offensive action of this nature for other reasons, the limits of the power of the Tanks are very broad. Even taking an average rate of progress during an attack of not more than one mile per hour, over a sector of country without natural obstacles, an advance of 12 miles forward could be carried out during the daylight hours, by those Tanks which are not knocked out by gunfire. A movement of this scale would take our troops past the enemy's main artillery positions and would, if successfully effected, would imply the capture or withdrawal of their guns. This being the case, it appears that when Tanks are used the contingency of such an extended bound forward being made, should be most carefully legislated for in the way of preparation to send forward reinforcements, guns, ammunition and supplies. In regard to the replenishment at the end of the first day's fighting of the Tanks themselves with fresh crews and ammunition in the event of such progress being made, schemes have yet to be worked out.[32]

The paper was sent to Haig who told Swinton, at a meeting in France on 14 April. that he endorsed the contents. Lt Gen Launcelot Kiggell (Haig's chief of staff) also told Swinton the same at the end of May but, remarkably, this key document was never circulated to the GHQ BEF staff.[33]

Finding the Tank Crews

The tanks' crews would require to be trained not only in the operation of the main armament and machine-guns but in driving, steering and maintaining the machines. Fortunately, the surplus MMGS personnel, identified by the TSC, had been recruited from those with the necessary mechanical aptitude and were used to working in small teams. The MMGS had been formed in response to Army Order 480 dated 12 November 1914 which had approved the addition of a MMG battery to each infantry division. These batteries comprised a headquarters, and three machine-gun sections, each consisting of 18 motorcycle side-car combinations, with additional motorcycles and lorries as domestic transport. The combinations were grouped to provide two detachments, each of two Vickers machine-guns, two ammunition carriers and two spare combinations which could either transport the Vickers or ammunition in the event that one of the primary load-carrying vehicles became inoperable.

Although the MMG batteries were initially effective, the stalemate of the Western Front in late 1915 appears to have stopped further deployment of more batteries to France. In early 1916, when No. 22 Battery was sent to India, members of other units, including Nos. 21 and 27 Batteries, were mostly kicking their heels.[34] The initial order for 100 tanks would require more than 75 officers and 750 men, proposed at the Christmas Eve inter-departmental conference, to

32   Swinton's footnote stated 'Each machine will carry enough petrol for a journey of 60 miles.'
33   Pidgeon, Tanks at Flers, p. 26.
34   For more on the formation of the MMGS and the actions of No. 22 Battery, see Paul Macro, *Action at Badama Post* (Oxford: Casemate, 2019).

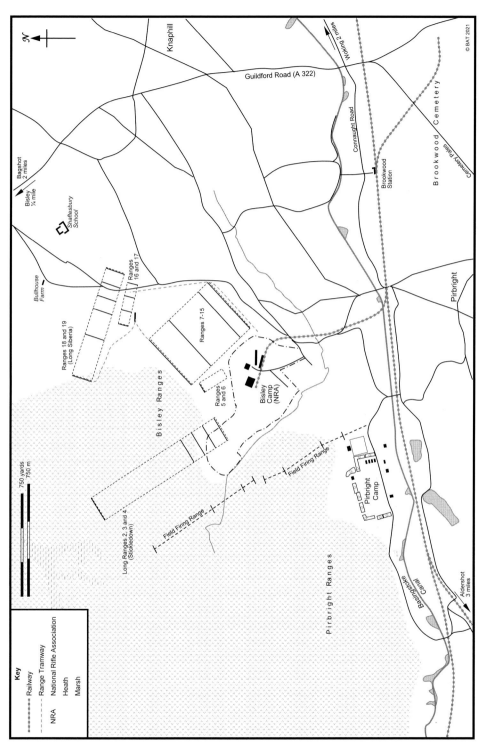

Bisley Camp and ranges. (Barbara Turner)

be trained as crewmen.[35] There were only 700 machine-gunners at Bisley, so MMGS recruiting recommenced. This was primarily undertaken through the *Motor Cycle* newspaper recruiting section in Coventry working under the auspices of the editor, Geoffrey Smith. The *Motor Cycle* had a world-wide circulation and its staff developed a very slick system for screening applicants, undertaking medical checks and forwarding suitable candidates to the depots of Corps equipped with motorcycles and light vehicles such as the RE, the ASC and the RFC as well as the MMGS. These cap-badges were able to turn on recruiting pipelines as and when required. The pay, and terms and conditions of service were superior to infantry units. Volunteers readily presented themselves initially at Coventry and later in London, Manchester and Scotland for assessment. As a result, it was simple for Bradley to obtain the raw material needed to fill the new tank detachment's needs.

The MMG Training Centre had been established in the TF accommodation lines of the National Rifle Association (NRA) at Bisley Camp. The Centre had the advantage that it was less than two miles from Brookwood Station, on the London and Southwestern Railway line to Southampton. Since the declaration of war, the ranges at Bisley were under-utilised and were ideal for machine-gun training. The training provided to the MMGS crewmen was significantly less complex than that delivered to infantry recruits, and the training centre staff were well practiced at delivering initial training. As a result, the formation of the new tank companies was relatively quick.

Lionel McAdam (left) undertaking MG training at Bisley. (Sue Handley)

---

35   Author's note: One officer and eight Other Ranks (OR) per tank crew (900) plus unit commanders, headquarters and support staff.

On arrival at Bisley, the recruits were initially housed in large sheds, each capable of housing 70 men. Each man was assessed and then allocated to one of 12 companies which were initially expected to operate six tanks each. The OR were then instructed in the operation of the Vickers and Hotchkiss machine-guns. They also completed foot and arms drill, to instil discipline and a military bearing, and route marches to improve the men's physical fitness.[36]

On 28 February, Swinton was formally notified that he 'should assume command of Tank Detachment to which you have been appointed at Bisley.' Others appointed to the MMGS over the next month included Lts Stern, Symes and Wilson from the RNAS and Capts Frank Summers (RMLI), Cecil Tippetts (SWB) and Graham Woods of the York and Lancaster Regiment (Y&L).[37] On 9 March, Swinton accompanied by Summers travelled to White City in west London which was the base of 20 Squadron RNAS. His aim was to recruit experienced armoured car crewmen and mechanics as members of the Tank Detachment. Swinton gave outline details of the new unit, which he described as 'an epoch-making service', and told them they would be paid 1/6d a day. He then ordered all volunteers to step forward – not one moved. Unfazed, Swinton again addressed the assembled men, reminding them of the fact that they would be paid 1/6d per day which was 50 percent more than that paid to the infantry. Again, he ordered all volunteers to step forward and again not one man moved. It was at that point that Swinton noticed that Summers was smiling broadly and that something was wrong. It was only later that Summers informed Swinton that the RNAS crew were being currently paid between four and five shillings a day.[38]

On 1 April 1916, the Tank Detachment was renamed the Armoured Car Section which caused confusion as 'there are already armoured car units in existence belonging to the MMGS. Would it not be better to call it the Heavy Section of the MGC, the cycles and light cars forming the "Light Section"?'[39]

Frank Summers. (TMA)

36   Information on the initial training of tank crewmen can be found in the letters sent by Atkins to his mother.
37   Stern and Wilson were appointed majors, Symes as a captain. *London Gazette*, 3 April 1916.
38   Extracted from a report by 'Beveren' in the *Sketch*, 1 May 1922 of a lunch given to celebrate Summers' retirement from the Officers' Appointments branch of the Ministry of Labour.
39   Handwritten memo to DASD from Lt. Col. P.E. Lewis (AG1) dated 20 April 1916. The name of the Armoured Car Section would be changed to the Heavy Section by the end of the month.

Swinton had realised that Bisley and the areas around Aldershot were unsuitable for tank collective training so he requested Maj Maurice Tandy to look further afield.[40] Having investigated areas around Bournemouth and then in East Anglia, Tandy identified Elveden in early March as being more suitable for training.

Although the *Motor Cycle* recruiting section could provide suitable volunteers to train as tank crewmen, there were only a limited number of MMGS officers available to command them and the new tank companies required many more. Swinton requested the WO to send a memorandum to home-based infantry battalions and depots, seeking officers with mechanical expertise to volunteer for 'a secret and dangerous mission.' Amongst the volunteers were two who had been injured in action: Eric Purdy who would command *Challenger*,[41] and Archie Walker who would command *Clan Leslie*.[42] The CO of 3rd (Depot) Battalion East Kent Regiment especially selected Lt Basil Henriques and Lt George Macpherson for interview. Both were accepted by Swinton, following an interview at Chelsea Barracks, despite the fact that neither had combat experience, mechanical aptitude or knowledge of either the Vickers or Hotchkiss machine-guns.

There were also potential skippers amongst officers under training at the three officer cadet battalions which had recently been established at Oxford and Cambridge.[43] Clough Williams-Ellis wrote that 'certain officer cadets with engineering experience drawn from 18th, 19th and 21st Battalions of the Royal Fusiliers were asked to volunteer for an experimental armoured car unit.[44] They were interviewed by Swinton and Bradley who gave no clue as to the result.'[45] Swinton also interviewed other officer cadets including former NCOs, who had sought commissions after being wounded in action but who were now fit for active service.[46]

Having carried out the interviews at Oxford and Cambridge, Swinton then drove to Elveden and confirmed its suitability for tank training.[47] Swinton visited the owner of the majority of the land, Lord Iveagh, to gain permission for its use and also visited Maj Gen F H Kelly, the

---

40   Tandy was a RE survey officer on home leave from India as a result of illness. He was the right man in the right place at just the right time. The training area requirement was for a large rural and unpopulated area with good railway connections. Elveden, in the heathlands on the border between Norfolk and Suffolk fitted the bill.

41   Eric was commissioned in the field in March 1915 into the Northants Regiment. He had been wounded in the shoulder at Hulluch whilst commanding a company of 1st Northants. Pope, *FTC*, pp. 41 to 45.

42   Archie had served with 2nd Kings Shropshire LI and was wounded during a counter-attack near St Julien in Apr 1915. His elder brother Allen would command C Company; Archie commanding No. 4 Section. Pope, *FTC*, pp. 54 to 57.

43   2nd Officer Cadet Battalion at Pembroke College, Cambridge; 4th Officer Cadet Battalion at New and Keble Colleges in Oxford; and 5th Officer Cadet Battalion at Trinity College in Cambridge. Information provided by Charles Fair.

44   These Public School Battalions had been deployed to France in November 1915 and had undertaken some limited time at the front holding the line. Although these potential officers had been trained by The Junior Division of the Officer Training Corps as school boys, it was decided that they needed a further one months' training. None of them had any real combat experience.

45   Clough and Amabel Williams-Ellis, *The Tank Corps* (London: Country Life, 1919), p. 16.

46   These included Arthur Blowers, who would command *Dolly*, and Harold Darby who would command *Dinkum* on 15 September 1916.

47   It is highly likely that Bradley also was with Swinton during this initial visit to the future tank training area.

GOC of the local Home Defence formation, 59th Infantry Division. Swinton briefed Kelly on the purpose of the training area although Kelly's staff were not informed. Returning to London, Swinton then contacted Drivers Jonas, an estate agent attached to the WO, who visited Iveagh to arrange compensation for use. He obtained entry to the area within a week and, in mid-April, the families living within what became known as the 'Elveden Explosives Area' were ordered to evacuate their properties to alternative accommodation outside the area.

Male and Female Tanks

As Swinton gave further consideration about the tactical use of tanks, he became concerned about their potential vulnerability to attack by large numbers of infantry.[48] As the Hotchkiss light machine-guns provided insufficient fire power to prevent them being overwhelmed, Swinton proposed that a second variant be developed which would be fitted with twin Vickers machine-guns.[49] The two types would operate in pairs; the original design for Mark I prototype, fitted with the 6-pounder Quick Firing (QF) gun which he designated Male, would destroy enemy machine-gun positions and hard targets whilst the other, known as Female and fitted with two Vickers machine-guns in each sponson, was to kill enemy defenders in their trenches and counter-attacking Germany infantry in the open. On 3 April 1916, the TSC contact for tank production was uplifted from 100 to 150 tanks; 75 being Male and 75 Female. The contract for the production of all the Females was placed with Metropolitan, which also built half of the Males (serials 701-738); Fosters building the remaining Males at Lincoln. The sponsons were all to be built in Birmingham – they would be sent to Elveden, on trailers specially designed for movement.

On 14 April, whilst visiting GHQ in France, Swinton met Haig who asked to investigate tanks being in France by mid-June. Unsure of the details, he asked to defer his answer until he had spoken to the TSC and had consulted Stern. Swinton was also tasked to provide establishments for

Hugh Knothe. (IWM)

---

48   Swinton, Eyewitness, p, 226.
49   The Hotchkiss light machine-gun, based on the French *Modelle 1909*, was issued to British cavalry units. The variant fitted to Mark I tanks fired 0.303-inch ball ammunition loaded into strips each holding 30 rounds. In tactical terms it is an automatic rifle and less effective for delivering sustained fire than the Vickers.

three workshops (on the basis of one per two companies) to support the tanks. As he had no experience of tractors, he contacted the BEF Directorate of Transport to seek assistance. They selected Hugh Knothe, a mechanical engineer who was commanding one of the two Holt tractor units supporting RA siege batteries.[50] Knothe returned to England, and Swinton '...explained the situation and what was required, I sent him to Lincoln, where *Mother* lay dismantled, with orders to live, eat, and sleep with her until he knew her inside out, and then, when he was ready, to work out in full detail what he considered necessary for workshops. This he did.'[51]

Move to Siberia

In the second week of April, the other ranks of the Armoured Car Section set up a tented camp on the Long Siberia range and, on 17 April, moved under canvas. On 20 April (Maundy Thursday), successful officer cadets, interviewed at Oxford and Cambridge, were notified of the results and offered commissions in the MMGC. Those who accepted were directed to report to Bisley the same day and, on arrival, were notified of the need to obtain their field kit and were granted leave until the following Tuesday (25 April) to do so.[52]

On Easter Monday, all officers already based at Bisley moved under canvas at the Siberia range. The unit then consisted of small companies commanded by captains each having a strength of 12 officers and 120 men; each company being established to operate two sections of six tanks. On Monday 24 April range training recommenced. 'Instruction was concentrated on the two machine-guns and each officer, NCO and man was required to pass the training test. With the above exception, physical drill and the occasional route march, no further training of military character was imposed.'[53] On 25 April, the newly commissioned officers reported back to Bisley and the next day, the officers selected from infantry battalions, arrived at Brookwood Station only to be informed that the companies had moved to Siberia. This caused some concern for Henriques until it was revealed that this referred to the range complex and not the east of Russia.[54]

As for the availability of tanks, Swinton notified Haig on 28 April that some would be available in June to train crews but not to deploy by 1 July. The original contract allowed the two companies ten weeks to set up their factory for production, which would then ramp up to a specified level. There were problems obtaining the armour plate as well as special parts. The tank production timetable would slip and Haig's plans to have tanks available for the summer Somme offensive would not be achieved.

---

50   Surprisingly, it appears that Knothe was *not* the ASC officer who Swinton met in France in June 1915.
51   Swinton, *Eyewitness*. p. 229. Born in Jesmond, near Newcastle-upon-Tyne, in 1886, Knothe was commissioned into the ASC Special Reserve on 29 August 1914. He was promoted to temporary captain on 13 March 1915, Mentioned in Despatches on 30 November 1915 and awarded the Military Cross prior to being attached to the Heavy Section.
52   Unlike other ranks, officers were responsible for purchasing all of their own clothing and personal equipment.
53   Williams-Ellis, *The Tank Corps*, p. 27 quoting Cyril Renouf who initially served with B Company. Renouf was appointed a major in 1918 and was awarded the OBE in the 1919 New Years' Honours List for his service with the Chief Mechanical Engineer's staff in Jan 1919.
54   BLQ Henriques, *The Indiscretions of a Warden* (London; Methuen & Co, 1937) p. 123.

4

Growing Pains

The Tank Detachment of the MGC was redesignated as the Heavy Section on 1 May 1916. This was confirmed in a memorandum sent from the WO to the C-in-C Home Forces that same day. It stated that 'The Tank Detachment of the MGC is a detachment of the MGC in the same way as the MMGS is, and for the present the two are located together at Bisley.' But, whilst the MMGS was under the orders of GHQ BEF for training etcetera, the Tank Detachment '... will be directly under the WO for training, organisation and equipment and under Aldershot Command for discipline and administration. For official communications it is considered advisable to change the name of this detachment to Heavy Section MGC (HS MGC).'

The establishment of the HS MGC was fixed at 184 officers and 1,610 ORs, formed into three battalions, each of five companies.[1] Each tank company was to consist of ten tanks which meant that there were none available as replacements, in the event of any being lost in battle. There was also no training fleet – the crews had to use the same vehicles in combat on which they had learned to drive and manoeuvre in England.

Tank Company Organisation

The manpower came from the Armoured Car Section with new recruits arriving at Bisley on a weekly basis. They were then allocated to one of the three battalions, with 1st Battalion HS MGC receiving their first men from 4 May.[2]

GHQ BEF did however not support the idea of three-tank battalions. As a result, six large independent companies were established with twice the number of sections and tanks in each unit. These six companies, denominated 'A' to 'F', were under command of Majs Cecil Tippetts of the South Wales Borderers (SWB), Thomas McLellan (Cameronians), Allen Holford-Walker

---

1   Swinton, *Eyewitness*, p. 226.
2   Individual soldiers' records show that the officer approving recruits for service with 1st Battalion from 4 May was Graham Woods (later adjutant of D Company). Officers approving recruits, from 15 May, for service with 2nd Battalion were Tippetts (later CO of B Company) and Blampied (later adjutant of A Company). Ralph Mansell, the future adjutant of B Company, approved recruits for service with 3rd Battalion on 25 May 1916.

of the Argyll and Sutherland Highlands (A&SH), Frank Summers of the Royal Marine Light Infantry, Norman Nutt of the RNAS and W.F.R. Kyngdon RA.[3]

The headquarters of the HS MGC consisted of Swinton and a staff captain, five other ranks and two vehicles. This organisation which, whilst just suitable for the management of training, proved to be wholly insufficient to manage even two companies once they deployed to the Somme in September 1916. The HS MGC organisation also included the Park, a unit which managed the tanks at Elveden, and three quartermaster's (QM) departments, each one supporting two tank companies. Driver training, maintenance, modifications and repair at Elveden was undertaken by 711 MT Company ASC which also, as the tank companies deployed overseas, was to provide three static ASC workshops, each supporting a pair of companies.

Each of the six tank companies consisted of a HQ, four tank sections and a reserve section. The headquarters had three other officers – the adjutant, the park officer, and a reserve skipper, plus the sergeant major, a QM's department, and ASC attached personnel who drove the unit's wheeled Mechanised Transport (MT).[4] The Reserve section included 48 MGC soldiers, 12 per section, who would act as immediate Battle Casualty Replacements.[5]

Each tank section was commanded by a captain who also commanded one of the six tanks, while the other tanks' skippers were subalterns. The OR consisted of six NCOs (with at least one sergeant), 30 gunners and a cook.[6] Each section operated three Male and three Female tanks enabling them to work in pairs or in two sub-sections of three tanks.[7] The section was also allocated one 3-ton lorry, one box body car and four bicycles. Three motorcycles were established in each company headquarters for use by despatch riders and a Sunbeam motor car for use by the major. Despite the changes, this allocation of tanks was again such that there were no dedicated training vehicles either in England or in France; there was only one spare tank per company which was insufficient to replace those tanks damaged in training, transit or later in battle.[8]

During initial tank training at Elveden, a few MGC crewmen were trained as tank drivers. However, as the majority did not have the skills to handle large and heavy vehicles, it was decided that the ASC would provide experienced drivers from tractor units. An increase to 711 MT Company establishment was approved on 14 July 1916. The majority of the tank drivers came from the ASC Tractor Depot at Avonmouth where the men were used to operating Holt tractors. Some were also found from units in France from ASC MT companies supporting RA siege batteries although the driver of *Delilah*, Private Alfred Bloomfield, described by his

---

3   Four of these were Regular officers. Summers and Nutt had served since the beginning of the war. Holford-Walker's youngest brother Archie had joined the Armoured Car Section on 14 April 1916 and would command No. 4 Section of C Company. See below.

4   C Company landing lists show that the unit also deployed with one Army Ordnance Corps (AOC) armourer sergeant and one Royal Army Medical Corps corporal. D Company had an armourer but I have been unable to locate a RAMC NCO.

5   Extracted from WO 121/Stores/4446 (SD2) dated 3 May 1916.

6   One of these was also appointed as the officer's batman,

7   In most cases, the section commander's vehicle was a Male tank – Mann and Sellick in D Company being the exceptions.

8   One of C Company's tanks damaged during at Yvrench could not be repaired and was cannibalised for spare parts. In early September, eight 'spare tanks' were sent to France for use in the first tank actions. However, these were vehicles which should have been allocated to B Company, which deployed without any tanks.

skipper Billy Sampson as a diminutive Geordie staff car driver, had been a chauffeur in civilian life. The tank and MT drivers were under command of an attached ASC road officer in the tank company HQ, the tank drivers being allocated to individual crews after deployment. This did not allow any esprit de corps to be built amongst the crews during training; a lesson learned quickly and, when the Heavy Branch (HB) MGC was formed in November 1916, tank drivers all wore the MGC cap badge and were commanded by MGC officers.[9]

Providing enough men to man the first 50 tanks went well, mainly due to the sustained efforts of Geoffrey Smith and the Recruiting Section of the *Motor Cycle* magazine. The recruits, who were all volunteers, were either trained mechanics or experienced drivers and motorcyclists able to maintain their own machines. As such, they had the necessary aptitude to operate machine-guns and maintain tanks. In March and April, the *Motor Cycle* had identified more than 450 potential candidates for employment with either the HS MGC or one of the trades requiring mechanically trained personnel such as the RE and ASC. As a result, there were enough men to start forming the tank companies in May. In the first two weeks of June, another 186 were selected at which point recruiting was paused.[10] Some MMGS battery personnel, who were posted back to Bisley after illness or injury overseas, were re-allocated to the HS MGC and warmly welcomed by crewmen like Walter Atkins and Roland Elliott who had absolutely no military expertise. Atkins noted that, one Friday in the middle of May, a 'grand parade' was held at Bisley where 1,500 men were inspected by 'the colonel' – probably Bradley.[11]

Training undertaken by the HS MGC crews was, as with MMGS gunners, much simpler than that undertaken by the average infantryman. It consisted of foot and arms drill, designed to instil discipline and provide the crewmen with the ability to work together as a group. It also included route marches to improve fitness and develop physical stamina. Every officer and crewman had to pass practical tests on the Vickers medium machine-guns, which would be fitted to the Mark I Female tanks, and the Hotchkiss light machine-guns which were fitted on every tank.

Selected crewmen were trained to operate the 6-pounder guns; each company requiring at least 24 qualified gun-layers to fight their twelve Male tanks. Three 6-pounder guns were obtained by Swinton (two from the Mark I Prototype *Mother* and the third from the RMA at Woolwich) which were positioned on logs at the Stickledown range, the longest and largest of the Bisley ranges.[12]

The 6-pounder guns fired the largest calibre (57mm or 2.233-inch) of ammunition used on the Bisley ranges. The rounds fired were solid shot, not high explosive, which penetrated the

9   These included some of the attached MT drivers from 711 MT Company who retrained as tank drivers in 1917. Not every ASC driver who drove a tank in action in 1916 remained with the HB MGC. Some decided not to transfer and at least one was posted to an ASC MT unit having been deemed as unsuitable for service with the HB MGC.
10 Author's note: Data extracted from archive copies of the newspaper.
11 See Atkins correspondence serial 1985-129-18 held at the Herbert Art Gallery and Museum in Coventry. The letter is undated but, from other items in the collection, it was probably written on 12 May 1916. This colonel may have been Swinton but it was more likely to have been Bradley.
12 The tank sponsons, which were built at Birmingham, were not available until July 1916 and were shipped directly to Elveden for fitment to the tanks.

mantlets to a depth of three feet and put those working in the range butts at risk.[13] This caused the Secretary of the NRA, Lt Col C.R. Crosse, to request that the firing of the 6-pounder to be restricted to the Long Siberia range, permanently allocated to the HS MGC, to minimise damage to the other ranges.[14] The crewmen's bell tents were pitched between the 600- and 800-yard firing points on the Long Siberia, which reduced the distance firing parties had to walk. However, it created a further difficulty when 6-pounder ricochets left the range safety template and fell outside the range boundary, some landing close to cottages near Chobham.[15] As a result, live fire training was restricted to the medium Vickers machine-guns, fitted to dummy Female sponsons erected on the Short Siberia range, or individual Hotchkiss light machine-guns on the Long Siberia range to its north.

Dry training on the 6-pounder continued at Bisley on the Stickledown Range with selected crewmen undertaking live firing practices courtesy of the Royal Naval Gunnery School at Whale Island in Portsmouth Harbour. Atkins described the training regime in a series of letters written from 4–10 July. The crewmen travelled to Portsmouth by motor vehicle on the Sunday and were accommodated in HMS *Excellent's* NCOs' Mess. This provided much better food than that cooked at Bisley and Walter Atkins commented that the beds were provided with sprung mattresses. Land-based training started at 0900 and finished by 1530 hours daily; the first two days were simulated live firing using a gun fitted with a sub-calibre device based on an air rifle. On the third day, the crewmen undertook seaboard gunnery training and then live firing from a warship in the English Channel the following day. The newly qualified gun-layers then returned to Bisley on Friday afternoon.[16]

Walter Atkins wearing the gun-layer's sleeve badge. (Herbert Art Gallery and Museum)

13   This level of penetration shows why the Male tanks were able to neutralise German machine-gun emplacements in France, their construction being designed to defend their crews from indirect fire.
14   Christopher Bunch, Bisley at War, *NRA Journal,* Vol. XCIV 2015 No 2, pp. 14 and 15.
15   Pidgeon, *Tanks at Flers,* p. 22.
16   Atkins correspondence serials 1985-129, 51, 30–34, Herbert Art Gallery and Museum in Coventry.

Company Formation

By the middle of May 1916, there were plenty of crewmen either in training or in the recruiting pipeline, and sufficient subalterns to command and man the tanks. There were, however, insufficient captains to command the sections. Few of the officers who transferred from the MMGS to the HS MGC were sufficiently experienced and only a handful had seen combat.[17] The company commanders, who had seen action, therefore used their regimental contacts to obtain suitably experienced officers and by the end of the month, the establishment was filled. The key postholders were:

Role (rank)	A Company (original unit)	B Company (original unit)	C Company (original unit)	D Company (original unit)
CO (major)	Cecil Tippetts (SWB)	Thomas McLellan (Cameronians)	Allen Holford-Walker (A&SH)	Frank Summers (RM LI)
Adjutant (captain)	Bertram Blampied (R West Kents)	Ralph Mansell (RA)	Richard Williams (MMGS)	Graham Woods (Y&L)
OC No 1 Section (captain)	Percy Jackson (MMGS)	James Bennewith (MMGS)	Arthur Inglis (Glosters)	Harold Mortimore (RNAS)
OC No 2 Section (captain)	Maurice Miskin (Staffords)	Richard Clively (South Lancs)	Herbert Hiscocks (North Lancs)	Graeme Nixon (KLR)
OC No 3 Section (captain)	Arthur Jacobs (MMGS)	Frank Vandervell (South Lancs)	Richard Trevithick (ASC)	Stephen Sellick (MMGS)
OC No 4 Section (captain)	David Raikes (SWB)	The Lord Rodney (Scots Greys)	Archie Holford-Walker (KSLI)	George Mann (MMGS)
Sergeant Major (WO II)	John Campling (SWB)	Unknown	Joseph Hackett (Northamptons)	Thomas Walsh (5 DG)

Nutt was appointed to command E Company in June and deployed with half his company to Egypt in December 1916 (see Volume 2). Kyngdon, who was appointed to command F

---

17   Allen Holford-Walker made specific reference to this problem in a letter to the official historian in 1935.

Company, deployed from Elveden in early August as a member of HQ HS MGC to France; this company never deployed for operations, its men instead joining F and G Battalions in 1917.[18]

The HS MGC headquarters and officers' mess was established at Bullhouse Farm, 500 yards north of the Long Siberia range and half a mile from Bisley village.[19] This village had a post office, a small number of shops and a hall which hosted a small YMCA canteen. Later, as the number of crewmen living on the ranges increased, two marquees were erected at the Long Siberia range; one providing refreshment and the other for reading, writing and quiet relaxation. In the evenings, the crewmen could also visit Knaphill, where there were a number of shops, pubs and even a professional photographer, or the town of Woking which was either a five mile walk or a short train journey from Brookwood. Weekend leave was granted in limited numbers with priority given to those who had passed weapon training tests. Those who failed to return to Siberia Camp before the nightly curfew of 2200 hours or return on time from weekend leave were automatically charged for absence.[20]

On 27 May 1916, the crewmen were formally transferred to the new six companies.[21] The next day, after Sunday lunch, Swinton briefed the company officers on their new role, explaining what tanks were and how they would be used. This informal briefing took place in an orchard south of Bullhouse Farm, which was well away from the crewmen who were only told that they would be operating a new type of armoured car. Despite the briefing, the officers and most crewmen were wholly unprepared by the design and capability of the tanks.

The Elveden Explosives Area

At the end of May, C Company started to move to the tank training area located south of Elveden. The companies travelled in groups, although not always as complete crews, by rail from Woking to Waterloo railway station, across London to Liverpool Street and thence by rail to Thetford Bridge station. The final stage of the journey was on foot, C Company's headquarters being located at Bernersfield Farm in the southwestern corner of the training area. Walter Atkins, who arrived later in June, recorded his march to Canada Farm as eight miles long which means the party took the direct route through Elveden along the London road, before heading south down the Seven Tree road towards Iklingham.[22] Bernersfield Farm was also the location

---

18   Kyngdon, who had spent many years on secondment in West Africa, had been serving in the Cameroons with the Anglo-French force which defeated the German forces. He was one of three officers posted to the HS MGC on his return to England. The others were Maj John Brough, who would command the training ground at Elveden and then at Yvrench, and Capt Arthur Inglis who assumed command of No. 1 Section of C Company.

19   Now known as Bullhousen Farm, the farm is located off Shaftesbury Avenue, southwest of Bisley and north of HM Prison Coldingley.

20   Individual soldiers' conduct records show that a late return in the evening was normally punished by being Confined to Camp. Those returning late from weekend leave were also Confined to Camp or sentenced to No. 2 Field Punishment as well as having their pay reduced to reflect the amount of time spent absent on leave.

21   This date appears in the individual service records of soldiers of all six companies but many were already serving in these units; Walter Atkins first used the name of D Company as a correspondence address in a letter dated 14 May 1916.

22   HQ D Company's location (Canada Farm) is approached via the Iklingham Road and is to the north of Bernersfield Farm.

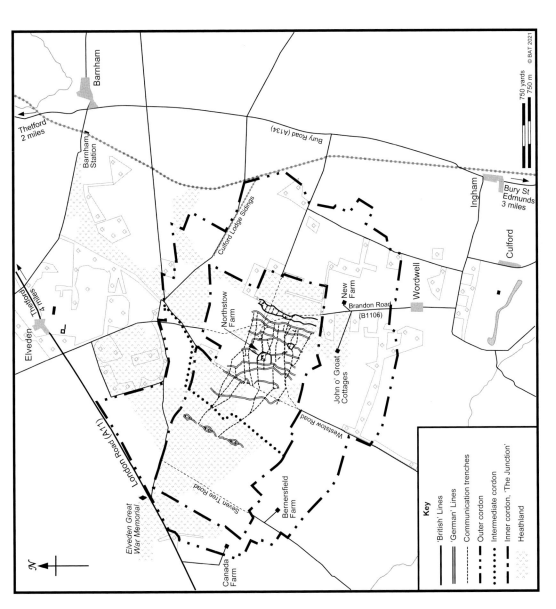

The Elveden
Explosives area.
(Barbara Taylor)

© BAT 2021

Key

'British' Lines
'German' Lines
Communication trenches
Outer cordon
Intermediate cordon
Inner cordon, 'The Junction'
Heathland

of HQ 711 MT Company ASC and where the crewmen were given preliminary instruction in the principles of tank construction driving and maintenance, by Knothe, in a barn illustrated using a magic lantern. On 4 June, the two prototype tanks *Mother* and *Little Willie* arrived at the training area. They had been loaded on rail wagons at Lincoln the previous day and off-loaded at Barnham Station sidings the previous night. They were then driven to Bernersfield Camp, the local villagers having been told not to look out of their windows.

As mentioned in Chapter 3, the area to the south and west of Elveden had been initially identified by Tandy in late March. The area was generally heathland, poor in agricultural terms, but popular during the shooting season. Elveden Hall had been owned by Prince Duleep Singh who regularly hosted the Prince of Wales (later King Edward VII) for game shoots. After Duleep Singh's death in the 1890s, the Hall was purchased by the 1st Earl of Iveagh and high society, including the future King George V, continued to shoot on the estate. The owners of Culford Hall also had hosted large shooting parties, including other members of the Royal Family, in the early 1900s. The land was virtually flat, and generally unenclosed, which made it suitable for tank training; the soil was also light and there were few large areas of woodland.[23] The area had been used for a major army exercise in 1911 and, with HQ 69th (2nd East Anglian) Division based in Thetford and three infantry brigades in the area, the arrival of the HS MGC should not have attracted much attention.[24]

The new training ground, named the Elveden Explosives Area to disguise its real purpose, covered some 25 square miles of mainly agricultural land. To its east was the Bury St Edmunds to Thetford Bridge railway line, a single-track branch line operated by the Great Eastern Railway (GER) Company. There were two local railway stations; one at Ingham and one west of Barnham, which included two freight sidings used for the movement of animals.[25] At Thetford Bridge station, the branch line connected to the Norwich to Cambridge mainline which ultimately led to London. To the north and west of the training area, the ground was bounded by the Thetford to Mildenhall Road, which passed through Elveden village. The southern boundary ran north of the River Lark which passed through West Stow and Iklingham. Within the outer cordon. which was patrolled by Indian cavalry and guarded by Royal Defence Corps units, were Bernersfield and Canada Farms in the west, Culford Lodge, West Farm and New Farm in the east. North Stow Farm, in the centre, was the focus for tactical training, the farm buildings being converted to form a strong point.

Access to the area was strictly controlled to those holding individually-issued passes. As with current MOD range areas, warning signs were erected informing locals of the danger within the area from explosives. Rumours as to exactly what was taking place in the area included that it was the western end of a tunnel under the English Channel which would allow the British Army to invade Germany. Crewmen were regularly reminded of the need for secrecy regarding tanks;

---

23   The area is now heavily forested; this results from a plan to provide work for the unemployed in the 1930s as well as to meet the needs for commercial timber.
24   HQ 69th Division commanded three home defence infantry brigades based at Thetford, Bury St Edmunds and Newmarket.
25   In an article entitled *The Secret Siding*, written in 1998, Trevor Pidgeon stated that the western siding was 300 feet at Barnham whilst the eastern one was 600 yards long and used for offloading cattle. The siding had the advantage that it was connected by a track to the main Norwich to London Road at Elveden which gave ready access to Bernersfield Camp.

however, it is clear that some relatives did press their loved one for information. The officers and crewmen, who described the tanks as 'cars' or 'buses', tried to obfuscate but the mother of one officer, who met Swinton at a dinner, made it clear she knew more than she should. Swinton quietly told her that, should any secret information be divulged to the Germans, her son would be charged with treachery and she would be jailed.[26]

The inner area, which contained a detailed replica of a German defensive system and a driver training area with challenging obstacles, was constructed over a period of six weeks. There were also shooting ranges although weapons training appears to have featured little on the programme. The main workforce for the construction of the training areas were two Home Defence pioneer battalions; however, as the arrival date of the first production tanks approached, they were reinforced by a pioneer battalion from a Welsh regiment whose men were mainly miners. Their CO, who was unaware of the nature of the task other than it was an urgent operational requirement, brought his men fully equipped for war. After some natural disappointment, the training area was ready for use in the third week of June.

The replica battlefield had been designed by Major Giffard Martel, another RE officer acquired by Swinton.[27] It was based on the most up-to-date information about German defensive systems. A strongpoint was constructed around North Stow Farm, which became known as the Citadel, behind a simulated German frontline, protected by barbed wire, with support and reserve trenches all being linked by interconnecting communication trenches dug to a minimum depth of six feet. The frontline consisted of five-foot-high breastworks, similar to those used near the French and Belgian borders, barriers made of felled trees and, of course, machine-gun emplacements – the primary target for the tank crews. The trench system, which was over one and a half miles wide, included trench blocks, dugouts and magazines, with signs in German, enabling the crews to be instructed in their meaning. These defences required the filling and placement of over one million sand bags, miles of barbed wire, and several viewing platforms so that the training could be observed.

Of equal importance was the driver training area. The course included an initial descent down a 1 in 4 slope into a wide

Giffard Martel. (TMA)

---

26   Swinton, *Eyewitness*, p. 228.
27   Martel would join HQ HS MGC in France in the autumn. See Chapter 9.

pond, filled with water to a depth of 30 inches. Having negotiated these two obstacles, the driver would then drive up a 1 in 3 slope to flat ground, then descend another long slope with an even steeper gradient of 1 in 1½ to another pond. Having forded that, he would exit by driving up another slope measuring 1 in 2½. This was extremely challenging and would require that the driver could confidently use the tank's gears to make progress. Tanks in the Great War had no suspension and, whilst the steering tail did aide the driver in coping with climbs, it required wholly different skills to that normally used to drive a wheeled vehicle on a road or over normal terrain. There was however little opportunity for drivers to train on unprepared routes and virtually no training undertaken at night.

In addition to the tactical training areas, work was required in the tented camps which housed the tank companies. The men of C and later B Companies camped at New Farm whilst A and D Companies were billeted in tents at John O'Groats Cottage which were located south of North Stow Farm and outside the battle area.[28] An ASC camp was also built to the east close to the new, purpose-built, railway siding near Culford Lodge Farm. Finding that there was no local water supply, and unprepared to accept the WO's suggestion that vehicles be used to bring water into the area every day, Martel arranged for a well to be sunk. It produced a plentiful supply for the companies and the training staff but it had to be boiled for safety; the taste was unpleasant and loathed by the soldiers. Having lived under canvas at Siberia, the relocated bell tents presented no hardship to the officers and men under training, but the men's bedding soon became infested with earwigs. There were also only limited facilities for bathing, something essential for the crews after operating in the tanks' fighting compartments. The River Lark, which was a couple of miles south of the campsites, was used however for both washing and relaxation. There were no pubs within the training area, although there were a few in the

Unidentified tank skippers at Elveden. (TMA)

28   *War History 3rd Light Tank Battalion*, p. 1A.

surrounding villages. An officers' mess was established in the stable at Elveden Hall and the OR messes were in disused tobacco drying sheds. As at Bisley, there were also large marquees containing YMCA recreational facilities, the main beer available being Bass.[29]

Training Limitations

Mother was used for the first sessions of driver training for the crewmen. The prototype was no longer fitted with her main armament and, when the production tanks started to arrive, these also were not fitted with sponsons, their manufacture in Birmingham being constrained owing to a shortage of armoured plate and also the sighting systems. The lack of sponsons and associated armament taught the crew false lessons about the operation of their tanks. Tanks were never driven at their full combat weights before they deployed from the Loop on 13 September 1916 and the crews never experienced the difficulties of operating fully closed down until that time.[30] The use of the tanks without their sponsons also allowed the engine heat and exhaust gases to dissipate. This did not assist their commanders to understand just how debilitating the fighting conditions would be for their crews. It also permitted the hull frames to become distorted, which created problems for the crews when attaching the sponsons. On their arrival in France, it was, at times necessary to drill additional holes to enable their refitting.[31]

Male tank No. 713 crossing a low obstacle at Elveden. (TMA)

29 Roger Pugh, *The Most Secret Place on Earth*, p. 38.
30 'That is to say, with all hatches closed and dependent on the visibility afforded by two periscopes fitted in the vehicle cab and a small number of glass vision blocks.' Henriques, *The Indiscretions of a Warden*, pp. 115 and 116.
31 Author's note. It is also possible that the loading and offloading of the tanks into the hulls of ships, using cranes, may have exacerbated this problem.

It was difficult for the 6-pounder gun-layers to undertake continuation training at Elveden although some limited live firing was undertaken when attacking the replica strongpoint at North Stow Farm. This was partly overcome by visits to the Salisbury Plain artillery ranges at Larkhill. Atkins described the regime in letters written to his mother at the end of June:

> Thursday night. Did not know we were coming to Bisley until last night – will be going to Salisbury Plain for live firing practice tomorrow and will return to Thetford on Sat so no chance of leave this weekend. We left [the training area] at 7.15, arrived Thetford at 9.30. Officer allowed us to go for a stroll as train did not leave until 11.45. Got to London at 2 and marched across London. Arrived at Waterloo at 3.15. Stayed at Soldiers' buffet and then departed at 4.5. There were lorries at Brookwood to collect us (only 45 out of 250). Don't write to me at this camp [Bullhouse] as I will leave before the letter arrives. Write to me at Canada Camp.
>
> Friday night 8-15 – Bullhouse Camp. Have arrived at Bullhouse Camp safely. We got up at 5.00; had breakfast at 5.15 and started at 06.20; two lorries waiting at the camp gates to take us to Woking [station]. Got there just before 7 and caught the 7.0 train. Arrived at Salisbury at 9.00 where we met by two more lorries and then we had a ride by road for 12 miles. We were taken by Stonehenge to fire and we had only 5 rounds [each]. We started back at 4 and got to Salisbury by 4.30. Then we went into a restaurant and had a good tea. We caught the 5.10 train back, reaching Woking at 7.30. Again, we were met by a motor lorry and brought here. We must have travelled 32 miles by road and 100 by train.
>
> Sunday morning – Thetford. Have arrived back safely from Bisley. Started at 9.15 and caught the 10.00 train from Woking to London. We arrived just before 12.00 and had wait until 2.30 for the train to Thetford. We arrived at Thetford at about 6.00 and got back at camp at 9.00 and had a good meal waiting for us. Today I am mess orderly and I have just finished cleaning up after breakfast 9.30 and have nothing else to do until 12. Glad to know you are getting my bike ready as it will be useful down here. I see in the papers that the English had made a good advance and I hope they keep it up.[32]

Atkins had, like many other crewmen, identified that a motorcycle would enable him to get away from the training area, visiting Thetford and Bury St Edmunds at weekends, and to reach home when granted weekend leave. In early June, the crewmen were not permitted to leave the training area but, after a couple of weeks, this stricture was relaxed. Atkins was not the only person to bring his machine as there are several images of members of the Heavy Section on their motorcycles amongst the tented camps at Elveden.[33] Those without their own transport could reach both Thetford and Bury St Edmunds by rail although there were only four trains

---

32   This last sentence refers to the starting of the Battle of the Somme on 1 July 1916. The newspaper reports were so written as to hide the tremendous losses suffered by the British Army that day, concentrating on the very limited success in the areas near Montauban. See Atkins correspondence serials 1985-129-46, 47, 50. The letters were usually undated but, based on other items in the collection, it was composed at the end of June.

33   Many of the officers and soldiers, who had joined the MMGS before the Heavy Section had formed, had used their motorcycles at Bisley when off duty.

each day, and unit transport was probably also used when permitted. The officers tended to gather at the Angel Hotel[34] whilst NCOs used the less grand Suffolk Hotel. It is highly unusual to this day for different ranks to use the same public houses.

That said, relationships between officers and other ranks were much less formal than in other units due to close relationships built up working in such a confirmed space. Gnr Archie Richards, a member of the D7 crew who lived until he was 101, told Richard van Emden: 'Our officer [Alfred Enoch] used to treat us as a friend. Talking to us like he would talk to his own rank. He used to call me Arch, he used all our Christian names. I'm sure he thought that we might all go up [would be killed] together so we'll be pally, pally until the end.'[35] It was certainly not appreciated by Capt Henry Steedman of 711 MT Company who commented that the tank units were 'over-officered and under-disciplined.'[36] *Daphne's* skipper, Harry Drader, for example rewarded his crew for their progress during training by buying cakes. In addition to the formal

Casa Crew at Bury St Edmunds:
John Witty, J. Stewart, William Scott, George Caffrey.
Douglas Gardiner, Victor Smith, John Webby.
Harry Greenberg. (TMA) #

34   Stanley Clarke witnessed Arthur Inglis' will on 13 August at the Angel Inn, jut before they deployed to France.
35   Richard van Emden and Steve Humphries, *Veterans: The Last Survivors of the Great War* (Barnsley: Leo Cooper, 1998), pp. 94–101.
36   H.P. Steedman, *Historical Account of 711 MT Company ASC attached to Tanks in France*, 17 Jul 1917. NCOs did not formally command tank crews until the Battle of Amiens when the Corps establishment

unit photographs arranged by HQ D Company, the whole crew of the Female tank *Casa* was photographed whilst visiting Bury St Edmunds – a unique image in that it includes the driver Private Stewart.[37]

On 4 June, Bradley and Brough were appointed to Assistant Adjutant General (AG) staff appointments even though both were controlling crew training, Bradley at Bisley and Brough at Elveden. 4 June was also the date of the formation of 711 Mechanical Transport (MT) Company ASC. One officer, a mechanical staff sergeant and about a dozen men were initially sent with a mobile workshop to OC HS MGC at Elveden but the numbers quickly grew.[38] The Company's role was to control, and keep in order, all transport and tanks, to maintain their efficiency and to provide and train tank drivers.[39] Knothe, who had devised the Workshop's establishments, was appointed to command 711 Company; Steedman was in charge of the Park and Second Lieutenant (2Lt) Henry St John commanded a small Albion lorry-based workshop. The unit drew its men from the ASC Depots in London, from the Holt Tractor Depot at Avonmouth plus a number of experienced drivers from France.[40] The officers were generally newly commissioned but had engineering backgrounds.

Driver training was initially designed to use skippers and key crewmen who then trained their own crews. However, it was quickly decided that the tank would be driven by ASC MT drivers and by 14 July, the 711 Company establishment was increased accordingly. Henriques later wrote that the allocation of individual drivers to crews did not take place until the unit was in France and he had the choice of two men, choosing the quieter one.[41] As the number of tank companies at Elveden increased, so did the size of 711 MT Company. By the end of August, the unit comprised a total of 303 of all ranks, operating nine cars, thirteen box vans, twenty-seven 3-ton lorries, fifteen 30-cwt lorries, three motor coaches, seventeen motorcycles and three Foster-Daimler tractors, in addition to supporting the vehicles and equipment used by the six tank companies.

Tank Production

The first production tank was not completed until 7 June.[42] There had been slippage in the programme due to design modifications, engineering problems, a shortage of factory space at Lincoln, and a lack of trained fitters. In May, a party of MGC crewmen deployed to

was changed to permit this.

37   Author's note: Unfortunately, despite many years researching the FTC, I have still to identify this crewman.

38   TNA WO 158/805: War History of the Central Workshops.

39   HP Steedman, *Historical Account of 711 MT Company ASC Attached to Tanks in France*, 17 July 1917.

40   One of these was 2934 Cpl Robert Parker who deployed to France on 23 September 1914. In the summer of 1916, he was serving with a Holt tractor unit supporting a Siege Artillery Battery in France when he was identified with 30 others. Parker would remain with the tanks for the remainder of the war, although he was a private soldier at the end of his service. He related his experiences in 1974, the recording being held at the IWM Catalogue number 492. Pugh *Most Secret Place on Earth*, p. 21.

41   Henriques' papers do not identify any of his crew although his wife's papers, held at Southampton University, do mention Paterson, Fisher and Raynor. Pope, *FTC*, pp.61 and 62. Gnr. 'Harry' Hayward was identified through an article in the *Evesham Standard and West Midlands Observer*, 20 December 1919.

42   Glanfield, *The Devil's Chariots*, p. 276.

the Wellington Foundry to assist and men were also sent to the Metropolitan works near Birmingham.[43] On 14 June, Swinton provided an update to GHQ_BEF on the availability of tanks. He reported that 25 machines would be available by the third week of July, and by the end of the month, a further 25 would be delivered – this would be sufficient to equip C and D Companies. A further 50 would be available by the middle of August (A and B Companies) and another 25 by the end of the month. The final 25 would be available by the beginning of September – exactly when was not specified. Of the 150 tanks, the majority (113) were built by the Metropolitan factory at Oldbury near Birmingham, the remainder (37 Male tanks) were built at Lincoln by Fosters and by Robey and Co. at the nearby Globe Works. Swinton does not however state whether 'available' meant available for use in France or for training in England. This would cause a wealth of correspondence in July.

The now-famous rhomboid shaped Mark I production tanks were 9 feet in height, 32 feet 6 inches long including the steering tail, with an overall width of 8 feet. The sponsons were not fitted to the tanks whilst in transit by rail but, when added, the width of the tank was 13 feet 9 inches.[44] The tank was designed to cross a gap of 10 feet and climb a vertical step of 4 feet 6 inches. The Daimler Knight 105 bhp engine was connected to a primary gear box containing two forward and one reverse gear with secondary gears providing two speeds to each track. The tank was protected by armour-plated steel, the thickest being 12mm on the cab.[45] The armour could, however, be defeated by German armour-piercing bullets. The combat weight of a Male tank was 28 tons and 27 tons for the Female variant although these weights were never achieved at Elveden. Eight men made a crew; the skipper, the driver and two gearsmen to drive and manoeuvre the vehicle plus four gunners to fight the tank. The engine was driven by petrol from two internal fuel tanks, within the horns of the tank, on either side of the skipper (seated left front) and the driver (right front). The driver steered the vehicle using cable which linked a steering wheel to the tail whilst the skipper operated the brakes on the tracks. The driver gave orders using hand signals for the gears to be selected to cope with the ground over which the tank would travel. The tanks sent out to France were not fully equipped; for example, there was no armour to protect the hydraulic steering pump and the oil tanks, which would lubricate the tanks' track, were not fitted before deployment. Full technical details of the Mark I tank are in Appendix IV.

On 17 June, the first batch of production tanks left the Oldbury factory, arriving at Barnham station the next day. They were unloaded at night and driven along the public roads to Elveden and thence to Bernersfield Camp – the villagers once again being told to keep their curtains closed. The problem of keeping the movement of tanks in and out of the area secret was resolved by the construction of an 850-feet long, double-track, siding running northwest from the railway line near Culford Lodge (now Lodge) Farm. The siding was built with end ramps for loading the tanks and a single platform between the two tracks to enable access to the wagon

---

43   Amongst them was Cpl Charlie Ironmonger whose family have a photograph of the detachment. Sadly, the quality of the image is too poor to allow reproduction in the Volume.

44   The limited gauge of both British and French railways required the sponsons be removed for transit. They were placed in specially designed trailers which accompanied the tanks on the rail flats.

45   Plans were produced to fit a second skin to the roof of the tank but only 23 sets were to be sent to France. There are no photographs of these being fitted to tanks used in action.

Male tank 743 being loaded onto a rail flat at the Fosters factory. (TMA)

beds. The whole area was screened from view by canvas sheeting to prevent activities being seen by anyone travelling on the Thetford to Bury St Edmunds branch line.

On 20 June, the Ministry of Munitions, which was responsible for tank production, contacted the Great Eastern Railway (GER) asking that they produce a plan for the siding; their request was endorsed by the Board of Trade two days later. The following day, Lt Col Pelham von Donop indicated that he had no objection to the proposal.[46] The plan was produced two days later but, although the GER stated that the siding was complete by 8 July, von Donop did not approve the siding for use until 29 July.[47]

Unsurprisingly, the construction of the training area, and the arrival of the tanks and crews, did not go unnoticed by RFC pilots who were based close by at Snareshill. On 24 June, Swinton visited their aerodrome and briefed them on the purpose of the training; as a result, unwanted RFC low level sorties ceased. Other observers at Elveden included Colonel Jean-Baptiste Estienne who was driving forward the formation of the *Artillerie Spéciale*: the French Army's tank arm.[48] Estienne had visited the Fosters factory at Lincoln, presumably to see tanks being

46   Pelham von Donop, a retired RE officer who had played Association Football for England, was appointed a railway inspector for the Board of Trade in 1899. He was promoted to Chief Inspecting Officer in July 1913 and held that position until his retirement in 1916. Pelham was the godfather of the author P.G. Wodehouse.

47   Trevor Pidgeon, *The Secret Railway*. p. 2.

48   Tim Gale, *French Tanks of the Great War*, p. 15.

manufactured, his visit on 26 June being noted by one of C Company's crewmen.[49] Swinton, meanwhile, was in London with Bradley and Brough, at a WO conference attended by Maj Gen Richard Butler (Deputy COS GHQ BEF) and Brig Gen John Burnett-Stuart (BG GS BEF).[50]

Amongst the subjects discussed was one which would create issues over the next three months. It was agreed that:[51]

The command and control of the Heavy Section, both as regards to personnel and materiel, up to the moment when companies are handed over for actual operations to the tactical commanders concerned, will be the responsibility of OC HS [Swinton] and his staff. For this purpose, the OC Heavy Section can take out to France whatever staff he finds necessary to maintain and produce the companies in condition to take to the field. The OC Heavy Section will coordinate the training and give instructions to the officers commanding companies up till that moment, receiving his own instructions from GHQ and where necessary assisting, by advice based on previous experience, the higher commanders under which the companies will operate.

The OC Heavy Section will command the whole unit in the usual way but naturally cannot be responsible for the tactical handling of the unit as a whole, or any part of it during operations. Companies will operate tactically under the orders of the formations to which they are attached but the OC Heavy Section must always exercise control and supervision of the whole under the General Staff GHQ and will be responsible for all the arrangements up to the moment of attack precisely in the same way that the Officer Commanding the Special Brigade is responsible.[52] His responsibilities include:

   a   Cooperation with the higher commanders concerned regarding all details connected with the employment of his companies.

   b   Arranging with Armies and departments for the maintenance of his companies when detached, for the provision of additional transport and for the repair of his machines and the replacing of casualties.

GHQ also confirmed that the tanks would be used to support attacks which would take place shortly before dawn. To that end, the crews were to be trained to drive at night, following tapes marked with luminous paint, laid to guide the tanks from their Points of Assembly to their Starting Points for a distance of 1,000 yards and that guides also be provided with belts fitted with lights to give directions to the drivers. Shortly before Zero, the tanks would then advance in line, 100–150 yards apart, and ahead of the infantry. This would place the vehicles on the enemy frontline at first light protecting the attacking units as they crossed no man's land.

Swinton proposed using small kite balloons to pass instructions to tanks from behind the British frontline. GHQ agreed that the RFC would supply 600 cubic feet of gas for the signalling balloons but three weeks' notice was required. They agreed that the manpower to

49   Diary of the unidentified crewman of Female tank 510 *Challenger* reprinted in Pidgeon, *Tanks at Flers*, p. 70 and translated by Karl-Heinz Pfarr.
50   By this time, the GHQ staff had been split with key elements deployed to an Advanced HQ located at the Chateau de Val Vion near Beauquesne 12 miles northwest of Albert.
51   unreferenced Digest of Discussions at Conference on 26 June 1916 - TNA WO 168-844'
52   The Special Brigade RE was responsible for the provision of poison gas.

operate the balloons was to be provided by the HS MGC but the source of the pressure gauges was yet to be confirmed.

Tank Training at Elveden

On 28 June, the first training exercise involving a group of tanks took place.[53] Collective training was undertaken at Elveden, such as following simulated routes from Places of Assembly to Start Points, using the scheme outlined above. Red lamps were fitted to the rear of tanks to act as a convoy light and to reduce the likelihood of accident. Other drills considered were communications between tanks and local units as well as their headquarters. Using his Sapper connections, Swinton had, in March, contacted the RE Wireless Experimental Establishment at Woolwich to design the equipment to allow messages to be passed back to the tank company headquarters. He also asked the Commandant of the RE Wireless Training Centre at Worcester to 'earmark' a few specially selected operators to be transferred to the Heavy Section when required. Following visits to Lincoln and Thetford, a small spark transmission set was developed, using the 200-metre wavelength with a range of three miles. It had a small folding mast designed to fit within the confined space of a tank. Although messages could be sent from the crew to the headquarters, reception in the tanks was not possible owing to the noise and vibration within the tank when the engine was running.

Another communication system trialled was tank-to-aircraft messaging using special daylight signalling lamps provided by the RFC at Snareshill. It was found that the amount of information which could be conveyed by code was extremely limited and the chain of transmission was so slow and cumbrous as to be almost useless.[54] As a result, only two signals were to be used: a series of Ts indicating 'Out of action' and a series of Hs meaning 'Am on objective.'[55]

A tank-to-tank signalling system was trialled using coloured discs raised through the tank roof hatch but these were vulnerable to artillery and small arms fire. The use of signal balloons, discussed with GHQ BEF, was also trialled and signalling sections formed within tank companies.[56] These balloons however proved to be impractical other than as a means of providing a fixed point for navigation back across the battlefield when tanks were rallying. Another trial conducted at Elveden was the laying of an armoured telephone cable across the battlefield – a small plough being attached to the tanks, so that cable would be buried six inches below ground.[57] In the end, however, long distance communications to headquarters were undertaken by using messenger pigeons and inter-tank communications using flags and lamps. The former worked well in battle, the latter less so.

It was suggested that compasses be fitted to the tanks to aid navigation when operating with the tank hatches closed. Most people would think that, using such a device, was impractical owing to the fact that the tank's hull, being made of steel, would prevent a true reading

---

53   See Pidgeon, *Tanks at Flers*, p. 70 translated by Pfarr.
54   Swinton, *Eyewitness*, pp. 250–251.
55   See Appendix VI, paragraph 9.
56   D Company's Balloon Section comprised an officer (Sampson), one corporal, two lance corporals and 13 gunners. See Woods' notebook p. 15 at the TMA.
57   *Crème de Menthe* laid a telephone cable on 15 September after the capture of Courcelette. See Chapter 8.

being given. However, the RN had developed a demagnetised version and happily provided reconditioned compasses together with an expert in their use. The cases were fitted and some skippers were instructed how to use them. Whilst they coped with the ground conditions at Elveden, the deeply rutted soils of the Somme battlefields made their use impractical as was shown during the attack by No. 1 Column supporting the Guards Division on 15 September – see Chapter 6.[58]

Another device tested was a grapnel, towed behind the tank, to rip out German barbed wire. This again worked at Elveden but grapnels were not deployed on the Somme or Ancre battlefields in 1916. They were however used very effectively during the Battle of Cambrai, the wire-pulling tanks being crewed by instructors from the Driver Training School – some of whom were originally crewmen who had seen action at the Battle of Flers–Courcelette.[59]

The arrival of tanks at Elveden caused a mix of emotions amongst the crews. Gnr William Dawson said of his first sighting: 'Early one morning we were awakened by a rattling and rolling. In great excitement, everybody rushed out and there they were – the first of the tanks passing our tents to the practice driving ground. We were almost too excited to bother about breakfast.'[60] Capt Basil Groves, who initially served with B Company and in 1941 commanded 7th Royal Tank Regiment in North Africa, was struck with awe:

> On arrival in the restricted area, our company was used as [enemy] infantry to hold a farm and its locality. I was in a building and we were not allowed to look out until a signal was given. I opened the top of a stable door and there, 50 yards away, was a colossal monster moving along at 3 miles an hour with guns sticking out from all sides. It really made me think.'[61]

Another crewman, who had seen action in France, saw one whilst running on his second evening in the area:

> Suddenly, around the bend in the lane, I heard a grinding and a grunting and, a few seconds later, I was confronted by the awful apparition of a Mark I tank with its weird, wheeled tail. I drew up, petrified, wondering if this was another manifestation of the condition that caused me to be invalided home from France.[62]

58 The compass in Male tank No. 765 *Daredevil*, used on 15 September 1916, was removed by her skipper after the first action. It has been loaned to the Tank Museum, by the Mortimore family, and it is currently (2021) on display as part of the Tank Men exhibition.
59 The tanks were under command of Hastie, who commanded *Dinnaken* at the Battle of Flers on 15 September 1916. Amongst the crews were Arnaud who commanded *Male tank 722*, William Hopkins of B Company, and Cpl Roy Reiffer MM who had been a crewman in *Dinnaken*.
60 WT Dawson, 'Reminiscences of My Experience with the First Tanks', an unpublished manuscript held at the TMA. Dawson first saw combat with tank crew C20 at the Quadrilateral and was in action on five occasions in 1917 before being commissioned into the Tank Corps in May 1919. Pope, *FTC*, pp. 65–68.
61 HBM Groves' papers. TMA.
62 Pugh, *The Most Secret Place on Earth*, p 39. Unfortunately, the individual is not identified but it is likely to have been an officer.

Some of the ASC drivers posted from the Tractor Depot at Avonmouth experienced major difficulties with their new role:

> The problem was that nothing in their past had prepared them for the shock of seeing the tanks and many were alarmed at the thought of driving these monsters. Those who were extremely unhappy were returned to Avonmouth, having been assessed by Major Knothe as incompetent, probably because they pretended to know nothing about internal combustion engines, which was obviously not true.
>
> There were some men who believed that their return to unit was unfair since they were the best qualified people available. With good management, fear of the tanks could probably have been overcome and they could have developed the same sort of pride in their work as the others who remained. It was perhaps quite unnecessary of the Tractor Depot to be asked by the War Office for an explanation but that was probably caused by the embarrassment felt by senior ASC involved. [63]

On 10 July, a second group of production tanks arrived at Elveden, bringing the total to 50 which was just sufficient to equip two companies.[64] Stern, who was now chairman of the TSC, had been concerned that, should no further orders be made beyond the original 150, then the manufacturing capability would be lost. His fears were probably heightened when, on 10 July, Burnett-Stuart wrote to Bird, the DASD at the WO, asking for further tank orders to be delayed.

> It is hardly possible with the knowledge at our disposal, whether more tanks should be ordered or the type changed. Before any judgement can be formed, it will be necessary to have at least twenty tanks, fully equipped and manned, functioning in some definite tactical scheme. It will also be necessary to view the French experiment which they have informed us they propose to hold shortly with the tanks. Can you say please for how long a decision may be delayed without affecting the continuity of manufacture?[65]

Responding two days later, on behalf of DASD, Swinton replied: 'The decision as to the supply of tanks, if it is affirmative, should be immediate. As regards manufacture, it is a question of engines, gun mountings, gun ammunition and various small parts. The absolute continuity of supply is already broken but so far, the skilled men have not been dispersed.'

Swinton also expressed concern about the lack of suitable manpower for further crews, recruitment having been paused, and he believed that obtaining men of the right education, intelligence, physical development and mechanical aptitude could not be guaranteed. To expand the HS MGC, Swinton therefore recommended using men from a unit such as the Royal Marine Artillery, who already were trained in gunnery, machine-gunnery and machinery. His final paragraph indicates that, if GHQ required a significant increase in the number of British tanks, perhaps to match the French plan to use tanks in numbers in the spring of 1917, it would 'necessitate a tremendous expansion in the manufacture of ancillary services connected to the

63   Young, *ASC 1902-1918*, pp. 100–101.
64   Pugh, *The Most Secret Place on Earth*, p. 38.
65   It is interesting to note that this request occurred only 14 days after the visit of Estienne to Elveden.

maintenance and repair of the unit, the importance of which we are only now just beginning to be in a position to gauge.'[66]

Tactical Demonstrations

GHQ's desire to see twenty tanks operating in a tactical scheme was achieved within a fortnight. On 21 July, a mock attack involving 25 tanks was observed by Lloyd George, the new Secretary of State for War,[67] and the Honourable Edwin Montagu,[68] plus Robertson (CIGS), Maj Gen Frederick Maurice (Director Military Operations), and representatives of GHQ. Swinton arranged for Robertson and Maurice to be accommodated at Elveden Hall the previous night. Having heard that Earl Iveagh had been kept in ignorance of the activities on his land, Robertson arranged a briefing that evening by Maurice about the tanks and their role in the next major offensive.

The next morning, as Lloyd George and his party made their way by train from London to Elveden, Robertson and Maurice visited the various training schools and reviewed the battleground. On Lloyd George's arrival, the party moved to the observation platform, just behind the 'British frontline'. A rocket was fired to signify Zero, eight kite balloons were launched at the tanks' Starting Points and the 25 tanks then advanced in line. As they crossed no man's land, they were followed by Lloyd George and the other observers on foot. The tanks were observed smashing down the protective barbed wire and attacking the dummy machine-gun positions which were located in the enemy frontline parapet. Both Male and Female tanks fired blank rounds from their weapons, the latter's target being an enemy counter-attack launched from a depth position once the tanks had penetrated the frontline. Throughout the attack, RFC aircraft flew overhead, taking photographs. The GHQ staff arrived as the demonstration was underway, their journey having been delayed by a car breakdown. Lloyd George, who was presented with photographs of the event as he returned to London, was convinced of the tanks' potential as were the GHQ!

Next day, at a meeting between the WO and GHQ staff, it was agreed that one section of six tanks, with a workshop, should deploy by the end of the first week in August, the remainder of the tanks following in groups of twelve at weekly intervals. The tactical idea underlying this was the employment of six tanks at a time. Swinton disagreed with the proposal, since it would break up the companies and cut down the time available for effective collective training, but he was over-ruled. It was agreed that a further 100 tanks should be built and 75,000 rounds of special 6-pounder ammo be ordered.[69] The conference also agreed detailed arrangements for equipment support in France including the establishment of a Tank Park at Le Havre.

Four days later, a second but smaller demonstration was arranged at Elveden, this time for a 'Russian General.' Only five tanks took part whilst other training continued. It was only when

---

66   Stern, *Tanks 1914–1918,* pp. 83–85.
67   Kitchener had drowned on 5 June 1916 en route to Russia and Lloyd George replaced him as Secretary of State for War. He maintained his support for the new weapons system in his role.
68   Recently appointed Minister for Munitions.
69   The additional 100 tanks were to be built on the completion of the initial order. In fact, they were not manufactured until after many of the Mark I machines had been destroyed in action and were of the Mark II and III design. See Chapter 9.

the Russian officer reached the grandstand that someone realised that the visitor was King George V. The news of his presence quickly spread and, after the demonstration, as the monarch drove back to the local station, the road within the area was lined with cheering crewmen. As the Royal party returned to London by train, accompanied by Swinton and Brough, the King 'expressed his gratification at what he had seen.'[70]

D Company officers at Canada Farm 1916:
Rear row: Reginald Legge, Arthur Blowers, Eric Robinson, Leonard Bond, George Bown, Harry Drader, Jack Bagshaw, Arthur Arnold, Stuart Hastie, Harold Darby, Hugh Bell, Charles Storey and Herbert Pearsall.
Centre: Edward Colle, Alfred Enoch, Graeme Nixon, George Mann, Stephen Sellick, Frank Summers, Graham Woods, Harold Mortimore, unknown, Jeff Wakley and Walter Stones
Front row: Vic Huffam, Sandy Sharp, Reginald Court and Harold Head. (TMA)

In his book, *Eyewitness*, Swinton describes that the training programme was expanded in July as the companies prepared to deploy. The key activity was driver training, in particular obstacle crossing, and vehicle maintenance. However, there was no time for training the tank crews in

---

70   Swinton, *Eyewitness*, pp. 262–265.

accordance with any identified tactical scheme, and there was no infantry formation with which to practice.[71]

One of the forms of individual training used by the British Army is called a Tactical Exercise Without Troops (TEWTs). This is usually undertaken on a training area or another piece of land where officers or NCOs can work through the problem – an answer having been already agreed by the training staff. Swinton placed the responsibility for this training, and other basic skills, on the company commanders (see Part II of Appendix V). This document is comprehensive and is worthy of reading. Unfortunately, time constraints and a shortage of fully equipped tanks made it impossible to achieve. Swinton stressed the need for map reading, working to a timetable and giving orders. He also required that skippers and drivers be practised in having to work out how to cross various pieces of ground by day and night, something which could be achieved without using the tanks. Furthermore, the mechanical skills needed to keep the tanks fit for action were not mastered by the crews and there was a shortage of spare parts for repairs.[72]

Tank Tips

Swinton also developed Tank Tips to ensure that every crewman knew what to do in action.[73] They were published and individual crewmen required to memorise them. They were:

- Remember your orders
- Shoot quick – shoot cunning.
- Shoot low. A miss that throws dirt in his eyes is better than one which whistles past his ears. Shoot the enemy when they are rubbing their eyes.
- Economise ammunition and don't kill a man three times.
- Remember that trenches are curly and dug-outs deep – look round the corners.
- Watch the progress of the fight and your neighbouring tanks.
- Watch the infantry whom you are helping.
- Remember the position of your own line.
- Smell out the enemy's machine-guns and kill them with your 6-pounders.
- You will not see them for they will be cunningly hidden.
- You must ferret out where they are, judging by the following signs: Sound, smoke, dust, a shadow in the parapet, a hole in the wall, a haystack, rubbish heap, a pile of wood or line of bricks.
- One 6-pounder shell which hits the loophole of a machine-gun emplacement will do it in.
- Use the 6-pounder with care, shoot to hit and not to make a noise.

71 GHQ did not publish such direction until 15 August 1916. See Appendix VI. Until then the tank companies' only tactical guidance was Swinton's note developed earlier that February. See Appendix III.
72 The fact that detailed orders for the drivers were issued on 14 September in manuscript form indicates that there was concern over the training and practice completed at Elveden. See Appendix XI. It may, however, have been developed in Great Britain as the orders refer to the track oil tanks which were not fitted to the tanks used by C and D companies.
73 Swinton, *Eyewitness*, pp. 272–274.

- Never have a gun, even when unloaded, pointed at your own infantry or another tank.
- Never mind the heat, never mind the noise, never mind the dust, think of your pals in the infantry.
- Thank God you are bullet-proof and can help the Infantry who are not.
- Have your [gas] mask always handy.

These Tank Tips would prove to be a valuable aide-memoire for the crewmen in battle.

5

Preparing for Battle

On 2 August, BEF GHQ issued directions to the Fourth and Reserve Armies on its future objectives including a 'wearing out battle' starting in mid-September 1916. This gave a six-week period for the tank companies to deploy, complete their tactical training and prepare for battle. The French Government had sought a delay for the use of the tanks until the spring of 1917 when their own vehicles would be ready for use. Lloyd George understood the French position but political pressure at home, following the unprecedented losses on 1 July, made it necessary to defeat the Germans on the Somme. He therefore agreed that the tanks could deploy in the autumn, rather than wait until the following spring. However, D'Eyncourt and Stern were keen that the tanks should not be used in small numbers and approached Robertson about the matter.

On 3 August, Stern wrote to the Ministry of Munitions concerning the availability of the 150 tanks, which had been ordered at the same time identifying the spares problems which would be experienced by C and D Companies. 'I was under the impression that these would not be used until the order had been completed, therefore the spares would not, in the ordinary way, be available until the 150 machines had been completed.' He did, however, state that he had made arrangements that 100 tanks, with appropriate spares, would be completed by 1 September and that the sending out of partially-equipped machines was courting disaster.[1]

Also on 3 August, Brough left England for France to establish a new tank training area, north of Abbeville, between St Riquier and Yvrench (map 2, map square C4).[2] Shortly after his arrival, Brough found it necessary to wire home for support as he had been ordered to take over command of the units in France. Kyngdon was sent out to assist him, with two clerks and a motor car. This small group became known as HQ HS MGC and it sent and received signals from GHQ and from the WO. Brough was required to make regular visits to the Advanced GHQ near Beauquesne, which was about an hour's drive away, as well as to the main headquarters, at Montreuil, which was a three hour return drive. Sadly, however, he did not develop a good rapport with the GHQ staff and this would ultimately lead to his dismissal.

---

1   Stern, *Tanks 1914–1918*, pp. 87-88. This would have provided sufficient for the three tank companies to deploy to France whilst allowing some training for other crewmen to continue at Elveden. The tanks were not however fully complete when they deployed. See chapter 9.
2   Fuller, *Tanks in the Great War*, p. 34.

The training area, described by GHQ BEF as being at Riquier, is generally known as Yvrench as this was the village where the tank companies were billeted. The tanks were to be off-loaded at Conteville, which is three miles east of Yvrench. The railway stations at St Riquier and Conteville had been regularly used by infantry divisions to access the training area in the past. However, the GHQ Movement Staff identified that off-loading tanks on the single-line track at Conteville could take up to 24 hours so they put Conteville out of use to other units when it was required by the tank companies. The Movement Staff also realised that the railway wagons, which transported the tanks, would have to be dedicated to their carriage and therefore assembled two rakes of rail flats, each capable of moving two sections of tanks, so that a company could be loaded and moved over two days from their port of entry at Le Havre to Conteville and then from Conteville to the new tank base at the Loop railhead between Bray sur Somme and Fricourt.

Officer instructors in early 1917:
Standing: William Hopkins, Sir John Dashwood, Gerald Philips, Alec Arnaud and 'Mick' Wheeler.
Sitting: Stuart Hastie, Percy Jackson and Hugh Swears. (TPA)

On 5 August, an advance party, led by Lt Sir John Dashwood, left Elveden for France.[3] Dashwood's selection reveals the lack of depth within HQ HS MGC which consisted of

3   *War History 3rd Light Tank Battalion.* p. 3A.

Swinton and one staff captain. The company headquarters establishment also did not provide a second captain to undertake such tasks so Holford-Walker utilised Dashwood who was his Reserve section commander.[4] The party arrived at Le Havre on 8 August, most deploying to Yvrench although at least one joined 17 (Supply) Company AOC at the port – this was also the location of the Stores Park which would handle the material needs of the HS MGC in France.[5] Coincidently, that same day, Swinton wrote to the DASD concerning the spare parts and other accessories. Stern's previous statement about a shortage of spare parts was confirmed as it was clear that none would be available on 1 September other than those for the tanks' engines which were readily available from the Daimler company.[6]

ASC Officers at Elveden:
Centre rank: Philip Johnson, Frederic Bracey, Henry St John, Hugh Knothe, Beresford Edkins, Henry Steedman and Alfred Woodhams. (*The Sphere*)

4   Holford-Walker and Dashwood had served together in 10th Argyll & Sutherland Highlanders (A&SH) and 'claimed' Dashwood shortly after joining the HS MGC. Dashwood would serve with the tanks for remainder of the war, acting as assistant adjutant of C Battalion in the spring of 1917 and, when Mortimore became too ill to remain in his role as adjutant of F Battalion, succeeded him in August 1917. Dashwood stayed in that post for a year, leaving after the Battle of Amiens to serve at the Inter-Allied Tank School. He then returned to 3rd Light Battalion and served as a company commander. Pope, *FTC*, pp. 39–42.
5   The route used is unknown. Based on information in individuals' records, crews travelling without equipment usually travelled by the daily packet boat sailing from Folkestone to Boulogne, with those travelling with equipment moved via Southampton to Le Havre.
6   The Daimler Knight engine, which had been in production for several years, had the necessary supply chain already in place and could easily meet the needs of the tank companies from its factory in

An advance party of ASC workshop personnel also moved to France two weeks before the first tank shipment. Knothe deployed with three officers, a mechanist sergeant major (MSM) and 25 other ranks. With them went two trailers, one containing a 60-ton press whilst the other carried lathes, drilling machines and emergency wheels. The ASC advance party deployed via Le Havre where they were provided with two Holt caterpillar tractors, before driving to the Loop. In September, they were joined by Capt Beresford Edkins, who had assumed commend of 711 Company after Knothe's deployment and who, like Knothe, was used as a technical advisor.[7]

Following Swinton's warning on 31 July about the poor state of the tanks, the steering tails were removed and sent to Lincoln to be reinforced. The vehicles also needed 'tuning-up', a task which it was calculated would take two months if undertaken by the reduced number of experienced artificers now present at Elveden.[8] Stern, who visited the training area with Col Frederick Sykes to review the situation, informed the WO that he would guarantee to complete the task in ten days.[9] Stern then visited the Metropolitan factory at Oldbury to seek assistance from amongst their staff. Forty men immediately volunteered and travelled to Elveden where local billets were found by the Chief Constable. However, feeding was a problem so Stern approached Lt Col Henry Thornton, the General Manager of the GER, who provided a restaurant car which was positioned at the new Culford Lodge siding.[10] The 'tuning-up' was completed in under ten days although how this impacted on ongoing crew training is not recorded.[11]

Whilst Brough was based at the new training area, he visited GHQ to ascertain whether any plans had been developed for the tactical employment of the tanks. His visit was fruitless, for no ideas apparently existed on the subject and he had to rely on what was taught at Elveden.[12] On 10 August, CIGS' office confirmed Swinton that he was to command the HS MGC at home with Brough commanding the units in France – his actual control of them was however limited as command remained with the GHQ staff. At Elveden, some training continued under Bradley but it had major limitations owing to the lack of tanks. According to Henriques:

Coventry.

7   Young, *ASC 1902-1918*, p. 100.
8   Stern, *Tanks 1914-1918*, pp. 86–87.
9   Sykes had commanded the RNAS in the Eastern Mediterranean in 1915. On 9 June 1916, he was appointed an Assistant AG, a staff post at the WO, with responsibility for organising the MGC and manpower planning. One of his former staff officers in the Dardanelles was Summers who was now commanding D Company. Sykes would later be appointed Second Chief of the Air Staff in the rank of air vice marshal.
10   As civilians there was no entitlement for the workers to be brought on ration strength.
11   Thornton was an American businessman who had previously managed the Long Island Railway Company. Appointed to manage the GER in 1914, Thornton was commissioned as a lieutenant-colonel in the Royal Engineers in 1916, serving as Deputy Director General of Movements and Railways and, later, as Inspector General of Transportation, with the rank of major-general. He became a naturalised British citizen in 1919 and was knighted for his wartime service.
12   Fuller, *Tanks in the Great War*, p. 34. Swinton's original tactical proposals, written in February 1916 (see Appendix III) were still unknown at the HQ Heavy Branch at Bermicourt when Fuller developed the new Branch's training system in January 1917. Fuller, remarkably, also did not refer to GHQ's produced provisional notes published on 16 August. See Appendix VI.

Training had its strengths and weaknesses. One great asset was the calibre of the crews – practically all picked mechanics of above average intelligence, extraordinarily keen on their work. They knew and understood the tank, and its engine, and had a thorough knowledge of, and confidence in, the Vickers machine-gun. They felt great pride in their Company, in their section and in themselves as a crew. There was a healthy competition among crews but were able to tell the men, whom we trained ourselves and whom we got to know thoroughly, that *our* tank was going to go through at all costs.

But we had to work under tremendous pressure. The tanks did not arrive until the last minute and we could not possibly get through many of the things on our programme. Our own tank developed a fault on the day it arrived so we were without one for the whole time we were in in Britain, except on one occasion. We had no instruction on reconnaissance, map-reading, signalling or the use of the compass. We had insufficient instruction on the use of our gas masks, our revolvers and, because we had no tank of our own, we had no opportunity using the actual [Vickers machine] guns we would use in action until we *were* in action. Only once did we fire from a tank whilst it was in motion.

Especially important was the lack of any practice in driving over an unknown course. Although we had no tank, my crew were attached to different tanks at different times but they never drove over a course which had not been driven over, carefully and step by step, beforehand. They had no practice driving with visors [hatches] closed down and having to use the periscope. The first time we did this was when we crossed the British front line in battle. Nor did we have much training in moving in darkness. The only time we did this was on a bright, moonlit night, so it was not much use. We had insufficient physical training and insufficient discipline was instilled in the crews. We officers were given no instruction on the rapid comprehension of long divisional orders and in the extraction of those parts of most concern to our crews.[13]

C Company's Deployment

With deployment fast approaching for the first half of C Company, 11–12 August was to be their last weekend in Great Britain.[14] Most packed their kit at New Farm Camp whilst the Tank Park personnel were undertaking final checks of the tanks; their sponsons and weapons, and their limited supply of spares. On Sunday 13 August, the diarist Gnr Victor Archard and two chums walked to Culford Arms public house at Ingham for lunch and, having played music afterwards, stayed that afternoon for tea.[15] That evening, Swinton addressed all members of C Company; it was an informal briefing with crewmen being seated with pipes lit rather than a formal parade.[16] At 2200 hours, as it was becoming dark, the tank loading parties marched to the Culford Lodge siding and 13 Male tanks were loaded onto a rake of flat wagons. The work was conducted under the command of Capt Herbert Hiscocks, OC No. 2 Section, who was to deploy with the tanks and their drivers. After the tanks left the siding, the tank loading party

---

13 Henriques, lecture script given on 6 March 1917 (TMA).
14 The tanks and their crews did not deploy in sections as proposed by GHQ BEF but in half-companies.
15 Archard, *Diary* and *Letters 1916*. The pub is called now the Cadogan Arms.
16 Swinton, *Eyewitness*, p. 275.

returned by lorry arriving back at New Farm by 0400 hours; the tanks, meantime, headed for Avonmouth Docks, near Bristol. The next day, Archard rode three miles to Bury St Edmunds to have a tooth extracted before visiting Wordwell Church near New Farm Camp as he had been unable to attend a service the previous day. There was a severe thunderstorm that afternoon, after which Bradley inspected the first C Party main body (MB1) dressed in full kit, ahead of their departure the next morning.[17]

On Tuesday 15 August, C Company's Male tanks arrived at Avonmouth and were loaded onto SS *Ilston Grange*. The ship was due to depart for Le Havre the following day but this was delayed owing to the threat of German U-boats operating in the English Channel. Meanwhile, at New Farm Camp, after Reveille on Wednesday 16 August at 0400 hours and breakfast 30 minutes later, the Company HQ and Male tank crews assembled at 0530 hours and moved by lorry to Thetford Bridge railway station. Here MB1 caught the 0715 hours train which took them to Liverpool Street Station in London. Having made their way to Waterloo Station, MB1 left London at noon and travelled to Southampton Docks where they embarked on SS *France* at 1730 hours. The ship, which was a former Atlantic liner, sailed two hours later and travelling under the cover of darkness, arrived at Le Havre by 0200 hours the following morning.

Initial Battle Plans

On 16 August, GHQ notified HQ Fourth and Reserve Armies that tanks were available for the next major attack in mid-September. An initial allocation of 36–42 tanks was made to the Fourth Army and 18–24 tanks for the Reserve Army (see Appendix VI).[18]

Fourth Army was warned for an attack between Leuze Wood, Ginchy, Delville Wood and High Wood, as far as Munster Alley (the Army's left boundary) between Bazentin-le-Petit and Pozières (see Coloured Map 4). The Fourth Army's objective would be the German third line trench system from Morval to Le Sars, a village on the old Roman Road from Pozières to Bapaume, and possibly the German gun positions beyond. The Reserve Army would be required to attack from Munster Alley to the River Ancre, with a view to securing the German third line system west of Le Sars to Pys and then form a defensive flank along the River Ancre.

GHQ also directed army and corps commanders, and their staff, to study the new weapon system at the St Riquier training area so that 'they can adapt their plans for using [tanks] to best advantage.' To that end, details of combined exercises for infantry and tanks would be notified shortly. The instruction stated that several points required to be considered when using tanks:

> An assembly place under cover [of fire]. These should not be difficult to find behind the ridge we presently occupy.

---

17   MB1 mainly consisted of the Company HQ and the crews of the Male tanks.
18   This allocation was more than could be provided by two tank companies; it may have been based on the anticipated arrival of 100 tanks in France as mentioned earlier. Haig was hoping for at least fifty for the next attack. In a letter to Robertson, written on 25 August, he stated, 'Even if I cannot get so many as I hope, I shall use what I have got as I cannot wait any longer for them and it would be folly not to use every means at my disposal in what is likely to be the crowning effort for this year.' Miles, *OHGW*, pp. 234–235.

Their use with infantry. It will be necessary to train those divisions who may be earmarked to work with the tanks. [19]

Although the recommendation is that the tanks should be 100 to 150 yards apart, it may probably suffice, in view of the nature of German defences opposite us, to use these tanks on a wider interval from 200–250 yards. One section of tanks would thus appear to be a suitable distribution for an infantry division covering 1,000 to 1,500 yards of front. [20]

The infantry will have to work close behind the tanks, occupying, clearing out, and consolidating successive positions after these have been reached by the tanks. Some tanks might be required to work with the infantry in clearing up strong points overrun by the leading tanks and troops.

The working of our artillery barrage in conjunction with the tanks will require careful consideration.

It is for consideration whether the tanks could not move a short distance in the darkness, say as far as the Switch Line where that line is close to our front line. They would then move forward to the German third line in the grey dawn. [21]

The objectives of the tanks must be clearly stated and as simple as possible as it is difficult for the tanks to manoeuvre.

Notes on Tank Employment

With that warning order, GHQ also issued a paper on employment of the weapon system; see Appendix VI. It includes information on the organisation of the HS MGC, the size of each tank company, as well as their integral but limited support capability. The paper warned that the latter were immobile units, located by a railhead, and that the Workshop could not be sub-divided. [22] The paper also explained the method by which ammunition, technical stores and other combat supplies were to be provided by local formations.

The notes gave outline details of an individual tank's capabilities and limitations, stressing:

The chief attributes of the tank are its power of crossing obstacles, its fire power, its momentum and its invulnerability to shrapnel and small arms fire. Its chief weakness is its liability to be knocked out by artillery and heavy trench mortars.

The machine weighs 28 tons. Its speed is from 4–5 miles per hour on the level to 2 miles per hour when climbing or over very rough ground. It can reverse. It can surmount a revetted parapet 5 feet high and cross a gap 10 feet wide. Wire entanglements, hedges and walls etc do not interfere within its progress. It can push down and pass over single

19 This was not achieved: only 56th (London) Division had sight of, and the opportunity to train with, any of the Tank Companies – see below.
20 It appears that the GHQ staff were unaware of Swinton's recommendation that tanks should be used in pairs; one Female supporting each Male.
21 The GHQ staff were referring to the German's main defence line (the Switch Trench) rather than the third line of trenches such as The Flers Line.
22 The inability of the Workshops to be split also caused difficulties which became apparent when individual sections were allocated to III Corps and the Reserve Army on the western flank.

trees up to 10 inches in diameter and it can traverse ordinary fir plantations or coppices of young trees. In close woods, however, there is considerable risk of the sponsons and guns coming into contact with trees and being wrenched off.

Whilst GHQ gave provisional instructions on the tactical use of tanks, it was not overly proscriptive. It gave the formation commanders options for use in support of the infantry stating:

> There are four ways in which tanks may be employed:
> The advance in line in large numbers.
> The attack in groups, or pairs, against selected objectives.
> Employment singly, or in pairs, for special purposes.
> Employment as mobile light artillery.

It also provided detailed guidance as follows:

> Within the limits of the objective given to an attack, it is generally possible to pick out the points from which the greatest resistance is to be expected. An allocated number of tanks should be told off to deal with each of these points of defence. They should be closely supported by bodies of infantry told off for the purpose, who will advance under the cover of the tanks, clear up behind them and eventually consolidate the locality when taken. In the case of a village of wood, the tank may find sufficient cover to enable them to remain and help / hold the location. If not, they would either go on to a further objective, or go back, according to their original orders.
>
> Each tank attack will be a definite operation against a limited objective allocated to a selected number of tanks and a select body of infantry. In certain cases, a pair of tanks, supported by a platoon might suffice. Wherever tanks are to be employed, special attention must be paid to counter battery work, and the tanks should move under cover of a close barrage which should not lift from the objective until the tanks are close to it. Whether the tanks should deal with only the perimeter of the objective, or penetrate into it, depends on the circumstances, but their primary task will consist of preventing the locality with which they have to deal from interfering with the main infantry attack.

Unfortunately, this direction was not incorporated into the training undertaken at Yvrench, the direction provided by Fourth Army to the formations on 11 September (Appendix VII) or any of the extant divisional orders. Nor was any time available for training divisions and their allocated tanks in the rear areas near the Loop after 10 September and before they deployed on 12 and 13 September to their Places of Assembly.

C Company's Arrival in France

On 0700 hours on Friday 17 August, C Company's MB1 disembarked at Le Havre and then marched for two miles to a tented rest camp. For almost every crewman, this would have been their first experience of being part of the huge BEF organisation. They would have been briefed on the regulations, which limited their access to civilian establishments. The town of

Le Havre was in bounds but strictly controlled, and there was a large YMCA which provided refreshments and entertainments. The next day, the crewmen undertook a five-mile route march and that evening three men per section were granted access to Le Havre. On Sunday 20 August, the C Company men were marched four miles to a pebble beach and allowed to bathe in the sea – probably most welcome as the weather that day was very warm.[23]

On 19 August, GHQ BEF issued further instructions to the Fourth and Reserve Armies regarding a mid-September offensive.[24] This confirmed memoranda issued over the past two months but reduced the total allocation of tanks to 50 with the possibility that should more tanks became available, one or two more sections would be allocated to the Reserve Army. Based on this, the two army commanders, Rawlinson of Fourth Army and Gough of the Reserve Army, were directed 'to submit their proposals for the execution of the operations by 28 August. The plans of attack should state in detail how it is intended to employ the tanks.' This requirement was challenging as neither Rawlinson nor Gough would see the tanks being used until they attended a small demonstration at Yvrench on the afternoon of 26 August – see below.

Also on Monday 19 August, the C Company Male tanks left Avonmouth on the SS *Ilston Grange,* having been delayed four days by U-boat activity. As a result, Swinton prepared a revised shipping plan. This showed that the remaining twelve C Company tanks, having been loaded overnight on 21–22 August at Barnham, would now sail on a 'special' ship as SS *Ilston Grange* would not be available. C Company's second main body (MB2) would depart from Southampton on 24 August; the first half of D Company's tanks would be loaded at Barnham on 25–26 August and then be sent to Avonmouth for loading to SS *Ilston Grange.* HQ D Company and No 1 and 2 Sections would sail on a separate vessel leaving Southampton on 28 August.

The remainder of D Company's tanks would also be transported on SS *Ilston Grange,* having been loaded at Culford Lodge siding overnight on 2 September, with their crews departing Southampton on 4 September. Swinton also gave details of the planned movement of A Company. Half of their tanks would leave Elveden on 8–9 September, although Swinton stated that the dates 'may possibly be brought forward a few days' with their crews deploying via Southampton on 11 September. The remainder of A Company's tanks would leave the Culford Lodge siding on 15–16 September for Avonmouth with the crews travelling on 18 September via Southampton. This timetable was sent to GHQ, under the cover of a letter from DASD, which confirmed that only 50 tanks would reach Le Havre by 10 September providing the Channel stayed open.[25] This change in programme significantly reduced the training time for D Company at Yvrench. The workshop supporting C and D Companies was planned to depart from Barnham for Avonmouth on 28 August although Swinton stated they might move earlier. This was a modification to the original plan which saw them being loaded at Southampton. The

---

23   Archard's diary for the period 17 to 20 August 1916.
24   OAD 116 dated 19 August 1916. See Trevor Pidgeon, *Tanks at Flers,* p. 228.
25   WO 121/Stores/4446 dated 22 August 1916. This letter must have created significant concern at GHQ as Kiggell sent a memo to the WO the next day (sadly not held on file but mentioned in a letter from Butler to Whigham on 26 August). This letter stated that all of D Company's tanks must be in France by 4 September, if they were to be utilised for the planned attack on 15 September.

fact that the vessel was not named signifies Swinton was relying on the WO trooping staff to charter a ship from the open market.[26]

On 21 August, the SS *Ilston Grange* arrived at Le Havre carrying the first tanks. The French dock workers were asked to unload the tanks at night for security reasons but refused.[27] The task took them three days, during which two tanks were damaged.[28] Also on the evening of 21 August, C Company MB1 paraded at 2100 hours and two hours later, marched to the Gare Maritime at Le Havre. At 0100 hours, they boarded trains to take them to Rouen. That same night at Elveden, the remaining twelve C Company tanks were loaded onto rail flat wagons at Barnham for their move at Avonmouth and they left the next morning.

New Railhead at the Loop

On 22 August, at Val de Vion, the GHQ Operations staff tasked the QMG staff to establish two tank detraining points near the Somme battlefield.[29] One was to be at Dernancourt, on the mainline from Amiens to Albert, and the other on the British standard gauge 'Maricourt line', built to provide artillery units with ammunition.[30] The GHQ staff requested that location be in a sheltered spot west of the Plateau siding. The location selected was the Loop, an existing railhead halfway between Bray sur Somme and Fricourt, close to a camp known as Happy Valley. The Loop railhead was well drained, under-utilised and with a network of roads which could be used for deployment and replenishment, albeit some five miles from the locations where most of the tanks would operate. The Directorate of Rail Transport (DRT) therefore worked with Deputy Director RE, in the same way that the WO worked with the GER Company to build the new siding near Culford Lodge Farm. The Loop became the base of HQ HS MGC as well as the location of the QM's department and ASC workshops under Knothe. Later that day, DRT issued Movement Order 111 which confirmed the plan of C and D Companies' tanks journeys to the training area at Yvrench. The tanks would be transported on two rakes of flatbed wagons, each capable of moving 13 tanks and their sponson trailers, being off-loaded

---

26 Author's note: As a movement planner during the Persian Gulf War of 1991, I understand Swinton's difficulties. The delay to an early part of a programme impacts on the remainder unless it is possible to charter an appropriate vessel to fill the gap – from my experience this is far from easy.

27 Author's note: I have some sympathy for the dockyard workers. Off-loading a 25-ton load, from a ship's hold through a hatch and onto a quayside, requires skilled crane operators, specialist hawsers and tackle, well-practised teams on board and on the dockside, and good visibility. My first experience of off-loading Challenger tanks at St John in New Brunswick taught me that it is a task best taken steadily and can only achieved at night with the type of lamps used at major modern sporting stadia.

28 Unreferenced letter from Butler to Whigham dated 26 August 1916. The *3rd Battalion War History* p.3a states Smith's tank was the first to be offloaded followed by Henderson's.

29 GHQ OB/83 dated 22 August 1916.

30 Trevor Pidgeon, *Tanks at Flers*, p. 47, states that the request for facilities at Dernancourt was prompted by the need to off-load the six tanks from No 1 Section of C Company, close to northeast outskirts of Albert where they were to be based. However, Victor Archard, who was a member of that section, reveals they were off-loaded at the Loop and later drove via Meaulte to Aveluy arriving on 12 September. See TMA E2006.3104.

and on-loaded at Conteville, the crewmen disembarking at St Riquier. The rakes were retained for future tasks.[31]

C Company MB1 arrived at Rouen at 0700 hours, their 44 mile rail trip taking six hours.[32] In France and Belgium, British troops normally travelled in box wagons, originally designed for the movement of up to eight horses. Up to 20 men could be transported in such wagons with officers travelling in a third-class coach. However, on this occasion, the crewmen travelled in a coach which Archard described as being narrow, dark and very uncomfortable. The C Company crewmen then had to wait at Rouen until 1500 hours but they were permitted to leave the station, and at least one sent a postcard home to loved ones.[33] In England, A and D Companies continued to train at Elveden, with D Company's crewmen being issued with their distinctive leather tank helmets. Although these provided protection from head injury whilst in action, they were apparently disliked due to reports that some crewmen were mistaken for Germans and almost shot by British troops. Certainly, they gave no protection from shrapnel on the battlefield. As for B Company, it was difficult for them to undertake effective crew training, due to both a lack of tanks and insufficient drivers.[34]

C Company MB1 at last arrived at St Riquier at 0830 hours on 23 August. They had left Rouen at 1500 hours the previous afternoon, and were routed via Abbeville, stopping at one station for four hours, before travelling the last few miles on the single-track railway to the tiny halt. The crewmen then marched through Oneux for five miles to their new billets at Yvrench. The men were accommodated in barns and the local café was, in Archard's view, as good as a third-rate public house in England. Also, on 23 August, at Elveden, D Company formed a balloon signalling section under 2Lt Billy Sampson. Consisting of one corporal, two lance corporals and 15 men, its task was to send flag signals to the tanks, the balloons also acting as reference points to enable the tank crews to navigate their return to British lines. C Company MB2 were making their final preparations for deployment. They departed early the next morning from Thetford, travelling to Liverpool Street Station, then marched across Southwark Bridge to Waterloo, in order to catch the train to Southampton Docks. Coincidently their tanks also left Avonmouth the same day although, sadly, the name of the ship is not recorded.

As part of his personal equipment, each man carried a First Field Dressing (FFD) pack. This pack consisted of two large gauze pads and bandages, with two waterproof covers and safety

---

31 Movement Order No. 111 makes it clear that the off-loading and entraining of tanks at Conteville could take up to 24 hours. Other units being routed to that location would be held at Abbeville as the route was single track. It also foresaw that the entrainment of tanks, on completion of their field training, would take place on 7–8 and 10–11 September. In fact, the tank crews became so practised in loading or off-loading they could complete the task, in daylight, in about an hour.

32 Author's note: This seems an exceedingly slow journey given that the two locations were linked by a main railway line but it may indicate the difficulty the DRT staff had in obtaining a train path at short notice.

33 40006 Gnr. Fenwick Styan, a chauffeur from Hull, sent a postcard showing an aerial view of Rouen to his fiancée Doris Shipley who lived in Driffield. Styan was discharged from the army the following year as a result of sickness. The couple married and ran a successful taxi firm in Beverley for many years. Pope, *The FTC*, pp. 346–347.

34 B Company crews, who deployed as BCRs on 18 September, did not include ASC personnel; the shortfall was found from amongst drivers already allocated to C and D Companies whose tanks had been knocked out.

C Company crews marching across Southwark Bridge:
The officers are (left to right) Archie Holford-Walker, George Macpherson and Basil Henriques; the fourth officer remains unidentified. (TMA)

pins, which could be placed directly over wounds and then secured. Swinton was concerned that a FFD alone was insufficient to cope with the sort of injuries which would be sustained by a tank crew in action and tried to obtain first aid kits for each tank.[35] On 24 August, he sent a memo to the QMG staff stating: 'It is desirable that crews have a scaling more than First Field Dressing, the First Aid Bag as used by armoured cars of RNAS might be suitable.' He received the unhelpful reply: 'No info held on them, Med authorities in France to make arrangements.' This added another task for the minute HQ HS MGC, now in France, who were concentrating on training crews for battle and their support at the Loop; they now had to organise life-saving equipment for their men at very short notice.

On 25 August, C Company's Female tanks arrived at Le Havre, the Male tanks having left that morning by rail for Conteville. The Male tanks travelled much more quickly than their crews, arriving at 1940 hours. They were offloaded, fitted with their sponsons, and then driven to their camp near Yvrench that evening although two tanks broke down en route. A small workshop had been assembled at Yvrench but there were very few tank spares or specialist tools, which would create problems during training.

---

35   Author's note: I have only found a record for one RAMC SNCO travelling with C and D Companies; I therefore assume that it was expected that any wounded crewmen would be treated by his own section and then evacuated either as 'walking wounded' or by stretcher-bearers from the infantry units being supported.

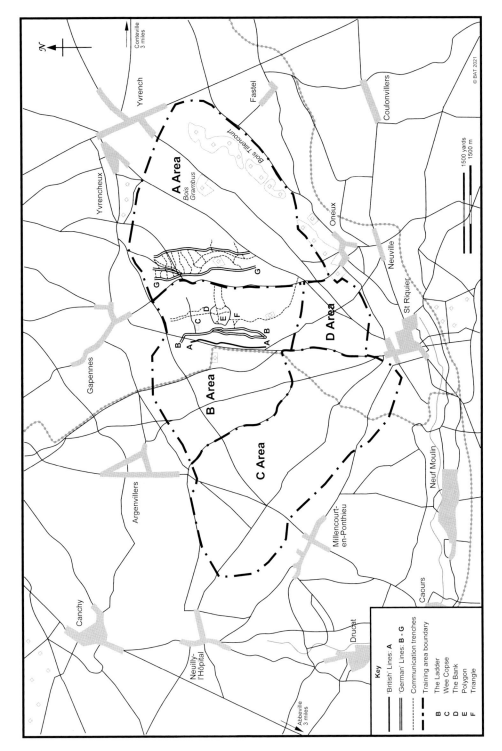

Yvrench training area (Barbara Taylor).

Tank Training at Yvrench

The following afternoon, five Male tanks supported a simulated attack on Le Bois Grambus by 7th Middlesex. The infantry were told that the tanks would cross the British trench at Zero hour, after which the battalion would advance as usual in four waves; the first wave at Zero plus one minute; the second at Zero plus three; the third at Zero plus five and the final wave at Zero plus six minutes. The infantry were ordered to advance in short rushes, up to but not beyond the advancing tanks unless one of them broke down in which case they were to proceed as though it was not there.[36] The exercise was observed by Haig, his chief of staff Lieutenant-General Lancelot Kiggell, and the two army commanders, Rawlinson and Gough, who would employ tanks for the first time. Haig recorded in his diary: 'At 3.00 p.m. I was present at a demonstration on the use of tanks. A battalion of infantry and five tanks worked together. The tanks crossed ditches and parapets, representing several lines of a defensive position, with the greatest of ease and one entered a wood which was made to represent a strong point, and easily walked over fair-sized trees of six inches diameter. Altogether, the demonstration was quite encouraging but we require to clear our minds as to the tactical use of these machines.'[37]

C Company's Female tanks arrived at Conteville on 29 August, as did Swinton, who visited the training area in the pouring rain.[38] The next day, he observed an exercise and later commented in *Eyewitness*:

> It consisted of an advance of much the same nature as that carried out at home five weeks earlier but over an inferior battlefield. I did not discover if there was any more elaborate tactical scheme underlying the scheme.
>
> The antics of the tanks caused amusement and, by many of the spectators, the exercise was not taken seriously. After the advance it became a circus. Some of the machines were asked to force their way through a wood and knock down trees; tricks they were not designed to play and which were likely to damage them seriously.
>
> I protested against these 'stunts' and the frequent exhibitions which were wearing out both machines and personnel. In addition to the almost continuous work of repairing, cleaning and tuning up the tanks, the men had barely time to eat, sleep and tend themselves. I speculated as to how many machines would be 100 per cent fit to go into action when their day arrived and wondered how the Royal Flying Corps would have fared if it had made its debut during the war with 50 machines of the first type produced and had to submit to similar preliminaries before it went into action.
>
> As had been the case in England, it seemed impossible to establish a realisation of the fact that the New Arm was a mass of complicated, and in some ways delicate, machinery in an embryonic state, and not the fool proof product of long trial and

36 CH Dudley Ward, *History of the 56th Division* (Uckfield: N&MP facsimile, 2001) p. 51.
37 Author's comment: It appears that Haig was unaware of the Tactical Notes issued on 16 August by the BEF Operational Analysis staff. See Appendix VII.
38 Archard recorded in his diary: 'It poured all day and the wind blew a hurricane. Six of us had to work with sleepers, picks and crowbars. By 9 am, we were all soaked but were forced to continue as the track had to be on the Willie by that evening. Eventually we were finished and we started back but stopped halfway for want of petrol. We waited for nearly an hour before some was bought from the Park.'

experience. Most of the ignorance in regard to the capabilities and limitations amongst the senior officers would have been dispelled if my memorandum of February [Appendix III] had had even limited circulation.[39]

Archard took part in this exercise which included a large number of infantry and several aeroplanes. His view was that it was very realistic but his tank fell into a ditch at the outset and the crew had to dig it out, all the time being observed by staff officers. It was a harbinger for his tank's debut on the battlefield when *Cognac* ditched twice on 15 September and bellied on 26 September.[40]

Rawlinson's Initial Plans for the Attack

Having seen the tanks in action, Rawlinson presented his plan to GHQ.[41] He proposed attacking in three phases in order to reach the Butte de Warlencourt (map 4, map square E2). He would use three corps, each attacking on a two-division front, to take three lines. The first (Line A) was from Combles (F3), though Bouleaux Wood, then south of Flers (E2), to High Wood and Martinpuich. This would require an advance of between 200–600 yards. The second attack, on Line B, would take place a few days later after the original attackers had been relieved. They would capture a point 1,000 yards south-southeast of Flers, and then proceed to take the German trench system known to the British as the Flers Line. This double trench system started at the southwest outskirts of Flers and ran in a north-westerly direction to the fortified farm complex at Eaucourt l'Abbaye and onto Le Sars (E2) which controlled the Albert to Bapaume Road. The third attack, again a few days later, would capture Line C running from a point west of Morval (F3), to Lesboeufs, then southwest of Gueudecourt (F2) then northwest to the Butte de Warlencourt (E2), presumably taking the Gird Line trench system between Flers and Gueudecourt. and the remainder of Le Sars as part of this operation.

Rawlinson saw tanks offering new possibilities but also potential difficulties. 'Should [the tanks] be successful, we might lose valuable time and miss an opportunity by confining our operations only to the capture of Line A. On the other hand, we may, by expecting too much of the tanks, be tempted to undertake an operation which is beyond our power and might cause very heavy losses to the tanks themselves and *to the infantry engaged in their support*.[42] Moreover, if the attack failed, the secret of the tanks would be given away once and for all.'

Rawlinson therefore proposed that the tanks should attack at night, on 11 September when there was a full moon. Their objective was to be Line A plus the village of Martinpuich and part of Flers. The tanks would be withdrawn before first light, without giving the Germans a chance

---

39 Swinton, *Eyewitness*, p 278. Glanfield, *The Devil's Chariots*, p. 153, states that the paper was held at the highest level for security grounds, and states it was remarkable that it had not been passed to Elles. He was also apparently unaware of the instructions reproduced at Appendix VII. Given that he had attended the original trial at Hatfield and was the GHQ representative at the conferences which proceeded the September Offensive, this is almost beyond belief.

40 The term 'bellied' describes the situation when the ground is so bad that the tank rests on its belly plates and the tracks make no progress.

41 Fourth Army 329 (G) dated 28 August 1916 described in Pidgeon, *Tanks at Flers*, pp. 51–52.

42 Author's italics: Rawlinson's proposal envisages the tanks taking the main role, rather than being in support of the attacking infantry; something which had not been made clear in earlier papers.

of seeing them in daylight or risking one of them falling into the enemy's hands. Rawlinson was concerned that their first use in battle should not be too difficult a task, or over too great a distance. He stated that 'their mysterious appearance on system A and withdrawal under cover of darkness after their task had been accomplished, without any sign or indication of what they are, or what their powers are, except the somewhat distorted reports that are bound to drift back to higher [German] authorities from the demoralised survivors of the garrison of system A, would most certainly have a great effect on an army already shaken in morale.'

Limiting the use of tanks in support of the capture of Line A would, in Rawlinson's view, truncate the timetable for the subsequent attacks of Lines B and C. He proposed that the initial attack on Line A take place on 11 September. Once Line A was taken southeast of Flers, this would enable an attack on Line B to start the next day (12 September) attacking up the Flers Line to Le Sars. That same day, a foothold would be made in the southern part of Line C, near Lesboeufs and, on 13 September, the attack would continue northwest towards the Butte de Warlencourt. The distances to be achieved were considerable (Line B required two miles of double trenches to be taken and Line C almost four miles) and the plan did not include the capture of the villages in which German troops were based, which would free them to undertake counter-attacks with their usual ferocity.

However, on 30 August, Kiggell visited Fourth Army's headquarters at Querrieu and told Rawlinson that Haig had rejected his proposals. On 31 August, GHQ issued a further instruction concerning the mid-September attack.[43] This directed that 'all arrangements are to be made with a view to overwhelming the enemy at the outset by a very powerful assault and by following up every advantage gained with rapidity and vigour.' It also stated that 'it is necessary then to impress on all leaders that the slow methods of trench warfare are unsuited to this kind of operation they will be required to undertake once the enemy has been driven from his prepared line of defences.' To assist Rawlinson, HQ Fourth Army was temporarily allocated a cavalry corps headquarters and a further three cavalry divisions in addition to the two already under his command. The allocation of tanks remained as before, that is, two companies with up to 50 tanks for the Fourth Army with up to two sections to the Reserve Army should these become available.

Rawlinson's Revised Plan

Rawlinson briefed his corps commanders the same day, at Querrieu, of the need for a detailed proposal for a complete penetration of the defence line opposite Fourth Army. He would allocate a section of tanks to support each attacking division in XIV and XV Corps but only one section in support of the three divisions of III Corps; a second being attached if enough tanks were available. III Corps, on the left, which was still under the command of Pulteney,[44] would provide a western flank guard, holding a line between Flers and Martinpuich. In the centre and

---

43   OAD 131 dated 31 August 1916. See Pidgeon, *Tanks at Flers*, p.229.
44   Pulteney been appointed GOC on III Corps' formation during the Retreat from Mons – see Chapter 2 of this Volume.

the east, XV and XIV Corps would capture the four villages and create gaps in the German lines to allow the cavalry to attack German artillery positions in their rear areas.[45]

The tanks would be used in groups, rather than in line, advancing ahead of the infantry to clear known strong points and trench junctions. Once the infantry had secured each objective, the tanks would move forward and assist the infantry take the next line, and so on until all objectives had been taken.

Haig's reaction to this proposal was mixed. He wrote, 'it strikes me that the infantry and tanks should start and advance level to the first objective, tanks going for strong points whilst the infantry rush the intermediate lengths of trench [with a] Barrage of 18-pounders as usual to cover the infantry advance.' Haig also commented, 'Will it not greatly help to push forward in some cases, a group of two or more tanks against the Support of Reserve Line, to prevent the enemy using machine-guns from his back lines during this period and the subsequent infantry advance?' Notwithstanding Haig's comment following the demonstration at Yvrench, it is clear that no-one had a clear idea as to the best way to employ tanks for their debut which would be in a fortnight's time.

Formation Training at Yvrench

C Company, which was now complete at Yvrench, had to undertake three days of brigade level training on 1–3 September.[46] These exercises took place west of Le Bois Grambus over a more demanding set of defences; a simulated trench system called the Ladder, 100 yards east of the British 'frontline', with a strong point in Wee Copse to its north, another set of defences to the east with the Bank and the Triangle strongpoints to the north and south, and then more 'enemy' support lines. The exercising brigades were from 56th (2nd London) Division who would be supported by tanks on the Eastern Flank on 15 and 25 September (see chapter 6). On 1 September, 169th Brigade took part in an exercise, supported by tanks, which was observed by the Prince of Wales (later Duke of Windsor). He drew a diagram of the exercise in his diary, which showed the tanks advancing in an extended line between the first and second waves of the infantry. He also recorded that two tanks broke down during the exercise, which left him (and probably several others) unimpressed by their performance. His one-liner is very revealing: 'They are good toys but I don't have much faith in their success, tho' their crew of one officer and seven ORs are d*mned brave men.'[47]

On 2 September, Rawlinson watched 168th Brigade in action; this time the tanks were a great success and cooperation with the infantry was excellent.[48] On 3 September, Haig brought

---

45   The four villages were Flers, Gueudecourt, Lesboeufs and Morval. The XIV Corps would create a gap for the cavalry to break through the German line northeast of Ginchy, where the enemy were furthest to the British frontline, whilst the capture of Flers and Gueudecourt, by XV Corps, would allow the cavalry to exploit due north towards Bapaume.

46   Archard records that it took two days to replace one tank track, after the previous exercises, owing to a lack of equipment and the dreadful weather conditions on 30 and 31 August.

47   Pidgeon, *Tanks at Flers*, p. 45 quoting from the Prince of Wales' Diary held at the Royal Archives at Windsor Castle.

48   Author's note: The diary of a crewmen in Female tank 510 *Challenger*, found by the Germans on 20 September, states that he had taken part in a large exercise on 2 September with 15,000 men. See Pidgeon, *The Tanks at Flers*, p. 70. The German translator presumably made an error as it is more likely

the French C-in-C, Field Marshal Joseph Joffre, to the training area to see 167th Brigade with eleven tanks in support. *The History of 56th Division* records that 'the tanks also demonstrated their ability to attack obstacles including breaking down trees and they filled the infantry with hope.'[49] The soldiers' reaction, according to Rifleman Aubrey Smith who was at Yvrench during this time, was that the tanks 'could run across any trench and tear up barbed wire like paper. They will run into any house and crush it flat; and trees less than sixteen inches in diameter will bend like matchwood when they run against it.'[50]

Allen Holford-Walker. (Alan Holford-Walker)

Despite the positive feedback from observers, C Company's commander Allen Holford-Walker was unimpressed with the training, and lack of equipment support, during the time at Yvrench:

Instead of the time being spent in proper overhauling, show stunts were done, and invariably resulted in some being broken – and no spare parts were available. I emphasise this for when our Company was moved to join XIV Corps, one tank had to be stripped to complete the rest for action. This tank had only broken one track plate but, as there were no spares, had to be left at Conteville, and parts taken from it to make the remaining 24 serviceable.

So badly tended were we that one man had to be sent back to England to bring back necessary small articles (spanners etc) and bring them back to prior to the action on the 15th. My wife bought 15 sets of spanners, which were unobtainable through Ordnance, and sent them out with this man.[51]

It was not just equipment which became unserviceable during the exercises; there was

49   Dudley Ward, *History of the 56th Division*, pp. 47–49.
50   *A Rifleman* (Aubrey Smith), *Four Years on the Western Front* (London: Odhams, 1922) p. 157. If the latter part of the report was believed, then a very false lesson was learned from this training.
51   Letter to the Official Historian (Brig Gen James Edmonds), 22 April 1935. Holford-Walker papers at the National Army Museum (NAM), Chelsea.

also at least one crewman injured. Capt Richard Trevithick, who commanded No. 3 Section, badly injured his knee and was hospitalised; he was replaced by Dashwood.[52] Although the training was limited, it did give the C20 crew a chance to get to know their tank and also their driver. Henriques was given the choice of two men. One must have been overly confident as the skipper chose 'the quiet man' and on 3 September, Henriques had his first experience of collective work with his crew:

> We did a show before Joffre and Haig, together with large numbers of staff, but that did not give us much confidence. The experience did however allow me to place my crew to best effect in the tank – senior NCO as the port side gearsman so he was at my beck and call and could help control the guns to some extent. Two best gunners on the front Vickers guns in each sponson, two second best behind them and the best mechanic as the starboard gearsman so that he could, at the same time, look after the engine.

It was the only time his crew would practice together before going into action.

Whilst C Company was at Yvrench, the move of the HS MGC to France continued. An unidentified officer and five other ranks arrived at Le Havre on 27 August and were sent the next day to GHQ to join Brough.[53] D Company's first heavy train, carrying 13 Female tanks, was loaded at the Culford Lodge Siding on the night of 25–26 August and left in the early hours for Avonmouth with a small party under the command of Lt Jeff Wakley. Later a second 'heavy train' containing sponsons for the 13 tanks, spare guns and all ammunition and stores for the entire Company was loaded up and despatched on Saturday 26 August. Not all of the crewmen were present at Elveden that weekend as many tried to see their families before deploying. On 25 August, Gnr Frank Divall (later of D13 *Delilah*) married Winifred Maybanks at West Ham Registry Office and, on Sunday 27 September, LCpl Laurence Upton ASC married Bertha Smith at their parish church in Barnby Dun near Doncaster. The 33-year-old schoolmistress would be widowed less than three weeks later – Upton being killed in action on 16 September at Gueudecourt when D6 was hit by enemy shellfire (see chapter 7).

D Company Deployment to France

On 28 August, the men of Nos. 1 and 2 Sections, the majority of D Company Headquarters, spare crewmen and attached personnel, entrained at Thetford Bridge Station at 0600 hours. Reaching Liverpool Street Station, the party marched to Waterloo where they entrained at noon for Southampton. Three hours later, they arrived at the docks and, at 1715 hours, embarked on

---

52 *War History 3rd Light Tank Battalion* p. 3A. Trevithick, who was the great grandson of the famous Cornish engineer, remained in France until December 1916, when he was graded unfit to active service. He was then employed by the Ministry of Munitions for the rest of the war, initially as the resident engineer for the Southwest of England in Bristol and later at the Ministry offices in Whitehall. Demobilised in February 1919, he returned to work for the engineering firm, Dewrance, and then worked as an independent Chartered Engineer based in Pall Mall. He married Marie Miller at St Margaret's Church in Westminster on 19 June 1919 and they had a daughter Noel born in 1925. Richard Trevithick died, aged 82, on 10 April 1973. Pope, *FTC*, pp. 319–320.

53 This may have been A Company's advance party.

the troopship *Caesarea*. Although it was a stormy night, their journey was uneventful and they arrived at Le Havre at 0500 hours. After breakfast on board, the men off-loaded their stores at 0700 hours and then marched off to the docks' rest camp. Meanwhile, back at Elveden, No. 3 Section were preparing their tanks for moving by train and, presumably with others in No. 4 Section, Gnr Walter Atkins was issued his revolver, ID discs and paybook. Atkins had been unable to get pre-deployment leave and was struggling to get his motorcycle back to his home in Coventry. He was also trying to convince his mother not to travel to see him at Bury St Edmunds as he had been warned he was departing for France on either Thursday or the following Monday.[54]

There was positive news about tank movement on 29 August in a signal sent to GHQ by the WO Trooping staff. This not only confirmed the sailing of D Company MB1 the previous day (see above) but also that the second half of the workshop and two spare tanks would sail on 1 September. Later that day, the DASD staff reported that four Male and four Female tanks could be despatched, complete with all their stores by 4 September, or alternatively one of A Company sections could move on 7 September. They also were advised that a second workshop company (presumably due to support A and B Companies) could deploy on 7 September and GHQ were asked to confirm if this was required.

Burnett-Stuart sought direction from Kiggell stating that two companies would be in place for battle on 15 September with a third (A Company) at the end of the month. There was no forecast for the arrival of the remaining three but Burnett-Stuart thought it unlikely to be before the end of the fighting season (mid-October). As initial casualties were likely to be heavy, and there was no reserve except the company establishment, Burnett-Stuart proposed concentrating on using the first three companies only, with the 15–20 tanks at Elveden being sent out to France. Kiggell agreed and GHQ gave the following shipping priorities for movement; D Company's second main body (MB2) should depart England on 1 September followed by the eight spare tanks on 4 September. The second workshop should leave as soon as possible, on 7 September, and then A Company deploying by sections if necessary.[55]

On the evening of 30 August, HQ D Company was ordered to move to Conteville at 0400 hours the next morning. D Company MB1 left Le Havre at 0600 hours, leaving Mortimore and 25 men to off-load the tanks and equipment en route to Le Havre.[56] Although it was planned MB1 would travel directly to St Riquier, the journey was broken at Rouen; the men's kit was moved to a siding and men transported by lorries to a rest camp. The party entrained at Rouen at 1530 hours and spent all night on the train, arriving at St Riquier at 0630 hours on 1 September. The crewmen cooked their breakfast at the station whilst the officers ate at a local *estimanet*.[57] The party then marched to their new billets at Yvrench and settled in.

The last D Company 'heavy train' left the Culford Lodge siding that same morning and the remaining crewmen left Thetford Bridge station at 0600 hours on 2 September. The next three days saw tanks, men and road transport steadily moving to the new training area, with

54 Atkins' letters are held in the Herbert Art Gallery and Museum at Coventry.
55 Deployment by sections had been proposed by GHQ staff in late July and rejected by Swinton.
56 Mortimore had initially been employed as the Park officer, responsible for the tanks and their equipment, whilst training at Elveden, but had subsequently been appointed No. 1 Section commander.
57 An *estimanet* was a cafe selling alcoholic drinks and was often out of bounds to other ranks but not to officers.

all elements of D Company eventually concentrating at Yvrench on 6 September – this left virtually no time for collective training.[58]

Brough's Dismissal

On 4 September, having been removed as OC HS MGC in France, Brough returned to the WO. Brough was concerned that the tanks and their crews were not ready for battle and presumably made this clear to the BEF staff. He was therefore considered to be 'difficult' and was sent back home for doing the most difficult staff job of all – 'speaking truth unto power.' Brough was replaced by Bradley, an effective trainer but, unlike Bough, without the staff experience on which to call in the difficult weeks ahead.[59]

Tank Trial at Fricourt Farm

There must have been an early arrival at the Loop Railhead as, on 4 September, a tank undertook field trials at Fricourt Farm which was observed by Elles.[60] The purpose of the trial was to determine the speed of a tank across the battlefield; the area around Fricourt Farm being considered to be equivalent to no man's land. The tank was able to drive 'a maximum 100 yards in 5 minutes without check' although, according to Holford-Walker, the ground between the British and German frontlines was significantly worse than that at Fricourt. This derived planning speed of 20 yards a minute, provided to formation headquarters by GHQ, proved to be optimistic at best.

Ammunition

With only ten days until Zero, serious consideration was being given to ammunition requirements. The provision of ball rounds for their machine-guns was not an issue but the HS MGC were unique in requiring 6-pounder shells for the main armament of the Male tanks. On 18 August, the WO staff had notified GHQ BEF that 1,000 rounds of 6-pounder ammunition per gun (that is, 2,000 rounds per Male tank) had been ordered which was expected to be more than adequate. Given that each Male tank could only carry 376 rounds, this allowed for more than five complete loads, which indicates the scale of usage expected. Ten days later, GHQ BEF asked for an update as the stocks in France were less than 13,000 rounds, that is, 4,352 with HS MGC, presumably at Yvrench, and another 8,123 in the supply chain. Given that A, C and D Companies would deploy with a maximum of 36 Male tanks, this was more than enough to

---

58   D Company's War Diary and the Adjutant's notebook, both written by Captain Graham Woods, provide full details. Both are held at the TMA.

59   Swinton visited the Loop on 16 September and noted that 'Bradley was in a state of great perturbation. In addition to the legitimate work and excitement attendant on the fighting of the previous day, he was almost distracted by numerous peremptory inquiries for all sorts of information which it was quite impossible for him to collect quickly from the two companies spread out over a considerable stretch of front.' *Eyewitness* p. 287.

60   Elles later reported that he had nothing to do with tanks after having first investigated them in January until their arrival in France. This is not strictly true as Swinton states he was in correspondence with Elles in the summer.

cover immediate demands but, when HQ BEF staff were again prompted on requirements on 5 September, the HQ staff stated, 'it is not possible to say what requirements will be' and asked that a reserve of 20,000 rounds be held in readiness for shipment to Rouen on demand. The ammunition was to be sent to established depots and not to Le Havre.

That same day, GHQ BEF staff were warned by the WO about a manufacturing issue amongst the Male tanks built at Birmingham. 'Pigeon holes for 6 pdr ammo found to be badly fitted. HS MGC to ensure all racks are to be tried before being used.' This was more work to be undertaken by the workshops personnel who were beginning to assemble at the Loop. Initial plans were for the men and all their vehicles to move by rail. However, the Fosters tractors and the trailers which carried their machinery were too tall to be transported on a standard freight wagon. As a result, they had to drive 150 miles from Le Havre to the Loop; a task which the Movement staff calculated as a four-day trip.

On 4 September, GHQ issued the outline movement plan for the tanks and their crews from Conteville to the Fourth Army area. The advance party would move by road on 7 September with the units then moving in half companies, with two sections of tanks and their crews travelling on each train. The first C Company train would leave Conteville on the evening of 7 September and the second the next morning. The empty wagons having returned to Conteville, the first half of D Company would leave on the morning of 9 September and the remainder on the morning of the tenth. The movement order stated that one spare tank would move with each half company which seems to indicate that additional tanks had reached Conteville whilst the units were training at Yvrench. HQ HS MGC was ordered to move to the Loop under arrangements with HQ Fourth Army, presumably by road, whilst the small ASC workshop at Conteville was to travel with D Company by rail.

That same day, Rawlinson held a conference at Querrieu, which confirmed that the 42 tanks allocated to Fourth Army would be divided so that XV and XIV Corps had 18 tanks each with the remaining six to III Corps. He also announced that the tanks were to be used in groups of four, advancing in a diamond formation, with the artillery barrage between them. The tanks were to advance at 100 yards every five minutes, based on the timings from the trial undertaken the previous day at Fricourt.

At Yvrench, a new pattern of gas mask was issued to C Company crewmen and the tanks' guns and sponsons were removed ready for entrainment. [61] D Company's crews continued to load .303 bullets to the Vickers machine-gun belts ahead of a firing practice at Yvrench but the crews were not to undertake any exercises supporting infantry formations of the type undertaken by C Company. Wakley, with a party of ten men, moved by road to Le Havre to collect the eight spare tanks and accompany them to the Loop. That evening, Nos. 3 and 4 Sections of D Company and their tanks departed Le Havre for Conteville.

---

61   This was probably the Large Box respirator, which gave better protection that the previously issued Phenate Helmet (P Helmet) and alternatively the Phenate-Hexamine (PH) Helmet developed originally for artillerymen which incorporated sponge-rubber tear-gas goggles with an elastic strap that fitted around the head. Both the large box respirator and PH Helmet were lighter in weight, provided better vision and were less uncomfortable than the P Helmet.

Equipment Shortcomings

The first production tanks had been sent to France without any armoured protection for the hydraulic system which raised and lowered the steering tail. There was also concern that the tanks' roofs were vulnerable to penetration by artillery shrapnel and grenades. A modification had been developed and, on 6 September, the WO notified GHQ BEF that 'Hydraulic ram covers (15 sets) to Le Havre, 23 sets with first half of A Company. 23 bullet proof plates for double roofs will accompany A Company.' A Company was not due to arrive until after 15 September 1916. As a short-term measure, to provide some protection from enemy grenades exploding on top of the tanks, 'roofs' made of wood and wire, were constructed and sent out to France but there were insufficient for all 50 tanks with C and D companies. Whilst most equipment was being moved through Le Havre, and sent to the Loop by rail, HQ HS MGC was informed on 7 September that six packages, containing 122 Hotchkiss machine-guns for D Company and twenty-six 6-pounders for C Company, were being sent to Boulogne.[62] These stores would have to be collected, which required a 200-mile round trip, mainly travelling on minor roads, using the four lorries held by the companies, which were fully laden and preparing to deploy to the Loop.

Dinkum showing unprotected hydraulic steering gear. (Simon Jones)

---

62   Author's note: This signal is extremely puzzling as the Male tanks of C Company should have deployed with the sponsons fitted with the guns and 122 Hotchkiss machine-guns for D Company was far in excess of the unit's requirements.

Clan Leslie fitted with an anti-grenade 'roof'. (TMA)

Nos. 3 and 4 Sections of D Company arrived with their tanks at Conteville on 6 September at 0935 hours. The tanks were off-loaded in under two hours due to help from 1 and 2 Sections. Drader arrived with the remainder of the road transport the same day, having driven from Le Havre, and D Company was complete at Yvrench. The workshops, which would support C and D Companies, arrived at le Havre but had to move by road to the Loop as their vehicles were too tall to fit under bridges.

Company Redeployment to the Somme battlefield

That next day, 7 September, C Company's tanks were named, driven to Conteville and loaded by sections onto two trains, the crews travelling with the tanks. The first train left Conteville for Abbeville at 1400 hours then left Abbeville four hours later for Méricourt l'Abbé (south of Albert) arriving at 2100 hours that evening. The second train was to depart Conteville at 2100 hours and reach Abbeville at 0030 hours, stopping overnight. It would then leave at 0600 hours and arrive at Méricourt at 0900 hours.

Some of No. 1 Section's tanks were seen at a railway station near Amiens, on 8 September, by Maj Raymond Brutinel, the HQ Canadian Corps machine-gun staff officer. He had been tasked by Lt Gen Julian Byng to look at some tanks which were allocated to the Canadian Corps.[63] When Brutinel asked whether they were water tanks, Byng replied that he did not

---

63   Michael R. McNorgon, *Great War Tanks in Canadian Service* (Service Publications, Ottawa, 2009) pp. 3–4. In September 1914 Brutinel had created, from scratch, the 1st Automobile Machine-Gun

know as they were a secret but Brutinel was to let him know how they could be employed. Brutinel saw two Male tanks, *Crème de Menthe* and *Cupid,* and spoke to a major in charge of them who described the tank's potential and the trials that had been completed. Brutinel, who knew the conditions around Pozières, did not believe that the tests had been sufficiently severe and recommended that the tank officer accompany him to look at the ground. Once there, the officer, who Brutinel described as a clear headed, resolute man, indicated that it would be very difficult for the tanks to be at the Canadian jumping-off trenches, by the Old German line, by zero. He would try to do so and, if successful, the tanks would do their best to support the attacking troops.[64] Returning to the Canadian Corps HQ, Brutinel briefed Byng on the potential of the tanks and what had been arranged; the noise and slow speed of the tanks not giving rise to undue expectations.

The tanks were also seen, in transit, by a newly commissioned infantry officer named Teddy Winder. He recollected:

> During the afternoon, we reached Amiens and turned north-east on an even slower line to our destination. On the way we passed a siding in what was drawn up a long train of trucks carrying what appeared to be outsize travelling cookers covered in tarpaulins. These quaint vehicles had extraordinary long chimneys. We came to the conclusion they must be cookers to deal with the feeding of the troops in the advance which we expected. Later we found out that this was our first glimpse of tanks.[65]

Whilst C Company was travelling to the Loop, Nos. 1 and 2 Sections of D Company completed a living fire exercise at Yvrench, which was observed by the British Prime Minister Asquith. The crews then removed their tank sponsons in preparation for the rail move to the Loop. Unlike C Company, there was no opportunity for the sections to practice field exercises with the infantry they would support on 15 September. The D Company War Diary makes no mention of either No. 3 or No. 4 Sections completing any training in France.

On 8 September, at Elveden, A Company started loading their tanks to rail at the Culford Lodge siding. In France, at noon, C Company's first train arrived at the Loop, in broad daylight and more than 15 hours later than the planned time. One of *Challenger's* crew recorded that the area was under hostile fire; this was probably because the location was surrounded by British gun positions and well within range of the German counter-battery units. After 1500 hours, the first train crews started to refit the sponsons to the tanks. Archard noted C Company's second train left Abbeville at 0630 hours that morning, travelling via St Roch, Amiens, then Heilly (two miles southwest of Méricourt l'Abbé) to Happy Valley; two locomotives were required to pull the train up the steep incline to Happy Valley. Archard was in new billets at Happy Valley,

---

Brigade, a company-sized units consisting of 120 personnel, eight armoured cars each carrying two Colt machine-guns, and twelve support vehicles. Two year later, he was in command of Canadian Corps' machine-gun batteries. The following year, he was appointed brigadier general to command the Canadian Machine-gun Brigade.

64   Author's note: The tank officer was probably Inglis.

65   These are likely to have been the second D Company train on 10 September. Winder saw the tanks before he reached Dernancourt, where he left the train in order to report to HQ 41st Division. Winder would join 12th East Surreys with whom he would attack Flers on 15 September. Extracted from '*A Subaltern on the Western Front*' a lecture to the South African Military History Society, 10 March 1977.

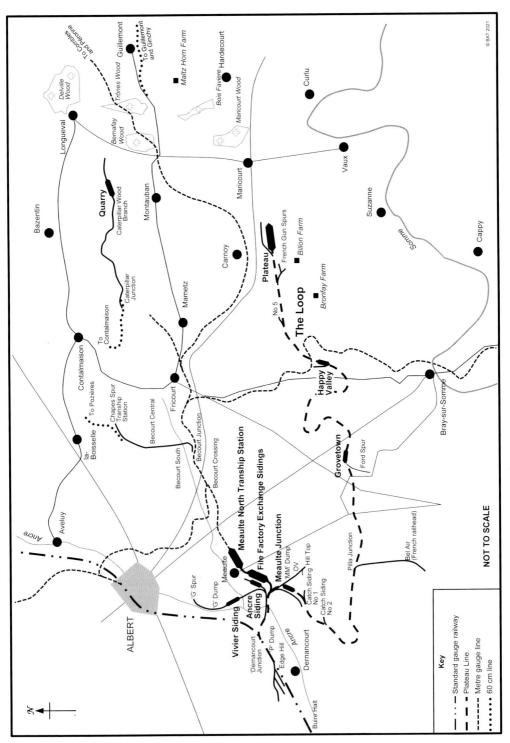

The Loop. (Barbara Taylor)

a camp to the west of the Loop by 1600 hours and, after his evening meal, assisted in off-loading the tanks.

Although the Loop position was well arranged for off-loading the tank companies, it was not well placed to support the 50 tanks in several locations across the six miles from Combles to Courcelette. The equipment support plan had been based on the premise that the tanks would operate close to the workshops at the railhead and that broken-down tanks were to be bought back for repair; this was despite the fact that there were no recovery vehicles. Knothe therefore started to develop plans to support the tanks at their advanced bases at Aveluy (seven tanks supporting Canadian Corps), near Bazentin-le-Petit (eight tanks for III Corps), Green Dump near Longueval (18 tanks for XV Corps) and Trones Wood (18 tanks supporting XIV Corps) – all of which were between six and eight miles from the Loop.

On Saturday 9 September, the WO movement staff notified HS MGC that eight tanks and trailers (carrying their sponsons) plus a tractor had left by water transport.[66] At the Loop, C Company fitted their gun sponsons to their tanks; one of *Challenger's* crew recorded in his diary, 'Hundreds of officers and other ranks come to see the vehicles. In the afternoon firing practice.' This range practice was likely to have been for the Vickers and Hotchkiss machine-guns, the valleys south of the Loop being suitable for the purpose. The Prince of Wales also made a visit, this time accompanied by an ADC.[67]

Following up his work the previous day, Knothe sent a signal for the GHQ QMG staff: 'In order to generate HS MGC on a section basis, the following is required: one lorry and trailer per section with one NCO fitter, three fitters, one blacksmith and 2 drivers plus one x 3-ton first aid lorry with one fitters' bench.' At 0330 hours, the next morning, Director General Transport replied: 'Can provide 8 Peerless lorries but not artificers or fitters' tools. These should be found from in-theatre Corps Heavy Artillery units but personally I do not think the provision of this outfit is required.' Realising he was unlikely to provide every tank section with integral support, Knothe decided to despatch his engineer officers and ASC fitters to the main tank bases at the Briqueterie and Green Dump to undertake forward repair.

At Yvrench, D Company moved all of their tanks to Conteville station by 0935 hours. The first train, carrying Nos. 1 and 2 Sections, started loading at 0800 and departed at 1500, one hour later than planned. It then left Abbeville at 1800 hours and arrived at Méricourt at 2100 hours. D Company's second train started loading at 1330 hours and moved off at 2000 hours, one hour earlier than planned. The company's wheeled transport left Yvrench at 1930 hours, the OC and adjutant travelling in the Sunbeam car which arrived at the Loop at 2200 hours; the remainder, led by 2Lt Bill Brannon ASC, arrived at 0300 hours the following morning.

On Sunday 10 September, at Elveden, the first half of A Company's crews made their final preparations to deploy to France. At Le Havre, the commandant's staff reported the departure by road at 1000 hours 'for Alpaca [HS MGC] of 1 officer, 14 other ranks, 1 car and 1 tractor due to arrive Middleham [Méricourt l'Abbé] at 6 pm 15 Sep 1916'; this was A Company workshops' advance party. At the Loop, D Company's first train arrived at 0600 hours and off-loading commenced at once. The second train, due at 1000 hours, failed to arrive. At 1500 hours,

66 Author's note: This signal must have caused total surprise to its recipients as all other internal movement of tanks was undertaken by rail. They arrived by rail at the Loop on 10 September.
67 The ADC was Capt WTC 'Bill' Huffam; his cousin Victor Huffam commanded *Dolly* and the D9 crew.

Wakley and his party arrived at the Loop on a train with the eight spare tanks which were unloaded as previously notified. The tanks were four Females and four Males.

For C Company there were demonstrations to staff officers at 0900 hours and again at 1400 hours for one hour. This was the first time that the divisional and brigade staffs would see the tanks which they would have to integrate into their attacks five days later. At last, they laid eyes on the hush-hush weapon which until now they had only known through a single photograph and the limited information provided by GHQ on 15 August (Appendix VI). However, there was no opportunity for collective training or even familiarisation for the battalions which would be accompanied by the tanks into the attack five days later.

The Prince of Wales again visited the Loop on the Sunday afternoon, this time on a bicycle, joining the D9 crew for a cup of tea. Two members of the C20 crew met up with relatives and friends who had heard about their arrival. Gnr William Dawson spent the afternoon with his two brothers who were serving with the Coldstream Guards whilst his skipper, Lt George Macpherson, was joined by his best friend from Winchester College, Geoffrey Wyatt who had also served in the East Kent Regiment.[68] The College's archives contain a letter from Geoffrey's brother Oliver to their former housemaster, Horace Jackson dated 14 November 1916 which mentions Macpherson. 'I think it was exceedingly kind of you to write to me to sympathize about Geoffrey. Of course, it has made another great gap in the family, and it is very sad. But the Christian side makes so much of it seem wright [sic]. I don't know if you realized that he and George died on the same day in the same district. As you know, they were the greatest friends in the world, and it is very wonderful and beautiful that they should have died together. They met in France on the Sunday, before for the first time for some months, and Geoffrey sat in his "tank" and talked for a good deal of the afternoon. I am sure they would have liked to die together as they did.' Sadly, that was not the case.

On Monday 11 September, A Company MB1 left for France. One of their despatch riders, Gnr Frederick Cutting, recorded in his diary: '3.00 A Coy departs New Farm [Camp] Elveden in Leyland Lorries, embarked trains at Thetford Bridge, then by train to Liverpool Street; by tube to Waterloo, then train to So'ton arriving at 12.00 hours. Depart So'ton at 15.00 hours and arrive Le Havre by 19.00 hours.'[69] It appears that the party remained on board overnight as the crewmen's records show them disembarking the next day.

D Company's second tank train had arrived at the Loop overnight but did not start to be unloaded until 0600 hours, twenty hours late. The sponsons were again refitted and more ammunition belts were filled. D Company's box body van was sent to Le Havre, not to Boulogne as previously warned, to collect a supply of Hotchkiss machine-gun ammunition strips. C Company's crews were issued with spare parts, tools and track spanners and started loading their tanks with petrol, oils, rations and the rest of their other combat supplies. After this was completed, Macpherson and Henriques used bicycles to explore their route to their Place of Assembly in the Chimpanzee Valley just to the east of the Briqueterie.

At the Loop, a petrol fire broke out onboard *Campania* possibly as a result of the crew trying to clean the tank. It was extinguished within 10 minutes and, whilst no significant damage was

---

68   The Guards Division had arrived at Happy Valley on 9 September.
69   Cutting's diary is held at the TMA.

done to the tank, two gunners were burnt. They were rescued by Sgt Robert Hillhouse, No. 3 Section's SNCO, who was subsequently Mentioned in Despatches.[70]

The first tank deployment to a Place of Assembly occurred when No. 1 Section of C Company, who were to support the Canadian Corps, left the Loop. Seven tanks left at 1400 hours that afternoon. They took two and a half hours to reach the village of Meaulte where they would spend the night. The tanks were named *Champagne, Cognac, Chablis, Chartreuse, Crème de Menthe, Cordon Rouge* with a spare Male known as *Cupid*. The distance was only five miles cross country but their passage was delayed by men en route wanting to see the new invention, so it was not a true reflection of the tank's deployment speed. That said, another tank trial had taken place at Fricourt that morning, which was again witnessed by Elles. This showed that, where shellholes overlapped, tanks could only move at only 15 yards a minute; 25 percent slower than the trial held on 4 September.

Detailed Battle Orders

Also on 11 September, HQ Fourth Army confirmed the allocation of six tanks to III Corps, 18 to XIV Corps and the remaining 18 to XV Corps. The tanks were to operate in groups of three, in column on route, following well-defined tracks or trenches. HQ Fourth Army also issued Instructions for the Employment of Tanks (see Appendix VII) which covered the move to the Assembly Areas and using aircraft, flying over the forward areas, to mask the sounds of the tanks' engines. The orders for the tactical use of the tanks did not wholly reflect those issued by GHQ on 15 August 1916 (Appendix VI). The key elements in the Fourth Army instruction were that for:[71]

5. The Attack of the First Objective. Tanks will start movement at a time so calculated that they will reach their objectives 5 minutes before the infantry. The infantry will advance as usual behind a creeping barrage in which gaps, about 100 yards wide, will be left for the route of the Tanks.[72] The stationary barrage of both heavy and field artillery will be timed to be lifted off the objectives of the tanks some minutes before their arrival at these objectives.

6. After clearing up the First Objectives, a proportion of the Tanks should be pushed forward a short way to pre-arranged positions as defensive strongpoints.[73] If necessary, a Tank may be sent to assist the infantry in clearing such points in the line which may be holding them up.

70 Hillhouse was killed in action on 11 April 1917 during the capture of Monchy-le-Preux. He was initially reporting missing, giving his widow Janet some cause for hope. Having heard nothing from the Red Cross, the WO notified her in April 1918 that Robert must be presumed dead. Janet never remarried, bringing up her two young daughters alone. Pope, *FTC*, p. 287.

71 Issued with Fourth Army Instruction 299/17(G) of 11th September 1916

72 Tanks were directed to move in column, rather in a line at 100 yard intervals as originally suggested by Swinton in August 1915 or in one of other options identified by GHQ in August 1916. This system kept the number of lanes within the barrage to the minimum and should have provided tank skippers with a designated route for movement between the first and second objectives.

73 No such direction appears to have been given in divisional orders.

7. The Attack of the Second Objective. Tanks and infantry will advance together under the creeping barrage. Tanks will move, as before, in column and on well-defined routes. The pace will be regulated to tank pace (30-50 yards per minute) but the infantry must not wait for any Tanks that are delayed.[74] The action for the Tanks will be as for the First Objective.

8. The Attack on the Third and Subsequent Objectives.
There will be no creeping barrage.
The Tanks will start sufficiently far in front of the infantry to reach the Third and Fourth Objectives before the infantry.
The Tanks will move as before in column. Their action will be as to crush wire and keep down hostile rifle and machine-gun fire.
The infantry must not wait for any Tanks that are delayed.

9. The following signals will be used from the Tanks to Infantry and Aircraft

Flag Signals	Red flag	Out of action
	Green flag	Am on objective
	(Other flags are inter Tank flags)	
Lamp Signals	Series of Ts – Out of action	
	Series of Hs – Am on objectives	

A proportion of Tanks will carry pigeons [for communication to higher formations].

10. If Tanks get behind timetable, or get out of action, the infantry must on no account wait for them.

11. If the Tanks succeed, and the infantry are checked, the Tanks must endeavour to help them.

12. Any Tanks, that may be in reserve, should be moved to positions of assembly vacated by the front line Tanks on night Y/Z. They should be in telephonic communications with Corps.

13. After the capture of the most distant objectives, Tanks will be withdrawn under Corps arrangement to previously selected positions some way to the rear of these objectives. Arrangements must be made for replenishing the petrol and ammunition supply.

14. General Notes.
   a. Recent trials show that, over heavily shelled ground, a greater pace than 15 yards a minute cannot be depended on. This pace will be increased to 33 yards a minute over good ground and downhill on good ground it will reach 50 yards a minute.
   b. Tank officers are without exception strange to the ground and to the conditions of the battle. They will require a good deal of assistance from staffs of formations, particularly in the study of the ground over which they are to advance.

---

74 Fourth Army staff were expecting the tanks to move at least twice as fast as had been achieved at the second tank speed trial at Fricourt on 11 September.

c. Every Tank going into action should be provided with a map shown its track clearly marked and the objectives of the infantry with time-table.[75]

That afternoon there was another conference at HQ Fourth Army at which the corps commanders explained their attack plans to Rawlinson. It was attended by Bradley, now responsible for the coordination of the two tank companies, but who did not make any contribution. Elles was also present and he was the only one to comment when Pulteney stated that the four tanks supporting 47th Division should drive through High Wood. Elles told Rawlinson that the tanks could not have got through Trones Wood. Commenters, including Trevor Pidgeon, have found this statement odd. Elles was however a relatively junior officer, and not on Rawlinson's staff, so he could not directly challenge the III Corps Commander about his plan.[76] I believe that Elles was suggesting to Rawlinson, who knew Trones Wood well, that Pulteney's plan would not work. Sadly, Pulteney was not directed to review his plans by Rawlinson but Elles was proved to be right.[77]

The next morning, 12 September 1916, No. 1 Section of C Company left Meaulte at 0630 hours, driving to the northeast of Albert where they were spotted by Lloyd George who spent some time with the crews. The section arrived at their advanced base: 'arriving half hour after dinner, huge crowds came to see tanks and Canadians show keen appreciation.'[78] At the Loop, the remainder of the tank crews were preparing their tanks for action, with one of *Challenger's* crewmen recording in his diary that, 'Further preparations for use. The tanks create great interest amongst the infantry.' The preparations included fitting the C Company tanks with the recently arrived roof frames, covered with chicken wire, designed to counter grenade attack.

At 1100 hours on 12 September, HQ HS MGC, now located at the Loop, signalled the Camp Commandant at Le Havre regarding A Company: 'Send by rail to CHEAM [Conteville] as many officers and ORs of Alpaca as can be spared, leaving sufficient party to deal with Armadillos [tanks].' By this time, the first half of A Company's tanks were being loaded to SS *Ilston Grange* at Avonmouth and were due to sail for Le Havre the following day.

Corps Conferences

Also, on 12 September, three corps conferences were held, these being attended by Holford-Walker (XIV Corps), Summers (XV Corps) and Captain George Mann (III Corps) who commanded No 4 Section of D Company. At the XIV Corps conference, Cavan confirmed the allocation of nine tanks to the Guards Division, three to 6th Division, and three to 56th (1st

75 This was not actioned for either C or D Company who were only issued maps on the basis of one per section / sub section.
76 Pidgeon, *Tanks at Flers*. p. 54.
77 Author's note: Elles may have read Swinton's 'Notes on the employment of tanks' written in February 1916, which stated that 'woods and plantations are an absolute obstacle to their movement'. The advice to formations, published by GHQ BEF on 15 August, was not so specific and the demonstration of tanks entering woods at Yvrench may also have persuaded the commanders that using tanks in woods was practicable. There was no copy of Swinton's 'Notes' at HQ HB MGC when Fuller joined the Branch in December 1916.
78 Archard's diary for 12 September 1916. He does not record the exact location of the new tankodrome but Trevor Pidgeon, in *Tanks on the Somme* p. 90. places it south of Aveluy Wood on the Chemin d'Authuille.

London) Division. The Guards were to attack north and east from Ginchy and take Lesboeufs; 6th Division would attack east from the Quadrilateral to take Morval; whilst 56th Division, located in Leuze Wood, would clear Bouleaux Wood, the ground to its northeast and that to the southeast on the outskirts of Combles. The aim was to provide a defensive flank, which would stop any attempts by the Germans to retake the ground to the west. The remaining three C Company tanks would form a Corps Reserve – one of which was to be allocated to Mann.[79]

The C Company War Diary records that, 'All details with regard to points of assembly and starting points were fixed in Conference with staffs concerned and Tank Group commanders were immediately put into communication with their divisions who issued them with orders direct.'[80] It also states that 'arrangements for replenishing tanks and men in petrol, oils etc. were made under Company arrangements.' These did not prove satisfactory, mainly due to a lack of transport within the tank companies and a lack of support from XIV Corps.

What the report does not record, for obvious reasons, are the meetings Holford-Walker had with Rawlinson at Querrieu and with Brig Gen Francis Gathorne-Hardy, COS at HQ XIV Corps.[81] Rawlinson asked him three questions; firstly, whether his men were trained to which Holford-Walker replied that his men 'were not fit to fight immediately as I had not officer or man who had seen a shelled area.' The second question was the pace at which the tanks could move and, thirdly, the distance they could accomplish on average ground and return for replenishing.

At his interview with Gathorne-Hardy, Holford-Walker 'was given a map showing the preconceived tank routes which had been arbitrarily fixed with no reconnaissance by any officer who knew anything about a tank at all.' He later had interviews at various division headquarters but their orders for the tanks were given directly to the section commanders. 'The net result was that the indefiniteness [sic] of the [needs] of the unit was literally disastrous because, whilst I was actually in command of the unit, orders were being issued direct by divisions to sections and I knew nothing about it whatsoever.'[82]

By comparison, Summers wrote the orders for Nos. 1, 2 and 3 Sections which he issued at 1400 hours on 13 September, just before the tanks deployed from the Loop. We also know that Summers received amendments to the initial plan and that he had to re-brief the tank skippers on 14 September at Green Dump, after they had carried out their route recces and just before they were to deploy to their starting points (see chapter 7). Summers had detached Mann's section under command HQ III Corps for the next month whilst he retained command of 1, 2 and 3 Sections to support XV Corps.[83] The breakdown of these 18 tanks was: ten sent to 41st Division who were to capture Flers, four tanks to the 14th Division who were to take Gueudecourt and four to the New Zealand (NZ) Division who were to capture the ground northwest of Flers (see map 5). Lt Gen Henry Horne (GOC XV Corps) was concerned about the German position

---

79   Another of the Reserve tanks was later allocated to the Guards Division – see Chapter 6.

80   TNA WO 95/96.

81   Second son of the second Earl of Cranbrook, Gathorne-Hardy had been on the staff of II Corps in 1914.

82   Typed copy of his letter to Brig Gen James Edmonds dated 22 Apr 1935 p. 2 (NAM Chelsea).

83   HQ D Company had been previously notified of the allocation, ordering officers commanding the tanks to get in contact with the relevant divisional headquarters. HQ XV Corps 43 GX dated 10 September 1916 (NZ Archives R2598529).

east of Delville known as the Brewery Salient. This was on the route which would be taken to get to their starting-off points for 42nd Brigade of 14th Division. The main attack would then be supported by all 18 tanks, mainly operating in groups of three but with three singletons operating on the divisional flanks. The routes to be used by the tanks were shown on a coloured map and by means of route cards issued by HQ XV Corps on 12 September.[84]

Mann was told to provide eight tanks to III Corps; two more than he had been allocated. He was to provide two tanks for 15th (Scottish) Division to aid the masking of Martinpuich, two to 50th (Northumberland) Division who were to capture the land northeast of Martinpuich, and four to 47th (2nd London) Division who were to clear High Wood and capture the ground to its northeast. It was later agreed that D Company would provide a scratch crew under Sampson with one of the spare tanks whilst C Company was ordered to send one of its reserve tanks to Mann.[85] However, no action to detach the C Company tank was taken until 14 September. There is no record that Mann expressed concern about the plan to send tanks through High Wood at the conference. However, his tank skippers subsequently did so with GOC 47th Division, who endorsed their view, but the III Corps staff did not permit Barter to use the tanks on the edges of the wood.[86]

On Wednesday 13 September, the remainder of A Company deployed from Elveden to France. The first two sections of tanks were due to have sailed from Avonmouth on the SS *Ilston Grange* that morning but this was delayed until nightfall owing to the threat from German U-boats which were active in the England Channel. This information was received by GHQ BEF at 1545 hours with the warning that the remaining tanks would not sail until the night of 15–16 September. The Camp Commandant at Le Havre also notified HQ HS MGC on 13 September that 15 officers and 123 other ranks (the first Main Body of A Company) had left Le Havre by a scheduled train for Conteville.

Inglis and one other officer (probably Wheeler) attended a briefing at HQ 2nd Canadian Division, which at which they were told how the tanks would be employed and then they walked forward to look at the ground north of Pozières over which the tanks would operate. Three tanks (*Champagne*, *Cognac* and *Cordon Rouge*) were to support 6th Canadian Brigade by driving along the Sugar Trench whilst *Chablis*, *Chartreuse* and *Crème de Menthe* would follow the line of the Pozières to Bapaume road and assist 4th Canadian Brigade capture the Courcelette Sugar Factory and Candy Trench which linked the Factory to Martinpuich. Unlike the formations in the Fourth Army, Inglis' tanks would follow the first wave of the infantry assault, rather than proceed it, thereby allowing the Canadian infantry to follow the creeping barrage as closely as possible – this also avoided leaving a gap to be used by the tanks in the protective shrapnel curtain. Meanwhile, back at their tankodrome, the majority of the crewmen carried out pre-battle preparations and tank maintenance which included tightening the tanks' tracks. Another party established a refuelling point by the Advanced Dressing Station on the road from La Boiselle to Pozières which would be used on the way forward to their Places of Assembly.[87]

At the Loop, the ASC workshop discovered that the newly arrived armoured shields for the hydraulic cylinder rams were unaccompanied by either fitting brackets or instructions. The

84   HQ XV Corps 41/5 dated 12 September 1916 (NZ Archives R2598529).
85   HQ XIV Corps S74/2 dated 12 September, copied to III Corps.
86   Terry Norman, *The Hell They Called High Wood* (Wellingborough: Patrick Stephens, 1989) p. 217.
87   Author's note: This Place of Assembly is now the site of the Pozières Memorial to the Missing.

General Staff at GHQ were quickly notified and they sent a signal to the WO. Also, to quote Knothe, 'the tracks of every machine were adjusted before the machine left this camp; I myself checking the adjustments. Every machine's guide rails were taken down and examined and new ones put in where necessary. I may add here that the officers, NCOs. and fitters worked continuously for five days and five nights, only snatching an hour's sleep whilst they were waiting for parts.'[88] As part of this work, the fitters also identified that the vehicles had been manufactured without the oil tanks which lubricated the tracks – in fact by 26 September, only fifteen of these oil tanks had arrived at the Loop.

That afternoon, C Company received copies of the orders issued to the group commanders by the divisions in XIV Corps. At 1155 hours, the Guards Division issued a further set of orders for a tenth tank to carry out a preliminary operation between Ginchy and Delville Wood starting at 0540 hours. Summers, in the meantime, was writing, checking and issuing orders to eight tank groups; the section commanders and tank skippers had not been taught how to extract orders from higher formations and this task would have been beyond them. He also ordered that Sampson and his scratch crew, many from the (unused) Balloon Section, to join No. 4 Section under Mann.

At 1500 hours, Bradley attended a final confirmatory conference at HQ Fourth Army at Querrieu. The corps commanders were happy with their plans for the attack; Horne informed Rawlinson that he would use two tanks to clear the Brewery Salient in a preliminary action. The majority of D Company's tanks left the Loop from 1500 hours. All bar one deployed to Green Dump which was situated in a shallow valley one mile west-southwest of Longueval (map 5, map square D4). Their route was northeast to Carnoy and then north to the line of old French light railway (map square B5) then east to the Quarry (map square C5 where the railway line crosses the road from Montauban to Bazentin-le-Petit) and then north east to Green Dump. The dump was also the site of the New Zealand (NZ) Division's Advanced Dressing Station and within 500 yards of the headquarters of 122nd and 124th Brigades (41st Division). The exception was Mortimore's tank *Daredevil 1* which had a separate place of assembly due east of the Montauban Quarry on the road from the Briqueterie to Longueval.[89]

At 1600 hours on 13 September, the artillery preliminary bombardment started – an activity which gave the Germans a clear signal that a major assault was to take place in the next few days. From 1700 hours, Nos. 2, 3 and 4 Sections of C Company left the Loop for their assembly areas near Trones Wood, which was also the site for C Company's dump.[90] The route was across firm ground and the tanks should have made good progress, as can be seen from the image of C8 pictured over. Several of the tanks were however delayed by crowds of soldiers. The ten tanks from Nos. 2 and 3 Sections, supporting the Guards Division, moved to the west of Trones Wood. Two tanks from No. 3 Section and four tanks of No. 4 Section, which were to support

---

88   See Appendix XVI
89   Map reference S23c 1,6. See Pidgeon, *Tanks at Flers*, p. 147.
90   According to C Company's War Diary, the XIV Corps dump was to hold 70 gallons of petrol, five gallons of Vacuum A oil, ten gallons of heavy steam cylinder oil, 30 pounds of grease and two gallons of gear oil. The ammunition dump was to contain 320 rounds of 6-pounder and 9,000 rounds of .303-inch small arms ammunition per Male tank; the stock for the Females was 27,500 rounds per Female tank. There were also 200 gallons of water and one day's worth of rations. Sadly, the exact location of the dump is not given but it is likely that it was the same as the assembly place for the ten tanks supporting the Guards Division.

C8 'going into battle' – the image was probably taken near the Loop. (TMA)

6th and 56th divisions, drove to Chimpanzee Valley which was 1,000 yards south of the Guards Division Assembly area. The remaining three Reserve tanks were sent to the Briqueterie (map square D5) south of Bernafay Wood which was also the site of C Company's headquarters.[91]

That evening, HQ C Company was informed that one of the Corps Reserve tanks, L tank commanded by 2Lt Reginald Cole, was to carry out a preliminary task, clearing the area west of Ginchy at first light in concert with two D Company tanks. Cole's orders were not however received until the following day – see Appendix VIII. C Company's tanks had trouble getting to their destinations in a timely fashion as they were competing for road space with other units. At 0530 hours, a report was received at the Loop that one tank was still held up by traffic.[92] This was probably Henriques' tank, who described his journey as follows:

> We moved off from our camp behind the lines at 5.00 p.m. on the 13th. We went in a long procession and progress was slow as corners would take some time in manipulating. Some troops rushed to the side of our route and stood open eyed, staring at us. Thousands swarmed round us and the remarks were very humorous. We were seemed to cheer people up as we went.

91 The tanks allocated to III Corps and Guards Division had not been informed of their tasks at this stage.
92 C Company War Diary. WO 95/96 (TNA).

Then, at about 8, we got onto the main road [now the D64]. We covered 1½ miles in 8 hours. To add to the joy, it was pouring with rain. The number trees I broke and the motor lorries damaged and ammunition waggons I jammed was high. Here the remarks were rather different. No language seemed too strong and I think they used the strongest. The traffic was jammed for both miles for miles and the Military Police and A.P.M. [assistant provost marshals] were getting frantic. However, at last we got off the main road and, about 6.30 a.m., reached our place of assembly behind the Front Lines.[93]

The tanks supporting III Corps, under Mann's command, also had three different Places of Assembly to the north of the Loop. Mann and Drader, who were to support 15th (Scottish) Division, assembled on the southern outskirts of Contalmaison (map square A4) alongside HQ 46th Brigade. Stones and Colle, who were to support 50th (Northumbrian) Division, were to assemble north of the Contalmaison to Longueval road between Bazentin-le-Petit and Mametz woods (map square B4), whilst Sampson, Robinson and Sharp assembled at Flatiron copse (map square C4) between Mametz Wood and Bazentin-le-Grand wood. Although the moon was supposed to be full, drizzle started in the early evening and this turned to heavy rain. Two of 4 Section's crews had a particularly miserable night as Mann's tank broke down and Colle's broke a track. They and half their crews had to return on foot to the Loop to collect one of the spare tanks and then drive back, cross-load the 30,000 rounds of ammunition, rations and water, fuels and stores from their stricken tanks to their replacements at night in the pouring rain, and then drive north again to join the other tanks in their sub-sections. It also does not mention the problem which it caused the ASC fitters who had to recover the stricken vehicles back to the Loop.

As for A Company, the Camp Commandant at Le Havre reported on 13 September that 11 officers and 95 other ranks left that morning on scheduled train 159. This was the MB1 party which travelled by Rouen and Abbeville, reaching Conteville at 2200 hours the same day and then marched to Yvrench. Their tanks were also on their way but there was still the risk of their being sunk by German U-boats in the English Channel.

93   Lionel L Loewe, *Basil Henriques: A Portrait* (London: Routledge & Keegan Paul, 1976), pp. 40–41.

6

Tank Actions on the Eastern Flank

Situation

By mid-August 1916, the Fourth British and Sixth French Armies were fixed on the Eastern Flank of the Somme battlefield (see map 6). Allied success in the first weeks of July had stalled and, despite British and French attacks in August and early September, the Bavarians continued to hold the villages of Guillemont (map square B5) and Combles (D5) as well as Leuze and Bouleaux woods (C5) between them.[1] Guillemont was eventually captured by 20th (Light) Division on 3 September although an attack on Ginchy (B4) the same day failed. The village was finally taken on 9 September 1916 after extremely hard fighting, by 16th (Irish) Division.

Combles, which was one of the larger villages on the battlefield, had housed a German garrison since its initial capture in September 1914. Its houses acted a rest area for German units holding their frontline at Hardecourt and Montauban to its west. From 22 July 1916, Combles had been bombarded and was now severely damaged. As a result, the Germans found shelter in cellars as well as in the catacombs which ran to the north of the church.[2] The French Sixth Army attacked the area on 3–4 September and their I Corps took the high ground to the south of the village. The British capture of Falfemont Farm (C6), on 5 September, enabled the British and French Sixth Armies to link up southwest of Combles; their boundary is shown in map square C6.[3]

The Guards Division relieved the Irish Division on 13 September 1916 but they were unable to do more than consolidate their position. The Germans remained in firm control of the trench lines northeast of Ginchy and the roads leading to Lesboeufs (D2–D3) and Morval (D3–4). Their artillery targeted Ginchy and its approaches as the preparatory bombardment by the British Fourth Army showed a major attack was imminent.

---

1   The woods were known by the soldiers as 'Bully Wood' and 'Lousy Wood'.
2   Paul Reed, *Combles* (Barnsley: Leo Cooper, 2002), pp. 34–36.
3   Known to the locals as Faffemont Farm.

Ground, German Defences and Dispositions

The Eastern Flank consisted of open farmland with a few woods. The southern edge included a series of generally shallow valleys although Combles was situated in a deeper valley which rose as it went west towards Wedge Wood (B6). Leuze and Bouleaux Woods had been heavily bombarded and were a tangle of trees and shellholes. The relatively unscathed villages of Lesboeufs and Morval, in the northeast, provided bases for Bavarian units in their depths, in west-facing defensive positions.

The battlefield northeast of Leuze Wood. (TMA)

The German defences were formed by a series of trench lines, with strongpoints established in their frontline at the Park (see C3, the Triangle, and C4 and the Quadrilateral directly to its south). The defences were mainly on the high ground, often on the 150-metre contour line. The juncture of Leuze and Bouleaux woods (C5) was also at 150 metres whilst Morval and Lesboeufs, the final objectives for 6th and Guards divisions respectively, were on slightly lower ground at 130 metres. Combles, in its valley, was between 110–120 metres. The Germans also had the advantage that, except for 56th (London) Division's advances in the southwest near Combles, all British attacks were uphill over unfenced fields. There was no cover from view, enemy fire or the weather. According to the 56th Divisional history, 'the field of battle was a field of mud, the resting area of the division was a field of mud, the roads and tracks were rivers of mud. The Army had simply blasted its way forward so that the shell holes cut one another in the mud.'[4]

4   Reed, *Combles*, p. 80.

In the northern part of the sector, *5th Bavarian Division* occupied a trench line running southeast of Flers containing three strong points: the Park on the boundary between 14th and Guards Divisions 1,000 yards north of Ginchy; the Triangle 1,000 yards northeast of Ginchy on the road to Lesboeufs; and the Quadrilateral 1,000 yards south along Straight Trench. South of the Quadrilateral, the Bavarians held the first 200 yards of Bully Trench which had formerly linked to the Quadrilateral to the southwest edge of Bouleaux Wood (C4–5). British attacks by 6th Division had managed to capture the rest of Bully Trench but the Bavarians held Beef Trench which ran 200 yards to its northeast. They also secured the gaps between Middle Wood and the Quadrilateral using machine-guns and artillery fire. South of Bouleaux Wood, the Bavarian's frontline was Stew Trench, which ran along the road to Combles, and then, at right angles, Loop Trench which ran southwest 300 yards (C5) before turning, again at right angles, southeast along the Combles Trench, which protected the western approaches to the village.

The German troops on the Eastern Flank were part of *III Bavarian Corps*. *5th Bavarian Division* had arrived on the Somme in early September 1916, having spent the previous nine months in the trenches between the Meuse and Moselle rivers. *7th Infantry Regiment* took over the area around Ginchy on the night of 11–12 September whilst *21st Infantry Regiment* took over the area around the Quadrilateral the following night.[5] *185th Reserve Division* held the area around the Bouleaux and Leuze woods northwest of Combles.

The Quadrilateral, Bouleaux Wood and Loop Trench, 15 September 1916

Development and Summary of the Plan

The attack on the Eastern Flank on 15 September was designed to provide flank protection to the British and New Zealand (NZ) Divisions who were to take the villages of Gueudecourt and Flers. The plan was issued on 11 September,[6] with a series of objectives specified for the morning of 15 September and strict timelines laid down to ensure that artillery and tank support was integrated.[7] The number of objective lines varied; in the south (56th Division) there was one; in the centre (6th Division) there were three and, in the north, the Guards Division had four.

The Guards Division, supported by ten tanks, would attack north and east from Ginchy.[8] They would advance 1,000 yards to capture the German trenches on the high ground (Green Line between the Park and the Triangle), allowing the British cavalry to advance. In the northwest corner, they would also link up to 14th Division (Second Objective or Brown Line). The Guards would then advance for a further 750 yards downhill to take Cow Trench, the eastern German trench lines on the Somme battlefield, which was the division's Third Objective or Blue Line. Finally, the Guards would advance for a further 500 yards to take the village of Lesboeufs and establish a defensive flank 200 yards to its east; this was their Fourth Objective or Red Line.

---

5   Miles, *OHGW*, p. 277, fn. 3.
6   XIV Corps Operation Order No. 51 dated 11 September 1916. See Appendix VIII which was transcribed into Appendix I to C Company War Diary (TNA WO 95/96).
7   Appendix IV to C Company's War Diary which is reproduced in Appendix X of this volume.
8   The original allocation was nine but Cole's tank was added on 12 September to undertake a preliminary operation. The details of the role were adjusted by two further sets of orders.

They were selected for this demanding role by the Earl of Cavan, who commanded the Guards Division from its formation in August 1915 until he was appointed XIV Corps Commander in January 1916.

In the centre, 6th Division, supported by three tanks, would advance from the Quadrilateral and the former German frontline trenches on either side: Straight Trench to the north and Bully and Beef Trenches to its south.[9] Their First Objective (Green Line) was 4–500 yards to the northeast; this objective was not easily recognised on the ground. Their intermediate objective (Blue Line), which required an advance of 1,000 yards, was the most easterly German trench (Bovril Trench which linked to the Cow Trench to its north). The Final Objective (Red Line) was a further 1,500 yards in the north and centre, but only 1,000 yards in the south, beyond Morval and Lesboeufs. As with the Guards, this Red Line was designed to form a protective flank about 400 yards east of the village.

To their south, 167th Brigade of 56th Division would initially clear Bouleaux Wood, and the ground to its north supported by a pair of tanks. This task was to be undertaken in two stages; the first included the capture of the German frontline (Beer Trench) and ground 200 yards to its northeast but their objective (Green Line) was not easily identified as a location. Secondly, after 50 minutes, 167th Brigade would continue to follow the barrage, at a pace of 20 yards per minute, clearing the rest of the Bouleaux Wood, and the ground beyond, until they reached the French narrow gauge railway line (Blue Line in D4–5) by 0828 hours. 167th Brigade would then secure the area, setting up a defensive flank southeast of Bouleaux Wood, and 168th Brigade would take over the advance to Morval.

Whilst 167th Brigade cleared Bouleaux Wood, 169th Brigade in the southeast, supported by single Female tank, was to capture the southern end of Loop Trench and the northern end of Combles Trench (Green Line). They would then advance up the Loop Trench, to the road linking Combles to Bouleaux Wood. 167th Brigade would then form a defensive flank against German counter-attacks from Combles; the tank in the meantime would drive to the northeast corner of Bouleaux Wood to take part in the final stage of the attack on Morval.

168th Brigade, proceeded by all three tanks, was then to advance east-northeast of Bouleaux Wood, taking the German trench system (Red Line or Fourth Objective) which protected the south-eastern part of Morval. Like the other two brigades, 168th Brigade would then set up a defensive flank to prevent any German counter-attack from Combles sweeping up the new British flank from the south.[10]

9   The 6th Infantry Division was a Regular Army formation which had deployed to France in September 1914. Two years later, having spent most of its time in the Ypres Salient, it was dispatched to the Somme.

10   The exact position of the defensive flank between Morval and the north-eastern corner of Bouleaux Wood is not recorded.

Objective	Lesboeufs	Morval	North and West of Combles
Opposing formations	*5th Bavarian Division* *7th Bavarian Regiment*	*5th Bavarian Division* *21st Bavarian Regiment* *7th Bavarian Regiment*	*185th Reserve Division* *28th Reserve Regiment*
Assaulting Division	Guards Division GPT Feilding	6th Division C Ross	56th (1st London) Division - CPA Hull
Assaulting Brigades and positions	1st Guards Brigade (south) 2nd Guards Brigade (north)	16th Brigade (south) 71st Brigade (north)	167th and 168th Brigades (northeast) 169th Brigade (southeast)
Divisional Frontages	1,200 yards	1,100 yards	400 yards (north) to 450 yards (south)
Distances to objectives			
1st Objective (Green Line)	1,000 yards (north) to 750 yards (south)	1,300 yards (north) 1,700 yards (centre) 650 yards (south)	400 yards (northeast) to 240 yards (southeast)
2nd Objective (Brown Line)	Up to 600 yards (north)	None	500 to 750 yards (north east); None (southeast)
3rd Objective (Blue Line)	1,250 yards (northeast)	850 yards (north) 1,050 yards (south)	None
4th Objective (Red Line)	1,300 yards (southeast)	1,250 yards	None
Tank Units	Nos 2 and 3 Section C Company	No. 4 Section (-) C Company	No. 4 Section (-) C Company
Tanks	10 × Mark I (6 failed to start)	3 × Mark I (2 failed to start)	3 × Mark I (1 failed to start)
Field Artillery	244 × 18-pounder; 64 × 4.5-inch (308)		
Howitzers	1 × 15-inch; 2 × 12-inch; 20 × 9.2-inch; 8 × 8-inch; 40 ×inch (71)		
Heavy Guns	2 × 9.2 inch; 28 × 60-pounder; 4 × 4.7-inch (34)		
Higher Formation	XIV Corps - The Earl of Cavan		

The Infantry

The three British divisions committed to the attack on 15 September were all battle-hardened. 56th Division had taken part in the diversionary attack on Gommecourt on 1 July 1916 where they had sustained major casualties. They then held the frontline for a month, whilst they were reinforced with drafts to replace their losses and undertook some rest. They then retrained at St Riquier where they gained some experience of operating with C Company's tanks.[11] Moving into the frontline at Leuze Wood on 6–7 September, they launched their first attack on 9 September at the same time that 16th (Irish) Division attacked Ginchy. 169th Brigade, commanded by Brig Gen ES d'E Coke, assaulted from Leuze Wood in a south-easterly direction towards the Loop Trench (the German frontline) which protected the north-western approaches to Combles. The attacking troops, who came from the London Rifle Brigade (LRB), were almost stopped in their tracks as they emerged from Leuze Wood and crossed into the open ground. Despite the heavy losses, the lines reformed and pushed on. Some of the bombing parties managed to get forward using an old German trench but the advance stalled as it reached the Loop Trench; the LRB took almost 400 casualties. Those who stayed on the battlefield overnight consolidated in the former German communications trench known as Combles Trench. However, at 0500 hours the next morning, the Germans drove the Londoners back to Leuze Wood using stick grenades. On 11 September, it was suggested at a Fourth Army Conference that 56th Division should once again attack towards the Loop Trench. The proposed attack was designed to be coordinated with the French who were to attack northwards on 12 September. However, GOC 56th Division (Maj Gen CPA Hull) declined; it being agreed that the next attack be delayed until 15 September when tanks would be available.

By this time, 6th Division had taken over the ground southeast of Ginchy, which enabled 56th Division to consolidate in Leuze Wood and the Guards to concentrate in Ginchy village. On 12 September, patrols found that there were no Bavarian troops manning the trenches to the southeast of Ginchy and it was decided to capitalise on this opportunity. At 0600 hours on 13 September, 16th and 71st Brigades attacked the Quadrilateral from the southwest, using the narrow-gauge railway line as their boundary. 71st Brigade was north of the railway and 16th Brigade was to its south. 71st Brigade got to within 250 yards of the Quadrilateral but were unable to hold it in strength.[12] They therefore withdrew to the line of a track which ran from the northern corner of Leuze Wood to the southern outskirts of Ginchy. One company of 8th Bedfords held the old German frontline, south of the Quadrilateral, and 16th Brigade also managed to form a flank from the northern corner of Leuze Wood, along a track running northeast, which was also occupied by the Bedfords. In the view of Maj Gen C Ross, the attack failed because the artillery did not neutralise the objective. The problem was that Quadrilateral sat in dead ground beyond the brow of a ridge, overlooking the ground to the east and south.

---

11   The 56th Division was the only formation which completed any sort of collective training with the tanks in France before the Battle of Flers–Courcelette. None would take part in tactical training after 15 September.

12   Soldiers from 2nd Nottinghamshire and Derbyshires (Notts & Derby) held a line of shellholes 250 yards from the Quadrilateral to the north of the railway line. Small parties from 9th Suffolks held a similar line similar position south of the line but most troops withdrew 500–1,000 yards to the line of the track linking Ginchy to the junction of Leuze and Bouleaux woods.

The British believed that the main part of the Quadrilateral was on a reverse slope whereas much was forward of it; however, this could not be seen by the artillery observers in the frontline. As a result, the British artillery barrage, which was targeting the ground behind the frontline trenches, failed to neutralise the defenders. A further attack at 1800 hours that evening also came to nothing.

The Guards had taken over Ginchy from 16th (Irish) Division who had finally captured the village on 9 September.[13] On 0600 hours on 12 September, 1st Grenadier Guards pushed the Bavarians back along the road running northeast toward the Quadrilateral. However, the units which remained in the village were in sight of the German artillery observers on the high ground northeast of the village and there were machine-guns on their lines of advance particularly towards Flers. Ginchy was a desperate place to occupy and even worse as a Forming Up Place from which to attack.

The Artillery

Some 389 artillery pieces were in direct support of XIV Corps which was also allocated 34 heavy guns to target known strongpoints, lines of communications and rear areas – see above. The Corps Artillery Instructions were that:

a   At the hour of Zero an intense fire will be opened by the Field Artillery and the creeping barrage will be advanced at the rate of 50 yards per minute in front of the Infantry, gaps being left open to allow movements of the Tanks. When the creeping barrage reaches the stationary barrage, the stationary barrage will lift on to the next barrage line.

b   At Z + 45 minutes the barrage in front of that portion of the XIV Corps which is to advance to the second objective, will again become intense, to cover the further advance of the Infantry.

c   For the attack of the third and fourth objectives there will be no creeping barrage immediately in front of the Infantry.

The lane left for the tanks was 100 yards wide. This meant that the enemy units, positioned where the railway ran north of the Quadrilateral, were not neutralised. The instructions also did not reflect the various starting positions of the attacking brigades and their relative distances to the German frontline. Units in 56th Division had to advance between 240 and 400 yards on the right (south); in the centre, 6th Division had to advance 350 yards in the south, 1,300 yards in the centre and 900 yards in the north where they would link up with the Guards. The Guards Division had to cross 750 yards of no man's land where they joined 6th Division but a full 1,000 yards in the north where they would link up with 14th Division. No formations in the Central

---

13   7th Division started the attack on 3 September, their initial assault being badly disrupted by German machine-gunners in the Brewery Salient to the east of Delville Wood (map square 4B). Although they managed to enter the northwest part of Ginchy, they were quickly ejected by a German counter-attack. Over the next four days, 7th Division carried out further assaults but were unable to hold any ground taken near the village. On 9 September 16th (Irish) Division took over the attack and succeeded, after much fierce fighting, to take the village. They were relieved that night by the Guards Division.

area and the Western Flank were required to cover such large distances between the jumping off trenches and the German frontline as those on the Eastern Flank.

The problem was compounded when, despite objections from Ross, 6th Division's First Objective line was moved back 200 yards so that it abutted the Guards' First Objective. As a result, 71st Brigade would now have to advance 1,300 yards to the Green Line. The artillery could still not observe and adjust fire on their initial objectives as they were in dead ground. Furthermore, as the Green Line in the 6th Division area was just a line on the map, it did not fall on any German position. As a result, this stationary barrage caused no damage to the enemy and was a complete waste of ammunition. Hull objected strongly to this plan at the Corps Conference on 13 September and managed to convince Cavan, after comments by the Guards, that one quarter of the available 18-pounders would target a line 100 yards on the near side of the German frontline before creeping to the rear at twice the predicted level. It was some assistance but not sufficient.

The Tanks

Coloured map No. 6 will assist in following the tank groups on the Eastern Flank. The ten tanks supporting the Guards Divisions comprised three groups (known by the Guards as Columns), each of three tanks with a single Female tank on their Western Flank. In the east, No. 1 Column was to start on the road which linked Ginchy to Lesboeufs; it comprised two Male tanks and one Female tank. The Male 741 (known as Tank A) commanded by Lt Jethro Tull, was manned by the C15 crew; 746 *Campania* (Tank B) was commanded by 2Lt Jack Clarke and the C17 crew whilst Tank C, the Female 508 named *Casa*, was manned by 2Lt Victor Smith and the C18 Crew.[14] The tanks would initially advance, north of the road to Lesboeufs, between 1st Grenadier Guards and 3rd Coldstream Guards along the inter-brigade boundary. The tanks' First Objective was the southeast part of the Triangle, the strongpoint on the enemy frontline which was to the south of that road (see map square C4). The allocation of two Male tank indicates No. 1 Column's main targets were German machine-gun positions within the strongpoint.

No. 2 Column, operating in the centre of the Guards Division, was to support 2nd Coldstream Guards attack on the Serpentine Trench/Flers Line to the northwest of the Triangle. The group, commanded by Hiscocks, consisted of two Female tanks and a Male tank which indicates their primary role was suppression of the German troops in the trench lines. The first Female 507 (D Tank) was commanded by Hiscocks; the second Female 513 (F Tank) was commanded by 2Lt Tom Murphy and the final (E tank) was the Male 722, commanded by 2Lt Alec Arnaud (see page 102). The Starting Point for No. 2 Column was northeast of Ginchy and they were to advance on the right flank of 2nd Coldstream Guards.

The tanks of No. 3 Column, operating on the western side of the Guards' divisional area, were two Males and a Female, so allocated because of the number of German machine-gun emplacements in their area. Lt Leonard Bates was in command of Male 714 (G Tank) whilst Lt Benbow Eliot commanded 760, which was known as *Centurion*.[15] The Female 554 was

---

14   Smith's tank was named after his family home in Reading.
15   Unfortunately, few crew numbers are recorded for this section.

commanded by 2Lt Charles Ambrose and known as K tank. The three tanks were to advance on the left flank of 3rd Coldstream Guards. The machine-gun positions on their route also threatened the advancing infantry of 14th Division moving northwards to clear the German frontline trench called Tea Support. There were also a series of machine-guns, 600 yards further north along the Flers Road in the Pint Trench, which created the same danger for 41st Division as they advanced towards Tea Support Trench from Delville Wood.

The single tank allocated to the Guards Division was the Female tank *Clan Cameron*, commanded by 2Lt Harold Cole.[16] Designated L Tank, she was to operate on the west flank, undertaking a preliminary operation against the Brewery Salient in the open ground between Ginchy and Delville Wood. Cole was subsequently given additional tasks on the road running north of Ginchy towards Flers.[17]

The orders from HQ Guards Division gave timings for the tanks' deployment as well as their start times. Leaving their Position of Assembly at Trones Wood (map square A5), all three columns were to reach their various Starting Points near Ginchy by Z - 4 hours (0220 hours).[18] At Z - 50 minutes (0530 hours), No. 3 Column was to advance to the Green Line on the left, the other columns starting their advance 10 minutes later. The orders for Cole were that he was to assist in the area northwest of Ginchy but gave no times.[19] As a result, Cole was ordered by Holford-Walker 'to report to Brigade Major, Left Guards Brigade and ask him for any information which may aid you.'[20]

The second stage of the Guards' attack would start at Z + 90 minutes (0750 hours) when the three columns were advanced towards the Blue Line. No. 1 Column was ordered to pass into the 6th Divisional area in map square T9 Central as this area contained a group of six parallel trenches, bounded on each side by a connecting trench, which would create a major threat if not cleared of enemy troops. The third stage of the attack, for Nos. 2 and 3 Columns only, would start from the Blue Line at Z + 3 hours 30 minutes (0950 hours) to advance northwest to the Red Line northeast of Lesboeufs.

16 Cole, who was originally was part of No. 4 Section, commanded one of the XIV Corps Reserve tanks. A SNCO motorcyclist in the RE Signals Section, which supported Plymouth Garrison in 1915, Cole was awarded the MBE for his services in the Baltic States in the summer of 1919. Pope, *FTC*, p. 32.

17 See Appendix IX.

18 The tanks were initially to use a route which followed the narrow gauge French railway line through the centre of Trones Wood and then north-easterly, north of Guillemont, to a rendezvous 750 yards southwest of Ginchy (Guards Division memo 2228 dated 12 September 1916). However, it appears that the tanks actually travelled around the southern edge of Trones Wood to their Starting Points. This required an approach march of two miles for No. 3 Column and over 3,750 yards for Nos. 1 and 2 Columns.

19 The original instructions to C Company, issued at 1155 hours on 13 September, stated that Cole was to attack the area of the Brewery Salient at 0550 hours, but these were not sent to him. See Appendix IX.

20 The left brigade was 1st Guards Brigade. Its headquarters was located 400 yards southeast of Waterlot Farm (Map 6 map square A4) in trenches just south of the Guillemont to Longueval road. It therefore would have been perfectly feasible for Cole to be briefed on his role shortly before getting to his Position of Assembly.

6th Division's three tanks were from No. 4 Section under the company commander's brother Archie Walker.[21] Walker also commanded Male tank 705 *Clan Leslie*[22] and the C19 crew.[23] The other two tanks were both Female: 523 commanded by Macpherson with the C20 crew and Henriques with 533 and the C22 crew. These tanks, which had reached Chimpanzee Valley in the early hours of 14 September, were to attack in column of route (Line ahead).

The other sub-section, which supported 56th Division, consisted of Male 716 commanded by Dashwood with the C13 Crew and two females; 509 *Corunna* commanded by 2Lt Frank Arnold (C14 crew) and Lt Eric Purdy, who commanded the C16 crew in the Female 510 known as *Challenger*.[24] Purdy, who was tasked to initially support 169th Brigade, was referred to as the Right Tank whilst Dashwood and Arnold, who initially were to support 167th Brigade as a pair, were respectively known as the Centre and Left Tanks. This placed Dashwood closest to Bouleaux Wood, where his 6-pounder guns could destroy the machine-gun positions at a range of less than 200 yards. Arnold was on the Left Flank close to the German communications trenches and stronghold in Middle Wood, where *Corunna's* Vickers' machine-guns would neutralise the German defenders in Beef Trench and then aid 167th Brigade to their objectives. Thereafter all three tanks would rendezvous at the northern end of Bouleaux Wood and support the final attack by 168th Brigade on Morval – see Appendix X.

Preparations for Battle

Despite their lack of sleep the previous night, the tank crews had a full day of work on 14 September with only limited sleep expected the following night. The skippers supporting the Guards Division had to meet their guides at 0600 hours and check the route to Ginchy which had been selected the day before. That morning, it became apparent that many of the tanks were short of petrol. At 1100 hours HQ C Company, at the Loop, received a message requesting replenishment. The planned dump at Trones Wood[25] had not been in-loaded so a reply was sent that 500 gallons of fuel would be sent forward immediately.[26] The crews also had to top up the lubricants in their engines, transmissions and running gear then tighten their tracks. This activity can clearly be seen in the picture of the four tanks leaguered at Chimpanzee Valley.[27]

---

21   Walker had seen action in April 1915 with 2nd Kings Own Shropshire Light Infantry at Ypres shortly after the Germans used poison gas for the first time. His battalion was sent forward to fill gaps left in the line; he was wounded on 26 April during a counter-attack, his injuries being sufficiently severe that he was evacuated to England. Pope, *FTC*, pp. 54-55.

22   The tank was named after Walker's Scottish family clan.

23   The Tank Museum has painted the sole remaining Mark I tank to represent *Clan Leslie* (see colour photograph 1). However, the tank on display *is not* that commanded by Walker on 15 September 1916.

24   Dashwood replaced Trevithick after the latter had injured his knee at Yvrench.

25   See Chapter 5.

26   Author's note: Notwithstanding this entry in the War Diary, several vehicles later reported that they were short of fuel. It is therefore unlikely that all the crews topped up before moving to their Starting Points.

27   Author's note: It is not possible to positively identify all the tanks in the photograph over. The four in the area were the three supporting 6th Division (Henriques, Walker and Macpherson) and Purdy's tank *Challenger* which would support 56th Division. The Male tank, second from the left, has been positively identified by Karl Heinz Pfarr as *Clan Leslie* from its camouflage pattern.

C Company tanks at Chimpanzee Valley, 14 September 1916. (TMA)

As the tanks were being prepared for battle, HQ 6th Division issued revised orders, reflecting the failure to capture the Quadrilateral on the previous day:

> Section will assemble about A5d 2,6. in the neighbourhood of Chimpanzee Trench on W/X night and will be in position at the Point of Departure at cross-roads east of Guillemont Cemetery T20c 2,3 two hours before Zero [0420 hours] on X day.
>
> A Section will move from Position of Departure at Z – 1½ hours [0450 hours] and move to first objective T15 central [Green Line] along the railway. German strong point about T15c 0.4 [the Quadrilateral] to be dealt with en route.
>
> A Section will move to Morval (T16b 5.8) in front of infantry under cover of a creeping barrage at Zero + 3 hours 30 minutes [0950 hours].[28]

The requirement to 'deal with' the Quadrilateral was a major change in orders to the crews.[29] This would have required that Walker speak with the Divisional staff and agree tactics for the preliminary action before they advanced to the Green Line. Fortunately, 16th Brigade staff

28   Amendment to 6th Div G/18/13/1 Special Instructions Regarding Action of Tanks dated 14 September 1916. The time the orders were issued are not recorded in C Company's War Diary nor does it indicate if the orders were sent to the section commanders. The orders show that Caterpillar Valley was not the original Place of Assembly.

29   Author's note: The distance from the Starting Point to the Quadrilateral is 1,050 yards. Assuming an approach speed of 15 yards a minute, the tanks would reach their new objective at 0600 hours (Z – 20

were already positioned in their HQ position at Wedge Wood, which was just over a mile from Chimpanzee Valley. There is no record of any discussions but I think it highly likely that Walker went forward and discussed how the tanks were to be used. Alternatively, he could have discussed the matter by telephone from the forward C Company headquarters located at the Briqueterie but this seems less likely.

At 1900 hours, as dusk approached, the C Company tanks set out for their different Starting Points. The Guards Division's tanks had a demanding route: 'A great deal of difficulty was experienced in getting the tanks from their position of assembly southwest of Trones Wood to the forward positions during the night. Tapes had been laid on the ground from a point southwest of Guillemont to the forward position on the outskirts of Ginchy. The ground over which the tanks had to travel was as bad as possible and, without the existence of the tapes, the tanks would have been unable to reach their forward positions.'[30] Despite having the furthest to travel, all three tanks in No. 1 Column successfully reached their Starting Point to the east of Ginchy on time. No. 2 Column was one tank short before they started as it had been impossible to repair Murphy's tank. Arnaud very nearly reached Ginchy but *Centurion* became ditched in a shellhole on the southwestern outskirts of the village; as a result, only Hiscocks' tank reached

Clan Leslie deploying on 14 September 1916. (TMA)

mins). They would then have been wholly unprotected from enemy attack, on an insecure location, until the artillery bombardment commenced.

30   Report by GOC Guards Division quoted in Pidgeon, *Tanks at Flers*, p. 92.

its Starting Point. All three tanks of No. 3 Column got to their Starting Point west of Ginchy, as did Cole after he had been briefed by HQ 1st Guards Brigade at their headquarters near Waterlot Farm.[31]

Several photographs depict *Clan Leslie* leaving Chimpanzee Valley on the evening of 14 September. In *Tanks at Flers*, Trevor Pidgeon states that the three tanks travelled due east towards Angle Wood and then northeast to Wedge Wood. However, since Trevor's death, a map of the deployment route has been found.[32] This shows the group must have driven northeast towards Guillemont to reach their Point of Departure east of the village cemetery. After half an hour's drive, it was discovered that the carrier pigeons had been left behind so a crewman was sent to collect them. About this time, Macpherson's tank started to develop engine trouble, the crew worked on the problem for half an hour and the three tanks started off again. A short distance further on, Macpherson's tank broke down again and the crew was left to fix it – which they successfully did. Meanwhile, Henriques followed his section commander towards Guillemont. As they reached the south-eastern edge of the village, *Clan Leslie*'s steering failed whilst traversing a steep slope.[33] Unable to proceed, Walker directed Henriques to continue, not to the Guillemont crossroads, but to HQ 16th Brigade presumably to let them know of the problems the crews were experiencing.

Arriving at Wedge Wood at midnight, accompanied by Macpherson whose tank which had managed to catch up, Henriques found out that his tank had only half of his fuel remaining.[34] Henriques immediately reported this to his section commander, who also had walked down to Wedge Wood leaving his crew to repair the steering using the tail from Murphy's tank. Walker immediately went to find petrol, possibly from the Trones Wood Dump. At 0115 hours, HQ C Company at the Loop received the message that fuel was needed and the C Company Commander delivered 16 gallons of fuel reaching Wedge Wood in his Sunbeam car at 0230 hours after 'a very rough ride.'[35] Henriques and Macpherson used the time, whilst fuel was being located, to walk north up the road from Wedge Wood to the Guillemont Crossroads (map square B5), onto the railway line (map squares B5–C5), and then eventually up to the frontline, returning to Wedge Wood feeling doubtful about the attack. At HQ 16th Brigade, Henriques was told that he should depart for his Starting Point at 0400 hours, 50 minutes earlier than planned, which meant he would have arrived at his Starting Point by 0510 hours.[36]

31 Cole was originally ordered by his company commander to join Hiscocks at his Place of Assembly. It is likely his orders were changed when he visited HQ 1st Guards Brigade; either during the afternoon of 14 September or as he deployed to his starting point.
32 The map, attached to a second copy of Henriques' script for a presentation given in February 1917, is held in the Tank Museum archives in the C Battalion box.
33 The tank was recovered and allocated to Morris Henderson on 25 September.
34 Presumably Henriques did not manage to refuel from the cans sent to Trones Wood earlier that day.
35 It is not clear where Holford-Walker was located when the message was received. The C Company War Diary shows the HQ was at the Loop overnight but, in order to get the fuel to Wedge Wood in 75 minutes, he must have been much closer, possibly at Trones Wood. Holford-Walker was certainly at the Briqueterie later that morning as a signal was sent to him from HQ 56th Division regarding the follow-on attack on the Quadrilateral.
36 In the 'Indiscretions of a Warden', written in 1930s, Henriques mentions that he was accompanied on this forward reconnaissance by Macpherson, walking into no man's land, and that the two tanks set off together from Wedge Wood to support the attack. Macpherson's tank then broke down again at Z-40 minutes (0540 hours), leaving Henriques' crew to tackle the first objective alone. Henriques'

The three tanks supporting 56th Division also had problems getting to their Starting Points.[37] They left Chimpanzee Valley at 1900 hours travelling east towards HQ 169th Brigade which was 700 yards from their Assembly Place. Here they were met by a guide, Rifleman Gray,[38] who led them on to Leuze Wood. Gray commented that: 'the run between Brigade HQ and Battalion HQ would normally take something like 20 minutes but, owing to the unsuitable ground, a longer route had to be taken which should have been travelled in 30 minutes.'[39] After a struggle of 3½ hours, the first tank [*Challenger*] got into position. The ground over which they had to travel was very soft and nothing but a mass of shell holes, some of which were very large in deep, and as it was dark, the drivers could not see where they were going. Before long they were in difficulties.' The ground conditions can be seen in monochrome photograph on page 136.

Gray does not mention that one of Dashwood's tracks broke as it approached Angle Wood, about one third of the way along its deployment route.[40] Gray continued:

> Our battalion was on the right of the British Line and linked up with the French; the ground we were travelling over was where the French supports [trenches] were. The track was still bad and the tanks were spitting fire, making no end of a row with their engines attracting the Poilus' attention. They poured out from their dug outs to see what was going on and soon there were quite a number gazing in amazement at the new engine of war.
>
> We were not far from Battalion HQ and naturally I did not like the idea of continuously showing a light to guide the tanks, so only gave a flash now and again. The officer alighted and wanted to know what was the matter? I explained that we were getting close to the [front] line and the light would attract some whizz bangs.[41]
>
> The Officer replied that we were very late and as they must bring the tanks up at any cost, they must take the risk.

Dashwood stopped at HQ 167th Brigade at Falfemont Farm (map 6, map square C6), to inform them that only one tank was available to support the northern attack. He then probably accompanied *Challenger* and then *Corunna* to their differing Starting Points at Leuze Wood. It is also likely that Arnold visited the 1st Londons' HQ, which was on the northern edge of Leuze Wood and en route to his Starting Point, to receive an update on the enemy situation and how his tank, now working alone, could support the initial stages of the attack.[42]

---

recollections do not reflect the entries in C Company Diary; that said, several reports in the War Diary appear *not* to have been contemporaneous.

37   Appendix V to the C Company War Diary states that the North Group Point of Assembly was Wedge Wood but this is not where they stayed on 13–14 September.

38   Rifleman W.J. Gray of 9th London (Queen Victoria's Rifles) – see Pidgeon, *Tanks at Flers*, pp. 60-61.

39   Probably travelling in daylight hours.

40   The news of the breakdown reached HQ 56th Division at 0045 hours on 15 September.

41   Probably 77mm field artillery used in close support of German units.

42   The C Company War Diary records that their HQ was not notified of the situation until 0730 hours; Dashwood reported that his tank had suffered a split track but that Purdy and Arnold had reached their Starting Points on time. This indicates that Dashwood was able to get his message to them from HQ 167th Brigade.

Zero

Zero was at 0620 hours – there was some early morning mist in the valleys but later the morning broke into perfect autumnal weather.[43]

Final Moves

There was a further loss of tanks supporting the Guards Division when Hiscocks' tank, the sole remaining member of No. 2 Column, ditched as it moved up to the frontline. As a result, there were no tanks to lead 2nd Coldstream Guards to their First Objective or counter the enemy machine-gun fire coming from the Triangle and the Serpentine trench. Work continued on Macpherson's tank, which would ultimately prove successful but, despite the fitting of the steering tail from Murphy's to Walker's tank, *Clan Leslie* did not get into action. Henriques left Wedge Wood at 0400 hours and reached a set of trenches 500 yards behind the British frontline at 0500 hours. There he waited there until he judged it was time to move forward again.[44]

Assault on Combles

169th Brigade's attack on the northwest of Combles was led by *Challenger*. At Z - 20 minutes (0600 hours), in accordance with the timetable,[45] the Female tank left the southwestern edge of Leuze Wood and obliquely crossed the heavily crumped fields for 500 yards to the junction of Combles Trench and the German frontline Loop Trench.[46] *Challenger* drove obliquely across the battlefield (see colour photograph 2) to the junction of Loop and Combles trenches; A and B Companies of 2nd Londons advancing on their left from the north with C and D Companies advancing at a right angle from the west, enabling a full battalion to reach the first objective at one time. The ferocity of the German bombardment, and their machine-guns firing across the battlefield, slowed the advance and caused severe casualties, which created difficulties in taking the Loop trench.

An RFC aeroplane reportedly saw *Challenger* circling in the area of the First Objective. This is surprising, given that Purdy's machine-gunners could have enfiladed attacks along either Combles Trench or Loop Trench if the tank had remained at the trench junction. *Challenger* then started to drive along the south-eastern side of Loop Trench northwards towards a strongpoint half way to the 'sunken road' which linked Ginchy to Combles. As the tank got to within 100 yards of the strongpoint, it stopped. The reason was not reported at the time

---

43 Weather condition recorded by Andrew Carbery, *The NZ Medical Service in the Great War 1916-1918* (Auckland: Whitcomb & Tombs 1924) p. 198. See <http://nzetc.victoria.ac.nz/tm/scholarly/tei-WH1-Medi.html> (accessed 1 November 2020).

44 At 0550 hours, HQ 71st Infantry Brigade, located at Arrow Head Copse (map 6, map square A5), received a message informing them that the tank had passed through its forward lines. The time at which the message was sent was not recorded but it is likely that this message was sent by telephone or wireless telegraphy.

45 C Company's War Diary records that, at 0730 hours, Dashwood reported both *Corunna* and *Challenger* had left on time.

46 *Challenger* was driven obliquely, across no man's land, to reach its objective which is why the crew needed to start twenty minutes before Zero (0600 hours).

Challenger abandoned on the battlefield, winter 1916. (TMA)

but Holford-Walker, writing to Edmunds in 1935, stated that the tank track had been hit by a 'short'.[47] This makes sense as the British artillery were laying down a barrage, 200 yards beyond Loop Trench, to prevent German reinforcements reaching their frontline trench from Combles.

The German infantry, recognising that *Challenger* was immobilised, attacked the tank. The Londoners, who were still trying to subdue the defenders, were unable to approach the position due to German trench blocks and uncut wire entanglements above ground. The C16 crew fought off their attackers, using their Vickers machine-guns and revolvers, initially to good effect. The battle raged for five hours by which time *Challenger's* crew had virtually exhausted their ammunition (some 30,000 0.303-inch rounds).[48] By this time, the Londons had advanced to within a short distance from the tank and the crew were able to escape, Purdy setting fire to *Challenger* as required by his orders as he abandoned the tank. The Londoners fought on, trying to bomb the defenders out of Loop Trench for almost 24 hours, but eventually withdrew at 0500 hours the next morning as first light was approaching. The Germans retained the Loop Trench for 100 yards south of the Sunken Road.

In his subsequent report on the attack, Hull said that 169th Brigade had failed to make much progress; this comment by GOC 56th Division seems unfair as only one battalion was engaged

---

47   Holford-Walker letter, 22 April 1935.
48   *Challenger* was unusual in that she was able to use all five of her machine-guns to beat off the attack; most other tanks which broke down or ditched on 15 September were unable to use guns in both sponsons to engage their German attackers.

and there seems to have been no action to reinforce it. As for the tank crew's contribution, Holford-Walker reported seeing 150 German bodies in the area where *Challenger* had been hit. The Official Historian[49] states that all of the crew were wounded and Purdy was later admitted to hospital.[50] The tank could not be moved, despite determined efforts by the British and French Armies, as neither the tank companies nor the ASC workshops were equipped for such a task. *Challenger* remained where she was until the battlefield clearances when she was broken up.

Assault at Bouleaux Wood

Corunna also left its Starting Point on time, driving northeast from the northern tip of Leuze Wood, parallel to the northern edge of Bouleaux Wood (see colour photograph 3). The tank crossed the British frontline (Bully Trench) on time at 0608 hours but further north than ordered.[51] *Corunna* advanced ahead of the infantry across the 250-yard-wide no man's land to the German frontline (Beef Trench). The infantry of 1/1st Londons advanced on time but could not enter Beef Trench as the protective barbed wire had not been destroyed.[52] Rather than waiting for the infantry to capture and consolidate the Beef Trench,[53] Arnold drove on, running parallel to a communications trench known as Gropi Trench,[54] towards Middle Wood which was on the Green Line (the First Objective). Realising the infantry were not following the tank, Arnold turned *Corunna* back to Beef Trench in order to lead the Londons forward. He then drove northeast again and was seen just north of the Green Line at 0705 hours within 100 yards of the wood edge. In his letter to Edmonds in 1935, Holford-Walker states that Arnold 'moved down the edge of Bouleaux Wood, shooting at every living thing he saw.' Assuming his starboard Vickers guns did the same thing, this may have caused heavy casualties amongst the German defenders. By this time, some elements of D Company 1st Londons had cleared Gropi Trench and taken Middle Wood so *Corunna's* position would have offered them some protection. However, the rest of the advancing infantry were well behind, the advance through

---

49   Mills, *OHGW*, p. 309.
50   Purdy was awarded the MC which was presented at Buckingham Palace on 13 May 1917. He served with C Battalion, successfully commanding sections in the Ypres Salient and at Cambrai. In 1918, he remained with 3rd Light Battalion, leading a section of Whippets into attack on 26 March 1918 at Colincamps – the first time they were used in action. Purdy also led a section on the opening day of the Battle of Amiens and was in that role when wounded in the left arm and thigh on 25 August 1918. Pope, *FTC*, pp. 43–46.
51   The tank was ordered to cross the trench at T21c 9,9 whereas Trevor Pidgeon shows she crossed 250 yards further along at T21a 8,2.
52   The Battalion's War Diary records that the enemy trench was undamaged and fully manned. See Reed, *Combles*, p. 80. This was possibly due to the British artillery targeting the Green Line which was 200 yards further north.
53   Holford-Walker, writing in 1935, stated that Arnold had never seen a shot fired in anger in his life. He joined 19th Royal Fusiliers as a rifleman in 1915 and had a maximum of four months' experience in France. The attack at Bouleaux Wood was his first battle and the first in which he commanded a tank. The limited training at Yvrench had probably not included such battle drills and Arnold's lack of experience meant he followed his orders to advance without confirming the infantry were following him.
54   Gropi Trench was just inside the inter-divisional boundary with 6th Division and would have provided a useful reference to Arnold when crossing the overwise featureless ground.

Bouleaux Wood being delayed by the German defenders whilst machine-gunners on its edge destroyed the Londons as they advanced to the First Objective.[55]

Corunna returned towards the German frontline but then set off northeast again. At 0800 hours, the tank was spotted 200 yards from the end of Bouleaux Wood, which ties into the timings given in the 56th Division timetable.[56] Turning east at the top of the wood, presumably in order to start his advance towards Morval, Arnold must have realised that 168th Brigade infantry were not in position. He therefore followed his tracks back to the original German frontline, passing Middle Wood which was still in British hands. By this point, the tank's differential was damaged which required the driver to lock it. Approaching Beef Trench, Arnold ordered Private Sleath to turn *Corunna* round and back the tank towards the trench. This was a difficult manoeuvre, especially with the differential locked, and *Corunna* drove into a large shell hole, next to the German frontline. The Female tank slipped onto its right-hand side so that only two of its four Vickers' machine-guns were effective.

Corunna ditched north of Bouleaux Wood (TMA).

55   This objective, which was just a line on the map, would have offered no protection to the Londons. Casualty reports showed 60 officers and men killed, 143 wounded and 84 missing in action on 15 September. Paul Reed has identified that 128 men of the Battalion were killed on that day. See Reed, *Combles*, p 81.

56   Trevor Pidgeon states that Arnold's orders had been amended on three occasions. See Pidgeon, *Tanks at Flers*, p. 56.

What happened next was recorded by Gnr Tom Bernard in his diary.[57]

> Unfortunately, at 9.16 our diff [differential] got stripped and we can only proceed with the diff locked which caused our steering to jam. The officer, 2Lt Arnold consulted us on the matter and we decided to stick [continue] the action. We were signalled by a sergeant of our infantry that they were being attacked by a party of bombers from Leuze Wood[58] so we came stern first to attack these bombers and, just when we got within 20 yards of them, the car[59] got stuck in a large shell hole, which, had our steering gear been in order, we would easily have got out of.

Arnold realised that he could not stay where he was so asked for volunteers to try to dig the tank out. Bernard continued:

> Corporal Pattinson, Winter, Williams and I went out of the back door and made a start. The shell hole in which we were stuck was connected to the trench in which there were German bombers. After about ten minutes digging, a bomb [German stick grenade] fell at Corporal Pattinson's feet. He picked it up and tried to throw it away but it exploded in his hands, killing him and wounding Winter. Williams and I rushed down the trench towards the bombers and, at the corner of a traverse trench, came onto one [German] who had a bomb in his hand and was in a position to throw it. I had my revolver ready and let him have two [bullets]. Unfortunately, Williams had left his revolver in the car so we rushed back to it. Winter had also just got wounded through the shoulder by a sniper.

The Germans continued their attacks. Realising the crew needed assistance to extract the tank, Arnold left *Corunna* and made his way back across no man's land and having found an infantry captain, asked for a working party. He then returned across no man's land in an attempt to reach his tank. Whilst Arnold was away from *Corunna*, two crewmen manned the machine-guns which could be used whilst Bernard fired his pistol from the loopholes in the tank. He observed in his diary:

> At about 4 pm we decided to abandon the car and we made for the short trench forty yards away, which had been made by connecting a few shell holes. We were sniped at all the way. I got nearly to where Mr Arnold was and reported to him. He then told me that the locks would have to be removed from the car to make the guns useless in case the enemy should get inside, in which event they would have been able to sweep the [battle] field. I went back and took Gunner Williams with me and left Gunners Richie, Giles and Winter in the Trench with Mr Arnold and Private Sleath. We got back to the car and effectively jammed the guns, fetching the locks back with us, not without difficulty. We arrived where Mr Arnold was but he had left.

---

57 This was written on 13 October at Acheux. The complete entry is reproduced in Appendix XIII.
58 More likely to have been from Bouleaux Wood as Leuze Wood was occupied by British units.
59 Many of the crewmen referred to their vehicles as 'cars' or 'buses' in their diaries and letters. It was not until later that the term 'tank' became commonly used.

Arnold had taken Sleath with him, possibly to try to get some help from the ASC in recovering the tank.[60] Bernard waited with four other crewmen until dark when a bombardment started. At 1950 hours, Bernard, Williams and six infantrymen who were also sheltering in the shellhole, dashed back 250 yards to the British second line trench, dropping to the ground every time a star shell illuminated the battlefield. The others followed but two were shot on route.[61] The surviving crewmen got back to the Briqueterie the following morning.

Tom Bernard (standing centre) with his crew. (TMA)

60   Lt. Theodore Wenger, one of 711 (MT) Company's engineering officers, was at Guillemont Station working on one of the Guards Division's tanks by this time.
61   Three *Corunna* crewmen died. Gerald Pattinson was buried on the edge of Bouleaux Wood but the body of 'Bag' Giles, killed whilst trying to get back to the British Second Line, was never identified. Arthur Ritchie died of sepsis, on 14 November at Abbeville; his mother and sister were present at his bedside. Pattinson's body was moved to the Combles Community Cemetery after the war, his parents paying for the following to be inscribed on his grave marker: 'He, taking death on himself, saved his comrades'. Pope, *FTC*, pp. 47–53.

Assault on the Quadrilateral

Henriques' tank was the only tank now available to support 6th Division's attack on Morval. The route was along the line of the French 1-metre gauge railway which ran obliquely across the fields up to the Quadrilateral (see colour photograph 4). At 0535 hours, the Germans started to bombard the waiting infantry, the reason being attributed to the tank's presence. Ten minutes later, the tank reached the frontline and Henriques was asked to withdraw for fear of attracting fire onto the waiting troops of 71st Brigade. Reversing a tank today is not difficult – the driver only has to select the right gear. However, the driver was very inexperienced, there were no reversing mirrors and the drill had probably not been practiced. It was now well after first light and Henriques states he only reversed 20 yards, which would have made little difference. The British Official History records that, at some time before the attack, the tank fired into the waiting infantry, creating casualties amongst the 9th Norfolks which was only stopped when an officer approached the tank and pointed it towards the enemy.[62]

At 0550 hours, 1st Leicestershires, who were on the left flank of 71st Brigade, recorded that a tank was seen moving quietly towards the German frontline. At the same time, two German aeroplanes flew over the area, trying to identify what was taking place in the half-light and the key element of surprise, underpinning the first use of tanks, was lost. Henriques was following the railway on its northside when the Germans opened fire using machine-guns.[63] These were concentrated on the tank's cab and they soon smashed the vision blocks and one of the periscopes. Both Henriques and his driver, who is not identified, suffered wounds to their faces and had to stop at one stage when they could no longer see.[64]

Henriques reached the German lines at 0600 hours and then turned north, presumably to follow Straight Trench towards the Triangle. The Norfolks recorded this, no doubt with some relief, as Straight Trench was the German frontline which they were to assault. The tank continued north suppressing the defenders as it went but it drew fire from the Bavarians with the sides of the tank being penetrated with armour-piercing bullets.[65] Realising his machine-gunners had stopped firing and had taken cover on the floor of the tank, Henriques left his position and got them back into action. There are no reports of how far the tank got but the driver must have been able to turn the tank as it was seen by an RFC pilot heading back south towards the Quadrilateral. At this point, realising that no infantry were attacking the German

---

62   Miles, *OHGW*, p. 310; the officer is named as Capt AJG Cross. However, Trevor Pidgeon states that the incident is not recorded in the War Diaries of the battalion, the brigade or the division – *Tanks at Flers*. p. 81.

63   Henriques later wrote that the tank went into action with its front hatches open, the crew having never driven the vehicle during training with them shut or having used the periscopes. *Indiscretions of a Warden*. p. 116.

64   Henriques did not name his crew and, whilst his wife mentions three in her papers, the driver is not identified.

65   Armour-piercing bullets were issued to German frontline units to enable them to counter British snipers who used an armoured shield as protection. It is likely that the number of armour-piercing rounds was increased after German intelligence had identified that armoured cars would be operating in the area.

frontline, Henriques decided to withdraw and he returned to Wedge Wood where the crewmen were treated for their wounds.[66]

Henriques' initial attack, however short, paid dividends. The *OHGW* records that 71st Brigade advanced in fine style first against Straight Trench and then, out of sight, over the crest.[67] Although they were later stopped by uncut German wire, the Norfolks and the Leicestershires were the only element of 6th Division to penetrate the German defences that morning. The attack by 16th Brigade, to their south, stalled owing to enfilading machine-gun fire from the Quadrilateral and the German frontline trenches north of Bouleaux Wood to the south. The view that the defenders in the Quadrilateral had over the surrounding countryside can be discerned at colour photograph 5. Leuze Wood is on the extreme left, in the centre is the Guillemont crossroads whilst the route used by the tanks is just left of the right electricity pylons. The large wood on the central horizon, left of that pylon, is Trones Wood whilst Delville Wood breaches the horizon on its right.

The 16th Brigade again attacked at 0830 hours but were no more successful. Cavan, realising that the attack in 6th Division's area had stalled, ordered a third attack starting at 1330 hours. Macpherson's tank, whose engine problems had been resolved, was available as was the sole XIV Corps Reserve tank, Male 740 commanded by Lt Harold Vincent. At 0930 hours, Vincent was ordered forward to the Guillemont crossroads to join him. Macpherson saw Henriques' tank arrive at Wedge Wood and exchanged looks with his great friend after Henriques had been debriefed at HQ 16th Brigade. Macpherson is recorded as looking anxiously at the cuts to Henriques' eyes and they parted.[68] Vincent reached Guillemont but, whilst moving east towards the crossroads, the tank became ditched. Vincent and his men took cover in a nearby shellhole and sent a signal notifying HQ C Company of the situation.[69] Their War Diary records that, at 1030 hours, Murphy was ordered to drive to the crossroads to support the renewed assault despite its missing steering tail.[70]

6th Division's plans for the attack at 1330 hours was a repeat of that which had failed seven hours earlier. In a signal sent at 0950 hours, HQ C Company was told that the two tanks were to advance against the Quadrilateral down the railway, clear the Quadrilateral and then continue their advance eastwards along the road to cut the wire in front of the Blue Line. It was this plan which was explained to Macpherson at Wedge Wood, the tanks being required to reach the German strongpoint thirty minutes before Zero (1300 hours). Macpherson and Murphy subsequently joined up, presumably at the crossroads, and then started their final approach not

66   Most were minor. Henriques was, however, evacuated to England and his facial injuries treated in London. He made a full physical recovery.

67   Miles, *OHGW*, p. 310.

68   Henriques was convinced, before he deployed to France, that he would lose his eyesight in the fighting and had practised trying to operate blind. Given the close relationship between the two men, it is likely that Macpherson fully knew of his fears and feared the worst for his friend.

69   The Guillemont crossroads can plainly be seen from the Quadrilateral and the shellholes, used by Vincent, were no doubt caused by German artillery who had registered the position which was a major way point for any attacking unit. Miles, *OHGW*, p. 310.

70   The crew had no experience in driving without the steering tails and some believed it was impossible. Although it was found that the tanks could be steered using their tracks on 15 September, Mark I tanks sent out from the factories in October arrived with them fitted. Murphy's tank was also refitted with the tail in time to take part in the subsequent attacks on 25 September.

knowing that the attack had been cancelled in an order issued at 1235 hours. By this time, the two tanks were on their way, travelling in broad daylight with no accompanying barrage, up a route which had been registered by the German artillery and against a very aware garrison of Bavarian infantry in the Quadrilateral. It was a recipe for disaster. There is no record of the tanks' action in the *OHGW* nor in 6th Division's or C Company's War Diaries. There is, however, a near-contemporary record, written by one of Macpherson's crewmen William Dawson, who indicates that the two tanks operated independently after they reached the Quadrilateral:

> The briefing and instructions regarding the objectives were quite inadequate and there was little or no cooperation between the infantry and the tanks.[71] We reached a point which we believed was our objective and, after a while when our petrol was getting low, we were joined by the other tank in our section [Murphy]. Both it and ourselves came up against machine-gun fire with armour piercing bullets and, while we had a few holes, I counted upwards of forty in the other tank.[72]

Both tanks successfully returned to the British lines and Macpherson reported to HQ 16 Brigade where he was debriefed. Shortly afterwards, he suffered head wounds and died later that day at the Grove Town Casualty Clearing Station west of the Loop.[73] Henriques was sent back to London for treatment to his wounds.[74] Despite being penetrated by bullets, Macpherson and Murphy's tanks were operational and allocated to the follow-on attack which took place ten days later.

Guards Division Assault

The Guards Division were to the northwest of 6th Division on the western flank of XV Corps. The three tanks of No. 1 Column, supporting 2nd Guards Brigade, set off from their Starting Point on time but not without difficulty. The first problem concerned the route to reach their target which was the south-eastern corner of the Triangle (map square C4). Unlike other groups, No. 1 Column tanks were not to follow a track or trench but the skippers should use their tank compasses to reach their objective. Based on Holford-Walker's subsequent comments, the crew had been told to use a bearing of 42 degrees by Bradley.[75] However, this was impractical as the compass was affected by the jarring movement of the un-sprung vehicle. The Company Commander had advised against the use of compasses before the attack but was told it was not

---

71   Dawson had, by the time he wrote his manuscript, fought in tank actions at Tilloy, Frezenberg, Bleak House and Fontaine Notre Dame.
72   Dawson was commissioned in March 1919. He wrote 'Reminiscences of his experience in the early tanks' whilst undertaking officer training. The manuscript is held at the TMA.
73   An officer of 16th Brigade later wrote that Macpherson tried to commit suicide. Dawson however stated that the injuries were caused by shellfire and Macpherson's pistol was with another member of the crew.
74   Henriques was to serve as a Recce officer with G Battalion and was awarded the Italian Silver Medal of Valour for his service during the Battle of Cambrai. He later became an eminent youth and social worker and magistrate in London. He never forgot his 'brother in arms' and dedicated a lectern to his memory at the St George's Settlement and Synagogue in East London. Pope, *FTC*, pp. 62–65.
75   He was the senior Heavy Section officer in France at this time.

his concern.[76] Furthermore, as can be seen from colour photograph 6, there were few landmarks to aid them, the tree lines having grown since the tanks went into action.

The Guards in 2nd Brigade advanced behind the creeping barrage at Zero. They moved across the open ground for 850 yards. Latterly, 1st Grenadier Guards, on the left, pursued a northerly direction perhaps to conform to 1st Guards Brigade's advance. By 0715 hours, despite woeful casualties, 2nd Guards Brigade had secured its First Objective at the Triangle.

They were preceded by the tanks. Setting off in a thick mist at 0540 hours, led by Male tank 741 commanded by Tull, the tanks' advance towards the Triangle was immediately compromised. 741's steering wheels became damaged as the tank moved across no man's land and Tull turned back towards his Start Point as did Clarke in *Campania* who was following him. Fortunately, Hiscocks was in the area and intervened, ensuring that *Campania* and *Casa* drove north-eastwards toward the Triangle. The Germans were made fully aware of the impending attack when, at 0600 hours, British heavy artillery bombarded their rear position. As a result, the Germans bombarded Ginchy village, especially the northeast area where the infantry were waiting to attack, as well as Leuze Wood and the men of 6th Division.[77]

The time at which the tanks reached the German frontline is not recorded. *Campania* turned north along Serpentine Trench, where her crew engaged a number of machine-guns, firing 60 rounds of 6-pounder ammunition. Clarke, who claimed he knocked out six machine-guns, waited until the Guards arrived and consolidated their position. He was then told by an infantry officer to return to his Starting Point. Clarke, who was concerned about the lack of fuel in *Campania*, returned to Ginchy even though he had not completed his mission.[78]

Casa reached the Triangle (his First Objective) although Smith could not identify exactly where he had gone when he returned. Smith stated that he was near a line of trees which the Guards Division staff concluded was in the T15a map square. A map, showing tank location's based on RFC sighting reports, also shows a tank in that area.[79] This confirms that *Casa* not only breached the German wire and frontline at High Road Trench but worked its way east into 6th Division's area.[80] Smith was concerned about the *Casa's* engine bearings.[81] There was no infantry close by and Smith had to decide whether to push onto the Third Objective (Blue Line), wait where he was until the infantry appeared, or withdraw.[82] Eventually Smith decided to return to his Starting Point and *Casa* reached HQ 1st Guards Brigade near Waterlot Farm at some point after *Clan Cameron* did so at 0904 hours.[83] Meanwhile, Tull (A Tank) made his way back from

---

76   Letter to Edmonds dated 22 April 1935.
77   See 3rd Grenadier Guards War Diary.
78   This is third reported shortage of fuel in C Company. Henriques and Macpherson had similar concerns and Tull would have as well.
79   Pidgeon, *Tanks at Flers*, p. 94 states this map was held in the Public Record Office but does not provide the reference, so I have been unable to confirm the location.
80   The wood in the T15 grid square is in the northwest corner.
81   The two semi-circular linings made of white metal, fitted between the bottom ends of each piston connecting rod and the crank shaft, became fused by heat when there was insufficient lubricant. Whilst this was uncommon on road-going tractors, where oil levels were constant, those tanks moving across country experienced problems. Pidgeon, *Tanks at Flers*, p. 100 en. 9.
82   The closest recorded infantry was a small group of Leicestershires, the most forward element of 71st Brigade, who were located 300 yards southwest of Smith's position. Pidgeon, *Tanks at Flers*, p. 94.
83   Smith sent a message by pigeon to his headquarters, reporting he had reached Cole's location and asked that Wenger be sent and for more instructions.

Ginchy, perhaps trying to reach HQ 1st Tank Brigade or the section assembly area at Trones Wood. He reached neither location but sent a message to C Company stating, 'Have arrived at S24b 85,60. Steering gear out of order and need petrol.'[84]

To their west, 1st Guards Brigade set off at Zero; they were joined by 2nd Coldstream Guards wheeling northwest and came into line with their third battalion to their left, and then advanced. Owing to the failures in No. 2 Column, they had no tank support on their right flank. Ambrose in K Tank also failed early on following engine and steering problems, and probably did not travel further than 300 yards.[85] The other two tanks in No. 3 Column (Elliot and Bates) started at 0530 hours, right on time, and were 'seen moving forward on the left flank of the Brigade but apparently, they did not attract any fire, nor did they arouse suspicion amongst the Bavarians.'[86]

L Tank, commanded by Cole who was also ordered to move at 0530 hours, set off to clear the Brewery from the southeast. Exactly what *Clan Cameron* actually achieved is unknown. The Female tank was, for example, not seen by Mortimore in *Daredevil 1* which was operating in the same area. Feilding, GOC Guards Division, later stated that L tank did not fire at all although it may have gone to approximately the right position. The C Company War Diary states that *Clan Cameron* reached its First Objective but, with the officer being given at least four sets of orders, he was probably unsure of where he was to go.[87] What is certain is that he did not engage the machine-guns along Pint Trench and the Bavarians did not engage *Clan Cameron*, probably to avoid giving away their position. The other piece of confirmed information is that the tank got back to HQ 1st Guards Brigade at 0904 hours by which time one tank track required replacement owing to the lugs being bent on one side.[88]

That left the Male two tanks in No. 3 Column (Bates in No. 714 and Elliot in *Centurion*) to support 1st Guards Brigade on the left flank. They appear to have travelled up the road to Flers, in line ahead, driving alongside of Pint Trench but not engaging any of the machine-gun posts. Given the half-light and the mist, it is quite possible that the crews did not see the posts and, as the German machine-guns did not reveal themselves by opening fire whilst the tanks were in the area, they remained uncrushed. At 0743 hours, a tank was seen at the southern end of Watling Street moving north up the left flank of the Guards. The location was 200 yards south of the First Objective near the Park. Bates later sent a pigeon message stating that he had passed this objective and was advancing with the infantry. The two tanks were observed at 0855 hours, still moving north, about 200 yards north of the Park. They had left the Guards' area and were now operating within 14th Division's area. Bates ditched just north of the Brown Line and Elliot drove a further 300 yards, presumably to provide local protection. By this time, however, the Guards had stopped and were consolidating their positions on the Second Objective. They

84 The grid reference quoted by Tull is north of the road between Guillemont and Longueval, 300 yards southeast of Waterlot Farm.
85 That afternoon an RFC pilot reported a tank stationary 200 yards north of the start point on King's Street. It is possible that this was Ambrose's tank as no other tanks were in that area. Pidgeon, *Tanks at Flers*, p. 97.
86 Brig Gen GCE Pereira commanding 1st Guards Brigade. See Pidgeon, *Tanks at Flers*, p. 97. The Bavarians may have held their fire so as to ensure that their positions were not compromised and attacked.
87 Appendix XI (TNA WO 95/96).
88 Writing to Edmunds in 1935, Holford-Walker does not give any detail of what Cole achieved, only where he was ordered to go. He does however state that, after the action, Cole was in a very jumpy condition and was sent back to Great Britain to recover. Pope, *FTC*, pp. 32 and 33.

had taken dreadful losses from the undisturbed machine-guns and, like their comrades in 6th and 56th divisions, faced the daunting prospect that their next battle would be for the ground they had failed to take on 15 September.

Casualties and Awards

Casualties amongst C Company tank crews on 15 September were light.[89] Pattinson and Giles were killed and Ritchie died of his wounds almost two months later. Williams was also reported

missing (he suffered from shell shock and had been taken to hospital) whilst Macpherson died of wounds at Grovetown. In addition to the five members of *Challenger's* crew, Henriques and four crewmen were taken to hospital whilst Cole was evacuated owing to shell shock. The formations they supported suffered badly: 56th Division took 4,485 casualties, the Guards 4,150 and 6th Division 3,600; respectively the second, third and fifth highest of all divisions in action that day.[90]

Amongst all the crewmen who went into action on the Eastern Flank on 15 September, only members of *Challenger* and *Corunna's* crews were honoured with medals. *Challenger's* skipper, Purdy, was awarded the MC whilst Gunners Bernard and Williams of *Corunna* received the MM for putting the machine-guns out of commission. *Corunna's* skipper Arnold also received the MC but only after Holford-Walker had followed the tank's tracks, having heard conflicting accounts about his action.[91] The C Company Commander also recommended that Corporal Pattinson be awarded the VC; it was not however granted because 'there was

Eric Purdy. (Paddy Lilley)

89 According to Appendix 12 of the C Company War Diary which is *not* contemporary to the action as Ritchie survived until 14 November 1916, when he died of his wounds.

90 R. Prior and T. Wilson, *Command on the Western Front: The Military Career of Sir Henry Rawlinson 1914–1918* (Barnsley: Pen & Sword, 2004) p. 243.

91 Holford-Walker letter dated 22 April 1935. Arnold later served with C Battalion, commanding tanks at the Battle of Arras and Third Battle of Ypres. He served on with 3rd Light Battalion and commanded a section of Whippets from 1 September 1918. He spent some time in Mexico in the 1920s before returning to England and marrying. On the outbreak of the Second World War, Arnold was commissioned into the Royal Armoured Corps and served with the 8th Army in North Africa. He remained with the Army Reserve of Officers until the maximum age limit of 55 and died aged 61 in 1957. See Pope, *FTC*, pp. 49–50.

no other unit evidence which shows that the infantry were a considerable distance behind the tank when this was going on.'[92]

Tank Effectiveness

Challenger achieved its initial task of providing protection to 169th Brigade crossing no man's land to the Loop Trench but, although its crew killed 150 Germans in the area where *Challenger* had been hit, they could not prevent the Londoners being ejected from the ground they had taken. *Corunna* suppressed machine-gun fire, after it crossed the German frontline at Beef Trench but, like *Challenger*, after it was ditched, its crew played no effective role in assisting the advance of 167th Brigade Division. Henriques also suppressed the machine-gunners, for a short period, along Straight Trench to the north of the Quadrilateral, which enabled 71st Brigade to take their first objective but his withdrawal made further progress impossible. Regrettably, none of the ten tanks supporting the Guards Division could be considered as being effective as, although four did reach their initial objectives, the Bavarian machine-gunners were not deterred from firing on the attacking infantry.

Aftermath

Section Commanders bore the brunt of work for the next 24 hours, getting their men back to Trones Wood which also became the base for the fit tanks. Of the 17 tanks which deployed from the Loop, only two were destroyed[93]. However, four more had ditched and seven suffered mechanical faults, mainly due to problems with tracks and steering tails.[94] Two were extremely low on petrol but were fit for action. Wenger and the ASC artificers managed to get those with minor faults back into action; they were however operating three miles from their main base at the Loop and had no major assemblies, few spare parts and no means of transporting them. The ASC and the tanks' crews succeeded in getting eight tanks fit for action before the next attack but they remained fragile.

There were also problems in getting supplies forward to the tanks. Three more dumps were established to support the follow-on actions; the dump at Trones Wood was retained for ammunition and water whilst petrol and lubricants were sent forward for the sub-sections who were to support the Guards, 5th and 56th divisions.[95] As each sub-section was working directly to their divisional staff, they had to seek carrying parties from the infantry to move these stores. Holford-Walker sent a consolidated list to HQ XIV Corps seeking assistance.[96] Gathorne-

---

92 Gerald Pattinson's body was exhumed from its original grave during the battlefield clearances and reburied at Combles Communal Cemetery Extension in plot VII A 21. Pope, *FTC*, pp. 48–49.

93 *Corunna* and *Challenger* were behind enemy lines until 27 September and suffered such damage that they could not be repaired in situ or recovered.

94 See the report by OC 711 (MT) Company ASC in Appendix XVI.

95 The dump locations were at Ginchy (Guards Division), east of Guillemont near the crossroads (5th Division) and a quarry just west of Leuze Wood (56th Division). Each dump held 120 gallons of petrol; 6 drums of track oil and 2 cases of engine oil. A water point was also set up at Wedge Wood. See Appendix V to C Company War Diary (25 to 27 September 1916).

96 In his letter to Edmunds dated 22 April 1935, Holford-Walker blamed himself for not thinking out this problem to the end. However, no one else on the staff had considered it either, although Swinton

Hardy, the COS, 'jibbed at the requirements after 12 hours fighting, pointing out that a section of 6 tanks required 5 ×3-ton lorries for full replenishment.' No vehicles were however available as the ASC Divisional Trains were only equipped with horse transport.[97]

As ever, one of the worst tasks was writing to the families of those killed or seriously wounded. This was mainly the role of the individual skippers although section commanders would have written to the crewmen's families if the skippers were injured or dead.[98] C Company had fewer casualties than D Company but the task was no less daunting. The personal effects of the dead and seriously wounded had to be gathered and also sent back to Britain and systems established to monitor the whereabouts of those wounded men, still in France, so that mail could be sent to them.

With only eight tanks fit for use, C Company now had several skippers with no immediate role. Holford-Walker decided to use these to good effect, allowing Nos. 2 and 3 Sections' commanders to concentrate on that role. This enabled them to move where and when they were required across the battlefield to exercise effective command of the tank groups. Holford-Walker also reinforced his company headquarters with an officer to deal with requests for information from divisions and formed spare crewmen into a group of runners to provide more effective communications with his tank sections.

Capture of Lesboeufs, Morval and Combles, 25–27 September 1916

Plan Development

On 19 September, at a Fourth Army Conference at Querrieu, Rawlinson explained his concept for the next attack to his corps commanders. 5th, 6th and Guards divisions would launch the main assault on Morval and Lesboeufs whilst 56th Division would form a defensive flank facing southeast towards Combles. The first three divisions were to attack in three stages, against three objectives. The attack on the Green Line (First Objective) would start at Zero (1235 hours); the attack on the Brown Line (Second Objective) was to start one hour later and the Third Objective (Blue Line) would be attacked at 1435 hours. Three of the divisions would be supported by tanks, but not in the initial stages of the attack. Rawlinson required that 'they should where possible be placed in covered positions from which they can be bought up to assist in the capture of the villages of Gueudecourt, Les Boeufs and Morval after the troops have reached the Brown Line, but they should not be moved across the open in daylight to the attack of the Green and Brown lines.'

Rawlinson was concerned that tanks, such as those in the open near Flers on 15 September and near Gueudecourt the following day, were vulnerable to artillery fire. Haig, writing the following day in his diary, stressed that the threat was from direct fire such as that used by the

had identified the issue of post battle replenishment in February 1916 (see Appendix III paragraph 36).
97 Presumably every 3-ton lorry allocated to the tank sections were laden and unable to undertake the task.
98 D Company's adjutant wrote to some of the relatives of wounded officers – copies are in the Correspondence Book which was copied and is held in the TMA. The letters for the relatives of dead officers would have been written by their company commanders.

Saxons to knock out *Dolphin*.[99] Haig stated that, for this reason, Rawlinson could use tanks during the attack on Morval and Lesboeufs but not against Gueudecourt. Haig's analysis was however flawed: every tank knocked out on 15 and 16 September, except D5 and D6, resulted from indirect fire, with four being hit whilst stationary and four whilst mobile.[100]

On the afternoon of 20 September, HQ XIV Corps issued the operation order for the attacks on Morval and Lesboeufs.[101] The specific direction was that:

> Tanks allotted to 56th Division should be used to assist in the neutralisation of Bouleaux Wood, and may be used in daylight, but should not move from their assembly positions until after the hour of Zero [1235 hours].
>
> Those allotted to 5th and Guards divisions should be brought up into covered assembly positions previous to the day of attack and might be usefully employed at dusk in Morval and Lesboeufs, should these villages not by then have been cleared.
>
> Guards, 5th and 56th divisions will reconnoitre assembly positions and lines of approach and will make all arrangements directly with the OC C Coy HMG Corps to have the Tanks allotted in the positions by daylight on the 23rd.

Preparation for Battle

On 23 September, Holford-Walker confirmed the allocation of tanks to the three divisions. The Guards Division would be supported by A Group which consisted of Male 722 (Arnaud), Female 505 (Murphy) and Male *Centurion* (Ambrose) again under the command of Hiscocks. Their Position of Assembly was southwest of Trones Wood and their forward position was west of Ginchy, collocated with the forward dump,[102] which was screened from view from German defensive locations.[103] Their journey was one and a half miles across a very heavily crumped battlefield, criss-crossed with old trenches. On arrival, Hiscocks and two orderlies were to report to HQ 1st Guards Brigade and await orders from the Divisional HQ, the tanks being held in reserve and only being deployed when they were needed.

HQ 5th Division was allocated three Male tanks, known as B Group, consisting of 746 *Campania* (Clarke); 741 (Tull) and 740 (Smith) commanded by Walker. The tanks' Position of Assembly was again at Trones Wood and their forward position was east of Guillemont, between the cemetery and the crossroads, where the dump had been formed. This was only a one and a half mile journey but it would prove to be difficult in the pre-dawn light on 25 September. 5th Division's orders were that 'at 1235 hours (Zero), the tanks were to advance from their Position of Assembly towards Morval. Their route was south of the railway, then to the south of Quadrilateral to the old Green Line, thence along north side of railway cutting and then to

---

99   See Chapter 7.
100   A single tank was subsequently used against Gueudecourt on 26 September and was extraordinarily successful. See Chapter 7.
101   XIV Corps Operation Order No. 59. See Appendix XIV.
102   T13 Central was on the western side of Ginchy on a track to the southeast corner of Delville Wood.
103   The Germans had a number of observation balloons in the area.

the cross-roads west of Morval.'[104] The orders then stated, 'After reaching the neighbourhood of our frontline troops, the further action of the Tanks must depend on the tactical situation. The officers in command must necessarily act very largely on their own initiative; the main task allotted to them being to assist the infantry in every possible way by dealing with any local strong points which may be met with and which are seen to be worrying our troops, and generally by clearing up the situation in Morval by moving down Moor Street and along Main Street.'[105]

56th Division were to be supported by C Group comprising Male 705, now commanded by Henderson,[106] and Female 523 now commanded by Dashwood who was also the sub-section commander. Their Place of Assembly was at Wedge Wood and their forward position was in a quarry, west of Leuze Wood, where their dump had been in-loaded. Their approach route was only 800 yards and the tanks would have been screened from the Germans' view by the lie of the land and the remains of the woods. The tanks were ordered to rendezvous at the Quarry on the night of the 24–25 September, their route to the rendezvous having been taped out by 1000 hours on 24 September.[107]

56th Division's orders were that, on receipt of the message 'Tanks Advance', C Group were to proceed, along the Guillemont–Combles road between Bouleaux and Leuze woods, to clear the northern end of Loop Trench, Stew Trench and the orchard and trenches to its north and, finally, to block the sunken roads which formed the north eastern exits from Combles.[108]

Deployment and Ditchings

By 1700 hours on 24 September, all three groups had rendezvoused at their respective Positions of Assembly. Holford-Walker had deployed from the Loop and was once again established at the Briqueterie. Deliberately disobeying orders and 'being roundly cursed and threatened with arrest by Gathorne-Hardy for leaving his HQ', OC C Company made sure his tanks got to their position, personally leading one from its Position of Assembly.[109]

In the early hours of 25 September, leaving another officer to answer requests for information from higher commands, Holford-Walker went forward with a section of runners and signallers, to monitor the marrying-up of the tanks with the infantry. At 0430 hours, an hour before first light, B Group started to move towards Guillemont. *Campania* ditched midway between Trones Wood and Guillemont and her crews started digging out. Ninety minutes after setting

---

104 5th Division Operation Order No. 127 Appendix III Instructions for Tanks (No. 2) dated 25 September 1916 – incorporated in C Company War Diary (TNA WO 95/96).

105 The divisional staff seemed unaware that the Group had a separate officer as a subsection commander.

106 He had returned from his detachment with D Company; his tank however remained ditched at High Wood and was never recovered.

107 The 56th Divisional artillery and signals staff were ordered that telephone wires were buried. To ensure communications were maintained, in the event of loss of telegraphy, HQ 167th Infantry Brigade was also ordered to arrange for visual signal communication direct from the location at Maltz Horn Hill to the tanks in the quarry for use in case of the wires being cut.

108 'Instructions as to Employment of Tanks associated with 56th Division.' Order No. 48 dated 22 September 1916, issued on 23 September which were subsequently attached to C Company's War Diary.

109 Holford-Walker's letter to Edmonds dated 22 April 1935.

off, Tull in 741 stopped with engine trouble, the platinum having come off the contact breakers. Repairs were undertaken and, after 90 minutes, Tull could manoeuvre. It was a beautiful day,so Holford-Walker told Tull to proceed as far as possible towards his starting point without being seen by the German observation balloons.[110] At 0800 hours, the third tank in B Group, Male 740, crashed through the roof of a dugout.[111] Smith's crew eventually extracted the tank but it took more than five and a half hours before the Male tank could move forward. Thus, at Zero, only one tank in Group B was fit to deploy.

At 0700 hours, C Company contacted HQ 56th Division for an update on their tanks but received no reply. At 1000 hours, C Company were instructed that Tull was to move to the Starting Point, so Holford-Walker cancelled his earlier orders. A Group were still at Trones Wood, manoeuvring before setting off. At 1250 hours, Murphy's tank became ditched, after falling into a dugout in an old trench. The C Company War Diary recorded that these dugouts were frail and long disused and, like Smith's earlier ditching, there was nothing for Murphy to distinguish them. Twenty minutes later, Arnaud stopped as a result of water in the petrol.[112] The crew emptied the contaminated fuel from the internal tanks and refilled them. The remainder

Male tank C15 on 25 September east of Guillemont. (TMA)

110 The weather was fine and sunny with some haze. Miles, *OHGW*, p. 373.
111 His OC later noted that these were not easy to see which indicates that the skippers were mounted in their tanks and not leading them forward on foot.
112 Holford-Walker, writing in 1935, stated that water had been added to fuel on two occasions causing tanks to fail to cross the Starting Points. He laid the blame at the hands of ASC drivers, some of whom were not volunteers and did not wish to serve with the tanks. A number were later returned to the ASC

of A Group started to move forward at Zero hours to Ginchy and Arnaud was able to catch up with the other tanks before the scheduled time of their departure from Ginchy.

At Zero + five minutes (1240 hours) OC B Group (Walker) was ordered by HQ C Company to move forward at Zero and to find out what time the barrage lifted. C Company's War Diary also states that it was 1255 hours (Zero + 20) by the time tanks moved but this entry does not reflect that only one was fit to move. At 1445 hours, *Campania* was extracted and moved forward to the Starting Point east of Guillemont, arriving there 15 minutes later. Clarke was ordered by HQ C Company to halt at the Starting Point and await orders. Reports also came through to C Company HQ that Tull and Smith had moved forward and were advancing on Quadrilateral Ridge. At 1400 hours, HQ C Company received a message from Dashwood asking for a replacement skipper for *Clan Leslie* as Henderson sprained his ankle and could not walk. Bates, who must have been at the Briqueterie, was sent forward to the quarry to replace Henderson. However, neither of the C Group tanks were ordered forward that day.

Holford-Walker again went forward to the Quadrilateral Ridge, arriving at 1700 hours, where Tull's tank had stuck after yet another trench had fallen in. He obtained a fatigue party and started to dig out. Meanwhile Smith had reached the valley facing Morval and had halted, hearing that the objectives had been taken and consolidated. Smith was subsequently recalled to his Starting Point at Guillemont by his company commander.

None of the eight C Company tanks saw action on 25 September because the infantry achieved their objectives without needing their support. The German artillery had fired a good deal overnight but there was little shelling of the packed assembly trenches the following morning. This was because British counter-battery work went well, with 124 German batteries being located, 47 engaged and 24 silenced.[113] However, the enemy artillery did cause casualties to both the British and French infantry as they attacked and to those crews when their tanks were stationary, eight men being hospitalised and one later dying of his wounds.[114] By the end of the day, XIV Corps had overcome the last of the German defences on a frontage of nearly 2,000 yards; German artillery batteries were withdrawing and most of the German infantry were retiring out of contact. Although the British reached their objectives, the French I Corps had more difficulty. They were initially held up by machine-guns situated in Combles and were unable to take the hamlet of Fregicourt to its east.

At 2030 hours, on 25 September, Tull and Murphy were still digging out whilst Dashwood had pulled his tanks back to Wedge Wood. At 2200 hours, a German officer was captured who revealed that Combles was being evacuated that evening. HQ 56th Division acted immediately and 1st London Scottish started to push south into the village whilst 1/4th Londons worked their way through the northern half of Bouleaux Wood, finding no Germans but that the French and the British Armies had linked up at the northeast exit from Combles.

On the morning of 26 September, C Company's War Diary noted that two tanks of A Group were to the east of Delville Wood, presumably by their dump, whilst Murphy was ditched east of

although most served with distinction with the tanks being awarded gallantry medals and/or being killed in action.
113   Miles, *OHGW,* p. 373.
114   Individual soldiers' records indicate wounds linked to shrapnel injuries were generally received outside of tanks. Gnr. Frank Bull later died at the Casualty Clearing Section at Grove Town on 28 September 1916.

Trones Wood. Tull was also ditched on the Quadrilateral Ridge whilst Clarke and Smith were at their rendezvous near Guillemont crossroads. Only C Group were together, probably in the quarry by Leuze Wood.[115] The French now sought assistance to advance north; having captured Fregicourt, they planned to capture Haie Wood that afternoon. However, some Germans who had left Combles had taken control of Mutton Trench, which dominated the ground between Morval and Fregicourt.

Two British infantry battalions were tasked to expel them and, at 1340 hours, C Group were sent forward 'to clear up situation South of Morval in Mutton Trench.' The two infantry battalions were 1/12th Londons (the Rangers) attacking from the southwest and 12th Gloucestershires (5th Division), attacking from Morval. There are no records of orders given to the tanks but based on their approach routes, Bates was in support of the Rangers whilst Dashwood supported the Gloucestershires.

The tanks likely started at the Quarry, Bates driving 2,200 yards before ditching northeast of Bouleaux Wood, about 1,200 yards from his objective. Dashwood, whose tank became stuck on a tree stump in the sunken lane on the south-eastern edge of Morval outskirts, got to within 400 yards of Mutton Trench, having driven two miles from the quarry. Interestingly, with the ditching of both tanks, the attack was called off. Later that afternoon, XVth Corps gave orders to the tanks to concentrate at their Places of Assembly and, at 1900 hours, Hiscocks reported he had arrived at Trones Wood. Walker reported he was in map square T19 which probably means B Group was back at the dump near the Guillemont crossroads.

At 0200 hours, on 27 September, C Company received a request from Dashwood for petrol and lubricants. Probably because there were no suitable vehicles, the cans and drums were sent on mule transport at 0300 hours. It appears, from later entries in the C Company War Diary, that news that Dashwood was stuck south of Morval never reached his company headquarters.[116] Meanwhile, orders were received for A Group at Trones Wood to support a follow-on attack on Mutton Trench. Hiscocks was ordered to report to HQ 60th Brigade who were to undertake the attack. The tanks set off at 0300 hours for the Quadrilateral but, realising they might not arrive on time, Holford-Walker walked to B Group's location east of Guillemont, and ordered the two remaining tanks (Male 740 and *Campania*) to move there as well.

As Holford-Walker pondered the orders, he realised that the plan had shortcomings. He therefore walked with his brother, still in command of B Group, to HQ 60th Brigade for orders. They arrived at 0400 hours and briefed the Brigade HQ about his concerns. As a result, the GOC decided to walk to Morval, accompanied by OC B Group, to see the situation for himself and to talk to CO 12th Rifle Brigade who were to attack from the northeast. OC C Company meantime walked to Leuze Wood to see HQ 168th Brigade who were to carry out the attack from the southwest. Arriving at 0500 hours it was only then that Holford-Walker found out

---

115 Although the C Company War Diary states Wedge Wood, Dawson records he spent three days at the Quarry.

116 With hindsight, this is probably not surprising. Dashwood would have concentrated on getting his own tank free; knowing that no equipment held by C Company or the ASC Workshops could extract him, Dashwood would decide to limit his request to the petrol and lubricants that he would need to attack once the tank was free.

that Dashwood was stuck at Morval. Realising that this would turn the plan to chaos, Holford-Walker decided he must go to Morval and see GOC 60th Brigade.[117]

At 0830 hours, Tank 740 and *Campania* arrived at the Quadrilateral; it had taken them over four hours to move 1,300 yards, with the three tanks from A Group arriving 30 minutes later. At 0900 hours, Holford-Walker reached the Sunken Road at Morval where he met GOC 60th Brigade and OC B Group, warning both of the likely chaos. A new plan was agreed (sadly the map giving details is not with the War Diary) and Holford-Walker returned to the Quadrilateral to bring the three A Group tanks to their Starting Point which was reached by 1100 hours. OC C Company decided to keep 740 and *Campania* at the Quadrilateral as a reserve but, when at noon the German artillery started to bracket the position, he ordered the tanks back, presumably to Guillemont.

In fact, the A Group tanks never moved all day and were withdrawn by OC C Company to Trones Wood at 0600 hours the following morning. At 0700 hours on 28 September, HQ C Company received orders that all tanks should rendezvous at Loop. They left Trones Wood four hours later and, by 1700 hours, all had arrived back at Loop except Dashwood who was still stuck at Morval and was not be extracted until 30 September.

Tank effectiveness

None of the tanks were called into use on 26 September. On 27 September, the two tanks tasked to support the attack on the Mutton Trench failed to reach their Starting Points.

Lessons Learned

No formal list of lessons learned were produced by C Company but the actions of the previous few days confirmed the need for the Company HQ to have more staff for command and control as well as better communications to their sections and the units they were supporting. The actions undertaken by Holford-Walker, during the night of 25–26 September, also revealed that tank officers needed to be involved in battle planning by corps, divisional and brigade staffs. The weaknesses in replenishment, and in the repair and recovery capability, were revealed. Above all, the frequency of ditching indicated that a reconnaissance capability was required in each company headquarters and that tank drivers needed more training to be able to cope with the type of ground experienced on a battlefield.

Visiting the Battlefield

It is possible to see the key locations on the Eastern Flank in about four hours. The best starting point is at the Briqueterie, the site of C Company's Headquarters. It was located, just south of the junction of the D64 and the D197 roads, about half a mile east of Montauban and one mile south of Longueval. There is no off-road car park, so I suggest you pull in at the Y-junction with the unsigned metalled track which heads southeast to Hardecourt. The buildings and chimney of the brickworks were located to the west of the D197 road with some working areas on the

---

117 Directly quoted from C Company War Diary entry for that time. (TNA WO 95/96).

eastern side in the space between the road and the track heading southeast. C Company reserve tanks arrived here overnight on 13–14 September and C Company HQ established itself the following night; the Briqueterie remained the focus for C Company until 28 September 1916 when the tanks returned to the Loop.

Bernafay Wood is the thick wood to your north on the other side of D64; Trones Wood can be seen, to the northeast, poking out from the edge of Bernafay Wood. If you wish to visit the location where tanks supporting 6th and 56th divisions assembled on 13 September, drive carefully down the metalled track toward Hardecourt. After 700 yards, you will be in Chimpanzee Valley and, if you look carefully on the left-hand side of the road, you will see the remains of a track heading north towards Trones Wood which is on the skyline. This track was almost certainly the start of the route used by Walker, Henriques and Macpherson to deploy on the evening of 14 September. The other three tanks supporting 56th Division, led by Dashwood, would have driven east from here, along a track over the hill, east for a mile to Angle Wood and then northeast, past Falfemont Farm, to Leuze Wood. The current track to Hardecourt does not however allow you to drive to these locations so return to the Briqueterie for the next element of the tour.

Leaving the Y-junction, turn right and then turn right again at the crossroads, following the D64 signed for Guillemont. After a half mile, on your left-hand side, you will see the western edge of Trones Wood where the tanks supporting the Guards Division assembled overnight on 13 September. This was also probably the site of the first C Company stores dump. Drive on, through Guillemont, ignoring the right-hand turn which takes the D64 to Combles, and continue north for 200 yards. Turn right on the minor road (C1) to Ginchy; the Guards Brigades' headquarters were in the field 200 yards north of you but there are no remains to be seen.

Now drive northeast towards Ginchy, noting the large wood and a prominent water tower which is in the distance to your left. That is Delville Wood and Cole had instructions to clear the Brewery right of the water tower in the open fields. The road you are now following was probably used by Nos. 1 and 2 Columns in the early hours of 15 September.

Drive into Ginchy, which is where the Guards' Division had their forming-up place and turn left following the Grand Rue past the church, heading north towards Flers. As you leave the village, the road followed Pint Trench which linked Ginchy to Tea Support which was the German frontline on 15 September. Just after the cemetery, there is an unmetalled track on your right which was the boundary between the Guards and 14th Division late that morning. Two hundred yards further up the road was the site of several machine-guns which fired across the field to your left on the advancing British infantry; these were a target for Cole and also for the tanks of No. 3 Column which none of them located.

As you pass under the powerlines, you are close to Tea Support, the German frontline. As you cross over the next hill (about 500 yards or 0.4 miles), you are near the First Objective for the Guards and a German defensive position known as the Park, a triangle of trenches, which is 200 yards into the fields on the right-hand side of the road. A single tank, probably from No. 3 Column, was seen here at 0743 hours on Friday 15 September. It was also just to the northwest of the Park, at 0855 hours, that Bates and Elliot were seen to advance towards the Second Objective. Drive up the road to the major bend, which has a track leading to your right, and stop. Bates became ditched 600 yards east (right) along the track. Elliot reached a point 900 yards to your east-northeast before he realised that he was ahead of the infantry and running out of fuel. The tank therefore returned to Ginchy; you should follow his example and drive south back into the village.

When you reach the crossroads in the centre of Ginchy, turn left on the road signed C5 to Lesboeufs. You are once again following the route taken by Nos. 1 and 2 Columns. After 200 yards, as the pylon comes into sight, turn left and drive for 200 yards then stop. You are now at the Starting Point for No. 1 Column who travelled northeast (half right) towards the open fields towards the Triangle. That defensive position is out of sight to you (and the tanks' skippers) and you can understand why Hiscocks had to direct them in the early morning mist on 15 September. The start for Hiscocks' own group (No. 2 Column) was a further 400 yards north, his tank being the only one to reach its Assembly Point.

To follow No. 1 Column, drive on up the road to the right and then up the hill. You are driving parallel to the boundary between 1st and 2nd Guards Brigades which was on your left. On your right, at two o'clock, you will see a long tree line which is in the area where Smith stopped. As the ground flattens out, and before you reach the Guards memorial, the Triangle was in the fields on your right. Halt at the Guards Memorial and get out of your car. With your back to the memorial, you are looking south at a track which roughly follows the line of Straight Trench towards the Quadrilateral where Henriques, Macpherson and Murphy were in action. Clarke stopped about 200 yards south down the track and Smith in *Casa* was operating about 500 yards away to the southeast. If you look in the far distance slightly right, you can see Leuze Wood on the horizon, which you will visit later.

Getting back in your car, turn around and drive back towards Ginchy. As you reach the first T-junction, turn left and drive up the hill to the site of the Quadrilateral. The railway line, which guided the 6th Division's tanks, was in the fields to your right and the Quadrilateral is at the top of the rise. On arriving at the top, turn right onto the hard surface and park up. With your back to the Ginchy Road, there is a track on your left (north) which roughly follows Straight Trench and leads to the Guards Memorial. This is the route taken by Henriques once he reached the German frontline at about 0600 hours on 15 September. We do not know where Murphy and Macpherson were operating at 1300 hours that afternoon but it is possible that one continued along the road towards Morval towards the Green Line or First Objective which was 500 yards further northeast.

Now turn around and walk back to the top of the hill, looking west to Ginchy and then southwest (half left) where you will see Guillemont church spire surrounded by trees. Looking across the fields, to your right, you can imagine how Bavarian machine-guns, firing from the Straight Trench, enfiladed 71st Brigade as they advanced uphill over the open fields in the morning mist on 15 September. Guillemont crossroads may be located by watching traffic heading south from Ginchy; the vehicles will stop as they reach the crossroads. At about 1230 hours on 15 September, Macpherson and Murphy would have been seen by the Bavarians from your position as they reached that crossroads. If you look left from the crossroads, observing the traffic left (east) travelling across the open ground, you will see Leuze Wood on the horizon. Where the vehicles are lost to sight is Bouleaux Wood. This gives you an impression of how clear the view of the Bavarian machine-gunners was, in the Quadrilateral, of 6th Division's soldiers advancing across the open flank towards the German Bully and Beef frontline trenches to our south.

Now return to your car, drive down into Ginchy, turn left, and drive south for 500 yards. You are now in the area where the railway crossed the road and made its way up to the Quadrilateral.

You can barely see the large German position but you can appreciate how much the tank commanders relied on the railway line to guide them to their objective. Continue driving to the crossroads, stop and then carry straight on down the hill for 1,000 yards (0.7 miles). This was the route taken by Henriques and Macpherson from and to HQ 16th Brigade, which was located at Wedge Wood which still exists on the left (eastern) side of the road. It was in this area that Henriques refuelled his tank in the early hours of 15 September and, about six hours later, where Macpherson saw his friend for the last time.

Driving on, you can turn your car as the road starts to go uphill, then head back to Guillemont crossroads. As you come up out of the valley, Leuze Wood is on your right at three o'clock. If you look carefully, at 11 o'clock on the skyline, you will see a long wood with a water tower on its right which is Delville Wood.

At Guillemont crossroads, turn right (east) and follow the D20 to the point where the road bends right (southeast) between Leuze Wood and Bouleaux Wood. *Corunna* drove along the edge of Leuze Wood in the early hours of 15 September and then crossed the road at 0600 hours on her way into action; if you stop, on the right-hand side of the road at the track where Leuze Wood meets the road, you are at *Corunna's* staring point. There is an unmetalled track directly opposite heading northeast; if you walk along it, you can see the ground over which *Corunna* drove – she was operating about 200 yards from the edge of Bouleaux Wood, reaching its north-eastern end. If you have stout shoes, and you wish to get closer to where *Corunna* ditched, walk back to the road, then follow it to the edge of Bouleaux Wood and follow it east for 400 yards. Pattison was originally buried 200 yards further along the wood line.

Returning to your car, drive 300 yards to the southern edge of Leuze Wood; there is normally hardstanding where you can pull off. You are now in the area where *Challenger* was in action in the open fields to your right. You can see a water tower on the edge of the road; this is in the area where Loop Trench met the road and which was *Challenger's* second objective. If you have stout shoes, you can walk 600 yards along the southern edge of Leuze Wood to its corner; this is where *Challenger* crossed the British frontline and then headed southeast, across the field for 400 yards to the junction of Combles and Loop trenches. Only one Company crewman, Corporal Gerald Pattison, was buried in the area but his remains were relocated after the war. To see his grave, drive though the village of Combles and then, when you reach the major fork, ignore the signs to the motorway, and bear left to the Combles Communal Cemetery Extension. Pattison is buried close to the entrance on the right-hand side of the central pathway in grave VII A21. His epitaph on his grave marker tells the story of his only battle: 'He, taking death unto himself, saved his comrades.'

Returning to your starting point at the Briqueterie is simple. Follow the D20 west, back through Combles to Leuze and Bouleaux Woods towards Guillemont and go straight on at the crossroads. When you reach the centre of Guillemont, turn left following the Route D64 back to the crossroads; this final part of the drive will take about 12 minutes.

7

Tank Actions in the Central Area

Situation

As on the Eastern flank, the Fourth Army was fixed in the Central Area of the Somme battlefield (see colour map 7). Allied success in early July had stalled and the Bavarians continued to hold High Wood (map square A4) and Delville Wood (C5), both of which had been turned into fortresses. The Bavarians also held the village of Guillemont, to the south of Delville Wood, and Ginchy to its northeast (D6). Follow-on British attacks had little success owing to insufficient supporting artillery, understrength infantry battalions and few reserves. Delville Wood, which was first entered by the South African Brigade on 15 July, was the scene of bitter fighting for over a month and was not cleared until 25 August when 14th (Light) Division expelled the remaining Bavarian defenders. Even then, the trenches to its east, Hop Alley with Beer Trench and Ale Alley, collectively known as the Brewery Salient (C6), and the village of Ginchy remained in Bavarian hands. Guillemont, to the south of Delville Wood, was captured by 20th (Light) Division on 3 September although an attack on Ginchy the same day failed. The village was eventually taken by 16th (Irish) Division but the Bavarians still held trenches to the west and north, dominating the ground over which 14th and 41st Division would attack on 15 September.

The Ground, Bavarian Defences and Dispositions

The Central Area consisted of unenclosed farmland; high ground in the south falling away to the north.[1] The villages of Gueudecourt (D2-D3) and Flers (C3-4) in the centre controlled the routes to the north as did High Wood and the large farm complex Eaucourt l'Abbaye (B2) to its north. Flers was protected from attack by three trenches, Tea Support, the Switch Trench (A4–D5) and Fat/Gap Trench. It also had two German field defence systems: Box and Cox to its north with the Hogs Head to the northeast. Flers and Eaucourt l'Abbaye were also shielded

---

1   The 150-metre contour line in the Central Area encompasses High Wood to the west, Longueval and Delville Wood in the centre and Ginchy to the east. Flers and Gueudecourt sit on low ridges at about 130 metres whilst Eaucourt l'Abbaye is about 120 metres above sea level.

from the southwest by a double trench system consisting of the Flers Trench and Flers Support Trench (A1–C3). Another trench system, known as the Gird Line (B1–D3), protected the southwestern approach to Gueudecourt as well as the German rear areas around Ligny-Thilloy and Le Sars (A1).

The German frontline (Tea Support Trench south of Flers and Crest Trench to its west) was severely damaged but the Switch Trench and Flers Line were in good order and well protected by barbed wire. The German trenches were generally sited in dead ground to the attackers but had excellent views over their field of fire especially to the east of Flers (see colour photograph 8). The German also had a number of tethered balloons in the northern sector of the area, which enabled artillery observers to bring indirect fire to bear on developing threats should the British attack penetrate the various German defence lines. The Bavarian formations in the Central Area had doggedly defended their positions but were tired; indeed a relief in place was planned for the night of 14–15 September. Furthermore, other Bavarian units at High Wood, in III Corps' area, protected the southern western approaches to Flers and Eaucourt l'Abbaye (see chapter 8).

The 41st Division Report on the capture of Flers lists the defending enemy formations on 15 September as *3* and *4 Bavarian Divisions,* part of *II Bavarian Corps,* which had been in the line for 20 days and had suffered considerable losses. The initial assault on Flers on 15 September identified soldiers of *9* and *14 Bavarian Regiments.* Later that day, soldiers of *11 Bavarian Regiment* were captured, these being part of the advance party of *6 Bavarian Division* which were due to replace *4 Bavarian Division* as part of a relief in place operation.

Flers and Guedecourt, 15 September 1916

Development and Plan Summary

The Central Area was the main focus for the attack by Rawlinson's Fourth Army. He allocated XV Corps (Horne) to break through the second line of Bavarian defences, that is, the Switch Trench, and then capture the villages of Flers and Gueudecourt by noon. This would enable two cavalry divisions to exploit northwards, capturing German heavy artillery positions around Le Sars and disrupting the arrival of enemy reinforcements at Bapaume which was five miles north of Flers. Notwithstanding Haig's view that the Bavarians would fold, Horne was concerned that the machine guns in the Brewery Salient would inflict severe casualties on his advancing troops, as they had on 3 September, and planned a preliminary attack to clear them before Zero.[2] At his planning conference on 12 September, Horne specifically directed that a tank was to support that operation; this would later be increased to a pair of tanks.

Four objective lines were specified by Fourth Army for the attack on 15 September (see map 5). In XV Corps area, the First Objective (Green Line) ran from east of High Wood, along the Switch Trench south of Flers and then in a south-easterly direction, as far as Gas Alley, which formed the boundary between 41st and 14th (Light) Divisions on the Flers to Ginchy road.

---

2   The 7th Division had attacked the nearby village of Ginchy on 3 September, their initial assault being badly disrupted by German machine-gunners in the Brewery Salient. Ginchy was eventually taken by 16th (Irish Division) nine days later but the Germans still held the Salient.

The Second Objective (Brown Line) initially followed the Starfish Line, 500 yards north of High Wood, in an easterly direction, then south along the communications trench called Fish Alley for 300 yards, and then travelled east along Fat Trench, to the southern entrance to Flers, along the Ginchy to Flers road (map square D4) and then east along Gap Trench to the eastern boundary of 14th Division.

The Third Objective (Blue Line) ran from Prue Trench (which linked Flers to Martinpuich) towards the Cough Drop (B3), then northeast along Drop Alley to the Flers Support Trench, which it followed to Grove Alley 800 yards northwest of the village of Flers. The Blue Line then travelled in a south-easterly direction, north of Flers village, to the Bulls Road (D3). The Fourth Objective (Red Line), within the central area, started at the Abbey Road (D3), travelled in a north-easterly direction across country (just northwest of a German communications trench known as Grove Alley) until it reached the road from Flers to the Factory Corner (D2). The Red Line then ran northeast to the Gird Trench, then east to the northern edge of Gueudecourt before turning southeast towards Lesboeufs. Its capture would provide flanks protection to the east and the west.

HQ Fourth Army laid down timings for the capture of all four lines before midday. The Green Line was to be attacked at 0640 hours (Zero + 20 minutes) and occupied ten minutes later. At 0720 hours (Zero + 1 hour), proceeded by a creeping barrage, the infantry and tanks would advance towards the Brown Line, which they would reach at 0745 hours and occupy in 20 minutes. At 0805 hours, (Zero + 1 hour 45 minutes) the tanks would advance towards the Blue Line with the infantry advancing 15 minutes later (Zero + 2 hours).[3] The tanks and infantry then had two hours to capture the Blue Line. At 1035 (Zero + 4 hours 15 minutes) the tanks would advance northeast towards the Red Line with the infantry again following 15 minutes later. The capture of the Gird Trench was expected to take 30 minutes and the Red Line, including the village of Gueudecourt and the road to its north, was to be secured by noon so that the cavalry could exploit northwards to Le Sars and Bapaume. The plan turned out to be overly ambitious.

---

3   Author's note: It is unclear whether these timings were designed to allow the tanks to reach the new objective ahead of the infantry (the best option) or that they reflected the fact that the infantry moved quicker across the grounds than the tanks.

Photo 1: The only remaining Mark I tank. (TMA)

Photo 2: *Challenger's* route towards Combles. (Geoffrey Vesey Holt – GVH)

Photo 3: *Corunna*'s route north of Bouleaux Wood. (GVH)

Photo 4: Henriques; Macpherson and Murphy's route to the Quadrilateral. (GVH)

Photo 5: Looking south west from the Quadrilateral towards Guillemont. (GVH)

Photo 6: *Campania* and *Casa's* route to Lesboeufs. (GVH)

Photo 7: *Daredevil*'s approach to the Brewery Salient. (GVH)

Photo 8: The Saxon gunners' view of the battlefield. (GVH)

Photo 9: The last part of *Dolphin*'s route along Watling Street. (GVH)

Photo 10: D6's route from Flers to Gueudecourt. (GVH)

Photo 11: D8 gunners' view from the Fork towards Flers. (GVH)

Photo 12: D24's location with High Wood on the horizon (Mike Haspey)

Photo 13: *Daphne*'s route to Martinpuich. (GVH)

Photo 14: Looking along the route of 26th Avenue trench towards Courcelette. (Mike Haspey)

Photo 15: Courcelette from the Sugar trench. (GVH)

Photo 16: Remembering Gnr Cyril Coles on the centenary of his death. (Pam Wilkins)

Allied Formations attacking in the Central Area on 15 September 1916

Objective	Northwest of Flers	Flers	Gueudecourt
Opposing formations	*4th Bavarian Division* *5th Bavarian Regiment* *3th Bavarian Division* *18th Bavarian Regiment*	*4th Bavarian Division* *9th Bavarian Regiment*	*5th Bavarian Division* *14th Bavarian Regiment*
Assaulting Division	NZ Division A H Russell	*41st Division* S T B Lawford	*14 (Light) Division* V A Couper
Assaulting Brigades	2nd NZ Brigade 3rd NZ Rifle Brigade	122nd Infantry Brigade 124th Infantry Brigade	41st Infantry Brigade 42nd Infantry Brigade
Divisional Frontages	800 yards (start line) 1,400 yards (Red Line)	1,100 yards	1,000 yards 1,600 yards (Red Line)
Distances to objectives			
1st Objective (Green Line)	350 yards	650 yards	1,000 yards
2nd Objective (Brown Line)	900 yards	450 yards	600 yards
3rd Objective (Blue Line)	1,000 yards	1,050 yards	1,000 yards
4th Objective (Red Line)	950 yards	1,200 yards	1,500 yards
Tank Units	No. 2 Section (-) D Company	Composite from Nos. 1–3 Section D Company	No 1 Section D Company
Tanks	4 x Mark I	10 x Mark I (4 failed to start)	4 x Mark I (2 failed to start)
Field Artillery	248 x 18-pounder; 72 x 4.5-inch (320 pieces)		
Howitzers	2 x 12-inch, 16 x 9.2-inch 24 x 8-inch; 24 x 6-inch (66 pieces)		
Heavy Guns	4 x 6-inch; 34 x 60-pounder, 8 x 4.7-inch (46 pieces)		
Higher Formation	XV Corps - HS Horne		

The Infantry

HQ XV Corps committed three divisions to the attack in the central area on 15 September, each using two brigades with their third in reserve. The NZ Division were on the left, 41st Division in the centre and 14th Division on the right. 14th Division had been fighting on the Somme, including at Delville Wood, for the previous two months whilst 41st and the NZ divisions were to attack for the first time ever as formations. Both divisions were inexperienced but fresh; the troops of 14th Division were battle-hardened but tired as was some of their equipment.

The Artillery

The bombardment of Bavarian positions started at 1600 hours on 13 September.[4] More than 350 artillery pieces were in direct support of XV Corps which was also allocated 46 heavy guns (see table above). The artillery provided a mix of creeping and lifting barrages which generally worked well. However, the creeping barrage supporting 14th Division was not as heavy and well-defined as others. The Official Historian commented that this 'may be explained by the fact that they had been in action on the Somme for two months and many of the 18-pounders were having trouble with their buffer springs and their rate of fire was reduced thereby.'[5]

The tanks were to advance, either in groups of three or as singletons, along major tracks and communication trenches to aid the skippers' navigation.[6] The artillery plan incorporated 100-yard-wide lanes in the creeping barrage along the tank routes during the attack on the First and Second Objectives. This gave the Bavarian defenders in those gaps an advantage as positions were not neutralised. The war diarist of 8th Battalion King's Royal Rifle Corps (KRRC), which led the assault on the First Objective, also commented on the slowness of the advance 'owing to the barrage being timed to slow to allow the tanks to come up.'[7] Certainly, the ground conditions were such that the infantry were much quicker across the ground than the tanks.

The Tanks

Eighteen tanks from D Company were allocated to support the XV Corps attack in the Central Area (see colour map 7). The NZ and 14th divisions were allocated four tanks each whilst 41st Division, tasked to capture the village of Flers, was allocated ten. A further tank from C Company, known as L Tank, was allocated to support the preliminary attack on the Brewery – see chapter 6. The tanks would operate either in groups of three or as singletons protecting the flank of the infantry's attack.

4   D Company War Diary (WO 95/110) dated 13 September 1916.
5   Miles, *OHGW*, p. 321 footnote 2.
6   A route map was issued by XV Corps and route cards had been prepared for each tank group (copies of these are held in the NZ Division 'tanks' file at their National Archives). However, it appears that detailed maps were not provided for each tank skipper.
7   8th KRRC War Diary (WO 95/1895).

The final orders, as recorded in the D Company War Diary, reveals that all four tanks allocated to 14 Division were from No. 1 Section.[8] The section commander, Mortimore, also commanded Male tank No. 765 and tank crew D1 in *Daredevil I*. This singleton tank, known as A Group, would operate just inside 14th Division's right boundary and would clear the eastern side of Gueudecourt.[9] The other three (B Group) would initially operate on the left of the Divisional area as far as the Green Line, then move to the Divisional centre by the Brown Line, then head for the Blue Line (Bulls Road) and finally attack the south-eastern side of Gueudecourt.

B Group consisted of the Male tank No. 728, with the D3 crew commanded by Lt Harold Head[10] and two Females; No. 516 with the D4 crew under 2Lt Charles Storey[11] and No. 540, known as *Dolphin*, manned by the D5 crew commanded by 2Lt Arthur Blowers.[12] Before the main attack, *Daredevil I* and *Dolphin* were to clear the Brewery Salient in a preliminary operation as directed by Horne. Mortimore's orders were 'to proceed to SE corner of Delville Wood and at 5.30 am on Sept 15 to attack and clear Hop Alley. Then endeavour to overtake advancing Infantry and proceed with them to further objectives.' Blowers in *Dolphin* was ordered to 'proceed to point just East of Cocoa Lane [200 yards north of Delville Wood][13] and attack preliminary objective at the junction of Ale Alley and Edge Trench in conjunction with Tank D1 at 0530 hours on Sept 15. Position to be thoroughly cleared and after to catch up advancing infantry and deal with subsequent objectives.' Ale Alley ran parallel with *Dolphin's* objective 200 yards north of *Daredevil I's* objective at Hop Alley, with Blowers in *Dolphin* attacking from the northwest and Mortimore from the southwest.

Head and Storey had a single task: to 'proceed to point just East of Cocoa Lane in advance of infantry to attack and clear Tea Support Trench [the Bavarian frontline] and then proceed again in advance of the infantry to Switch Trench [the Green Line]. To remain with infantry until position consolidated and advance with infantry on 2nd, 3rd and 4th objectives.' Their route followed the German communications trench known as Gas Alley (which was a continuation of Cocoa Lane) northeast to its junction with Watling Street (just north of the Brown Line),[14] and then northeast along Watling Street to the Bulls Road (Blue Line) and then onto the southwest entry into Gueudecourt.

Ten tanks were allocated to 41st Division in the centre: a singleton tank on the Eastern Flank and the other nine operating in groups of three. C Group was the singleton, the Male No. 747 commanded by 2Lt Reginald Legge and manned by the D6 crew. According to the D Company War Diary, Legge was 'to proceed along edge of Delville Wood, [along the] Flers

---

8   TNA WO 95/110.

9   The routes are depicted on a colour map reproduced in Pidgeon, *Tanks at Flers*, p. 137.

10   Head, who had married on 12 September 1915 aged 18, was the father of a young son and was known by his fellow skippers as 'Daddy'. Pope, *FTC*, pp. 91 to 95.

11   Storey, who was unmarried and 39 years old, had served as a cavalry trooper in South Africa in 1900. He was known as 'Father'. Pope, *FTC*, pp. 88 and 89.

12   Blowers had served as a Territorial soldier in the Devonshire Regiment whilst training as a schoolmaster. He volunteered to join the Suffolk Regiment on the outbreak of war, deployed to France in November 1914 and had seen 6 months' active service as an NCO. Pope, *FTC*, pp. 35 and 36.

13   Cocoa Lane was a short element of the Gas Alley communications trench, which linked the centre of Delville Wood to Watling Street and hence onto on towards Gird Street.

14   Watling Street was a major track linking Ginchy to Gueudecourt.

Road to Switch Trench, from Switch Trench to Gap Trench [the Brown Line]. Thence to Flers and North to Gird Trench and Gueudecourt.'[15]

D Group consisted of three tanks: the Male tank No. 759 called *Dinnaken* commanded by Lt Stuart Hastie; and two Female tanks, No. 546 known as *Dolly* commanded by 2Lt Victor Huffam (D9) and No. 534 commanded by Second Lieutenant Gordon Court (D14).[16] Their Starting Point was close to Legge's on the Flers Road, north of Delville Wood. Their orders were 'to proceed from starting line at 5.45 am ahead of infantry to Tea Support, then 1st objective Switch Trench. Thence to Flers Avenue [the Brown Line east of the Flers Road] onto Flers Village and on from there to Gird Trench, Gird Support to Gueudecourt.' The route map for D Group shows they were to follow the Flers Road to a point 400 yards north of the Switch Line (Green Line) and then, bearing right at the Y-junction 350 yards south of the Flers Trench (Brown Line), support 124th Brigade who were fighting on the east side of the village.[17]

The other two groups of tanks supporting 41st Division were ordered to clear the western edge of Flers village. E Group consisted of three tanks under No. 3 Section Commander, Capt Stephen Sellick, who also commanded crew D19 in the Male tank No. 753 called *Duke*. There were also two Female tanks: crew D2 commanded by Lt Hugh Bell in tank No. 539 and Lt Jack Bagshaw commanding crew D15 in tank No. 537 known as *Duchess*. The D Company War Diary does not record the orders given to Sellick and Bell; however, they are likely to have been identical to Bagshaw's which were 'to leave starting line at Z-35 [0545 hours], proceed to Switch Trench [Green Line] and thence follow route W of Flers Road to 2nd and 3rd objectives.'

The final three tanks allocated to 41st Division, known as F Group, consisted of the Male tank No. 743 with the D7 crew under Lt Alfred Enoch, Lt Arthur Arnold with the D16 crew in the Female tank No. 538 known as *Dracula* and the D18 crew, in the Male tank No. 743, commanded by 2Lt Leonard Bond.[18] Their orders were: 'on leaving starting line [to] advance on Tea Support, passing the junction of Switch Trench [the Green Line] to eventually reach N20c 1.4 [the Gird Line east of Factory Corner].' This route would have taken F Group along the western side of Flers, in support of 122nd Brigade, as they took on the clearance of the village.[19]

---

15   An unreferenced extract of the initial orders issued by 41st Division, held in the D Battalion box in the TMA, reveals that Legge would then attack a large farm in the centre of Gueudecourt.

16   There is doubt as to the spelling of the tank's name *Dinnaken* which is Scots for 'I do not know'. The traditional spelling is 'dinnae ken' but there are no images of the tank with the name painted on it. Liddell Hart consistently uses the spelling 'Dinnaken' as does Reiffer in a letter to Hastie dated 8 November 1963. Trevor Pidgeon's archives includes a type-written copy of a latter from Hastie to Charles Staddon received on 23 November 1963, which gives the spelling as 'Dinniken'.

17   TNA WO 75/2617 and 2619. This route is, however, is at variance with later accounts of the attack by Huffam and Hastie.

18   Arthur Arnold was one of three brothers who served in the Tank Corps. Bill and Clem were later awarded the Distinguished Service Order in 1919, Clem for commanding the Whippet tank *Musical Box*. Frank Arnold, who commanded C14 *Corunna* (see Chapter 6), was not a relative.

19   This route is confirmed by the maps attached to 41st Division 'Report on the attack on the 15/16 September including the capture of Flers Village' which forms part of the Divisional War Diary.

The open ground west of Flers was to be captured by the NZ Division, which was allocated four tanks, a group of three operating on the outskirts of the village and a singleton on the division's western boundary. The crews came from No. 2 Section which was commanded by Capt Graeme Nixon. Nixon also commanded a Male tank No. 719 known as *Dreadnought* which was grouped with two Female tanks; No. 535 manned by the D10 crew in *Dinkum* under Lt Harold Darby and No. 547, known as *Diehard*, manned by the D11 crew commanded by 2Lt Herbert Pearsall. The orders for the three skippers were identical: 'from starting line just northwest of Delville Wood to proceed to Crest Trench and to remain there till this point was cleared.[20] Thence to proceed to Switch Trench and advance ahead of infantry to the west of Flers on 3rd objective [Blue Line west], thence to 4th objective, viz Gird Trench and Gird Support' (shown on the original XV Corps map as a point northeast of Factory Corner).

The fourth tank, the Male tank No. 720 under 2Lt George Bown with the D8 crew, had a separate task. Its crew were to move 'along the left boundary of XV Corps' which was also the western flank of NZ Division. Bown's route was 'from starting line just northwest of Delville Wood to proceed to Switch Trench before infantry, to stay at this point for one hour and deal with any opposition.[21] Then to proceed to Flers Trench [800 yards northeast of the Cough Drop] with the infantry. From thence to push well ahead before infantry again advanced and assist in capture of 3rd objective [Blue Line]. Thence ahead of infantry to 4th objective [Red Line].[22]'

Deployment for Battle

With the exception of *Daredevil I*, all tanks supporting XV Corps left Green Dump after 2000 hours on 14 September.[23] Several of the tanks were late arriving at their Starting Points due to traffic congestion near Longueval. Rather than travel cross country, as is current practice, the tanks were required to follow roads and tracks northeast from the Green Dump and they were held up by other units deploying that night. The tanks were driven in first gear, to keep engine noise to a minimum with a speed of five yards a minute, and they caused major delays as they negotiated the road junctions around Longueval and the roads to the west of Delville Wood.[24] A report sent to HQ NZ Division that day stated: 'The tanks left their final assembly point at about 9.0 p.m. 14/9/16. The road metalled most of the way. Progress was good [about 1 mile per hour] until the shell pitted ground on the West of Longueval was reached. Progress

20 The starting line was at the junction of the Longueval to Flers Road with a major track (known as the North Road) leading north to the Fork.
21 Bown's position at the Fork (now the site of the NZ Memorial) provided a first-class view over the ground to the north-western outskirts of the village to Factory Corner and beyond.
22 A type-written set of orders for this Tank Group, by the General Staff of HQ NZ Division, including detailed routes with grid references and timings, has been recently discovered in the New Zealand National Archives.
23 Mortimore and his crew spent to the night at S23c 1,6, about 300 yards north of Bernafay Wood on a track due east of the Montauban Quarry. Pidgeon, *The Tanks at Flers,* p. 147.
24 Arnold arrived in *Dracula* at the Longueval crossroads at 0330 hours, having taken six hours to travel 1,500 yards from Green Dump. See Appendix XIII.

then became very slow owing to leading tanks becoming fixed and other routes having to be reconnoitred for the remainder of the column to pass them.'[25]

The final stage for most of No. 1 Section was through Delville Wood itself, which was almost impassable due to the fallen tree trunks, stumps about four feet high and the ground criss-crossed with damaged trenches, dead bodies, fallen branches and unexploded munitions. Before *Daredevil I* started to move towards Delville Wood, Mortimore was visited by Brig Gen P C B Skinner who commanded 41st Brigade, who wished him well.[26] *Daredevil I* had a shorter and simpler route than the tanks in Group B,[27] and reached South Street, on the southern edge of Delville Wood, by 0230 hours.[28] The other three tanks had more difficulty; Head described this in the 1980s:

> Everyone wanted to move off at the same time: infantry, limber wagons, tanks and everyone associated with the next morning engagements. The engineers had the job of laying white tapes for the destination or starting point for each tank.[29] The engineers, not knowing the capabilities of the tanks, laid the easiest route along the edge of the trenches which was a big mistake as a tank must cross as near right angles as possible. So, we found our own way to our kicking off points and through the sunken road. The site of my destination was Delville Wood and it [the tape] was laid over the top with mortar shells. We tried to pull them out, not knowing if they had detonated or not. Eventually the Germans sent over some gas shells, on came our masks and you couldn't see a thing so we had to do without. It would have taken all night to move them so I had conflab with the fellow following me and we decided to go over them. The ground was so soft that the bombs sank in very slowly. At the end of the wood, we had to turn right [east] and pass along the [northern] front of the wood and wait until dawn. The fellow following me [probably Blowers] got into the wood too far and got his track stuck on the stump of a tree. The stumps were not more than four feet high and we manoeuvred into such a position that we could pull him out, which we did just before dawn.[30]

Most of C, D and F Groups reached their Starting Points on time but, in E Group, only *Duchess* was successful. According to the History of the New Zealand Division, the Bavarians to the west of Flers undertook a Relief in Place during the early hours of 15 September. Stewart also notes that the four tanks in G Group were delayed by traffic and one broke down.[31] Nixon's section

---

25   The full report is also at Appendix XIII.

26   Pidgeon, *Tanks at Flers*, p. 147.

27   The exact routes are not recorded. A Group (Mortimore) would have driven approximately 2,000 yards following communication trenches with no other traffic whereas B Group had to drive 1,800 yards along crowded tracks from Green Dump to Longueval Village and then a further 1,000 yards through the centre of Delville Wood. All distances calculated by the Author.

28   Mortimore's post-battle Report. See Appendix XIII.

29   Gnr. Charles Bond states Bagshaw undertook this task for *Duchess*. See *Bridgwater Mercury* 25 July 1917.

30   David Fletcher *Tanks and Trenches* (Stroud: Alan Sutton, 1997) p. 8. This account was given by Head at the Tank Museum on 15 September 1982 and is probably less accurate as the accounts in Appendix XIII.

31   Hugh Stewart, *The New Zealand Division 1916 – 1919 – a popular history based on official records* p. 72. <http://nzetc.victoria.ac.nz/tm/scholarly/tei-WH1-Fran-t1-body1-d3.html> (accessed 23 March

had been the last to leave Green Dump and Pearsall, commanding *Diehard*, later reported: 'I left GREEN DUMP at 9.10 PM on Sept 14th and reached position SW of LONGUEVAL where a delay of more than one hour caused by a tank in front of column becoming immobile.'[32] The steering tail of Bown's tank was hit by artillery fire en route to the Starting Point which also probably delayed their arrival. However, the main difficulties encountered were that the steering tail had to be raised at each junction, to allow the tanks to pivot on their tracks and make the turn; sponsons being caught on the edge of shell craters; tracks losing traction in the associated loose spoil with the result that the crew had to dig out the tank; and their little experience of working a tank over the ground of a recent battlefield.[33]

Zero

Zero was at 0620 hours: 'the morning broke in perfect autumn weather but with a slight mist lying in the valleys.'[34]

Final Moves

Mortimore's post battle report states *Daredevil I* started to move from Delville Wood at 0445 hours.[35] He was to leave the Starting Point, possibly at Pilsen Lane, at 0510 hours[36] which gave him 20 minutes to reach his preliminary objective.[37] *Dolphin* had started to move at 0500 hours but became ditched on the edge of the wood and had to be pulled out – as a result, Blowers was too late to take part in the preliminary attack.[38] The 'left-hand group' of Head and Storey moved at 0527 hours but Storey ditched en route and his tank could not be recovered until 26 September. Huffam and Court of D Group became ditched in a British trench, before crossing into no man's land, and were not recovered until later that afternoon. Bell and Sellick's tank never reached their Starting Point, Bell through ditching and Sellick for mechanical reasons, and G Group were so late that they did not reach the British frontline until well after Zero.

2021).

32   See Appendix XIII. Pearsall's report was written about 29 September 1916.

33   The report to HQ NZ Division (see Appendix XIII) stated that they reached a point 600 yards north of the main road junction in Longueval at 0530 hours. They still had to negotiate the village itself.

34   Weather conditions recorded in *The NZ Medical Service in the Great War 1916 -1918* <http://nzetc. victoria.ac.nz/tm/scholarly/tei-WH1-Medi-t1-g1-t1-body-d9-d2.html> (accessed 8 November 2020).

35   See Appendix XIII. This account is in Woods' correspondence book which only became available in summer 2016.

36   42nd Infantry Brigade War Diary (WO 95/1897) records the tank attacking Ale Alley started at 0500 hours and that attacking Hop Alley started at 0510 hours. However, D Company's War Diary states that Blowers did not get to Ale Alley.

37   The exact location of his starting point is uncertain. On p. 147 in *The Tanks at Flers*, Pidgeon states that Daredevil's starting point was 150 yards southeast of the wood south of the Rue de Ginchy. However, the XV Corps planning map on page 150 of his book shows the approach from the southwest of the wood. Mortimore's post operational report (Appendix XIII) states the start was at Pilsen Lane, a trench on the northern side of the road linking Delville Wood to Ginchy and the tank's Route Card states it was at the south-easterly corner of Delville Wood.

38   D Company War Diary (WO 95/110) also states that *Dolphin's* steering tail was damaged.

The Clearance of the Brewery Salient

Coloured photograph 7 depicts the area south of the Brewery, taken from Pilsen Lane (the communication trench which ran from Longueval to Ginchy) with Delville Wood to its west (left). Hop Alley and Ale Alley are in dead ground beyond the skyline but Mortimore would have been able to locate the western end of Hop Alley by following the edge of Delville Wood. The D Company War Diary records that D1 'cleared HOP ALLEY and had caught up and passed infantry when tank was hit by shell in rear starboard sprocket and put out of action.'[39] This however does not tell the whole story for, at the end of September, Mortimore gave a full report to Woods in which he stated:

> Arrived at SOUTH STREET – DELVILLE WOOD at 2.30 AM on 15th SEPT. My orders were to attack HOP ALLEY (supposed strong post of enemy) at 5.30 AM in conjunction with KOYLI [King's Own Yorkshire Light Infantry] bombers.
>
> Started at 4.45 AM for first objective and arrived astride HOP ALLEY at 5.30 AM precisely. During this period, it was quite dark and, to add to the difficulties of observation, we were forced to wear gas masks. Proceeded along HOP ALLEY but found the trench devoid of enemy although there were many traces of recent occupation. Then proceeded along ALE ALLEY for a certain distance but encountered no resistance and in conjunction with the bombers the whole of this area was scrutinised.[40]
>
> I then commenced my attack on the first main objective viz SWITCH TRENCH but had proceeded but a short distance when the tank was hit by artillery on the starboard sprocket and this rendered it out of action. Was forced to abandon D1 as the enemy commenced to range upon it with heavy guns. The 4 Hotchkiss automatic guns have since been salved and are at GREEN DUMP. 6-pounder ammunition has been removed and placed at a safe distance from the car.

This report was never sent to a superior headquarters and its existence was unknown in the UK for almost a century.[41]

On 6 September 1957, Gnr Albert Smith wrote to Victor Huffam describing the preliminary action. He recalled that:

> ...we came to the left hand side of Delville Wood. White tapes had been laid down to Hop Alley, at one time one of our crew got out and guided our driver with red

---

39 The exact final position of *Daredevil* is uncertain. Pidgeon, using RFC photographs, places the hulk at T13a 30,95 (*Tanks at Flers,* Map 8) whilst Woods' tank location report, as of 29 September 1916, states the tank was at T7c Central. A contemporary map 'British Front from High Wood to Ginchy' (1st Printing Section RE IV Army 645 with printed corrections dated 10 Sep 1916 and manuscript markings dated 16 Sep 1916), shows a hulk at T7C 0,4 i.e., 200 yards north of Ale Abbey and 400 yards NNE of the northeast corner of Delville Wood.

40 This may indicate that Mortimore realised that Blowers had not undertaken his element of the preliminary operation. Mortimore's original orders were for his tank to undertake this task.

41 The D Company Correspondence Book was sent to the Author by the grandson of D Company's CSM Thomas 'Paddy' Walsh in the summer of 2016. The first person to hear the report was Mortimore's daughter Tilly; it was read to her, at Delville Wood on 15 September 2016, by Morty's grandson Max.

and green lights showing from a belt he had round him, the going was very bad. We arrived at our starting point, Sergt Davies was in charge. Davies was gunner on the starboard side, Hobson loader. I was gunner the port side, with Day loader. Doodson and Leat were on the machine guns and Wateridge driver. At zero we moved off to the roar of artillery and machine gun fire. I think we all had the wind up but we were a good crew and collected. We were getting along very nicely, all guns manned, when there was a crash and we stopped dead. A shell had hit us on the starboard side and Davies was shell shocked.

It seems odd that Smith did not mention Mortimore but his letter was written 40 years after the event.[42] John Foley interviewed *Daredevil's* skipper whilst finalising *The Boilerplate War* in the early 1960s. In the postscript, Foley quotes Mortimore saying that two crewmen were killed when the shell hit the starboard sprocket.[43] Mortimore

Harold Mortimore. (Tilly Mortimore)

must have conflated two events as none of the crew of *Daredevil I* died on 15 September 1916.[44] Sadly, however, Gnrs Ewart Doodson and Harry Leat were killed six months later during the Battle of Arras.[45] Although Smith stated Davies suffered from shell shock, he had recovered sufficiently to be reallocated to the D3 crew by 20 September and served on with D Company until early December.[46] Despite being the first tank skipper to see action on 15 September, and his sustained work as a section commander until December 1916, Mortimore was not decorated. He was, however, Mentioned in Despatches in January 1917.[47]

42   D Company box in the Tank Museum archives.
43   John Foley, *The Boilerplate War* (London: Virgin Books, 1981) p. 191.
44   Mortimore was seriously ill by this time. He had just been appointed, in absentia, Vice President of the newly formed Devon Branch of the RTR Association but was never able to attend its meetings. He died aged 76 on 17 July 1967. Pope, *FTC*, pp. 25 to 28.
45   Ewart Doodson was fatally wounded by an artillery shell during No. 12 Company's attack on Thelus on 9 April 1917; Harry Leat was killed two days later, probably during No. 11 Company's attack on Bullecourt. Sadly, the locations of both men's graves are unknown. Pope, *FTC*, pp. 28–31.
46   In December 1916, Davies was admitted to hospital with gunshot wounds and was subsequently discharged from the army in November 1917.
47   Mortimore was badly gassed at Beaumont Hamel in November 1916 (see Chapter 10). Appointed adjutant of F Battalion in January 1917, he returned to France but his health was so poor he was sent

Attack on Gueudecourt

At Zero, the Light Infantrymen of 41st Brigade advanced towards the Switch Trench, their First Objective. The non-appearance of *Daredevil* and *Dolphin* did not slow their assault as they had orders to keep up with the creeping barrage and not wait for the tanks.[48] The two lead battalions, 8th Rifle Brigade and 8th Kings Royal Rifle Corps (KRRC), suffered severe casualties from two machine-gun posts in Pint Trench,[49] which ran along the Ginchy to Flers road, as well as taking casualties from the British creeping barrage. Whilst the Tea Support trench was taken quickly, Switch Trench (the Green Line) was only cleared by 0700 hours, ten minutes later than required. However, two machine-guns were captured, the German dug-outs cleared using grenades, and many prisoners were taken. 6 KOYLI, on the right advancing from Pilsen Lane, also took their objective.[50] 41st Brigade then sent skirmishers forward to clear out enemy snipers and the Switch Trench was made ready to defend against counter-attacks.

The attack on the Second Objective (the Brown Line) was delayed as the deployment of 7th Rifle Brigade and 7th KRRC was disrupted by a German bombardment as they exited Delville Wood. The battalions also had difficulty in forming up near the Switch Trench which was full of wounded Bavarians as well as the remnants of 8th Rifle Brigade and 8th KRRC. The attack on Gap Trench did not start until 0800 hours, some 40 minutes behind schedule, but the battalions quickly gained the Second Objective after the Bavarians swiftly surrendered.[51] Remarkably, once the two battalions consolidated on the Brown Line, they did not link up with units of 41st Division on their left, despite the fact that the Londoners had captured the Brown Line (Flers Trench) by 0750 hours and held the position for the rest of the day.

42nd Brigade, the other attacking formation in 14th Division, were tasked to capture the Third Objective (the Blue Line at Bulls Road and Needle Trench), then the Gird Line trenches, and finally, the Red Line (Fourth Objective) including the village of Gueudecourt. 42nd Brigade had left their place of assembly in the Caterpillar Valley on a 3,000-yard approach, passing through Delville Wood, before deploying into their attack formations south of the Brown Line at Gap Trench. On the way, 9th KRRC came under the fire of a Bavarian machine-gun which should have been destroyed by the Guards Division tanks.[52] 9th KRRC's CO was killed, his adjutant wounded, and six other officers were killed, meaning that command and control was severely weakened. Although the machine-gun was silenced by two Lewis guns and a party of bombers, the advance was delayed by 40 minutes. It was not until 0900 hours that 42nd Brigade started for the Third Objective (Blue Line) along Bulls Road.

---

back to England in June for treatment. He was later served later as the adjutant of two convalescent hospitals. Pope, *FTC*, pp. 25–28.

48   See Appendix XIII.

49   These machine-gun posts were mentioned in the orders by HQ Guards Division. See Chapter 6. They were also on the planned route for Mortimore but *Daredevil* had been knocked out before Zero.

50   This route would have been fatal if *Daredevil* had failed in her task.

51   The German artillery did not respond to request for assistance from the defending *14 Bavarian Regiment* as the British bombardment had cut all the telephone lines and their light signals were obscured by smoke over the battlefield. See Miles, *OHGW*, p. 320 fn. 1.

52   The battalion HQ was hit at 0730 hours but tanks were not in the area until 0743 hours. See Chapter 6.

As they advanced, 9th Rifle Brigade's CO and every officer in the battalion headquarters, except one subaltern, was wounded. The 42nd Brigade attack petered out about 200 yards south of the Bulls Road with most soldiers taking cover in shellholes. One party of 9th KRRC, however, did reach the Third Objective using the track, known as Watling Street or *Hohwegzug*, and destroyed two artillery pieces which were in a sunken part of the track.

Watling Street was also used by *Dolphin* to reach the Blue Line and which it then followed north towards Gueudecourt.[53] Having failed to take part in the preliminary action, Blowers drove straight to the First Objective (Switch Trench) and then followed Gas Alley to the 14th/41st inter-divisional boundary on the Ginchy to Flers road.[54] The time when *Dolphin* arrived at the Second Objective (the Brown Line) is not recorded but it was probably after it was secured by 41st Brigade (0900 hours). Blowers' route along Watling Street enabled him to use a sunken section for about 500 yards south of the Blue Line. This kept *Dolphin* partially out of sight of the Saxon gunners[55] who were manning 77mm artillery pieces, located along the Bulls Road (colour photograph 8). Furthermore, the sunken road (see colour photograph 9) must also have aided the driver, Private George Thomas, as *Dolphin's* steering tail had been damaged earlier in the morning.

According to the D Company War Diary, Blowers 'engaged a German battery and the gunners of this battery disappeared into their dugouts' after which the tank then flattened the guns. These were probably the same guns attacked by 9th KRRC mentioned above. By now Blowers was using his Webley pistol[56]

Arthur Blowers. (Roger Blowers)

---

53   *Dolphin* was the only tank from A and B Groups to get so far north. *Daredevil* was knocked out south of the German frontline, D3 reached Tea Support where she was hit by German artillery and D4, having pulled *Dolphin* from the wood edge, became stuck on a tree stump. She was not recovered until 26 September.

54   A German communications trench which linked Delville Wood to Watling Street.

55   The guns were manned by men of *1 Battery, 7 Saxon Field Artillery Regiment*. Pidgeon, *Tanks at Flers*, p. 151.

56   Blowers later told his youngest son Roger 'I fired over a hundred rounds. None of the targets was more than about 10 yards away, so I didn't miss many.' Pope, *FTC*, p. 35. The revolver is now on display at the Tank Museum.

rather than his Hotchkiss machine gun.[57] *Dolphin* was well ahead of the majority of 42nd Brigade, who were dead, wounded or sheltering in shellholes south of the Bulls Road owing to the Bavarian machine guns on the eastern side of Flers and at Point 91.[58] Despite this, *Dolphin* advanced towards Gueudecourt to clear the way for the final assault.[59] The remaining 350 soldiers of 9th KRRC and 9th Rifle Brigade started to attack the Gird Line at 1120 hours but their advance was again stopped by machine-gun fire which forced them to take cover. Blowers pushed on and reached a point about 100 yards from the Gird Line and 'after waiting for a long while for infantry to come up decided to return.'

Despite being in full sight of the German artillery observers in balloons to the north of Flers, and with a damaged steering tail, Thomas turned *Dolphin* using her gears and followed Watling Street south, via the sunken section, to a point 500 yards south of the Bulls Road where the road levelled out. As the tank emerged, some sheltering riflemen asked Blowers to destroy a Bavarian machine-gun which was still active on the eastern edge of Flers. Blowers did not hesitate despite the presence of the 77mm guns located along on the Bulls Road (see colour photograph 9). As the tank could only move at walking pace, and at a range of less than 700 yards, the Saxon gunners could not miss. *Dolphin* was 'hit several times, one shell exploding within the tank and the tank eventually caught fire.'[60] Gnr Leslie Gutsell was killed and Blowers suffered from head injuries and burns. Despite this, Blowers and Gnr William Hodgson lifted Gnr Robert Barnsby, whose legs were shattered, out of the tank and placed him in a nearby shellhole. Cpl Ted Foden, the tank NCO, and the driver George Thomas were also wounded as they got clear. Unable to move Barnsby, Blowers asked the infantry to assist Barnsby but he died shortly afterwards.[61] Blowers was subsequently awarded the MC with Foden and Thomas were awarded the MM.[62]

As for the remainder of B Group, Storey and the D4 crew remained stuck, probably on a tree stump, at Delville Wood.[63] Head and the D3 crew got into action, advancing ahead of the infantry across no man's land. The tank's arrival at Tea Support Trench, the German frontline,

---

57   According to Arthur Arnold (see Appendix XIII), the commander's Hotchkiss machine-gun was vulnerable to German small arms fire. Given Blowers used his revolver, it is likely that his Hotchkiss was also out of action.

58   This position at the junction of Gird Trench and Gas Alley was the target of the follow-on attack on 25 September.

59   Trevor Pidgeon mentions that Gird Trench was being bombarded at the time presumably in preparation for the final assault. From this we can determine that *Dolphin* must have been at the location no later than 1115 hours when the barrage would have lifted in this area.

60   D Company War Diary – consolidated list of tank actions (TNA WO 95 /110).

61   Woods' diary records he buried Barnsby and Gutsell on 30 September. The graves were subsequently lost and both men are commemorated on the Thiepval Memorial to the Missing.

62   Blowers recovered from his wounds, although he suffered from headaches for the rest of his life. He returned to France with H Battalion but was knocked unconscious shortly afterwards when an explosion occurred in a tank he was inspecting. Ted Foden, who had been shot in the ankle, recovered but the injury was such he was not fit for active service. He remained at Bovington as an instructor for the rest of the war. Pte George Thomas was transferred to the Heavy Branch and was killed in action during No. 12 Company's ill-fated assault on Bullecourt on 3 May 1917. Sadly, the location of his grave is unknown, Pope, *FTC*, pp. 34-8.

63   This tank was not recovered until 26 September; one crewman Gnr Fred Horrocks being killed and three injured whilst trying to extract it the previous day. Storey and his crew were provided with a replacement which they used to remarkable effect at Gueudecourt on 26 September – see below.

was observed by Sgt Norman Carmichael of 21st KRRC, 'lumbering past on my left, belching forth yellow flames from her guns and making for the gap where the Flers Road cut through the enemy trench [Switch Line].'[64] The D Company War Diary records that the Male tank 'crossed [the] starting line near DELVILLE WOOD. At Tea Support Trench [the Bavarian frontline] the tank was hit by a HE shell and splinters became wedged in the track and, when the tank was moved, track was damaged. As efforts to repair damage were unsuccessful, the tank took no further part in the action on Sept 15.' The war diary mentions that one of Head's gunners (George Bentley) was wounded in his hand by a splinter but it does not record the determined efforts by D3's crew, for the next 12 hours, to get their tank back into action. The D Company correspondence book records a citation for two of Head's crew, Cpl William McNicoll and Gnr William Steer. This states that 'when the car became ditched these two men worked from 7.30 a.m. till 8 p.m. continuing under heavy shell fire, digging and repairing, and it is only due to the efforts of these two men that the car got clear.'[65] The tank then drove westwards, following Tea Support Trench, towards the Flers Road and reached the Rideau des Filoires, a bank 600 yards north of Delville Wood, where *Dinnaken* was awaiting recovery. The ASC bought Head's tank back to Green Dump on 18 September, and she was deployed again on two occasions before the end of the month. *Dinnaken* was not brought in until 1 October owing to engine problems which are described below.

Tank Effectiveness

As *Daredevil* successfully achieved the preliminary objective, by ensuring that Brewery Salient was cleared in concert with the KOYLI bombers, *Daredevil's* action was effective. Similarly, *Dolphin's* actions after she had reached the second objective were effective as they caused the death of defenders in the depth positions and the destruction of artillery equipment.

Capture of Flers Village

The attack on Flers was undertaken by 41st Division supported by ten tanks. The inter-brigade boundary was along the Flers road to the centre of the village with 124th Brigade on the right (east) and 122nd on their left. 124th Brigade had captured the Switch Trench (Green Line) slightly late at 0700 hours but took Flers Trench (Brown Line) by 0750 hours according to schedule. Thereafter they made limited progress as, according to the *OFGW*, they were unsure of the situation within Flers village.

122nd Brigade had made a good start, 'the [creeping] barrage was excellent, just what the men expected.'[66] Some casualties were suffered from machine-gun and rifle fire at Tea Support Trench but the First Objective (the Switch Trench) was taken by 0640 hours. As 18th KRRC advanced towards Flers Line (the Second Objective) their CO, second in command, adjutant and three officers of his HQ were killed. This caused a delay in the advance but the CO of 12th

---

64   Pidgeon, *Tanks at Flers*, p. 151.
65   Neither crewman was awarded a gallantry medal but McNicoll later won the Distinguished Conduct Medal for commanding a tank at Cayeax on 8 August 1918. Pope, *FTC*, pp. 91–95.
66   Miles, *OHGW*, p. 322.

East Surreys,[67] who were following them, took 18th KRRC under command and they eventually cleared the Flers Line, with the assistance from *Dinnaken*, taking hundreds of prisoners – the Regimental History of *9 Bavarian Regiment* noting that most of *I* and *III Regiment* were captured that morning.

Flers was one of the key targets for the Fourth Army that morning and several tanks played a role in its capture. To the east, the singleton Male No. 747 commanded by Legge followed *Dinnaken* up the Flers Road. She got behind schedule early into the action. Legge was expected to be at the Green Line (the Switch Line) at 0645 hours; however, at that time, he was seen by an RFC at the bend in the Flers Road some 600 yards south of his First Objective. Legge's Second Objective, at the eastern end of Flers Avenue on the Brown Line, was over 1,800 yards away. Reaching the Switch Line, Legge turned east for about 200 yards then followed the disused German communications trench Gate Lane north east for 700 yards to the eastern end of Flers Avenue. An RFC contact aircraft noted a tank in this area at 0855 hours – there were no other tanks east of the village so it can only have been Legge.

It seems likely that Legge was operating on revised orders as, instead of continuing northeast towards Gueudecourt, the tank turned northwest towards the eastern edge of Flers. This was useful as *Dinnaken*, part of the D Group which had been tasked to clear this area, was now fighting its way up the village High Street.[68] Legge's crew may have been late but their arrival was timely. Like 14th Division to the east, the leading battalion of 124th Brigade, 26th Royal Fusiliers, were pinned down by a number of German machine-guns on the edge of the village. At 0928 hours, Legge's tank was observed due east of the village cemetery, about the time that *Dinnaken* was by Flers Church. Legge's 6-pounder gun layers soon identified and targeted the machine-gun posts enabling the Fusiliers to advance. The CO of 26th Royal Fusiliers, Lt Col George North, later reflected, 'This tank was of the greatest material use and the party in charge of it distinguished themselves considerably.'[69]

Arriving at Bulls Road, close to the site of the post-war CWGC cemetery, Legge decided to push on. The exact time of his arrival is unknown but, based on his earlier progress, he was on schedule to support the final attack on Gueudecourt. Initially driving east along the Bulls Road, the tank turned north just before the crest of the ridge possibly having engaged and destroyed one of the Saxon artillery pieces which dominated the ground to the south.[70] The tank then drove north towards the eastern edge of the German defensive position known as Hog's Head, and then northeast towards Gueudecourt (see colour photograph 10) where, according to the D Company Diary, she 'engaged a German battery, putting one gun out of action with 6-pounder guns, but was put out of action by a direct hit from a German field gun.' The tank later caught fire and became a total wreck.

The skipper helped as many out of the tank as possible and was seen standing by the tank. Legge, who was wounded, was later taken prisoner by the Bavarian defenders and died the following day. This was, of course, unknown when Summers wrote to Legge's mother on

---

67   Lt Col Henry Walmisley-Dresser, an officer of the Warwickshire Regiment who retired as a lieutenant in 1912. See *London Gazette* (LG), 26 November 1912. He was very seriously injured during the attack on Flers and died of his wounds on 17 September 1916.
68   See D Group's confirmatory orders in Appendix XII.
69   Pidgeon, *Tanks at Flers*, p. 165.
70   Pidgeon, *Tanks at Flers*, p. 165.

18 September – see Appendix XIII. Another of his crew, Gunner Herbert Clears, was also captured, interrogated and spent the rest of the war as a prisoner. Three crewmen were reported missing after the battle and later declared killed in action, one of whom, Gunner Bardsley, was reported as dying whilst he was trying to crawl to safety.[71] The three remaining crewmen, Brooks, Beesley and Thacker, made their way across 900 yards of no man's land until they met up with NZ troops near Flers.[72] LCpl Wilfred Brooks was awarded the MM as was the tank's driver, Sgt Herbert Thacker ASC.[73] Legge's death was recorded in the war diary of *1st Battalion, 10th Bavarian Regiment* although sadly not the location of his burial.[74] His ID disc was subsequently sent to the German Red Cross at Munich who forwarded it to the WO where his name was added to the list of war dead.

D Group, which was to attack the eastern side of the village, encountered problems before Zero.[75] As they moved forward, Court's tank became ditched in an old dug out in a support trench, north of Delville Wood, before crossing the British frontline.[76] Huffam drew his tank *Dolly* alongside Court's tank but, whilst trying to extract the stricken vehicle, the two became stuck together. They were recovered later in the afternoon by 4th South Lancashires (a pioneer battalion) and the two skippers were castigated by Summers. Meanwhile Hastie and *Dinnaken* pressed on alone. The D Company War Diary states that 'orders were carried out as given as far as Flers where tank was hit, putting tail out of action. Lt Hastie decided to bring his tank back and on return journey was hit again which put his engine out of action.'

This wholly understates what *Dinnaken* achieved as does Hastie's own description of the attack recorded by the BBC in 1963.[77] As the tank crossed no man's land, her steering gear was damaged by German artillery shells. Hastie therefore raised the trailing wheels off the ground and thereafter the driver, Pte Charles Wescomb, steered by braking the tracks. Hastie recalled in 1963 'that the need to use the brakes to steer the tank put pressure on the Daimler engine bearings and that the engine was in a sorry state.'[78] An RFC contact pilot observed a tank at the Switch Trench at Zero, fifteen minutes ahead of schedule, which can only have been *Dinnaken*. However, the tank's progress was thereafter very slow. The road was 'bad and much cut up by

71 The other two were John Garner and George Goodwin Cook – none of their bodies were identified and they are remembered at the Memorial to the Missing at Thiepval. See Pope, *FTC*, pp. 100-101.

72 In a HQ NZ Division unreferenced letter dated 17 September 1917, Maj. W.H. Hastings records 'L/Cpl Brooks was quite cool and seemed to think what had happened was nothing out of the ordinary'.

73 Thacker, who suffered from shell shock following the action, was evacuated to England. After three months at Aldershot, he trained at the Officer Cadet unit at Grove Park before being commissioned into the ASC on 4 March. Appointed as section commander of a transport company supporting a RA siege battery in the Middle East, Thacker drowned on 15 April 1917 after the ship in which he was travelling to Egypt was torpedoed. Pope, *FTC*, p. 103.

74 The Adanac British Cemetery, north of Courcelette, contains the remains of an unknown tank officer but this is unlikely to be Legge.

75 Their detailed orders are at Appendix XII. They were to leave their Starting Point at Z-35 [0545 hours] travelling 60 yards apart, in column of route, at a speed of 10 yards per minute.

76 Harry Sanders' letter to Liddell Hart, 1 September 1959 stated *Dolly* had travelled 800 yards. (Liddell Hart Archive 9/20/63 extracted by Trevor Pidgeon on 2 January 1991). This distance would place the two tanks in the area of the old German trench (Map ref 12a 7,4) southwest of Brown Street.

77 IWM catalogue number 4126. Hastie gives two descriptions of the event which vary slightly.

78 Undated letter by Wilfred Staddon (Liddell Hart collection LH 9/28/63 extracted by Trevor Pidgeon).

shellfire and crossed by three or four trenches.'[79] As *Dinnaken* drove on towards Flers village, the tank was stopped by an infantry runner, who asked Hastie to help clear up a machine-gun strongpoint. According to Gnr Roy Reiffer, Hastie stated that Flers was his objective and the tank drove on. [80] As *Dinnaken* did so, she was probably observed by Arnold in *Dracula* who was operating to his west.[81] As they travelled north, *Dinnaken's* starboard gun layer Gnr Percy Boult engaged one of the German observation balloons flying to the north of the village; the balloon descended and Boult claimed it as a direct hit.[82]

As *Dinnaken* got within 300 yards of Flers, Hastie did not bear northeast at the fork, but continued due north up the Flers Road. This was fortuitous as he arrived at the Second Objective (the Brown Line), where the Flers Trench protected the southern entrance to the village. Hastie was 25 minutes behind schedule at 0810 hours but the advance of 122nd Brigade had been halted at the barbed wire obstacle. Hastie therefore followed the procedures identified at Elveden in July 1916, using *Dinnaken's* weight to crush the wire and, having placed the tank astride the German trench, used his guns to enfilade the Bavarian defenders.[83]

By 0820 hours, 12th East Surreys had crossed the obstacle and started to clear the village. Reiffer recollected:

> As we came into the village, which was a heap of rubble with, in places, a few skeletons of houses still standing, Boult of the eagle eye spotted a couple of machine gunners at first floor level, who were firing at us. Four rounds of 6-pounder aimed at their only visible means of support, at almost point blank range, was enough to put them *hors de combat*.
>
> A few yards farther on, Lt Hastie stopped the tank and told us to strip to the waist on the starboard 6-pounder as we were approaching a crossroads in the centre of the village and 100 yards to our right [along the Rue de Gueudecourt] there was a battery of German field guns. As we crossed this road, we were to engage the enemy guns with the starboard 6-pounder.[84] We stripped to the waist and then the tank lumbered on up the main street of Flers.
>
> We were within 50 yards of the crossroads when we were stopped by a runner, who informed us that we were in our own barrage and we had orders to retire. The infantry had apparently run into stiff opposition and the second objection [Flers trench] had been abandoned, Lt Hastie turned us about and I think we all heaved a sigh of relief.

Dinnaken was seen by an RFC contact patrol at 0845 hours in the main street with a large number of troops following it. This report would form the basis for newspaper headlines: 'A tank is walking down the High Street of Flers with the British Army cheering behind.' *Dinnaken*

---

79   The road conditions were described in 41st Division's route briefing notes, copies of which survive in the NZ Division's 'Tanks' file (R25968529) held at the National Archives at Wellington.
80   Letter from Reiffer to Hastie dated 8 November 1963.
81   See Appendix XIII. Arnold does not give an exact timing; he was in the area by 0850 and no other tanks crossed the Flers trench before *Dinnaken*. *Dreadnought* entered the village later, after 0915 hours.
82   Accounts written by AHR Reiffer MM 14-16 September 1916 (TMA).
83   See paragraph 11 of the paper 'Handling the Heavy Section Machine-gun Corps' in Appendix V.
84   In fact, the German 77mm guns would *not* have been visible to *Dinnaken's* crew as they were hidden from view by the buildings in the village.

was observed at the church at 0925 hours; the tank's progress seems slow if you walk through the village today but it reflects the ferocity of the fighting.[85] Arriving at the village square, *Dinnaken's* crew destroyed a machine-gun post which was holding up the attack. This was observed by Second Lieutenant Teddy Winder of 12th East Surreys who recalled:

> We continued to Flers. It was there that we realised the true value of the tank. House-to-house fighting is always a beastly job, even though the houses are but shambles, and it was then that a tank came to the rescue. Suddenly, round a corner, guns firing, it came and, ambling up the main street, went straight for a machine gun nest in the cellar of what had been the village school, admirably sited on a Y-shaped corner. Right over the ruins it went, drew back and then went forward again. The garrison were scrambling out of the back of their nest running for their lives and Flers was taken.[86]

Dinnaken arrived at the village square at about 1000 hours, which was being bombarded by British artillery. Hastie sought directions to Gueudecourt but he was in a quandary as his orders were to support the final attack by 14th Division on Gueudecourt. However, his was the only tank of D Group to reach this position and he was concerned about the condition of *Dinnaken's* engine. At 1020 hours, the tank was still in the square by which time Box and Cox Trenches, the German field position to the north of the village, were occupied by 18th KRRC and 12th East Surreys. Hastie decided to return to Green Dump and, by 1100 hours, *Dinnaken* had reached the southern edge of the village. Here Hastie was asked to drop off a machine-gun to assist in the defence of the area. The Hotchkiss machine-guns were not, however, accompanied by ground mounting kits so this was impossible.

Hastie pushed on slowly south towards his Starting Point but, as the tank approached a bank called Rideau des Filoires on the left hand side of the Flers Road, he directed *Dinnaken* off the road, enabling other traffic to use the road should the engine fail. This it did, just as the tank reached the bank. According to Reiffer, Head's tank was already at The Rideau and, as *Dinnaken* was

Stuart Hastie. (TPA)

85   The villagers had been removed by the Germans in 1915; the church was being used as a first aid post.
86   *The Springbok*, December 1976 pp. 3 and 4. The village school was situated on the northern side of the village square, a position which provided the machine-gunners with a first-class view of the main street south towards the church and of the entrance to Abbey Road.

being targeted by enemy fire, the crew evacuated the tank and took cover in Head's machine.[87] *Dinnaken* remained at the location until the end of the month, being used for a while as a brigade headquarters, and was finally recovered to Green Dump on 1 October 1916.[88]

Despite the heavy fire directed at *Dinnaken* in Flers, only Gnr William Sugden was wounded, early in the action in the left hand, but he stuck to his post.[89] Hastie, who remained at Green Dump after the rest of D Company withdrew to the Loop on 28 September, was awarded the MC for his actions on 15 September. He deployed again on 18 October to take part in the attack on the Bayonet Trench – see below. Hastie had recommend his NCO, Cpl Edward Sheldon and Sugden for gallantry awards on 29 September but these were not granted. Reiffer was however awarded the Military Medal for his actions in clearing the hulk of *Dolly* on 23 September (see below). Boult, who was commissioned in 1917 and later fought with 9th Battalion Tank Corps, was awarded the MC and Bar; the first for an action on 1 October 1918 and the second on 4 November 1918; almost the last time tanks were in action.[90]

D7 broken down on 15 September 1916.
The crewmen can be identified by their leather helmets. (TMA)

---

87   This is contrary to Head's later citation for Cpl William McNichol and Gnr William Steer of his crewmen: 'When the car became ditched these two men worked from 7.30 a.m. till 8 p.m. continuing under heavy shell fire, digging and repairing and it is only due to the efforts of these two men that the car got clear.' Woods *D Company Correspondence Book*, Medal Citations dated 291930 September 1916.
88   Woods *D Company Correspondence Book*, Disposition of tanks dated 29 September 1916.
89   Sugden, who was evacuated for treatment of his wounds, returned to France with G Battalion, fought with them at Ypres and Cambrai, and was commissioned in September 1918. Pope, *FTC*, p. 107.
90   Pope, *FTC*, pp. 109–110.

When Arthur Arnold, commanding *Dracula*, arrived at his Starting Point on the North Road at 0600 hours, he reorganised the four tanks present from E and F Groups into pairs.[91] Bagshaw in *Duchess* (D15) would operate with Bond (D18) whilst Arnold in *Dracula* (D16) would work with Enoch (D7). The tanks then moved in a north-easterly direction towards Tea Lane, a British communication trench, which led across no man's land. Sadly, Enoch's tank had engine problems and the tank became stuck before reaching the British frontline. It was therefore Bagshaw who led the way, followed by Arnold then Bond, into action. One of *Duchess*' crew, Gnr Charles Bond, recorded that the tank was engaged by machine-gun fire well before they reached the German frontline.[92] The bullets smashed the glass observation prisms and entered between gaps in the armour.

As Bagshaw's tank crossed a German trench, Arnold saw *Duchess* hit by artillery fire and emit smoke.[93] *Duchess*' front hatches were also penetrated by fragments from high explosive shells. Bagshaw and LCpl Jung were wounded in the face ('cut to ribbons' according to Bond) and several other crewmen injured whilst in the tank. When *Duchess* stopped, Bagshaw waited for the infantry to pass and then ordered the crew to *Abandon Tank*. The Bavarians, however, continued to fire at *Duchess* and Gnr Cyril Coles was shot in the head after he left the tank.[94] Gnr Charles Hoban was killed shortly after whilst Gnr

Arthur Arnold. (Nel Gilbert)

91 The timings for *Dracula*'s action are taken from a letter written by Arnold to Summers on 19 September 1916 (see Appendix XIII). The remainder of the account is drawn from an article written by Arnold in early 1963. Both the letter and the article were published in the *Tank Magazine* Vol 45 May 1963 pp. 183-184, 200-201. Unfortunately, the two accounts vary regarding timings.

92 See Appendix XIII. Bond, who was wounded in the tank, contracted trench fever in October 1916. He was evacuated to England and recovered. Posted to Bovington, Bond joined G Battalion but later contracted pulmonary thrombosis. Discharged from the army as no longer being fit for service, Bond died on 10 September 1918. He was buried by his family at Wembdon Road Cemetery in Bridgwater where his grave is lovingly maintained. Bond's name was placed on the Bridgwater War Memorial and action is underway to add his name to the CWGC list of War Dead.

93 The exact location is in doubt: Miles (*OHGW*) p. 32 states the tank was hit at the Switch Trench; Pidgeon (*Tanks at Flers*, p. 106) states it was at Tea Support whilst the D Company Location Report of 29 September places *Duchess* at grid square S6 Central which is 350 yards north of the Switch Trench. *Duchess* was later recovered to the Green Dump on 1 October by a D Company salvage party.

94 I have analysed available information about the tank crew fatalities on 15 September and Cyril Coles was undoubtedly the first crewman to be killed that day. He and Hoban were buried near the tank but, after the Armistice, Coles' body was moved to the Bulls Road cemetery. See colour photograph No.

Tom 'Tippo' Wilson was fatally wounded – his leg almost being severed by bullets. He died of his wounds on 22 September at the Casualty Clearing Section at Heilly.

Arnold in *Dracula*, followed by Bond and tank crew D18, reached the Switch Trench ahead of the infantry and remained there until 0700 hours.[95] Driving north, Arnold observed a tank entering Flers, which was probably *Dinnaken*. Arnold states that he arrived at the Brown Line at 0745 hours, which was right on time, and reached his next objective, at Fort Trench, west of the church on the edge of the village by 0850 hours. He states that, ten minutes later, the NZ infantry entered the village and cleared it of Bavarians and had completed their entrenching one hour later. This is much earlier than other reports and may reflect an entry by the New Zealanders into the southwestern edge of the village. Arnold then became concerned that *Dracula* could be seen by German artillery observers from their balloons. He moved the tank behind some trees on the edge of village and stopped; the crew then refuelled their tank and had breakfast. Later, the crew fought a fire in *Dreadnought* which had reached the western edge of the village but had been hit by German artillery fire. Despite the two crews' efforts, *Dreadnought* was burnt out.

At 1045 hours, expecting to advance in accordance with his orders, Arnold consulted the local infantry commander about moving north of Abbey Road towards the Red Line but was told they had no instructions; this is probably because the NZ unit was not tasked with the final part of the attack. As a result, Arnold again moved *Dracula* to avoid being shelled by the Germans. Later, whilst again talking to the NZ commander, Arnold observed a large party of German soldiers enter a sunken road about two miles northwest of the village.[96] Although he wished to deal with this potential counter-attack, Arnold realised that the area was outside his boundary and it was too far for *Dracula* to reach in a timely fashion. *Dracula's* crew remained 'stood to' until 1430 hours when the NZ commander asked Arnold to deploy north and assist in breaking up an expected Bavarian counter-attack. The tank crossed the sunken section of Abbey Road and, using her portside Vickers machine-guns, engaged lines of advancing Bavarians at a range of 900 yards. Although Arnold was unable to estimate the Bavarian losses, the tank's action apparently checked the advance.

Whilst *Dracula* was patrolling the open ground north of the village, she was engaged by a German field gun which scored a near miss, so Arnold moved back to the village. At 1515 hours the serviceable tanks were ordered to withdraw. As she moved south, *Dracula* was joined by the tank crew D8 who had been supporting the New Zealanders on the left flank. En route to Green Dump, Arnold saw a wounded rifleman in front of *Dracula* and got out in order to move him to safety. Arnold was then hit in the knee by a bullet. Gnr Jacob Glaister took charge of *Dracula* and ordered the driver to pick up their skipper before continuing towards the Starting Point. *Dracula* was being targeted by German artillery fire, and was being very effectively bracketed, which confirmed Arnold's fears that the tanks would be destroyed. On the way south, *Dracula* joined up with Bond's tank. Having located a NZ medical officer, the wounded

---

16. Hoban's grave was lost and Wilson is buried at Heilly Station Cemetery, a few yards from Lt Col Henry Walmisley Dresser, CO 12 East Surreys, who died of his wounds on 17 September.

95   The timings, however, are at variance with other reports. See Appendix XIII.

96   This was probably along the line of the D74 road from Factory Corner to the Fiveways track junction which is sunken for part of its route.

Kiwi soldier was removed from *Dracula* and the three tanks continued south.[97] The shelling stopped, probably as the tanks crossed the ridge near the Flers Road and were lost to the sight of the balloon mounted observers, and they eventually reached Green Dump at 2000 hours. There,

Arnold was greeted by Summers who, having given the wounded skipper a large glass of whisky, sent him to the collocated Dressing Station from where he was evacuated. Arnold was later awarded the MC and Glaister the MM;[98] the first of two decorations he was to earn in a month.[99]

Leonard Bond. (TPA)

Other than Arnold, there were no casualties amongst *Dracula's* crew. Bond, in tank crew D18, was however suffering from splinter wounds and shell shock as was his NCO Cpl John Paul, an artillery shell having penetrated the tank. The D Company War Diary states that 'Bond's tank had reached the Flers Trench (the Brown Line) but was not able to proceed to the third and fourth objectives as the infantry in his sector were hung up.[100] The tank remained with the infantry until positions were consolidated, during which it was hit by an artillery shell putting the steering tail and one brake out of action.' There is little information about where D18 was operating but the citation for the MC awarded to Bond states his tank put 'a machine gun out of action capturing the team. Later, he went to the support of a party of infantry, and finally safely brought his tank out of action.'[101]

97   The Medical Officer of 1 Battalion NZ Rifle Brigade established a Regimental Aid Post at a point south-west of Flers. See *The NZ Medical Service in the Great War 1916-1918*, p.199 <http://nzetc. victoria.ac.nz/tm/scholarly/tei-WH1-Medi-t1-g1-t1-body-d9-d2.html> (accessed 8 November 2020).

98   Having recovered from his wound in the UK, Arnold was posted to Bovington and joined F Battalion, no doubt having been claimed by its new CO Frank Summers. Arnold was appointed a section commander and fought at Ypres where, after being shot in the chest, he was captured on 22 August 1917. He spent the rest of the war as a POW and later met his brother Clem who was captured on 8 August 1918 commanding the Whippet tank Musical Box. Both men survived the war; Arthur moved to South Africa where he died, aged 77, on 26 May 1977. Pope, *FTC*, pp. 146–147.

99   Glaister also won the Distinguished Conduct Medal at Eaucourt l'Abbaye. See below.

100 This may refer to the difficulties experienced in crossing the Blue Line on the western side of the village at around 1030 hours.

101 Bond recovered from his wounds and also joined F Battalion serving under Summers. He was wounded in the lung on 29 July 1917 after which he served at Bovington as an instructor. In 1920, he

As the tanks were withdrawing from Flers, and the depleted attacking brigades dealt with prisoners and casualties, HQ 41st Division sent its reserve (123rd Brigade) forward and they joined up with the New Zealanders. That afternoon and through the night, supported by 233 Company RE, the Londoners and the Kiwis improved the northern defences of the village ready to beat off German counter-attacks. Flers was secured; the attack by 41st Division was a total success.

Tank Effectiveness

Reginald Legge's crew were undoubtedly effective in destroying the machine-gun positions along the eastern edge of Flers and attacking the Saxon guns along the Bulls Road. It is difficult to gauge their effectiveness against Bavarian field artillery near the Gird Line owing to a lack of information. *Dinnaken* was also effective in clearing the obstacles for the infantry at the southern entrance to Flers, engaging German troops along the High Street and thereby enabling the East Surreys to clear the houses and, finally, destroying the machine-gun emplacement in the school. On the western edge of the village, *Dracula* engaged a series of targets as she led the advance towards the Abbey Road as did Bond and the D18 crew, successfully destroying machine-gun position. *Dracula* also assisted in deterring counter-attacks by the Germans in the afternoon by actively patrolling north of the village.

Capture of Western Flers

The final four tanks allocated to the attack on Flers, known as H Group, supported the NZ Division. The Kiwis only had an initial front of 800 yards compared with 1,200 yards for 41st Division on their right. They therefore only used two battalions for the initial assault, 2nd Otago (left) and 2nd Auckland (right) from 2nd NZ Infantry Brigade, whereas 41st Division used two brigades (four battalions) in line. The Kiwis had the advantage that their forming-up trenches were out of sight of the German artillery observers which limited the ability of the Bavarians to target their follow-on units. At Zero (0620 hours), the Kiwis quickly advanced; in fact, some elements of the Otago Battalion crossed the Starting Line 30 seconds early and took casualties from the protective creeping barrage. Both NZ battalions also took losses from Bavarian machine-guns, located in High Wood, which enfiladed the Crest and Switch Trenches. The two battalions pushed on, hardly pausing at the Crest Trench, which was smashed to pieces, and down the hill for 250 yards to their First Objective, Switch Trench. This trench was well defended but, after some hard fighting, was captured by 0653 hours. The Auckland and Otagos then consolidated, digging a new trench 70 yards north of the Switch Trench, in order to minimise casualties from the expected German artillery counter-attack bombardment.

The four tanks in H Group were, as previously described, late in deploying and crossed the British frontline at 0710 hours. They then joined up with the Kiwis at Switch Trench. Bown in D8 had been ordered to wait for an hour to deal with any opposition, his location at the Fork on

transferred to the Regular Army and served with Archie Holford-Walker and Billy Sampson in 10th AC Company on the North West Frontier. In 1928, he transferred to the Royal Indian Army Service Corps, serving as a major, and died of a pontine haemorrhage in 1942 near Karachi. Pope, *FTC*, pp. 150–152.

the North Road (see colour map 8, map square B4) giving the 6-pounder gun-layers a first class view across the battlefield – see colour photograph 11.[102] Nixon in *Dreadnought* then led Darby in *Dinkum* and Pearsall in *Diehard* to the east until they reached the German communications trench known as Fish Alley, which was also the boundary between the NZ and 41st divisions.

The 3rd NZ Rifle Brigade now took over the attack.[103] The tanks then followed Fish Alley north, moving more slowly than the advancing infantry, possibly because of the poor state of the ground. Shortly after 0915 hours, as *Dreadnought* reached the lower ground near the village of Flers, the tank was stopped by an infantry runner, Rifleman Joseph Dobson. He carried a message from Lt Charles Butcher who was commanding a company of 2nd Battalion NZ Rifle Brigade. Butcher had seen that German machine-guns were stopping the advance and sent Dobson to *Dreadnought* with the message 'Enemy machine guns appear to be holding up infantry to your right. Can you assist us in pushing forward?'[104] Entering the tank, Dobson guided *Dreadnought* to a farm building which housed the machine-guns. Rather than waste 6-pounder ammunition to destroy the guns, Nixon ordered his driver to use the tank's weight to crush the building, forcing twenty Bavarians to flee.[105] Nixon then directed his driver to the village, which *Dreadnought* entered, and the crew assisted the attacking infantry who were being targeted by snipers and machine guns.[106]

According to the *OHGW*, *Dreadnought* also assisted another tank to break through the German defences on the Blue Line west of Flers.[107] *Dreadnought* then came under artillery fire, possibly from the same guns which engaged Arnold. The tank was hit by a shell and the steering tail was damaged as she withdrew south. *Dreadnought* ditched on the edge of the village to the west of the church near Fort Trench and, as the crew tried to extract it, the tank caught fire. Despite the help from *Dracula*'s crew, see above, the flames could not be extinguished and *Dreadnought* was burnt out. Nixon later led his crew back to Green Dump, during which time Gnr William Debenham became detached from the party. He was initially reported as missing and later declared Killed in Action. On 29 September, Nixon recommended his tank NCO, Sgt John Vandenburgh, and Gnr Horace Allebone for the MM but neither were decorated.[108]

---

102 Bown's position is now the site of the NZ Memorial, from where you can see the north and western outskirts of the village as far as Factory Corner and the northern approaches to High Wood.

103 The nomenclature of these NZ formations can be confusing. The 3rd NZ Brigade consisted of four infantry battalions, all of whom were part of the NZ regiment known as the Rifle Brigade who based their traditions on the 95th Regiment of Foot (Rifles) formed in 1803.

104 The original message, which is first record of infantry-tank cooperation, is held in the TMA. Butcher wrote the message at 0915 hours.

105 Nixon clearly remembered the direction on dealing with machine-gun posts given during training at Elveden. See Appendix I, para 10.

106 *Hull Daily Mail* dated 30 November 1916 quoting one of *Dreadnought*'s crew, Gnr Harry Zimmerman. See Appendix XIII.

107 Miles, *OHGW*, p. 325. However, this is not supported by the Official NZ History, D Company's War Diary or by Zimmerman's Report. It probably refers to Bown's action – see below.

108 Nixon moved with D Company north of the Ancre in October, commanding a section until November 1916. He also commanded sections in D Battalion at Arras, Ypres and Cambrai and then a company in 4th Tank Battalion. He was awarded the MC in May 1918. Allebone received Cards of Honour, as a tank driver, on two occasions firstly at Arras in April 1917 and then at Poelcapelle in October 1917.

Dinkum's crew at Elveden:
Lionel Britt (standing second left), Leonard Haygarth (sitting far left), Harold Darby (sitting centre) and Horace Ellocott (standing rear right). (TMA)

The two remaining tanks of H Group, *Dinkum* commanded by Darby and *Diehard* commanded by Pearsall, were still in action.[109] Following Fish Alley, they reached Fat Trench which was the southernmost part of the Brown Line (Second Objective) at 1030 hours – almost two hours after they were due to arrive. However, their appearance was timely as 3rd NZ Rifle Brigade was held up by the barbed wire protecting the trench system. As *Dinkum* followed Fish Alley to the north heading for Flers Trench, she was hit by German artillery fire, the first shell shattering the tank's prisms and temporarily blinding both Darby and the driver LCpl Ernest Phillips.[110]

A second shell smashed two track plates, the blast also buckling the armour plating and smashing all the controls mounted on cast iron inside the tank.[111] *Dinkum* stopped dead and

He was killed in action, driving a D Battalion tank, at Flesquieres on 20 November 1917. Pope, *FTC*, pp. 15–164.

109 The identification of *Dinkum* is shown by a drawing of D10 by Gnr Horace Ellocott, one of her crew.

110 Phillips rebadged to the Tank Corps, was promoted corporal and was Mentioned in Despatches in December 1917. Serving with 1st Tank Battalion as a sergeant, he was promoted to Mechanical Staff Sergeant and awarded the Belgian Croix de Guerre in July 1918, probably for actions at Cambrai. He was killed in action during the attack on the Hindenburg Line on 29 September 1918. His body was never found and he is remembered on the Memorial to the Missing at Vis en Artois. Pope, *FTC*, p. 169.

111 Described by Gnr Robert Frost on the Westward Television programme 'Fear Naught' screened in 1968 –Pidgeon, *The Tanks at Flers*, p. 158.

Darby ordered his crew to take shelter in Fish Alley. Taking one of the tank's machine-guns (probably a Hotchkiss), the crew then supported the NZ infantry from the trench. Darby was later evacuated to England for treatment of his wounds and awarded the Military Cross.[112]

Diehard's skipper described the attack on Flers in a report dictated at the end of September 1916.[113] Pearsall does not mention the attack on the Brown Line, although he does say he crossed the Flers Line at 0945 hours. Both the *OHGW* and the History of the NZ Rifle Brigade state that *Diehard* reached the Flers Line and found 3rd Battalion NZ Rifle Brigade held up by the German barbed wire.[114] *Diehard* flattened the wire and engaged the Bavarian machine-guns, after which the infantry stormed the trench and captured 100 prisoners. The Bavarian Regimental Histories records the arrival of the tanks and the inability of their men to do anything about them.[115] Pearsall then moved *Diehard* eastwards into Flers village to undertake the final part of his orders.

Whilst this was underway, Bown and the D8 crew remained on the left flank of the

Ernest Phillips (John Phillips).

New Zealanders' advance. Leaving their position at the Fork, the Male tank followed North Road to the Starfish Line (the Second Objective) and then northeast towards the Abbey Road which linked Flers to Eaucourt l'Abbaye. En route, despite the damage to the steering tail, Bown and his crew put two machine-guns out of action. After this, a recently discovered report reveals that Bown played a key role in helping the NZ Rifle Brigade continue north. 'Our attacking troops were held up for some time in front of the Flers Line at M36a 0,6 by wire and enfilade machine gun fire. It is doubtful whether we should have succeeded in carrying this line except by re-bombardment, had it not been for the fortunate arrival of a tank which demolished the wire and placed itself astride the trench, raking it both ways. With this assistance, we

---

112 Having recovered from his wounds Darby joined F Battalion at Bovington under Summers. One of Inglis' section commanders, Darby commanded B Company 6th Light Tank Battalion until seriously wounded on the Bray Road on 22 August 1918. In 1939, he was again commissioned and served in Europe from 1944. He died aged 89 in 1978 at Hove. Pope, *FTC*, pp. 165–6.

113 See Appendix XIII. The report is not dated but, from its position in the Company Correspondence Book, it was written on either 29 or 30 September.

114 WS Austin, *The Official History of the New Zealand Rifle Brigade*, p.127 <http://nzetc.victoria.ac.nz// tm/scholarly/tei-WH1-NZRi-t1-body-d6-d2-d2.html> (accessed 9 November 2020).

115 Miles, *OHGW*, p. 325 fn. 1.

carried the trench.'[116] The grid reference, which is just south of the Flers trench, was just 100 yards to the right of D8's designated route. She then continued in a north-easterly direction, crossing the Flers Support Trench, to read the Third Objective (Blue Line) and then onto the Abbey Road reaching a point about halfway between Flers and the Fiveways crossroads. This enabled Bown to be in a position to protect 3rd NZ Rifle Brigade from any counter-attack from the north. As a result, the tank was targeted by artillery fire which smashed the tank's prisms and caused Bown and his driver Pte Bertram Young (ASC) to be temporarily blinded. Despite this, the tank remained in the area until ordered to withdraw at 1515 hours. Young then drove down the Abbey Road to the edge of Flers and joined *Dracula*, and later Bond with the D18 crew; the three tanks arrived at Green Dump at 2000 hours. Bown was subsequently awarded the MC,[117] and Young the MM 'for his actions which included driving for 10 hrs using only the brakes and gears.'[118]

D Company's War Diary states that, when *Diehard* reached the north of Flers, 'a New Zealand officer asked that tank might protect his flank. Pearsall took up this position and remained there till 7.45 pm. Tank was then asked to go forward to meet expected counter attack and remained forward till 6 am next day (16 Sept).' Trevor Pidgeon understood from this that *Diehard* stayed on the western side of the village although he mentions that a tank, seen by an RFC contact pilot to the northeast at 1330 hours, could have been Pearsall. He also mentions a report of a tank seeing seen 200 yards from the southern entrance to Gueudecourt between 1825 and 1845 hours which HQ Fourth Army did not believe; the RFC confirmed the report and stated that several other aircraft had seen the tank.[119] Pearsall's recently discovered report, included in Appendix XIII, reveals some of what actually happened:

> Moving northeast, I crossed Flers Support [trench] and the Abbey Road, reaching the third objective at 11.45 a.m. Passed on towards road north of Flers and, failing to locate enemy forces, returned to the north end of Flers where British infantry were digging and reported to Capt Jardine [of the] New Zealanders who was in charge there at 12.45 p.m. I was placed in reserve at 1.00 p.m. and I was sent to the east end of Flers village to protect exposed flank. At 1.20 p.m. the infantry were sent forward and I went with them to protect them whilst digging in. I remained on the infantry front line until 7.45 p.m. when I was sent forward a short distance out of the village to meet expected counter attack. I remained in this position until 6 a.m. on 16 Sept.

Diehard was the only operational tank to remain on the battlefield overnight, although its position in no man's land, between Flers and Gueudecourt, put its crew at risk of capture. The

116 HQ NZ Division report on Tank Effectiveness dated 23 Sep 1916. (R25968529) held at the National Archives at Wellington.
117 Bown was in action again on 1 October at Eaucourt l'Abbaye. See Chapter 8. Wounded on 7 October whilst carrying out a recce near Hebuterne, he served with F Battalion as a section commander until October 1917 when he was again injured. His brother Cyril was killed in action on 30 November 1917 whilst serving in H Battalion. Pope, *FTC*, pp. 155–156.
118 Young, who was transferred to the Tank Corps, was killed during the attack on Flesquieres on 20 November 1917. The location of his grave is unknown Pope, *FTC*, p. 157.
119 Pidgeon, *The Tanks at Flers*, p. 160.

Bavarians did not press home any counter-attacks in that area but, when they did the following morning, *Diehard* and the New Zealanders were waiting for them.

Tank Effectiveness

Although none of the tanks were of any benefit to the NZ Division during the initial attack on Crest and Switch Trenches, all were later to support attacks on the Second and Third Objectives. *Dreadnought* saved lives by demolishing the two storey building identified by Rifleman Joe Dobson and dispersing the machine-gunners within it. The crew later engaged Bavarian soldiers on the western edge of the village, before *Dreadnought* was damaged and subsequently knocked out by German indirect fire. Pearsall in *Diehard* and Darby in *Dinkum* also reached their second objectives, *Dinkum* being knocked out as she manoeuvred in support of the NZ Division whilst *Diehard* broke through the barbed wire that was preventing the Kiwis' advance. Similarly, Bown and the D8 crew broke down the barbed wire obstacle which protected the more northerly Flers Line, and both tanks remained in support of the units as they dug in, patrolling in no man's land and thereby deterring counter-attacks.

Flers and Guedecourt, 16 September 1916

Preparation

At 1500 hours on 15 September, Rawlinson gave orders that the Fourth Army advance would continue the next day with Zero at 0925 hours. The aim of the attacks in the Flers area was the same as the previous day; to enable the Cavalry Corps to push through and complete the enemy's defeat. 43rd Brigade (14th Division Reserve) was tasked to capture the village of Gueudecourt whilst 64th Brigade (21st Division) was to take the Gird Line trench system north of Flers.[120] At the same time, 1st NZ Infantry Brigade (the NZ's reserve) was to capture the German communications trench, known as Grove Alley, between the Flers Line and Gird Lines, and thus provide flank protection to the villages of Flers and Gueudecourt. In a separate action, albeit unsupported by tanks, 47th Division was to seize the spur to the southwest of Eaucourt l'Abbaye.[121]

At 2345 hours on 15 September, Summers received orders that five tanks were required to support the attacks on Gueudecourt and north of Flers, which was more than the company had available. Bell's was still ditched and Sellick's had water in its fuel; Enoch's engine was knocking badly which left only Huffam in *Dolly* and Court with the D14 crew fit for action. Pearsall and the D11 crew were still at Flers but Summers did not factor *Diehard* into his plan

---

120 Trevor Pidgeon (*The Tanks at Flers,* p. 180) states that the commander of 64th Brigade did not receive his orders until 2330 hours on 15 September. These orders would have been given at his divisional HQ at Bellevue Farm on the eastern edge of Albert, more than eight miles from where his brigade was located.

121 The only mobile tank in No. 4 Section of D Company, commanded by Robinson, was still en route back from High Wood. The D22 crew had taken 14 hours to extract the tank from the former British frontline after it ditched and it did not reach the Assembly Area, south of Bazentin-le-Petit Wood, until 16 September. See Chapter 8.

for the attack on Gueudecourt – presumably, he expected Pearsall to support the NZ attack. Summers was ordered to allocate two pairs of tanks: one to 43rd Brigade and the other to 64th Brigade. Both brigades were well to the south of Green Dump but it is likely that Summers spoke to their staff by telephone.[122] Faced with having to provide some protection for each element of the attack, Summers decided to allocate one tank to each brigade, Court supporting 43rd Brigade and Huffam supporting 64th Brigade.

Zero

Zero on 16 September was at 0925 hours. The weather was fine although cloudy.

Deployment

The infantry commenced moving forward at 0200 hours in the pouring rain, not long after their brigadiers had received their briefing and several hours before formal orders were issued. They had a five-mile approach march along tracks to Longueval and then across the torn-up battlefield, to their start points along the Bulls Road. 43rd Brigade was delayed and only reached the southern outskirts of Flers at first light. It was decided that their men should take shelter in the old German trenches along the old Brown Line. The attack plan was quickly revised so that their advance would start from there before Zero; the troops deploying to Bulls Road in time to get behind the creeping barrage. It was a recipe for disaster as the Germans still held the ground to the east of Flers; the machine-guns along Gas Alley and Point 91 had not been knocked out; there was no protection from their fire and the initial advance was 800 yards in broad daylight.[123] Fortunately, the men of 64th Brigade were able to reach their Starting Points, north of Flers, by marching through the village and were therefore screened from the sight of the Bavarians.

In the early hours of 16 September, Huffam and Court's tanks left their Starting Points, presumably somewhere near Delville Wood, and drove under the cover of darkness presumably straight up the Flers Road.[124] Huffam later recalled that his tank's arrival was not welcomed because the noise of the tanks could warn the enemy that an attack was forthcoming and the jumping-off locations would be bombarded.[125] Reporting to an Australian colonel at dawn, Huffam was told the attack had been cancelled which was apparently confirmed by Court.[126]

---

122 The brigades were located at the Pommern Redoubt, just north of the Mametz to Montauban Road, approximately two miles southwest of Green Dump. There was almost certainly communication between the two locations as Green Dump was the site of two NZ brigade headquarters.

123 It is possible that the artillery supporting 14th Division did target the known Bavarian machine-gun positions but I can find no record of this.

124 It is unlikely that the tanks would have been withdrawn to Green Dump after they have been dug out on 15 September. The crews had sufficient rations and they were behind the old British frontline, albeit not out of danger from harassing fire.

125 Fletcher. *Tanks and Trenches.* pp. 14-17.

126 This officer is likely to have been a New Zealander. Huffam's memory of events on 15/16 September, which was recorded by the BBC almost fifty years after the event, may not be completely accurate and they vary from the D Company War Diary.

However, Huffam was told by Summers, who had moved forward from Green Dump to Flers, that the attack would go ahead despite there only being two tanks available.

At 0600 hours, in the half-light before dawn, Pearsall withdrew *Diehard* back to the eastern outskirts of Flers. The tank then drove back to the western edge of the village to re-join the New Zealand Division. Pearsall may not have seen Court and Huffam's tanks which would been to his north on the higher ground. Huffam had been ordered to clear the Box and Cox practice trench system, and then drive in a north-easterly direction towards the junction of Grass Lane and the road which linked Gueudecourt to Eaucourt l'Abbaye.[127] Court was tasked to move in a roughly parallel direction, his objective being the western edge of Gueudecourt village behind the Gird Line system (see colour photograph 7). A single tank was seen by an RFC aircraft at 0645 hours on the road leading out of Flers towards the Bulls Road but it has not possible to determine whose tank this was.

1st New Zealand Brigade Advance

The defences to the northwest of Flers were attacked at 0900 hours by the Bavarians, a classic German counter-attack, down the road from Factory Corner. According to Stewart: 'Just prior to the 1st Wellington attack, an attempt by 2 enemy companies against our right flank was crushed by rifle fire and that of the 4 machine guns allotted to Wellington, together with the help of a tank which was on its way to cooperate with the troops on the right.'[128]

Diehard would have been visible to the German artillery observers, still located in balloons to the north of the village and, at 0905 hours, a German high explosive shell burst over the tank.[129] A small piece of shrapnel pierced the roof of the tank, wounding Gnr James Lee in the shoulder who refused to quit his post. The follow-on attack went ahead, as planned, at 0925 hours. 1st NZ Brigade, who had also moved up overnight, advanced northwest towards their objective at Grove Alley, the German communication trench which ran about 400 yards to the northwest of Flers. They secured and held it, their right flank being just short of the road to Factory Corner. According to the *OHGW*, Tank D11 advanced some 300 yards before being hit by an enemy shell.[130] Pearsall states that *Diehard* was knocked out at 0910 hours after a German shell burst underneath the tank, smashing its belly, the gear box and base of engine. Unable to manoeuvre, Pearsall removed his crew and took one machine-gun out of tank, setting it up in the trenches.[131] The crew remained on watch throughout the day whilst Pearsall returned to *Diehard* from time to time to use the Vickers machine-guns on Bavarians as they were observed.

At some point, *Diehard's* NCO LCpl Harry Nixon and Gnr Charles Leeming were also injured, the latter in the knee. At 1600 hours, having been ordered to return to Green Dump,

---

127 This was in fact still in British and New Zealand hands.

128 Stewart, *The New Zealand Division 1916-1919: A Popular History Based on Official Records*, p. 87.

129 It may also have been part of the supporting fire for the German counter-attack.

130 Miles, *OHGW*, p. 352. The exact final position location of *Diehard* also is in doubt. The Michelin Battlefield Guide for 1919 states it was at the northern entrance to the village south of Factory Corner; Trevor Pidgeon states it was at N31a 23.87 (*Tanks at Flers*, p. 181). Pearsall's report (Appendix XIII) places the tank at N31a.8.2 which is on the Bulls Road east of Flers. The D Company Tank Disposition Report also gives this location which probably results from a transposition error.

131 Probably a Hotchkiss machine-gun but fully in accordance with the training given to the crews at Elveden (see Appendix III).

Harry Nixon on commissioning. (Mike Nixon)

Pearsall secured *Diehard* and handed the tank over to the local commander. The crew then walked back three miles across the battlefield to Delville Wood and then on to the D Company base at Green Dump. By the time they returned, they had been in action for almost 48 hours. Nixon, Lee and Leeming were then admitted to the NZ Advanced Dressing Station, collocated at Green Dump, and sent down the medical evacuation chain. Lee returned to the Loop two days later and Leeming on 21 September; Nixon was evacuated to the UK and, after recovering, was commissioned into the Tank Corps in July 1917.[132] Pearsall was awarded the MC and Nixon the MM.[133] *Diehard's* ASC driver, Frank Still, was also awarded the MM, the citation stating he 'stuck to the wheel for 36 hours continuously and both in action and afterwards, when the car was blown up, he showed exceptional coolness.'

Attack on Gueudecourt

The attack by 43rd Brigade on Gueudecourt on 16 September failed. The Bavarians' machine-guns, located at Point 91 and along Gird Trench, decimated the infantry as they moved from their revised starting point towards Bulls Road, the planned start line, and again as they advanced towards Gueudecourt. The *OHGW* also states that the creeping barrage was again weak, possibly because the artillery was in poor condition, having been in use for over a month.[134]

D14's route was to the north of the Hog's Head trench system (D3) and on to the southwest approach of Gueudecourt. There was absolutely no ground cover and the tank was in full view of artillery observers positioned in balloons north of Flers. Court's tank overtook the attacking

---

132 Lee was again wounded by shrapnel, with two other gunners on 25 September, whilst trying to recover Story's original tank at Delville Wood. The same shell killed Gnr. Fred Horrocks who was buried near Green Dump. Woods' Correspondence Book memo dated 25 September 1916.

133 Pearsall served on with D Battalion until the end of 1917 when he was posted to 1st Tank Battalion. He commanded A Company, returning to 4th Battalion after the Armistice. Pearsall died of Spanish influenza on 19 March 1919, just six weeks after he was demobilised. Harry Nixon was presented with the MM at Aldershot by King George V on 25 July 1917. He served with 13th Battalion Tank Corps until he was gassed and crushed on 24 April 1918. He survived the war. In 1940, he was commissioned into the RAF, eventually relinquishing his commission in 1954. He died at Fairford in 1964. Pope, *FTC*, pp. 170-174 and subsequent information provided by his grandson, Mike Nixon.

134 Miles, *OHGW*, p. 561.

infantry and, as it made its way up the slope towards the Gird Line, his tank was 'smothered' by German artillery fire. Remarkably, the tank stopped as it reached the German's protective barbed wire entanglement which protected the Gird Line.[135] The tank NCO, Sgt Robert Pebody, and driver LCpl Lawrence Upton dismounted, possibly to determine how to cross the trench. The tank then suffered a direct hit from German heavy artillery and caught fire; all the crew were killed. Pebody and Upton's bodies were found close to the tank and were later buried; the bodies of the remaining six crewmen were left in the tank.[136]

The D Company War Diary records that, as *Dolly* reached the defensive location known Box and Cox (D3), Huffam was asked by the CO of a NZ battalion to clear Glebe Street which runs northeast from Cox and Box. The tank was targeted by German artillery and penetrated by shell fragments; her driver LCpl Arthur Archer was wounded. Huffam replaced him with another NCO, Harry Sanders and opened his hatch to confirm his location.[137] Huffam recalled *Dolly* was almost astride the German-held Flea Trench,[138] and that the two starboard Vickers gunners inflicted heavy casualties.[139]

As *Dolly* moved on, Huffam states he saw Court's tank stop and then almost immediately explode. *Dolly* drove down into the valley for a further 650 yards into Grass Lane where she was knocked out by German artillery fire. The two portside gunners were killed and Sanders lost both legs.[140] The tank was then subjected to further heavy enemy fire, which caused an explosion, and Huffam was knocked out. He woke to find himself lying on Sanders to whom he administered morphia and bandaged him with field dressings. Huffam left the tank to check the rest of the crew, sending two for help. After Sanders had got himself out of the tank, Huffam dragged him for 300 yards back across no man's land using his belt.[141] Only one of Dolly's crewman escaped injury but all eventually reached the British lines.[142]

---

135 Trevor Pidgeon places the tank hulk in the area of N26c 3,7 (*Tanks at Flers* map 12) and remains have been found at that location. The Tank Disposition Report for 29 September gives the location as N32b 4,9 (400 yards further southeast) which is incorrect.

136 All of the D14 crew were single except Lawrence Upton; he had married Bertha Smith, a 33-year-old teacher, on Sunday 27 August, the weekend before he deployed to France. Pope, *FTC*, pp. 119-121.

137 In the *Tanks at Flers* p. 183, Trevor Pidgeon confuses Harry Sanders with M2/104198 LCpl George Sanders, an ASC driver who was attached to HQ D Company as a MT driver. George Sanders' name does not appear in the Woods' list of crewmen, Woods' notebook, nor the list of casualties recorded in Woods' Correspondence Book. *Dolly*'s allocated ASC driver was M/194832 Pte. George Mullis; Woods' notebook shows Mullis did not go into action on 15 September.

138 Pidgeon's archive contains several undated and differing accounts of the action by Huffam.

139 Pidgeon believes that Huffam is mistaken as Flea Trench was held by the British. See Pidgeon, *Tanks at Flers*, p. 182. It is more likely to have been a German trench north of Flers, from where Huffam would have a clear view of the destruction of D14.

140 Gnrs Alfred Andrew and Ronald Chapple were reported as missing and later declared Killed in Action. Sanders was discharged from the army on 31 May 1917 but lived at his home in Birmingham until he was 74. Pope, *FTC*, pp. 116-117.

141 Sanders' unsigned manuscript dated 11 Sep 1957 found in Trevor Pidgeon's archive.

142 Archer suffered gunshot wounds to the skull, right shoulder and the left forearm. Discharged from the army on 28 Apr 1917, he found work in his home town of Stoke on Trent where he died, aged 43, of tuberculosis. Both Huffam and Gnr Reg Laverty were both hospitalised due to shell shock. Pope, *FTC*, p 117.

Aftermath

The attack on Gueudecourt once again failed; the destruction of the tanks by artillery being seen by the Germans as key. The War Diary of *5 Infantry Regiment, 4 Bavarian Division* records:

> With direct hits from our artillery, the tanks were neutralised. The attacking spirit of the British troops were thus broken and the main assault came to a halt. Under the heaviest of fire, from machine guns and artillery, the remainder of our battalions held out. Again, and again the enemy tried to advance and to break through the barrier we had set in front of him but again and again our men, standing up to fire, repelled him.[143]

D Company's losses in both tanks and men in the Central Area were significantly greater than those of C Company to their east. Ten tanks were knocked out or badly ditched; the remainder required repair and replacements amongst the crews. Of the 43 officers and men in No. 1 Section, one officer and six men were reported Missing in Action, two officers and four crewmen were wounded whilst the Section SNCO, Davies, reported as suffering from shell shock; he was however assigned to replace the second in command of the D3 crew. Of Mortimore's six tanks, only *Duke* was fit for action. Four of No. 2 Section's tanks were wrecked and never recovered, Enoch's tank engine needed major repairs,[144] and Bown's steering tail was damaged.[145] *Dolly* had lost all but two of its crew and the skipper and driver of *Dinkum* were wounded; the tank was irrecoverable as was *Diehard.* No. 3 Section's commander Sellick had to write to the relatives of every member of D14's crew as well as most of *Duchess* crews' next of kin. He also needed replacements for Arnold and Bond as well as a new NCO for D18; he did however have three tanks fit for tasking.

'On the evening of 16th September, the weather broke. Occasional showers fell on the 17th but by midnight, heavy rain set in, which continued for the rest of the night and the whole of the 18th dying away to fitful squalls on the 19th.'[146] As a result, the Germans were able to relieve their troops and improve their defences in preparation for the next attack. The weather made matters much worse for the attackers; trenches became ditches and, without duckboards, these soon were filled with ankle-deep and in some place, knee-high mud. Tracks, even in the rear areas, became difficult for the infantry to use and impossible for despatch riders. The work of stretcher bearers taking wounded men to safety, and ammunition and ration parties taking stores forward, was exhausting. The Bavarian machine-guns, still in place on the ground to the west and south of Gueudecourt made movement by day north of Delville Wood perilous whilst

---

143 Pidgeon, *Tanks at Flers* p. 183.
144 Enoch's original tank was not recovered to Green Dump until 29 September – see Woods' report to Summers of the same date, recorded in the D Company Correspondence Book.
145 The steering tails were highly vulnerable to shell fire and there were still insufficient armoured shields for the hydraulic rams. The workshops at the Loop ensured the tails of those to be used on 1 October at Eaucourt l'Abbaye were serviceable but the drivers now knew that they could steer their tanks using their track brakes. Tails were not fitted to subsequent Marks of British tanks.
146 Weston. *The New Zealand Division 1916-1919*, p. 89.

artillery harassing fire against track junctions and dead ground at night slowed movement even more.

At Green Dump, Woods reallocated the uninjured men to available vehicles, filling gaps with spare crewmen and shuffling officers and NCOs to man the eight operationally-fit tanks.[147] He also organised three composite crews in support of the Reserve Army. On 22 September, four of the eight tanks were sent to reinforce No. 4 Section in support of III Corps on the Western Flank.[148] The other four tanks were tasked to support a new attack on Gueudecourt as part of an Anglo–French advance which would start on 25 September. On 23 September, the crews of the ditched and damaged tanks started to salvage guns, ammunition and stores from the immobilised tanks, a task that continued until the end of the month. Field artillery was sent forward to Flers to destroy the hulk of D14 hulk as it was feared a German machine-gun at its position would disrupt the next attack on Gueudecourt. That afternoon, whilst a working party was removing *Dinnaken's* equipment, Hastie was asked to provide two men to clear the machine-guns from *Dolly*. She was located in no man's land on what is now Grass Lane, about 50 yards from a German trench and some 300 yards from the nearest British trench. The local commander wished to ensure that *Dolly's* Vickers machine-guns could not be used to disrupt the forthcoming attack. Hastie called for volunteers; Roy Reiffer from his own crew and Albert Smith from *Daredevil* were persuaded and they made their way towards Flers for an unrehearsed operation.[149]

Having been briefed by the local brigade commander, the two crewmen were stripped of all identifying equipment. They moved forward, with an infantry escort, to clear *Dolly* just after midnight when there would be a pause in the bombardment. The infantry took up protective positions whilst their officer led Reiffer and Smith towards the tank. It was a misty night, with the darkness punctuated by star shells, and silence was disrupted by machine-gun fire and occasional shelling. Smith opened the port sponson door whilst Reiffer opened the starboard; both men then entered the tank. Dolly's floor was covered with spent machine-gun bullets and scale from the overheated armour plate. The crewmen ensured the gun locks were removed and Smith also removed the skipper's Hotchkiss gun.[150] On leaving the tank, the crewmen were observed by the Bavarians who used star shells to illuminate the area and fired machine-guns at the hulk. The two crewmen went to ground and waited, eventually making their way unharmed back to the British lines; both were subsequently awarded Military Medals for their bravery.[151]

147 See D Company's Correspondence Book held at the Bovington Tank Museum.
148 Woods' Diary states these were commanded by Bell (D2), Enoch (D7), Bown (D16) and Wakley (D18). Their actions are described in Chapter 8.
149 Woods' notebook contains an undated account of the night reconnaissance of the abandoned tank.
150 This weapon was later sent to Huffam who was in hospital, presumably as a keepsake.
151 Smith served with D Battalion, then 4th Battalion eventually serving as a despatch rider for the battalion HQ. In September 1917 Reiffer became a driving instructor, under the command of Stuart Hastie, before joining the staff at Bovington. In 1920, he set up the Red Garage at Bovington; one of his regular customers being T.E. Lawrence, whom he served for 12 years until his fatal motorcycle accident. Reiffer later ran a garage in Wales before returning to Dorset and running a boarding house in Weymouth. He died in 1970, aged 74. Pope, *FTC*, pp. 111 and 112.

Fred Horrocks. (Bacup Natural History Society)

In the early hours of 25 September, Woods sent two of the composite crews to the Loop for transfer to the Reserve Army. Mortimore was instructed to allocate them to one Male and one Female tank and take them to Bradley. Later that morning, Woods submitted a reinforcement request to HQ HS MGC for eight officers and 59 other ranks as Battle Casualty Replacements. Woods also asked for an additional four subalterns to ensure that section commanders were not trying to control both their sections and a tank in action. This request was out of date by 1400 hours when one crewman was killed and three wounded by harassing fire while trying to extract Storey's original tank from Delville Wood. These four men were members of the third composite crew, identified in Woods' notebook, for use by the Reserve Army. The body of Gnr Fred Horrocks was bought back to Green Dump and buried close by whilst the injured men were treated at the NZ Advanced Dressing Station. After the war, Horrocks' body was moved to the Quarry Cemetery near Montauban.

Storey's crew, in a different Female tank 541, had been amongst the four sent that evening to Flers; they would be in action at Gueudecourt on 26 September with spectacular results. [152]

Capture of Guedecourt, 26 September 1916

Allied Plan

The renewed Fourth Army offensive, which was to be supported by the French Sixth Army on its Eastern Flank, was to capture the villages of Eaucourt l'Abbaye, Gueudecourt, Lesboeufs, Morval and Combles. The plan once again included using cavalry to exploit success by attacking rear German positions.[153] XIV Corps, on the right, had four divisions in the line whilst XV

---

152 Disposition of tanks 29 September 1916. See Woods 'Correspondence Book'.
153 Two brigades of 1 Indian Cavalry Division, located at Mametz, were to move east of Gueudecourt and advance upon Tilloy and Ligny Tilloy supported by III Corps. The cavalry was to cross a line between Lesboeufs and Gueudecourt by 1830 hours to give them 90 minutes before it became dark. Miles, *OHGW*, p. 372.

Corps in the centre would again use three divisions. Similarly, on their left, III Corps also had three divisions involved. 1st Division, which had replaced 47th Division, was to clear the Flers Line trenches north of High Wood; in the centre 50th Division was to take further objectives to the northeast of Martinpuich, whilst 23rd Division, which had replaced 15th Division was to clear 26th Avenue – this action being described in chapter 8.

Owing to the losses on 15 and 16 September, HQ Fourth Army gave specific instructions of the tanks' employment at the Corps conference on 19 September. 'Each Corps is to hold as many tanks as possible for the attack. They should, where possible, be placed in covered positions from which they should be brought up to assist in the capture of the villages of Morval, Lesboeufs and Gueudecourt after the troops have reached the Brown Line but they should not be moved across the open ground in daylight to attack the Green and Brown Lines.' Rawlinson informed Haig of this direction on 20 September who wrote in his diary that evening 'I have arranged for [Rawlinson] only to use tanks in the next attack where they can be hidden until the time for using them has come, and not to move them across the open in daylight for fear of them being knocked out, by a direct hit by enemy guns. Under these conditions, he can use them against Morval and Lesboeufs but not against Gueudecourt.'[154]

The Plan

On the right 21st Division would take Gueudecourt.[155] Their commander, Maj Gen David Campbell,[156] planned a three-stage attack using 64th Brigade on the right and 110th Brigade on the left supported by two tanks.[157] The brigades were to capture the Gird Line immediately in front of Gueudecourt, then take the village, after which the tanks were to destroy the German machine-gun positions, in the Gird Line and at Point 91, which had created such carnage on 15 and 16 September. In the centre of the attack, 55th Division were to take the Gird Line and the ground as far west as (but not including) Factory Corner – no tanks were allocated to support them. On the left of the attack, the NZ Division was to take Factory Corner and also Goose Alley, one of their original objectives on 15 September. One of the tanks allocated to 21st Division was also on call to the NZ Division and to deploy if available and urgently required.[158]

154 If Haig had made this decision independently of Rawlinson, he made it on incorrect grounds. Analysis of tank losses for 15–16 September shows that only *Dolphin* was definitely destroyed by direct fire. Every other tank knocked out by shellfire on those two days was struck by British or German indirect artillery.

155 Miles, *OHGW*, p. 380 footnote 2. The tanks were allocated to 110th Brigade.

156 Campbell was a successful amateur jockey as a young officer, riding *Soarer* to victory in the 1896 Grand National at Aintree.

157 This brigade had taken part in the abortive attack on Gueudecourt on 16 September.

158 Annex D to 21st Division G298 dated 22 September. The request for tank support was to be passed to HQ 110th Division which was at the Rideau des Filoires where *Dinnaken* was still located. OC Tanks was also tasked to place himself at the brigade headquarters. It is assumed that this was Summers rather than the section commanders who would have been forward with his tanks at Flers.

Zero

Zero was 1235 hours to conform to French tactics. The French did not attack at dawn, preferring to use daylight to ensure the maximum effectiveness of the pre-attack bombardment.

Preparation

The preliminary artillery bombardment commenced at 0700 hours on 24 September. The weather was dry but a persistent heavy mist curtailed planned counter-battery work. That day RFC aircraft bombed the villages of Le Sars, Warlencourt and Tilloy as well as German artillery positions and the railways in Lille and Douai area in order to delay the despatch of German reinforcements to the Somme. Although only two tanks were allocated, Summer sent all four available tanks to Flers. These four D Company tanks were commanded by Head, Nixon, Sellick and Storey.[159] They left Green Dump in the late afternoon on 24 September and drove to their Assembly Point at Flers Church.

HQ 21st Division orders stated that the tanks were to then move up as soon as it got dark and move then to a 'Position of Readiness' on the Bulls Road on the eastern edge of the village (N31a 7,1), with the tanks' escorts arriving at 2130 hours.[160] With Zero at 1235 hours the following day, this should have given the crews some opportunity to rest before the attack. However, 21st Division ordered that one of the tanks was to move under the cover of darkness to N26a 9,1 to be ready to be employed at Gueudecourt.[161] Despite Summers' decision to send all four available tanks forward to Flers, only Storey's tank was available to 21st Division and none to support the NZ Division.[162] One of Head's tracks broke en route to the Flers, Nixon's replacement tank was disabled by artillery fire and Nixon subsequently hit,[163] whilst *Duke* dropped out after Sellick was injured.[164]

At Zero, as the men of 64th Brigade attacked, they were immediately targeted by machine-gun fire from Point 91 as well as other positions along the German held parts of Gas Alley. The attack on Gueudecourt village failed although some elements of 110th Brigade secured the Gird Line west of Gueudecourt and the sunken part of Watling Street, north of the Bulls Road, establishing trench blocks and holding their gains overnight. At 1700 hours, HQ XV Corps ordered Campbell to use Storey's tank as part of an attack to be carried out that evening.

---

159 Woods' personal diary. Woods' Correspondence Book shows that the D4 crew were manning a replacement tank Female No. 541, his earlier Female tank No. 516 being extracted from Delville Wood on 26 September.

160 100th Brigade were ordered to provide 15 men as escorts for each tank, the task being to move the dead and wounded out of its way during the advance.

161 Author's note: The original 21st Division order (Annex D to G298 dated 22 September) was not carried out. Whilst it conformed to HQ Fourth Army's direction that the tanks should not move across open ground in daylight, it required one tank should locate itself overnight east of the Gird Line (which was still in enemy hands) on the western edge of Gueudecourt. It appears the order must have been cancelled at some stage

162 'The tank was damaged by shellfire in Gueudecourt before it could leave.' HQ NZ Division SG6/17 dated 30 September 1916.

163 Nixon quickly returned to duty and was supervising salvage work on 4 October near the Green Dump.

164 Sellick was hit by a shell fragment in the knee and evacuated to England. On recovery, he served in a variety of staff appointments as a tank engineer until September 1920. Pope, *FTC*, p. 129.

Campbell, recognising he had less than two hours to get his troops organised and into action before dusk, recommended to his corps headquarters that the attack be postponed and Horne agreed.

Tank action at Gueudecourt

At 0630 hours on 26 September, Storey's tank left the north-eastern edge of Flers and advanced along Pilgrims' Way, north of the Hog's Head, towards the southwest corner of Gueudecourt.[165] His tank was followed by two infantry companies and a large bombing party carrying 1,000 hand grenades. Reaching the Gird Line without incident, the Female tank turned right and drove south-eastwards following the trench, her machine-guns engaging the defenders. Those Bavarians, who took cover in dug-outs, were bombed out by the accompanying infantry. RFC aircraft also flew low over the trench lines, engaging the enemy as they streamed along the deep trenches. There was a slight delay when Storey reached Watling Street, but the driver managed to cross the sunken section by Bulls Road successfully and then pushed on to the southeast. The tank then turned north and drove towards Gueudecourt village to attack another position before it ran out of fuel.[166]

A part of one crewman's account of the action was published in his local newspaper.[167] Gnr Frederick Hobson, who was seriously injured by shrapnel,[168] had written to his parents stating that the Germans:

> …ran in front of us in hundreds and we were just taking another trench when the engine stopped for want of petrol. Well, they bombed us and pumped lead from machine guns at us but we slaughtered them alright. That was at 1030, when I was wounded, and the infantry came up and took the trench at 1100 with very slight losses.[169]
>
> When I was making my way back, I saw dead Bosches three and four dead in the trenches and the smell was terrible.

Tank Effectiveness

Despite the fact that the tank ran out of fuel, overall the D4 crew's action was a singular success. Eight Bavarian officers and 362 other ranks were captured as the Gird Line was taken. The exact numbers of dead and wounded are unknown but the *OHGW* quotes German records

---

165 Miles, *OHGW.* p. 383.
166 The D Company Correspondence Book includes a report which shows Storey's tank was found at N33a 2,7. This indicates that Storey drove east for 500 yards having successfully crossed the Gird Line. A salvage party managed to restart the tank on 29 September but it was then hit by artillery fire and one track was broken.
167 *Lancashire Evening Post* dated 6 October 1916. The Hobson family lived in Preston.
168 Hobson suffered 24 wounds to the back, mainly of a superficial nature, but with one serious injury in the lumbar region which resulted in his being discharged from the army in February 1918. In 1931, whilst living at Stockport, he married Dora Allinson but died aged 39 on 29 December 1932 as a result of heart failure. Pope, *FTC*, pp. 28 with subsequent research by the author and Susan Chifney.
169 Haig's Second Despatch on the Battle of the Somme, 23 December 1916. Hobson's account shows that the tank was in action for two hours after Flers Trench was cleared at 0830 hours.

which state *1/6th Bavarian Regiment* was annihilated in the action. British infantry losses were minimal with only two dead and three wounded. However, five of the tank crew were injured, Storey losing the sight in one eye. Storey was awarded the second Distinguished Service Order given to a tank skipper; it was, to quote the citation for the award, 'the best tank performance to date.'[170]

Attack on Bayonet Trench, 18 October 1916

Introduction

The fighting along the Fourth Army Front north of Flers continued into late September. Woods' diary for 26 September states, 'Head goes up to position for tomorrow' which indicates that there was a plan to provide support for the attack on the following morning. However, there is also an entry on 27 September which states 'Head withdrawn' – no reason is given. Despite the lack of tank support, 55th Division captured both trenches of the Gird Line, north of Gueudecourt, on 27 September with '...little loss. The enemy appeared to be demoralised and his dead were numerous.'[171] The NZ Division attack was also partially successful, allowing a trench to be dug from Goose Alley to the area near Factory Corner, but the capture of Goose Alley as far as the Gird Line did not take place despite desperate fighting.

An early morning attack was planned for 28 September, north of Factory Corner, using 1st NZ Brigade supported by Head in the Male tank No. 728. Head was tasked to rendezvous at Factory Corner by 0300 hours but, as he deployed, the tank was knocked out by a German shell within 20 yards of *Die Hard's* position. Remarkably, No. 728 was also disabled by a shell which exploded under the tank replicating Pearsall's loss on 16 September.[172] The failure of Head's tank to reach the rendezvous at Factory Corner, and a heavy German bombardment which prevented the NZ infantry reaching their assembly area, resulted in the attack being cancelled. HQ 2nd NZ Brigade had previously recommended that the bellies of tanks should be armoured to prevent a reoccurrence – a prescient suggestion but one which was never implemented.[173]

Preparations

On 29 September, Haig had issued orders for the advance into the German depth positions. He was trying to maximise gains within his limited resources, particularly of artillery ammunition and aircraft. With winter approaching, Haig was aiming to use favourable weather usually

---

170 Storey was the oldest tank skipper in 1916 at the age of 39. He had served as a trooper in the Imperial Yeomanry during the Second Boer War and as a private with 18th Battalion Royal Fusiliers in 1915. Having lost the sight in his right eye on 26 September, he was evacuated to England. When fit for action, he was posted to Bovington and joined F Battalion under Summers' command. On 31 July 1917, whilst commanding a section, Storey sustained an injury to left eye from enemy shell fragments and was again evacuated to England. He married a widow the following year and they later had a daughter. Storey died of lung cancer, aged 66, on 27 July 1943. Pope, *FTC*, pp. 89–90.

171 Miles, *OHGW*, p. 387.

172 Head's interview at the Tank Museum on 15 September 1982. Fletcher, *Tanks and Trenches*, p. 8.

173 ZBM 340 dated 24 September 1916.

Diehard (left) and Male No. 728 (right rear). (TMA)

experienced in early October to best effect. Although the first week was not good, rain stopped on the morning of 9 October and remained dry for two days, thereby allowing the relief of battle-weary divisions to take place only hindered by the unrelenting mud.

The focus for the C and D Company's activities now switched north of the River Ancre (see chapter 9). On 29 September, Summers with the majority of D Company and its surviving tanks, returned to the Loop. Sellick's and Storey's original tanks were brought in the next day and two crews, under Hastie and Pearsall, were formed at Green Dump. A small working party was also left behind under Nixon. Dumps started to be cleared the following day and the remaining tanks, which required major repairs, were handed over to 711 (MT) Company ASC.[174] *Duchess* and *Dinnaken* were brought in on 1 October; Storey's replacement tank was refuelled but not recovered when a track broke after it was hit by artillery fire. *Dinkum* also could not be moved as it had a broken track and the workshops did not have the capability to repair or replace it. Head was still on salvage duties at the Green Dump on 4 October.[175]

174 The engineering officer was Lt. Harold Strange who continued salvage operations for two months and was Mentioned in Despatches in May 1917. He transferred to the Heavy Branch MGC in January 1917 and posted to Bovington as an instructor. In 1919, he became a Chief Instructor, transferred to the RE and served on, with the Royal Tank Corps, until 1929.

175 Memo to Head timed 0540 hours seeking an update on the recovery of Storey's tank. See Woods' Correspondence Book.

On 13 October, Rawlinson issued orders to his corps commanders to attack all along the Fourth Army front. The attack was to start with a night attack; Rawlinson had proposed such an attack on 15 September but the plan had been rejected by Haig. This time, Rawlinson won through; the attack would take place on 18 October with Zero at 0340 hours. There would be only limited natural light that night as the moon would be in its last quarter. The main objective, Bayonet Trench, ran east to west behind the Gird Line about 900 yards north of the road linking Factory Corner to Eaucourt l'Abbaye (Map sheet 6). A series of meetings was held on 15 October, at which senior officers considered how the breakthrough could be achieved. It was attended by the new GOC XV Corps, JP du Cane,[176] and GOC 30th Division, Maj Gen JSM Shea whose formation had replaced the exhausted 41st Division. Inglis was also present.[177] It was decided that the attack would *not* include a direct attack up the Flers–Tilloy Road which was dominated by the Bavarians. Rather, 12th Division would take the ground to the east of the road. In the centre, gas was to be used to keep the defenders quiescent whilst, in the west, 21st Brigade (part of 30th Division), supported by three D Company tanks, would take the western parts of Bayonet Trench and Bite Trench.[178]

The night attack would take place without tanks, these being held back until after first light, and then committed if the initial assault failed. The tanks would operate in two groups, both deploying via the Fiveways junction (map square A1); two would travel northeast and start at the western end of Bayonet Trench; the third would travel northwest towards La Barcque Road and eliminate a German machine-gun post which was well forward of the Gird Line.

The next day the three skippers went forward to locate where they would be briefed (HQ 21st Brigade), the deployment route to the Fiveways crossroads 400 yards east of Eaucourt l'Abbaye and their individual start points.[179] The weather was clear and crisp although the ground was in poor condition. That afternoon, Inglis attended another Corps conference at which it was revealed that a new German trench had been identified. It was 150 yards to the north of Bayonet Trench and the embryo plan, agreed with GOC 21st Brigade (Brig Gen RW Morgan), had to be adjusted so that the attacks on the two trenches were sequential. It was also decided that one tank should support 12th Division.[180] Inglis may have been able to brief the three skippers on the changes but 30th Division's divisional orders were not signed until at 0345 hours on 17 October, just over 24 hours before Zero. The orders did not leave the divisional headquarters after 0815 hours that morning and HQ 21st Brigade did not receive them until the afternoon.

Modern battle procedure, in particular operation planning and extraction of orders, seems to be wholly opposite with what occurred in this case. According to 30th Division's account:

> Battalion orders were issued before brigade orders. Brigade orders were at Divisional Headquarters before divisional orders were issued. It was not possible to issue Divisional orders until after the conference on the afternoon of the 16th. Corps orders did not reach Divisional headquarters until the morning of the 18th [i.e., after Zero]. Had the

---

176 The former GOC, Henry Horne, had been selected for promotion and took command of First Army.
177 No. 1 Section of C Company returned to the Loop on 15 October and remained there until 1 December. Inglis was allocated a car for his personal transport – see Archard's diary and letters. (TMA)
178 The skippers were Hastie, Head and Pearsall.
179 This was located 300 yards south of Abbey Road to the west of Flers Church.
180 Pearsall was allocated to this task.

Division waited to write orders until after the receipt of Corps orders, the companies in the front line would have received no orders at all.[181]

Morgan directed that 21st Brigade should attack Bayonet Trench from Gird Trench, where it crossed the Le Barque Road, to a point 900 yards east, due north of Flers village. The direction to attack Bank Trench, as a follow-on attack, was not included – presumably, its existence was unknown at the time the orders were written. Indeed, it is possible that its existence was never shared with the battalions although it is more likely that battalion commanders were briefed by Brigade staff once the Divisional Orders were interpreted.

Battle preparations were further disrupted by a short notice bombardment of the German frontline by the British artillery for two hours on the afternoon of 17 October. This required the battalions in the line to leave their forward position as the bombardment would result in a counter-bombardment by the Bavarians.[182] Morgan succeeded in getting the bombardment reduced from three to two hours, warnings were issued to battalions and forward positions evacuated. However, as the infantry returned to the front, German artillery struck the British communications trenches creating casualties. Worse was to come; at 1800 hours it started to rain, gently at first but, as the evening progressed, it became torrential. The troops in the open had no protection, as they were dressed for the assault and they were soon soaked to the skin. Those in the trenches were caked with mud as were their weapons. The ground become a mud bath, shellholes quickly filling with slime, and the grassy areas become like moss.

The tank crews were fortunate in that they had shelter whilst in their vehicles. They had left the Loop on the afternoon of 17 October for their old base at Green Dump,[183] where Pearsall's tank broke down.[184] Hastie and Head moved forward to Flers, probably after dark, and the crews may have got some rest on their arrival. Hastie and Head reportedly left Flers at 0240 hours to travel 900 yards to Morgan's brigade headquarters where Inglis was located; however, they had not reached him by Zero.

Zero

Zero was at 0340 hours. The rain had stopped in the early hours of the morning but, until shortly before Zero, the moon was blanketed by thick cloud.

Pre-dawn attacks

The night attack went ahead as planned, just as the moon appeared. On the right hand side of the attack, 12th Division was initially successful with one company occupying the eastern end

---

181 Pidgeon, *Tanks at Flers*, p. 64.
182 Counter-bombardment of British lines was a standard German procedure, designed to target attacking units and their reinforcements.
183 This was a change from the initial plan which saw the tanks deploy to Flers on the night of 16/17 October and then remain in the village during daylight hours. The orders must have been amended, possibly because such a plan was unachievable. Pidgeon, *Tanks on the Somme* (Barnsley: Pen and Sword, 2010) p. 69 fn. 2.
184 Pidgeon, *Tanks on the Somme*, p. 65.

of Bayonet Trench; they were however bombed out. To the left, 21st Brigade advanced across the heavily water-logged no man's land which was between 65 and 180 yards wide. They were however spotted by the Bavarians who stopped part of the initial advance with grenades. 21st Brigade reformed and continued the attack, one group reaching Bite Trench. Some troops lost direction in the dark and moved northwest away from their objective. Others were stopped by uncut barbed wire defences and machine-guns in the German strongpoint known as the Maze. Some who did reach Bayonet Trench were unwilling to enter it and were then forced back to their own lines by German fire.

Tank Action at Bayonet Trench

Morgan received news that the first assault had failed at 0416 hours. He ordered Inglis to bring the tanks forward so that they could support a follow-on attack. Morgan planned that the pair would reach the British frontline at 0530 hours and the attack should recommence on its arrival. However, Head's tank did not arrive at HQ 21st Brigade until 0630 hours. After being briefed by Morgan, Head took 30 minutes to return to his tank and then paused for 20 minutes. The reasons for this delay are unknown; Pidgeon believes it possible that Head was waiting for Hastie to arrive so that they could travel together, alternatively there may been some mechanical problem with his tank. A third (and in my view most likely) explanation is that Head's new orders were so at variance with those he had originally received, he had to rebrief his crew as well as trying to sort out the new route on his maps.

Head drove the 850 yards to the Fiveways junction, and then north for a further 600 yards to the German frontline arriving at 0804 hours, a speed of less than one mph which confirms the poor ground conditions. There is no record of the Start Point of his attack but the tank's arrival caused the Bavarians to withdraw along the Gird Line and their communication trenches to the Gird Support Line. The tank remained at its initial position for 20 minutes, engaging the Bavarian positions and causing over 50 casualties. The tank's 6-pounder gunners also identified and destroyed a German machine-gun position in the Gird Line. After 20 minutes, Head got out of his tank and signalled to the British infantry to come forward and take control of the newly cleared position. However, there were few surviving officers and their men were so exhausted that no one responded and an extremely useful opportunity was lost. Head then got back into his tank, crossed the Gird Line and followed it northwest for another 500 yards, driving the Germans before him and eventually reaching the road to La Barque. According to the 21st Brigade War Diary, Head waited for ten minutes, signalling the infantry to come forward, before turning southwest and following the road toward Eaucourt l'Abbaye, to assist units operating to the west of 21st Brigade. Having achieved all he could, Head's tank then turned southeast and made its way back to the brigade headquarters arriving at 1000 hours.

Meantime, Hastie had left Flers but did not pass HQ 21st Brigade until 0840 hours. Here the story gets confused. According to the 30th Division account, Hastie was to move to the same location from which Head started his attack but move eastwards and then subdue the Maze, to the northwest, in order to allow the infantry to advance. Knowing that Hastie was on his way, Morgan gave orders for the attack to be supported by 19th Manchesters, who were in reserve, and sent his brigade major forward at 1030 hours to see that orders were carried out. Hastie never reached the Starting Point, becoming stuck in mud south of the Gird Line some 300 yards southeast of the location specified by Morgan.[185] Hastie's failure to get to the Start Point resulted in the attack being cancelled with the blame for the failure to take the Bayonet Trench being placed on the tanks.

It appears that the brigade major checked the map in Hastie's possession and the orders which he was following, which did not agree with those given to Inglis at HQ 21 Brigade. Trevor Pidgeon comments that Inglis, who was an experienced and decorated infantry officer, may have had good reason to change the orders given to him by Morgan.[186] These could have been explained in a report, written by Inglis, which is mentioned as an appendix in C Company's War Diary on 23 October. The reference has however been struck through and the report is not amongst Holford-Walker's papers held by the National Army Museum. Nor is there any reference to Inglis in 30th Division's report. Some might suggest there may have been an attempt to whitewash the tanks but I wonder if there is another, simpler explanation. It is possible that the map and orders in Hastie's possession related to the original attack plan and that, by not stopping at the brigade headquarters to make up lost time and thereby not meeting up with Inglis, Hastie did not receive the revised orders. We shall of course never know.

Tank Effectiveness

As for Head's successes, these were acknowledged. Haig's diary for 18 October concludes with the following entry: 'Results of the attack by Fourth Army at 3.45 a.m. were meagre. A tank moved out along the German trenches, demoralised and killed a good few many Germans without the infantry taking advantage of it. The tank returned safely.' The Official History mentions the tank's action positively although Head is not named.[187] He was awarded the Military Cross, the citation stating he '...handled his Tank with great courage and skill, remaining out for over an hour under heavy fire, and accounting for many of the enemy.' The award, when published, was celebrated at Head's old school in Bournemouth; the boys were granted an extra half day's holiday on 15 February 1917.[188]

Aftermath

The Bayonet Trench attack was the last in which tanks took part in the Central Area. Fighting would however continue for a further month as Fourth and Fifth Armies tried to reach Bapaume. As it was, the ground conditions were such that the troops became exhausted and it was virtually impossible to make progress. What few tanks remained fit were sent north of the River Ancre, where the Poor Bloody Infantry and their supporting artillery engaged in a ghastly failure to make progress. The weather won the battle but the level of human casualties and losses in material suffered by the Germans forced the *Oberste Heeresleitung* consider how to cope with

---

185 Given that Hastie's tank particulars are unknown, it is impossible to say whether it was eventually recovered. It must have been a very weary crew which made the five mile walk to back to Green Dump and thence on their base at the Loop railhead. The attacking infantry would have had even further to reach warmth and shelter.

186 Pidgeon, *Tanks on the Somme*, p. 63.

187 Miles, *OHGW*, p. 446.

188 *The Bournemouthian* April 1917. See Pope, *FTC*, pp. 91 to 94.

ascendant Allied armies who had driven through their well-constructed defences. Their answer was to build a new defensive line, known as the *Siegfriedstellung*, about 15 miles to the northeast and withdrew to it in the spring. It became known by the British as the Hindenburg Line.

Visiting the Battlefields

The best place to start your tour of the Central Area is at Delville Wood, near the South African Memorial, to the east of Longueval. There is an off-road car park, alongside a small information centre which includes lavatories – these are the only public conveniences in the area. The Rue de Ginchy, which runs alongside the southern edge of the wood, is generally free of traffic but it is unwise to park on the verge.

Stand on the verge, with your back to the information centre. Mortimore states that he arrived at South Street, a trench which ran along the Rue de Ginchy, at 0230 hours on 15 September and then set off for the Starting Point at 0445 hours. *Daredevil's* starting point is to your left at the southeast corner of the wood. Walk along the wood edge, following the Rue de Ginchy, then bear left by the water tower and follow the wood edge for 250 yards.

You are now standing in the area where Hop Alley met the edge of the wood; *Daredevil* arrived here at 0530 hours and then turned east (parallel to the Rue de Ginchy) for 250 yards. She then turned north following Beer Trench to Ale Alley which also ran parallel to Rue to Ginchy. *Daredevil* then drove along Ale Alley following it east, for an unspecified distance, before turning north and heading towards Flers. If you continue walking up the wood edge, you will come to a prominent corner; this is where Ale Alley met the wood line. Keep following the wood line, away from the road for about 500 yards to the next corner, which is the northeast corner of Delville Wood. You will easily see the village of Flers in front of you, about one mile away to your north. The infantry advanced from the wood edge to your left from 0620 hours onward; it is also where Head and Blowers started their drive towards the German frontline at Tea Support trench. By this time, *Daredevil* had stopped after a shell hit the starboard rear track sprocket. Mortimore does not record the location in his report but Woods' Correspondence Book states it as grid reference T7c Central which is 300 yards northeast of your current position.

Return to your car and then drive east, following the route you have just walked, toward Ginchy. Shortly after you enter the village, you will see a road entering from your right; as there is no priority sign, give way to any traffic and then bear left to the crossroads. Now turn left and drive up the Grand Rue, past the church, heading north. As you leave the village, you are following Pint Trench, a communications trench which linked the village to Tea Support which was the German frontline on 15 September. Just after the cemetery, there is an unmetalled track on your right which was the Guards Division and 14th Division boundary. Two hundred yards further up the road was the site of several machine-guns which fired across the field to your left at the advancing British infantry. You can see the outline of Delville Wood clearly; this was the Start Point for Blowers and Head. The concrete track on the left is close to the line of Ale Alley; *Daredevil* was hit about 200 yards further north.

As you pass under the powerlines, you are close to Tea Support Trench which was the German frontline. The place where Head's tank was hit by a shell is 300 yards to your left. As you cross over the next hill, you are on the line of Tatler Trench which linked to the Switch Trench and was the Green Line or First Objective for 14th Division. Blowers crossed this road on his way to Gueudecourt about 200 yards further on, that is, as you start to drive downhill. As you reach the left-hand bend, pull onto the track which goes off to your right. You are now on the Second Objective (Brown Line) for 14th Division and Flers village is half left (you can easily see the church spire). In 1916, a track went straight ahead; this was known as Fosse Way and formed the boundary between 41st Division on the left and 14th Division on the right. 14th Division's final objective, Gueudecourt, is half right ahead, on the horizon, albeit masked by a large wood.

Now drive into Flers village remembering the Bavarian infantry were in deep trenches along this road. On your right is the open ground across which Legge drove, clearing out the German machine-guns on the edge of the village. It is also where Blowers' tank was knocked out after *Dolphin* had returned from the outskirts of Gueudecourt. If you look left, you can see Delville Wood on the horizon and how the advancing British troops would have been sky-lined as they moved across the fields.

At the crossroads by the Calvary, stop. Be careful as you are crossing the main road from Longueval to Flers as the sightlines are normally poor. Drive for about 100 yards and park up. The track to your left and right was used by Arnold and Bond to attack the western edge of the village. You are also in vicinity of the machine-gun post destroyed by *Dreadnought*; sadly, its exact location is not recorded. Straight ahead, 900 yards across the fields, is where *Dinkum* was knocked out and where *Diehard* smashed through the wire which restarted the NZ Division's attack. If you walk up the track to your right for 400 yards, along the edge of the village, you will reach the point where *Dreadnought* caught fire. This is also the area where Arnold and the crew of *Dracula* had breakfast.

Returning to your car, drive back to the Calvary crossroads; *Dinnaken* smashed down the wire protecting the south entry to the village 100 yards to your right, before leading the East Surreys into the village. You should turn left and follow *Dinnaken's* route into the centre of Flers. It will only take two minutes to reach the church and then another minute to reach the village square. On 15 September, it took 90 minutes for Hastie and his crew to cover this route. Park up in the square by the memorial to 41st Division. To the left of the memorial is Rue de l'Abbaye, which was used by Head to get Bayonet Trench. The main road continues north to Factory Corner and, after five miles, reaches Bapaume. On the corner is the site of the school where the machine-gun post was flattened by *Dinnaken* after she arrived in the village square. To the right is the Rue de Gueudecourt, leading to the Bulls Road cemetery which you will visit later.

If you wish to see the routes taken by G Group, supporting the NZ Division, drive up the Rue de l'Abbaye to the T-junction, then turn left ignoring the Rue de Poirier and take the second turning on the left, which is unsigned. Drive for half a mile to the next turning on the left; this track junction is on the Brown Line. The track to the left, which is rough in parts, was used by D8 on 15 September. *Dinkum* was knocked out 200 yards to your left and D8 broke through the Flers Line about 250 yards to your right.

Now turn around and drive back towards Flers. You are now following *Diehard's* route towards Flers. When you reach the junction with Rue de l'Abbaye, carry straight on and follow the Rue de Tourrier to the point where Pearsall halted having reached his Third Objective – the junction with the D197. Turn left and drive north, away from the village, passing a small wood with high ground on your right; the Box and Cox position is on that high ground. Head's and Pearsall's tanks were knocked by German artillery after another 100 to 200 yards. The ground now becomes more open and, to the right, you will just see, on the horizon behind a wood line, the village of Gueudecourt. The road then enters a shallow S-bend in a slight dip; this is the point where the Red Line (Fourth Objective) crossed the road on 15 September.

Dinkum after her guns had been removed. (Simon Jones)

Turn left when you reach the next crossroads which was known as Factory Corner. This was the site of the original NZ Memorial which was a large wooden cross. Follow the D74 west for 1,200 yards, to the road bend and stop on the left-hand side. This is the Fiveways junction, which was used by Head and Hastie on 28 September as a waypoint. There are two tracks on the left; the one from southeast is the Abbey Road leading to Flers, which was used by Head and Hastie. On the other side of the road is a poor track leading going north. You can follow the track on foot to reach Bayonet Trench is 500 yards to the north, but you should **not** use a vehicle.

Now turn your car and follow the D74, which heads towards Gueudecourt. Do **not** turn right, at Factory Corner, but take the next junction. You are now on the track known as Grass Lane – drive to the AEF Burial Ground on your right and park up. Please visit the graves of Sgt Pebody (grave III J 12) and LCpl Upton (III E 2) who were the only D14 crewmen whose bodies were recovered. Now walk 300 yards south along Grass Lane. This is the area where *Dolly* was knocked out of 16 September and where Gnrs Chapple and Andrews were killed. It is also where Gnrs Reiffer and Smith won their Military Medals one week later. You cannot see Gird Line, where D14 was destroyed, from this point; it runs across the fields on the slope to your left (east).

Returning to your car, drive down Grass Lane, away from the Burial Ground, turn left at the T-junction and park up by the Bulls Road cemetery. I recommend that you get out of your car and walk up the hill east to the crest line. You are now on the Blue Line (Third Objective) where the Saxon artillery was located. If you look right (south), you see the open fields across which the tanks and infantry advanced from Delville Wood. *Dolphin* was hit 400 yards south of the road in the open ground – the site of so many deaths and injuries amongst 14th Division. If you look half left, you can see Gueudecourt – 500 yards across the open ground. Now follow the Bulls Road eastwards and you will enter the sunken element of Watling Street; Blowers used this to approach Gueudecourt on 15 September and Storey managed to cross it without difficulty eleven days later. The Saxon gun, which was crushed by *Dolphin* on 15 September, was positioned in the lane to your right. Gueudecourt is to your left and, if you walk north towards the village, you will reach the Gird Trench after 400 yards. This is where *Dolphin* turned around and the site of D6's destruction is another 100 yards further north.

Head back to Bulls Road cemetery to your car. Before departing, please visit the grave of Gnr Cyril Coles (III E 6) whose body was moved here after the Armistice. He was the first of the tank crewmen to die on 15 September but the others lie, unmarked, in the fields around you. To reach your starting point at Delville Wood, drive straight into Flers village and, having reached the 41st Division once more, drive south along the D197. Leaving the village at the Calvary Crossroads, carry straight on and you will notice the road starts to rise after 750 yards. As you pass under the power lines, there is a large bank in the field on the left hand side of the road. This is where *Dinnaken* reached on her way home about midday on 15 September and also where Head and the D3 crew arrived later than evening. As the road bears right, reaching the high ground with Delville Wood to your left, you are passing the Starting Points for C and D Groups.

You will next see the entry sign for Longueval. Turn right at the forked junction (signed for the New Zealand Memorial) and stop; this was the starting point for the twelve tanks of E, F and G Groups. Now follow the road up the hill; you are following North Road, the final part of the approach march for Nixon's section. As you pass the small Calvary, you will see a wood on the horizon to the left which is High Wood. You will also see, as you drive up the hill to the crest, how machine-guns in the wood enfiladed the New Zealand infantry as they attacked over the crest. Drive around the Memorial and park up; you are now at the site of Fork and the Switch Trench, the First Objective. It was here that Bown was ordered to remain for an hour to assist the advance. Here you will also find a magnificent view across the battlefield and an interpretation board which includes locations of the New Zealanders' attacks from 15–28 September.

That completes your short tour of the battlefields around Flers. If you wish to visit the site of D Company's HQ at Green Dump, drive back into Longueval and turn right at the major crossroads. Follow the D20 towards Bazentin, passing the memorial to 9th (Scottish) Division. After 450 yards you will see a small crossroads; turn left and then immediately right at the junction of the two unmetalled tracks. This was the route used by all D Company tanks, except *Dinnaken,* to reach their start points near Delville Wood. If you wish to visit Green Dump, walk 500 yards southeast to where the track bends; this is close to the site of D Company's base and the NZ Advanced Dressing Station. It was here that the wounded crews were bought after 15 and 16 September and also where Gnr Fred Horrocks was buried on 25 September. If you wish to see Fred Horrocks' final resting place, return to your car and drive west along the D20, past the Caterpillar Valley Military Cemetery to the next junction on your left (it is unsigned as you approach it but there is a direction sign to Montauban). Follow that road south, over the ridge, and down into the valley to the Quarry Military Cemetery. The track, which crosses the road north of the cemetery, was part of the route used by D Companies' tanks on 13–14 September as they deployed to the Green Dump. Fred's body was moved here during the battlefield clearances and is buried in grave II H 9 – We Remember Him Still!

8

Tank Actions on the Western Flank

Background

During August 1916, Fourth Army had slowly pushed the Germans north from the twin villages of Bazentin towards the Switch Line Trench south of Martinpuich (see map 8, map square E3). The Reserve Army had captured the German second line trenches (known as the OG Line) located 400 yards to the north of Pozières (A4–5). The Australians then held the ground against sustained German counter-attacks in the area of the Windmill (B4) on the Pozières to Le Sars road. They were relieved by the Canadian Corps on 2 September who were tasked to evict the Germans from Courcelette (C2) and capture the strong point at Mouquet Farm located 800 yards northwest of Pozières. III Corps were ordered to do the same at Martinpuich and complete the capture of High Wood (G4–5). This would open the way for the capture of Le Sars, Eaucourt l'Abbaye and the rear areas around Bapaume.

The Ground, German Defences and Dispositions

The ground around Courcelette and Martinpuich was open fields north of a ridge, 150 metres above sea level, running between High Wood and Pozières. Martinpuich was tucked into a valley and not easy to observe; Courcelette was similarly shielded from view albeit by a row of trees. The areas through which the trenches ran had been turned into a wasteland by the artillery bombardments of the previous two months. Some of the shellholes were over nine feet deep, many were over six feet deep and the smaller ones often overlapped. The buildings in Courcelette and Martinpuich were damaged but habitable with the cellars used as shelter for the German garrisons. As well as a series of trench lines which were generally well-hidden from view, the Germans had constructed two defensive positions to the east of Martinpuich known as Tangle South and Tangle North (E4) which provided flank protection both to the defenders in the village and those in High Wood. High Wood dominated the approaches to Martinpuich from the east as well as the south-western approaches to Flers.

High Wood had been the scene of almost non-stop fighting since the middle of July and was very heavily defended. The Germans had also fortified a sugar beet processing plant known as the Sugar Factory (C3) which dominated the Pozières to Le Sars road. There were German practice trenches to the north of Courcelette whilst a communication trench, known as 26th

Avenue (D2 to G1), linked Courcelette to the Flers Line trench system near Eaucourt l'Abbaye. Finally, Candy Trench (D3) linked Courcelette to Martinpuich where it was known as Factory Trench.

High Wood was defended by *23rd Bavarian Regiment* of *3rd Bavarian Division*. Martinpuich was defended by *17th Infantry Regiment* of *3rd Bavarian Division* whilst Courcelette was held by *210th, 211th* and *212th Regiments* of *45th Reserve Division*. The ground to the southwest of Courcelette was also defended by *210th Regiment* of *45th Reserve Division*.

Capture of Courcelette, Martinpuich and High Wood, 15 September 1916

Development and Summary of the Plan

The attack on the Western Flank was to be carried out by two corps from two armies. On the left was the Reserve Army, commanded by Gen Hubert Gough, who tasked the Canadian Corps under Lt Gen Julian Byng to take Courcelette. On the right, part of Fourth Army, was III Corps, still commanded by Lt Gen William Pulteney, which was tasked to take High Wood, Martinpuich and the ground to its north. As with the attacks on the Eastern Flank and the central area, infantry divisions, supported by creeping artillery barrages and tanks, would break through the second line of Bavarian defences, capture the villages of Courcelette and Martinpuich and, having finally taken High Wood, push north into the valleys which would then open the route between Martinpuich and Flers. This initial attack would be followed by further actions to take the defended locality at Eaucourt l'Abbaye and the village of Le Sars.

The Fourth Army plan for the break-in, developed by Rawlinson in August, was that Martinpuich would not be attacked on 15 September to avoid mass casualties. Rather, he directed that the village should be enveloped by III Corps and then pinched out as a follow-on operation.[1] By early September, Haig was convinced that the German troops' morale was so low that defenders would give way in the face of a sustained assault. His view was supported by Gough who proposed that Canadian Corps advance in a north-easterly direction beyond Courcelette whilst III Corps capture Martinpuich on 15 September. Rawlinson held to his original plan but, on 14 September having spoken once more to Gough, Haig ordered Rawlinson to capture Martinpuich the next day.

There were two objective lines for the Canadian Corps and three in the III Corps area. The First Objective (Green Line) for the Canadians ran across country from the track between Courcelette to Ovillers to the Sugar Factory (map squares 3A–C) then along Candy Trench to the southwestern edge of Martinpuich. The Second Objective was the village of Courcelette and its northern environs. The three objective lines for III Corps did not link up with those of the Canadians. The First Objective (Green Line) started 1,000 yards due east of the Pozières Windmill on the track from Martinpuich to Pozières. It then travelled in a north-easterly direction to the east of Martinpuich, turned south-easterly to exclude the Tangle North defensive position before travelling in an easterly direction, along Hook Trench, and onto the tip of High Wood. The Second Objective (Brown line) at Martinpuich ran through the southwestern edge of the village until it met up with the Canadian Green Line at Candy

---

1   This was usual practice and one recommended in Field Service Regulations.

Trench. East of Martinpuich, the Brown Line ran north of the Tangle North across country until it reached the Starfish Line in the 47th Division area. The Blue Line (Third Objective) started near Tangle North, following Martin Alley North until it reached the area of the Prue Line which it followed east into the 47th Division area until it reached the Cough Drop.

Allied Formations attacking on 15 September 1916

Table 1. Reserve Army

Objective	West of Courcelette	Courcelette
Opposing formations	*4th Guards* and *45th Reserve Divisions* *212th Reserve Regiment*	*45th Reserve Division* *211th Reserve Regiment* *210th Reserve Regiment*
Assaulting Division	3rd Canadian Division LJ Lipsett	2nd Canadian Division REW Turner
Assaulting Brigades	8th Canadian Brigade	4th Canadian Brigade (right) 6th Canadian Brigade (left)
Divisional Frontages	1,000 yards	1,600 yards
Distances to objectives		
1st Objective (Green Line)	300 yards	400 yards (left) 1,000 yards (right)
2nd Objective (Brown Line)	1,000 yards (central)	1,000 yards (central)
3rd Objective (Blue Line)	None	None
4th Objective (Red Line)	None	None
Tank Units	None	No. 1 Section C Company
Tanks	None	6 × Mark I (2 failed to start)
Field Artillery	196 × 18-pounder; 48 × 4.5-inch howitzer (244 in total)	
Howitzers	16 × 9.2-inch; 12 × 8-inch, 20 × 6-inch. (48 in total)	
Heavy Guns	16 × 60-pounder	
Corps and Commander	Canadian Corps – JHG Byng	

Table 2. Fourth Army

Objective	Martinpuich	East of Martinpuich	North of High Wood
Opposing formations	*3rd Bavarian Division* *17th Bavarian Regiment* reinforced by *24th Reserve Division*	*3rd Bavarian Division*	*3rd Bavarian Division* *23rd Bavarian Regiment*
Assaulting Division	15th (Scottish) Division FWN McCracken	50th (Northumbrian) Division PS Wilkinson	47th (2nd London) Division CStL Barter
Assaulting Brigades	45th and 46th Infantry brigades	149th and 150th Infantry brigades	140th and 141st Infantry brigades
Divisional Frontages	1,100 yards	1,200 yards	1,300 yards
Distances to objectives			
1st Objective (Green Line)	800 yards (central)	300 yards	650 yards
2nd Objective (Brown Line)	250 yards	750 yards	700 yards
3rd Objective (Blue Line)	None	450 yards	450 yards (west) – 950 yards (east)
4th Objective (Red Line)	None	None	None
Tank Units	No. 3 Section (-) D Company	No. 3 Section (-) D Company	Composite sub section
Tanks per Division	2 × Mark I (One knocked out during deployment)	2 × Mark I	4 × Mark I
Field Artillery	228 × 18-pounder, 64 ×.5-inch howitzer (292 in total)		
Howitzers	1 × 15-inch; 4 × 12-inch; 12 × 9.2-inch, 16 × 8-inch, 28 × 6-inch (61 in total)		
Heavy Guns	1 × 12-inch, 1 × 9.2-inch, 40 × 60-pounder, 80 x 4.7-inch (122 in total)		
Corps and Commander	III Corps – WP Pulteney		

The Infantry

The Canadian Corps plan, developed by Lt Gen Julian Byng, was that 2nd Canadian Division, using 4th and 6th Canadian Brigades, would capture the Sugar and Candy Trenches to the south and east of Courcelette, and the Sugar Factory (First Objective). 8th Canadian Brigade, which was part of 3rd Canadian Division, would protect the Western Flank from attacks by the German units in the northwest. 2nd Canadian Division's reserve, 5th Canadian Brigade, was tasked to exploit the capture of the Sugar Trench, and take Courcelette village, should the opportunity arise. Similarly, 7th Canadian Brigade (3rd Canadian Division's reserve) was to be prepared to capture the German trenches to the northwest of Courcelette should the conditions allow.

The capture of Martinpuich would be undertaken by 15th (Scottish) Division who would break through the German defences from the south and then fight their way northeast to Factory/Candy Trench and then form a protective flank. 50th (Northumbrian) Division would take the open country between Martinpuich and High Wood, reaching the Blue Line (E3–F3) south of Prue Trench. Finally, 47th Division would first clear High Wood and then capture the German trench lines in the valley to the north, also securing a line just south of Prue Trench (G3).

47th (2nd London) Division was a Territorial Force formation formed in 1908. It had mobilised in August 1914 and some units were sent independently to France during the winter of 1914. The bulk of the Division arrived in France in March 1915 and fought at the Battles of Aubers Ridge, Festubert, Loos and the subsequent Actions at the Hohenzollern Redoubt. It spent the winter of 1915–16 in the defensive lines around Loos. In the spring of 1916, 47th Division was badly pressed by the Germans at Vimy Ridge but held the position at a cost of more than 2,000 casualties. They remained in the line until the end of July when they moved to St Riquier,[2] rebuilt their units from drafts of troops and practised open warfare close to the Crecy battlefield. On 20 August 1916, 47th Division joined III Corps and, from 1 September, 140th and 141st brigades started rehearsing for the attack on High Wood. The Division moved into the British frontline, south of High Wood, on the night of 11–12 September.[3]

The 50th (Northumbrian) Division deployed to France in April 1915 and was immediately thrust into action during the Second Battle of Ypres. It held the line against several German assaults but did not take part in any offensives before it was sent to the Somme. 50th Division became the III Corps' Reserve formation in August and, on 9 and 10 September, two of its brigades took over part of the British line between 47th (2nd London) Division and 15th (Scottish) Division. Meanwhile, 161st Brigade, which was 50th Division's Reserve, undertook training to prepare for an exploitation task to the northeast of Martinpuich.[4]

The 15th (Scottish) Division had arrived in France in July 1915 and, on the opening day of the Battle of Loos, stormed two German defensive lines, captured the village of Loos and then took Hill 70. The Division then remained in the area for the next nine months. In July 1916, it moved south to join the Fourth Army and took over the III Corps trenches to the north of Bazentin on

---

2   This was the same training area used by the tanks in August–September 1916. See Chapter 5.
3   Alan Maude, *History of the 47th Division* (London: Amalgamated Press, 1922), Chapters 2–5.
4   Edward Wyrall, *History of the 50th Division 1914-1919* (Uckfield: N&MP facsimile, 2012) pp, 138–139.

8 August. 15th Division then took part in the systematic capture of German trenches between Bazentin and Martinpuich during the third week of August. Two of its brigades (45th and 46th Brigades) were then withdrawn from the frontline on 7 September and spent several days rehearsing the attack on Martinpuich.

The 2nd Canadian Division arrived in England in May 1915 and then completed pre-deployment training at Shorncliffe. It reached France in September 1915 and served in the Ypres Salient for nine months.[5] The Division arrived on the Somme in late August and took over the OG trenches from the Australians to the north of Pozières on the night of 11 and 12 September. 3rd Canadian Division, which had formed in France in December 1915, had fought alongside 2nd Canadian Division during the Battle of Mont Sorrel in early June 1916. In early September, the 2nd and 3rd Canadian Divisions took over the frontline to the north and west of Pozières, including facing Mouquet Farm. With 1st Canadian Division as its reserve, the Canadian Corps was to take part on their first major offensive on 15 September.[6]

The Artillery

The attacks on Martinpuich and High Wood were supported by III Corps' artillery group. These consisted of 292 artillery pieces (see table 2 above) with a further 60 heavy howitzers and 112 heavy guns allocated in support. The attacks by 2nd and 3rd Canadian Divisions were supported by three groups of heavy artillery (see table 1 above). 2nd Canadian Division was to receive close support by one hundred and fourteen 18-pounder guns and twenty-eight 4.5-inch howitzers whilst 3rd Canadian Divisions was allocated seventy-two 18-pounders and twenty 4.5-inch howitzers.

The III Corps artillery plan was similar for 15th and 50th divisions. It was, however, impossible to use the guns to best effect in High Wood as the Bavarian and British trenches were extremely close. Pulteney directed that the guns concentrate their fire on the northern part of High Wood and the tanks be used in close support to the infantry in the wood itself.[7] Despite Elles' comment at the III Corps Conference on 12 September (see chapter 5), this plan was implemented.

The preliminary British bombardment by Fourth Army started at 0600 hours on 12 September. The Reserve Army artillery preparation began at 1300 hours on 14 Sep 1916. 'From that hour until 3 o'clock in the morning of the 15th, the enemy's position was subjected to a deluge of high explosive. At 3 o'clock this fire diminished in intensity. At 4 o'clock it ceased abruptly. A sudden calm fell upon the opposing lines—a calm as full of menace in its sinister

---

5   2nd Canadian Division was commanded by Richard Turner who had been awarded the VC and the DSO during the Second Anglo-Boer War. He had not performed well as a brigade commander in April 1915, when the Germans used gas for the first time, nor when initially in command of 2nd Canadian Division at St Eloi twelve months later. He was, however, secure in his post as he retained the confidence of the Canadian government.

6   The 4th Canadian Division had formed in Great Britain in April 1916. It would soon see action, as part of British II Corps, on 21 October during an attack on Regina Trench which linked Le Sars to Stuff Redoubt.

7   'Notes on Tank Organisation and Equipment,' issued by GHQ on 16 August 1916 (see Appendix VI, Paper B, Paragraph 6) made it clear that the tanks could be severely damaged when operating in close woods.

suggestiveness, like the core of silence at the heart of the cyclone, as the devouring roar of the bombardment.'[8] The German counter-bombardment was typically ferocious and, by the next day, the Canadian Corps had suffered 97 officer and 2,724 other rank casualties.

At Zero on 15 September, the 18-pounders were to fire shrapnel 50 yards short of the German frontline trenches thus restricting the view of the defenders. One minute later, the barrage would lift onto the German positions and remain there for three minutes. After that, the barrage was to creep northeast 100 yards every three minutes until it reached the Canadian's First Objectives at Sugar and Candy Trenches. There it would stay for six minutes before moving on in three more lifts, every three minutes, to a final barrage line between Courcelette and Martinpuich. Whilst this was happening, the howitzers would deliver stationary barrages upon the Germans' rear areas.

Throughout the assault, 2nd Canadian Division would also be supported by 1st Canadian Motor Machine-Gun Brigade and 4th, 6th, and 9th Canadian Machine-Gun Companies. The Canadians were using Vickers medium machine-guns for the first time. Hitherto they had used the lighter Colt machine-gun but, rather than withdrawing all the Colts, two were issued to each infantry battalion in addition to the newly-issued fourteen Lewis guns. The belt-fed Colt provided a much better rate of fire than the Lewis which used drum magazines and the fire of the Colts was probably key to the breakup of a German counter-attack on the afternoon of 15 September.[9]

The Tanks

No. 1 Section of C Company, commanded by Inglis, was tasked to support 2nd Canadian Division; each of its two assaulting brigades were allocated three tanks.[10] The left or Western detachment, supporting 6th Canadian Brigade, was allocated one Male tank and two Females. Male tank No. 709, known as *Champagne*, was commanded by Lt 'Mick' Wheeler with the C1 crew. C2 crew manned the Female tank No. 522 *Cognac*, under Lt Will Bluemel, whilst the C6 crew in Female tank No. 504 *Cordon Rouge* was commanded by 2Lt John Allan. Their orders were to follow the line of the Sugar Trench in a north-easterly direction, one Female tank to the south of the trench and the other to the north, to a point due north of the Sugar Factory. Their task was to cover the left flank of the advancing infantry and to assist with the mopping up.

The right or Eastern detachment, supporting 4th Canadian Brigade, also consisted of three tanks. The two Male tanks, No. 721 *Creme de Menthe* commanded by Inglis and No. 701 *Chartreuse* commanded by 2Lt Stanley Clark, were grouped with one Female tank, No. 504 *Chablis*, commanded by 2Lt Geordie Campbell. These tanks were to follow the infantry along the line of the Pozières to Le Sars road, one tank by the road and one tank 30 yards to the left

---

8   G.D. Roberts, *Canada in Flanders: The Official Story of the Canadian Expeditionary Force (CEF) Vol. III,* (Hodder & Stoughton, 1918), Chapter 4 <https://www.gutenberg.org/files/46114/46114-h/46114-h.htm> (accessed 1 February 2021).

9   This weapon was air cooled, making the Colt more portable than the Vickers. The air cooling however made it less effective for sustained fire tasks such as barrage firing.

10   No tanks were allocated to 3rd Canadian Division as the section's spare, a Male known known as *Cupid*, was held in reserve.

and right. Once the artillery barrage lifted from the First Objective at 0703 hours, one Male tank was to aid the attack on the Sugar Factory whilst the other two were to follow Candy Trench (D3) southeast into Martinpuich and neutralise machine-guns in that village. The tanks would then withdraw to their Rallying Point at the Pozières Windmill.

Initially, No. 4 Section D Company were to support the attack on Martinpuich using all six tanks using three separate routes. When Pulteney informed Rawlinson of this on 10 September, the Fourth Army Commander replied: 'You will have to put your tanks right in the village in front of your infantry, they will have to start very early as the infantry will move faster than they will.'[11] On 13 September, the section commander Capt George Mann was ordered to detach two tanks to 47th Division in support of the attack in High Wood. Of the other four, two were allocated to 15th Division and two to 50th Division. Mann, who also commanded crew D23 in the Female tank No. 528,[12] was tasked to support 46th Infantry Brigade with 2Lt Harry Drader and the D20 crew in the Male tank No. 744 known as *Daphne*, their objective being the southwest approaches to Martinpuich. The remaining two crews, D24 commanded by Lt Walter Stones in Male tank No. 751 and D25 commanded by Second Lieutenant Edward Colle in a Female tank No. 511,[13] were allocated to 150th Brigade which was ordered to capture the high ground to the east of Martinpuich. The transfer of the two tanks to support 47th Division meant that no tanks were available to support 149th Brigade who were to capture the ground northwest of High Wood as far as Prue Trench.

Pulteney's requirement for four tanks, to support 47th Division's attack on High Wood, was achieved by using two reserve tanks: one each from C and D Company plus the two remaining from Mann's section. These tanks were formed into a scratch sub-section organised on 13 September. The three tanks from D Company were the Female tank No. 512 named *Delphine*, manned by crew D21 under Lt Sandy Sharp; a Male tank No. 756 manned by crew D22 with their skipper Lt Eric Robinson; and D Company's reserve tank, the Female No. 548 commanded by 2Lt Billy Sampson.[14] His tank was named *Delilah* – one of the few circumstances where a tank's name can be clearly linked with the identity of its commander. Sharp and Robinson's Place of Assembly on 13 September was the same as Stones and Colle, south of the Bazentin-Le-Petit Wood. It is likely that Sampson moved there directly from the Loop rather than travelling via Green Dump. Orders for the fourth tank, provided by C Company, were given on 12 September but the tank, known as *Clan Ruthven* under 2Lt Morris Henderson, did not deploy from its base at the Briqueterie until 1130 hours on 14 September.

11   Pidgeon, *Tanks at Flers*, p. 118.
12   This tank broke down en route to its Place of Assembly at Contalmaison; it was replaced but the details of new vehicle are not recorded. Pidgeon, *Tanks at Flers*, p. 119.
13   Like Mann's tank, this vehicle broke down during the night of 13–14 September and had to be replaced; its details are also not recorded. D Company War Diary.
14   Sampson with three members of the Balloon Section and four spare crewmen formed the scratch D13 crew.

Allied Plans

According to the D Company War Diary, Sampson's orders were 'to proceed from High Alley S4c 6,2 to Flers Lane M29d 6,6.' This latter grid reference is where Flers Support Trench met the Drop Alley communications trench and the route would take *Delilah* across the broadest part of the devastated wood. Robinson was ordered to 'proceed from Anderson Trench S4c 8,0 to Flers Lane' whilst Sharp was ordered to 'proceed from S4c 7,0 to Flers Lane.' Robinson and Sharp would therefore start at the most southern point of High Wood and travel inside the wood to reach the Bavarian frontline one minute before Zero. There the pair would then remain for three minutes, firing on the defenders, after which they were to exit the wood and drive to their First Objective (the Green Line) just beyond the Switch Trench at 0652 hours. The tanks were then to drive to Brown Line, at the Starfish, by 0802 hours. They would cross into 141st Brigade's area and, joining up with Sampson and Henderson, all would attack the Cough Drop, just south of the Blue Line. Finally, they would then follow the Drop Alley, to their Third Objective (Blue Line) which was the junction of Flers Support Trench and Goose Alley. These orders were at variance with the III Corps' Operational Order of 12 September as they were amended in the 47th Divisional Order on 14 September which was not issued until 0100 hours on 15 September.[15] Given that the tanks were moving from their Point of Assembly to their Starting Points at this time, it is difficult to know what orders were eventually given to the tank commanders and if they were able to assimilate them.

To the west, Sampson would drive through the centre of High Wood whilst Henderson would operate to his left also driving through the wood. Sampson's original Starting Point was initially in a field just 200 yards from the southernmost corner of the wood but this was changed to the point where Glasgow Trench exited the wood. Henderson would start from the same place but drive 400 yards up the edge of the wood to the remains of a ride or break. He would then turn right into the wood and drive through it to the Bavarian frontline trench. Sampson was also tasked to reach the Bavarian frontline trench one minute before Zero. After remaining on the trench for three minutes, giving covering fire to 141st Brigade, *Delilah* would then drive through the wood to the Switch Trench (also the Green Line), which ran through the northern part of the wood, and then to the Starfish Line (their Second Objective or Brown Line) by 0745 hours and then, joining up with Robinson and Sharp, attack the Cough Drop and eventually reach the Blue Line at Flers Support.[16]

Pulteney's decision to send the tanks through High Wood created significant concern amongst the tank commanders. They understood that the tanks could be damaged by fallen trees, that their visibility was minimised and that the tank drivers would have extreme difficulty in getting their underpowered vehicles through such a heavily shelled place. Pulteney has attracted much criticism for his decision to insist on this, rather than to allow them to skirt it, and then support the infantry as they made their way across the open ground north of the wood. However, as his

15   Pidgeon, *Tanks at Flers*, p. 111 fn. 6.
16   Author's note: These orders are exceedingly complex and significantly more demanding than anything practiced at Elveden.

artillery could not neutralise the Bavarian frontline and support trenches, Pulteney probably felt he had no choice.[17]

Mann and Drader's orders were to leave their Starting Point at Pithie's Post (C3) at Z - 48 (0532 hours) and reach the German support trench, known as Tangle Trench, where it crossed the track from Pozières to Martinpuich by Z + three minutes (0623 hours). The tank's Second Objective was the Factory Line (known in the Canadians' sector as Candy Trench) which linked the southwest corner of Martinpuich to the Sugar Factory; this was only 250 yards north of Tangle Trench. The tanks were then to return to Contalmaison as soon as the infantry had secured the area. Overnight on 14–15 September, in light of Haig's direction, 15th Division were ordered to capture the whole village but these orders do not appear to have reached Drader.

Arthur Inglis and Jock at Wailly, October 1917. (TMA)

The orders for Inglis' section were distinctly different to those supporting Fourth Army. His section was to follow, not to advance ahead of, the infantry and suppress German defenders' fire. The Canadian infantry were to advance as closely as possible behind the artillery barrage, the tanks following to mop up. 2nd Canadian Division's orders stated that, if the tanks were unable to keep up with the infantry, the latter were not to wait for them.

17   Author's note: Pulteney may have been influenced by seeing an example of a tank felling a tree, an event which appears to have been common in demonstrations by tank crews for senior officers.

Deployment for Battle

According to Gnrs Victor Archard[18] of *Cognac* and Lionel McAdam[19] of *Crème de Menthe*, No. 1 Section of C Company left their base at 1900 hours on 14 September. Having driven to La Boisselle, the tanks then followed the old Roman Road towards Pozières, arriving at the dressing station at 2120 hours. Here they refuelled the tanks, a task which took two hours to complete as each petrol can had to be passed by hand, up to the roof of the tank and then poured into petrol tanks located within the horns of the tank, either side of the commander and driver's position. The task, undertaken in darkness, was made more difficult as the road was subjected to enemy harassing fire. After refuelling their tanks, the crews were given hot cocoa and biscuits which were, according to McAdam, 'most welcome.' McAdam also recorded, just as they were about to deploy, one of *Crème de Menthe's* crew was wounded so badly by a splinter that he could not take part in the action.[20]

Victor Archard. (Graham Archard)

The six tanks started to move forward at midnight, in two groups led by Canadian guides who followed white tapes, to their Starting Points. On the western edge of the battlefield, *Champagne* reached her Starting Point close to the boundary between 2nd and 3rd Canadian divisions, at 0200 hours. Whilst her crew waited the four hours until Zero, the tank's steering tail was damaged by artillery fire. One of *Cognac's* stub axles was also damaged as she moved forward but she

---

18   Archard's diary and letters (TMA). Victor was wounded on the opening day of the Battle of Arras (9 April 1917) and evacuated on SS *Donegal*. This ship was torpedoed as she made her way to Southampton. He recovered but was not sufficiently fit to return to active service. He became a gunnery instructor at Bovington until his discharge in June 1918. He returned to the teaching profession in Hampshire. Pope, *FTC*, pp. 228–229.

19   *The Motor* Magazine Aug 1919 (Toronto) pp. 27–50. Scanned extracts provided by the McAdam family. Lionel was wounded in January 1917, probably whilst undertaking salvage duties. On recovering, he was also posted to Bovington where he quickly joined F Battalion and returned to France as part of the Workshop Company (Lionel was an electrical engineer by trade). In January 1918, on the organisation of the Tank Corps repair system, he was posted to the Central Stores at Erin and then to No. 1 Tank Stores from March 1918 which was deployed to support forward tank battalions. Lionel returned to his home in Toronto when he was demobilised in May 1919 and granted a pension by the Canadian Government. Pope. *FTC*, pp 260–262.

20   The casualty was Gnr. Laurie Rowntree. See below.

reached her designated position, 500 yards to the southwest of *Champagne's* position, by 0200 hours. *Cordon Rouge's* skipper John Allen reported that, after very considerable difficulty, his tank did not join *Cognac* until 0415 hours. At their Starting Points, each tank was joined by a detachment of five Canadian infantrymen whose task was to remove any wounded men away from their tracks of the tanks as they advanced.

The right-hand group (Inglis' sub-section), whose deployment route was to the east of Pozières, were also subjected to artillery fire. They reached their rendezvous northeast of the village without difficulty but then *Chablis* and *Chartreuse* were damaged by shellfire. *Chartreuse's* steering gear was damaged and *Chablis'* tracks had become loose. Corp Charles Harrison and the ASC driver, Pte Daniel Cronin tightened the tracks, despite being under fire. The tank then halted about 170 yards from the Starting Point. *Crème de Menthe* was hit by shellfire on two occasions as she waited for four hours south of the ruins of the Pozières Windmill. The explosion caused the whole tank to be lifted onto her nose which, according to McAdam, shook the crew thoroughly. This shelling could well have been part of German barrage fired at 0300 hours in support of a trench raid on the trenches occupied by 4th Canadian Brigade. The raid, which was designed to capture Canadian prisoners and gain intelligence about their plans, was fiercely beaten off by the waiting troops.

To their east, south of Contalmaison, Mann and Drader had set out from HQ 46th Infantry Brigade by dusk on 14 September. Passing through the village, they followed the Martinpuich road for 1,000 yards as far as Contalmaison Villa and then drove north across the old OG Line towards their Starting Point at Pithie's Post. Mann's Post-Operational Report states that his tank was hit by an artillery shell which broke a track after he reached the Starting Point; however, a message received by HQ 15th Division at 0200 hours indicates that Mann's tank was damaged before reaching the position. Whatever the true story, *Daphne's* crew then prepared to go into action alone.

Stones and Colle's tanks left their Point of Assembly, south of Bazentin-le-Petit Wood, and drove eastwards to the five way junction north of Bazentin-le-Grand Wood. They then turned north and, following a recently repaired track, drove to the Bazentin-Le-Petit communal cemetery. They waited there, as ordered, alongside HQ 149th Infantry Brigade until 0320 hours. The tanks then followed the track north to the next junction and then north across country to their Starting Point at Swansea Trench (E4). This position was 250 yards behind the jumping-off trenches where 149th Brigade, to the east, and 150th Brigade to their west, were waiting for Zero.

All four tanks supporting 47th Division's attack at High Wood should have reached their Starting Point on time. It was a short journey from their Place of Assembly, from Bazentin-le-Grand, along the Longueval road east to Crucifix Corner.[21] They then turned northeast and followed the track which led directly to the southern corner of the wood. Sampson was in position by 0420 hours but the other three were later,[22] possibly because of the requirement for all the tank skippers to be briefed again after orders had been issued by 47th Division at 0100 hours.

21   Crucifix Corner is a T-junction (map reference 16a 4,9) where the road running north from Montauban meets the Contalmaison to Longueval Road (D20) approximately 1¼ miles west of Longueval.
22   They were seen travelling up the track at 0545 hours.

Zero

Zero was at 0620 hours; dawn was at 0622 and first light at 0549. There was an early morning mist over the ground at both Courcelette and Martinpuich. The weather was fine and slightly cooler than the previous few days.

Chartreuse ditched with *Chablis* immobilised to her rear. (TMA)

Final Moves

As *Chartreuse* approached the Pozières Windmill, the driver was unable to steer away from a large shellhole which was full of tree trunks. After the tank ditched, the crew worked for three and a half hours to extract it but the tank would not move as the engine had seized due to poor lubrication.[23] *Chablis* also did not cross the start line, despite the crew's earlier attempt to tighten the tracks, as the left-hand track had become so loose that it fell off before reaching the Windmill. Campbell therefore sent his crew to the rear and then joined the crew of *Crème de Menthe* replacing the wounded Gunner Rowntree.

---

23   Splash lubrication only worked if the vehicle remained level which was impossible owing to the shell holes across the battlefield. If the tank were tipped onto its side, as a result of becoming ditched, the oil did not reach all elements of the engine and it would seize.

Capture of Courcelette

The Canadian Corps' initial assault was successful due to their effective use of the creeping artillery barrage. The Canadian battalions quickly crossed no man's land and were on top of the German frontline positions before the Bavarians could man their defences. By 0700 hours, 4th Canadian Brigade reported it had occupied Candy Trench and had taken a substantial number of prisoners. *Crème de Menthe* followed the next wave of infantry forward, shrouded by mist, with her progress slowed by the overlapping shellholes and groups of surrendering Bavarians. The tank's presence, however, raised the spirits of Canadians whilst creating a degree of panic amongst some Germans who were in the forward positions. The machine-gunners however remained resolute and after the mist cleared, targeted *Crème de Menthe* as well as the accompanying infantry.

On the left, all three tanks supporting 6th Canadian Brigade crossed no man's land and reached the western end of the Sugar Trench which was their First Objective. Both *Champagne* and *Cognac* drove northeast, reaching the communications trench (known to the Canadians as McDonnell Trench) which was the boundary between 2nd and 3rd Canadian Divisions. When the tanks were about 100 yards beyond the First Objective, both drivers lost control due to steering problems and became ditched in the trench. *Champagne* stuck fast but, after a short while, *Cognac's* driver Pte Herbert Ledger managed to extract his tank. However, instead of following Sugar Trench towards the Factory as ordered, Ledger could not get the tank to turn eastwards. His skipper, Bluemel, was forced to follow the McDonnell Trench towards the southwestern edge of Courcelette. When *Cognac* reached the track junction on the outskirts of the village (map square C2), the tank again became stuck in the communications trench, this time 200 yards behind a German trench protecting Courcelette and more than 500 yards from the Canadian infantry in the recently captured Sugar Trench.

Champagne's hulk. (TMA)

Cordon Rouge, which was heavily shelled as she crossed no man's land, made her way along the Sugar Trench assisting the infantry on her way towards the Sugar Factory. The tank's gunners engaged the enemy as they advanced 'guided by a foot soldier who miraculously escaped a rain of fire now diverted from us toward the new arrival. On it came, a dragon spouting fire in all directions. The ground was pitted with thousands of shell holes, but the dragon dipped and rose and just came on relentlessly until it stood astride the trench. Some of the Germans fled but most of them stood rooted to the spot on which they stood; hands held high in surrender. We casually took over the trench and then proceeded on down the hill in the wake of our good friend. The tank then moved across to the Sugar Factory, which was resisting a very vigorous attack. Walls and emplacements were pushed aside or mounted and this redoubt was speedily reduced.'[24]

By 0740 hours, 6th Canadian Brigade had occupied Sugar Trench and having cleared the enemy dug-outs, prepared it for defence by reversing the parapets. They also started to establish two strongpoints equipped with Colt machine-guns: one between the Sugar Factory and Courcelette and a second to the west of the Pozières to Courcelette road. Inglis' report and McAdam's article both mention that they were delayed by German prisoners as they advanced. According to McAdam, *Crème de Menthe* and *Cordon Rouge* moved forward towards the Sugar Factory on parallel courses about 100 yards apart. The defenders of the Sugar Factory fought hard against 21st Battalion CEF whose mission was to capture the strong point. They had broken into the complex at 0655 hours and, after close quarter fighting, captured the position taking 125 prisoners.

There are conflicting reports as to whether *Crème de Menthe* was engaged in the action. 6th Canadian Brigade's after-action report stated that the tank did not arrive until 0750 hours but the original Canadian Official History says that the tank was of direct benefit to 21st Battalion CEF.[25] Inglis reported that the infantry were in the Factory as he arrived but that he used his Hotchkiss guns to good effect.[26] McAdam also stated that the 6-pounders were used against the Factory as they approached. Other contemporary Canadian accounts state that the tank used its weight to enter the Factory and destroyed machine-guns but this could have occurred after 21st Battalion CEF entered the Factory.

In the meantime, Allen ordered *Cordon Rouge* to the northwest to cut off Germans fleeing from the Sugar Factory towards Courcelette. Inglis later reported *Crème de Menthe* skirted the southern and eastern side of the factory before arriving at a trench where the Canadian infantry were consolidating (probably Candy Trench).[27] According to McAdam, *Crème de Menthe* then turned right and drove for 1,500 yards, patrolling the area. He does not specify their route but it is likely the tanks reached Gun Pit Trench (D3). A tank was reported to be at that location

24 HRN Clyne, *Vancouver's 29th: A Chronicle of the 29th In Flanders Fields* (Vancouver: Tobin's Tigers Association, 1964), pp. 20-21. Quoted by David Campbell, 'A Forgotten Victory: Courcelette, 15 September 1916', *Canadian Military History* 2007: Vol. 16: Issue 2, Article 4 <http://scholars.wlu.ca/cmh/vol16/iss2/4> (accessed 14 December 2020).

25 'The unexpectedly swift collapse of this stronghold of the Sugar Factory – which the enemy had thought to make impregnable – was hastened, no doubt, by the intervention of one of the "Tanks"'. Roberts, *Canada in Flanders Vol III*, Ch. 4.

26 Although *Crème de Menthe* was equipped with three Hotchkiss light machine-guns, Inglis was probably referring to the 6-pounder guns which were also designed by Hotchkiss.

27 See Inglis' contemporary report in Appendix XIII.

at about 0900 hours by a party of 20th Battalion CEF who captured two prisoners and two machine-guns.[28]

Cordon Rouge on the Albert Road. (TMA)

Once the Canadian infantry had consolidated their initial objectives, both *Cordon Rouge* and *Crème de Menthe* were sent to the rear. As they travelled to the Rallying Point at the Windmill, *Crème de Menthe* deployed an armoured telephone cable in order to provide communications between the newly gained positions and the old Canadian frontline. Regrettably, the cable drum, which was fitted to the back of the tank, was destroyed by artillery fire as *Crème de Menthe* approached its rallying point south of the Windmill.[29] One of *Crème de Menthe's* tracks was also damaged but both tanks successfully made their way back down to Albert Road to the tankodrome southeast of Aveluy.

Meanwhile the crews of *Champagne* and *Chablis* were still trying to extract their ditched tanks despite being bombarded by German artillery. Wheeler, who had sent the Canadian escorts back to their unit, realised that his crew were not going to extract their tank. At 1055

28 'Greatly daring—and profiting, no doubt, by the demoralising effect of the Tank's peregrinations in the neighbourhood—the little party bombed several dug-outs and returned with two captured machine-guns and two prisoners to show for their splendidly insolent exploit.' Roberts, *Canada in Flanders, Vol. III*, Chapter 4.
29 Now the site of the Tank Corps Memorial.

hours, just as he was about to tell the crew to stop working, shrapnel from a German shell fatally wounded *Champagne's* driver, Pte Horace Brotherwood. Wheeler and the other members of the crew carried his body back to the dressing station, south of Pozières where it was buried. The tank was never recovered.[30]

Mick Wheeler. (Steve Butcher)

At 1100 hours, Byng decided that conditions were such that 5th Canadian Brigade could attack Courcelette village and sought assurance from HQ 2nd Division's headquarters that they were ready to move. Brig Gen AH MacDonell, GOC 5th Canadian Brigade who had positioned himself at Turner's location, agreed and, at 1110 hrs, Byng gave orders for the attack to start at 1800 hours. At the same time, the commander of 7th Canadian Brigade Brig Gen AC MacDonell was tasked to capture the German trenches to the northwest of the village.[31]

At about noon, elements of the *212th Reserve Regiment*, who were holding the line between Courcelette and Mouquet Farm, started to reinforce the defenders of Courcelette.[32] Later that afternoon, the Germans launched their long-expected counter-attack from Courcelette village towards Sugar Trench, which was comprehensively repulsed by the Canadians. Meanwhile, *Cognac's* crew, still well behind enemy lines, were continuing to dig out their tank. At 1800 hours the crew was forced to take shelter from the bombardment which preceded 5th and 7th Canadian Brigade attacks on Courcelette and the ground to its northwest. The initial assault was successful and *Cognac* was behind the new Canadian frontline within an hour. At 1930 hours, Turner was informed that the village was in Canadian hands.[33] At 2000 hours, as it became dark, Bluemel told his men to cease work. Once *Cognac's* crew had removed the locks from the Vickers machine-guns, and secured the tank, Bluemel led his men back down the communication trench towards their Starting Point. The Germans were continuing to shell the trench, which followed the

---

30   All the other members of the crew survived the war. Wheeler was one of the first officer instructors (see photograph 28), and commanded a section at the Battles of Messines, 3rd Ypres and Cambrai, before serving the remainder of the war as an instructor.

31   The two brigadiers were cousins and the communications trench along the track from Ovillers to Courcelette was probably named after them.

32   It is likely that, given that the 3rd Canadian Division had not launched an attack westwards, the German regimental commander was ordered to reposition his troops at Courcelette.

33   It did however take two days for the defenders to be cleared out of the dugouts and cellars of the houses.

track towards Ovillers, so the crew made their way across country to another trench which was full of body parts. It took them four hours to reach their base near Aveluy, arriving at midnight. Whilst the crewmen slept, 5th Canadian Brigade fought to hold their newly-held ground against a series of German counter-attacks. It was the start of a month-long struggle to clear the Germans from the outskirts of the village and the trench lines to its northwest.

Capture of Martinpuich

Three brigades were tasked to capture the village and environs of Martinpuich with a fourth tasked to take the ground between the village and High Wood. The first three were successful whilst 149th Brigade, which had no tank support and more open ground to traverse, was unable to hold their Second Objective.

Daphne's crew at Elveden:
Standing rear left Frank Styring then Walter Atkins.
Sitting centre left, Roland Elliott then Harry Drader and Owen Rowe. (TMA)

On the left, closest to the Canadians, were 15th (Scottish) Division. The initial attack on the southwest of Martinpuich was completely successful with *Daphne* playing a part. According to Mann's post-operation report, she 'left starting point on time. Shelled from starting point until return. Engaged enemy on hostile frontline trenches, the majority of who threw up their hands, the remainder retreated in disorder to the top of the crest where the tank guns destroyed many. Destroyed enemy machine guns near 1st line. Enemy machine guns and infantry concentrated fire on tank and then surrendered.'[34] The final part of the route taken by *Daphne* is shown in colour photograph 13. Drader had stopped the tank on the southwest outskirts of the village where he could observe, and presumably engage, any Bavarians trying to escape along the Factory/Candy Trench north-westwards towards Courcelette. *Daphne* was at this point only 500 yards east of the Sugar Factory where *Crème de Menthe* was in action. 8th and 20th Canadian infantry battalions had taken Candy Trench, which was 400 yards from his position.

Expecting to be called upon to support the follow-on attack, and presumably unaware of the overnight change in orders, Drader left the southern edge of Martinpuich at about 0720 hours to refuel and replenish ammunition. *Daphne* was hit by German artillery fire during her return journey, which damaged the steering tail, and one crewman was severely wounded by shrapnel whilst replenishing the tank.[35] At 0947 hours, a further order was issued to Mann by HQ 46th Brigade. This was that the tanks were to move round to the north of the village and 'clear up the situation.' The damage to the tank's steering, and the fact that the tank's driver, Private Alfred Bowerman, was suffering from shell shock, made this impossible. The infantry attack on the rest of the village was, however, a complete success, the Scots driving the Bavarians out of the village to the north and the east being secured by 150th Brigade. When *Daphne* failed to reappear, HQ 46th Brigade directed CO 10/11th Highland Light Infantry to interview Mann.[36] The purpose of the interview is not recorded but it is likely that the aim was ascertain *Daphne's* availability for action. The report must have been favourable as orders were given, after midday, that Drader take ammunition to the nearer part of the village and then proceed around the south side to assist 45th Brigade who were being targeted by German machine-guns.[37] As there was no other trained driver amongst *Daphne's* crewmen, this was not possible. The problem was resolved when Mann swapped over the tank crews, using his own men from D23, and sent *Daphne* into the village twice to carry out replenishment including machine-gun ammunition which was used to break up a German counter-attack the next day.[38] It was the first time a tank was used in this role, a task which would become common from June 1917 onwards. *Daphne* then returned to Contalmaison.[39]

---

34   See Appendix XIII.
35   Gnr Walter Atkins from Coventry. He recovered from his wounds but died five months later, on 9 February 1917, during an appendectomy at Worgret Camp hospital near Wareham. He was buried by his parents at Foleshill United Reform churchyard.
36   Pidgeon, *Tanks at Flers*, p. 122. He also states that *Daphne's* steering tail wheels had been damaged by artillery fire on the return journey.
37   Presumably, this was after Colle had left his position at the Third Objective. See below.
38   Mann's report. See Appendix XIII. He must, however, have retained Drader in command of *Daphne* as he would have known the route into the village; this is confirmed by the citation for the MC subsequently awarded to Drader.
39   Images of D20 and D23 cleaning *Daphne's* guns and undertaking vehicle maintenance after the battle appear in Geoffrey Malins' 1917 film *The Battle of the Ancre and the Advance of the Tanks*. Although Malins had been sent forward to film the battle, to a point where he should have been able to see *Daphne* in action, he did not record this historic event.

To the east of Martinpuich, the Male and Female tanks commanded by Stones and Colle crossed the British frontline at 0603 hours. Crossing the jumping-off trenches at 0618 hours, the D24 and D25 crews quickly reached 50th Division's First Objective, Hook Trench. The tanks suppressed the German defenders as the British infantry crossed no man's land and, by 0650 hours, 150th Infantry Brigade had cleared Hook Trench.[40] The infantry had to wait there until the creeping barrage started moving north. During this enforced halt, 149th Brigade was under continuous machine-gun fire from the German defenders in High Wood.

At 0709, the two tanks moved northwest leading 150th Brigade towards their Second Objective near the road from Martinpuich to High Wood. Stones' Female tank was struck by an artillery shell as it passed the eastern edge of the Tangle North position (see colour photograph 12), which protected the Second Objective.[41] A shell penetrated the tank's hull but none of the crew was killed. The tank pushed on until it was hit by a second shell which smashed one track and damaged the steering tail. Stones, who had received a head wound after the periscope was hit by a bullet, ordered his men to abandon the tank.[42] Taking machine-guns from the immobilised tank, the crew took cover in shellholes. They were pinned down on a forward slope and could not get back to British frontline trench until after 1300 hours, that is once High Wood and the north-eastern edge of Martinpuich had been secured. It took them a further eight hours to return to their Place of Assembly.[43]

Colle's route towards his Second Objective was broadly the same as Stones although, given the position at the German frontline, he probably followed the track between Tangle North and Tangle South. His tank was spotted by an RFC pilot as it sat on the furthest north trench of the Tangle North complex. This position enabled the tank's gunners to dominate the German communications trench which led from High Wood to Martinpuich and protect 150th Infantry Brigade as they consolidated their position at the Second Objective. At 0801 hours, as the creeping barrage started again, Colle set off northwards towards the Third Objective (Blue Line), putting three machine-guns out of action as his Female tank travelled through the remains of the orchards and gardens on the eastern edge of Martinpuich.[44]

149th Brigade on their right, which had no tank support, was unable to reach their Second Objective which was further north than that allocated to 150th Brigade. They were subjected to continuous machine-gun fire by *23rd Bavarian Regiment* from their positions in High Wood. Although some of the brigades' leading elements did reach a small trench line known as the

---

40 Pidgeon states that the first tank (probably Stones) stopped at M32d,7,0 whilst Colle was 150 yards to his left at S2b70,75, See Pidgeon, *The Tanks at Flers* p.113.

41 This location was not only visible to the German units in High Wood, which is in the background of the photograph, but also to those on the north-eastern edge of Martinpuich.

42 Stones' injuries were treated at the Royal Free Hospital in London. Having recovered, he was posted to Bovington where he was claimed by Summers and joined F Battalion as a section commander in No. 17 Company and, again, then as a company commander in 15th Tank Battalion. Stones left the post, as a result of neuralgia and insomnia caused by his head wounds in August 1918 and was discharged in January 1919. He returned to Doncaster where he developed the family's farming business. Walter Stones died, aged 91, on 1 April 1972. Pope, *FTC*, pp, 210-211.

43 See *The First Tanks* by Gnr William Foster in Appendix XIII <http://www.oucs.ox.ac.uk/ww1lit/gwa/item/3815> (accessed 1 May 2021).

44 Given the enemy machine-guns were probably in protected positions, this was a significant achievement by a Female tank crew.

D24 crewmen at Elveden:
Fred Rule (standing rear left), Billy Foster (standing rear right)
and Walter Stones (kneeling centre). (TMA)

Bow, they were forced back to a sunken road only 300 yards north of their First Objective. 150th Brigade however reached their Third, and final, Objective where they were joined by Colle's tank. He remained with them, on the north-eastern edge of Martinpuich (E3), providing protection against the expected German counter-attack. Three of the crew were injured during the attack and, once the infantry consolidated their position, Colle returned to the Brigade Headquarters at the cemetery. Here Colle signaled for help to repair the tank's steering tail and the steering pump which had been damaged during the action.[45]

Tanks at High Wood

Three of the four tanks, which supported 47th Division, reached their Start Points with little time to spare before Zero.[46] Robinson and Sharp's tanks entered the southernmost tip of High Wood and, in accordance with their orders, drove about 50 yards apart on a route parallel to the southeast edge of the wood towards the German frontline. The ground conditions were so bad that *Delphine* became ditched in a British support trench, 100 yards behind the British frontline at 0630 hours after a track became broken.

---

45   Author's note: The fitting of the armoured shields, which arrived on 12 September without fixings, may have prevented this damage. See Chapter 5.
46   Three tanks were seen driving up the track from Crucifix Corner at 0545 hours.

D21 *Delphine's* hulk. (TMA)

Robinson, realising that his tank was also in danger of becoming ditched, drove to the edge of the wood, crossing Anderson Trench which ran down its length, and then moved to the British frontline. Mann states that Robinson 'engaged enemy East of High Wood at about 6.45 a.m. on 15' [September] but there is also a report that his crew, mistaking waiting soldiers from the Londons for Bavarians, inflicted casualties although the exact number is not recorded.[47] Robinson's tank then became stuck in the British frontline known as Worcester Trench. After hard digging for 14 hours, the D22 crew managed to extract the tank and return later to their Assembly Area that night, the only crew who did so that day.

Of the other pair, the crew of Male tank *Clan Ruthven* drove along the south-western edge of the wood, entering well short of the planned entry point at 0615 hours. It is possible that Henderson decided, as he was extremely late, to get ahead of the British troops who were 150 yards to his north in their jumping-off positions in Queen Trench. Owing to the damage caused by previous artillery fire, *Clan Ruthven* ditched on tree stumps just 40 yards in from the edge of the wood. The tank was never recovered.

The remaining tank, *Delilah* and the D13 crew under Sampson, was in position on the edge of the wood at 0420 hours. Sampson contacted the infantry who told him that Zero had been brought forward by thirty minutes. Sampson however did not start early but entered the wood at 0600 hours. As *Delilah* went forward, she attracted the attention of the defending Bavarians

47   *The Battlefield Debut of the Tank 1916* <http://www.eyewitnesstohistory.com/tank.html> (accessed 24 May 2021).

Billy Sampson. (Stuart Sampson)

who opened fire with machine-guns. As she advanced, one of the tank sponson doors was removed from its hinges by a tree stump. One of the crew, Gnr William Chandler, got out of the tank whilst it was crossing no man's land and refitted the armoured plate door despite the tank being subjected to machine-gun fire. *Delilah* was moving very slowly so, although Chandler was a large man, this was some feat.[48] In a letter written to his sister,[49] Divall tells that *Delilah's* progress was slowed by her engine sparking plugs becoming covered in soot.[50] However, the tank put two machine-guns out of action as she travelled across no man's land. Once they had crossed the German frontline trench, two Bavarians got onto *Delilah's* roof to attack the crew. Another Bavarian fired into the crew compartment through a pistol port which wounded a crewman. *Delilah*, however, drove on reaching the Bavarian Support Trench where she stopped. Whilst the driver tried to clean the sparking plugs, the rest of the crew continued to fight their tank. The German artillery was now firing into the wood and hit the tank. Given that *Delilah* was sitting in the Bavarian Support Trench, it is possible that the German guns were deliberately firing on their own positions.[51] The crew bailed out and thereby avoided being burnt alive when *Delilah* caught fire. The Bavarians in the Support Trench tried to surrender to the crew, who were armed only with pistols. Fortunately, the timely arrival of some British infantry prevented the crew being overwhelmed; Sampson handed the problem over to their sergeant major and then led his men back to the wood edge.

Despite the disabling of all four tanks and the initial losses suffered by 47th Division, a second attack on High Wood starting at 1100 hours was successful. It was proceeded by the Division's trench mortars firing 750 rounds in 15 minutes, which broke the will of the defenders, and the wood was at last taken.[52] 47th Division then advanced down a forward slope without any fire support to attack the Starfish Line (their Second Objective) and Flers Line, both formidable objectives. Despite their determined efforts, the defences proved too strong and the attack

48   His enlistment papers show that Chandler was 6 feet and one quarter inch tall.
49   Published in the Kent and Sussex Courier on 30 March 1917.
50   Author's note: It appears that the orders regarding the maintenance of tanks prior to their use, issued on 14 September 1916, did not reach all crews.
51   It is now common practice for defenders to call down fire on their positions to disrupt an attack.
52   This was not the first time that 140th Brigade's mortars had been so effective. Supporting a trench raid on 3–4 July, they fired 750 rounds in 30 minutes despite two tubes being damaged and four men injured. See Maude, *The 47th Division*, p. 58.

failed.[53] Barter was subsequently relieved on his command, by Pulteney, for causing too many casualties amongst his own men.[54]

After-Action Reports

On 19 September, 2nd Canadian Division's commander submitted a report to this Corps HQ which included a separate report written by Inglis.[55] Turner noted that the poor state of the ground, coupled with the fact that Zero was virtually in daylight, prevented the tanks taking an active part in the capture of the German frontline trench.[56] Turner stated that the two tanks, which reached the final objective, did very good work in assisting the infantry to mop up. He noted that the tanks were immune from everything but a direct hit by something larger than a field gun but that the steering gear and tails were weak spots. Turner also stated that future actions would require larger numbers of tanks as it was unsafe to assume that more than a third would reach their objectives. Turner saw the future role of tanks as being used to mop up enemy positions once the leading waves had passed.[57] He also recommended that a proportion of tanks should be sent beyond the final objectives to enable the infantry to establish posts well in front of their own positions and also to capture further objectives.[58]

In his report to HQ Reserve Army on 21 September,[59] Byng stated that the tanks provided moral support to the infantry when they were in action; they were, however, liable to break down and were susceptible to damage from shellfire. He noted that it was not possible for the infantry and tanks to advance at the same pace over the type of ground encountered near Courcelette but that *Cordon Rouge* and *Crème de Menthe* had been very useful at the Sugar Factory. His conclusion was that no infantry action should be subservient to that of the tanks, 'tanks being a useful accessory to the infantry and nothing more.'

Tank Effectiveness

On 19 September, HQ Fourth Army sought details of the work done by the tanks during the period 15 to 18 September. Responding on 22 September, Mann gave an outline of the action by four of his tanks.[60] He noted that the tanks gave the attacking infantry greater confidence and caused considerable local panic amongst the enemy. However, the tanks were shelled by

---

53 The attack was made down a forward slope in clear view of German artillery observers and with heavy enemy machine-gun fire from the left flank. A follow-on attack, launched at 1800 hours, without preparatory artillery registration, was also unsuccessful.

54 The Divisional History ascribes the losses by the decision by Pulteney not to use artillery in High Wood. It states that insurmountable obstacles existed in the wood and that Barter's proposal to use tanks on the edges of the wood would have aided the infantry. Maude, *The 47th Division*, p. 68.

55 Turner's Report was HQ 2nd Canadian Division G.345 dated 19 September. Inglis' unreferenced report is reproduced in Appendix XIII.

56 He appears to have overlooked the fact that the tanks were ordered to follow, not proceed, the infantry.

57 This contradicts his earlier comment about tanks leading the infantry.

58 Author's note: This is the first suggestion of tanks being used in the exploitation role previously undertaken by cavalry.

59 HQ Canadian Corps G.167b, 21 September 1916.

60 See Mann's report in Appendix XIII. Unfortunately, the report from HQ D Company regarding the tanks supporting XV Corps has not survived.

German artillery from the start to the finish of the action and any abandoned tanks continued to draw enemy fire. The Female tanks inflicted considerable casualties on the Bavarian infantry by enfilading trenches and firing on retreating enemy troops whilst Male tanks were particularly good at destroying machine-gun emplacements, the fire from the 6-pounder guns 'being on the whole very good.' He concluded that, once the enemy discovered that their small arms and machine-gun fire was ineffective, they surrendered or retreated.

Casualties and Prisoners

The 4,000 casualties sustained by 47th Division were the highest in III Corps and this led to Pulteney's sacking of Barter.[61] In comparison, 50th (Northumbrian) Division sustained the least (1,207) of all the attacking divisions on 15 September even though 149th Brigade was under fire from High Wood throughout their attack. 15th Division sustained only 1,853 casualties on 15 September whilst clearing Martinpuich but was understandably withdrawn on 18 September, having been in the line since 8 August.

The 2nd Canadian Division lost 1,283 men on 15 September in capturing Courcelette; their opponents in *211 Reserve Regiment* lost 59 out of 75 officers and 1,820 other ranks whilst *2 Battalion, 210 Reserve Regiment* was annihilated. Sadly, the casualties amongst the Canadians would increase as they attempted to capture the German held trenches to the west and north of Courcelette over the next two months.

Casualties amongst the tank crews were extremely light. The only fatality, *Champagne's* driver Horace Brotherwood, was buried by the dressing station where the tanks refuelled on 14 September and his grave can be found within the Pozières Military Cemetery. The first casualty in No. 1 Section, Gnr Lawrie Rowntree who was injured as the tanks deployed, recovered and was commissioned in the Royal Field Artillery; sadly, he was killed in action near Dochy Farm on 25 November 1917. There were no other serious casualties in No. 1 Section although Inglis mentions the skipper and five men in *Cordon Rouge* suffered injuries from shell splinters and bullet splash. No. 4 Section suffered no fatalities but one skipper and eight crewmen were hospitalised.[62]

Gallantry Awards

Inglis was awarded the Distinguished Service Order (DSO) for his leadership at Courcelette, the first such awarded to a tank officer. His driver Sgt George Shepherd was awarded the Distinguished Conduct Medal; again, the first of its type to a tank crewman. Colle, Drader and Stones, the three skippers whose tanks got into action at Martinpuich, were each awarded the

---

61   Barter was unfairly dismissed; he continued to be well regarded by his men and he was present at the unveiling of the statues to 47th Division in London as well as post-war reunions.

62   Casualty returns for 15 September (Woods' Correspondence Book) records Stones (D24) gunshot wound to head; Atkins (D20) shell splinters in right shoulder; Bell (D25) unspecified; Bowerman (D20) shellshock; Divall (D13) shrapnel wound to knee; Lowson (D22) scalp wound; Petrie (D25) unspecified; Pick (D13) burns and Private Wood ASC (D25) splinters in eyes.

MC. Campbell, who joined *Crème de Menthe* in action, was also awarded the MC as was Allan, who commanded *Cordon Rouge*.[63]

Allan's tank NCO, Cpl Frank Vyvyan, was awarded the MM as was Gnr Ernest Hunt. Gnrs Ernest Bax and William Smith were awarded the MM for trying to extract *Champagne;* Gnr George Simpson of Chartreuse was also awarded the MM for bravery under fire; the circumstances are not recorded.[64]

Honours were awarded to the tank crews who fought at High Wood. Robinson and Sampson were awarded the MC whilst Chandler was awarded the MM for replacing a sponsor door displaced whilst moving through the wood. Two of Robinson's crew were also awarded the MM – his driver Pte Cecil Howes, and Gnr Percy Raworth, for extracting the tank after 14 hours constant digging.[65]

Conclusions

Crème de Menthe and *Cordon Rouge* did useful work at Courcelette. The three tanks supporting 15th and 50th divisions assisted their brigades in breaking though the German frontlines. Colle did further good work destroying machine-gun posts on the eastern side of Martinpuich, reducing the number of 50th Division's casualties to the lowest of the divisions on 15 September. The misuse of the tanks at High Wood taught a lesson which was never forgotten.

Recovery, Repairs and Reinforcement

Both Inglis and Mann were operating in direct support of their respective corps, as demonstrated by the reports mentioned above. They remained in that situation until their companies moved back to the Loop, although both units provided them with reinforcements to allow them to provide effective support. The immediate priority for the section commanders was preparing for the next operation which had initially been expected to commence within days. However bad weather conditions and a lack of artillery ammunition delayed these for ten days.

The section commanders notified corps headquarters of their casualties, the death of Horace Brotherwood being notified to his parents by a WO telegram. A letter was also received expressing the condolences of the crew, which was probably written by Wheeler.[66]

---

63   Allan died of wounds received at the Battle of Messines whilst commanding a section of A Battalion.

64   Vyvyan was awarded the DCM for commanding a tank on 9 Apr 1917, after his skipper was killed. He was later commissioned in the Tank Corps. Hunt was also commissioned and served with 3rd Light Battalion. Bax was commissioned in the HB MGC in May 1917 as an Equipment Officer. In May 1940, he was commissioned into the RAOC, was awarded the MBE in 1942 and rose to the rank of colonel in 1946.

65   Robinson recommended James Anderson and Arthur Lowson for medals. Anderson was awarded the DCM for his actions at Bullecourt on 3 May 1917 but survived the war. Raworth died of wounds on 23 September 1917 after D Battalion's transport lines were bombed by German aeroplanes. Lowson was reported Missing in Action on 11 August 1918 near Parvillers; his was one of three 4th Battalion tanks knocked out by an anti-tank gun and all of his crewmen less one were later declared Killed in Action. His body was never found.

66   The *Woking News and Mail* of 6 October 1916 reported 'Mr and Mrs Brotherwood of 1 Elm View Villas, Goldsworth Rd, Woking have received news of the death, in action in France, of their son Pte H Brotherwood of the Heavy Section Machine-gun Corps. It is understood that Pte Brotherwood has

The priority for those crews, whose tanks had ditched or broken down, was their vehicle's recovery and Inglis' section was similar to the other sections in C Company. *Champagne* and *Chartreuse* were too well-ditched to be dug out; furthermore *Chartreuse* was lying at an angle which caused her engine to seize.[67] Track problems of the sort affecting *Chablis* were beyond the capabilities of the ASC fitters based at the Loop owing to a lack of spare parts and machinery available to move major assemblies. The crews were at risk during such recovery operations, especially those near the Pozières Windmill as this area was clearly visible to the artillery observers working from balloons southeast of Le Sars. Fortunately, Bluemel and his crew managed to recover *Cognac* from the communication trench near Courcelette on 16 September without interference as she was screened from view. When she returned to the section base south of Aveluy, Inglis had four operational tanks including the spare known as *Cupid*.[68]

Mann, commanding No. 4 Section, had a similar problem. Although Robinson had managed to extract his tank on the evening of 15 September, *Delilah* had been burnt out and was never recovered. *Clan Ruthven* was impossible to move and her crew were therefore sent back to C Company. *Delphine* was only 50 yards from the eastern edge of High Wood but had broken a track. As there was no means of moving track sections or equipment by vehicle, and mule transport was at the time unavailable, a SNCO artificer and three ASC other ranks carried a number of plates, links and pins for a mile across country from Green Dump to the stranded vehicle. Their repairs were initially unsuccessful but *Delphine* was recovered at the end of the year.

Mann was expecting to support further operations by III Corps north of Martinpuich and at Le Sars and Eaucourt l'Abbaye. By 19 September, D Company had reorganised the available tanks and men at Green Dump into eight crews and, on 22 September, four tanks were detached to Mann's section commanded by Bell (D2), Enoch (D7), Bown (D16) and Wakley who had replaced Bond as skipper of the D18 crew.[69] Robinson, Colle and Drader were still commanding fit tanks but Mann's own tank continued to suffer track problems. The location of Mann's base is not recorded but it is likely to have been near Contalmaison, where *Daphne* was replenished, probably at the quarry 800 yards north of the chateau.[70]

been engaged with the famous tanks.' The reference to the HS MGC indicates the author was from C Company rather than an officer of 711 MT Company on whose establishment Brotherwood remained.

67   The splash lubrication system, used on the Daimler Knight, did not work when at an oblique angle.

68   One of *Cupid*'s crew was 38225 Gnr. Maurice Voile, the details being recorded in his New Testament. Voile was killed during the attack on the Harp defensive position on 9 April 1917, whilst driving tank C39; his body is buried at Tilloy British Cemetery.

69   Wakley had been D Company's Park Officer on arrival in France. Pope, *FTC*, p. 22.

70   Location identified by Dr Gerald Moore, a Canadian researcher with detailed knowledge of the first tank actions. The quarry benefits from being out of sight of the German artillery observers whilst being located on a major track connecting Contalmaison to Martinpuich, within 100 yards of a trench railway line.

Tank Action at Martinpuich, 25 September 1916

Local Situation

On 16 September 150th and 151st brigades of 50th Division attacked and captured the German trenches to the northeast of Martinpuich. 15th Division and 2nd Canadian Division also linked up the defences between Courcelette and Martinpuich along Gun Pit Trench; they also established posts overlooking the German communication trench '26th Avenue' which linked Courcelette to the Flers Line near Eaucourt l'Abbaye. On 17 September, the Germans reinforced the group of trenches in the east of Courcelette to prevent any further advance in that area. This was timely as, at 1700 hours, 5th Canadian Brigade tried to evict them but the Germans held them off.

Initially Rawlinson's plan was that Fourth Army should press ahead, with its divisions completing the capture of the final objectives on 18 September. A combination of a lack of artillery ammunition and bad weather delayed these attacks until 20 September. On 18 September, 1st Canadian Division took over the Courcelette defences, permitting 2nd Canadian Division to withdraw and prepare for the next attack. At the same time, 23rd Division relieved 15th Division as well as elements of 50th Division holding the Starfish Trench and Prue Trench to the east of Martinpuich. More heavy rain on 18 September, which prevented forward troops being resupplied, and the inability of French troops to participate in the attack in the east, caused Haig to delay Fourth Army's attack a further 24 hours.

On the afternoon of 19 September, at 1720 hours, the Germans launched a bombing raid against 69th Brigade (23rd Division) east of Martinpuich but it was repelled. On 20 September, HQ III Corps held a planning conference at which it was decided to provide two tanks each to 1st Division and 50th Division for the next attack.[71] Later that day, after no improvement in the weather, it was decided that the attack would be delayed by another 24 hours.

Meanwhile, Haig visited HQ Reserve Army and reviewed plans to take the village of Thiepval, the German redoubts to its north and the high ground to its east including Mouquet Farm (see Map 9). This attack was to be a preliminary action which would be followed by an attack north of the River Ancre to take the ground which the Germans had retained despite the original attacks on 1 July. Gough, in command of the Reserve Army, needed tanks to assist in this attack so Haig directed Rawlinson to replace those lost on 15 September. On the night of 20 September, the Germans made two attempts to reoccupy Courcelette which were rebuffed by 3rd Canadian Division. The next day, orders were given that the Reserve Army would attack the Thiepval Ridge on 26 September. Rawlinson reviewed his plans and agreed to provide eight tanks to Gough. These were a mix of four tanks from No. 1 Section of C Company provided by Inglis, a pair from No. 4 Section of D Company provided by Mann, as well as two manned by crews formed from spare crewmen in unused tanks at the Loop.

---

71   The 1st Division replaced 47th Division which had been withdrawn to absorb replacement drafts. Tanks, however, were not provided.

The Ground and German Defences and Dispositions

Ground conditions were starting to improve, rain having stopped on 21 September. The Germans continued to hold the trenches to the south west of Courcelette where 3rd Canadian Division had been in action since 15 September. This included Mouquet Farm which was transferred to the operational area of II Corps. The Canadians still held Courcelette village but not the practice trenches to the north east of the village. The Germans had also retained field defences to the east of Courcelette as well as the 26th Avenue Trench which enabled the reinforcement of the village as well as preventing movement along the road from Pozières to Le Sars. The ground either side of the Sugar Trench and the road is depicted in colour photograph 14.

The 23rd Division had taken over the positions on the high ground northwest of Martinpuich, overlooking 26th Avenue and, on 23 September, took more ground to the east of the village. That same day, 1st Canadian Division reported that they had captured the trenches to the east of Courcelette and requested that 23rd Division occupy 26th Avenue. That afternoon, 68th Infantry Brigade launched a quick attack and, at 1645 hours, reported that they had occupied two positions; however, the Brigade was unable to build on its initial success. At 0130 hours the following morning, 68th Brigade reported that the overall attack on 26th Avenue had failed; the Germans remained firmly in control of the ground between Martinpuich and Courcelette as well as the road from Pozières to Le Sars, and they retained their means of reinforcing the remaining troops near Courcelette.

The Plan

At 1910 hours on 24 September, 23rd Division received HQ III Corps' Operation Order to take 26th Avenue, confirming that two tanks were at their disposal for the attack the next day. The attack was to be carried out by 10th Northumberland Fusiliers. One tank would drive up Gun Pit Lane to the Pozières to Le Sars road then drive northeast to its junction with 26th Avenue (known as Point 29), then clear the trench northeast for 400 yards to the centre of the M26 grid square before returning down the hill into Martinpuich. The other tank would start half way between Gun Pit Lane and the Mill Road. It would then drive north, uphill then across the open ground to 26th Avenue as far as the centre of the M26 grid square and then, turning right, clear the German communications trench to the east as far as Point 53. This was a junction between 26th Avenue and a communications trench, known as Park Alley, which led back into Martinpuich. Here the tank would turn right and drive south back into the village. Enoch was to command one tank; the name of the other skipper is not recorded.

The Infantry

HQ III Corps directed that 23rd Division capture 26th Avenue on 25 September whilst 50th Division would take the Crest, just south of Prue Trench. To their right, 1st Division, who had relieved 47th Division north of High Wood, would capture a further 300 yards of the Flers Trenches to the northwest of that village.

The Tanks

Mann had six tanks available. Initially III Corps allotted one to 1st Division but this was later withdrawn. Two were allocated to support the Canadian Corps attack on 26 September; this left three, two being allocated to 23rd Division under Maj Gen JM Babbington.

Deployment

The two tanks supporting 23rd Division had to deploy overnight on 24–25 September as the southern approaches to Martinpuich were visible in daylight to the German artillery observers located in balloons to the north of the village. The exact approach route taken by the tanks is not recorded other than it was from the west – it probably followed the route used by Drader on 15 September. Enoch arrived at Martinpuich in the early hours and concealed his tank in Gun Pit Lane.[72] At 0245 hours, 68th Brigade reported both tanks had reached their rendezvous in Gun Pit Lane but this was untrue.

After first light, Enoch recced his route from Gun Pit Lane to his start point, no doubt wondering where the other tank was. At 0915 hours, 68th Brigade informed 23rd Division that the second tank had ditched on its way to the rendezvous. They also stated that it would not be able to take part in the attack as its approach to the village would be visible to those in the over-watching balloons.

Zero

In common with the other Fourth Army units attacking on 25 September, Zero was at 1235 hours. It was a cloudless day with temperatures reaching 73 degrees Fahrenheit.

Final Moves

At 0920 hours on 25 September, Babbington spoke by telephone to Brig Gen Colville who commanded 68th Brigade. Babbington directed that, should the second tank not be available, Colville was to cancel the attack eastwards from Point 29 towards M26 Central and Enoch was now to undertake a portion of both tanks' tasks. His route would follow Park Alley to Point 53, then follow 26th Avenue for 900 yards as far west as Point 29 destroying the German machine-gun posts en route, then turn south west into the village using Gun Pit Lane. Enoch, who must have checked his new route, asked to leave five minutes ahead of 10th Northumberland Fusiliers' attack due to the poor state of the ground; this was approved.

Tank Action

When Enoch's tank appeared over the horizon at 1220 hours, she became visible to the Germans in 26th Avenue who fired rockets to call for artillery support. At 1230 hours, the

---

72   Author's note: This was a different tank to that which he commanded on 15 September 1916 but, so far, it has not been identified.

Germans launched heavy artillery fire on the British trenches. At Zero (1235 hours), two companies of 10th Northumberland Fusiliers attacked in two waves, each of two platoons 50 yards apart, with two platoons in reserve. They immediately came under heavy artillery fire as well as machine-gun fire from 26th Avenue when they topped the rise about 150 yards from the enemy trenches. They initially pressed home their attack but were forced to take cover; the reserve platoons were also committed but did not get far before they were recalled. The first wave of Fusiliers reportedly got to within 55 yards of 26th Avenue.

Meanwhile Enoch drove to within 200 yards of Point 53 and destroyed a German machine-gun post before turning west along 26th Avenue in accordance with his revised orders. At 1259 hours, 23rd Division received a report from Royal Artillery observers that both tanks were going well, which makes no sense whatsoever. A subsequent report received at 1340 hours from the RFC stated that one tank had been seen at Zero 200 yards to the west of Point 53 which is also contrary to other reports. What exactly happened next is impossible to determine. An RFC report stated that the tank had made a complete circuit before coming to rest in British-held territory. Enoch must however have turned round in no man's land as he returned to Park Alley where his tank became ditched. The tank was subjected to heavy artillery fire and the crew abandoned the tank; it was subsequently destroyed by shellfire.[73]

Tank effectiveness

Enoch's tank partially fulfilled its mission of destroying the machine-guns along 26th Avenue but it was incapable of completing the task of two machines. Its early appearance from Martinpuich also added a trigger for the Germany artillery to engage the infantry as they attacked across a completely uncovered piece of ground.

Casualties

The number of casualties sustained by 10th Northumberland Fusiliers, which advanced on a two company front, is not recorded in reports by III Corps, 23rd Division or the brigade or battalion war diaries. However, the CWGC records show 65 officers and men of the Battalion were killed or died of wounds between 25 and 27 September, the Battalion being withdrawn following the attack on 26th Avenue. D Company's War Diary records that three crewmen were injured in the tank although HQ III Corps recorded that four crewmen were wounded in the tank.[74]

---

73   Enoch, who was unwounded, continued to serve with D Battalion, then 4th Tank Battalion eventually serving as adjutant. Whilst undertaking occupation duties, he was awarded the MC in May 1919. Enoch then served with the Rhine Army Tank Company until Spring 1920. He returned to Wolverhampton where he managed an engineering company. He died, aged 68, on 22 May 1959. His only son, Russell, and his grandson Alfie are well-known actors. Pope, *FTC*, pp. 138–141.

74   The tank's NCO Cpl Charlie Ironmonger recorded that he, Gnrs. Franks and Lapthorne were wounded outside the tank, presumably as they attempted to reach safety. Ironmonger had shrapnel wounds to the chest, knee, face and arm but was back in action at the Battle of Cambrai. Alfred Lapthorne's right hand was however so seriously damaged that he was discharged on 5 April 1917 but lived until he was 89 near Plympton. I have not yet been able to identify Gnr. Franks. Ironmonger's diary is now held by the Tank Museum Archives.

Conclusions

The Post-Operational Report written by 23rd Division states that, as a result of the loss of the tanks, that 'the infantry failed to gain the ground.' It is possible that they based this view following the success of 50th Division on 15 September when Stones' and Colle's tanks had aided one brigade to clear its objectives to the east of Martinpuich. Their opinion may also have been coloured by Storey's exceptional success at Gueudecourt on 26 September which indicated that a single tank could make a crucial difference.[75]

Tank Action at Courcelette, 26 September 1916

Introduction

The next day, the Canadian Corps took part in the Reserve Army attack designed to capture Thiepval, Mouquet Farm to its east and the trenches to the north of the Thiepval Ridge (Map 9). The 6,000 yards of frontage was divided equally between the Canadian Corps on the right and II Corps (Lt Gen CW Jacobs) on the left. At the extreme left, 18th (Eastern) Division, under Maj Gen FI Maxse, was to capture Thiepval (map square B3) and the Schwaben Redoubt to its north (B1) supported by four tanks. In the centre, 11th (Northern) Division, under Lt Gen Charles Woollcombe, was to take Mouquet Farm (D3) then Zollern Redoubt (D2) then Stuff Redoubt (C1), supported by two tanks. On the right, 1st Canadian Division was to take three trench lines; Zollern Graben, Hessian Trench and Regina Trench, the last of which was linked by a road north of Courcelette (G2) to the Schwaben Redoubt. Remarkably, no tanks were allocated to 1st Canadian Division whilst two were allocated to 6th Canadian Brigade who had the easier task of first clearing 26th Avenue as far as the boundary with 23rd Division (G3) and then supporting an attack on the German practice trenches to the northwest of Courcelette (G1).

The Ground and German Defensive Positions

To the northeast of Courcelette, the ground was open fields which provided no cover whatsoever for the attackers. The Germans had converted the old communications trench 26th Avenue into a defensive line with a series of machine-gun positions which dominated the ground to the east as well as the road from Pozières to Le Sars. They had also converted the practice training trenches, northwest of Courcelette, into a defended position. Again, these trenches were in open fields. Their artillery positions, near Le Sars, dominated the open farmland; observers in balloons had a clear view as far as the Old German Lines, by the Pozières Windmill, from which the Canadians had attacked on 15 September.

---

75   See Chapter 7 of this volume.

Local Plan

HQ 6th Canadian Brigade directed that 28th Battalion CEF, supported by two tanks, would capture 26th Avenue as far as the Pozières to Le Sars road. This plan was probably based on the premise that 23rd Division had captured the remainder of the trench the previous day. The tanks, which were commanded by Colle and Robinson, would then drive north to support the attack by 29th Battalion CEF on the German practice trenches to the northeast of the village.

Deployment

The 6th Canadian Brigade moved into Courcelette on the night of 25–26 September with 28th and 29th Battalions CEF taking over the front line on the east of the village. D Company's War Diary states that Colle and Robinson's tanks were to proceed from Albert to Courcelette.[76] As they moved through Pozières (E5), Colle's tank became ditched. As it could not be freed, Robinson pushed on alone and arrived in the centre of Courcelette well before daylight. His Place of Assembly was just east of the church on the Grand Rue.[77]

Zero

Zero was 1235 hours, the same time as the Reserve Army's main attack on the Thiepval Ridge. The weather was fine with a trace of rain; temperatures were warm, reaching almost 75 degrees Fahrenheit.

Final Moves

Robinson moved to his Starting Point using the sunken lane which left Courcelette in the northeast and went towards Martinpuich. His Starting Point was 275 yards west of the crossroads with Pozières to Le Sars Road, and Gunpit Lane. The time when he arrived at his Starting Point (M25b 65,10) is not recorded.

Tank Action

At 1154 hours, Robinson started his attack along 26th Avenue in an easterly direction. As soon as the tank appeared, the German infantry withdrew, knowing that their artillery would stop the tank's advance. Robinson pushed on, along the northern side of 26th Avenue covering 250 yards in about three minutes; this was good progress given that the planning speed for actions on 15 September was a maximum of 50 yards a minute. Having got within 100 yards west of the Pozières to Le Sars road, which was his First Objective for the attack, Robinson stopped

---

76   This is a puzzling description as there are no records of any D Company tanks being based in the town although Archard describes the location used by No. 1 Section of C company as Albert. It is more likely that Colle and Robinson were based near Contalmaison and approached Pozières from the east. Robinson then later drove down the track from Ovillers used by *Champagne and Cognac* on 15 September.

77   Grid reference M25b 2,4. See Pidgeon, *Tanks on the Somme*, p. 79

and remained there until 1205 hours, presumably to prevent the trench being reoccupied before Zero. Highly visible to the German observers, Robinson's tank was targeted by artillery fire. Rather than heading north to undertake the second element of his mission, Robinson either reversed or turned to get back to his Starting Point with the German artillery fire pursuing it. The crew remained with the tank until 1220 hours when, after it was hit, they abandoned the stricken vehicle. Their only supporting tank having been destroyed, 28th Battalion's attack was abandoned.

To the northwest, despite the lack of tank support, 29th Battalion CEF advanced at Zero and occupied the German frontline in ten minutes. It was not, however, able to take the practice trenches to their northeast. To their south, Robinson's tank, which continued to be targeted by German artillery fire, was set on fire at 1412 hours and its ammunition subsequently exploded. As a result, the tank was never recovered. 28th Battalion CEF engaged the German infantry as they began to filter back into 26th Avenue during the afternoon but did not attempt to occupy the trench. It was taken the next day, without fighting, by 23rd Division after an attack by 1st and 20th divisions penetrated the Flers Line near Eaucourt l'Abbaye and the Germans withdrew to avoid their troops being cut off.

Summary

Employing two tanks to aid the task of clearing the two groups of trenches was reasonable; sadly, the ditching of Colle's tank during the deployment through Pozières reduced the odds of success significantly. The loss of Robinson's tank on 26 September confirmed the lesson learned on both 15 and 16 September at Gueudecourt and on 25 September at Martinpuich: that tanks operating near enemy trenches were highly vulnerable to well-directed indirect artillery fire. The failure of 28th Battalion CEF to attack was probably due to the recognition that their starting position and objective was now registered by German supporting artillery. Any attack would have been suicidal.

Capture of Mouquet Farm and Thiepval, 26 September 1916

Introduction

The fortified village of Thiepval (map 9, map square B3) had been one of the original British objectives on 1 July 1916. To its north was a German field defence position known as the Schwaben Redoubt (B1) which dominated the village; to its east, Mouquet Farm (D3) was part of the Second Line whilst to its south of Thiepval was the Wonder Work,[78] another field defence system which dominated not only the front line but also to the rear towards Mouquet Farm.

The attack on 1 July by 32nd Division on Thiepval village failed and, whilst 36th (Ulster) Division took the Schwaben Redoubt that morning, they were evicted that same afternoon. On 2 July, responsibility for the area between Thiepval and Pozières was transferred from Rawlinson's Fourth Army to Gough's Reserve Army. Initially the Reserve Army had been tasked

---

78 *Wundt Werk* to the German troops.

to undertake the exploitation of the Somme offensive, once the Fourth Army under Rawlinson had captured the German frontline trenches. It gradually started to operate separately, taking Pozières in late July, but was not in a position to attack Thiepval until early September.

On the evening of 14 September, 11th (Northern) Division, which was part of Jacobs' II Corps, captured the Wonder Work to the south of the village as well as 250 yards of the Hohenzollern Trench to the east. The II Corps' formations were only 500 yards south of Thiepval but the Germans had, by now, constructed three major trenches to its south through which they would have to break through.

The Ground, German Defences and Dispositions

Thiepval sat at the western end of a plateau above the River Ancre. Attacks from the south and west were uphill (the latter being a 44-metre climb up from Thiepval Wood) and the German defences utilised the ground to optimum effect. The CO of 12th Middlesex subsequently wrote to his wife that the ground was 'absolutely shell torn for three months. It was, I considered, an impossibility.'[79] In addition to well-placed machine-gun positions on the frontline, and within the Chateau, the Germans had placed advanced posts in no man's land where the crews could use enfilade fire against any units attacking from the west. To the north, the village remained protected by the Schwaben Redoubt and to the east, along the Thiepval Ridge, by Mouquet Farm and the Zollern Redoubt.

Three German formations held the line between Courcelette and Thiepval. *7th Division* had three formations to the east: *393rd, 72nd* and *26th Regiments*. In the centre, holding the ground from the Zollern Redoubt (D2) to the eastern edge of Thiepval was *8th Division* comprising the *93rd, 165th* and *153rd Regiments*. In the west, the village was held by *26th Reserve Division* with the *77th Reserve Regiment* and *180th Regiment* under command. According to Maxwell: 'The Prussians and Württembergers, who held the line for a year [and] were supposed to have been relieved, were found out at the last minute to still be there!! An enormous advantage to the enemy who thus knew every inch of the ground which they had themselves prepared for our annihilation when we should attempt to attack it.'

Plan Summary

The plan for the capture of the Thiepval Ridge required the Canadian Corps to capture trenches to the northwest of Courcelette unsupported by tanks. The II Corps, supported by six tanks, would capture Mouquet Farm which had been under constant assault for six weeks,[80] as well as the fortified village of Thiepval and three redoubts and a series of interconnecting trenches, which sat on the high ground north of the Pozières to Thiepval Road.

On the right, 34th Brigade of 11th (Northern) Division was to capture Mouquet Farm, then take the Zollern Redoubt, which was 500 yards to its north, and finally the Hessian Trench

---

79   Lt Col Francis Maxwell VC. Letter dated 27 September 1916: (NAM 1974-02-31-13).
80   The farm was first attacked by the Australians on 8 August 1916. They then attempted to capture the farm on another six occasions before they were relieved by the Canadian Corps who had also attacked the farm complex on 15 September. All of these assaults had been from Pozières whereas the attack by 34 Brigade was from the south.

(C2 to E1) and Stuff Redoubt (C1) which required a final advance of 500 yards to the highest part of the ridge. From there, strong patrols were to advance and, if possible, occupy Stuff Trench which joined the final Canadian objective Regina Trench (B1 to F1). This final task was complicated by the fact that Stuff Redoubt could not be observed from the south and therefore accurate artillery supporting fire could not be guaranteed.

In the centre, 33rd Brigade would advance from the head of Nab Valley on a frontage of 1,000 yards. Two battalions would take the first objective (Schwaben Trench) which linked Mouquet Farm to Thiepval. The second objective, Zollern Trench (B2 to D2), would then be taken by three companies of infantry, after which the final objective Hessian Trench, which had a frontage of less than 500 yards, would be taken by two more companies.

To their west, 18th (Eastern) Division would clear the village of Thiepval and then secure the Schwaben Redoubt which was a further 750 yards to the north and in line with Stuff Redoubt. 53rd Brigade would assault on the left flank of 33rd Brigade from the south, starting at Nab Valley, and negotiating the heavily bombarded ground as far as their first objective at Schwaben Trench. They would then push north and west, clearing the eastern side of the village of Thiepval before pushing onto their final objective, Midway Trench (B2 – C2), which linked Hessian Trench to the Schwaben Redoubt. 54th Brigade had the most unenviable task of breaking into Thiepval from the west, clearing a previously unpenetrated frontline trench system, then the heavily fortified Chateau and the western side of the village. Two battalions were allocated to this task; 12th Middlesex would clear the chateau and village whilst 11th Royal Fusiliers would clear the trench line and mop up any defenders left behind in the remains of the village. These two battalions would push on to a line just north of the village, at which point 6th Northamptons would assault and clear the Schwaben Redoubt.

The Infantry

Both 11th and 18th divisions had already achieved success on the Somme. 11th Division, which had seen action in Gallipoli, arrived in France in early July 1916 and initially served under Third Army. They arrived on the Somme on 2 September and, as part of the Reserve Army, on 14 September captured the *Wundt Werk* position, south of Thiepval. Two days later, they relieved 8th Canadian Brigade to the south of Mouquet Farm. The II Corps had been in the line for two weeks whilst the Canadians had been in the line for three. 18th Division was one of the few formations to take and hold its objectives on 1 July when it took Montauban. It then captured Trones Wood and took part in the battle to clear Delville Wood on 19 July.[81] Having been withdrawn, to reorganise and be reinforced by new drafts of men near Ypres, it undertook three weeks of battle training in the Third Army area before joining II Corps on 8 September. The division was commanded by Ivor Maxse, who was one of the best unit trainers in France.[82]

---

81 This task was achieved by 12th Middlesex under Maxwell. They walked steadily in extended line through the trees, like beaters at a pheasant shoot, firing into every position which could provide the defenders with cover.

82 In January 1917, Maxse was promoted and took command of XVIII Corps. He then, in June 1918, was appointed Inspector of Training for the BEF. See John Baynes, *Far from a Donkey: The Life of General Sir Ivor Maxse* (London: Brassey's, 1995).

The Artillery

The ratio of guns supporting the Reserve Army attack on 26 September was broadly the same as that provided to Fourth Army on the opening day of the Battle of Flers–Courcelette. 230 heavy guns, howitzers and mortars, together with 570 field guns and howitzers, were allocated to support the attack. Artillery units from 11th, 25th, 48th and 49th Divisions were in direct support of II Corps. V Corps' artillery to the north of the Ancre, in particular those of 2nd and 39th divisions, also bombarded the river crossings to prevent the Germans reinforcing Thiepval as well as destroying German defences and communications to the rear. Some of the artillery north of the Ancre were able to fire at right angles to the attack, which aided the attackers considerably. There was no preliminary bombardment.

The Tanks

Six tanks were allocated in support of the attack.[83] Two were to support 34th Brigade attacking Mouquet Farm and the ridge in the centre whilst 18th Division was allocated four in support of the attack on Thiepval, the Schwaben Redoubt and the ridge to its east.

The four tanks were divided into pairs;[84] the western pair was *Crème de Menthe* and *Cordon Rouge* supporting 54th Brigade whilst the eastern pair, allocated to 53rd Brigade, was the Female *Cognac*, skippered by Bluemel, and another whose name has not been recorded but was probably the spare Male tank *Cupid*.[85] The commanders of the pair supporting 34th Brigade at Mouquet Farm are also not identified; they were probably drawn from spare tanks held at the Loop – one of which (Female No. 542) was allocated to C Company and fitted with a grenade roof.[86] The tanks' orders, like those for the Reserve Army for the attack on 15 September, were to follow the infantry during the first stage of the attack, who were to stay as close as possible to the creeping barrage.

Preparation for Battle

The tanks left for their Starting Point on the afternoon of 25 September. Archard, who was again a member of *Cognac's* crew, described the deployment of the Eastern Pair in his diary.[87] They left their base at 1400 hours and, passing the lakes near Aveluy, paused at Authuille Wood (A4) where they had a meal. After dark, *Cognac* then drove north to their Point of Assembly which was a quarry near the Nab (B4). The journey was delayed by the problem of negotiating old barbed wire. The tank arrived after midnight, after which it was camouflaged and the crew rested. They made their own breakfast at 0830 hours and took their camouflage sheets to a camp

---

83   Miles. *OHGW*, p. 393 fn. 3.
84   See Appendix XV for 18th Division 'Orders for the Employment of Tanks', 25 September 1916.
85   It was probably manned by crewmen who did not see action on 15 September. Two of those recorded as injured in C Company's War Diary for the period 25–27 September were originally members of *Chablis* crew.
86   The tank had not been previously allocated to an earlier attack. The remains of the grenade roof can clearly be seen in a painting of the tank produced in the winter of 1917.
87   Tank Museum acquisition number E2006.3104.

about a mile away, before they prepared for action. [88] At 1200 hours, an officer and a section from 8th Norfolks met up with the eastern pair, their task being to act as escorts and move any wounded men out of the paths of the tanks. The Starting Point for the western pair was the Caterpillar Dump at the southern end of Thiepval Wood (A3). Their deployment route probably used the road from Aveluy to Authuille, which 18th Division had screened from observation using brushwood hedge, [89] to the southwest corner of Thiepval Wood before driving east up the hill to the dump.

The final pair, which was to support 34th Brigade's attack on Mouquet Farm, was tasked to deploy from a point west of Pozières. They may have deployed from the tankodrome near Aveluy or they could have deployed directly from the Loop. They are likely to have waited near Ovillers (south of B5), where a brigade headquarters was located and which was out of enemy sight in accordance with 11th Division's direction. The assaulting troops of 34th Brigade (8th Northumberland Fusiliers on the left and 9th Lancashire Fusiliers (right) were positioned on the British frontline by daybreak (0527 hours). 53rd Brigade of 18th Division moved forward at 0600 hours and the assaulting units were in their jumping-off trenches by 1000 hours. Keeping the troops out of sight, and preventing the Germans disrupting the assembly, was well organised and war diaries record that there was no effective artillery fire on the concentration of troops in those trenches until Zero.

Zero

Zero was at 1235 hours. The weather was fine and clear with temperatures reaching a maximum of 75 degrees Fahrenheit.

Capture of Mouquet Farm

On the right flank, bombing parties quickly crossed no man's land whilst an initial artillery barrage neutralised High Trench and 34th Brigade Trench Mortar Battery bombarded Mouquet Farm. Within 30 seconds of Zero, bombers had secured the entrance of the cellars underneath the farm, preventing the German garrison disrupting the assault. The assaulting battalions successfully reached High Trench, which sat 200 yards to the northeast of the farm, and 34th Brigade had taken their First Objective within 15 minutes. The Germans quickly laid down a barrage on the British frontline to prevent a further advance. Having been concealed until Zero, the tanks drove north via Mouquet Farm in order to assist the attack on Zollern Redoubt. According to the Brigade post-operational report, both tanks drove into deep holes at 1330 hours and were still stuck three days later; the Female (No. 542) became ditched within 50 yards south of the farm and was never recovered.

Despite the Germans' attempts to delay the advance, the attacks by 34th Brigade on the Second and Third Objectives were successful. Zollern Trench was cleared by 1318 hours and, at 1500 hours, an Artillery Observation Officer reported that the infantry were in Stuff Redoubt and more than 100 prisoners had been taken. As expected, the Germans bombarded

88   Possibly in Ovillers
89   GHF Nichols, *18th Division in the Great War* (Uckfield: N&MP facsimile) p. 80.

the Redoubt and the attackers had to fight for their lives. It was not until 1825 hours that it was confirmed that Stuff Redoubt had been captured. Mouquet Farm was captured in the late afternoon, having been masked since Zero. At 1630 hours, the Germans were causing so many casualties that an ad hoc party, including the crew of Female tank No. 542, lined the top of the mound which was all that remained of the farm. They placed two machine-guns from the tank to cover the western and north entrances of the farm whilst grenades were thrown into the cellars with no obvious effect. One hour later, smoke bombs were thrown down the entrances into the farm and shortly afterwards the garrison surrendered. One officer and 55 other ranks came out and, when the complex was cleared, three machine-guns, two flame throwers and two gas canisters were found. The Brigade War Diary states that the final taking of the farm could not be claimed by a single unit as men from 6th East Yorkshires, 11th Manchesters, 5th Dorsets and the crew of tank No. 542 were all present. Sadly, the name of the tank officer and the members of his crew were not recorded.

Capture of Thiepval

In the centre, 53rd Brigade attacked with 10th Essex deploying against the eastern side of Thiepval village whilst 8th Suffolks on their right cleared the open ground as far as the Zollern Trench. Following an excellent creeping barrage, the infantry quickly reached the German frontline, known as Joseph's Trench, arriving at Zero. They captured the position by 1241 hours and then took the First Objective (Schwaben Trench) by 1247 hours.

According to Archard, *Cognac* made good progress towards the frontline and was traversing a large hole when a German shell burst just in front of the tank; this made the ground so soft that the tank became bellied and the tracks were unable to gain purchase. *Cognac's* crew, who had plenty of experience of digging on 15 September, extracted the tank just before dark and returned to the quarry where they had spent the previous night. They arrived back at the tankodrome on 27 September and returned to the Loop on 1 October.[90] The second tank (probably *Cupid*) became ditched in a massive crater in the German frontline but the driver managed to extricate it. The tank pushed on north, arriving at the First Objective which followed the road from Pozières to Thiepval. Here the tank stuck again, Inglis reporting on 27 September that it had engine trouble but it was recoverable.[91] Sadly, the ditched tank was later hit by two or three large German shells which set it on fire and it was abandoned.

Despite the lack of tanks, the infantry successfully reached Zollern Trench, their Second Objective, by 1315 hours. At this point, casualties amongst the attacking battalions were light and more than 400 German prisoners were taken. At 1415 hours, 53rd Brigade started their advance towards the Schwaben Redoubt. Although successful for the first 250 yards, the attack was slowed due to machine-gun fire from Bulgar Trench. At 1535 hours, the lead battalions

---

90   Author's note: It was the only tank from No. 1 Section to return. See C Company's War Diary. Sadly, it was badly damaged two weeks later after it had been assigned to A Company. See Archard's diary for 13 October.

91   Archard's diary for 1 October describes an attempt to extract a tank near Thiepval. The approach route was across a ploughed field which indicates the tank was *Crème de Menthe*. On their arrival the area was shelled by the German so the unditching party took cover in one of the deep bunkers built by the Germans in the village.

were still 600 yards short of the Final Objective. By 1642 hours, 54th Brigade pushed into 53rd Brigade's area where the attacking units started to consolidate their position on the Second Objective. At 1751 hours, 53rd Brigade was warned to attack towards Schwaben Redoubt, preceded by a new barrage. However, at 1830 hours, the assault was cancelled and orders were given for the troops to consolidate on Zollern Trench.

In the west, 54th Brigade's initial assault on Thiepval's western defences was disrupted by a German machine-gun hidden in no man's land. It was located and silenced by *Crème de Menthe* which was following the British infantry as ordered. The tank was also behind the initial assault as its route across no man's land was to reach the Chateau; this required an 800 yards advance climbing almost 44 yards in height. *Cordon Rouge*, which broke through the frontline trenches further south, became ditched as she tried to push north toward the Chateau. The attacking infantry were held up again by machine-guns located in the remains of the Chateau, which had been turned into a pile of bricks by previous artillery bombardments. The enemy stoutly resisted 12th Middlesex's efforts but it was eventually cleared after *Crème de Menthe* arrived and neutralised the position. The Male tank then moved north towards its First Objective, the road which ran west to east through the village but ditched as she crossed a communication trench which followed Mill Road. Maxwell, who commanded 12th Middlesex, believed the tanks' failure was not the crews' fault:

> We had two tanks with us, but they failed us as they only could fail in such country; both arrived on the scene behind us not in line with us; one got ditched hopelessly almost immediately and was left behind – the other was panting along boldly, but trying to dodge wounded men, lost ground and fell behind and finally got ditched also.[92]
>
> I wonder if anyone has learnt the lesson about them viz those monsters must precede troops and not follow. Nobody seems to have thought of the wounded men difficulty; some were, I fear, rolled over.[93]

Maxwell's last comment seems unfounded given that HQ 18th Division had given clear orders that escorts should be provided by the attacking brigades exactly for that purpose (see Appendix XV, paragraph 6).

The 11th Royal Fusiliers, assaulting with 12th Middlesex on the right, painstakingly cleared the German trench system and the associated 144 dugouts. Thiepval village was eventually cleared at 1700 hours. 45 minutes later, after HQ 54th Brigade identified that 6th Northamptons could not attack the Schwaben Redoubt that evening, 18th Division gave direction to its units to consolidate the ground they held. As a result, *Crème de Menthe* remained where she was, covering the approaches to the north and west. The clearance of the bulk of Thiepval Ridge defences was not achieved until 29 September; removing the Germans from the defences to northwest of Thiepval and Courcelette took a further five weeks.

92 Author's note: The first mentioned was *Cordon Rouge*, the other was *Crème de Menthe*.
93 Maxwell's letter dated 27 September 1916: NAM 1974-02-31-13.

Tank Effectiveness

Creme de Menthe's actions in no man's land and at Thiepval Chateau undoubtedly saved lives. Whilst none of the tanks played a significant role on 26 September, Haig took a more positive view: 'On the left of the attack fierce fighting, in which tanks again gave valuable assistance to our troops (18th Division), continued in Thiepval during that day and the following night, but by 8.30 a.m. on the 27th September the whole of the village of Thiepval was in our hands.'

Casualties

The official history gives no details of overall casualties sustained by II Corps on 26 September, other than 54th Brigade which suffered 840 from the 2,240 officers and men who went into action. Nor is there any detail of German casualties although Maxwell observed:

> It was an extraordinarily difficult battle to fight owing to every landmark, such as a map shows, being obliterated – absolutely and totally. The ground was of course the limit itself, and progress over it like nothing imaginable. The enemy quite determined to keep us out as they had so many times before. And I must say that they fought most stubbornly and bravely: and probably not more than 300 to 500 put their hands up. We accomplished three quarters of it, and were extraordinarily lucky at that, and it seems to have surprised the high command, which at least is something. But the price has been heavy; how heavy I don't know as regards men yet, but as regards officers I have, of the 20 who went over, nine killed, seven wounded and four (including myself) untouched, I lost all my regimental staff, with three officers and RSM killed.[94]

Whilst *Cognac* was quickly recovered, *Crème de Menthe* and *Cordon Rouge* were firmly stuck. They and the other three ditched tanks were subsequently destroyed by enemy artillery fire. There were three recorded casualties amongst the tank crews: Gnrs Bill Boylin and William Cheadle who originally were members of *Chablis'* crew, and Gnr William Jones of *Cordon Rouge*.[95] 2Lt Robert Aitken, who was C Company' reserve skipper, suffered injuries to his first and second fingers of right hand when his tank was hit and he was evacuated to the Queen Alexandra's Military Hospital at Millbank.[96] Boylin recovered and was commissioned in September 1917. He served with 11th Tank Battalion until 2 October 1918, when he joined HQ Tank Corps as an equipment officer. Cheadle who also returned to England, did not redeploy and later served with the Labour Corps.

---

94   Letter dated 27 September 1916 (**NAM** 1974-02-31-130 and diary (NAM 1978-07-25-1).
95   Jones suffered gunshot wounds to his leg and was evacuated to Glasgow. He applied for a commission in Jan 1917 and returned to France with G Battalion. He was commissioned in the Tank Corps on 13 July 1918.
96   Aitken suffered from neuralgia for the rest of his service. He relinquished his commission on account of ill-health contracted on active service and was granted the hon rank of lieutenant on 25 August 1918. He initially settled near Bovington, married a woman from Milton Abbas and they had two children. The family made their way to Australia but returned in 1926. They moved to Norfolk and then established a turkey farm in Taverham. He died, aged 77, in 1971. Pope, *FTC*, p. 277.

Conclusions

The tanks contributed little to the success achieved on 26 September. However, *Creme de Menthe*'s actions in no man's land saved lives and her timely arrival at Thiepval Chateau turned the battle for 12th Middlesex. The main difficulty for the tanks was the poor condition of the ground and the lack of expertise amongst drivers. In spring 1917, training was increased to provide skilled drivers, who generally coped with the ground during the Battles of Arras and Messines. Sadly, no amount of training would have helped the drivers of tanks in the Ypres Salient, which became known as 'The Graveyard of the Tanks'.

Capture of Eaucourt L'Abbaye, 1 October 1916

Preparation

By the end of September, the majority of D Company had moved back from their advanced base at Green Dump to the Loop. Three tanks were still with Mann supporting III Corps,[97] whilst three more, under the command of Inglis who had been detached from C Company, were to support operations north of Flers.[98] Salvage work continued, under the control of 711 MT Company, supported by working parties initially under command of Captain Graeme Nixon.[99]

Mann was tasked to support III Corps' ongoing advance northeast towards Bapaume. The next attack, on 1 October, would be on the fortified farm complex of Eaucourt l'Abbaye (map 7, map square B2), which sat just behind the Flers Line, and the village of Le Sars (A1), which secured the main road from Albert to Bapaume. Exactly where Mann's section was based at this time is unknown; it may have still been near Contalmaison but it is possible he had moved his headquarters forward to Martinpuich.[100]

The Plan

HQ III Corps' plan was for 50th (Northumberland) Division was to capture Le Sars on the Pozières to Bapaume road; in the centre, 47th (2nd London) Division to attack to Eaucourt l'Abbaye whilst the NZ Division was to take the ground to the east of Eaucourt l'Abbaye including a feature known as the Circus. The former abbey was now a substantial farm; the cellars of the abbey and the outbuildings had been fortified making it a formidable objective. Two of the three available tanks were allocated in support of the Londoners but no support

---

97 These three tanks were commanded by Bell, Bown and Wakeley; two other tanks had been destroyed at Martinpuich and Courcelette whilst Enoch's original was still at the Loop.

98 These tanks were commanded by Hastie, Head and Pearsall - see Chapter 7.

99 Four tanks were recovered to the Dump: 753 (initially commanded by Sellick), 515 (Storey's original tank), 742? (Enoch) and 559 (Hastie). Disposition of tanks as of 29 September 1916 with pencilled updates in Woods' Correspondence Book.

100 Mann had visited Woods at Green Dump on 29 September; Woods later wrote that day asking Mann to accompany him to the Loop the next morning to see Summers. Summers wished Mann to provide a tank to Woods at Green Dump to bring the total there to three. Two memos dated 29 September in Woods' Correspondence Book.

to the other divisions.[101] Bown was again in command of the Male tank 720, with tank crew D8, whilst the Female tank 538, probably still known as *Dracula*, was commanded by Wakley. The D16 crew included a new driver, LCpl Wilfred Brookes, who was also be the second in command but it meant that there was no NCO supervising the gunners.[102]

The tanks were to move from their base under cover of darkness on 30 September–1 October, driving along the north-western edge of High Wood (A4), to the Starfish Redoubt, where they would lay up under camouflage. The skippers were ordered not to deploy from their hide until Zero, presumably to maintain surprise. (It appears the lessons from Enoch's action at Martinpuich had been quickly learned). The tanks were then to drive to Cough Drop (B3) and then follow the communications trench (Drop Alley), to the double trench system of the Flers line. The tanks would then drove in a north-westerly direction to the fam built on the remains of Eaucourt l'Abbaye. The tanks and the infantry were to be supported by aircraft of 34 Squadron RFC in the contact role.[103]

Zero

Zero was 1515 hours on 1 October; it was a fine autumn day.[104]

Tank Action

The tanks' initial approach started well, covering 1,100 yards in only 40 minutes,[105] which was later reported as a 'record sprint for the tank.'[106] Bown's Male tank successfully crossed both elements of the Flers Line and, then having achieved a right angle to the line of the infantry advance, opened fire on the farm at 1631 hours at a range of 450 yards. Wakley, who had followed in *Dracula*, crossed the first trench and then drove northwest, his crew using the Vickers machine-guns in both sponsons to suppress the German defenders in the front and support trenches.

Unfortunately, as the Female tank reached the vicinity of the former abbey, the most westerly 47th Division troops were still in no man's land. Their battalions had got into difficulty from the start, not leaving their jumping-off trenches in good order nor using the creeping barrage to best effect. On the right, 1/19th Londons was checked by machine-gun fire when 50 yards from the frontline trench and waited in shellholes for the arrival of the tanks. As the tanks went past, the Londoners advanced, cleared both trench lines and joined up with the Kiwis. In the centre, 1/20th Londons were also able to advance after the tanks had passed along the two trenches, sweeping through the farm buildings without clearing them, and joining up with the 1/19th Londons.

---

101 The third tank was commanded by Bell. See below.
102 This indicates the shortage of trained drivers amongst the ASC company.
103 The tanks' progress was recorded by Maj JA Chamier, it was 2 Lt Pearson who observed Bown's tank in action. Pidgeon, *Tanks on the Somme,* pp. 39–43.
104 Miles, *OHGW,* p. 429.
105 Twenty-seven yards per minute, although less one mile per hour, was almost double the original planning speed for movement across a damaged battlefield.
106 *The Daily Sketch,* 6 October 1916.

Having reached the farm complex, Bown attempted to smash through the wire defences. However, the tank became entangled within it and the D8 crew had to abandon it, Bown setting fire to the tank in accordance with his orders.[107] According to D Company's War Diary, *Dracula* became stuck at M23c 2,4, which was also in the wire but south of the farm. Wakley may therefore have been trying to break down the obstacle and allow the attacking battalion to get forward. Wakley ordered Brookes to disentangle the barbed wire with nippers, but he was unsuccessful, so the skipper ordered Brookes to set fire to the tank. Wakley meanwhile left the tank to find a way out for the D16 crew but was hit, almost immediately, by shell fragments.[108]

The German defenders. northwest of the abbey, then counter-attacked down the Flers Line and *Dracula*'s crew became trapped;[109] Brookes was shot in the right forearm, sustaining a compound fracture. They spent the remainder of the afternoon, and overnight, in shellholes taking cover.[110] HQ 47th Division, realising 1/19th Londons were incapable of attacking again, sent 1/23rd Londons into action at 0630 hours on 2 October but they made no progress and took 170 casualties. Rain started at 1100 hours which continued for the next two days, the conditions being described by Gnr Cecil Frost in a letter to his parents:

> I had such a frightful experience last week, lost all my clothes, equipment etc and nearly got captured or killed by the Huns. I stopped in a huge shell hole for two days without any food or drink, and all manner of shells dropping round me. Only in the darkness could I escape. If ever I thought of home and all our little ups and downs it was then.
>
> Of course, you will have read the accounts of our doings. It almost makes me sick to read about them. Nobody has described our affair correctly; probably they could not but they are not allowed to. We lost two officers in our crowd and two men are wounded. I dared not move for snipers; their bullets whistled and pinged around me for hours.
>
> You should see our airmen; they are just grand. No wonder we lose a few planes; they come down to about 40 feet, just to see what is going on. Very rarely does a Hun plane come over our front line and, if he does, he gets it hot.
>
> My words I have seen some sights. They would have made me sick at home. How they smash up the villages and countryside; hardly a brick left standing. It's a good job it is not in dear old England.[111]

It was not until 3 October that the crews were able to get Wakley and the other casualties back to the British lines. Bown had remained in the area throughout and did not return to the Loop until 4 October. On the left, the attack by 50th Division on 1 October at Le Sars failed although they did make some lodgements in the Flers Line. Despite the strength of the German

---

107 Gnr Eddie Williams was wounded as the D8 crew withdrew.
108 Wakley suffered a compound fracture above the left knee; his leg was subsequently amputated from just below the hip.
109 Part of *2nd Regiment, 17th Reserve Division*. See Miles, *OHGW,* p. 430 fn. 4.
110 Those known to have remained with Wakley were Brooks (wounded on 1 October), Glaister (wounded on 2 October), Cecil Frost, Charles Foot and Fred Roberts.
111 The letter was published in the *Western Morning News* on 20 October 1916.

positions, and lack of tank support on the right, the Kiwis managed to break through the Flers Line to the east of the abbey and quickly took the Circus. Their attack was not however without loss, one of their fatalities being Sgt Donald Brown who had won the Victoria Cross during the attack at the Switch Trench. The Germans withdrew from the abbey complex on 4 October but they continued to hold Le Sars which was not taken until 8 October.[112]

Jake Glaister. (TMA)

Tank Effectiveness

The pair were certainly effective up to the point when they became ditched in the German defences. Their guns and machine-guns engaged the defenders in both the trenches and defensive positions, enabling the infantry to advance and take most of the objectives. Bown once again showed his determination to flatten protective wire close to the final objective but on this occasion was defeated by its density. Wakley also employed *Dracula* in the final stages of the attack but was unable to smash down the wire and allow the attacking infantry to break through.

Losses and Gallantry Awards

The Official History does not detail the casualties suffered by 47th Division on 1 October, only stating that they were heavy. 1/23rd Londons suffered 170 casualties during the follow on attack on 2 October, which shows how effective the Bavarian defence at Eaucourt l'Abbaye remained. Wakley, Glaister and Brooks were so seriously wounded that they could not return to frontline duty.[113] Gnrs Charles Foot and

---

112 The Bavarians believed that Eaucourt l'Abbaye was lost on the afternoon on 1 October but they continued to deny the position for two further days. Miles, *OHGW,* p. 431.

113 Wakley served at the War Office, in a technical role, for the rest of the war. Glaister, who served at Bovington as an instructor, was awarded a 20 percent disability pension. Brookes was invalided home to the Bangour War Hospital, near Edinburgh, where he stayed for 11 months, latterly being employed in the X-ray department. He was then posted to the Tank Corps Depot, at Worgret Camp, where contracted Cerebral-Spinal Meningitis. He died at the Weymouth Isolation Hospital, aged 26, on 2 February 1918.

Jake Glaister were subsequently awarded the DCM,[114] whilst Corp Wilfred Brookes and Gnr Fred Roberts received the MM.

Capture of Le Sars, 7 October 1916

The Local Situation

Whilst 2nd and 3rd Canadian divisions were engaged in attacking the Germans to the north and west of Courcelette, in the area of Regina Trench, 1st Canadian Division had pushed northeast towards Le Sars. III Corps, to their east, continued a slow but steady advance into the German depth positions to the east of the Pozières to Albert road. On 1 October 23rd Division captured the Flers Line Trenches which protected the southwestern entrance to Le Sars. Elements of 69th Brigade captured the Flers Support Trench to the west of the Bapaume road, about 200 yards from the village whilst 70th Brigade made progress in taking the Support Trench. 47th Division and the NZ Division attacked the area of Eaucourt l'Abbaye on 1 October, and after three days of hard fighting, the German withdrew. The next objective was the village of Le Sars and the ground to its northwest and northeast.[115]

The Ground and German Dispositions

Le Sars is 1,200 yards from the northern outskirts of Courcelette and about a mile north of Martinpuich. The village sits on the Roman road between Albert and Bapaume and, in October 1916, was protected by the Flers Line and Flers Support Trenches which originally connected the village to Eaucourt l'Abbaye. The area around Le Sars was initially the site of German artillery positions, which had protected the German second line defences captured during the Battle of Flers-Courcelette. It was now a defended locality, protected by the Flers Line and a set of field defences known as the Tangle to its southeast. The area was held by three regiments of *4th Ersatz Division*.

Summary and Plan Development

Le Sars was to be assaulted by two brigades; 68th Brigade, which had relieved 70th Brigade on the right, whilst 69th Brigade were to attack again on the left. Tanks were at a premium as both C and D Companies were being sent north of the River Ancre. III Corps had only one tank available, all others in Mann's section having been destroyed in action. That singleton tank, commanded by Bell, was allocated to support 68th Brigade. The weather on 2 and 3 October was so foul that so the assault on Le Sars was postponed on 4 October. Despite the postponement of the main attack, soldiers from 69th Brigade tried to improve their hold on the Flers Support Trench northwest of the Bapaume Road. Attacking at 1800 hours that evening,

---

114 Foot, who was later appointed lance corporal, was killed in action on 20 November 1917 after his tank *Deborah* was knocked out of the northeast edge of Flesquieres. See Volume Three of this History.
115 III Corps Operation Order 143, October 1916.

their aim was to provide a jumping off position for the assault on the western edge of Le Sars but they were driven out by the German defenders after their stock of grenades was exhausted.

On 5 October 23rd Division issued orders in accordance with III Corps programme for the attack on Le Sars which would take place on 7 October. These stated that 68th Brigade was to cross 250 yards of open ground from the Flers Support Line northwards to the Tangle. Their route was dominated by machine-guns on the edge of the village and they were therefore allocated Bell's tank in support. 69th Brigade had to clear the remainder of Flers Support Trench, which protected to the southwest of the village, before fighting their way up the ribbon of houses along the main road. They were tasked to meet up with 68th Brigade at a crossroads in the centre of the village. The final Divisional objective was 500 yards northeast of the village close to, and dominated by, the Butte de Warlencourt.

Zero

Zero was 1345 hours on 7 October. Weather conditions were initially good but deteriorated overnight.

Allied Forces

The Infantry

The 23rd Division, which had arrived in France in August 1915, initially held the line in the area around Armentieres. In March 1916, the Division moved south of Loos to take over the line from the French forces. On 21 May, during the German assault on Vimy Ridge, the Division fought alongside 47th Division. 23rd Division was then withdrawn for intensive training and, joining III Corps, took part in the capture of Contalmaison. They had been in the field since relieving 9th (Scottish) Division at Martinpuich on 17 September. Their first experience of working with tanks on 25 September at 26th Avenue was not good. Despite this setback, they had successfully fought their way to the outskirts of Le Sars on 1 October and, as the action of 69th Brigade on the evening of 4 October revealed, their fighting spirit was undaunted. They cut their way through the thick barbed wire, protecting the Support Trench, and held it until their stock of grenades was exhausted. As they withdrew, 2Lt Henry Kelly of 10th Duke of Wellington's Regiment carried his wounded sergeant major for 70 yards across no man's land. He was subsequently awarded the Victoria Cross.[116]

The Tanks

The D2 tank crew, commanded by Bell, were probably still mounted in the Female tank No. 539. They were initially part of E Group supporting 41st Division during their attack on Flers on 15 September. The tank ditched on its way into action and Bell was wounded by a splinter from a high explosive shell as the crew extracted the vehicle. The D2 tank crew was allocated

---

116 Kelly was also awarded the MC and a Bar for actions in Italy in June and October 1918.

to Mann's section on 22 September as one of the replacements for those tanks lost or ditched on 15 September at High Wood. There is no record of the crew seeing action before 7 October although the tank may have been that which ditched on 24 September prior to the attack on Martinpuich.

Deployment for Battle

The two assaulting brigades of 23 Division were already in the frontline. On the afternoon of 6 October, soldiers from 68th Brigade got into the Tangle, in order to gain a jumping-off point for the following day but were forced to withdraw by a German bombardment.[117] Bell left his Point of Assembly at Martinpuich, at some time on the morning of 7 October, and drove alongside the track towards Eaucourt l'Abbaye. He stopped at the track junction 825 yards from the abbey and turned north to follow the track which skirted the east of Le Sars ultimately leading to the Butte de Warlencourt. According to the D Company War Diary, his Starting Point was 100 yards to the west of the track junction, which would have been easy for Bell to locate. His approach to his First Objective (the Tangle) was then due north, which in daylight, should have made navigation easy.[118]

Capture of Le Sars, 7 October 1916

The report on operations of 23rd Division,[119] and the Official History of the Great War,[120] provide a good description of the attack on Le Sars. The two lead battalions were 12th Durham Light Infantry (DLI) on the right, supported by Bell's tank, whilst 9th Yorkshires on the left led 69th Brigade into action. Both battalions advanced rapidly, Bell crossing the British frontline at 1346 hours despite having difficulty getting across the infantry jumping-off lines. This was very neatly timed as Bell would have been warned not to arrive early and provide the enemy with a clue as to the imminence of Zero.

The 12th DLI advanced with their left-hand company astride the communications trench which led from the Flers Support Line to the Tangle. Bell advanced behind the infantry, who were presumably following a creeping barrage, and 'did excellent service in assisting clearing the Germans from the Tangle.' The tank then turned west and followed the sunken lane which linked Eaucourt l'Abbaye towards Le Sars. As it advanced towards the village, the tank was struck by a German artillery shell and put out of action. It then caught fire before it was able to assist the DLI into the village. The 23rd Division report states that 'Bell showed great determination and pluck under very adverse circumstances.' Enfiladed by machine-gun fire, and unable to enter the village, 12th DLI dug defensive positions on the sunken lane. As a result, they could not marry up with 13th DLI who were clearing the south-eastern half of the village.

The 9th Green Howards, who took over the attack from 9th Yorkshires on the western side of the Bapaume road, succeeded in clearing the houses to the crossroads in the centre of the

---

117 Miles, *OHGW*, pp. 443–4
118 Author's note: I have no doubt, despite the lack of records, that Bell had recced the route, marked it with tape, and familiarised himself with it, on a number of occasions.
119 Report on the Operations of 23 Division from 19 September to 8 October 1916.
120 Miles, *OHGW*, p. 437.

village. On the right of 69th Brigade, the initial assault by 11th West Yorkshires was initially checked but later that afternoon, the battalion, supported by 10th Duke of Wellingtons, cleared the Flers Line to within 300 yards of the inter-army boundary. Also in the afternoon, 9th Green Howards and 13th DLI cleared the rest of the village and established posts of the northern outskirts of Le Sars. CO 13th DLI then sought reinforcements of two infantry companies, and a tank, in order to capture their Final Objective near the Butte but these were unavailable.

Consolidation

Overnight, the weather broke and the British battalions consolidated their positions, evacuating their wounded in the rain. An early morning (0450 hours) attack by 23rd Division caught units of *4th Ersatz Division* whilst they were reorganising and gains were made including the whole of the Flers trench system northwest to the army boundary. The Division also overran a German position in a quarry 750 yards northwest of the village, thereby securing the village against counter-attack.

Casualties and Prisoners

On 7 and 8 October 23rd Division sustained less than 750 losses. The casualties amongst their opponents in *4th Ersatz Division* are not recorded but, in 24 hours, 23rd Division captured 11 officers and 517 other ranks, including soldiers from two battalions of *360th Infantry Regiment* who were completing a Relief in Place when a pre-dawn attack struck at 0450 hours. Three of the tank crewmen were injured by shrapnel as they made their way to their own lines after their tank had been put out of action. All, however, made a full recovery after hospital treatment and they returned to duty.

Tank Effectiveness

Although only in action for a short period, the tank assisted the attacking infantry to take their First Objective and would have led them into the village had it not been struck by artillery fire.[121]

Summary

The victory of 23rd Division, in a one on one fight against a German Ersatz Division in a strong defensive position, was considered by the editor of the Official History of the Great War to be a striking success.[122] Bell's own action reinforced Swinton's original opinion that tanks were a useful auxiliary to the infantry when used for suitable tasks. They were not however invulnerable, especially when operating near defensive positions registered by German artillery.

---

121 Bell was again in action on 14 November, when his tank played a key role in the capture of a German strongpoint and its garrison at Hamel. See Chapter 9.
122 The usual ratio of attacking troops to defenders is three to one.

Visiting the Battlefields

This tour starts, and ends, at the Memorial to the Missing south of Pozières on the D929 road Route de Bapaume). It takes some two and a half hours to drive in a car, with a series of optional walks which will double the duration.

Park your car by the Memorial, facing north and cross the road. Walk downhill to its corner, looking down the road. The tankodrome, where No. 1 Section of C Company was based near the Aveluy lakes on the eastern side of the River Ancre, is half right. You can visit this as part of our tour of the Northern Flank (chapter 9). On the evening of 14 September, the six tanks drove from the Tankodrome to La Boiselle and then up the road towards you; it was in this area that the tanks were replenished and Gnr Rowntree was wounded. This is also the place where Horace Brotherwood, driver of *Champagne*, was brought after his death on 15 September. His body is buried in the cemetery within the Memorial; his grave marker, engraved with the badge of the RASC, is number II F 27 – please pay your respects to this brave crewman.

Return to your car and drive northeast, following the D929 through Pozières, passing Le Tommy and five pedestrian crossings. Fork left, at the Calvary, along the minor road (C6) signed Courcelette and you are on the battlefield. As you drive, you will see the main road to your right and a large television mast. This marks the frontline of the Canadian forces on 15 September. It is not advisable to walk on the fields, as they are private property, but the tracks may be used by pedestrians. On the left-hand side of Rue de Courcelette, you will see a track. Park in the area and walk to the track; you are now on the starting lines for 6 Canadian Brigade who would assault Courcelette village. You can see how light the soil is; it is very sticky when wet and, on 15 September, it was cratered with overlapping shellholes. The tanks from the Western Group started 500 and 600 yards to your north (left) along the line of the track.

Now return to your car and drive on for 800 yards – this is where Sugar Trench crossed the battlefield (see colour photograph 15). *Cordon Rouge* followed the trench from left to right towards the main road, and the Sugar Factory. You can no longer see the exact location of the factory from your current position as it is masked by trees. Continue on to the T-junction with Grand Rue and park by the sign to the Courcelette Military Cemetery. You are the exact spot where *Cognac* slipped into the communication trench which ran alongside track to your left. It is also where the crew worked for 12 hours to extract the tank; a task they achieved two days later.

Walk 1 (45 minutes). If you wish to see where *Champagne* and *Cognac* were first stopped on 15 September, follow the metalled road southwest towards the CWGC cemetery. At the first fork, where the metalled road bears right towards a group of trees marking the Cemetery, bear left and follow the track for 750 yards. The fields to your left are generally above a small bank; as the track rises to the level of the fields, you are in the area where *Champagne* ditched. The bank, and the communications trench on the side of the track, is probably the reason why both *Champagne* and *Cognac* could not turn east across the fields, as ordered, along the route of Sugar Trench. Now return to your vehicle, noting how open the battlefield was and how little cover there was from view and machine-gun fire.

Drive through Courcelette, passing the church on your left, to the T-junction. This was probably the route taken by the D22 crew on the morning of 26 September. Turn right and drive up the hill to the D929 crossroads and pause on the hardstanding to your left. The road opposite, leading down into Martinpuich, was Gun Pit Lane and it was probably the route taken by *Creme de Menthe* and *Cordon Rouge* on 15 September about 0800 hours. Now look left, across the roads and over the fields; these were crossed by the trench named 26th Avenue and they were scene of Enoch's action on 25 September.[123] On 26 September, around noon, Robinson and the D22 crew quickly drove along 26th Avenue but the tank was harried back to the Canadian lines by German artillery. The exact spot where the tank was destroyed was between the main road and the village, about 200 yards of your current position. Before you leave, remember the old Balloon Café at the crossroads as you will use it to navigate later in the tour.

The site of the Sugar Factory is to your right, 750 yards up the D929; it is privately owned and not accessible to the public – I **do not recommend walking** to see it owing to traffic speed. Follow the D929 up the hill; this route was used by *Crème de Menthe* to reach the Sugar Factory and the route back, with *Cordon Rouge*, to reach to their Rallying Point. (Now the site of the Tank Corps Memorial.)

If you need a comfort break, I suggest you drive into Pozières and stop at *Le Tommy*. If not, drive on up the D929, taking the D73 on the left signed Bazentin. Drive southeast and, after 0.8 mile, you will see a sign for a crossroads with a tree-lined track on the right-hand side. This track was used by Mann and Drader in the early hours of 15 September on their way from Contalmaison (to your right) to their Starting Point at Pithie's Post (to your left). Do not attempt to follow the route on the left as it becomes impassable to cars.

After a further 0.6 mile, just after the sign for Bazentin-le-Petit, there is another crossroads. Turn sharp left and follow the unnamed road (marked with a 10t limit) north towards Martinpuich. As you drive north, you will see High Wood on the horizon to your front and how it dominates the surrounding areas. Stones and Colle were driving parallel to your route, 300 yards to your right (east) following a minor track, at 0400 hours on 15 September heading for their own Starting Point which was 200 yards behind the British frontline. Follow the road downhill, slowing as you enter Martinpuich, and turn sharp left and **park**.

Walk 2 (More than 30 minutes). Follow the road northwest for 300 yards, passing the farm buildings, until fields are visible on your right. This road was used to guide *Daphne* to her Second Objective about 0700 hours on 15 September. *Daphne* drove parallel to the road, about 200 yards to your right in the fields, to a point where the tank's guns could dominate the German trench which linked Martinpuich to the Courcelette Sugar Factory. It was from here that *Daphne* returned to Contalmaison, two and a half miles south, to replenish her ammunition and fuel.

Now return your car, drive to the junction, giving way to traffic from the right, and stop at the next crossroads. Turn right and follow the D6 towards Longueval. As you leave Martinpuich, you will see a junction on the right-hand side, with ornamental hedges on each side on a metaled road. **Park** your car by the communal cemetery on your right.

Walk 3 (More than 20 minutes). Walk up the metalled road (it is a no-through road) towards the top of the hill. Pass through a line of trees in a sunken lane then, as the track levels out, stop and look to your left. The ground, which forms a shallow bowl, is the location of the German defensive position known as Tangle North; behind it, on the skyline, is High Wood. You are 300 yards from the German frontline which was to your south (right) just below the skyline. The attack on Tangle North was supported by tank crews D24 and D25, commanded by Stones and Colle. At about 0715 hours on 15 September, D24 was hit by two artillery shells, the second breaking the right-hand track, and the crew bailed out, taking cover amongst shell

---

123 You may see this location later in the tour.

holes and trenches about 150 yards from the road (see colour photograph 12). D25 pushed on down the hill and, having prevented German reinforcements moving between High Wood and Martinpuich, assisted 50th Division take the northeast side of the village. Colle's route was probably down the route you have just walked and then cross country towards the orchards and garden edge of Martinpuich where the Germans machine-guns were located.

Return to your car and follow the D6 road up the hill towards High Wood. There are two suitable places to park – the best is by the London Cemetery but there is also an unmetalled area at the far end of the wood on the right-hand side of the road. This unmetalled area is extensively used by farm machinery and entrances should not be blocked; the wood itself is also privately owned and cannot be entered. On 15 September 1916, four tanks were tasked to support 47th Division's attack. *Clan Ruthven*, commanded by Henderson, became stuck close to the southern face of the wood near the Memorial to The Highland Light Infantry 200 yards east (right) of the London Cemetery. Crew D13 in *Delilah*, commanded by Sampson, entered the wood to the west (left) of the 47th Division Monument. Now, walk or drive onto the eastern end of the wood. This is where *Delphine*, commanded by Sharp, and D22, commanded by Robinson, entered the wood. If you walk up the unmetalled track on the eastern (right-hand) edge of the wood, for about 200 yards, you will be in the area where Sharp's tank got stuck in the trees to your left. If you walk a further 100 yards, you will reach the area where Robinson's tank exited the wood. It crossed the track and then became stuck at Worcester Trench, which is about 50 yards south of the monument to the Cameron Highlanders and Black Watch. *Delilah* reached the centre of the wood but this area is not visible.

Returning to your vehicle, drive back into Martinpuich. At the crossroads, turn right and head north through the village for a mile to a sharp left-hand bend, where two small tracks go straight on. Park here on the right-hand side.

Walk 4 (More than 20 minutes). Walk up the main road up the hill for 400 yards. You are now on the line of 26th Avenue, running from Courcelette to Eaucourt l'Abbaye. Look to your left (colour photograph 14) and you will see Courcelette Church half right, the crossroads by the old Balloon café where D22 was knocked out, the line of trees screening the site of the Sugar Factory, and the TV mast which is next to the Tank Corps memorial where *Chartreuse* and *Chablis* were ditched. The view shows just how little cover from view was afforded to the attackers and how easily German artillery could target Enoch who was knocked out about 200 yards into the fields on your left. You can also see how easily D22 was observed as she advanced towards you from the Balloon Café crossroads. Then return to your car.

Drive straight on, following the left of the two unmetalled tracks north out of the village. You are now following Bell's route to Le Sars although you cannot follow it all the way as the road has been diverted for the last 500 yards. Passing the shrine on your right, follow the narrow road up the hill, with a line of trees and ditch on your right. The road surface gets uneven (there is also a 30 kph speed limit) so drive carefully. After 700 yards, you will reach a junction with a metalled track entering from the right. 200 yards further on, an electric power line crosses the road and then the road bears right, with a tree line going left across the fields; this is the line of the old track taken by Bell's tank on 7 October. As the tree line on your right stops, another track merges from the right. 500 yards ahead of you, on the right-hand side of the road, are some farm buildings; this is the site of Eaucourt l'Abbaye. Drive forward 200 yards and stop. You are crossing the Flers Line, and Wakley's tank was knocked out about 200 yards into the field on your right; Bown's tank was knocked out, 100 yards further down the road, about 50 yards on the right.

At the end of the road, by the farm entrance, turn left and follow the D11 road down the hill. After 500 yards, you will see a line of trees standing at right angles to the road. Immediately beyond the trees is a small stream; drive 200 yards further on and you will see a metalled track which joins the D11 at right angles. Pull into the side of the road; the Tangle was in the fields to your left and Bell's tank was knocked out just north (right) of where you have parked.

Continue into the village, stop at the crossroads, and then turn left on the D929 signed Courcelette. Drive down the D929 for one mile until you see an unsigned junction on the left; this is the area where Enoch and his crew were fighting on 25 September. Continue on the D929, passing the Balloon crossroads and then stop at the Tank Corps Memorial.

Memorial visit (30 minutes). The Tank Corps memorial is at the location of the Starting Point for the tanks of the Eastern Group on 15 September 1916, as well as the Rallying Point for the other three. *Chartreuse* got stuck in a huge shellhole here and *Chablis'* tracks came off about 100 yards into the fields to the southeast, leaving *Crème de Menthe* to attack alone. The Tank Memorial, construction of which was started during the winter of 1919,[124] is surrounded by a fence made from 6-pounder gun barrels linked by tank driving chains made in Coventry. These items came from the Central Stores and not, as sometimes stated, from Mark I hulks left on the Somme. The four bronze models of the Mark IV, Mark V, Whippet and Gun Carrying Tanks were cast in France, probably under arrangement of the Central Workshops. It is rather sad in my view, given the Memorial's location, that there is no model of a Mark I tank with its distinctive steering tail. The memorial lists the locations of battles where tanks were engaged in the Great War. Please feel free to leave a wreath or poppy cross to the memory of those who did not return home.

The tour finishes with a visit to Thiepval. Drive into Pozières and follow the sign for the Memorial. Travel north, along the D73, for one mile, pausing at the small memorial by Mouquet Farm. The track leads to the point where the Female tank 542 assisted 34th Brigade to clear the German held position – the tank becoming ditched only 50 yards from the farm buildings. Now drive on into Thiepval and park up in the Memorial car park.

Walk 6 (60 minutes). Go to the Memorial, walking up the stairs under the Arch and then stop on the terrace overlooking the cemetery. Where the hill falls away to your front, there is a wood line 800 yards away on the right – this was the Start Point for the attack by *Cordon Rouge* and *Crème de Menthe* on 26 September and also where the three tanks from A Company stopped before their attack on 13 November 1916. Now look right, along the terrace, and you will see a broad ride through the woods. *Cordon Rouge* became ditched on 26 September about 40 yards up this ride on the left-hand side. Before you return to your car, look up before you pass under the arch; the names of the crewmen whose graves are unknown are inscribed in the panels.

Now walk back towards your car, stopping where the paths cross by the café. Turn left and walk to the road – you will see the memorial to 18th Division on the far side – this provides a good view over the ground which *Crème de Menthe* crossed at the start of the attack. Turn right and walk alongside the road up the hill towards the farm complex on the left. This farm is on the

---

124 A progress report on the work was given by Charles Weaver Price, the QM for C and D Companies, who was working at HQ Tank Corps in Spring 1920 – the memorial was almost complete but not dedicated until 1922.

site of Thiepval Chateau where the timely arrival of *Crème de Menthe* ensured 12th Middlesex could take the location. Continue walking along the road, passing the church on your right, to the crossroads. Just down the hill is the final position reached by *Crème de Menthe*, the ground being such she became ditched and could not be removed. This is the end of the walk.

Crème de Menthe ditched at Thiepval. (TMA)

To return to your starting point, drive back to Pozières, turning right as you reach the D929 towards Albert. If you have not already done so, I recommend that you visit *Le Tommy*, which contains a group of fragments from *Chartreuse* and *Chablis*.

9

Tank Actions on the Northern Flank

The introduction of tanks during the Battle of Flers–Courcelette attracted criticism in that they were not used en masse but rather in small groups – even as driblets – contrary to Swinton's proposals.[1] Swinton's own view, later published in *Eyewitness* was that:

> The employment of a small number of Tanks during the Somme Battle was against the advice of those who had given most thought to the potentialities of the New Arm. So far, I have seen nothing to justify it, and personal inquiries have produced a similar negative result. No explanation is to be found in Sir Douglas Haig's published dispatches.
>
> To me the decision to give away the secret which had been so carefully kept for months and to squander the opportunity of a surprise was the more inexplicable, since both the Commander-in-Chief and his Chief of Staff had expressed their agreement with my memorandum—in which this course was specifically deprecated.
>
> It seems to have been brought about by disappointment at the lack of decisive results and the losses of the first days of the Somme offensive, and a desire to encourage our somewhat disheartened troops.[2]

Other adverse comments have been that their crews had insufficient training, the tanks were mechanically unreliable, that tactics had not been developed sufficiently for their effective use, that there was no formation training and there were insufficient spares to enable them to be used in more than one attack. Whilst these criticisms are perfectly fair, the C-in-C BEF's belief in the tank's potential was undiminished. On 20–21 September, Butler (Haig's deputy chief of staff) attended a conference at the WO in London, chaired by Maj Gen Robert Whigham (Deputy CIGS), for the expansion of the Heavy Section, based on Haig's request for 1,000 tanks which had been supported by Lloyd George.[3] Butler proposed that these tanks be arranged in five brigades (216 tanks each), each brigade consisting of three wings (later battalions) of

---

1 Swinton, *Notes on the Employment of Tanks,* February 1916. See Appendix III.
2 Swinton, *Eyewitness,* p. 294.
3 Liddell Hart, *The Tanks Volume One,* p. 79 states that an order for a further 100 tanks was made to keep the factories active; Stern in *Tanks 1914-18,* p. 106 gives the date as 16 October 1916. Glanfield, *Devil's Chariots* p. 146, links this order to the 100 made following the demonstration at Elveden on 21 July.

72 tanks, each consisting of three companies of 24 tanks. The meeting was also attended by Swinton and Brough who was now acting as Swinton's chief staff officer in Britain. The name of this enlarged structure was given due consideration. On 25 Sep 1916, Butler sent a memo to Whigham stating that the consensus at GHQ BEF was that the formation be called the Tank Corps. 'I do not care for the name very much myself but must confess I have not thought of anything better.' On 28 Sep 1916 Whigham agreed: 'I can think of nothing better than "Tank Corps".' That sobriquet has certainly come to stay.'[4]

Haig's Autumn Plans

By the end of September, the British Fourth and Reserve Armies built on the initial success of the Battle of Flers–Courcelette. Having achieved some success in the centre of the Somme battlefield, Haig sought to remove the stalemate which had existed north of the River Ancre since July. With its Eastern Flank secure in the hands of the Sixth French Army, the British Fourth Army would continue to attack north towards Bapaume. The areas to be tackled by the Reserve Army[5] on the Northern Flank (see map 10) were to be from Serre (map square C3), along the Redan ridge to Beaumount Hamel (B4), along both banks of the River Ancre (D4 to C6) and then the high ground to its south near Grandcourt (D4). With A Company now complete in France,[6] and the residue of B Company due to arrive in two weeks' time, Haig probably believed he would have the resources to provide infantry with the necessary support to capture the German positions north of the River Ancre.

On 20 September, Haig had paid visits to the headquarters of the Fourth and Reserve Armies. He told Rawlinson that Fourth Army must hand over some tanks to the Reserve Army to support their attack at Thiepval. Later that day, he instructed Gough to prepare plans for capturing the Serre Ridge as far north as Hébuterne (A1). Four days later, during a visit to HQ Third Army which held the line to the north of Gommecourt, Haig warned Lt Gen Edmund Allenby to prepare to attack the German positions to his east. Allenby would be allocated three infantry divisions, and possibly a fourth, supported by 50–60 tanks, but he was not to use a preliminary artillery bombardment.[7] Haig's thinking demonstrated a remarkable faith in the new weapon system and foreshadowed the tactics which would be used successfully at Cambrai fourteen months later.

However, despite his intention, Haig had to adjust his proposals in order to reflect the actual availability of tanks in France. By the end of September, C and D Companies had lost 27 tanks through enemy action, mechanical failure and ditching. Haig therefore decided that he would

---

They had not been completed due to the limited manufacturing capacity at the Fosters, Metropolitan and Robey works and were eventually produced as Mark II and Mark III variants.

4   TNA WO 158/836.
5   The Reserve Army was redesignated the Fifth Army in October 1916.
6   The A Company Main Bodies arrived at Le Havre on 12 and 15 September; their tanks arriving two days later. They initially moved to Yvrench in a similar fashion to C and D Companies and then, on 20 September, moved to Acheux where the men lived under canvas in an orchard. As a result, they had no opportunity to undertake any field training. Gnr Frederick Cutting's Diary (Tank Museum acquisition number E2006.2440) states that the tanks deployed on their tracks (a distance of 25 miles) although movement plans made in August stated they were to move by train.
7   Miles, *OHGW*, p. 392 fn. 1.

not allocate any tanks to Third Army but would concentrate those available to support the Reserve Army's attacks in the Ancre Valley and on the heights north and south of the river. On 29 September, he wrote to the three army commanders directing them to start planning to attack the German positions across the Transloy Ridges, the Ancre Heights, the Redan Ridge and the high ground near Serre on 12 October. The bulk of C Company was tasked to support V Corps (Lt Gen Edward Fanshawe) who were to attack the area near Serre whilst D Company would support XIII Corps from Hébuterne. A Company was allocated to Fourth Army to support attacks on the Transloy Ridges, south of the River Ancre whilst nine tanks under Inglis supported II, III and XIV Corps (See chapter 8).

Changes to Tank Command and Control

Whilst Swinton was at Beauquesne on the evening of 16 September,[8] he was informed that 'it was thought desirable that the command of the Heavy Section in France should be held by an officer who had been for some time on the Western Front and was familiar with the nature of the fighting and the existing organization and methods, etc., etc. After what had occurred to Brough I was not surprised.'[9]

On 25 September, Elles took command of the Heavy Section MGC in France in the rank of colonel.[10] Swinton later commented:

> When I was consulted as to the future commander of the Heavy Section in France, I felt that there was no one of the unit sufficiently senior to propose. Both my senior officers had by then failed to find favour in the eyes of GHQ. I therefore suggested Lt Col Hugh Elles, a brother Royal Engineer, whose name has already been mentioned. Elles had been remotely associated with the Tanks since the previous January, and after the Heavy Section had arrived in France had held a kind of watching brief as a liaison officer between it and the rest of the Army.
>
> He was to my knowledge a first class officer, and last, but not least, he was persona gratissima at GHQ, and knew everyone and all the "ropes." I could think of no one more suitable, in spite of the fact that he knew as little about the Tanks as his two predecessors did of the niceties of the tactics current in France. To meet the objection that he was not sufficiently senior I suggested that he should be given the temporary rank of colonel. Elles was obviously the best choice for the post, and I have no doubt that he would have been selected for it whether I had proposed him or had not done so.

Elles was also made responsible for the advanced training and tactical employment of tanks by the BEF despite his concerns that he did not have the necessary tactical expertise.[11] Elles established HQ Tanks in a hut in Beauquesne village square, close to the Advanced GHQ at the Chateau de Val Vion. A small staff was quickly assembled; a brigade major Giffard Martel, the

8   Earlier that day, Swinton had visited HQ HS MGC at the Loop and met some of the tank skippers who had been in action on 15 September.
9   Swinton, *Eyewitness*, p 287.
10   Swinton, *Eyewitness*, p. 288. Elles' appointment was published in the London Gazette on 16 Oct 1916.
11   Miles, *OHGW*, p. 371 fn. 1.

deputy assistant adjutant and quartermaster general Theo Uzielli, a staff captain Michael Tapper and an intelligence officer, Elliott 'Boots' Hotblack.[12] Bradley, supported by Kyngdon, continued to coordinate tank support by A, C and D Companies, but reported to Elles at Advanced GHQ rather than HQ Fourth Army as hitherto.[13] In early October, Bradley moved his team from the Loop to a new base at Acheux and, in the middle of the month, set up an advanced headquarters less than 875 yards from the frontline south of Hébuterne.[14]

The experience of the tank companies, in their first two weeks of action, had already led to changes in the company organisation. As previously mentioned, Holford-Walker had reinforced his company HQ with watchkeepers and established a team of runners to aid communications. On 25 September, Woods requested eight officers and 54 other ranks as Battle Casualty Replacements (BCRs) for D Company.[15] He also asked for an additional four subalterns as tank commanders, it being clear that the section commanders, who had previously doubled as tank skippers, had a full-time task in their primary role.[16]

Those tanks which were mobile were brought back to operational condition by the ASC Workshops at the Loop. Every track was removed, the running gear cleaned of impacted mud, serviced and, where available, lubrication tanks were fitted.[17] Damaged steering tails were also replaced by the fitters and crewmen working flat out to get the tanks ready to go into action north of the River Ancre.[18] On 28 September, Knothe produced a detailed report on the tanks' shortcomings in concert with Wilson who had temporarily deployed to France (see Appendix XVI). Although the weakness with the steering tails was mentioned, Knothe's main concern was about the tracks. Elles endorsed Knothe's comments; in a letter to GHQ Operations staff on 30 September (see Appendix XVI), he stressed the need for new tanks to have greater speed

12   The provisional establishment for HQ HS MGC was approved on 8 October 1916. In modern terminology, Martell was the Chief of Staff, Uzielli was Staff Officer Grade 3 (SO3) G1/G4 (personnel and logistics); Tapper was SO3 G3 (Operations) and Hotblack was SO3 G2 (Intelligence) although he seemed to spend most of his time on the ground not at a desk. The Headquarters would be expanded further when the Heavy Branch was formed.

13   This term was used by Holford-Walker in his letter to Edmonds in 1935. In September, the tank company commanders dealt with corps headquarters; from October, this continued but the company commanders also liaised with the divisions in place of the section commanders, to which their tanks were allocated. They appear to have dealt with Elles and his staff through Bradley.

14   A base location remained at the Loop until December 1916, supporting actions in support of Fourth Army and salvaging tanks and parts from abandoned hulks across the Somme battlefield.

15   HS MGC Min 42 memo dated 25 September 1916.

16   Appendices to the C Company War Diary also shows that two of its captains were selected to command sub sections on 25 to 27 September with subalterns taking their place as tank skippers. Holford-Walker had reinforced his company headquarters to enable more effective liaison with corps and divisional headquarters.

17   The first tanks issued at Elveden were not fitted with a track lubrication system; it was therefore impossible for the crews to apply the standard operating procedures. See Appendix XI. The first elements arrived on 26 September and the workshops installed the remainder as parts became available.

18   Although Murphy had demonstrated at the Quadrilateral on 15 September that his Female tank (513) could operate without one, steering tails appear to have been replaced on a routine basis. The Female tank C8 (tank number and skipper unknown) was photographed at a base location (probably the Loop) where the tail had clearly been removed. The date of the photograph is unknown but it was published in the French newspaper *Le Miroir* on 10 December 1916.

and better armour. Elles interestingly describes his own appointment as commanding the Corps of Heavy Armoured Cars rather than the Heavy Section MGC.

Tank Overall Effectiveness in September 1916

On 18 September, formation and tank unit headquarters had been ordered to comment on the effectiveness of the tanks in the first action. Mann, responding to a Fourth Army request, reported:

> …that male tanks were particularly good at destroying machine gun emplacements; enemy machine guns quickly put out of action by shell fire from male tanks. Female tanks inflicted considerable casualties to hostile troops, enfilading trenches and retreating enemy troops. Tanks were shelled from start to finish and abandoned tanks continue to draw fire. Tank[s] undoubtedly drew hostile machine gun fire and infantry rifle fire. On [the] enemy discovering the non-effect of this fire, they surrendered or retreated. [The tanks] gave our own troops greater confidence and, undoubtedly, caused considerable local panic amongst the enemy.[19]

The reports from the NZ Division were positive; HQ 2nd NZ Brigade stated that 'the tanks had a material effect on the enemy; specifically, in clearing up machine gun positions, strongpoints, enfilading trenches and generally dispersing the enemy.' They also commented that 'the tanks were particularly useful in village fighting and that "our tank" ran over an enemy machine gun in a street in Flers, the machine gun's crew attempting to stop the tank by using grenades which had no effect on the vehicle.'[20] HQ 3rd NZ Rifle Brigade noted that the Male tank appeared to have a greater morale effect on the enemy although, in the mind of their own troops, the Female eclipsed the Male in the terms of material damage done to the Bavarians. 3rd Brigade stressed that 'tanks were undoubtedly of the greatest use in destroying barbed wire entanglements and in dealing with strong points and machine guns in their emplacements.' They also recommended that the tanks should advance about 50 to 100 yards ahead of the first waves of the attacking infantry on clearly defined courses.'[21] In his covering letter, Maj Gen AH Russell commented that 'the moral [sic] effect on our troops was considerable; as far as can be judged, they had an extremely terrifying effect on the enemy.' Russell also stated that the 'tanks were generally speaking handled with great boldness and officers commanding some of the tanks in Flers displayed considerable tactical ability.'[22]

19   HQ Fourth Army No. 348 G dated 19 Sep 1916 (TNA WO 95/674). Mann's report was dated 22 September (see Appendix XIII) but sadly, the main responses from the companies HQ have not survived.

20   This tank must have been *Dinnaken* and the description indicates that the machine-gun post was much closer to the village previously than thought. See HQ 2nd NZ Brigade ZBM 340 dated 24 September 1916.

21   The destruction of barbed wire entanglements relates to the actions by D8 and D11. HQ 3rd NZ Rifle Brigade unreferenced letter dated 28 November 1916.

22   HQ NZ Division SG 6/17, 30 September 1916.

GHQ Direction on Future Tank Employment

The reports from the various formation and army headquarters were consolidated by the GHQ staff and signed off by Haig's Chief of Staff, Kiggell (see Appendix XVII). The opening paragraph re-affirmed Swinton's original view that tanks were an auxiliary to the infantry.[23] 'In the present stage of their development, the tanks must be regarded as entirely accessory to the ordinary methods of the attack i.e., to the advance of infantry in close cooperation with the artillery.' The paper however recognised the effectiveness of the tanks in action, for example:

> In cases where they have reached a hostile trench ahead of the infantry, Tanks have undoubtedly done good service. Their morale effect on the enemy's infantry has been considerable. They have also not only drawn a good deal of hostile machine gun and rife fire on themselves and, therefore off the attacking infantry, but they have been able to cause considerable loss to the enemy in the trenches, to knock out in many cases his machine guns and, by the combined morale and material effect, to bring about the enemy surrender or retirement.

As for future tactics, 'nothing can be laid down on the subject except that it is advantageous if things can be arranged so that the tanks reach the hostile trench just in front of the infantry.' Kiggell also stressed the importance of considering the state of the ground and that the infantry must use creeping barrage to best effect. Finally, he noted the need for formations to assist in marking suitable routes for tanks to get to their starting points, especially when operating at night.[24]

Future Tank Corps Structure

On 8 October, Martel arrived at the new Heavy Section HQ at Beauquesne where Elles was finalising the detailed establishments for the new tank battalions.[25] Elles recommended that the four tank companies in France be expanded to battalions in order to achieve the numbers of units proposed to the WO on 20 September. On 9 October, his proposals were sent to the WO,[26] with Haig recommending that a new arm be known as the Tank Corps.[27] This new Corps was to comprise an administrative HQ in England under the command of the WO. It was responsible for administration of Corps as a whole and dealing with the provision of personnel, technical material, the formation and training of units and unit maintenance in the

---

23   See Appendix III.
24   This had been the role of the section commanders but it would ultimately be undertaken by a dedicated branch of the Tank Corps with reconnaissance officers being established at battalion and company level.
25   Between the two World Wars, Martel commanded the RE Experimental Bridging Establishment, which researched the possibilities of using tanks for battlefield engineering purposes such as bridge-laying and mine-clearing, and he designed and built one-man tanks in his own time. In May 1940, as commander of 50th Northumbrian Division, he launched the British tank counter-attack at Arras, which halted the advance of *Gen Maj* Erwin Rommel's *7th Panzer Division*.
26   Letter signed by Burnett-Stuart (TNA WO 158/836).
27   As previously proposed by Butler (TNA WO 158/836).

field as regards personnel, vehicles, spares and materiel. There would also be a fighting HQ in France, commanding the Corps in the field and responsible for advanced training and tactical employment under orders of the C-in-C.

The BEF tank organisation was to consist of brigades, battalions, companies and sections. The primary organisation would be a battalion consisting of a headquarters, three fighting companies and a workshop company. There would also be a central depot and repair shop in France in addition to the workshops company in each battalion. Tanks, support vehicles and related equipment would be consigned from manufacturers direct to the Tank Corps in France through the 'Base Park', sections being formed at ports to receive and deliver them directly to the Corps. It was also proposed that a special uniform and special badges be adopted.[28] The WO accepted all the proposals except for the name Tank Corps on 20 October and, from 18 November, the Heavy Section was re-designated the Heavy Branch and the restructuring formally commenced.[29]

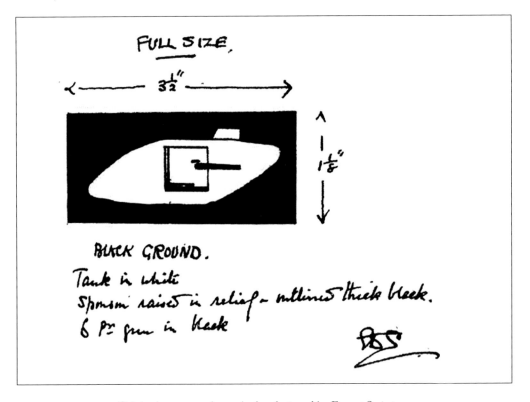

Original woven tank arm badge designed by Ernest Swinton.

28   Swinton had designed a woven arm badge which showed the side elevation of a Male tank without a tail. See image in *Eyewitness*, p.246, which is replicated above. A similar badge is still worn by members of the Royal Tank Regiment today.
29   Although the battalions were officially formed on 18 November, they were not fully established until the New Year. The Heavy Branch was redesignated the Tank Corps on 28 July 1917.

Preparations for Further Action on the Northern Flank

On 29 September, Advanced GHQ BEF issued orders requiring that all available tanks from Fourth Army,[30] south of the Albert–Bapaume Road, and those of the Reserve Army to its north, act in support Gough's planned operations on either side of the River Ancre.[31] On 30 September, C and D Company were each reinforced by a section of crewmen from B Company. These sections had deployed from Elveden to Boulogne on 18 September, in response to a request for BCRs from GHQ two days earlier,[32] and were initially held at the MGC Depot in Camiers. B Companies' reinforcing sections were only five crews strong and did not have drivers or tanks; the tanks were found from new tanks which had been delivered to the Loop and the drivers found by C and D Companies' tanks which were no longer fit for action.[33]

By 1 October, C Company had nine fit tanks at the Loop – six Male and three Females – which increased to ten when *Cognac*, the sole surviving tank from No. 1 Section arrived.[34] Unusually, D Company's diary does not specify how many tanks returned to the Loop on 29 September (there were only three fit) but it does state that all derelict and salvaged tanks were taken over by 711 (MT) Company ASC who became responsible for their recovery.[35] On 8 October, D Company were provided with a further seven officers from A Company.[36] As the number of tanks and the crews increased, so did the work of the sole quartermaster, Capt Charles Weaver-Price, who was now supporting three companies and expecting the balance of B Company to arrive shortly. Whilst his mind was mainly fixed on meeting their physical needs, Weaver-Price did not forget the troops' morale. He wrote to newspapers near his home in Brecon, 'seeking copies of books and magazines which the crewmen could read; the unit being far from any of the official canteens and institutes available to other units when they were out of the line.'[37]

30   GHQ OAD 159 dated 29 September 1916. A small number of D Company tanks remained in support of III Corps under Mann, using No. 4 Section tanks, whilst XV Corps was supported by a further three under Inglis' command which had been recovered from the battlefields near Flers. See chapter 8.

31   Mills, *OHGW*, p. 460. These operations were to be undertaken by V Corps, with assistance from XIII Corps to the north. V Corps comprised (from north to south) 3rd, 2nd, 51st and 63rd divisions.

32   The request had originated at 1130 hours from HQ HS MGC at the Loop: 'To Ops Branch. Several officers and men required to replace casualties at once. A Coy cannot be used as it is required for operations at once. Consider best arrangement would be to send out personnel of one complete section and then form new section at home.'

33   No. 2 Section of B Company, commanded by Capt Richard Clively, was allocated to C Company but the names of the tanks and crews are not recorded. No. 3 Section, commanded by Capt Frank Vandervell, was allocated to D Company: their five tanks being the Male No. 713 skippered by Charles Butcher, Female No. 532 (Lt Frank Telfor); Male No. 707 (Lt Chaloner Robinson); Male No. 712, known as *Dodo* (Lt Hugh Swears). See photograph No. 29) and the Female No. 515 *Donner Blitzen* (Cyril Renouf). All details from Woods' notebook, p. 10.

34   C Company War Diary. It was burned out by a replacement crew on 11 October – Archard's diary dated 13 October 1916.

35   The Adjutant's Correspondence Book lists all of these vehicles, complete with faults, and action underway to recover them. Although the ASC were in command of the salvage and recovery, Capt. Graeme Nixon remained at Green Dump with a working party of crewmen in their support.

36   The War Diary gives no mention of other ranks but the D Company reserve section crews in November did include SNCOs and others ranks from A Company.

37   *Brecon and Radnor Express*, 5 October 1916.

On 1 October, HQ HS MGC received a signal from the WO trooping staff that ten tanks, their trailers (presumably carrying their sponsons) and ten crewmen were on their way to Le Havre.[38] That afternoon, the attack on Eaucourt l'Abbaye took place on a fine day but the weather soon deteriorated (see chapter 8). On 2 October, in the pouring rain, lorries started to move D Company's stores from Green Dump to the new tankodrome near Acheux. That same day, Summers (OC D Company) was briefed on plans by the XIII Corps staff to attack the German positions opposite Hébuterne. He made an initial visit to Acheux that afternoon and, on 3 October, which was again very wet, undertook an initial recce to his proposed forward location at Hébuterne. On 4 October, Summers again visited Hébuterne, this time accompanied by Mortimore and they selected locations for the new battle headquarters and the unit dump.[39] On 5 October, the ten new tanks arrived at the Loop, five being allocated to C Company. An advance party of 21 other ranks from D Company moved by lorries to Acheux and the following day, the remaining C and D Company crews moved to Acheux; their tanks presumably moved by rail. On 7 October, Mortimore took D Company's officers to the forward trenches near Hébuterne, where he pointed out the company boundaries and key landmarks in the heavily shelled and now soaking ground. The party came under enemy shell fire; Lt George Bown was wounded and evacuated to hospital in England.[40]

On 8 October, Holford-Walker (OC C Company) visited HQ V Corps, where he was told that his tanks were to support attacks by 2nd and 3rd Divisions towards Serre. That afternoon, Holford-Walker issued an operation order (see Appendix XVIII) and briefed his tank skippers on their objectives and routes, using maps provided by the V Corps staff. His ten tanks were to operate in pairs; three pairs were allocated to 3rd Division under the command of Capt Richard Clively in No. 4 Section,[41] the remaining four to 2nd Division under Hiscocks who remained in command of No. 2 Section of C Company. A break in the bad weather coincided with a D Company working party, commanded by Enoch, establishing a battle HQ at Hébuterne. The working party also prepared dugouts for personnel, 'stables' for tanks and a dump for petrol, oils and other lubricants.[42] The C Company dump, which was located near La Signy Farm (A3), would contain 2,000 gallons of petrol, 160 gallons of Zeta heavy oil, 300 gallons of Heavy Steam cylinder oil, 300 pounds of grease and 40 gallons of Mobil oil. The dump also contained 480 rounds of 6-pounder ammunition, 50,000 rounds of .303-inch ammunition for the tanks' machine-guns and 1,000 rounds of 455-calibre ammunition for the crew's revolvers.[43]

On 9 October, HQ V Corps held another conference where Holford-Walker's plan was approved and issued as part of the Corps' operation order. This required that the tanks should

---

38 This was the first of several such messages and indicates that production tanks were now being shipped to France.

39 He retained command of No. 1 Section.

40 He recovered in England and, on recovery, posted to the newly formed G Battalion as a section commander. However, just before F Battalion deployed to France in May, he was claimed by Summers and appointed section commander in No. 16 Company. His new company commander was acting Maj Arthur Inglis DSO.

41 Clively was originally a section commander in B Company and was one of the reinforcements sent to France on 18 September.

42 Cutting states that A Company's Advanced HQ was also at Hébuterne.

43 There is no mention as to how these stores were moved but there was a comprehensive system of narrow gauge railways in the area supporting artillery and engineer units which could have been exploited.

start behind the infantry and their protective artillery barrage but it also required that the tanks would attack locations of known machine-gun positions to enable the infantry to take their objectives. C Company's tanks would leave Acheux on 12 October, that is, three days before the attack commenced. The tanks and crews would travel under the cover of darkness, halting at a 'halfway house' near Beaussart, and rest the following day. On the second night, they would drive to a Place of Assembly, some 350 yards to the west of La Signy Farm. Having camouflaged the tanks, the crews would then withdraw leaving the vehicles protected from 'interested onlookers' or pilferers by a small guard force. After resting as best they could during the day, the crews would return to the tanks and, between 1830 and 2230 hours on the night before the attack, would drive to their respective Starting Points along routes which had been identified and pre-reconnoitred by the tank section commanders.

Once the Corps plan was published, orders were given to Royal Engineer (RE) units to construct ramps or bridges to enable tanks to cross British trenches, in order to overcome some of the difficulties encountered on 15 September. Experiments were also undertaken to determine how to mask the sound of the unsilenced tank engines as they made their way to the forward locations. It was found that the tanks were only audible within 500 yards of an observer so a plan was developed to screen the noise from the enemy for their final approaches to the starting points. Artillery, mortars, rifle and machine-gun fire, as well as aircraft movement, was to be employed between 2030–2230 hours on the nights of 13, 15 and 16 October. This distraction was designed to make the Germans became accustomed to noises at that time, and not associate it with the unmistakable sounds of the tanks' engines.

On 10 October, eleven more tanks arrived from England and were off-loaded at the Loop. This might have occurred because there was still only one quartermaster available to serve the tank force but it seems odd considering the majority of tanks and crews were now based at Acheux, with some elements of C Company based at Louvencourt, which was on a different railway line.[44] Four of the new tanks were allocated to No. 2 Section under Hiscocks, who was ordered to transfer two older tanks to Clively commanding No. 4 Section. The fourteen C Company tanks were now grouped into seven pairs, four pairs under Clively supporting 3rd Division,[45] whilst Hiscocks had three pairs in support of 2nd Division.[46] On 12 October, two of the new tanks caught fire whilst deploying from the Loop; this was a significant loss, given the limited number of tanks available to the three companies, and a Board of Inquiry was immediately launched. A signal received the same day, from the Trooping Staff in London, reported that another 15 tanks had departed Avonmouth at 1000 hours which probably did something to lighten the mood of the staff at HQ Heavy Section in Beauquesne.

North of the Ancre, steady progress was being made. HQ D Company moved to its Battle HQ at Hébuterne on 12 October and completed in-loading their petrol, oils and grease stocks

44 C Company War Diary dated 15 October 1916. Louvencourt is two miles northwest of Acheux.
45 The skippers and tanks were Hallack (tank 758) and Atherton (549); Clarke (521) and Mills (511); Reardon (744) and Groves (528); Lambert (523) and Williamson (514), all originally of B Company. Three of the pairs consisted of a Female and Male tank.
46 The skippers were Arnaud (706) and Murphy (524); Bates (710) and Elliot (507 or 505); Ambrose (522) and Thompson from A Company (766).

close to the Points of Assembly where it was stored in underground pits.[47] The weather, which was bright, was also generally dry so the crews were able to complete the work to meet the planned attack date of 15 October. C Company meanwhile completed the route recce to the Half-way House at Beaussart.

In England, on 14 October, the remainder of B Company,[48] under Maj Thomas McLellan, left Thetford, reaching Southampton Docks that afternoon and embarking on the troopship *Caesarea*. They sailed that evening but were stopped at 2200 hours by an Admiralty patrol board and returned back to Southampton.[49] 15 October saw B Company remain in port, which probably was not too onerous for the crews.[50] C Company meanwhile received positive news regarding the work being completed by the RE to prepare the trench crossings and ramps, although it was found necessary to change route of approach for southern groups owing to the number of trenches which would have had to be negotiated.

Change in Orders

On the evening of 15 October, as B Company was making its delayed passage from Folkestone to Boulogne, HQ Reserve Army issued a new set of orders which gave D Company a new task in support of V Corps. The next day, as the good weather broke and Enoch and his working party started to outload the stores from Hébuterne back to Acheux, Summers was briefed that D Company was to support 51st (Highland) Division and 63rd (Royal Naval) Division.[51] D Company was to establish two forward locations; one at Auchonvillers (A4) supporting 51st Division's planned attack on Beaumont Hamel (B4) and the other at Mesnil (B6) supporting 63rd Division which was to push along the bank of the River Ancre towards Beaucourt sur Ancre (C4). That afternoon, Summers undertook an initial recce, accompanied by Vandervell, whose section was to support the Highlanders, and by Mortimore who was to support 63rd Division.[52] C Company meanwhile continued with its preparations for the attack towards Serre and, on 16 October, they were allocated another pair of tanks, bringing their total to 16 but with no reserve.

Moreover, on 16 October, A Company left Acheux with 20 tanks to support II Corps operating east and south of the River Ancre.[53] Their exact company location is unrecorded but Gnr Fred Cutting, one of their despatch riders, states it was a tented camp by some woods near

---

47   According to Cpl Forbes Taylor of A Company, in a letter written to the Tank Museum in 1974, this work took three days. The dump was just behind the front line; when the wet weather caused the proposed attacks to be cancelled all the stocks were dug out and withdrawn (RH.86 TC3719).

48   The company headquarters, the Mechanical Transport and Nos. 1 and 4 Tank Sections.

49   Previous sailings had been delayed because of the threat from German submarines in the English Channel.

50   The *Caesarea* was built in 1910 and operated from Southampton to the Channel Islands prior to the start of the Great War. It was capable of 20 knots.

51   63rd (RN) Division had relieved 2nd Division.

52   Both Summers and Mortimore had served with the RN Division in Belgium in September 1914; Summers as the adjutant of the Transport Company and Mortimore as a clerk. Summers was subsequently commissioned in the Royal Marine Light Infantry and Mortimore was commissioned into the Royal Naval Air Service.

53   Miles, *OHGW*, p. 461 fn. 2.

Aveluy.[54] On 17 October, Vandervell and Mortimore carried out their route recces, the latter with his tank skippers. The route identified by Vandervell from Auchonvillers down to the Starting Point east of Beaumont Hamel was passable but Mortimore, who also checked the routes from Mesnil to the front by night, found his to be unsuitable. This was probably due to the fact that his tanks would have to cross seven trench lines getting from Mesnil to the north of Hamel village (B5) and the final approach was up a major incline.[55] Mortimore explained this to Summers and, the following morning, they jointly reconnoitred a route from Auchonvillers to their Starting Point near Hamel. Satisfied that this was a viable option, the plan to establish a section base at Mesnil was abandoned and a single advanced company base was established at Auchonvillers.

Whilst Mortimore was carrying out his overnight route recces, B Company without their tanks and domestic transport moved by train to the Somme. The next day, there was another re-organisation of tanks within C Company. Two tanks were removed from Hiscock's section and detached to XIII Corps under Capt Archie Walker who remained in command of No. 3 Section.[56] The tanks were commanded by Capt the Lord George Rodney,[57] and Capt James Bennewith,[58] previously section commanders from B Company, with the crews being provided by A Company.

On 19 October, D Company's skippers were at Auchonvillers becoming familiar with their routes for the forward location whilst Mortimore and Vandervell discussed with the local RE the work needed to enable the tanks to cross trenches on the new routes. That evening, B Company arrived at Acheux, sleeping overnight at the railway station. The following morning, they were allocated a camp by HQ HS MGC which was, according to the B Company War Diary, very muddy.[59] On 20 October, all D Company officers completed their recces and maps were prepared under the guidance of Summers, the Company having learned the lessons about the need for effective recce and sufficient maps; a major failing on 15 September. C Company's skippers were also undertaking route recces from their Point of Assembly, at the crossroads east of the Sugar Factory (A3), to the frontline.

On 21 October, another 15 tanks left Avonmouth for Le Havre whilst five arrived at Acheux for C Company. That same day, Enoch and Huffam again left Acheux with a working party to prepare a stores dump and the Battle HQ for D Company, this time at Auchonvillers. The stores were brought forward the next morning; D Company's Adjutant (Woods) moving that afternoon to the halfway halt at Beaussart where a concentration area was established. Also, on

---

54   Forbes Taylor states the tanks were located in Aveluy Wood but the tents were pitched outside. Taylor was commissioned on 8 November 1918 and then served with 26th Tank Battalion.

55   The Germans dominated the area with a serious of strong points on the ridges overlooking the river; one at map square B5 was to prove particularly troublesome.

56   Having detached 51st and 63rd divisions to V Corps on 17 October, XIII Corps had only 31 Division holding the line for 1,500 yards south of Hébuterne (Miles, *OHGW*, p. 460). Holford-Walker allocated his younger brother's section to XIII Corps for this detached task as Walker was his most experienced section commander after Inglis had been detached to command tank operations in support of Fourth Army.

57   Lord Rodney was a Regular Army officer, having been commissioned into the Royal Scots Greys in December 1912.

58   Bennewith had been commissioned into the MMGS in September 1915.

59   It is possible that they took over A Company's old location at Acheux.

21 October, Lts William Hopkins and Gerald Phillips (see photograph 29) were detached from B Company, with thirty crewmen, to A Company and joined them at their base at Aveluy.

On 22 October, HQ B Company received orders that their OC, his adjutant Capt Ralph Mansell and 90 men were to proceed to Bermicourt; the remainder of the company remaining under Bennewith and Rodney were attached to C Company.[60] At 1800 hours that evening, C and D Company's tanks departed Acheux for Beaussart. Rodney and Bennewith's new tanks were delayed and Elliot's tank had engine problems but eventually all the tanks got into position at Beaussart before daylight except Elliot. The crews and ASC workshops party completed a pre-battle overhaul of the tanks in the fog and pouring rain. Elliot's tank eventually reached Beaussart at midday, his company commander telling him to drive forward as the foggy conditions made observation impossible for the Germans. The ground was now totally saturated and, that afternoon, Summers arrived at Beaussart to tell his crews that the attack, planned for 25 October, had now been postponed for 48 hours.

A Company meanwhile was preparing to undertake a series of attacks south of the River Ancre in support of II Corps (Lt Gen Claude Jacobs). II Corps had started to clear the area around Stuff Trench (northeast of Thiepval) in order to establishing jumping-off places for an attack on the Heights around Grandcourt. Nos. 1 and 2 Sections of A Company were to be allocated in support of 18th Division on the right. These ten tanks, commanded by Capts Percy Jackson (see photograph 29) and Maurice Miskin, were to advance 3,000 yards to the South Miraumont Trench and then push into Petit Miraumont; the way was barred by trenches, deep wire, deep mud and shell-torn ground. In the middle, 19th Division was to be supported by four tanks from No. 4 Section, under Capt David Raikes. Their objective was Grandcourt (D5) and their Starting Point was at Stuff Trench, just north of Stuff Redoubt. On the left, three tanks of No. 3 Section were to support 39th Division in clearing St Pierre Divion (C5) and the trenches to its south, which had resisted all attacks since 1 July.[61] Jacobs issued instructions on 23 October that 'every possible effort is to be made to get the tanks into position and to ensure their carrying out their task. However, divisional commanders are warned not to depend too much on the tank's assistance, and their plans must be made on the assumption that the tanks would not be available.' The section commanders started to recce the proposed routes and found them impassable.[62] The operation was consequently postponed until better weather allowed the ground to dry. As a final blow to morale, the tanks commanded by Hopkins and Phillips were knocked out by German artillery, on 23 October, whilst parked up on the Pozières to Le Sars road near the Sugar Factory at Courcelette.[63]

---

60   B Company would never be used as a formed tank unit; it spent the remainder of October and November at the newly formed Tank Administrative Area undertaking fatigue parties and labour for RE units erecting huts at Erin and Bermicourt. Their transport arrived from Elveden on 31 October and the Adjutant, Capt Mansell, moved under command HQ B Battalion at Wavrans on 8 November 1916.

61   Possibly under command of Capt Arthur Jacobs.

62   The routes to be used are not recorded. However, a trench map (57d SE2 dated February 1917) shows four derelict tanks sited on a track leading from the southeast of Thiepval towards Stuff Trench with one of the tanks being located less than 300 yards from their start point. It appears that the tank drivers did their best to reach the start point but ground conditions made it impossible.

63   The tanks were on route to an objective which was not recorded; they were hit whilst 'lying up on the Albert to Bapaume road' probably by German harassing fire.

Delays, Delays and More Delays

On 24 October, because of poor weather, HQ C Company gave instructions for a guard to be placed on the tanks and ordered the rest of their crews to shelter although they had no real cover.[64] A Company's new camp, near Aveluy, was targeted by German artillery on 24 October.[65] The crews took cover in the woods but there were a number of casualties including Lt George Steven who was killed.[66]

Also on that day, HQ A Company received detailed orders for the sub-section (three tanks) which was to support 39th Division's assault on St Pierre Divion (see Appendix XIX). Rather than just leading the infantry into the attack, each tank had a series of tasks with C tank, operating in the south, having the most demanding. This Female tank was first to flatten 500 yards of barbed wire protecting the German frontline trench north of Thiepval Wood (C6), and then destroy a set of machine-gun emplacements by the river (C5), thereby enabling the infantry to get into the German trench system. As the road leading north, alongside the river into St Pierre Divion, was believed to be impassable, C Tank would return back up the hill following the German frontline for 200 yards and then turn north to attack a strong point 200 yards behind the front line. The tank crew were then to clear along another trench for 200 yards before clearing another strong point, called the Summer House, on the river bank. The tank was then to move to the church, which was in the north of the village, for further orders, all the time ensuring that the tank was not hit by a moving barrage supporting the main attack which was moving east to west from their starting point in Schwaben Redoubt. This was to be the tank crew's first action and the tasks were in excess of their capabilities.

On 26 October, a further 48 hour delay was announced, Woods noting in his diary the following day that the ground was still unsuitable. On 28 October, a further two-day delay was ordered with Zero being pushed back to 1 November. C Company's crews were sent back to Acheux with their tanks being left at Beaussart in the care of a guard force. The conditions for the crews at Acheux had not improved, albeit it was better than with the tanks at Beaussart, but the men were living under canvas which started to impact on their health. Victor Archard sent a series of photographs back to his family, showing men huddled round improvised petrol fires wearing goatskins to keep themselves warm, in front of obviously soaking-wet bell tents pitched in the mud. It may not be a coincidence that several crewmen started to suffer from trench fever.

Activities at Home

As the tank crews were fighting to keep dry in France, the WO approved Elles' proposal to expand the original four companies in France to battalion-sized units and directed that a

---

64 C Company's War Diary states this was an officer and 12 men.
65 Gnr FS Cutting's diary (TMA).
66 Steven was a Glaswegian who studied engineering at the Royal Technical College and was a member of the Officer Training Corps. Commissioned into the Loyal North Lancashire Regiment in 1914, he was attached to the MMGS in April 1916. A member of No. 4 Section, he was 23 years old at the time he was killed; he is buried at the Blighty Valley Cemetery near Authuille Wood. The camp was screened from view but this did not stop German harassing fire, either alongside the river or on the locations further north.

further five battalions be formed in England.[67] As the tank training ground at Elveden was too small for such a task, Swinton recced sites which might be suitable, his preferred option being in Dorset near Wool which was rail-served.[68] There was already an infantry training camp on Bovington Heath capable of housing six battalions, complete with practice trenches and a rifle range constructed on sandy soil which could be used for driver training. There was also an area of coastal valleys, five miles to the south near Lulworth, which was highly suitable for gunnery training and tactical manoeuvre. Swinton's proposal was endorsed by Haig and the training centre at Elveden started to move to Wool on 27 October.

This was almost to be Swinton's last formal involvement with tanks until he was appointed Colonel Commandant of the Royal Tank Corps in 1934. A diligent and effective staff officer, who had brought the tanks into existence through persistence and his contacts in high places, the staff at Haig's headquarters wanted his replacement to be a proven formation commander.[69] The man selected was Brig Gen Frederick Gore-Anley,[70] who assumed the appointment of Commander Administrative HQ and Training MGC (Heavy Branch) on 10 November 1916.[71] Swinton's removal, and Gore-Anley's appointment in command of the new UK tank headquarters, created some resentment amongst members of the Heavy Section as well as embarrassment within the WO.[72] His service was however formally acknowledged by being appointed a Brevet Colonel and a Companion of the Most Excellent Order of the Bath in February 1917.[73]

'Greatcoats off, greatcoats on!'

In France, on 29 October, GHQ BEF delayed the planned attack again, the time until 5 November. However, on 2 November, HQ Fifth Army recommended that the attack should go ahead.[74] The same day, C Company's officers undertook route and ground reconnaissances, reporting that ramps and crossings in the 2nd Division area were good but those in the 3rd

---

67 Liddell Hart, *The Tanks Volume One*, p. 84.
68 One other option was near Hambledon, in the Meon Valley, which was rail-served and had access to the ports at both Portsmouth and Southampton.
69 Swinton was warned by Hankey, after Swinton returned to England from France on 8 October, by telephone. 'His [Hankey's] indignation was great, and he had not hesitated to give expression to it in high quarters. He was anxious that when free I should return to him at the War Cabinet Secretariat. Elles, who was with me at the time, informed me that he had known what was brewing, but of course had had no hand in it, and had been in a most uncomfortable position. To my question as to who was responsible, which I did not then know, he returned no answer.' Swinton, *Eyewitness*, p 302.
70 Gore-Anley had commanded 12th Brigade (4th Division) from October 1914 to June 1916. Although an experienced brigade commander, he apparently lacked the qualities for divisional command and had not been promoted. He commanded the Training Centre for a mere ten months after which he assumed command of 234th Brigade in Palestine. Shortly afterwards he became sick and returned home eventually commanding a demobilisation centre.
71 Swinton took Gore-Anley to Elveden to meet members of the HS MGC on 9 November; there were some 60 officers and 700 other ranks who would shortly move to Bovington, *Eyewitness*, p. 308.
72 Liddell Hart, *The Tanks Volume One*, p. 83.
73 *Edinburgh Gazette*, 26 January 1917. Bradley was appointed Brevet Lieutenant-Colonel in the same list.
74 The Reserve Army had been redesignated Fifth Army on 30 October 1916.

Division area were not. Two officers then accompanied the RE to locations where crossings had fallen in or been tampered with. Having received reports that the ground was very wet indeed, and two places were impassable, Clively visited HQ 3rd Division to obtain their views on redistributing the tanks.

On 3 November, HQ D Company returned to Auchonvillers and sent details of their planned routes to Bradley in his coordinating role.[75] Holford-Walker provided Bradley with a summary of reports by his tank commanders about the state of the ground and the crossing points where the tanks would cross British trenches before crossing no man's land.[76] That same day, GHQ directed that:

> in view of the difficulties involved by constant postponements of the operations by Fifth Army due to weather conditions, GOC Fifth Army is now authorised to make an indefinite postponement of those operations with the provision that arrangements are made to bring on the attack without delay as soon as the weather shows signs of becoming more settled.[77]

That same evening, GHQ amended its instructions stating that units should be prepared to attack on 9 November; this no doubt was met by some shaking of heads by formation and unit staffs and possibly negative comments about the GHQ staff.[78] On 4 November, C Company's War Diary records that the attack had been postponed indefinitely and the very bedraggled tank crews returned to their tents at Acheux.

On 6 November, amended artillery instructions were received relating to the various objectives. HQ C Company immediately issued an amendment to its Operation Order No. 7 and further details about locations of section and company headquarters as the advance took place.[79] Also on 6 November, Woods accompanied by a small advance party left D Company for Blangy to set up a winter base in the area west of Saint-Pol-sur-Ternoise with Mann assuming the role of adjutant.[80] From 7 November it started to rain continuously for two days. After a break in the weather on 10 November, Zero was fixed for 13 November. C Company received new orders from both 2nd and 3rd Divisions; the latter reported that three German machine-guns had been spotted due east of John Copse and machine-gun fire, from the tanks, was to be used to cover the infantry advance. This was difficult as the attack plan called for the infantry to advance immediately behind the creeping barrage with the tanks behind the infantry; it did however provide the tank commanders with some clear targets.[81] The crews moved up from Acheux and, at 1800 hours on 11 November, C Company's tanks started to move towards Beaussart, all arriving safely at their Place of Assembly south of the Sucerie except Bates whose Male tank ditched at the field cemetery owing to insufficient reconnaissance.[82] The tanks were

75 Bradley was probably at the Lyceum where he had identified a location close to HQ 3 Division.
76 Appendix XV to C Company War Diary.
77 OAD 199 quoted by Trevor Pidgeon *Tanks on the Somme* p 127.
78 There is a phrase, used amongst the British military, at an apparent loss of control by a headquarters: 'Order, counter order, bl**dy disorder!'
79 See Appendix XVIII.
80 D Company War Diary.
81 C Company Operational Order No. 8 incorporated within C Company's War Diary.
82 This would become the Sucerie Military Cemetery which is one mile east of Colincamps.

refuelled but the ground was very soft and some tanks sank in badly – where the route was along roads, the tanks could move well but where the ground was shelled it was impossible.[83] D Company's tanks in the meantime also left Beaussart at 1830 hours, reaching Auchonvillers about midnight, taking seven hours to drive less than three miles.

On 12 November, A Company prepared to send three tanks to their Place of Assembly, Paisley Dump, on the southern end of Thiepval Wood, prior to the attack on St Pierre Divion. That same day, D Company prepared their tanks for action and laid tapes along their routes to the Starting Points. At noon, Holford-Walker informed HQ V Corps his tanks could not operate owing to the state of the ground.[84] As a result, HQ C Company received an order to withdraw their tanks; this was achieved by 2030 hours except one which was left behind because of a broken track. At 1600 hours, HQ D Company was also informed that tanks were not to be used; as a result, the tapes were collected and the forward dump prepared for removal to Beaussart. The tanks started to move back at 1830 hours and the move was completed successfully. However, at 2300 hours, Mann was met by Summers who ordered the two tanks allocated to 51st Division to return to Auchonvillers under the command of Vandervell.[85] The tanks turned round and successfully made their way back the way they came. Arriving there, they prepared for action and got what rest they could; their sleep no doubt being disturbed by the crescendo of shells which occurred just at Zero.

Capture of St Pierre Divion, 13 November 1916

Situation

The capture of St Pierre Divion was part of the plan initially prepared by HQ II Corps in mid-October mentioned above but which was abandoned owing to the ground conditions.

The Ground

St Pierre Divion sits on the eastern bank of the River Ancre. There is a minor road along the eastern bank of the river, which acts as a boundary to the water meadows. 600 yards to its immediate south is Mill Road which provides a route westwards from the village of Thiepval to Hamel and to the south of Mill Road is Thiepval Wood. There are two river crossings over the Ancre; the southernmost one is at the end of Mill Road, the northern one, which reaches Beaucourt Station, is 400 yards north of the village. The ground contains meadows by the river, and rises steadily for 750 yards, gaining 76 yards in height from the meadows, and then becomes a small plateau (the Schwaben Redoubt) before rising again another 33 yards until it reaches the western end of the Thiepval Ridge. The ground north of Mill Road has no woods or fenced fields. There were also no fence-lines between Thiepval Wood and the village.

---

83   C Company War Diary (TNA WO 95/96).
84   Pidgeon. *Tanks on the Somme.* p 129.
85   Mann was now maintaining D Company's War Diary and would have been told by Summers of the task.

German Defences and Dispositions

The Germans continued to hold the defences from St Pierre Divion, on the south bank of the River Ancre to the east of the Schwaben Redoubt (D6), a position which had been established before the attacks on 1 July. The frontline trench faced southwest and ran parallel to Mill Road which ran northwest from Thiepval down to a bridge over the River Ancre (C5). There was a support trench running parallel and then a third trench, known as the Strassburg Line, which had originally linked St Pierre Divion to the Schwaben Redoubt. Seven hundred yards to the northeast, there was second communication trench known as the Hansa Line. The frontline trench contained a number of machine-gun emplacements, one group protecting the approach along the minor road which ran parallel to the river towards the village of St Pierre Divion, as well as strongpoints with the village.[86] Buildings in the village, as well as the protective dugouts, were believed to be mined. There was another defensive trench, known as Mill Trench, which ran from the northern end of the village to Grandcourt, which protected the Germans from assaults across the River Ancre, and a communications trench (the Serb Line) which linked the Strasbourg and Hansa Lines. The German defenders consisted of elements of *I* and *III Battalion* of *95th Regiment (38th Division)* and *I Battalion* of *144 Regiment (233 Division)*.[87]

The Plan

II Corps was to drive the Germans from the frontline system between Schwaben Redoubt and St Pierre Divion, clear the southern bank of the River Ancre, and then establish a line facing northeast opposite Beaucourt. Two road crossings across the River Ancre, at the Mill Road and near Beaucourt Station (C5) and Beaucourt Mill would also be taken.[88] 39th Division was to capture St Pierre Divion and the crossing over the River Ancre to its north, and then clear Grandcourt. The attack would start in darkness, the infantry following the artillery barrage to their first objectives.

The main assault was to be made by four battalions attacking northwest downhill from Schwaben Redoubt – these would not be supported by tanks. They would clear the village of St Pierre Divion including internal trenches and strong points, and on reaching the river, capture the crossing which led to Beaucourt Station. A subsidiary attack was made by two battalions northwards across Mill Road into the German defences close to the river. In addition to the usual creeping and stationary artillery barrages, two machine-gun companies would place a cordon behind the village, to neutralise German reinforcements, whilst two more machine-gun companies from the West would provide enfilade fire for the subsidiary attack from the south. It was this attack which would be supported by A Company.

---

86 Pidgeon, *Tanks on the Somme*, p.103.
87 Miles, *OHGW*, p. 485 fn. 1. The *223rd Division* was in the process of relieving *38th Division* as the assault took place.
88 Miles, *OHGW*, p. 478.

The Infantry

39th Division allocated 117th and 118th Infantry brigades for the attack; 117th Brigade on the left attacking northeast from Thiepval Wood (map square C6) towards St Pierre Divion whilst 118th Brigade in the centre would attack downhill from the Schwaben Redoubt. To their right, the 56th Brigade of 19th Division would attack from Stuff Trench towards the Grandcourt line and secure their northern flank.[89]

The Artillery

Gough's Fifth Army had been substantially reinforced to provide more artillery support than had been available on 1 July. II Corps had four hundred and five 18-pounders, one hundred 4.5-inch howitzers and thirty 13-pounder guns in direct support plus nine groups of heavy and siege artillery. As a result, II Corps had one field gun and howitzer for every 16 yards of front; twice that provided on 1 July but not quite as much available on 15 September for the opening attacks of the Battle of Flers–Courcelette. In addition, 16th Machine Gun (MG) Company and 4th Motor MG Battery were to fire in echelon from Hamel east into St Pierre Divion whilst 117th MG Company would provide covering fire during the opening stages of the assault.[90]

The Tanks

Three tanks from No. 3 Section of A Company were tasked to support the attack.[91] They were to attack from a point northeast of Thiepval Wood and, having captured St Pierre Divion, one of the three was to assist the seizure of the river crossings. Tank A, on the right, was to drive north to the Strasbourg Line; it was then to drive about 200 yards west towards the village, then turn northeast, making its way to the Serb Road and then onto the Hansa Line, following this trench northwest towards the river. At this point it would then receive new orders, either to attack targets in the river valley or press on towards Grandcourt. Tank B, in the centre, was to follow the same initial line as Tank A until it reached the German support trench. It would then turn northwest and follow the trench for 200 yards and then attack St Pierre Divion from the east. Once the village had been captured, the tank would then drive north and assist the capture of the river crossing near Beaucourt. The third tank, Tank C, on the left was tasked to follow the German frontline, crushing the wire protecting the trench and destroying German MG emplacements by the river. This tank would then retrace its tracks for 400 yards and drive north for 200 yards and destroy a strongpoint in a group of houses. It would then follow a trench west to a footbridge across the Ancre and clear another German position known as the Summer House before driving to the church in St Pierre Divion where the skipper would receive new orders.

---

89   Miles, *OHGW*, p. 480 and 481.
90   Miles, *OHGW*, p 482 and footnote 2.
91   There is an excellent map of the tanks' planned routes in the photographs in Pidgeon's *Tanks on the Somme* pp. 82 and 83.

Preparation for Battle and Deployment

No record is given about where the tanks completed their preparation for battle but this is likely to have been west of Aveluy, possibly in the same place used by No. 1 Section of C Company in September. The tanks' route to their Place of Assembly was through Authuille to Paisley Dump, on the southern edge of Thiepval Wood, close to where *Creme de Menthe* and *Cordon Rouge* had started their attack on Thiepval on 26 September.[92] In the early hours of the morning, the tanks were to drive to the southeast corner of the wood then turn left, driving north following Paisley Avenue (a communications trench) parallel to the eastern face of the wood, until they reached their Starting Point between the northeast corner of the word and the Mill Road.[93]

As the tanks moved toward their Starting Point, well before dawn, one broke a gear whilst the second sank into the mud.[94] The third tank, Female No. 544 with crew A13 under Lt Herbert Hitchcock, pressed on and successfully reached the Starting Point despite the thick fog over the battlefield.[95] The other two having failed to appear, it was tasked to undertake the role of C Tank on the western flank of the attack.

Zero

Zero was at 0545 hours; first light was at 0624 and sunrise at 0659 hours. Visibility was restricted, after 0600 hours, by thick mist which lasted until 0900 hours.

The Infantry Attacks

On the right, 56th Brigade advanced under the cover of the creeping barrage and took their objectives with little loss, the Germans having been surprised by the attack. Owing to the fog, one battalion advanced beyond their objectives but, by 0815 hours, they had been brought back to their correct positions and linked up with flanking units. The infantry then dug new defensive positions, to consolidate the positions. At noon, this was interrupted by some German machine-gun fire. As the day wore on, German artillery fire increased but it was erratic. The expected German counter-attack did not take place.

In the centre, all four infantry battalions of 118th Brigade attacked but had mixed fortunes. The right-hand battalion, whose objective was the Hansa Line and 500 yards of Mill Trench, made steady progress taking their objectives by 0730 hours, capturing 150 German defenders and four machine-guns. To their left, the other battalions lost direction and had to stop and reorganise. This was hampered by German machine-guns firing from the Strassburg Line;

---

92   This was also the site of HQ 110th Infantry Brigade.
93   This was at Map Reference R25a 6,4 according to the Battle Report at Appendix XIX. This is 400 yards southeast of the junction of the D151 and the D73.
94   Pidgeon, *Tanks on the Somme,* p. 112. Footnote citation 4 states that these tanks were probably commanded by Lts Houghton and Monro Phillips who were also members of No. 3 Section – his source is probably Gnr Fred Cutting's diary held at the TMA.
95   Pidgeon, *Tanks on the Somme,* p. 103 states that Hitchcock left his Place of Assembly at 0545 hours (Zero). The contemporary report is by his company commander (McLellan). See Appendix XIX. It indicates that this is when the tank left its SP which was only 200 yards from the frontline which appears more likely.

however, the battalions successfully reached Mill Trench and, by 1000 hours, had secured the Mill Road river crossing as well as Beaucourt Mill. Later that day, they met up with units from V Corps who were attacking north of the river.

On the left, 117th Brigade initially had difficulty in keeping up with the creeping barrage as they scrambled across the shattered German defences north of the Mill Road. They also lost direction owing to the fog. German machine-guns located on the Strassburg Line caused many casualties amongst the officers as they tried to get their men forward – as a result both battalion headquarters intervened, regained control of their troops and the advance continued. The clearance of the many deep dugouts overlooking the River Ancre was accomplished by 0615 hours and, by 0740 hours, the village had been taken. The German prisoners included the staff of a battalion headquarters caught in the cellars.[96]

Tank Action

At five minutes before Zero, LCpl Reginald Bevan ASC started the tank's engine and, at 0545 hours, Female No. 544 advanced across no man's land towards the German frontline. The tank had difficulty coping with the ground conditions and was unable to proceed at one stage. RFC reports show the tank carried out its orders fairly closely in that it smashed down the barbed wire, protecting the frontline, and tackled the machine-gun emplacements. At 0700 hours, the tank broke through the German frontline.[97] Again, the tank was temporarily unable to proceed as the tracks would not grip and, as the tank was unprotected by the British Infantry, it was soon surrounded by the Germans. About this time Hitchcock was wounded in the head with Bevan being wounded in the face by splinters.[98] Hitchcock decided to get help and handed command over to Cpl Arthur Taffs. After Hitchcock and three men got out of the tank, their skipper was killed by a grenade.[99] No more was seen of two of the men who left the tank but Gnr Clifford Ainley was pulled back into the tank after he had been wounded in the forearm.[100] The remaining crew opened fire on the enemy who retired and replied with machine-guns and rifles.

Rather than withdraw, Taffs decided to attack the second objective. Although Bevan had been wounded in the face by splinters from his prism, he and the gearsmen extricated the Female tank which showed some very skilled driving. The tank then drove forward 200 yards to the German second line where, at about 0800 hours, the tank crashed into a dugout. *We're All In It* became hopelessly stuck,[101] lying at an angle of 45 degrees with the result that the machine-guns on the left side were useless and the two guns in the right-hand sponsons were only capable of firing at a high angle. The tank was then again attacked by the Germans. Having realised the

---

96   Miles, *OHGW*, pp 480–484.
97   Pidgeon, *Tanks on the Somme*, pp. 103–105.
98   The tank front hatches had been fitted with bullet deflectors since it arrived in France (see photograph above). This reduced the damage from bullet splash but could not stop the prisms being smashed at close range.
99   *Balliol War Memorial Book* <https://www.flickr.com/photos/balliolarchivist/albums/72157625232059789/page2> (accessed 11 January 2020).
100 Probably Williams and Miles.
101 The name of the tank is clearly seen in photographs taken after the action. It was probably named after a popular musical play which opened in London in July 1916. Other tanks in A company were also named after musicals.

tank's machine-guns offered no threat to their safety, the German assaulted the tank with stick grenades from the sides, front and underneath.[102] As none of the British infantry could be seen, probably owing to the thick mist which prevailed during the whole action, Taffs sent a message by carrier pigeon asking for help. This message was passed by HQ II Corps to 118th Infantry Brigade who gave orders to the Black Watch to render all assistance possible. At about 0900 hours, the Germans were driven off and the A13 crew were relieved by a party of the Notts and Derby Regiment who were soon joined by the Black Watch.[103] Taffs and the remainder of the crew left the tank after the area was secured, the tank being safe from re-capture by the enemy. Owing to the dreadful ground conditions, it was however not possible to salvage the tank and it remained in place. As the tank's skipper was dead, A Company's commander produced a report with the assistance of the crew which is reproduced in Appendix XIX.

We're All In It ditched near St Pierre Divion. (TMA)

102 The tank crew only expended some 2,000 rounds of small arms ammunition that day; it should have been carrying in excess of 30,000 rounds for the four Vickers machine-guns.
103 The battalions had formed part of the subsidiary attack north across Mill Lane.

Tank Effectiveness

The ditching of two tanks and the mechanical problems suffered by the third did not prevent the infantry from succeeding in their mission. The tanks, however, were wholly ineffective.

Casualties, Prisoners and Awards

The 39th Division assault was totally successful. Casualties amongst the Division were only 78 dead, 454 wounded and 55 missing compared with 1,580 German prisoners plus an unknown number of dead and wounded.[104] The bodies of Hitchcock and Gnr William Miles were identified on 14 November and buried close to where they were killed.[105] Gnr William Stanley was evacuated to a casualty clearing station but he died of his wounds on 17 November 1916.[106] Each one of the remaining members of the crew was awarded the Military Medal; all survived the war and Taffs and Bevan were subsequently commissioned.

Capture of Beaumont Hamel, 13 November 1916

Situation

There had been no progress against the German position north of the Ancre since the carnage of 1 July 1916. The area around Serre and Redan Ridge to its south was, by now, a morass of water-filled shellholes, impossible for vehicle movement and extremely difficult on foot. There were no recognisable landscape features, the villages were smears of red brick dust in the all-pervasive mud, and metalled tracks were difficult to see.

North of the River Ancre, two divisions were allocated to take the villages of Beaucourt and Beaumont Hamel (see map 10). The latter had been attacked on 1 July 1916 after a mine was exploded under the German frontline but, despite the desperate attempts by 29th Division, the village remained in German hands.[107] The area was now to be attacked by 51st (Highland) Division, under the command of Maj Gen George Harper.[108] To their right, 63rd (Royal Naval)

---

104 The 39th Division report on the Battle of the Ancre dated 17 November 1916.
105 Their bodies were later exhumed. Hitchcock and Miles are now buried together at Mill Road Cemetery near Thiepval; Hitchcock in grave II. B. 10. and Miles in II. B. 9.
106 His body is buried at Contay British Military Cemetery in grace VIII. B. 18.
107 The explosion at Hawthorn Redoubt was photographed by Edward Malins and was included in the record breaking 1916 film *The Battle of the Somme*.
108 Harper, who was commissioned into the RE, attended the Army Staff Course and then served on the Directing Staff in 1908 for two years. During this time, he accompanied the Commandant, Henry Wilson on two recce trips along the Belgian, French and German borders in order to gain information which would be useful should the British have to fight on the continent. He then was appointed deputy to Wilson as Director of Military Operations and was responsible for supervising the production of railway timetables for the deployment of the BEF to France. In 1914, he joined the GHQ BEF staff with responsibility for operational analysis and then appointed to command 17th Infantry Brigade, again an unusual appointment for a Sapper, in February 1915. In September 1915, he took command of 51st Highland Division on the Somme; a post he would hold for 18 months during which the Division gained a reputation as a *corps d'elite*.

Division, under Maj Gen Cameron Shute, was to take the village of Beaucourt and the high ground to its north.

The Ground

Beaumont Hamel (B4) sits in a valley, well hidden from view. Its western approaches are dominated by high ground on either side of the Auchonvillers road, the Hawthorn Crater Redoubt to the south dominating not only the road but the high ground over which any attack on the Y Ravine (a deep valley which runs southwest of the village) must negotiate.

German Defence and Dispositions

The German formations dominated the approaches to Beaucourt both immediately north of the River Ancre, the disued Albert-Arras railway line (D4 – B6) and the road to its east, and the ridge north of Hamel where a strongpoint had been established in dead ground (B5). Any attack from the west had to take three lines of trenches, two of which were protected by barbed wire entanglements and machine-gun posts covering all approaches. The defenders lived in caves and concrete lined bunkers some 30 feet below ground level, and Y Ravine also contained many dugouts and stores for the defenders. The earlier artillery bombardments had created a wasteland of water-filled and interlocking shellholes which made the ground extremely difficult for attackers.

There was a second line of defences, based along the road from Beaucourt to Beaumont Hamel which included another strongpoint (C4) known as the Triangle which sat on the highpoint of that second ridge and dominated the areas to the east, north and west. The Triangle was also linked into a double trench system (Munich and Frankfurt), which was the depth position of the German trench systems which protected the defences at Serre, creating a major barrier to any unit attempting to advance towards Bapaume.

The Plan

Fifth Army's plan relied on the proven tactical combination of infantry and artillery; using the creeping barrage to protect the infantry assault, with tanks following to reduce previously identified machine-gun posts and strongpoints. In the south, 63rd Division was to capture the northern bank of the River Ancre, the high ground to its north and the village of Beaucourt sur Ancre (C4) whilst 51st Division was to take the village of Beaumont Hamel, the Y Ravine as well as the high ground to its east including the Munich and Frankfurt Trenches. There was a seven day preliminary bombardment and, as with the ill-fated attack on 1 July 1916, a mine was blown under the Hawthorn Redoubt which still dominated the western approaches to Beaumont Hamel. The key difference was between the two attacks was that, on 13 November, the mine would be detonated at Zero (0545 hours), rather than Zero minus ten minutes as on 1 July, which gave warning of the earlier assault. The bombardment of the German frontline would also only start at Zero.

There were five objectives at Beaumont Hamel; the first (Red Line) was the German frontline trench, the second (Blue Line) was the support line, the third (Purple Line) was the depth trench, just 200 yards behind the German frontline. The fourth or Green Line was to the east of the village and followed Station Road (C5) down the re-entrant towards Beaucourt sur Ancre; this was to be reached by Zero plus 40 minutes. The final objective, the Yellow Line, ran along Frankfurt Trench which was to be taken by Zero plus 70 minutes.[109]

The Infantry

The 51st Division had moved to France in early May 1915 and, two weeks later during the Battle of Festubert, was tasked to consolidate gains made by 2nd Division. It was a demanding role for an inexperienced formation and the Highlanders had to learn on the job. The Germans were expecting the assault and it was against unbroken wire defences. One brigade reached the enemy's frontline trenches but a German counter-attack, the next morning, expelled them. When the BEF was tasked to replace French units along the Somme, 51st Division took over the defences between Becourt, east of Albert, and the Ancre River at Hamel including La Boisselle and Thiepval. By the time Harper took command of the division in September 1915, it had acquired a dubious reputation. However, Harper inspired his men, imbuing them with such confidence that the Division gained a reputation for its effectiveness in defence and attack. They fought a fierce battle for High Wood in August 1916 and, after reforming and retraining, were selected to take Beaumont Hamel.

The Tanks

Two tanks were allocated in support of 51st Division: Lt Ewen Bruce possibly in Male tank No. 775 and Lt Frank Telfor again possibly in the Female tank No. 532.[110] Given the previous preparations in October, the deployment route would have been recced by Vandervell and his skippers. It probably followed the old Beaumont Road heading due east from Auchonvillers, which was mainly out of sight of the German defenders in Beaumont Hamel.

Zero

As with the attack on St Pierre Divion, Zero was at 0545 hours, first light was at 0534 hours and sunrise was at 0607 hours.

Action before Zero

Despite being urged to attack with all three of his brigades in line, Harper decided to use only two brigades, keeping his third in reserve. The original plan was for the attack to take place on 24 October but wet weather and bad ground conditions forced postponement after postponement. During this time, the Highlanders undertook patrols and raids to ascertain the strength of the resistance likely to be encountered and to inspect the enemy's wire. This activity identified the defenders were using knife-rests, made of heavy timber and barbed wire, to plug gaps where the British artillery had breached the German barbed wire defences.

---

109 Author's note: This timetable proved to be entirely unrealistic.
110 Tank details are as of 1 Oct 1916 as recorded in Woods' Note Book.

On 26 October, the Highlanders raided the German frontline trenches in order to confirm which units were holding the line. On 29 October, a patrol entered the enemy's frontline and then moved to the support line, which they found protected by an impassable belt of knife-rests but no sign of the enemy. On 31 October, a German deserter reached the British lines who revealed that his battalion was holding a front of only 700 yards, and that the rifle strength of the four companies was about 180 each.[111] This indicated that the enemy was holding the position in considerably greater force than was probable but, 'in view of his apparent poverty of intellect', the deserter was not believed. Further raids were carried out, on 4 November, which found the Germans holding the trenches in strength. The raiders were unable to enter the trench lines, not just because of the wire but due to the fact that the ground was so sodden that the troops found it a physical impossibility to keep up with the protective barrage.

Attack

The Highlanders used the darkness, and thick fog, to good effect. 153rd Brigade had initial success on the extreme right as their assault battalions broke through the frontline, passed the eastern end of Y Ravine and reached their First Objective (Station Road) by 0645 hours. However, in the centre, clearing the frontline took hard fighting and the infantry were then held up by positions in the Y Ravine, a re-entrant 30 feet deep with some 400 defenders, which could not be taken despite the deployment of a reserve battalion. The fighting went on until the early afternoon when the Germans started to surrender. The attack on the village by 152nd Brigade was also successful, the German support line eventually being taken by the afternoon. To their south, 63rd Division also forced the German defences along the River Ancre, albeit with serious losses, reaching Beaucourt Station. They were unable to take the high ground north of Hamel.

Tank Action

The fog and the terrain made it difficult for the Corps and Divisional headquarters to be kept aware of progress.[112] At 0930 hours, HQ V Corps proposed to HQ 51st Division that, if the village was not already taken, the pair of tanks standing by at Auchonvillers be used. This was agreed and the tanks successfully made their way to their Starting Point. According to the divisional history:

> At 10.30 a.m. two tanks were sent forward to clear up isolated pockets of the enemy still holding out in the village. This was the first occasion on which the Division had co-operated with tanks. The condition of the ground was, however, such that the tanks only just reached the German front line.
>
> By the time they had travelled this distance they had built up great mounds of mud under their bellies, which prevented their further advance. One of the tank officers, incidentally a Scot, refused to be prevented from joining in the fight. He therefore

---

111 'He was a miserable creature, described officially as "undersized and of poor physique."' E.F. Bewsher *The History of 51st (Highland) Division 1914-1918* (London: Blackwood & Sons, 1921) Chapter 7.

112 Harper was not informed that the right flank battalions had reached their first objective until 1030 hours, more than three hours after the event. Miles, *OHGW*, p. 492.

made some captured Germans carry his Hotchkiss guns and their ammunition up to the Green line, where he joined in the consolidation.[113]

One tank ditched on the Auchonvillers to Beaumont Hamel road, between the German frontline and the support trench north of the Hawthorn Crater. The Official History states that another reached the northern edge of Beaumont Hamel.[114] The news that both tanks had ditched reached HQ D Company in Auchonvillers at noon and, despite efforts at salvage, the tanks were still ditched on 19 November.[115]

Tank Effectiveness

The tanks were incapable of crossing the terrain near the German frontline; a task beyond them but one which was repeated throughout the Third Battle of Ypres. The lack of tanks did not blunt the attacks by 51st Highland Division who continued to fight for a further three days, clearing most of their objectives.

Capture of the Hamel Strongpoint, 14 November 1916

The Ground

North of the River Ancre (map 10), the ground rises quickly from 80 to 110 metres north of Hamel (D5) and 130 metres above sea level northwest of Beaucourt sur Ancre (C5). There are two re-entrants, one (C5) used by a minor road connecting Beaucourt station to Beaumont Hamel (known as Station Road). Another road (D4), north of Beaucourt, follows a re-entrant which eventually reaches Puisieux-au-Mont (D2). There is also a minor road (B4–C4) which links Beaucourt to Beaumont Hamel over the ridge which separates the two villages on which is located the Triangle Strongpoint.

German Defences and Dispositions

Southwest of Station Road, the Germans established three lines of trenches running southeast to northwest approximately 150 yards apart which linked to Y Ravine and then went due north

---

113   Bewsher, *History of 51st Highland Division,* Chapter 7. The Scottish officer was Ewen Bruce who was commissioned from Sandhurst into the Cameron Highlanders in 1910. He was Mentioned in Despatches in May 1917, probably for his action at Beaumont Hamel and awarded the MC for salvaging two tanks in full view of the enemy in July 1917, losing his left arm in the process. In the autumn of 1918, he led a tank demonstration team to Japan, subsequently being awarded the Order of the Rising Sun 4th Class. In June 1919, he commanded a British Tank Corps detachment, operating against Tsaritsyn (now Volgograd). On 30 June 1919, he personally led three tanks into action and destroyed a Bolshevik counter-attack. For this action he was awarded the DSO.

114   Miles, *OHGW,* p 494. This is likely to have been tank commanded by Bruce.

115   According to the D Company War Diary, all tanks were salvaged by 1 December and brought to Wavrans. There is no further record of 532 but 775 was used as a supply tank by No. 6 Company of B Battalion at Messines and also in late July 1917.

protecting Beaumont Hamel. They also constructed a communications trench, running parallel to, and south of, Station Road and a defence line, called Station Trench, which also ran parallel but to the north of the road. There were two strongpoints in the area. One was north of Hamel (B5) on the 110-metre contour which comprised a series of bunkers and underground store. The other strongpoint, called the Triangle (C4), was at the junction between the Munich and Strasburg Trenches and the Beaucourt Trench, 130 metres above sea level.

The capture of the village of Beaumont Hamel by 51st Highland Division and the road between Hamel and Beaucourt by 63rd Division on 13 November had surprised the Germans and they moved up reinforcements overnight. The remnants of *55th Reserve Regiment,* which had just held Beaucourt village, were relieved by *III Battalion 114th Regiment* whilst *II Battalion 29th Ersatz Regiment* took up position north of the village along the River Ancre, to prevent an attack from the east. At 0200 hours, *II Battalion 114th Regiment* took up position in the Puisieux Trench to the rear of the Ancre trench. The Beaucourt Road was a crater field and the ruins of the captured village were burning. In view of the uncertain situation, the Germans did not contemplate a counter-attack that morning.[116]

The Infantry

The 63rd Division, which had not seen action prior to 13 September, and was attacking without tanks, had acquitted itself well.[117] On the right of the attack, by the river, the German frontline position had been captured after very hard fighting with over 300 prisoners. Despite the fog, and the mass of shell craters, the attack continued according to the timetable after dawn with the result that another 400 prisoners were taken as the unit captured the dugouts along the Station Road as well as the railway station itself. On the high ground, however, on the left of the Division, the assaulting battalions were caught in no man's land by German machine-guns. Attacking formations were disrupted and cohesion lost; the deaths or wounding of commanding officers and company commanders meant reorganisation was difficult and, when the German frontlines were reached, the fighting became piecemeal attacks using rifles and bombs. However, by the afternoon, some elements of the German frontline were taken and 63rd Division linked up with 51st Division on its left.

Plan Development

The plan for 14 November was that, in the south, the attack would continue with the aim of taking Beaucourt and the ground to its northeast. On the higher ground, the German defensive lines would be taken using reinforcements provided by from two battalions from 37th Division supported by tanks and then take the original second objective.[118]

116 Miles, *OHGW*, p. 503.
117 The six tanks, which were from Mortimore's section, had been sent back from their forward base at Auchonvillers the previous evening.
118 Shute, who commanded 63rd Division, sought the tanks in the early afternoon of 13 September. Six tanks did return to Auchonvillers but arrived too late to be committed to the attack that evening.

Zero

Zero was at 0600 hours on 14 November; first light was at 0624 hours and sunrise at 0659 hours. There was a thin mist over the battlefield in the early morning which cleared as the day moved on.

Preparation for Battle and Deployment

At 1130 hours on 13 November, at the half-way halt at Beaussart, Mortimore was ordered to take six tanks back to Auchonvillers to support the ongoing attacks. They moved quickly and were back at D Company's forward base in four hours.[119] Whilst they were en route, Summers received orders to send two tanks to attack the strong point situated Q17b 7,4.[120] He decided to send three tanks, two commanded by Lieutenants Harry Drader and Eric Robinson with Lieutenant Hugh Bell in reserve.[121] When the tanks arrived at Auchonvillers, their crews carried out their final preparations for battle. Based on previous D Company operating experience, it is almost certain that the three skippers, accompanied by Mortimore, went forward to prove the routes to the rendezvous, where they would meet a guide from 63rd Division, and they then laid the tapes back to Auchonvillers which they would follow in the early hours of the following morning.

Shute described the tanks' objective as follows: 'The strong point was built in the form of a single communications trench and, from this cause, its presence had not been disclosed by aeroplane photographs beforehand. The dugouts which it contained were very deep and three concrete machine gun emplacements approached by steep ladders from the dugouts had been untouched by our bombardments. It appears that these machine guns could fire continuously in spite of our barrage.'[122] The War Diary of 10th Battalion Royal Dublin Fusiliers provides more details. 'The strong point extended from the German front line trench to their reserve trench and had four entrances in front and two each in the support and reserve lines. The dug out was capable of taking 1,500 men and had an electric plant installed. It also had ammunition stores to supply the three lines and a first aid station. Machine guns covered each entrance with various snipers in between.'[123]

The three tanks set off in the early hours of the morning, no doubt travelling very slowly to avoid arousing the enemy, and successfully reached the rendezvous one hour before dawn (about 0510 hours). Their guide from there was Lieutenant Allan Campbell RNVR of 63rd Division's Trench Mortar Battery. Campbell got into the leading tank (Drader's) which he then directed towards the enemy's frontline. It was 0600 hours but, before they could move, Robinson's tank was hit and knocked out by a German shell. As it was still dark, and also misty, the shot must have been lucky. Bell's reserve tank was brought into action and followed Drader towards the objective. Drader's driver found the planned route across no man's land difficult and had to drive south to find a suitable place to reach the frontline. He was successful and crossed the frontline,

119 The D Company War Diary records they arrived at 3.05p.m. (1505 hours).
120 This grid reference in the centre of the German lines, between the support and reserve trench
121 All three skippers had previously seen action; Drader at Martinpuich on 15 September, Robinson at Courcelette on 26 September and Bell at Le Sars on 7 October. See Chapter 8.
122 Pidgeon, *Tanks on the Somme*, pp. 141–142.
123 Pidgeon, p. 143.

the crew using their guns[124] to enfilade the defenders at a range of 50 yards.[125]

Having cleared the trenches, Drader's tank headed for the support trench but became ditched before reaching it. Bell's tank, which could not cross the German frontline, then ditched. However, it was now after first light and both tanks targeted the German position using their 6-pounder guns to good effect. Drader described what happened next thus:

> On opening the front flap [hatch] of the tank and obtaining a better view, it was seen that all the German garrison, some 400 in number, had found something white to wave in token of surrender. The situation was rather an embarrassing one for so small a number as the two crews to deal with. Fortunately, it was possible by signs, and the assistance of the infantry, to mop up these 400 before they realised that both tanks were stuck in the mud.

Drader's account is modest compared with the report in D Company's War Diary which states:

> At Zero (6 am) tanks advanced to the attack and at 50 yds range Lt Drader opened fire with 6 pounder guns. The tanks still advanced and crossed the first line of the strong point doing good enfilading work. Simultaneously the enemy hoisted the white flag. The tanks at this moment became ditched and an awkward situation arose, which was handled splendidly by both officers. A machine gunner was detailed to watch for any sign of treachery on the part of the enemy, and the officers and crews then left the tanks and entered the German trenches with loaded revolvers. They coaxed the enemy out of their dug-outs and, after about an hour, the prisoners who numbered over 400 were despatched to rear with an infantry escort. When the adverse conditions as regards ground are reckoned with, this must be considered a very fine performance and all ranks engaged in the operation are to be congratulated.

Not only had Drader and Bell's actions carried the front and support trenches, but the Germans were so demoralised that those in the reserve trench later surrendered. Sadly, neither Drader, who had been awarded the MC for his actions at Martinpuich, nor Bell, who was Mentioned in Despatches for his success at Le Sars, were recognised for their gallantry on this occasion.[126]

Tank Effectiveness

The tanks proved to be invaluable. They reached their objective ahead of the attacking infantry, suppressed the position, caused the garrison to surrender and then cleared the underground location with no British casualties. No tanks had been this effective since Storey's action on 25 September near Gueudecourt.

---

124 Drader was commanding Male tank No. 713; the number of Bell's tank is not recorded.
125 D Company's War Diary.
126 Lt Alan Campbell was awarded an MC and a Bar for his actions during the fighting in the Ancre Valley. The citation for the Bar states "he brought his guns into action with good effect. Later, he guided two Tanks to the enemy first line system, and materially assisted in taking over 400 prisoners". Campbell was promoted in 1917 and was killed, together with his CO on 30th December 1917, when a shell hit their battalion headquarters.

Tank Action Near Serre, 15 November 1916

Introduction

As previously mentioned, Holford-Walker informed HQ V Corps on 12 November that his tanks could not operate on the ground they were intended to cross and, after confirmatory orders, they started to withdraw to Beaussart after dark. Not only did these tanks start to move but, by some mistake, so did the pair allocated to XIII Corps.[127] At 2030 hours, Holford-Walker was informed that these tanks were required. The message was sent but the relevant tanks had left; there were however three remaining commanded by Clarke, Lambert and Reardon at the base at Jeremiah Trench near La Signy Farm (A3).

At 2300 hours, HQ C Company were informed that two tanks should report to their rendezvous – they were to support 31st Division who were attacking towards Puisieux in order to take the German front, reserve and support lines and then form a defensive flank for V Corps. Holford-Walker, presumably deciding to ensure there was a reserve in case of ditching or breakdown, ordered all three skippers to deploy; this was prescient as Clarke ditched on route.

At 0545 hours, an hour and a half before sunrise, the attack started as planned. Serre was protected by five lines of trenches and to its southwest, by a redoubt named the Quadrilateral (known to the Germans as the *Heidenkopf*). This was positioned on the German frontline so that machine-guns could enfilade no man's land to the northeast and south. XIII Corps was initially successful, reaching the front and support lines. A German counter-attack from the north was destroyed by machine-guns firing from the area of Hébuterne but the tanks were not sent forward. To quote the official historian: 'Serre on its little knoll commanded the ground to the west and the early morning fog was not so thick as to hide the British advance from the enemy. Starting in good order, the leading battalions were soon struggling in mud which was, in place waist deep, and when the German wire was found, there were few gaps in it.'[128] Despite their demands for the tanks to be made ready, HQ XIII Corps did not send them forward and, at 1700 hours on 13 November, released them.

At 1100 hours on 14 November, Holford-Walker was warned that the tanks would be required to support a limited operation by 2nd Division the following day. This was due to the moderate success achieved by the infantry earlier that morning. At noon on 14 November, Gough visited HQ V Corps, having received positive reports from Fanshawe and, after discussion, approved the resumption of the offensive the next morning.[129] Holford-Walker reported to 2nd Division's Advanced HQ at 1330 hours where he was told the Division would attack the Quadrilateral at 0600 hours the following morning. He immediately informed Clively to make all the necessary arrangements and for Hiscocks to tape the route to their start point.

---

127 Bennewith and Rodney, who were under command C Company's younger brother Archie.
128 Miles, *OHGW*, p. 498.
129 A copy of VI Operation Order was sent that evening to Haig who was in Paris preparing for an Inter Allied conference the next morning. He promptly telephoned Advanced GHQ stating he did not wish Fifth Army to undertake any further operation on a large scale before Haig returned to the Somme. Miles *OHGW*, p. 510.

The Ground

The ground was open farmland: sodden, pitted with overlapping shellholes, and mud so deep as to be almost impassable to the infantry. The roads had been heavily bombarded. Serre and the Quadrilateral were on slightly higher ground than the British frontline and therefore the attack was uphill.[130] The approach route for the tanks was completely visible to the Germans in daylight; there was absolutely no cover from view or fire.

The German Defenders

The *23rd, 62nd* and *63rd Infantry Regiments* of *12th Division* defended the area around Serre although the Official History does not indicate which unit actually held the Quadrilateral.[131]

The Plan

HQ 6th Infantry Brigade were ordered[132] to take the German frontline and then advance northwards up Serre Trench,[133] establishing two strongpoints against the expected German counter-attack. In a significant change from previous orders, the tanks were instructed to lead the infantry across no man's land. The tanks were to travel overnight to reach their rendezvous at HQ 6th Brigade at Vallade Trench.[134] They were then to travel east to the frontline and, at 0600 hours, drive across no man's land to breach the German frontline at 0630 hours.[135] The tanks were 'to pay special attention to enemy machine gun at K35c 40,85 [two-thirds of the way down the SW face of the Quadrilateral], which had been giving a lot of trouble to our infantry.

'Having crossed the German frontline, the tanks were to change course northwards along Frontier Lane and assist the infantry in forming a defensive flank on the line K35a 9,2 and K35a 6.3 [across Bowl trench].[136] After the position had been consolidated, the tanks were to return by route followed in the advance.' HQ 2nd Division concluded their orders by stating that 'every effort is to be made to take advantage of the assistance of the tanks in order to capture the Quadrilateral and make their defensive flank on the North secure.'

Zero

Zero was at 0715 hours – first light was at 0636 and sunrise was 0708 hours. A heavy mist formed at about 0600 hours which subsequently cleared.

---

130 It was at the north-western end of the Redan ridge.
131 They were relieved on 19 November 1916.
132 2 Division GS 1017/1/171 dated 14 November 1916. See Appendix XIX.
133 Serre trench runs from the southwest to the northeast.
134 The headquarters was located about 500 yards west of the British frontline, on the old Serre Road.
135 No man's land was 300 yards wide at this point; this required the tanks to traverse no man's land under cover of darkness at a speed slightly higher than planned for 15 September.
136 The flank position is actually northeast of the machine-gun position.

Deployment for Battle

Lambert and Reardon's tanks left Colincamps at 0200 hours, heading southeast along Sucerie Avenue to the Sugar Factory (A2) and then east along the old Serre road, known as Roman Road, to HQ 6th Brigade. The taped route was good, as it used formerly metalled roads, and the tanks reached a position just west of HQ 6th Brigade at 0500 hours. Having reported their arrival to the brigade commander, Clively asked that the infantry battalions COs should send any information of value by their scouts; however, no such details were received by the tank skippers.[137] At 0600 hours, Clively gave orders to his tanks to proceed; they moved off but were lost to sight when mist obscured the view from Vallade trench.[138]

Tank Action near the Quadrilateral

The infantry attack was successful, with some parties of 6th Brigade with 99th Brigade on their right getting into the frontline and then successfully constructing a strongpoint within the Quadrilateral on the high ground of the Redan ridge. At 1700 hours, Clively informed HQ C Company that 'both reported tanks were absolutely ditched and mud coming up to sponsons, all guns were salved, no casualties.' In his subsequent report, Clively wrote, 'I attribute the fact of the tanks failing to gain their objective to the extraordinarily bad ground they had to cross, which was worse than I had imagined possible. The officers and men under my command did all humanly possible to get the tanks into a successful action and I would like to bring their efforts to your notice.'[139] It proved impossible to recover either of the tanks and they were abandoned. The fighting however went on, with the infantry making modest success for another three days before the 1916 Ancre campaign was closed down on 18 November.

Tank Effectiveness

The tank crews were given an impossible task owing to the dreadful ground conditions. Holford-Walker's view, expressed three days earlier, was vindicated.

Attack on Frankfurt Trench, 18 November 1916

The final tank action of 1916 was in support of 37th Division who had relieved 63rd Division near Beaucourt sur Ancre. Their role was to assist the taking of the Munich and Frankfurt Trenches which were located on the high ground between Beaumont Hamel and Beaucourt.

---

137 Author's note: Provision of guides was, by now, a standard procedure; however effective marrying-up with the infantry, ahead of an attack, rarely seems to have taken place in 1916 or in the early stages of 1917.

138 It is unclear from Clively's report to C Company where the tanks were at this point. Given the previous instructions, they should have been at the British frontline.

139 Appendix XIX.

The Ground and British Dispositions

The ground over which the fighting took place was open, completely lacking in cover from view and enemy fire. The objective was on the summit of a broad ridge at more than 130 metres above sea level, at the southernmost extremity of the German Munich and Frankfurt trench system which was the German's second line in the area south of Puisieux au Mont. The initial objective, the Triangle, was a strongpoint located in a reverse slope position at the junction of the Beaucourt Trench, which ran along the southern side of the Beaucourt to Beaumont Hamel road, and the southern ends of Munich and Frankfurt Trenches. There were British communications trenches from the south (Station Alley), west (Beaumont Alley and Leave Avenue) and east (Muck Trench) but all required the attacking units to advance uphill over open ground.

Preparations

On Thursday 14 November, after his tanks captured the strongpoint above Hamel, Mortimore almost certainly went forward to determine how to recover Drader's and Bell's ditched tanks as well as Robinson's shell-damaged vehicle.[140] At 1500 hours, D Company received orders 'to move six available tanks to a forward position near Beaucourt Station. Tanks to be in command of Capt Nixon. This forward movement had to be done over our front line, across no man's land and across the original German front defensive system. There were no tracks or roads; accordingly, Capt Mann was detailed to find suitable route, and 150 men were placed at his disposal to build a defined route.'[141] Two hours later, Mortimore and Vandervell, with the tank skippers who had been in action, were relieved by Nixon.[142] The next day, D Company reported that there was no movement although route preparation must have started; C Company's diary stated they 'sent a working party of 3 officers and 80 men to make a road for 'D' Coy's attack and went to reconnoitre ground. Tape will have to be laid from No 1 Group Corps tanks. Possible position of assembly near batteries in White City.'[143]

By 0600 hours on 15 November 37th Division had relieved 63rd Division, and 32nd Division had started to takeover trenches east and north of Beaumont Hamel from the Highland Division. Anticipating that 37th Division would be sent into action shortly (16 November), Summers decided to immediately recce the possible approach routes.

---

140 2Lt Will Bluemel, who originally commanded C2 Cognac and who was later transferred to A Company and command of Female tank No 531 "Oh I Say" was seriously wounded near Auchonvillers on 14 November. Will suffered by splinters from 'a wiz bang' causing injuries to his Right Elbow, Left buttock, Left forearm and right thigh. He was hospitalised him until 22 Jul 1917 and then placed on light duties. Will never returned to active service, being downgraded to C2 medical status, and served with the Ministry of Munitions then the Department of Aero Supplies for the remainder of the war.

141 D Company War Diary.

142 Nixon had commanded No. 2 Section during its training at Elveden and supporting the NZ Division, west of Flers on 15 September 1916. He continued in this role as D Company moved north of the River Ancre.

143 The White City was situated north of the Auchonvillers to Beaumont Hamel road. At the start of the Somme campaign, it had been a major stores dump and was now being used by artillery supporting the attacks east and north of Beaumont Hamel. It had the advantage that it was protected from enemy view and fire by a ridge to its east.

The Plan

The official history gives no details of the plan, nor does D Company's records. However, it appears that the tanks were to advance from the south, crossing the Beaucourt Trench and then to assist the infantry to clear the trench system to its north. There are also no details as to whether the tanks would operate in pairs, although this had become common practice, or as singletons. Trevor Pidgeon states that the infantry would accompany from the south, and fire into the flanks of the German being pushed back.[144]

Zero

Zero was 0610 hours on 18 November, 30 minutes before first light. It had snowed overnight and the attack initially took place in whirling sleet, which later became rain.

Preparation for Battle

On 14 November, Summers 'reconnoitred [the] country into Beaucourt that morning.'[145] The task was extremely challenging as it required the tanks negotiate the severely damaged no man's land before they crossing the German defensive system running south of Beaumont Hamel. This consisted of three, and in places four, trench lines and the associated barbed wire entanglements. There is a slightly better route south of the Y Ravine and north of where Drader and Bell had ditched. However, it appears the route chosen was along the northern bank of the River Ancre, following the line of a minor road and the (then out of use) railway line to the tanks' rendezvous at Beaucourt Station. On his return to his headquarters at Auchonvillers, Summers met Bradley with orders for tanks to move forward to Beaucourt Station.

At 1800 hours, the tanks and the working party left 'taking all night to reach the Hamel Beaucourt Road.'[146] One of the officers participating later described the event to Williams-Ellis:

> Some of the worst of the ground was now in our line and an effort was made to get the tanks through this bad zone in order that they might continue the attack in the neighbourhood of Beaucourt. Efforts were made to prepare a track by means of a considerable digging party, but when the tanks reached the very broken ground just north of the Ancre, they became one after the other firmly stuck; with tremendous efforts they were dug out and, succeeded in getting a few yards further only to stick again. It was heart-breaking work. Finally, on the evening of the 17th, only one tank had succeeded in getting through this bad zone and reaching the comparatively good ground beyond. The crew, to whom great credit is due, had already been working continuously for some days and night, were not only exhausted but had no time to carry reconnaissance of the position to be attacked at dawn the next day.[147]

144 Pidgeon, *Tanks on the Somme*, p. 145 and Clough Williams Ellis, *The Tank Corps*, p. 36.
145 D Company War Diary.
146 D Company War Diary.
147 Williams-Ellis, *The Tank Corps*, p. 36.

The singleton was commanded by Lt Walter Partington.[148] His orders were 'to proceed to position 12 Central which will be the starting point for the attack on the following morning. At Zero proceed North to cross Beaucourt trench near the junction of Beaumont trench and Frankfurt trench. Continue along Frankfurt trench to Leave Alley. When position is consolidated, return by same route and park tank in the ravine near Beaucourt Station.' These orders fail to indicate that Partington's objective was actually a major strongpoint known as the Triangle.

Whilst Partington and his crew were preparing for battle, Hotblack recced the route from the Station, north and then northeast up the re-entrant for 700 yards to the tank's Starting Point. This was 300 yards south of the Beaucourt Road and out of sight of the Germans manning Beaucourt Trench which ran parallel to the road's southern side. The British infantry were fighting hard to gain control of the key German trenches, particularly Munich Trench (map square C4) and Frankfurt Trench, its support trench which ran about 200 yards to its east.

By the end of 17 November 32nd Division controlled Leave Alley, a key communication trench from Beaumont-Hamel towards the Triangle. Also on 17 November, three battalions from 37th Division had managed to fight their way from Beaucourt village up Muck Trench and establish a series of posts which overlooked Frankfurt Trench. This would enable them to kill any Germans trying to escape from 32nd Division's dawn attack the following morning.

Deployment for Battle

With Zero at 0610 hours, Partington's tank must have deployed well before first light. There is no record showing when he left Beaucourt Station but it was probably around 0300 hours.[149] Snow had fallen and covered the tape previously laid by Hotblack who therefore led the tank up the hill and onto its correct Start Point.

Tank Action at the Triangle

As the tank reached the open ground, Partington could not identify his route. 'Hotblack therefore went forward through heavy fire and led the tank forward, taking cover where he could in shell holes which were full of ice and water.'[150] At 0645 hours, just after first light, the tank was seen by members of 37th Division, crossing the German frontline at the junction of Beaucourt and Frankfurt Trenches. She then continued north following Frankfurt Trench to Leave Alley (a distance of 250 yards) led by Hotblack. 'The machine was now in the centre of the position so the German artillery did not dare open fire upon it. The tank poured devasting fire from its machine guns not only on the men in the trenches but also on some horse transport behind the enemy lines.'

Partington, rather than returning as ordered, drove north of Leave Alley for another 300 yards to the German communications trench known as the Glory Lane and then a further 100 yards to the Beaucourt to Serre road. His tank was then observed by members of 37th Division

148 Partington and his crew had deployed to France with A Company. It is unclear when they were attached to D Company but Woods' notebook shows they were initially operating female tank No. 560.
149 Author's note: This time is based on an average tank speed of 8 and a half yards per minute for the uphill approach march.
150 Williams-Ellis, *The Tank Corps*, p. 37.

in the area of map ref. Q6b 2,4, east of Frankfurt Trench and close to the Beaucourt to Serre road but sadly the time was not recorded. The 37th Division War Diary does however state that, from the time Partington crossed the Beaucourt Trench, his 'guns were firing continuously casing great havoc amongst the enemy. At one period he was attacked by thirty bombers; the port guns dealt with them and none escaped. A train of 25 pack mules was observed at a range of 400 yards and put out of action by machine gun fire. Many machine guns were encountered and dealt with.'

No British infantry were with the tank at this time which was more than 750 yards behind the German frontline, so Partington decided to return, following the Serre to Beaucourt road in a southerly direction. At 0855 hours, his tank was observed at Q6d 7,3 where the road met Muck Trench, which he then followed in a south-easterly direction. The tank eventually recrossed the Beaucourt Trench at 0907 hours after which the tank drove back down the hill to its starting point near Beaucourt Station. It was not called forward again for further action.

Tank Effectiveness

Partington's single tank action on 18 November stands alone; no other tank since 15 September 1916 succeeded in getting so far behind the enemy' frontline nor doing as much damage, before successfully returning to its Starting Point undamaged. Sadly, the infantry were not in a position to build on the tank's achievements.

Casualties and Awards

The Official History provides no details of casualties suffered either by 37th Division or the German units that day. The Division's War Diary records that two crewmen were wounded; these were the tank's SNCO Sgt David Davies and Gnr Harold Thomas whose head wounds were treated at a base hospital at Boulogne.[151]

Thomas and Davies[152] were awarded Italian bronze medals[153] for their gallantry and Partington was awarded the Silver Medal. His citation states that he 'commanded an isolated tank in action of the morning of 18 November. He remained in action for two hours under close fire from machine guns, trench mortars and bombers, out of touch with our own troops, and inflicted losses on the enemy. He continued to fight his tank after two of his crew were wounded and only retired in order to undertake a fresh attack in cooperation with the infantry.'

Hotblack was awarded the DSO 'for conspicuous gallantry on 18 December 1916. A tank being halted from uncertainty as to the proper direction, this officer went forward on foot

---

151 The *Brecon Radnor Express Carmarthen and Swansea Valley Gazette and Brynmawr District Advertiser*, 7 December 1916. He recovered from his injuries and trained as a pilot in the RAF.

152 Davies was later awarded the DCM whilst serving with A Battalion. The citation states 'on October 3, 1917, when his tank commander was wounded, he immediately took charge and guided the tank, with great coolness, through a heavy barrage to its place of assembly. On October 4, 1917, he took the tank into action and inflicted very heavy casualties on the enemy in the area of Reutel. He undoubtedly contributed to the success of the operations as before the arrival of his tank, the infantry were held up owing to heavy machine gun and rifle fire.' He was commissioned into the Tank Corps on 18 November 1918.

153 The awarding of allied countries' gallantry awards, though not common, was not unusual.

through very heavy fire and guided it to its objective by walking in front of it. He displayed great courage and determination throughout.' Hotblack was to be decorated on four further occasions in his service with the tanks over the next two years.

The End of the Beginning

D Company's war diary records on 18 November that 'preparations were commenced for D Coy's withdrawal to the winter training area and the first details of the reorganisation were made known.' The expansion of the companies had been foreshadowed two days earlier when C Company received three officers for instruction; Maj Joyce, Capt Tucker and Capt Gerald Hedderwick, the latter having commanded 24 MMG Battery which was disbanded on 10 November with many of its soldiers becoming crewmen in the new battalions.[154] D Company working parties, under Lt Philip Johnson of 711 (MT) Company ASC,[155] were still trying to recover ditched tanks; on 18 November, there were ten left, two at Beaumont Hamel, four at Auchonvillers and four at Beaussart.

On 18 November, Haig closed down the BEF's attacks across the Somme and Ancre battlefields as the ground and weather conditions were too bad to permit any further success that month. GHQ directed HQ Fifth Army 'to withdraw all tanks from their area, as quickly as possible, to the west of St Pol sur Ternoise'[156] this location around Bermicourt becoming the Tank Administrative Area. 'OC Tanks was to arrange this in concert with the QMG BEF staff who would provide the necessary rail movement.'[157] The location could not have been a surprise to the three tank companies as B Company had been employed there since mid-October and an Advance Party, under Woods, had left HQ D Company for their new home on 6 November. The formal direction to move north did not however reach C Company until 19 November when Bradley informed Holford-Walker that there were to be no more active operations and that orders for withdrawal had been issued.

Whilst the order was easy to give, it was more difficult to complete. The ditched tanks which littered the hills north and south of the River Ancre had to be extracted and moved to Acheux as well as the men and all their equipment. C Company's War Diary states that the lead for this work would lie with C Battalion but in fact it stayed with the three original tank companies.[158] It would take another two weeks for the units' withdrawal to be complete. On 23 November, D Company's salved tanks were taken to Varennes railway siding where entraining took place; they moved north overnight and were met at Wavrans the following morning by Woods. Meanwhile, No. 1 Section of C Company were at the Loop, under Inglis' command, clearing the location and undertaking salvage work across the battlefield. They were still living in tents

---

154 Hedderwick was awarded the MC for commanding a section in C Battalion on 31 July 1917. He lost his life commanding A Company 4 RTR on 21 May 1940; they were fighting to hold back the German advance over the Telegraph Hill, south of Arras, where he had been in action in April 1917.

155 Johnson was awarded the DSO for commanding D Battalion's workshop company in June 1917.

156 OAD 216 dated 18 November 1916 (TNA WO 158/844).

157 Possibly Elles but more likely Bradley.

158 This was not risk-free; the former tank NCO of *Daredevil 1*, Harry Davies, was admitted to hospital having been wounded by enemy shellfire on 3 December 1916.

but the weather was not as bad as it had been one month earlier, as can been seen from this photograph.[159]

C Company crewmen in November 1916.
(Graham Archard)

The final entry in D Company's War Diary, made on 1 December 1916, states 'the party entrained at Varennes and detrained at Wavrans. Marched to Blangy sur Ternoise where they were enrolled as D Battalion and the reorganisation commenced.' I am sure that it was no coincidence that the entry was signed 'Capt HW Mortimore', the skipper of the first tank to see action on 15 September 1916.

Touring the Northern Battlefields

The tour of the Northern Flank starts at the crossroads between La Boiselle and Aveluy. The best approach is from La Boisselle, driving east along the D20 'Au Chemin d'Aveluy'. As you drive down into the Ancre valley, there is a double bed in a sunken road. Slow as you get to the next junction, bear right and stop; there is a calvary in the trees and there is a sign to the CWGC cemetery at Blighty Valley, as well as local road signs to Authuille (2 kms) and Thiepval (4.5 kms). Leave your vehicle and walk back up the hill, following the D20 to the metalled track on the right, the 'Chemin d'Authuille', and follow it for 500 yards. On the left in the fields is the site of an old quarry, now overgrown, used by Inglis' section in September and by A Company in October. The raised walkways, which separated each tank pen, can sometimes be seen.

Now walk back to your car. As you approach the calvary crossroads, there is a track to the right, which follows the wood-line up the hill. This was probably used by *Cognac* and *Cupid* to reach their Starting Point at the top of Nab Valley on 25 September (see chapter 8). Their route will be parallel to you but is not passible in a vehicle. On reaching the calvary, drive your vehicle north, following the D151 north towards Authuille. The route is a series of bends until the end of the wood at which it straightens. Shortly afterwards, you will see the signs to Blighty Valley Cemetery on the right-hand side of the road. Park your car and walk up the grass path to the

---

cemetery – this sits at the western end of a long valley, the eastern end being Nab Valley – the destination for *Cognac* and *Cupid*. Lt George Steven, who was killed in A Company's location on 24 October, is buried in the cemetery at grave marker 1 H 11. The inscription 'These are they' from the hymn 'Follow the Lamb' was chosen by his mother.

Returning to your vehicle, drive north again on the D151, driving through Authuille, following the route used by *Champagne* and *Cordon Rouge* on 25 September and also by the A Company tanks which were tasked to take St Pierre Divion on 13 November. 150 yards after you leave Authuille, there is a minor track on the left which leads to a campsite. On 12 November 1916, it was used by the A Company tanks to reach their assembly point at Paisley Dump on the southern edge of Thiepval Wood.[160] Continue to follow the D151 up the hill and the massive red brick Memorial to the Missing will become visible. As the road flattens out, look left into the valley and you can see the bulk of Thiepval Wood tucked into the side of the hill. The road then passes between a wood on your right, and a small copse on your left. After the copse is a pillar which is the monument to the men of 18th Division, who took Thiepval on 26 September. You will then drive past a large farm on the left, built on the site of Thiepval Chateau, and the church to your right, before reaching a crossroads.

Turn left down the minor road (D73) signed Hamel 2.5 kms.; this is Mill Road and it was in no man's land on 13 November. As you look left, you can see the eastern edge of Thiepval Wood along which *We're All In It* drove in the misty dark. Its Starting Point was 400 yards down the road, 100 yards in the field to your left, close to the wood line. Drive on until Connaught Cemetery on your left, secure your vehicle and walk to Mill Road Cemetery. The grave of Lt Hitchcock is at marker II.B.10 alongside Gnr William Miles at II B 9. Return to your vehicle and drive down the hill looking right into the fields; this is where Hitchcock and his crew were fighting on 13 November; the infantry they were supporting advanced across the road from your left into the village of St Pierre Divion. The point where the tank finally got stuck is about 400 yards west of the Ulster Tower Memorial.

The next viewing point is on the high ground, above the Ancre British Cemetery, where Drader and Bell were in action the next day. Drive down Mill Road, go across the railway line, and turn right at the T-junction. Follow the D50 north for 300 yards and park by the cemetery. This is where many of those killed on the high ground above you are now buried, although their bodies were initially interred in battlefield cemeteries. More than 150 were killed on 1 July 1916; 180 on 3 September and more than 600 killed in November 1916; the remainder were mainly killed during the winter of 1916–17 when the advance stopped but the fighting continued. To see the location of the tank action at the Hamel strongpoint, follow the narrow track to the north of the cemetery; it will make a sharp left and then climb the ridge for 400 yards. You are now in the area where Draper and Bell forced the Germans holding the strongpoint to surrender and, as you can see, the German defences was superbly positioned. If you are using the internet to plan your route, you can also see the remains of the trench lines in the satellite view.

To see where Partington's crew was in action, on 18 November, return to your vehicle and drive north, along the D50, for 500 yards to Gare de Beaucourt. This hamlet is the location of Beaucourt station, now semi-derelict, where D Company's remaining tanks assembled on

---

160 The location was 300 yards west of the Starting Point for the attack by *Crème de Menthe* and *Cordon Rouge* on Thiepval on 26 September.

17 September after their nightmare journey across the German defences. It is not possible to follow Partington's route by car but he initially followed the road to Beaumont (D4151) from the crossroads by the snack bar. After 200 yards, he turned up a track and drove north to his Place of Assembly.

You should continue to drive north, up the D50, passing the memorial to the Royal Naval Division and Beaucourt church, to the next crossroads. Take the road to the left, which is oblique and you cannot see the sign before you turn; it is marked 'Beaumont 2.5 km'. Drive past the small war memorial, continue up the hill, leaving the village and passing the cemetery and the farm on your left, to the top of the ridge. Stop opposite the small farm track entering at right angles from the left. If you look along the track, you should see the Thiepval Memorial on the skyline just to its left. The track was used by Partington on 18 November; his tank came up the hill from Beaucourt Station to the D163 road along which ran Beaucourt Trench. His objective, the Triangle, is in the fields 200 yards to your right. You can see how well it sits on the reverse slope and how its defenders' fire would dominate the ground and repel any infantry attack from east, south, or west.

Now continue west along the D163, down the hill into Beaumont. Stop at the crossroads, then continue straight on, following the road as it bears left, and out of the village. You are now in a valley with higher ground on your left. As the ground on your right flattens, you will see a white memorial – turn onto the track signed Beaumont Hamel British Cemetery and park up. The memorial is to 1/8th Battalion Argyll and Sutherland Highlanders who were part of 152nd Brigade when they captured Beaumont Hamel in November 1916. With your back to the memorial, look up to the ridge on the opposite side of the road; the large clump of trees to the left is the site of the Hawthorn Mine crater, blown on 1 July and again on 13 November. You are just behind the British frontline; the two D Company tanks, commanded by Bruce and Telfor, drove down what remained of the road to your right and became stuck in the mud in no man's land to your left; one between the German frontline and support trench north of the Hawthorn Crater and the other on the northern edge of Beaumont Hamel.[161]

You are now going to visit the site of the Quadrilateral and the tank action on 15 November. Get back in your vehicle, drive back to the road and turn right, heading towards Auchonvillers. Drive west along the D163, up the hill to the next junction signed 'Hébuterne' and turn right. Follow the D174 north for three quarters of a mile to the next crossroads, which is located by the site of the now demolished sugar factory. Turn right and drive along the D919 in an easterly direction. You are now following the route used by Lambert and Reardon's tanks, in the early hours on 15 November, to reach their rendezvous at HQ 6th Brigade. This was located 600 yards east of the Sugar Factory (close to the roadside boundary marker). Their objective was a further 500 yards, near the Serre No. 2 Cemetery, which is on the next double bend. Park here and get out; then walk to the right-hand corner. You will immediately see how open the ground is to the west where the British defences lay, totally lacking cover from German view or fire. The cemetery sits on no man's land, its eastern corner on the German frontline boundary; the British frontline was at the western edge by the road. Lambert's tank became stuck about 50 yards into the field south of the road; the location of Reardon's tank was never identified.

---

161 Miles, *OHGW*, p. 494.

Your return journey to your starting point at La Boisselle is via Auchonvillers. Get back into your vehicle and retrace your route to the crossroads and turn left. Drive south again to the next T-junction and turn right (signed for the Newfoundland Memorial). You are now in Auchonvillers where, sadly, the location of HQ D Company is unknown. There is a tea room in the village,[162] which is on the former site of a headquarters and first aid station.

At the next crossway, give way to the traffic on the right and turn left towards Hamel. As you leave the village, there is a fork in the road; bear left on the D73, passing the communal cemetery, and continue towards Hamel. You are well behind British lines at this point, the Germans being on the higher ground to your left. You are probably following the route taken by Bell, Drader and Robinson on 14 September before they attacked the Hamel strong-point. After you pass the Newfoundland Memorial Park, look left and you can see the high ground on which the German defence lines and the strongpoint sat. The road downhill into Hamel is bendy, so be careful of your speed. At the T-junction with the D50, turn right and drive towards Aveluy.

You will follow the railway line for a while; ignore the signs for Authuille and continue following the D50 into Aveluy. At the major crossroads, turn left and re-join the D20 signed for Ovillers La Boisselle. The main road will bear left as the church comes into sight; should you reach the church, turn left and you will quickly reach the D20. Follow it across the meadows and you will see the Calvary junction where you parked at the start of the tour. Follow the D20 round the bends and up the hill; you may see the Golden Statue of the Virgin on the basilica in Albert, to your right, before driving back down the hill into La Boisselle.

162 Ocean Villas Tea Room run by Avril Williams. You will need to book in advance of visiting.

10

Lessons Learned During the Tank Actions of 1916

Tanks took an active part in 21 actions in the autumn of 1916. They were also held ready for deployment on 25 September at Flers, Ginchy, Martinpuich and Leuze Wood but were not utilised by their formation commanders. The majority of those tasked saw action although a lack of mechanical reliability and poor ground conditions limited their effectiveness. The most potent enemy counter-measure against tanks that autumn was indirect fire; often most effective when tanks were attacking German defensive positions.

Date	Location	No. of tanks allocated	No. which crossed the Allied frontline	No. knocked out by artillery fire	No. which broke down, ditched or bellied	No. of tanks which rallied	Notes
15 September	Courcelette	6	4		2	2	
	Martinpuich	3	3	1		2	
	High Wood	4	1		1		
	Flers and Gueudecourt	18	12	6		6	1 and 2
	Ginchy	10	6	2		4	
	Morval	3	1			1	3
	Bouleaux Wood and Combles	3	2	2			4
16 September	Flers and Gueudecourt	3	3	3			5
25 September	Martinpuich	2	1	1			

26 September	Thiepval	4	3		3		6
	Mouquet Farm	2	2		2		
	Courcelette	2	1	1			
	Gueudecourt	1	1		1		
1 October	Eaucourt l'Abbaye	2	2		2		7
7 October	Le Sars	1	1	1			
14 October	Bayonet Trench	3	1			1	
13 November	Beaumont Hamel	2	2		2		
	St Pierre Divion	3	1		1		
14 November	Hamel	3	2		2		8
15 November	Serre	2	2		2		
18-November	Beaucourt	6	1			1	

Notes:

1. *Daredevil* successfully completed its preliminary action at Delville Wood but was then knocked out by a British shell before reaching its Starting Point for the attack on Gueudecourt.

2. *Diehard* remained at Flers overnight and went into action again the following day when it was knocked out.

3. Two tanks, which did not get into action at Zero due to mechanical failure, undertook a follow-up attack at 1300 hours on 15 September. They reached their objective at the Quadrilateral and, although damaged, rallied.

4. Both tanks became stuck in the German barbed wire surrounding the objective.

5. *Diehard* disrupted a German counter-attack against Flers at 0900 hours but was knocked out as she advanced to support the NZ Division shortly afterwards. See note 2 above.

6. *Crème de Menthe* played a significant part in the capture of Thiepval Chateau.

7. The tanks were key to the infantry entering the fortified location. They subsequently became entangled in the German defensive barbed wire and were destroyed by their crews to avoid their capture.

8. After having ditched near the German frontline, both tank crews cleared their objective and took 400 prisoners. A third was knocked out by German artillery before it reached the Starting Point.

Casualties

Losses amongst the crews in action were generally light and mainly caused by artillery fire. There were a further four men killed and four others seriously wounded as a result of harassing fire on unit locations.

Date	Tanks crossed British frontline	Crewmen in action (8 per tank)	Killed / Died of Wounds	Seriously injured/ shell shocked	PoW	Total casualties	% of crew in action
15 September	31	248	14	35	1	50	20
16 September	3	24	10	7		17	71
25 September	1	8		4		4	50
26 September	8	64	1	5		6	9.5
1 October	2	16		3		3	18.75
7 October	1	8		3		3	37.5
14 October	1	8					Nil
13 November	3	24	3	1		4	16.7
14 November	2	16					Nil
15 November	2	16					Nil
18 November	1	8		2		2	25

Lessons Identified

The various army headquarters and units, which were supported by the First Tank Crews, learned lessons from the first deployment. Some immediate changes were made to tank company structures and procedures at the end of September 1916.[1] In December 1916, the expanded staff at the HQ Heavy Branch MGC, under Elles, started to provide the necessary direction to overcome many of the identified shortcomings. The first, and most important action, was the introduction of schools, both in the United Kingdom and in France, which provided a structured training programme for individuals and sub-units. Lessons were learned though

---

1　See Chapter 9. Following shortcomings identified during 15 to 26 September, company commanders reinforced their headquarters with watchkeepers and developed communication teams based on runners from spare crewmen. Section commanders became responsible for reconnaissance and in battle, the direct command of their crews; their previous responsibilites as tank commanders were undertaken by additional subaltern officers drawn from reinforcements or by from skippers whose tanks had been put permanently out of action. These were codified by Elles in early October and, along with further manning increases, approved by the WO staff as part of the new tank battalion and brigade structure.

the analysis of subsequent actions, the focus for this activity being Fuller who was appointed as COS in December 1916.[2]

In March 1917, Fuller wrote a paper entitled 'The history, organisation [and] training of tanks'. in which he included an overview of the first tank actions.[3] In his opinion, the Lessons Learned were:

> That the machine in principle was absolutely sound, that all it required were certain mechanical improvements.
>
> That it had not been given a fair trial. It had been constructed for good going and fine weather; it had been, unavoidably, used on pulverized soil, often converted by rain into a pudding of mud. Again, improvements were required to enable it to move over all types and conditions of soil.
>
> That the higher command had little or no conception of what tactics to apply to its use. That they adopted the very worst; dispersal of strength.
>
> That the crews require a thorough and careful training; the ones engaged had next to none.
>
> That tank operations require the most careful preparation and minute reconnaissances in order to render them successful. On 15 and 25 September, neither of these essentials were undertaken.
>
> That tanks require leading and controlling in battle, just the same as any other arm, and consequently communication is essential. No such system existed, tanks going into battle with pigeons and a few flags.
>
> That tanks, like every other arm, require supplying whilst fighting; no such system was arranged.
>
> That tanks must advance at Zero hour and not before, otherwise there would be a likelihood of their drawing the enemy's barrage onto our advancing infantry.
>
> That tanks do draw away fire from the infantry.
>
> That they have a great moral effect on our own troops and most demoralizing one on the enemy's.
>
> Taking into consideration the above lessons, it is truly surprising that the tanks had any success at all. Badly commanded, indifferently led, controlled by untrained men and used under conditions diametrically opposite to those for which they had been constructed, it is a wonder, almost a miracle, that they did so well.

The majority of these shortcomings were neither the fault of Swinton or the tank companies who did their best, within available resources, to field a brand-new and unproven weapon system in under eight months. Fuller's concluding comment, which was not published in 1919, must have caused anguish to some of the First Tank Crews who were now serving with the Heavy Branch. This, together with the failure of the Tank Corps Book of Honour to record the vast majority of

---

2   The first tactical planning exercise, developed by Fuller in January 1917, was based on the attacks near Hamel and Beaucourt sur Ancre undertaken by D Company in November 1916.

3   The Fuller Archive (Kings College London) file 1/8/1 pp. 25 to 27. Fuller published this list, albeit adjusted for public consumption in Chapter 5 of *Tanks in the Great War*.

those who were killed or honoured in 1916, was probably the cause of one C Company officer to comment 'We were an embarrassment and one to be forgotten.'[4]

Despite Fuller's last comment, the lesson learned by GHQ staff, and by the more perceptive of the formation commanders, were that the tanks, properly handled, made a difference when combined with the other arms. Haig's reaction to the tanks' use on 15 September was that 'we have had the greatest victory since the Battle of the Marne. We have taken more prisoners and more territory with comparatively few casualties. This is due to the Tanks. Wherever the Tanks advanced, we took our objectives and, where they did not, we failed to take our objectives.'[5] Despite these setbacks, and there were many caused by the staff's deployment of tanks in terrain which no machine could cross, Haig never lost faith and he was vindicated.

Furthermore, the initial experiences of the First Tank Crews were vital to those who served in other tank units over the next two years. The majority of the original officers served in command appointments or with the training organisations in France and at home until the end of the Great War. The same is true of the crewmen, who shared their experiences with those who joined after December 1916 and were often used as a cadre when new units were formed at Bovington. The First Tank Crews frequently appear in the TCBH, as the recipients of honours and awards for gallantry in action and dedicated service during 1917–18 and in the Roll of Honour.

They are Not Forgotten.

We Remember Them Still!

---

4   Author's note: Only three of 33 tank crewmen who were killed or died of wounds in 1916 are recorded in the TCBH. The only honours listed are Storey's DSO, awarded for the attack at Gueudecourt on 26 September, Hotblack's DSO at Beaucourt and Partington's MC for the same action on 18 November. The only crewmen's medals recorded were those awarded to A Company in November 1916 and Albert Smith's MM which was wrongly ascribed to actions near Delville Wood, rather than for the clearance of *Dolly* on 23 September. These extremely unfortunate omissions were probably due to the lack of records held at HQ HS MGC. A supplement was subsequently published, listing some of the omissions, but this was sadly not included in the recently published facsimile edition by the Naval and Military Press.

5   Stern, *Tanks 1914-1918*, p. 96.

Appendix I

The Need for Armoured Machine Gun Destroyers
Swinton's Memorandum to General Headquarters dated 1 June 1915 [1]

The Germans, possibly in order to release troops for offensive action on a grand scale elsewhere, have for some time been maintaining their front in France and Belgium with the minimum of men. They have been able to do this because they have fully recognised and exploited the principle that, on the defensive, numbers of men can be replaced to a very large extent by skilfully and scientifically arranged defences and armaments, and by machinery. They possess the knowledge, energy and skills to organise such defences thoroughly and have by now the time to do it.

By this time, their positions consist of a strong front firing line, of trench or breastworks, backed up by a zone which includes, besides communications, a network of subsidiary supporting trenches and points, such as works and houses, which are held by few men and yet provide a great volume of fire in different directions. Some of these works give fire to the front, others run fore and aft and give lateral fire to left and right against an enemy who may have broken through the front line and seeks to penetrate further. Most are so arranged that, if lost, they can be enfiladed or bombed. In this maze behind the front, the defenders unless absolutely paralysed and shattered by artillery fire, have all the advantages. For there the attackers, if they should succeed in penetrating find themselves fighting without much artillery support, on strange ground, at close quarters with the defenders who know every inch of the position and have marked every exposed spot, upon which they train their machine guns and rifles and shower bombs.

The chief feature of novelty in the German tactics does not lie either in the preparation of a strip of ground for fighting the attackers at a disadvantage, nor in the use of machine guns, hand-bombs or grenades. It lies in the number of machine guns employed. And not only is this the chief feature of novelty, it is the factor that has done most to make possible the economy of men practised by the Germans; it is also the chief factor which had rendered abortive our attempts to penetrate their positions.

So far, we have in all our offensive effort, been unable with our guns to shatter the German defensive zone to its full depth, over any considerable length and so blast a path for our advance. The machine guns have not been neutralised and it is our infantry, either caught up in the wire,

1   Described in French's letter to the WO of 22 June 1915 as Paper A.

in the open, or collected in the enemy's trenches, that have had to suffer from the undivided attention of these weapons shooting from protected and concealed positions. We have, so far, been unable to oppose anything to them except the bodies of our assaulting infantry.

Machine guns have caused most of our casualties in the attack and have stopped our offensive efforts. *And machine guns will do the same in future unless.*[2]

> We have sufficient artillery and high explosive ammunition to blast a way through the German positions (trenches, wire, trench mortars bombs, gas cylinders, land mines, vitriol throwers [3] and machine guns inclusive) preparatory to our assault **OR**
> We can have recourse to some other means of destroying these weapons or at least on meeting them on equal terms and diverting or neutralising their action so that it is not directed upon our infantry.

The first alternative is not at present within our power, though it may be so in the future. The second in believed to be possible through the employment of "Armoured Machine Gun Destroyers" which will enable us to engage with machine guns on an equality.

Armoured Machine Gun Destroyers (general description)

These machines would be petrol tractors on the caterpillar principle, of a type which can travel up to four miles per hour on the flat, can cross a ditch of 4 feet in width without climbing, can climb in and out of a broader cavity, and can scramble over a breastwork. It is possible to build such tractors. They should be armoured with hardened steel, proof against the German *steel-cored armoured- piercing and reversed bullets* [4], and armed with – say - two Maxims [machine guns] and a Maxim 2-pounder gun.

Construction. It is suggested that they be employed as a surprise in an assault on the German position to be carried out on a large scale. To enable the element of surprise to come in these machines should be built at home secretly and their existence should not be disclosed until all are ready. There should be no preliminary efforts made with a few machines, the result of which would give the scheme away.

Preparation for employment. The machines should be brought up to railheads by train or road, and then distributed at night along the front of action. They should be placed in deep pits with ramps leading from the rear and out to the front over our parapet, dug as required behind our front line.

Suggested Employment in Attack.

Say fifty destroyers are available. If they are spaced, say at one hundred yards apart on the average, it will enable a front of about 5,000 yards or about three miles, to be covered. The machines being in position ready, the wire entanglements in front of the hostile trenches will

---

2   Swinton uses italics in *Eyewitness* p. 130
3   Swinton understood the German had such devices, in addition to *flammenwerfers,* at the time of writing.
4   Swinton's italics. *Eyewitness*, p. 131.

be bombarded and cut early the night before the assault is intended to take place. After this during the night, nothing will be attempted except occasional outbursts of rifle fire to prevent the Germans from repairing their entanglements. At dawn of the morning fixed for the assault, at a given signal, the destroyers will start. Climbing out of their pits, and over the parapet, they will travel across the intervening space straight for the German lines. If this is 200 yards away, they will travel the distance in 2 ½ minutes travelling at a rate of 3 miles per hour. They can tear their way through any entanglement.

Wherever it has been possible beforehand to locate and mark down machine-gun emplacements in the German front line, the destroyers will be steered straight at them, will climb over them and will crush them. At other points they climb the enemy's parapet or trench and halting there will fire at any machine-gun located, with the 2-pounder gun and will enfilade portions of the trenches with their Maxims[5].

It is thought that the destroyers, even if they have not by this time actually accounted for the bulk of the defending infantry, will have succeeded in attracting to themselves the attention of the enemy and most of his fire, so that our infantry, who will leave their own trenches and assault, just as the destroyers reach the hostile parapet, will be able to cross the fire-swept zone between the lines practically unscathed.

After the destroyers have started out into the open and all surprise is over, our guns should at once start shelling the enemy's artillery in order to keep down its fire. There will be no need for them to bombard the German trenches. While our infantry is racing for the enemy's front line, the caterpillars will move on through the German defensive zone shooting left and right as they go. Those on the flanks of the section selected for the first assault will turn left and right and proceed along and behind the German defence zone to enable our infantry on either side of the selected section to advance also. The action of their 2 pounder guns will be reserved for the German machine-guns which cannot be rolled over, especially those in houses. Once through the zone of trenches, the destroyers will proceed forwards, backed up by and supporting the first waves of the assaulting infantry which will be moving forward with them, and followed by the mass of troops forming the main body of the attack. [6]

Employment in defence.

In defence the destroyers stationed behind the line, will move up if the Germans break though at any spot and will act as mobile strong points, which can be driven forward right amongst hostile infantry who have penetrated. When no general offensive or defensive is going on, their two-pounder gun can be used as mobile anti-aircraft artillery.

The attack, carried out as suggested, will probably result in the loss of a certain number of destroyers but not many, because the machines will be amongst the defending infantry before the German guns can be warned of their advance. Many details of design, such as contrivances to allow the destroyers to signal back to our own infantry, to attract the enemy attention, to repel boarders, etc can be suggested.

---

5   Author's note. Swinton is referring to the name of the weapon's designer; the machine guns fitted to the Male tanks were designed by Hotchkiss.

6   Swinton inserted a footnote in *Eyewitness*, p. 133: 'They may possibly get forward to with rifle range of the German guns.'

Gas operations.

The destroyers will be of great value in gassed areas since the crews will have their mouths at least ten feet above the ground and, not having to march, will be able to wear the most efficient masks, even if of heavy design.

Attack. In a gas attack, the destroyers could possibly move forward just in the rear of the gas cloud, where they would be hidden, in front of the rest of our infantry. But the employment of gas, in conjunction with destroyers, would prevent any surprise.

Defence. The employment of destroyers in obvious.

Engines. In case the gas should interfere with the engines, a small reservoir of oxygen could be carried as has been tried for aeroplanes.

Supplement dated 5 June 1915 [7]

The portion of the Engineer in Chief's minute marked refers to:

1. The possibility of building a machine such as described, and then to questions of
2. Speed,
3. Steering,
4. Weight.

1. **Possibility of Construction**. It was not strictly accurate to state that is possible to build a machine exactly of the type as suggested for the matter has not yet been definitely ascertained by trial. It would be more correct to say that, since tractors are now in existence which so nearly comply with the required conditions, that it is believed to be possible to construct a locomotive that will do all that is necessary sufficiently well to effect the purpose. On the other hand, the impossibility of producing destroyers of the type requisite will not be established until trials have been made and have all failed. Strictly speaking also, the proposed machine is not a tractor, for it will not be designed to draw anything. It will be self-propelling, climbing blockhouse or rifle-bullet-proof cupola.

2. **Speed**. There is a machine now on the market (the Holt Caterpillar Tractor of which 75 are on order by the War Office) which has two speeds and can travel on the top speed of something approaching 4 miles an hour.

   The exact maximum rate is not known here, and to be on the safe side, 3 miles an hour was assumed in the calculation for the time required to cross 200 yards. But speed is a question of gearing and there is no reason why a Caterpillar locomotive should not be designed and constructed to travel even fast than 4 miles per hour. It is believed that the Caterpillar tried at Aldershot (Hornby-Ackroyd type) some years ago moved at least 4 miles per hour

3. **Steering**. On dry ground, machines of the Hornsby-Akroyd type (which is an old one) having a long propelling base or wheel belt, can turn practically on the ground on which they stand through any angle. Such sensitiveness and flexibility of steering is far beyond

---

7   Author's note. Described in Sir John French's letter as Paper B.

what would be required of a destroyer. If it is found after experiment that all power of steering is lost in wet weather (which is unlikely), the fact will merely reduce the proportion of days on which the destroyer attack could be attempted. This would vitiate the principle no more than the principle of aviation is vitiated by the fact that there are some days on which aeroplanes cannot fly.

4. **Weight**. It is not possible to give the exact weight of a machine which is not yet in designed. As a comparison, it may be stated that the heaviest Holt Caterpillar tractor weights 14 tons while the old Hornsby type weighed between 7 and 8 tons. The destroyer could correspond in size to a large traction engine, boxed in with steel and might resemble in appearance a heavy motor lorry with caterpillar attachment carrying a large metal tank. The weight of the plate (half inch steel) to enclose a rectangular box 14 feet long, eight feet high, seven feet broad including floor and roof, would be under five tons. If the engine, gear and wheels could be built to weigh not more than ten tons, which would seem possible if steel be used, instead of the inferior metal used in the Holt tractor, - which is intended for agricultural purposes and has to be cheap - the total weight of the destroyer without machine guns, crew, ammunition, petrol and water would be 15 tons. Fully manned and laden it would be under 16 tons.

This weight would be distributed over two driving belts and would bring far less strain on bridges that some of the weights brought up from the bases to the front by road. Notably the tractor for the 15-inch howitzer (10 tons on a pair of wheels) or the 8-inch howitzer, (12 tons 14 cwt on a pair of wheels). The 6-inch gun Mark VII, which I believe is to travel by road though it has not yet come up, weighs as much as 16 tons on a pair of wheels.

However, if it is found on working out a design in detail that the weight of the whole machine is excessive for the existing bridges, there is no reason why the weight should not be subdivided, and the steel plating carried separately by lorry or train and then bolted together somewhere behind where the destroyer is required. This principle of subdivision is adopted for the 12 inch and 15-inch howitzers but it does not appear at this stage that the weight will be excessive and will necessitate the strengthening of the bridges.

I have written at some length in order to make clear in greater detail what is proposed and have confined my reply to the EinC 's minute marked. But I think that, to all his queries, answers can be given which will show that, if the employment of destroyers of the type suggested, in the manner suggested, is considered to possess any military value, their construction, is mechanically a sufficiently practical proposition to warrant the most earnest consideration of the whole scheme now merely outlined

GHQ
5.6.15

E D Swinton
Lt Col RE

Caterpillar Machine Gun Destroyer [8]

Suggested conditions to be adhered to, in design if possible.
(These are tentative and subject to modification).

Speed. Top speed on flat not less than 4 miles per hour. Bottom speed for climbing (Blank) miles per hour.

Steering. To be capable of turning 90 degrees at top speed on the flat on a radius of twice the length of the machine.

Reversing. To travel backwards or forwards (equally fast?).

Climbing. To be capable of crossing backward or forward an earth parapet of 5 feet thick and 5 feet high, having an exterior slope of 1 in 1 and interior slope vertical.

Bridging. All gaps of up to 5 feet in length to be bridged directly without dipping into them. All Gaps above 5 feet to be climbed up to a height of 5 feet with vertical sides.

Radius of action. To carry petrol and water for 20 miles.

Capacity. Crew and armament to carry 10 men, two machine guns and one quick firing gun.

Weight. Total weight of the destroyer loaded with armour, petrol, oil, ammunition and crew to be distributed on tracks, so as not to bring as greater strain on bridges than that produced by 14 tons on a single axle with a pair of wheels. The weight of armour, armament, ammunition and crew may be taken at 8 tons. This figure is an approximation and depend largely on the specific area of the armour carried, which is largely governed by the size of the enclosed space to contain the armament and crew under working conditions. The latter can be settled only by experiment with actual men and guns. It seems that a locomotive resting on long caterpillar tracks only (like the Hornsby-Akroyd type) would fulfil the conditions best; or, if another support in front must be given, it might take the shape of a fore carriage carried by a "skate", the skate to be an endless chain track running idle over rollers.

15/6/1915   E D S

---

8   Author's note. Described as Paper C in GHQ BEF letter of 22 June 1915. See Swinton. *Eyewitness*, pp. 146 and 147 which states the 'specification' was written on 15 June 1916.

Appendix II

Tank Operational Requirement – 11 September 1915

In July 1915, Swinton returned to London to assume the duties of Assistant Secretary to the Committee of Imperial Defence (CID) and had sight of progress being made, both privately and officially, of tracked fighting vehicles. In September he visited the Foster's factory at Lincoln where he saw the prototype known as Little Willie.

On 10 September 1915, he wrote to Maj Guest [secretary of the GHQ Improvement Committee] that 'the naval people are pressing on the first example caterpillar [and] have succeeded in making an animal which will cross [a gap of] 4 feet 6 inches and turn on its own axis. The following day, GHQ confirmed the operating requirement, in part stemming from Swinton's proposals made in June 1915, to the CID. These specified that:[1]

1. The object of the caterpillar cruiser or armoured fort is required for employment in considerable numbers in conjunction with or as an incident in a large and general attack by infantry against an extended front.
2. As a general principle it is desirable to have a large number of small cruisers rather than a smaller number of large ones.
3. The armour must be proof against concentrated rifle and machine gun fire but not proof against artillery fire. The whole cruiser should be enclosed in armour.
4. The tactical object of the cruiser is to attack; its armament should include a gun with reasonable accuracy up to a range of 1,000 yards and at least two Lewis guns which can be fired from loopholes to flank and rear.
5. The crew is to consist of six men: two for the gun, one for each Lewis gun and two drivers.
6. The caterpillar must be capable of crossing craters produced by the explosion of high explosive shells, such craters being of 12 feet in diameter [and] six feet deep with sloping side; of crossing an extended width of barbed wire entanglements; and of spanning hostile trenches with perpendicular sides and of 4 feet in breadth.
7. The cruisers should be capable of moving at a rate of at least 2 ½ miles per hour over broken ground and have a range of action of not less than six hours consecutive movement.
8. The wheels of the cruiser should either be of the "Pedrail" or the Caterpillar system, whichever is most suitable for crossing marshy or slippery ground.

---

1   Fuller, Tanks in the Great War, p.36.

Appendix III

Notes on the Employment of Tanks in February 1916

These notes, as to the measures of preparations and suitable tactics for Tanks, are not intended to imply that the whole of our offensive operations are to be subordinates to their action. They are put forward as a basis for early discussion of the possibilities and requirements of an entirely new weapon, so that that by the time it is ready for employment, everything possible may have been to ensure its success. [1]

1.   The use by the German of machine guns and wire entanglements – a combination which has such power to check the advance of infantry – has in reply brought about the evolution of the "Caterpillar" bullet proof climbing motor, or "Tank", a machine designed for the express purpose of assisting attacking infantry by crossing the defences, breaking through the obstacles and of disposing of the machine guns. It is primarily a machine gun destroyer, which can be employed as an auxiliary to an infantry assault.

DESCRIPTION

The Power of the Tanks now being made.

Progression

2.   The type of machine being constructed can travel at 4 miles per hour on the flat, forwards or backwards, and about 2 miles per hour over rough ground and when climbing. [2] It can

---

1   See *Eyewitness* pp 197-98. Swinton notes that this document was a development of an earlier memorandum drafted in October 1915 but which could not be completed in detail until the operating capabilities of *Mother* were confirmed. He also states that 'it was upon the lines here laid down that the epoch making Battle of Cambrai was fought on 20 November 1917, twenty months after it was written. At that battle, the Tanks were given their first chance. For fourteen months after they had reached France, until Cambrai, they were consistently misused, although copies of this memorandum were sent to the War Office in March 1916, and to GHQ'.

2   Swinton's footnote. 'Or 110 yards or 55 yards per minute respectively'.

cross parapets of up to 5 feet in height (even when revetted vertical) [3] and span trenches or gaps up to 10 feet in width and break through wire entanglements of British and German type. (The armament has not yet been absolutely decided upon un all details at present).

Offence

3.   The weapons of each Tank against personnel will be:
    a.   Fire from Hotchkiss machine guns. [4]
    b.   Possibly case shot from two 6 pounder quick firing [Q F] guns, one on each flank.
    Its weapons against hostile machine guns are:
    c.   Its own weight. This can, in favourable conditions where the enemy machine guns are situated in the trenches, be brought into play by rolling over the emplacements and crushing them
    d.   Fire from two Hotchkiss 6 pounder Q F [Quick Firing] guns, having arcs of fire from straight ahead to 30 degrees abaft the beam or 120 degrees on each side. The shell[s] are common, pointed, base fused, bursting on percussion or graze and filled with black powder of some other low explosive. With the reduced propellent charge used in the guns carried, the projectile will penetrate 2 inches of plate before bursting and will therefore pierce the ordinary German loophole plate and the machine gun and field gun shield.[5]
4.   Hostile machine guns, which are impossible or inconvenient to crush, will be attacked by gun fire. It is specially for the purpose of dealing with these weapons ensconced in houses, cellars, amongst ruins, in haystacks, or in other concealed positions behind the enemy's front line, where they may not be knocked out by our artillery, and whence they can stop our infantry advance, that Tanks carry guns. Being covered with bullet proof protection, and therefore to a great extent immune from machine-gun fire, they can approach sufficiently close to locate the latter and pour in shell at point blank range.
5.   Although the assumption is that long range fire will not be required for the above purpose, it may happen, owing to the speed of advance hoped to be rendered possible by the neutralisation of the holding power of the enemy's machine-gun fire (which has hitherto been the most important factor in checking the momentum of our assaults) that the Tanks, along with our infantry will be able, soon after the start of the offensive, to get within range of the German artillery positions. The 6 pounder guns firing with reduced charges will give accurate shelling up to a range of 2,000 yards, and they are being fitted

---

3   Author's note: The original design parameters were intended to permit tanks to deal with field defences which had been constructed by both British and German units in those areas where the high watertable did not allow trenches to be dug below ground level.
4   Swinton's footnote. 'Experiments are being made with special short, barrelled Hotchkiss machine guns which will give accurate shooting out to a range of 400 yards'.
5   Swinton's footnote. 'The Hotchkiss 6 pounder QF is a naval gun which has been adapted as being the only suitable weapon available. A reduced charge is employed because half of the guns being supplied will be of single tube construction and cannot fire full charges'.

with telescopic sights so that full advantage may be taken of a chance of this nature should it appear.

Defence (active)

6.   As detailed above for offence

Defence (Passive)

7.   The hardened steel plates (up to 12 millimetres in thickness) with which the Tanks are enclosed give complete protection against shrapnel balls and almost complete protection against rifle and machine gun fire of any nature that is likely to be encountered, and considerable protection against the splinters of high explosive shells that may detonate close by.

Communications with the rear.

8.   As will be seen, it is proposed that the Tanks will accompany the infantry in the advance. They will, therefore, to some extent, share any methods of communications adopted for the infantry. But, since they can convey any apparatus in safety from shrapnel and rifle fire, it may be an advantage to carry means of their own for communications with their headquarters in the rear, to supplement that used by the infantry. Experiments are being carried out, therefore, in the following methods of communications which will be alternative in their application.
    a.   Equipping a certain proportion for Tanks (say one in every ten) with small wireless telegraphy sets capable of action up to five miles.
    b.   Equipping a certain proportion of Tanks (say one of every ten) with apparatus for laying a field telephone cable either on the surface of the ground or possibly buried 12 inches deep. These could be used for communication in clear and would also serve for artillery observation purposes.
    c.   Installing a system of visual signalling to the Tanks from the starting point by means of miniature kite balloons. This would be limited in range and would work one way (forward) only and would serve to transmit a few pre-arranged orders.
    d.   Installing a system of signalling from the Tanks by smoke rocket. This would be more limited in scope and would also only work one way (Backwards) and would serve to transmit a pre-arranged signal.

Limitation to progress

9.   The exact size and nature of streams that can be negotiated by the Tanks are not yet definitely settled, and will form the subject of experiment, but it is certain that rivers and canals of a depth of 1 foot, having a muddy bottom or having banks over 3 feet in height steeper than a slope of 1/1 cannot be crossed by these until a crossing with ramps and a hard bottom has been prepared. The ordinary small bridges in the hostile zone, if not

destroyed, will not carry these machines. Woods and plantations are an absolute obstacle to their movement. Though Tanks can cross soft soil and muddy ground they will travel better in dry weather.

Vulnerability

10.   Tanks will be destroyed by a direct hit of any type of howitzer shell. They will probably be put out of action by all except the most glancing hits of high explosive shell fired by field guns.

    a.   They will probably be put out of action by all except the most glancing hits of shell fired from any form of high velocity small calibre Q.F. gun (such as the Germans are believed to have mounted in their defensive zone), which projectiles will, it is thought, penetrate the plating and burst inside the machine, thus immobilising it by putting the whole of the crew out of action. They may also be blown up by mines or land-mines.

    b.   Special stress is laid upon the vulnerability of Tanks to artillery fire of different natures, because it represents their greatest weakness, and because the simplest and most quickly organised method for the Germans to counter their employment will be by emplacing a large number of field and Q F guns in the defensive zone. Nevertheless, although there appears to be no direct method whereby they can escape the risks from the projectile actually fired against them, there are tactical measures which can (if properly thought out and prepared for beforehand) be taken to reduce indirectly the number of such projectiles fired i.e., the hampering by our bombardment of the activity of the enemy's artillery over the sector of the front concerned. Special allusion is made to this later on (see paragraph 39.)

Impossibility of repeated employment

11.   Since the chance of success of an attack by Tanks lies almost entirely in its novelty and in the element of surprise, it is obvious that no repetition of it will have the same opportunity of succeeding as the first unexpected effort. It follows therefore that these machines *should not be used in driblets* [6] (for instance as they are produced) but the fact of their existence should be kept as secret as possible until the whole are ready to be launched together with an infantry assault, in one great combined operation.

---

6   Swinton's italics.

MEASURES OF PREPARATION

Place of Employment

12.   The sector of front where these machines can best operate should be carefully chosen to comply with their limitations i.e., their inability to cross canals, rivers, deep railway cuttings with steep sides or woods and orchards. And this should be done, as long as possible before the moment of attack, so that the time may be allowed for the execution of the work on the lines of communications and in the shelled area behind the front line necessary to allow the machines coming up to position without delay when required.

Conveyance to the Front

13.   Once the most favourable sector for the action of the Tanks has been located, and the exact distribution behind the front line fixed, the best method of conveyance from the coast can be settled. This may be by road, by rail or by barge, or possibly by a combination of road, rail and canal, according to the communications available towards the chosen sector.

    In any case, however, certain preparatory measures will have to be taken beforehand. The roads to be followed will have to be reconnoitred and the bridges strengthened or ramps cut to the rivers or streams, and the possibility of collecting at the right time sufficient railway trucks or barges of the type necessary to carry the Tanks will have to be investigated.

Frontage in attack

14.   The exact distance apart at which the Tanks should move forward in the assault is a matter for experiment but it is thought that in order to assemble them to thoroughly search the ground for concealed machine guns, to support each other mutually by their own fire and to sweep the German parapets sufficiently to permit of our own infantry advancing more or less unscathed, they should not be more than 150 yards apart. It will serve to simply present calculations at present if the interval be taken at a round figure of 100 yards.

    As regards the total frontage, the number of Tanks under construction is less than 100 but, since it is not safe to assume that more than 90 per cent of the whole number available will be in line (to allow for machines to be told off to work outwards and to move laterally for destroying wire), the front of attack of that number with be 9,000 yards or 5 miles. For the sake of discussion, this distance will be assumed in considering an operation undertaken by the whole of the machines available, the reduction of front where a lesser number used is pro rata. [7]

---

7   Swinton's footnote. 'This calculation as to the extent of frontage will hold good whether the tanks move forward in one continuous line or in groups with intervals between the groups so that certain areas may be "bitten off" by lateral movement as soon as sufficient forward progress has been made. The selection of either method of attack is a matter of general tactics and not one specifically connected with the employment of tanks.'

Position of Assembly.

15. This may be a line parallel to our front line, and say, some two miles behind it. Here the machines should remain sufficiently long for the crews to reconnoitre, ease and mark out the routes up the points where they will actually cross the front defences, and to learn all that can be discovered of the German front line trenches and the defence zone behind it over which they will have to advance.

16. The officers and men will be trained at home, as far as possible, to steer and operate over an imitation British and German trench zone by the aid of trench maps similar to our aeroplane maps of the German defensive positions.

17. Along the positions of assembly, the Tanks will not be distributed at equal intervals so as to attract the notice of hostile aviators. But will be placed amongst trees, in villages etc so as to obtain concealment. [8] From it they can move up early on the night preceding the attack to their final positions or starting points., just behind where they will actually cross our trenches, and wait there until the moment (assumed to be just before dawn – see later); or if this procedure is considered impossible, owing to the intensity of the hostile bombardment directed in the vicinity of our front line, they can move straight from the position of assembly during the night so as to reach their starting points just before the time for the advance. The routes to the front line will have to be marked for night work with special lanterns to show light towards the rear of our position. [9]

18. If it is considered advisable for any reason that the machine should go up to their final positions still earlier, and remain there during daylight, suitable pits will have to be excavated for them before hand so that they are not visible to the enemy over our parapets. To confuse the enemy's air scouts, several more pits than necessary will have to be dug some considerable time before the attack.

19. The starting points will be 100 yards apart only, approximately, and should be carefully chosen as to be opposite some special enemy's points, such as a located field gun or machine gun emplacements and the forward end of communication trenches etc.

20. During the journey up from the coast, whether by road, rail or by canal, the Tanks will be encased in special tarpaulin covers marked "drinking water only" or some other misleading label. The guns and sponsons for each are to be carried on special trailers designed for the purpose and can be placed in position on board and bolted up at whatever state on the journey that is convenient. [10]

TACTICS (Only such points as appear to concern the use of Tanks are referred to.)

8   Swinton's footnote. 'Special tarpaulin covers coloured as to represent tile or thatch roofs can be made ready'.

9   Swinton's footnote. 'A certain number of such lanterns can be supplied as part of the equipment of each machine. Allowing for delays caused in the dark, to traverse the assumed distance of 2 miles from the position of assembly to the starting points should not take more than 2 hours'.

10 Swinton's footnote. 'The tanks are less noisy than had been expected, and it is thought that the sound of the bombardment from both sides and the noise from rifle and M G gun fire from the front line or behind will mask that of the tanks going from their position of assembly to the final positions'.

Time of the Advance.

21.   The most favourable time for the Tanks to advance, so as to avoid the chief danger to which they will be exposed i.e., hostile artillery fire, would be at night. But there are disadvantages in such a course which makes its adoption inadvisable. Firstly, no infantry could accompany the machines for the crews of the Tanks would not be able to distinguish between the flashes of our rifles from those of the enemy. Secondly it would not be possible for the drivers to see the obstacles in front of them, and they could not manipulate their clutches for climbing or steer the machines so as to avoid uncrossable spots. It seems that the best moment for the start will be just before dawn, as soon as there is sufficient light in the sky to distinguish objects to some extent. A start at such a time would also give the greatest number of hours of daylight for pressing on with the offensive.

Synchronization of the Advance of the Tanks with the Infantry Assault

22.   The Tanks, it is thought, should move forward together, say by rocket signal, sweeping the enemy's front line parapet with machine-gun fire, and after they have proceeded some three-quarters of the way across no-man's land and have succeeded in attracting to themselves the fire of the German infantry and machine guns in the front line, the assaulting infantry should charge forward so as to reach the German defences soon after the Tanks have climbed the parapet and begun to enfilade the trenches. [11]

23.   Since not much difficulty is usually experienced in rushing the German front line after a thorough bombardment [12], it may be thought it is unnecessary for the Tanks to precede the infantry assault, or even accompany it, and they should be kept behind our front line and only sent forward to help the infantry where and when they are held up by uncut wire and machine gun fire. There appears however to be drawback to such a course.

24.   It would result in unnecessary loss to the infantry who will only be able to discover the presence of uncut wire or of hostile machine guns only be finding themselves checked, shot down and unable to proceed. (It is to obviate such loss that the Tanks are being produced.)

25.   It would result, also, in delay, as a check would have to be experienced by the infantry, a message sent back for the assistance of the Tanks, and the latter sent forward to clear away the obstruction. This would entail the otherwise avoidable expenditure of a considerable amount of time and a consequent reduction of the speed of progress through the enemy's defensive zone (which may be some 3 or 4 miles in depth). It would therefore lessen the chance of the attack breaking through the defence whilst any beneficial effort which might be produced by its novelty was still in operation. This retardation of the advance might give the enemy time to reinforce the threatened section of the line with men, machine-guns and, what is more important from the point of view of this special form of attack, with field artillery.

---

11   Author's note: This paper was written before the advent of the creeping barrage.
12   Author's note: This paper was written before the losses inflicted on the attacking infantry on 1 July 1916.

26.   Lastly, it would result, it is thought, with greatly decreasing the chance of success of the Tanks themselves, owing to the fire of the German artillery which, it must be repeated is their greatest danger. The reason for this view is as follows: in whatever way the attack is made, whether it be infantry preceded by Tanks or infantry alone, as soon as it is launched and seen by the Germans to cross our parapets, the message will be sent back to the hostile artillery to put down a curtain of fire. This curtain, it is believed, covers no man's lands as well as our own front line so as to catch the assaulting troops and also cover the area between our front and supporting lines, so as to prevent our supports going forward. It takes place very quickly but there is nevertheless an appreciable interval between the moment when our assault is launched and its occurrence. [13]

27.   If the Tanks are kept back anywhere near our front line until after the assault has started, they may either be caught in this heavily shelled zone or, when required to go forward may be cut off by the [German] curtain of fire from our infantry who have gone ahead beyond the German front line and suddenly find themselves checked and in need of help.

28.   On the other hand, unless expectations are falsified, if the machines accompany the infantry, with it or just ahead of it, as sketched out above, both will be across the enemy's front line on their way to the second before the curtain of fire descends, and the latter will be behind them. It is hoped that, owing to the usual prevention of the checks to the advance that the Tanks will ensure, by the time the German gunners shorten their range in order to provide a second curtain in front of the second line, our assault will have swept beyond that point.

29.   The above anticipations are admittedly sanguine but, if the Tanks are employed and are successful, it is thought that they will enable the assault to maintain most of its starting momentum and breakthrough the German position quickly. To enable the expected rate of advance to be maintained will necessitate a very large force of infantry from the first, so that the successive lines of defence may be rushed by fresh troops and occupied and consolidated by others left behind.

30.   It seems, also, that the infantry should include an unusually large proportion of bombers, to supplement the Tanks which will not have any means of searching hidden ground.

The Extent of the Obstacle cleared by the Tanks

31.   Each Tank will clear only its own width through the entanglements and, although some of the assaulting infantry may make use of the gaps, the fact that an attack by Tanks is to be made will not preclude the usual wire-cutting fire of our guns and trench mortars across the sector over which they operate (see paragraph 39.)

Action of the Tanks after crossing the German Front Line

32.   Except for those few machines which are detailed to travel along the wire entanglements laterally (see paragraph 44), the Tanks will halt at the enemy's front line , keeping it under

---

13   Author's note: Here Swinton predicts the attack on 1 July 1916 when the BEF suffered almost 60,000 casualties.

enfilade fire, only until our assaulting infantry have reached it, when they proceed straight ahead at full speed for the German second line, as far as possible following up alongside the hostile communications trenches, which they will sweep with machine-gun fire, thus dealing with any German reinforcement and bombing parties coming up. Some of the infantry, armed with hand grenades, should follow in their wake, to assist to search out dead ground with bombs. At the same time, the "skipper" and gun crews of the Tank will keep a sharp look out for machine-guns in the second line. When discovered those will be shelled or, if possible, crushed. [14]

Extent to which the Attack is pressed

33.   The extent to which the attack is pressed, i.e. whether it is to be a step by step operation in which, after artillery preparation, a strictly limited advance is made over the front concerned and the gain of ground consolidated and then, after the necessary pause to give time for a renewed artillery preparation of the enemy's new front line, a further advance is made, and so on, or whether a violent effort is to be made to burst right through the enemy's defensive zone in one great rush, depends on the decision of the Commander in Chief and the strategic needs of the situation. But, as far as is known, a step-by-step advance, which has the drawback of giving the enemy time to reinforce the sector threatened, is not a course recommended for any positive advantages that it possesses. It is a course which has been forced on use by the inability, with the means hitherto at our disposal, of infantry even after immense sacrifice of life, to force their way through successive lines of defence, guarded by machine-guns and wire, of which none but the first can be thoroughly battered by our artillery.

34.   Not only, does it seem, that Tanks will confer the power to force successive comparatively unbattered defensive lines but, as has been explained, the more speedy and uninterrupted the advance, the greater their chance of surviving sufficiently long to do this.

       It is possible therefore that an effort to break right through the enemy's defensive zone, in one day, may now be contemplated as a feasible objective.

35.   Apart from the topographical limit, placed on an offensive action of this nature for other reasons, the limits of the power of the Tanks are every broad. Even taken an average rate of progress during an attack of not more than one mile per hour, over a sector of country without natural obstacles, an advance of 12 miles forward could be carried out during the daylight hours, by those Tanks which are not knocked out by gunfire. A movement of this scale would take our troops past the enemy's main artillery positions and would, if successfully effected, imply the capture or withdrawal of their guns.

36.   This being the case, it appears that when Tanks are used the contingency of such an extended bound forward being made, should be most carefully legislated for in the way of preparation to send forward reinforcements, guns, ammunition and supplies. In regard to the replenishment at the end of the first day's fighting of the Tanks themselves with fresh

---

14   Author's note: This is the first use of the term "skipper" I have identified in authoritative documents dealing with tank development. It indicates that the term had been used previously informally.

crews and ammunition in the event of such progress being made, schemes have yet to be worked out.[15]

Co-ordinated action of all arms

37. The necessity for the co-ordination of all arms, to work together in the offensive generally requires no remark here but the desirability of the especially careful consideration of the subject in the case of any operation by Tanks requires some emphasis, since the orchestration of the attack will be complicated by the introduction of a new instrument and one which changes the interdependence of all. A recapitulation of this chain will make the matter clear. The Tank cannot win battles by themselves. They are merely auxiliary to the infantry and are intended to sweep away the obstructions which have hitherto stopped the advance of our infantry beyond the German first line and cannot with certainty be disposed of by shell fire. It follows therefore that the progress of the attack, which depends on the advance of the infantry, depends on the activity and preservation in action of the Tanks.

38. The weapon by which Tanks are most likely to be put out of action are the enemy's guns. The only means by which we can, at the early stages of the attack, reduce the activity of the guns are by our own artillery fire or by dropping bombs on them from the air.

39. It follows therefore that in order to help our infantry in any operation in which Tanks take part (which is admitted to be the role of the artillery, also an auxiliary arm), the principle object of our guns should not be to endeavour to damage the German machine-guns, earthworks and wire behind the first line, task which they cannot with certainty carry out, and which the Tanks are specially designed to perform. It should endeavour to help the infantry by helping the Tanks i.e., by concentrating as heavy a counterfire as possible of the enemy's main artillery position and on any field or other light guns whose situation behind the front line is known. [16] For this purpose, i.e., of the spoiling of the enemy's shooting for the period of the advance, a free use of gas and poison shells might be very efficacious.

40. At the same time, any disturbance which should be used amongst the enemy gun detachments by the dropping of bombs of any nature would be valuable by every round which would be prevented from being fired.

41. If the above-mentioned assistance is given to the tanks by the action of our artillery and aeroplanes, it will necessitate considerable previous preparation to this end over and over that entailed for the normal offensive. It will include special air reconnaissance beforehand, in order to locate the enemy guns positions over the sector of the attack. The concentration of an extra allocation of heavy artillery for the purposes of making a special effort against those of the enemy guns which can be directed into the sector, the collection of special ammunition such as gas shells and of bombs for aeroplanes.

---

15 Swinton's footnote citation: 'Each machine will carry enough petrol for a journey of 60 miles.'
16 Swinton's footnote. 'This refers to the action of our guns after our attack has been launched and does not affect the question of the previous artillery preparation which should be of a normal nature, to avoid rousing suspicion, except that special pains must be made to knock out enemy light pieces emplaced in the defensive zone'

42.   These measures may appear somewhat excessive in their extent and scope, but it is thought that the trouble entailed in carrying them out will more than be justified if they enable the Tanks to perform their function of assisting the progress of the attacking infantry to an extent that seems possible.

Aids to the Attack by Tanks

43.   In order to increase the confusion which, it is hoped will be caused amongst the enemy by an attack by Tanks, and to assist in concealing the exact nature and progress of these machines, it would be of advantage if their advance was heralded by clouds of smoke. The employment of gas, it is thought, may be dangerous as the forward movement might be so rapid as to take our own men into their own gas. The release of smoke only on the sector where the Tanks are used might be accompanied by the release of gas and smoke elsewhere, so that the enemy would not know what was poisonous and what was not. Though the co-operation of smoke and gas will be an advantage, reliance on such assistance will introduce another complication into the operations since the movement of the attack will de dependant on the occurrence of a favourable wind as well as on the general prevalence of dry weather. [17]

More complete clearance of obstacles

44.   In order to clear away the obstacles over a broad front for the subsequent advance of reinforcements, or a burst through of massed cavalry, experiments are being made in trawling along the entanglements laterally by pairs of machines connected by a wire hawser. This would be done after the assault had passed over the obstacle.

Command and Control of the Tanks

45.   The frontage of the attack by 100 Tanks, as has been explained, would extend to some 5 miles, so the question of control will have to be worked out with some care. It seems, as the Tanks are an auxiliary weapon to the infantry, that they must be counted as infantry and in operation be under the same command.

E D Swinton   February 1916

---

17   Author's note: This paper was written before the wide availability of gas filled shells to artillery units. Gas was released by RE Special Companies from pressured cylinders or 4-inch Stoke mortars. The Livens projector was not used to throw chemical until September 1916 when it debuted at Thiepval.

Appendix IV

Inspection Department Royal Arsenal [Information about] Tanks and Ancillary Vehicles 1915-1918 dated January 1925 [1]

Mark I Description. The machine consists of a Hull, the exterior of which is of armour plate, with Tracks running all round on both the port and starboard sides known as Trackways. The Tracks themselves are built of armour plate Track Shoes, rivetted to Track Links, and these are joined by Link Pins. The Tracks are driven by two Driving Wheels in the rear of each Trackway, these being driven by the Track Pinions which mesh with them. The latter are driven from the Second Change Speed Gears, attached to the Worm Drive of a Daimler 105 hp Engine and Transmission Set. Four men are required to drive the machine.

The Driver's Turret is fitted in the roof of the forepart of the Hull and contains a front Outlet Door [Vision Hatch] for the Driver, who sits on the starboard side, and a smaller one for the Commander who sits on the left. Between the two is a Machine Gun Mounting. Six Pounder or Machine Gun Mountings fitted in Sponsons of armour plate are fitted on either side of the Hull according to the type of tank, i.e., Male or Female, and are removable for reason of movement by rail. There are four doors per Machine, thus - Rear Door in the back of the Hull, one door per Sponson and one Manhole in the Roof.

Reasons for introduction. The Machine was designed to fulfil the requirements of the Military Authorities.

1. All round Track
2. Gun sponsons.
3. 6-pounders and machine guns.
4. Armoured plate.

Name of designer. Maj Wilson and Sir W Tritton.
Date of commencement of design. October 1915.
No of machine built to 31.12.1918. Male x 75; Female x 75, total – 150.
Capabilities etc.
Speed at 1,000 rpm. 1st gear 0.75 mph; 2nd 1.5 mph; 3rd 2.1 mph, 4th 3.7 mph. Reverse 0.94 mph.

---

1   TNA WO 194/54.

Estimated Mileage on top gear without refuelling petrol ranks – 23.0 miles.
No of working hours on top gear without refuelling petrol ranks – 6.2 hours.
Width of trench which can be crossed without falling in – 10 fee**t**.
Vertical parapet which can be surmounted – 4 feet 6 inches**.**
Towing gear consisting of two towing eyes and shackles is fitted to the Hull front plate only.
Parts limiting reliability and life. Track Links, Rollers and Driving Wheels, Differential Locking Gear, Secondary Gear Shaft, Radiator, Engine.
Crew. Commander 1; driver 1, gearsmen 2, gunners 4.
Rations and water. No special provision made.
Armament. Sponsons to take 6-pounder or Vickers guns, also detachable, and may be carried on trolleys.
Turrets. One front or Drivers turret only.
Doors. Sponsons (Male) – one door each. Sponsors (Female) – one small oval manhole each.
    Rear door - one. Roof – one circular man hole – 18 inches diameter.

Equipment			Male	Female
Guns	6-pounder 40 calibre QF Hotchkiss guns		2	None
Machine Guns	Hotchkiss Portable Automatic guns		4	1
	Vickers light guns		None	4
Mountings	6-pounder recoil mountings		2	None
	Machine Gun Trunnion mountings with shutter.		5	1
	Vickers Turret mountings		None	4
Revolver ports			18	18
Ammunition	6 pounder shells		324	
	SAA (in strips of 14) rounds		6,272	6,272
	SAA (in belts of 80) rounds		None	24,960
Observation	Reflector Boxes (with glass prisms)		13	14
	Outlook Doors with flaps for officer and drivers		2	2
	Periscope openings		3	3
	Periscopes		3	3
Dimensions				
Hull	Length overall (with tail)		32 feet 6 inches	
	Length overall (without tail)		26 feet 5 inches	
	Length (within track centres)		23 feet 6 inches	
	Width in fighting trim (Male or Female)		13 feet 9 inches	
	Width for conveyance by rail		8 feet four inches	
	Width over side plates		8 feet	
	Height overall		8 feet ½ inch.	
	Height from ground to underside of belly		1 foot 4 5/8 inches	
	Height to top of tracks		7 feet 4½ inches	

Steering tail	Diameter of wheels	4 feet 6 inches		
Armour plate Thickness	Maximum	12 mm		
	Minimum	6 mm		
	Protecting crew	8 to 10 mm		
	Protecting engine and gear	8 mm		
	Track shoes	10 mm		
Weights		tons	cwt	lbs
	Hull frame	8	-	-
	Steering tail	1	-	-
	Engine and transmission to cross shaft coupling	3	10	-
	Coupling to track driving wheel	2	10	-
	Radiator with fan		10	-
	Armour	3	10	-
	Track shoes			41
	Track rollers			20
	Ammunition (Male)	1	-	-
	Ammunition (Female)	1	-	-
	General stores		10	-
	Total weight in fighting trim (Male)	28	-	-
	Total weight in fighting trim (Female)	27	-	-

Centre of Gravity relative to centre of length - 3 feet aft
Centre of Gravity relative to Ground line – 3 feet up.
Weight per horsepower – 597 lbs
Horsepower (hp) per ton – 3.75 hp

Power unit, ventilation etc.

Engine   Daimler [Knight] six cylinder sleeve valve engine 105 hp at 1,000 rpm
Ignition   One kw magneto with trip mechanism for starting
Carburettor   One Zenith 48mm, choke tube 32 mm,
                main jet 1.75mm, flow meter size 395 cc,
                compensating jet 1.45 mm, flow meter size 285 cc.

Engine control system: By hand levers on the right hand side of the driver's seat and by vertical governor driven by Skew Gear on the Half Time Shaft and operating a Butterfly Value in the Induction pipe.

Petrol system. Two Petrol Tanks of capacity 23 gallons are situated between the Trackways on each side of the driver's turret. The petrol is led by gravity through a pipe to the Carburettor, and a special funnel is provided for filling the tanks from the roof.

Lubrication. An Oil tank is connected to an eight Plunger Pump which delivers to the Main Bearings and Troughs below the Connecting Rods. Those Troughs are pivoted and can be connected to the Carburettor Throttle if required so that so the Dippers on the Connecting Rods can go deeper into the Troughs at high speed. The Pistons, Sleeves etc are lubricated by splash from the Troughs. The Oil is returned from the Sump by a two Plunger Pump delivering the bulk of the oil to the Oil Tank and the balance to the Governor Skew Bar and exhaust side of the Valves.

Starting System. A crank handle at which there is room for four men can be shipped between the Differential Case and the after end of the Engine Casing, where it engages with a Claw Clutch at the end of a Shaft passing over the top of the engine. At the other end of this Shaft is a wheel driving, by means of a chain, another Claw Clutch in line with the Engine Shaft. This can be slid into gear by the driver raising a handle at his side.

A Spring and Trip mechanism is fitted to the Magneto to give a delayed and fat spark when starting. Doping Cocks are provided on the cylinder heads.

Engine Cooling System. Radiator. Built up of 40 envelopes.
Radiator fan. (Keith Blackman) 17 1/8 inch diameter driven by a flat belt at 1,000 rpm [with a] capacity [of] 3,000 cubic feet per minute. Air is drawn from the inside of the tank thus ventilating it.

Lighting system. Lucas Dynamo driven by Whittle Belt off a Pulley fitted to the Flexible Coupling and sharing a 12 volt 75 Ampere -Hour Battery. Lamps: eight festoon lamps, two head lamps and one tail lamp.

Exhaust pipes. Exhaust [gases] taken up by pipes from the Manifold and exhausted straight into the atmosphere. Light metal covers deflect the gases to the sides. [2]

Transmission. The Clutch is of a Cone type, with the Male portion faced with *Ferodo*. It is operated by a Pedal from the Driver's seat and connected by the Clutch to the Gear Box Coupling, or spider and leather flexible couplings, giving two to the Gear Box consisting of Sliding Gear giving two speeds forward and one reverse. This drives the Worm and Worm Wheel which encloses the Differential Gear provided for use when steering with the Tail or the Hand Brakes. The Cross Shafts are driven by the Differential Gear and are fitted with a Sliding Sleeve operating from the Driver's seat, by means of which they can be locked together.

An Extension Shaft and Toothed Coupling connect the Cross Shafts to the Secondary Gears, which are two Sliding Gears meshing with the two Spur Wheels mounted on each side of the Chain Pinion (see below) and operated by Striking Forks with Interlocking Handles. A special Coventry Driving Chain connects the Chain Pinion with the Driven Chain Wheel, on each side of which are the Track Pinions engaging with the Track Driving Wheels. These are mounted on a fixed shaft with Floating Bushes and engage with the Track Links (see Track).

Gear Control – Secondary Gear. Arranged by Striking Lever and Interlocking Forks operated by Gearsmen at the rear of the Sponson ways.

Brakes (Track). *Ferodo* lined and hand operated, the Brake Drums are situated on the Second Change Slow Speed wheels.

Brake (Worm Shaft). Provided on tail end of Worm Shaft and pedal operated. Its effect is increased by the Worm and Worm Wheel reduction.

Steering System.
Sharp turns. After raising the tail, the tank is steered by locking the Differential. The Secondary

---

2   Author's note: The document stated there were no cut outs, lagging or protection for the crew.

Gear is put into neutral on one side and the Track Held by the Hand Brake. The other Track runs as usual.

Gradual turns. Made by unlocking the Differential and moving the Hand [Steering] Wheel which actuates wire ropes by which means the Steering Wheels are moved through an angle causing the Tank to turn. The Steering Tail consists of two Wheels (as above) mounted at one end of a frame, which is pivoted at the other. At this end are eight Springs in tension, which keeps the Wheels in contact with the ground. A Hydraulic Ram, actuated by a Pump, is also attached to this end, with Friction Drive off the Vibration Damper. And this raised the Tail when out of action.

Track. An assembled track consists of the following.;

Track Shoe - AP [Armour Plate] Special – 20 ½ inches wide.

Track Links – flanged and rivetted to the above. and

Track Link Pins – joining shoes to form the Track (45 ton Steel).

Tank Driving Wheels (see Transmission).

Track Adjusting Wheel. This is identical to the track driving wheel. [3]

Track Rollers. Below the hull and made of cast steel.

With Flange Plates and Springs – 10 pairs per track.

Without Flange Plates and Springs – 16 pairs per track.

Track Rails.

Angle irons – the tracks engage with these.

Switch Plates are fitted front and rear -to pick up the Track so that the Angle on the Hull engages below the lip of the Track.

Track Lubrication. Two Oil Tanks containing two gallons of oil each are situated on each side of the Hull at the foot of the Forward Diaphragm and feed oil to the Track Links through the Hull Floor by pipes fitted with Cocks. [4]

Track Brakes. (see Transmission above)

Track Pressures (in motion)	20 ½ inch shoe
Maximum pressure of hard ground	27.8 pounds per square inch
Pressure with 1 inch sinkage	26.2
Pressure with 2 inch sinkage	24.6
Pressure with 4 inch sinkage	16.9
Pressure with 6 inch sinkage	13.0
Pressure sunk to the belly.	11.6

Length of track on each side when on hard ground – 4 feet 7 inches

---

3   During initial employment on the Somme this was found to be unsatisfactory owing to the difficulties associated with the mud, On later Marks, it was replaced by a plain, rather than toothed, wheel.

4   These Oil tanks were not fitted prior to the arrival of tanks in France in September 1917. They were sent out and retrofitted by the Artificers of 711 Company workshop personnel. See Appendix XVI.

Appendix V

The Handling of the Heavy Section Machine Gun Corps and its Training

---

I - The Handling of the Heavy Section Machine Gun Corps [1]

The primary object of this unit is to assist the infantry by disposing of the principal difficulties in the way of their advance i.e., barbed wire and machine guns. Battles cannot be won by tanks alone and it is by infantry, and infantry alone, that a decision can be reached.

Definitions

1. **Concentration Area**: This includes any locality where the whole unit is concentrated under its own commander when it is not fighting.
2. **Positions of Assembly**: These are the positions where the companies are separately assembled and billeted when detailed for active operations.
3. **Position of Deployment**: This is the line on which Tanks are drawn up at their correct distances and preparatory to the battle. This will be from 2 -3 miles behind our own front trenches.
4. **Starting Line**: This is the line immediately behind our own front line trenches to which the Tanks move from the position of deployment, probably in the hours of darkness receding the attack.

Probable course of operations preliminary to the attack

(this is described for one HS company).
5. **From the Position of Assembly**: From the position of assembly, the company will proceed to its situation on the position of deployment by routes, which will be settled by the CO after consultation with the staff of the formation to which the company is attached.

---

1 Author's note: A confidential, undated and unsigned provisional paper held in the Fuller Archive at King's College London; a pencilled annotation on the first page indicates it was written by Swinton, Brough and Bradley in July 1916.

6. **Reconnaissance of the Position of Deployment**: As soon as the company commander is informed by higher authority of the directions and extent of his Position of Deployment, he will take steps to reconnoitre that position with a view to disposing his tanks along it at the ruling distance of 150 yards apart, the marking the spot at which each tank will take up its position. He will also make note of suitable locations where his Tanks can collect either for purposes of cover [from fire] or concealment if they are not at once required to be spaced at the proper distance at the Position of Deployment. When the general advance takes place, it is contemplated that the Tanks will move forward from the Position of Deployment in darkness, timed so as to arrive at certain points already marked out for them along the Starting Line, shortly before dawn, when at the pre-arranged moment, they will move forward to the attack over the British front line trenches.

7. **Selection of points on the Starting Line**: The responsibility for selecting the points in the British front line at which tanks will cross the defences to move across no man's land rests with the staff of the formation under which the Tanks will operate, working in conjunction with the Section Commanders. The latter will learn where the points are, arrange for them to be made practicable if necessary, and then take measures to select out the best route of approach to each from the Position of Deployment for each Tank.

8. **Marking out the routes for Tanks up to the Startling Line**: The actual marking of the routes for Tanks from the Position of Deployment to their points on the Starting Line will be carried out by the Tank Skippers working under the Section Commander.

Probable course of operations during the combat

9. **Progress and action up to the enemy front line trench**: At the appointed moment, the company will move over our front line of defence and drive across no man's land in advance of our assaulting infantry who will remain under cover until the Tanks reach the most suitable positions for enfilading the enemy front line with machine guns with the object of preventing the enemy from putting their heads up and firing on our infantry who will, by then, have left cover. This position may be on the enemy parapet or astride the trench, probably the latter.

10. **Attack on enemy machine guns**: It must not be forgotten that the Tanks can use their weight as well as their fire power and may, in some cases, be able to crush enemy machine gun emplacements. Enemy machine guns which cannot be rolled out should be destroyed by 6-pounder fire. And since it will often be impossible to locate with precision their guns, the Tank gun-layers must judge of their positions by flashes, dust etc. and must look out for them in what they know the most likely positions in the enemy defences.

11. **Progress beyond the enemy front line**: Directly our infantry reach the enemy front line, the Tanks will continue their advance, so as to ensure keeping ahead of the infantry and prepare the way for them. When and where possible, enemy communication trenches should be followed up and rapid fire should be poured by any machine guns that bear on the enemy who will probably be crowded in the trench.

    Successive lines of trenches will be dealt with on the same principles as those described for the attack on the enemy front line trench. It must be borne in mind that machine guns will be more in evidence the further into the position progress is made.

12. **Hostile artillery positions**: As progress as above outlined has been made for some 2,000 to 3,000 yards (approximately), the Tanks may find themselves within the area in which there are enemy artillery positions. Location of the enemy's batteries – probably concealed - however will be difficult and any, the positions of which have been plotted in the trench maps, should be closely watched for. In regard to the method to be employed by Tanks in attacking hostile guns, a certain amount of damage may be done by 6-pounder fire. Generally speaking, however, the best method will be to assist the infantry to get within rifle range of the gun detachments.

13. **Obstacles**. The line of Tanks as a whole will drive straight through wire entanglements or other obstacles. But certain specially fitted Tanks may be told off to tear up and destroy the entanglements by sweeping laterally or otherwise. (Details of this special work will be set forth later). Contingent on the above considerations, the tanks should be driven as straight as possible, dressing being kept so that fire is not masked.

14. **Halting**. No attempt should ever be made by one Tank to rescue a neighbouring tank which may in temporary difficulties and each Skipper must depend on his own resources to extricate his machine. If a Tank is forced to cease fire, it should not cease unless it is likely to damage other Tanks or our own infantry.

15. **Lateral inter-communication.** It is improbable that lateral inter-communication between Tanks can be established satisfactorily, so that even the Section Commanders will be unable to exercise any control once the attack has started. The success of the attack, therefore, will depend on the precision of the original orders issues, the way they are understood by those who have to carry them out, and the powers of initiative and observation of the Tank skippers and gun layers.

16. **Control.** Control by the Company Commander will probably cease directly his unit is launched. He must therefore remember that progress will depend on the clearness of the orders given by him to his Section Commanders.

17. **Special tasks.** It is to be contemplated that a definite task may be allocated either to a Section of Tanks or to a single Tank e.g., the attack of a particular locality. If this is done, the method of carrying out the mission must be considered with the general plan of the attack.

18. **Enemy counter attacks**. It is probable that hostile counter-attacks will take the shape of a sudden advance of a mass of enemy infantry in close order, possibly supported by artillery fire. The best method of dealing with such attacks will be for the Tanks to drive at full speed into the heart of the enemy firing as rapidly as possible from every available gun. It is considered that a Tank in action is more formidable than when stationary and that it will afford a more difficulty target than if it is halted in order to furnish a steady gun platform.

19. **Mutual support.** It must be born in mind that at all times, Tanks can give very valuable mutual support to each other by crossfire, that a Tank is a mobile machine gun emplacement and that every opportunity for bringing the power of machine guns to bear in cross or enfilade fire should be used. This opportunity, it is thought, is more likely to be presented when the hostile infantry attempt a counter-attack than at any other time, for in such a case, they will not attack the Tanks themselves but will attempt to get to close quarters with our infantry and, in doing so, will present a mass target which can be taken in flank by fire from the Tanks.

20. **Fire control**. The selection of targets, and method of engaging them, will depend almost entirely on the men handling the 6-pounder and machine guns. It is probable that the skipper can communicate by the means of an indicator with the gunners sufficiently to indicate the whereabout of suitable targets; but this does not absolve gunners from opening fire immediately upon any particular party of troops, individual or other objects within range of their weapons. It is important to remember than 6-pounders are for use against materiel and machine guns for use against personnel. Occasions may arise when the 6-pounder gun layers may wish to obtain a steady gun platform. In this case they will ask for a halt by the means installed. Whether this halt is made, or not, depends on the Skipper who alone is responsible for dealing with the tactical situation at the moment.

21. **Economy of ammunition.** It is essential that ammunition should be economised as far as possible at every stage of the operations.

22. **Abandon tank.** Should a Tank become immobile, for any reason, the guns should continue to fire o long as any useful result is obtained by their action. When this is no longer the case, or when the Skipper of the Tank decides that better effect could be produced by the employment of the machine guns outside of the Tank, he will order the crew to disembark, taking with them the machine guns. The small arms ammunition will if possible be thrown overboard. The Skipper must exercise his discretion as to opening fire with his machine guns at once to assist the infantry or collecting his command and joining the nearest infantry unit in the advance.

II - Notes on instruction of the Company

1. Before any preliminary collective exercise is undertaken, it is essential that all officers of the H.S. should be able to read a map - particularly a trench map - and understand the compass fitted in the Tank. They should also be in possession of luminous watches and trained to start engines and to move off at precise moments. They should be practised, in the case of an advance to be made in the dark, in synchronising their watches with that of the Company Commander who will obtain the correct time from the Signal Company.

2. All officers must be trained in the issue of precise and concise verbal orders to subordinates. They must also be taught to exercise their imagination and to inspire that of their subordinates, so that their unit may be handled in the most practical manner in contingencies both foreseen and unforeseen.

3. Much useful instruction can be imparted, independently of the tanks, by the rapid solution by Section Commanders of problems set on the battlefield in the training area under the guidance of the Company Commander. Officers and drivers should be exercised on foot over various portions of the manoeuvre ground and should be asked to decide exactly how they would overcome various obstacles. They should be taught to know instinctively what ground can be crossed and what should be avoided, for hesitation on the part of the driver may seriously imperil the Tank.

4. The crews of the Tanks should also be taken around the battlefield to learn to get a mental picture of what a battlefield looks like and the probable position of the principal targets. These tours should be made at different times of the day so that the aspect of the battlefield under all conditions of weather and light may be learnt.

5.   Company Commanders must understand that such tactical exercises must be based on a definite situation. They must issue precise orders to the Section Commanders who, in turn, must ensure that Skippers and each member of the Tank crew thoroughly understands the object of the exercise.

6.   Practice in laying out the routes of the advance from the Position of Deployment to the Starting Line must be carried out by day and by night. This must be done in conditions which obtain in war.

7.   When exercising with Tanks it is essential, in order to make the tactical exercise as realistic as possible, that some men should be detailed to act as our own infantry. To play this part, they must be instructed in the general principle that attacking infantry would follows and will not precede the Tanks in action (unless the latter break down).and that their progress will consequently be slow.

8.   When men are available, it will be very valuable if some are detailed to act as hostile infantry, particularly with a view to practising the gunners and gun layers with targets suddenly presented by counter attacking infantry, who will probably be in close formation. Vickers guns firing black ammunition from hostile trenches should be employed to represent enemy machine guns in action. Care must be taken that these guns are not rolled out by mistake.

Appendix VI

GHQ Instructions Regarding the Employment of Tanks

OAD 111 dated 16 August 1916

1. A number of 'tanks' (i.e., cars of the 'Heavy Section's' Armoured Cars) is expected to arrive during the next few weeks from England and it is hoped that make use of 50 to 60 of these about the middle of September in connection with offensive operations on a large scale.

2. The attached paper (marked B) is issued giving some description of the 'tanks' and the possible means of employment tactically. The 'tanks' on arrival will be concentrated at the St Riquier training camp. Army and Corps commanders should study these weapons on the ground, so that they can adapt their plans for using them to best advantage. Information will be given to Armies when any combined exercise with infantry and 'tanks' will take place at St Riquier.

3. As the time is short, it is of the paramount importance that Army and Corps commanders should study the use of these 'tanks' with the actual problem which will confront them on the ground. For this purpose, the following forecast of operations is given:
   a. The Fourth Army might be called upon to attack from a front Leuze Wood inclusive – Ginchy – Delville Wood and High Wood – to Munster Alley (left boundary of the Army). The objective would be the enemy's third line system, from Morval, inclusive, to Le Sars, inclusive and possibly the German gun positions beyond.
   b. The Reserve Army might be called upon to attack from a front Munster Alley (exclusive) to the River Ancre, with a view to securing the German third line system from Le Sars, exclusive, to Pys and thence forms a defensive flank along the River Ancre.
   c. The troops will be placed at the disposal of the Fourth and Reserve Armies; their training areas and period of training have already been notified to the Armies – see paper A [not copied].
   d. It is hoped that the following 'tanks' will be available for Fourth Army 36-42, for Reserve Army 18 – 24.

4. The following points require consideration in the use of the 'tanks':
   a. An assembly place under cover [of fire]. There should not be difficult to find behind the ridge we presently occupy.

353

b. Their use with infantry. It will be necessary to train those divisions who may be earmarked to work with the 'tanks.

c. Although the recommendation is that the 'tanks' should be 100 to 150 yards apart, it may probably suffice, in view of the nature of German defences opposite us, to use these 'tanks' on a wider interval from 200 – 250 yards. [1]

d. One section of 'tanks' would thus appear to be a suitable distribution for an infantry division covering 1,000 to 1,500 yards of front.

e. The infantry will have to work close behind the 'tanks', occupying, clearing out, and consolidating successive positions after these have been reached by the 'tanks. Some 'tanks' might be required to work with the infantry in clearing up strong points overrun by the leading tanks and troops [2].

f. The working of our artillery barrage in conjunction with the 'tanks' will require careful consideration.

5. It is for consideration whether the 'tanks' could not move a short distance in the darkness, say as far as the Switch Line where that line is close to our front line. They would then move forward to the German third line in the grey dawn. The objectives of the tanks must be clearly stated and as simple as possible as it is difficult for the tanks to manoeuvre.

Adv GHQ   16 August 1916
L E KIGGELL   Lt-Gen, Chief of the General Staff

Paper B

Notes on Tank Organisation and Equipment

1. The unit consists of: -
    Headquarters
    6 companies
    Quartermasters' Establishment) One for each
    Workshops) Two Companies
    (a) Headquarters.
         The Officer Commanding the Heavy Section will be directly under the General Staff at GHQs. His position in relation to the Heavy Section will be analogous to that of the OC Special Brigade in relation to the Special Battalions. His responsibilities include:
         a. The general control and supervision of the whole unit.
         b. Cooperation with commanders of formations concerned regarding all details connected with the employment of the unit.

---

1   Author's note: It appears that GHQ were unaware of Swinton's recommendation that tanks should be employed in pairs; one female supporting each male.
2   Author's note: This indicates that the tanks could operate in waves.

c.   Arrangements with formation and departments for the maintenance of such portions of the unit as may be detached, for the provision of special stores and for the replacement of casualties.

(b) Companies. Each company consists of a Headquarters and four Sections comprising six 'tanks' each, with one spare 'tank' per company. The establishment of a company is 28 officers and 255 other ranks including spare crews. [3] The 'tanks' are divided into two categories:

a.   The 'Male' carrying two 6-pounder guns and four Hotchkiss guns. [4]

b.   The 'Female' carrying five Vickers machine guns and one Hotchkiss gun. [5]

Sections are comprised of three 'Male' and three 'Female' tanks and are subdivided into [three] sub-sections containing one Male and one Female each. Each section has an establishment of six officers and 43 other ranks; the crew of each tank being one officer and six other ranks.

(c) Quartermasters' Establishment)

(d) Workshop)

A Quartermaster's Establishment and a Workshop, composed of one officer and four other ranks and three officers and 50 other ranks respectively, is provided for each two companies. These are immobile units and should be located in the vicinity of a railway. The Workshop cannot be sub-divided.[6]

2.   **Ammunition.**   The following is the approximate number of rounds carried in the tanks.

(a) 'Male' – 160 rounds per 6-pounder gun: 500 rounds per Hotchkiss gun.

(b) 'Female' – 4,800 rounds per Vickers guns; 3,000 rounds per Hotchkiss.

3.   **Allotment to Formations**.

Portions of the Heavy Section will be allocated to Armies for active operations in the same manner as the Special Brigade are now allocated. Units so allotted with be administered, as far as ordinary requirements are concerned, by the formation to which they are attached for fighting.

4.   Supply of technical stores.

The following arrangements have been made for the supply of special stores and spare parts, excluding ammunition.

A new section of the Ordnance Department is being formed at [Le] Havre to deal with stores peculiar to the Heavy Section. The Officer Commanding Workshop, with which the Quartermasters' Establishment should be located, will demand such stores through the Ordnance Officer of the formation to which he is attached in the usual way

---

3   Author's note: This did not include the drivers who were on the establishment of 711 (MT) Company ASC.
4   Author's note: One of the Hotchkiss machine guns was a spare.
5   Author's note: One of the Vickers machine guns was a spare.
6   Author's note: This was to create major difficulties during the first tank action when it was decided that the two companies were to operation over a six mile front, with two sections operating independently of their company headquarters on 15 September. On 9 September, Knothe sought additional vehicles, tools and equipment, from GHQ to form section fitter groups but these were not available.

and will form an advanced depot of those stores for these units. He will be responsible for keeping the two Companies provided which such special stores as they may require.

The replacement of guns and machine guns, and provision of spare parts for the same, will be arranged for in the same manner.

Under normal circumstances, a machine which requires repair will have to go back to the Workshop. If, however a machine is so badly damaged as to be unable to move, it might be possible to send a party from the Workshop to patch it up. [7]

5. **Ammunition Supply**.

The Officer Commanding the Corps Ammunition Park will be responsible for the supply of ammunition to the 'Tanks' working in the Corps area and will provide such lorries as may be necessary. These lorries will feed directly to the 'Tanks' or to dumps from which the 'Tanks' will pick up ammunition.[8] When 'Tanks' are transferred to another Corps, the Officer Commanding the Corps Ammunition Park which fed the dump will be responsible for emptying it.

6. **General Remarks.**

The chief attributes of the 'tank' are its power of crossing obstacles, its fire power, its momentum and its invulnerability to shrapnel and small arms fire. Its chief weakness is its liability to be knocked out by artillery and heavy trench mortars.

The machine weighs 28 tons. Its speed is from 4-5 miles per hour on the level to 2 miles per hours when climbing or over very rough ground. It can reverse. It can surmount a revetted parapet 5 feet high and cross a gap 10 feet wide. Wire entanglements, hedges and walls etc do not interfere within its progress. It can push down and pass over single trees up to 10 inches in diameter and it can traverse ordinary fir plantations or coppices of young trees. In close woods, however, there is considerable risk of the sponsons and guns coming into contact with trees and being wrenched off.

A photograph of a tank is attached. [9] All tanks are being "camouflaged" to render them as inconspicuous as possible. Efforts are being made to install means of signalling to tanks but it is doubtful how far these will prove efficient.

Issued by General Staff General Headquarters   August 1916.

---

7   Author's note: The inability to recover ditched or damaged tanks from their point of damage, or to be able to send parties of artificers forward to undertake forward repairs, would create a significant loss in capability after 15 September.
8   Author's note: This system did not work during the tank actions on 15 and 16 September.
9   Author's note: The photograph was an image of *Mother* taken at Burton Park near Lincoln.

Preliminary notes on the tactical employment of tanks

(Provisional)

1.   The object of the tank is to help the infantry forward and specifically to deal with enemy machine guns. The original concept of the employment of these machines was the advance of a large number in line at 100 to 150 yards interval, closely followed by the infantry. This implies an approach march and deployment under cover, a surprise start, accurate keeping of alignment and direction, and a suitable objective, such as parallel lines of trenches in open country; these considerations, combined with the extent and regularity of the target offered to the enemy's artillery, render this a difficult operation.

2.   A tank cannot, except at great risk, cross a heavy barrage of HE or gas shells and it cannot lie out in the open under shell fire. Its safety lies in its surprise, in rapid movement and in getting to close quarters. It must emerge from cover (either material or the cover of smoke or darkness), and it must return to cover, or find some other concealment or safety when its task is done. Also, it must have infantry with it. These considerations limit its employment, unless we are prepared to risk the loss of all the tanks by pushing them as far forward as they can go, if possible, up to the enemy's gun positions.

3.   The method of employment described in para. 2 entails this risk, and also requires that a large number of tanks should be available. As probably only small numbers will be available in the first instance, and as it may be required to use them as they arrive, it is necessary to consider how that can be employed under these conditions.

4.   The chief obstacle to any infantry advance is the villages, woods, strong points and hidden machine gun positions. No bombardment seems to succeed in obliterating these places so completely as to prevent the re-appearance of the machine guns as soon as the artillery lifts. The result is that the assault is checked in front of these points and that those elements, which continue to advance through the intervals, are taken in the flank.

What is wanted, therefore, is a means of supplying extra weight against their strong points, so that they may be overcome simultaneously with the other parts where the resistance is less. This weight cannot be applied by throwing in more infantry, as there is a limit to the density in which infantry can be used. The tank is designed to be a solution to the difficulty.

Within the limits of the objective given to an attack, it is generally possible to pick out the points from which the greatest resistance is to be expected. An allocated number of tanks should be told off to deal with each of these points of defence. They should be closely supported by bodies of infantry told off for the purpose, who will advance under the cover of the tanks, clear up behind them and eventually consolidate the locality when taken. In the case of a village of wood, the tank may find sufficient cover to enable them to remain and help / hold the location. If not, they would either go on to a further objective, or go back, according to their original orders.

Each tank attack will be a definite operation against a limited objective allocated to a selected number of tanks and a selected body of infantry all under one commander. In certain cases, a pair of tanks, supported by a platoon might suffice. Wherever tanks are to be employed, special attention must be paid to counter battery work, and the tanks should move under cover of a close barrage which should not lift from the objective until the tanks are close to it. Whether the tanks should deal with only the perimeter of the objective, or penetrate intò it, depends on the circumstances, but their primary task will consist of preventing the locality with which they have to deal from interfering with the main infantry attack.

5.   The tanks can move across country by night., but over unknown country it must be light enough for the driver to see where he is going. In our own lines, they can be assembled in complete darkness, by following a guide with a small light or luminous disc.

6.   There are also several purposes for which individual tanks may prove useful, for taking up stores, for hauling guns over trenches, for clearing up behind the leading lines of infantry, for removing captured guns, for destroying obstacles and possibly for reconnaissance. The closer the country, the more useful an individual tank is likely to prove.

7.   Finally, there are occasions which may arise when the 6 pounder tanks could be used as light mobile artillery in close support of the infantry, during the final stages of a successful advance until such time as field artillery can be brought up.

8.   There are four ways in which tanks may be employed:
   (a)   The advance in line in large numbers.
   (b)   The attack in groups, or pairs, against selected objectives.
   (c)   Employment singly, or in pairs, for special purposes.
   (d)   Employment as mobile light artillery

9.   The tank is a novel engine of war, and untried. Its use will require careful study and preparation on each separate occasion. Special care must be taken that tanks do not fall into the enemy's hands. It must be understood that one or more tanks by themselves cannot capture any hostile trench or position. As indicated in para 4 above, every attack by tanks must be accompanied with an infantry attack, and it will be the special duty of that infantry to co-operate closely with those tanks and to take special care that the tanks do not fall into the enemy's hands.

Issued by the General Staff
General Headquarters
August 1916.

Appendix VII

HQ Fourth Army Instructions for Employment of Tanks dated 11 September 1916 [1]

1. The 'Tanks' have been allocated to Corps as follows: [2]
   XIV Corps.   C Company less one Section (18 tanks)
   XV Corps.   D Company less one Section (18 Tanks)
   III Corps.   1 Section D Company
                    1 improvised section (12 tanks)
   Reserve Army. 1 Section C Company (6 tanks) [3]

2. Tanks should operate, as a general rule, in groups of 3 and will move in column of route (Line Ahead) along tracks or easily recognised trenches.

3. Tanks should be assembled on the night of X/Y in positions not more than 1 mile from points of departure.[4] Movement to be made during the hours of moonlight. On the night of Y/Z, tanks will move in hours of moonlight to points of departure. Very careful reconnaissance should be made of routes and positions of departure, and routes marked out by tapes. A pace of 15 yards per minute should be allowed for.

4. Aeroplanes will, if the weather permits, fly over the hostile front lines during the hours of moonlight on the night of W/X, X/Y and Y/Z, under Army arrangements, so as to cover the noise of the moving tanks as much as possible.

5. **The Attack on the First Objective**. [5]
   Tanks will start movement at a time so calculated that their will reach their objectives 5 minutes before the infantry. [6] The infantry will advance as usual behind a creeping barrage in which gaps about 100 yards will be left for the route of the tanks. The stationary

---

1 Author's note: Issued with HQ Fourth Army 299/17(G) dated 11 September 1916.
2 Author's note: This allocation requires a total of 54 tanks and crews; a maximum of 50 crews being available.
3 Author's note: This section was also allocated a spare tank bringing the total to seven.
4 Author's note: All Points of Departure and Starting Points on 15 September were significantly further than one mile from the Assembly Points.
5 Author's note: The first objective (Green Line) was generally to the rear of the German front line trenches.
6 Author's note: Given that the tanks had to reach the first objective five minutes before the infantry, the provision of a 100 yards gap in the creeping barrage along the tank routes served no effective purpose. Whilst it would have ensured that tanks running behind schedule be not fit by friendly fire, it also meant that German position in the gap were not neutralised.

barrage of both the heavy and field artillery will be timed to be lifted off the objectives of the tanks some minutes before their arrival on their objectives.

6.   After clearing the first objective, a proportion of the tanks should be pushed forward a short way to prearranged positions as defensive strongpoints. If necessary, a tank may be sent to assist the infantry in clearing such points in the line as may be holding them up.

7.   **The Attack on the Second Objective**. [7]

Tanks and infantry will advance together under the creeping barrage. Tanks will move as before in column and on well-defined routes. The pace will be regulated to the tank's pace (30-50 yards per minute) but the infantry must not wait for any tanks that are delayed. The action of the tanks will be as for the first objective.

8.   **The Attack on the Third and Subsequent Objectives**.

There will be no creeping barrage. The tanks should start sufficiently far in front of the infantry to reach the Third and Fourth Objectives some time before the infantry. The tanks will move as before in column. Their action will be arranged to crush wire and keep down hostile rifle and machine gun fire. The infantry must not wait for any tanks that are delayed.

9.   The following Signals will be used from Tanks to Infantry and Aircraft.

Flag Signals. Red flag – Out of action.   Green flag – Am on objective.

Other flags are inter-tank signals.

Lamp signals. Series of T's – Out of action. Series of H's – Am on objective

A proportion of the tanks will carry pigeons.

10.   If tanks get behind the timetable or get out of action, the Infantry must on no account wait for them.

11.   If the tanks succeed and the infantry are checked, the tanks must endeavour to help them.

12.   Any tanks, that may be in reserve, should be moved to the positions of assembly vacated by the front line tanks on the night Y/Z. They should be in telephonic communication with Corps.

13.   After the capture of the most distant objectives, tanks will be withdrawn under Corps arrangement to previously selected positions some way in the rear of those objectives. Arrangements must be made for the replenishing the petrol and ammunition supply.

14   General Notes

(a) Recent trials show that, over heavily shelled ground, a greater pace than 15 yards a minute cannot be depended upon. This pace will be increased to 33 yards per minute over good ground and downhill, on good ground, it will reach 50 yards per minute.

(b) Tank officers are without exception strange to the ground and to the conditions of the battle. They will require a good deal of assistance from staffs of formations, particularly in the study of the ground over which the tanks have to advance.

(c) Every tank going into action should be provided with a map showing its track clearly marked and the objectives of the infantry with timetable.

HQ Fourth Army   A. A. Montgomery

11/9/16   Major General, General Staff

---

7   Author's note: This paragraph is badly drafted as the number of objectives lines varied by corps and division.

Appendix VIII

XIV Corps Operation Order No 51 dated 11 September 1916 [1]

Reference   Map Sheet 57c 1:40,000; French Map 1:10,000 and special map attached.

1.
   a. Ginchy and the trenches N.E. of Leuze Wood have been captured by XIV Corps and it is anticipated that the situation between Leuze Wood and Ginchy will be further improved in the near future. The XV and III Corps have both advanced their lines.
   b. The Fourth Army will attack the enemy's defence between Combles Ravine and Martinpuich on "Z" day with the object of seizing Morval, Lesboeufs, Gueudecourt and Flers and breaking through the enemy's system of defence. The French are undertaking an offensive simultaneously to the South and the Reserve Army on the left of the III Corps.
   c. The attack will be pushed with the utmost vigour all along the line, until the most distant objectives have been reached. The failure of a unit on a flank is not to prevent other units pushing on to their final objectives as it is by such means that those units which have failed will be assisted to advance.
2. The objectives allotted to Divisions of the XIV Corps and the boundaries between Divisions and Corps are shown on attached map. [2]
3. The Infantry will advance to the attack of the Green Line at Zero, of the Brown Line at 0045, of the Blue Line at 01.30 and of the Red Line at 04.30. The hour of Zero and the date of Z will be notified separately.
4. The main action of the 56th Division on the right will be the clearing of Bouleaux Wood and the formation of a protective flank covering all the lines of advance from Combles and the valleys running N.E. from Combles. The capture of Morval and Lesboeufs will be undertaken by the 6th and Guards Divisions.

5 – 7 [omitted]

---

1   Author's note: The original was copied into C Company War Diary as the first appendix. Paragraphs 5-7 were not included nor was the map.
2   Author's note: This was not copied to the War Diary; the boundary lines, behind the Forward Line of Own Troops are shown however shown on Map 6.

8. Flares will be lit as follows:
    (a) On obtaining each objective
    (b) At 12 noon and 5 pm on September 15th
    (c) At 6.30 am on September 16th
9. Watches will be synchronised at 12 noon and 6 pm on September 14th by telephone from Corps Headquarters.

Appendix IX

Instructions for Tanks to be Attached to the Guards Division

Order No 76 issued on 12th Sept. 1916   G.D. No 17

1.
    (a) Tanks will reach assembly position about S29b 4.4 on the evening of X day.
    (b) Tanks will move from assembly position on Y/Z night in such time to allow of their being in their forward positions at Zero - 4 hours. On arrival at these positions, Tanks will be formed into three columns numbered from right to left, each consisting of three Tanks.

Tanks will be lettered:
A.B.C. in No 1 Column
D.E.F. in No 2 Column
G.H.K. in No 3 Column
and 'L' tank

During operations all references in messages to Tanks and Tank columns will be as above. All arrangements will be made by Divisional Headquarters for (a) and (b).

2.
Column No 1 will advance to the attack of the Green Line at Zero - 40.
Column No 2 will advance to the attack of the Green Line at Zero - 40.
Column No 3 will advance to the attack of the Green Line at Zero - 50.

Nos 1, 2 and 3 Columns will advance to the attack of the Blue Line (column No 1 passing into the 6th Division area about T9 Central) at Zero + 1 hour 10 minutes. Nos 2 and 3 Columns will advance to the attack of the Red Line at Zero + 3 hours 30 minutes.

3.   A special task is allotted to 'L' tank, viz., that of protecting the left flank of 1st Guards Brigade from hostile fire from the direction of T13a central. In this task, two tanks of XV Corps on our left will assist.

    'L' tank will, at Zero - 50, attack German Trench from T13b 2.5 to T13a 5.8 cruising in that neighbourhood and overcoming any opposition met with until the infantry of the 14th Division who are advancing N.E. at Zero from the line T13 central-T13a 0.0 have cleared up the situation. 'L' tank will, as soon as, but not before, the enemy's resistance in T13a has been completely overcome, withdraw to a position in reserve about S24 central. On arrival at this point O.C. 'L' tank will report the position to 1st Guards Brigade Headquarters at S24b 6.1½ and there await fresh orders from Guards Division.

4.   Orders as to withdrawal of tanks at the conclusion of operations or for the undertaking of fresh operations subsequent to the period dealt with in Guards Division No 76 will be issued by XIV Corps and repeated through Guards Division to Guards Brigades concerned who will transmit these orders to the tanks, care being taken that these orders are delivered to each individual tank on their Brigade frontage.

As regards local co-operation between tanks and infantry in carrying out the tasks allotted in Guards Division Order No 76, Company Commanders will notify tanks their requirements which will be met by tanks as long as it does not interfere with scheme of attack and times and routes laid down in Guards Division Order No76.

5.   Maps showing routes of the tanks and the special points in the enemy lines to be dealt with by them have been issued with Guards Division Order No76.

Sept. 13, 1916.

Supplementary orders for the preliminary operation by L tank

Four additional orders were issued regarding the tenth tank, operating on the western flank of the Guards Division.

The initial instructions were issued by XIV Corps on 12 September and stated that:

> One of the tanks in the Corps Reserve is allotted to the Guards Division for clearing up the situation immediately north of Ginchy in T7d and the trench front [at] T7d 1,5 and T7c 5,9. In this connection it should be noted from captured documents that it is clear there is a machine gun at T7d 1½,8 and two machine guns in the Triangle at T7d 9.8

Detailed orders were issued by HQ Guards Division at 1155 hours on 13 September: [1]

> A special task is allotted to L Tank, viz that of protecting the left flank of 1 Guards Brigade from hostile fire from the direction of T13a central [the Brewery Salient]. In this task, the two tanks of XV Corps on our left will assist. [2] L Tank will, at zero minus 50 minutes [0530 hours], attack the German trenches from T13b 2.5 to T13a 5,8 cruising in that neighbourhood and overcoming any opposition until the infantry of 14 Division, who are advancing northwards at Zero from the line T13 central – T13a 0,0 have cleared up the situation. L Tank will, as soon as possible but not before the enemy's resistance in T13 has been overcome, withdraw to a position in reserve about S24 central. On arriving at this point, the officer will report the position to 1 Guards Brigade Headquarters at S24b 6,1 and there await fresh orders from Guards Division.

---

1   Guards Division 2241/G dated 13 September 1916.
2   Author's note: The tanks allocated to this preliminary action were D1 *Daredevil*, commanded by Mortimore, and D5 *Dolphin* commanded by Blowers. See Chapter 7.

This order was not sent to L Tank's skipper 2Lt Harold Cole. However, an outline instruction was issued by HQ C Company at Loop Camp on 14 September 1916 but the time was not recorded.[3]

> You will proceed with your command to join Captain Hiscocks at his position of assembly. You have been detailed to cope with a special situation, explained verbally. A certain sector of ground, T13a [and] b, has enemy machine guns in it. This sector lies behind the left flank of the Guards Division in the attack. It is therefore necessary that you advance into this sector to keep down the fire of any machine guns which may open on the Guards Brigade or on the infantry attacking from Delville Wood.
>
> You must report to Brigade Major, left Guards Brigade, and ask him for any information which may aid you. After dealing with the organisation in T13a [and] b, you will come under the orders of Capt Hiscocks.

Finally, L tank was tasked to tackle machine guns posts on the Flers road, 800 yards north of Ginchy and then others in the area of the Park; both of which were in 14th Division's area.

> Herewith copy of information from Corps. One of the tanks in Corps reserve is allotted to Guards Division for clearing up situation in T7d immediately north of Ginchy and trench T7d 1.5 to T7c 5.9 [garbled]. In this connection it should be noted that from captured documents it is clear that there is a machine gun in T7d 1½.8 and two machine guns in Triangle at T7b 9.6. You must arrange to deal with these points. I suggest route as per attached map.[4]

> A H Walker.'

---

3   Recorded in the C Company War Diary. TNA WO 95/96.
4   Unfortunately, the map mentioned is not attached to C Company's War Diary.

Appendix X

Attack Timetables: HQ 56th Division and 12th Battalion East Surrey Regiment

---

HQ 56th Division [1]

Time	Barrage	169th Brigade [510 Purdy]	167th and 168th Brigades [509 Arnold and 710 Dashwood]	Pace (yards per minute)
Z-20 mins [0600 hrs]		Tank leaves south corner of Leuze Wood		25-30
Z-12 mins [0608 hrs]			Tanks cross our front line at T21c 9.9	20
Z-2 mins [0618 hrs]		Tank reaches German front line at T27b 1.5	Tanks reach German front line in T21a	
Zero [0620 hrs]		169th Brigade advances to Green Line	167th Brigade advances to Green Line	
Z+3 mins [0623 hrs]		Tank works up C.T. towards Sunken Road 169th Brigade reaches first portion of Line T27b 1.5	Tanks advance 50-100 yds in front of Green Line. 167th Brigade reaches Green Line where tanks cross.	20
Z+25 mins [0645 hrs]		Tank reaches Sunken Road about T21d 6.3		20
Z+70 mins [0730 hrs]	Creeping barrage advances to Blue Line		Strong patrols follow barrage through Bouleaux Wood	

---

1   Author's note. This table is based on Appendix IV in the C Company War Diary. See TNA WO 95/96.

Z+98 mins [0756 hrs]		Tank starts for Blue Line along SE edge of Bouleaux Wood		40
Z+103 mins [0803 hrs]			Tanks start for Blue Line along NE edge of Bouleaux Wood	40
Z+120 mins [0820 hrs]			167th Brigade advances to Blue Line	
Z+123 mins [0823 hrs]		Tank reaches Blue Line at T22a 4.8 (cutting)		
Z+127 mins [0827 hrs]			Tanks reach Blue Line at cutting T16c central	
Z+128 -132 mins [0828–32 hrs]			167th Brigade reach Blue Line on line of railway	
Z+210 mins [0850 hrs]	Barrage creeps to Red Line			50
Z+230 mins [1010 hrs]		Tank starts for Red Line	Tanks start for Red Line	25
Z+260 mins [1040 hrs]	Barrage clear of Red Line			
Z+265 mins [1045 hrs]		Right Tank arrives on Red Line wire	Left Tank goes onto wire on S. edge of village. Centre Tank arrives at wire on Red Line	
Z+270 mins [1050 hrs]			168th Brigade advances to Red Line	
Z+275 mins [1055 hrs]			Left Tank reaches wire on South edge of village	25
Z+282 mins [1112 hrs}			168th Brigade reaches first trench of Red Line	

12th Battalion East Surrey Regiment [2]

Before Zero	Tanks start as required in order to be reach Switch Line at 0.25 minutes east of Longueval – Flers Road and at 0.15 minutes west of that road.
Zero [0620 hrs]	Infantry leave their trenches and advance close up to the barrage which will begin creeping back in front of them at 0.6 minutes. Creeping barrage will go back steadily at 50 yards per minute until it joins stationary barrage on first objective (Green Line).
Z+15 mins [0635 hrs]	Tanks reach positions of first objective west of Flers Road
Z+20 mins [0640 hours]	Barrage lifts from the Green Line west of Flers Road
Z+25 mins [0645 hours]	Tanks reach positions of first objective east of Flers Road
Z+30 mins [0650 hours]	Barrage lifts from Green Line of Flers Road, Infantry capture first objective as the barrage lifts in each case. Barrage halts 300 yards beyond Green Line.
Z+60 mins [0720 hours]	Infantry and tanks advance together behind the creeping barrage. Creeping barrage goes back 100 yards in three minutes and, on arrival at Flers Line, joins stationary barrage.
Z+85 mins [0745 hours]	Barrage lifts from the second objective of 14th and 41st Divisions. 14th and 41st Division capture Brown Line.
Z+90 mins [0750 hours]	Barrage lifts from second objective of New Zealand Division. New Zealand Division capture Brown Line.
Z+105 mins [0805 hours]	Covering barrage goes back to allow tanks to advance from Brown Line.
Z+120 mins [0820 hours]	Infantry advance, complete capture of Flers and establish Blue Line.
Z+255 mins [1035 hours]	Covering barrage taken off to allow tanks to go forward.

Z+270 mins [1050 hours]	Barrage lifts from	(1) Right Boundary and Road N32b 3,8
Z+295 mins [1115 hours]	Gird Trench and	(2) Road N32b 3,8 and track N26c 4,5
Z+300 mins [1120 hours]	Gird Support between	(3) Track N26c 4,5 and left boundary.

Z+330 mins [1150 hours]	Bombardment of Gueudecourt ceases. Tanks push forward, and infantry complete capture of fourth objective [Red Line]

---

2   Author's note: This undated timetable is attached to Lt Stadden's report found in the 12th East Surreys War Diary held at the Surrey Records Office in Woking (File reference ES 23/2).

Appendix XI

Tank Crew Mechanical Duties[1]

The Tank Commander is responsible for the mechanical efficiency and cleanliness of the machine. He must satisfy himself that his crew have carried out the duties mentioned below.

Before Starting.

The leading driver will:
1. See that the petrol tanks are filled with petrol and the petrol used is strained.
2. Clean distributor and inspect Make and Break on magnetos.
3. Clean all plugs.
4. Check oil level in oil tank. Fill oil through strainer
5. Make certain that the fan belt is tight.
6. Clean petrol filter.
7. Clean and lubricate all the controls.
8. Trip the magneto, slightly open the throttle and switch on.
9. Fill cups on induction pipe.
10. Supervise the filling of the radiator.
11. Every seven days insert one drop of oil in every hole in the magneto.

The second driver will:
1. Charge clutch lubricators with grease and partially screw them down.
2. Fill up oil box on the differential casing.
3. See that the lighting etc is in working order and V belt tight.
4. Change and screw down the six oil caps on the fan drive shaft and two on the fan.
5. Assist the leading driver.

The third driver will
1. Fill up the track oil tanks and turn on the cocks at the moment of starting. [2]

---

1   Author's note: This undated manuscript document was issued, according to 32019 Gnr William Piper, on 14 September 1916 possibly in their starting positions "just a few hours before going over the top".
2   Author's note: These oil tanks were not fitted before the tanks deployed to France. See Appendix XVI.

2.   Inspect track and adjust if necessary
3.   Assist the leading driver.
The remainder of the crew will fill up the roller spindles with grease.

During Running

The leading driver will drive the tank.
The second driver will
1.   Keep the oil box on the differential casing filled.
2.   Squirt thick oil over the right-hand side secondary gears every half hour. [3]
3.   Deal with changing the right-hand side secondary gears as instructed by the leading driver.
4.   Will every half hour test plugs for misfiring.
5.   Be responsible for the temperature of the engine and report any signs of overheating to the commander.

After Running.

The leading driver will:
1.   Turn off both petrol cocks.
2.   Empty radiator, cylinder and cylinder head in severe weather if no anti-freeze is used.

The secondary driver will:
1.   Turn off three cocks on the oil box over the differential.
2.   Turn off the cocks drain track oil tanks on the right-hand side
3.   Pull out the charging switch.

The third driver will turn off the cocks from track oil tank on the left-hand side,

The remainder of the crew will work under the orders of the leading driver when oil, petrol and water is required for the engine and they will be responsible for the lubrication of the track rollers.

NOTE

The second and third drivers carry out the duties of ammunition numbers during action on the right and left sides respectively when required. They are also responsible during action for keeping a sharp look-out from the rear periscopes and prisms.
    In tank drill the leading driver will be No 1, second driver No 2 and third driver No 3.

---

3   Author's note: This order reveals that the second driver was located in the right rear of the engine compartment, visible to the driver, whilst the third driver was located at the left.

Appendix XII

Confirmatory Orders – D Group of tanks[1]

Hastie M[ale]   Court F[emale]   Huffam F[emale]

You will leave your Starting Line at Zero - 35 [0545 hours]. Distance is 480 yards but is taken at 600 yards [2] as you are in column i.e., at 10 yards per minute = 60 minutes. You must arrive at [Z] +25 as you are West of the Flers Road (60 – 25 + 35 minutes). Throughout the advance, you will follow the route laid down on map and adhere to times given you.

The following points in your advance are as noted:

The first Vickers Car [3] of the group that arrives at TEA TRENCH will stop there where he will deal with the German machine guns and advance posts until the arrival of the Infantry, when he will advance in line with them overtaking the group at the SWITCH TRENCH.

All tanks on arrival at SWITCH TRENCH wait until the arrival of the Infantry when the Group will advance 150 yards and then conform to the timetable.

The objectives, routes and responsibility for dealing with Strong Points encountered by Group of tanks D will be as follows: TEA SUPPORT (where 1 Tank MG will be dropped off until the arrival of the infantry) - SWITCH TRENCH - FLERS TRENCH – Sunken road at T1a 3.5 then to follow sunken ditch to the NE corner of FLERS village N31a 8,2 – HOGGS HEAD Strong Point.

During the advance to the Second Objective from SWITCH to FLERS TRENCH along the routes chosen. You will make every effort to deal with sunken roads and machine gun emplacement as far as FLERS Trench. Should any Strong Point want to indicate to Tanks their assistance is required (SIC)

In this Advance, tanks will proceed in conjunction with the Infantry, making every endeavour to keep up with them

Third Objective. From FLERS TRENCH forwards, the Tanks will again proceed the Infantry by the routes laid down and will do all possible damage to the enemy by destroying

---

1   Author's note: These orders are undated but are likely to have been issued on 14 September 1916 after Summers arrived at Green Dump.
2   Author's note: This distance indicates that the tanks would advance with a space of 60 yards between them.
3   Author's note: Female tank.

machine-gun emplacements and other defences. D Group will send one tank to N31a 8,2; one tank to N31c 8,4 and one to T1a 4,8.[4]

Fourth Objective. From HOGGS HEAD Strong Point, then under orders from 14 Div., detailed orders in respect of this are attached [they are missing]

---

4   Author's note: This indicates specific targets at the three locations, the eastern entrance to Flers village on the Bulls Road (N31a 8,2) one 400 yards east of Flers Church (N31c 8,4) and the third on the south east corner of the village, 400 yards from the road to Ginchy.

Appendix XIII

Contemporary Reports about tank actions on 15-16 September 1916

HQ New Zealand Division

Report on Tanks - Heavy Machine Gun Section.

The first tanks arrived at Road junction west side of MONTAUBAN at about 8-0 p.m. 13/9/16. It took approximately two hours to cover the 2,000 yards to the first assembly point [Green Dump]. The route followed two turns. The tanks left this first assembly point at about 9.0 p.m. 14/9/16. Progress was good (about 1 mile per hour) until the shell pitted ground on the ridge West of LONGUEVAL was reached. Progress then became very slow owing to leading tanks becoming fixed and other routes having to be reconnoitred for the remainder of the column to pass them. A point 600 yards North of the main junction in LONGUEVAL was reached at 5.30 a.m. on 15/9/1916.

The difficulties encountered and very slow progress made arise from the following facts: -

1. The process of turning in a very small space was an exceedingly slow one. Owing to the necessity of raising the tail before the tank can be swung round.
2. Large craters in loose earth that has been ploughed up by heavy bombardment present a very serious obstacle. If a tank gets tilted sideways and the sponson becomes embedded in loose earth, the tracks will race and it becomes a matter of digging out.
3. Owing to the fact that the personnel had very little, if any, experience of working the tanks over the ground of a recent battlefield, they are not sufficiently cognisant of the capabilities and limitations (especially the latter) of their machines in such circumstances.

The following suggestions are submitted.

1. Practice is required in manoeuvring under service conditions over difficult ground at night. The method of signalling by the guide who selects the course (should be a member of the crew) to the driver in the tank needs to be systematised.
2. When time permits, the tank officers should be taken over the route to the starting point sufficiently in advance of the contemplated date to allow of rough improvements being made, such as the filling of large and difficult craters with bricks, chalk and similar hard stuff. This should be done for a width of at least three tanks width to allow of passing

373

derelicts (tanks are liable to be hung up from other causes than difficult ground – mechanical trouble with gears etc).

3.   Tactical. Once tanks are launched in the attack, communication is very difficult and they cannot very well be controlled by any higher formation than the Battalion HQ. It would be well therefore that they should come under the command of O.C. battalion in whose sector they will be operating, from the time of their arrival at the Point of Assembly, in order that cooperation may be thoroughly worked out in detail.

D M Lapthorn[1]
Capt Artists Rifles

No 1 Section of C Company

Capt Arthur Inglis consolidated the reports by skippers of No 1 Section which were sent to HQ 2 Canadian Division on 16 September 1916.

Male tank no 709 – C1 *Champagne* - Lt AJC Wheeler.

We left the park at 7 p.m. Sept. 14th proceeding along POZIERES Road to 1st Dressing Station, which was reached at 9.20. Replenishments and adjustments were made here. We left the Dressing Station at 12 midnight following a track marked out by runners by means of tapes through POZIERES reaching point 34a 10,0 at 2.20 a.m. Sept 15th. A runner explained that this was the nearest point to our front-line trench to which the tank could advance without being visible to the enemy.

The steering wheel was damaged by shell fire during the night; tracks were tightened up and minor adjustments made by daybreak. We left our starting point at 6.30 a.m. reaching 35a 3,9 at 7.00 a.m. where the tank bellied, tracks turning round without moving tank. All members of the crew started digging out operations at once continuing up until 11 a.m. and being helped by three Canadians attached to the tank.

By 10.45 [a.m.] the [enemy] shelling had become so bad that after one more effort at digging out, I ordered the crew and attached Canadians to cease work, bringing back the crew back to park near POZIERES and ordering Canadians to Brigade Headquarters. One member of the crew [2] was struck by shell from direct hit at about 10.55 a.m. and died two minutes later. Gnrs Bax and Smith worked untiringly throughout the four hours digging and throughout the time covered by this report.

---

1   Author's note: The report is handwritten and the signature is not distinct. Lapthorn is the best fit I can make.

2   Author's note: The tank's driver Pte Horace Brotherwood ASC; his body was recovered and is buried at the Pozieres Military Cemetery II F 27.

Female tank no 522 – C2 *Cognac* – Lt FW Bluemel.

We had the stub axle of the tank 522 broken going through POZIERES and arrived in position to start off about 2 a.m. 15-9-16.

   We had to adjust tracks at Zero before starting off and proceeded to move off (6.20 a.m.); and at 6.50 got stuck at point 35a 3,9. owing to being unable to steer properly. The steering gear having been broken, and we had to steer on brakes which was difficult as the crump holes are so numerous and the tank slipped into a communications trench. We succeeded in digging ourselves out and started off again but owing to the difficulty of steering we could not get away from the CT [communications trench]. We then shoved the side up with timber and managed to get the tank on the ground. We were unable to carry on all the time as we were continuously under heavy shell fire.

   We eventually had to cease work at 8.00 p.m. (15th Sept) owing to the shelling caused by from our infantry reinforcements coming up. We removed our [machine] gun locks, fastened up the tank and brought the crew back. The work done by driver Ledger was very good, he worked from 6.50 a.m. right through endeavouring to extract the tank. The whole crew worked very hard all the time under heavy shrapnel and gunfire.

Tank 701 – C3 *Chartreuse* – 2Lt SDH Clarke.

Guided by scouts, we left the Advanced Dressing Station at 12 midnight and proceeded to a spot about 170 yards south of the Windmill and there stopped in a shell-hole. At 6.30. a.m. we proceeded towards our front line but owing to a shellfire the steering gear had been put out of action, which seriously inconvenienced the handling of the car. The car was taken forward till it stuck a large shell-hole with several tree trunks in it. The crew worked for three and a half hours to dig it out, but eventually the engine seized owing to the cars having become wedged underneath. The whole time the work was going on shells were dropping near the car.

Female tank no 503 – C4 *Chablis* – 2Lt GOL Campbell.

We left the dump at midnight and proceeded to point of deployment over heavily shelled ground and under heavy shell fire from the enemy. On the reaching the point of deployment, the left track came off owing to it being very loose. Both tracks were tightened as far as adjustment could allow by Pte Cronin and Cpl Harrison under shell fire just before point of deployment. The tank having been rendered useless; the Officer i/c ordered Cpl Harrison to take the crew to the rear whilst he proceeded in tank 721 to its objective. During the night, the tail of Tank 503 was hit by a shell and considerably damaged.

Male tank no 721 – C5 *Crème de Menthe* – Captain A McC Inglis.

We left the park at ALBERT at 7 p.m. on the night of 14 September and proceeded to the Advanced Dressing Station 300 yards South of POZIERES, on the POZIERES – ALBERT Road at which place I have made a dump for petrol, oils etc. Having replenished the tank we proceeded to our position of deployment at the Windmill via the eastern edge of POZIERES, which place we arrived at about 2 a.m. This route had previously been reconnoitred and tapes placed by scouts from the 2nd Canadian Division.

We remained at this point until 6.20. a.m. which was the time the attack commenced. During the whole of the time, we were subjected to heavy shell fire, and one of the wheels of the tail was blown off.   At Zero (6.20 a.m.) we commenced our advance and made for the SUGAR FACTORY which was my objective. Soon after crossing our front-line trench, a group of about 50 Germans came up towards the tank to surrender. Our infantry was well in advance of the tank and were in the Sugar Factory by the time I arrived but I was able to make use of my Hotchkiss [6 pounder] guns.

I skirted the southern and eastern side of the Factory and went up to the trench where the Infantry were consolidating. Having found an officer, who told me the position had been made good, I commenced my return journey and laid out about 400 yards of telephone cable which I carried on the tail of my tank. In this I was assisted by an officer of the Signals. Before reaching the Windmill, the wire drum was smashed in by a shell.

I eventually reached point on the POZIERES - ALBERT Road 300 yards from the camp when the track came off completely. The successful way in which we reached our object and eventually withdrew was due to the very fine driving of Sgt Shepherd ASC.

Female tank no 504 – C6 *Cordon Rouge* – 2Lt J Allan.

We reached the point of deployment at 4.15 a.m. the 15th instant after very considerable difficulty. At 6. 20 a.m. engines were started and we moved off towards our then front line. Between this line and the German front line we were very heavily shelled by the enemy artillery. Several parties of the enemy were engaged by us and finished off by the infantry. The course continued in the direction of COURCELETTE, which we did not enter, but turned in the direction of the SUGAR FACTORY. As this latter position had by this time been consolidated, we returned to camp for repair.

Slightly wounded; one officer and five men (one by shell splinter and five bullet splashes)

Female tank no 509 – C14 *Corunna* – 2Lt FJ Arnold.

Diary entry by Gnr Tom Bernard written at Acheux on 13 October 1916. [3]

We, that is C Company, were the first company of this Corps to go to France and eventually after going through Havre and [unreadable] went into action of 16 [sic] September 1916 with D Company and altogether 50 cars. My car no 509, which was a Female, went over [the British front line] on the left of Leuze Wood; the ground was awful, all shell holes and that very loose.

We went over our front line at 6.08 and drove about No Man's Land and over the enemy, backed up by our infantry. Unfortunately, at 9.16 our diff [differential] got stripped and we can only proceed with the diff locked which caused our steering to jam. The officer, Second Lieutenant Arnold consulted us on the matter and we decided to stick [give up] the action. We were signalled by a sergeant of our infantry that they were being attacked by a party of bombers from Leuze Wood so we came stern first to attack these bombers and, just when we got within

3   Author's note: Original held by his family.

20 yards of them, the car got stuck in a large shell hole, which, had our steering gear been in order, we would easily have got out of.

The officer then asked for volunteers to go out and try to dig the car out. Corporal Pattison, Gunners Winter, Williams and I went out of the back door and made a start. The shell hole, in which we were stuck, was connected to the trench in which there were German bombers. After about ten minutes digging, a bomb fell at Corporal Pattinson's feet. He picked it up and tried to throw it away, but it exploded in his hands, killing him and wounding Gunner Winter. Williams and I rushed down the trench towards the bombers and, at the corner of a traverse trench, came onto one [German] who had a bomb in his hand and was in a position to throw it. I had my revolver ready and let him have two [bullets]. Unfortunately, Williams had left his revolver in the car so we rushed back to it. Winter had also just got wounded through the shoulder by a sniper.

The officer then went out and managed to get to a captain of the infantry to try and get some men to assist dig the car out. During the time he was away, Gunner Ritchie took one machine and Williams took another and occasionally gave them [the Germans] a burst but, unfortunately, we were in such a position that we could not train them on the Germans but it reminded them that we were still awake, and I was potting away with revolvers through the loopholes of the conning tower. And all this time the artillery were giving us a very warm time.

At about 4 pm we decided to abandon the car and we made for the short trench forty yards away, which had been made by connecting a few shell holes. We were sniped at all the way. I got nearly to where Mr Arnold was and reported to him. He then told me that the locks would have to be removed from the car to make the guns useless in case the enemy should get inside, in which event they would have been able to sweep the field. I went back and took Gunner Williams with me and left Gunners Richie, Giles and Winter in the Trench with Mr Arnold and Private Sleath. We got back to the car and effectively jammed the guns fetching the locks back with us, not without difficulty. We arrived at where Mr Arnold was but he had left, we were in a small shell hole with a lieutenant and corporal of the infantry and stay there until dark, which was about 7.30. During this time, a chap was shot while crawling over my knees and it was rather cold.

At dark, the enemy artillery made a terrific bombardment on our second line trenches and we decided to wait a while. At 7.50 Williams, myself and about six infantrymen who had been wounded, made a dash across the 200 yards to the second line trench as the star shells came; we dropped to the ground so as not to be seen and then up and ran. I fell over the trench parapet but Williams had not arrived. Got long the communications trench, which was an awful sight with killed and wounded, and eventually got to the 8th Bedfordshire Headquarters and was directed to a valley where two of our tanks were waiting [4]. I was glad to see them at about 11 pm and managed to get some sleep.

In the morning, I proceeded to our headquarters and reported to the Adjutant [Capt Williams]. During the afternoon, the OC [Holford-Walker] sent for me and congratulated me on coming through. At night, Mr Arnold came and took me back to [Loop] camp. He and Private Sleath of the ASC had got through although both of them were shaken up. I have since ascertained that Gunner Ritchie is at present in Abbeville in hospital and hoping to get to England shortly.

4   Author's note: Probably at Wedge Wood.

Gunner Winter is in Boulogne Hospital and is almost blind in the left eye which I hope is only temporary, and the other wound in the shoulder is progressing satisfactorily. Gunner Giles was killed whilst trying to get back to our second line of trenches, Gunner Williams is also in hospital and suffering from shell shock. I have been to a dressing station and recovered the locks left there by him.

HQ D Company contemporary reports

Three reports were recorded in a Correspondence Book by Capt Arthur Woods. They are undated but, based on the dates of other items, they were entered in late September 1916 whilst Woods was still located at the Green Dump. As the Correspondence Book contains both the original report and the carbon copy, they were not passed to a higher formation. The original correspondence book is held by Geoff Donaldson of Long Island USA who has permitted me to publish the reports for the first time. Geoff is the grandson of D Company's Company Sergeant Major Thomas "Paddy" Walsh who emigrated to the USA in the 1930s. [5]

Male tank no 765 – D1 *Daredevil 1* - Captain HW Mortimore.

Arrived at SOUTH STREET – DELVILLE WOOD at 2.30 AM on 15th SEPT. My orders were to attack HOP ALLEY (supposed strong post of enemy) at 5.30 AM in conjunction with KOYLI [King's Own Yorkshire Light Infantry] bombers.

Started at 4.45 AM for first objective and arrived astride HOP ALLEY at 5.30 AM precisely. During this period, it was quite dark and, to add to the difficulties of observation, we were forced to wear gas masks.

Proceeded along HOP ALLEY but found the trench devoid of enemy although there were many traces of recent occupation. Then proceeded along ALE ALLEY for a certain distance but encountered no resistance and in conjunction with the bombers the whole of this area was scrutinised.

I then commenced my attack on the first main objective viz SWITCH TRENCH but had proceeded but a short distance when the tank was hit by artillery on the starboard sprocket and this rendered it out of action.

Was forced to abandon D1 as the enemy commenced to range upon it with heavy guns. The 4 Hotchkiss automatic guns have since been salved and are at GREEN DUMP. 6 Pounder Ammunition has been removed and placed at a safe distance from the car.

Female tank no 547 – D11 *Diehard* – 2Lt HG Pearsall.

I left GREEN DUMP at 9.10 PM on SEPT 14th and reached position SW of LONGUEVAL where a delay of more than one hour caused by tank in front of column becoming immobile. With difficulty passed through LONGUEVAL village and crossed British front line at 7.10 AM.

---

5   Author's note: A facsimile copy of the original book is now held in the TMA.

Taking a course due NORTH to SWITCH TRENCH, crossed SWITCH TRENCH at 8.25 AM following FISH ALLEY at 9.0 AM and crossed FLERS TRENCH at 09.45 AM. Moving NE crossed FLERS SUPPORT and ABBEY ROAD reaching third objective at 11.45 AM.

Passed on NE towards road north of FLERS and, failing to locate enemy forces, returned to NORTH end of FLERS where British infantry were digging and reported to Capt JARDINE [of] New Zealanders who was in charge there at 12.45 PM. I was placed in reserve at 1.00 PM. I was sent to EAST end of FLERS village to protect exposed flank.

At 1.20 PM Infantry were sent forward and I went with them to protect them whilst digging in.[6] I remained on the infantry front line until 7.45 PM when I was sent forward a short distance out of the village to meet expected counterattack. I remained in this position until 6 AM

16 Sept.

6 AM Stood by in front line.

9 AM Enemy opened fire. I was ordered forward by Infantry commander to engage enemy and help in countering [German] attack.

9.5 AM HE shell burst over tank, small piece of metal piercing roof and slightly wounding one man Gnr J Lee in the shoulder - Gnr Lee stuck to post right through.

9.10 AM Tank was put out of action by [a] HE shell bursting underneath and smashing tank belly, gear box and base of engine. I remained with my crew in the Trenches with the infantry. I took one Vickers gun out of tank and set it up for action in the trenches. I returned occasionally to the Tank to use on enemy when observed.

4 PM. Left Tank in charge of OC Troops FLERS and returned to GREEN DUMP

Map Reference of present Tank position is N31 a8,2. [7]

Female tank no 537 – D15 *Duchess* – Lt LJ Bagshaw.

Report by Gnr Charles Bond written on 29/30 September 1916. [8]

We were the first car [of our group] to go into action on Friday Sept 15th at 6.15 a.m. We crossed the [British] Line to the left of Delville. On approaching the enemy front line of trenches [Tea Support], we were met with very hot fire. Our prisms were smashed within few minutes, the glass getting into my eyes made it very difficult for me to detect exactly what was going on. A bullet struck the corner of the car between the Vickers gun and the [armoured] plate and went through my sleeve without touching my arm.

---

6   Author's note: As a result, Pearsall did not receive the orders, issued around 1500 hours, to return to Loop Camp that afternoon.

7   Author's note: This grid reference, which was also given in the Disposition of Tanks dated 29 September 1916, also in the Woods' Correspondence Book, is almost certainly a transposition error as it locates Diehard's location at the northern eastern edge of Flers on the Bulls Road.

8   Author's note: Bond made this report as every other member of the crew were dead or evacuated for medical treatment away from Green Dump. Having returned to the United Kingdom in October 1916, for treatment of trench fever, Bond wrote an article for his school magazine *The Morganian* which was published in the local newspaper *Bridgwater Mercury* on 25 July 1917. This article is much more journalistic in style than the original and adds no significant additional material other than the location of the crewmen; the name of his tank as *Duchess* and that of her pair was *Duke*. Bond died on 10 September 1918 as a result of tuberculosis contracted at Bovington Camp.

Immediately after this, I was knocked over by a piece of shrapnel or splinter from a HE [shell] hitting me under the shoulder and thigh. We could not determine where it went through [the side of the tank]. I continued to fire my gun which was the left-hand front and then a piece of shrapnel hit Mr Bagshaw's prism and igniting the lining to the shutter. Mr Bagshaw had his face cut to pieces as did the driver L/Cpl Jung, the latter's face bleeding badly. I then began to feel the effects of my wounds and asked Gnr Smith to take my place. Before many minutes Gnr Smith was wounded through the forearm and Gnr Hoban was also badly wounded.

We were still advancing under increased fire which became very hot when a shell pitched through the front putting the car out of action. At about this time Mr Bagshaw was wounded in the arm. We looked out to see if anyone was near us but could not see anyone. Soon after the infantry passed us, we were all ordered by Mr Bagshaw to jump out. We found that Gunner Wilson had been badly wounded in the leg. I left the car after taking over Gnr Coles' gun whilst the others got out except Mr Bagshaw and L/Cpl Jung.

On getting out I saw that Gnr Coles had been shot through the head - evidently by snipers - and getting to the back of the car saw Gnr Wilson badly wounded in the leg and unconscious, and the ASC driver who appeared to be suffering from shock. We tried to get some help to Wilson but the shelling was too much to expose oneself very much.

Mr Bagshaw and L/Cpl Jung then came out to see who was safe and on consideration decided to try to get the RAMC to bandage Wilson's leg which was bleeding badly. I saw Mr Bagshaw dive into a shell hole to render assistance to some of the wounded fellows so immediately decided get to the RAMC who were coming across the battlefield. A shell burst a few yards away and completely covered me.

After digging myself out, I proceeded to the trenches previously occupied by the New Zealanders, and there met a N.Z. officer who had been shot in the back. After attending to him until [soldiers wearing] the Red Cross arrived, he made them carry me with him to the nearest dressing station. I was attended to there and then sent to another station where they inoculated me and sent me to the Camp Hospital at ESBART. I asked to be allowed to enable on the following Wednesday 20th instant. They took me by car to Albert, from there I walked and rode to the Loop at 5.30 p.m. reporting to QMS Williams. Since then, I have had my wound dressed by the camp doctor.

Male tank No 747 – D6 – 2Lt RG Legge

Letter written by Maj Frank Summers on 18 September 1916. [9]
Dear Mrs Legge

You will now have heard, I fear, from the War Office that your son is missing. All of us here are quite convinced he is safe and sound but I want to send to you a few particulars of what he did and what happened. The whole Company did marvels but two officers absolutely stand out alone – your son and one other.

Your son went on alone ahead of the line: he got astride of one trench and the Germans surrendered en bloc as soon as he started on them. He finally, with this other fellow [10], got

---

9   Published in the *Mid-Sussex Times* on 26 September 1916.
10   Summers is referring to Arthur Blowers in *Dolphin*.

right up to a German battery, which he engaged at about 500 yards. One gun, and according to reports from some of his crew, two were put out of action. The German then turned their guns open him and a shell was put right through his tank at very short range.   This put the tank on fire and I believe two of the crewmen were killed but not your son.

Four of the others have returned and your son was last seen from some standing corn to which the others escaped, rescuing the rest of the crew from the burning tank. When he got them out, he too went in the corn. Our infantry were quite close and he would soon have got to them and, if wounded or injured in anyway, he would have been taken to a dressing station and I will not hear for a few days. But, of course, they will let you know at once.

He's a gallant fellow and I need not tell you that his behaviour has been reported by the General to the Commander in Chief. In the meantime, I know what your anxiety must be. My one son – my only child – who was but 17 was killed in the North Sea fight, so I hope you will allow me to offer my sympathy in this anxious time.

Male tank no 719 – D12 *Dreadnought* – Capt G Nixon.

Newspaper report quoting Gunner Harry Zimmerman [11]
We crawled in our tank onto our front line trenches just before dawn. The New Zealanders were our infantry. We then proceeded over no man' land to the German front line trenches. It was just then beginning to be dawn. We opened fire and gave them hell. I am sure I did my bit putting a few Germans out. We continued our advance killing Germans left and right. It was awful to see the wounded and dead, both Germans and English, but especially the Germans. There were heaps of their dead.

Anyway, we advanced for about three miles until we came to the village of [12], which is to the right of Delville Wood. Then the excitement occurred. It was simply swarming with snipers, and our infantry were being knocked over by them, so our captain gave the order to go through the village. There was a hail of bullets as we crawled up what had been the high street, and there was a hail of bullets on our tank, but they were harmless. We very soon put the blighters out of action and allowed our infantry to get through the village and make wholesale captures.

We advanced still further but, alas, we came in front of the German batteries and they evidently spotted us as they sent a few shells over. Anyway, things got warm and we had to take refuge in our front line trench and I was there for two nights. Our tank was known as HMLS *Dreadnought*.

Female tank no 538 - D16 *Dracula* - Lt AE Arnold.

Letter written by Arnold at No 6 Red Cross Hospital Étaples 19 September 1916. [13]
I am not making a formal report, as you did not ask for one, and you will have heard all the essentials of the movement of F Group from Bond, who kept close company with me all the way up to Flers.

---

11   *Hull Daily Mail* dated 30 November 1916.
12   The censor had removed the name of the village.
13   Author's note: First published in the November 1963 edition of the *Tank Journal*.

We were at the crossroads in Longueval at 3.30 a.m. and carried right through to our own Front Line with one short delay. As Bagshaw was the only remaining member of E Group I asked Bond to go with him, Enoch to carry on with me. We managed to reach and cross our own line at Zero time. This was over some of the worst of the ground and gives a speed of say 8½ yards a minute.

Bagshaw's tank [Duchess] was knocked out immediately in front of me and Bond became reattached to me. I had received a message from Enoch that his tail was broken and he was following as fast as possible. Although only crossing the frontline simultaneously with the infantry, we reached Switch Trench in front of them and bagged about a score. I unfortunately missed four sitters as my Hotchkiss Gun did not fire. I soon discovered this to be due to a shot through the handguard which caused it to foul the [gas] piston. Others may have had the same problem and, as the handguard serves no particular purpose on the tank mounting (except to cover the bright piston), I would respectfully suggest that they may just as well be removed before going into action.

We were [still] at Switch Trench at 7.00 a.m. (I could not distinguish Tea Support) and carried right on; the infantry overtaking us – they reaching Flers Trench first and lighting red flares. We passed through them and Bond and myself took up positions, as directed [Fort Trench], at 08.50. As we came up, I saw another tank entering Flers by the Flers Road. [14]

We got a few stragglers as we approached the village and from 09.00 a.m. it (the village) was under continuous enemy fire. The infantry, as far as I can see, entered the village at 9.40 and commenced to entrench beyond it at 10.00 am.

Further advance being timed for 10.45, I found the OC Infantry and he told me he had no orders other than consolidating the position. So, we stood by until 2.30 pm, when the infantry commander asked us to help him in front as the enemy was getting restless. We drew out of the village and opened fire on the enemy who could be seen advancing. It seems possible that our fire checked them.

It was whilst outside the tank that I received a bullet through the knee. Shortly after this, the shelling became so intense and accurate around the tank, that I considered it time to retire, especially as our supporting infantry were now arriving. This was about 3.15 pm and we arrived at Green Dump at 8 pm.

Work done by tanks (No 4 Section D Company) – 15 to 18 September 1916 [15]

Ref 4th Army 438 (G) dated 19 Sep 16.

Male tank no 744 - D20 *Daphne* – Lt H G F Drader - Route C - 15th Division.

15th. Left starting point on time. Shelled from starting point until return. Engaged enemy on hostile frontline trenches, the majority of who threw up their hands, the remainder retreated in disorder to the top of the crest where the tank guns destroyed many. Destroyed enemy machine guns near 1st line. Enemy machine guns and Infantry concentrated fire on tank and then

---

14   Author's note: The tank was *Dinnaken* commanded by Hastie.
15   Author's note: Extracted from TNA WO 95/673 180318.

surrendered. During evening and night of 15th, ammunition (303) was carried to the British front line

Shooting. Good results were observed at Martinpuich.

16th. Tank returned to Assembly Point [Contalmaison] to refuel and repair damaged tank

Female tank no 512 – 521 *Delphine* – Lt A E Sharp - Route A – 47th Division.

Broke track in High Wood about 6.30 on 15th. Crew withdrew from tank owing to heavy shelling. Shooting. Result of fire unknown. This tank is still in High Wood 22 September 1916

Male tank no 745 - D22 – Lt F A Robinson - Route A – 47th Division.

Engaged enemy East of High Wood at about 6.45 a.m. on 15th. Tank badly ditched. After about 14 hours digging, under heavy shell fire, managed to clear and return to Assembly Point on 16th.

1 gunner wounded – Lowson (scalp wound whilst digging).

Female tank D23 – Capt G W Mann – Route C - 15th Division.

15th [September]
Arrived at Starting Point. Shell hit and broke track. Crew remained with tank which was heavily shelled the whole time. Crew interchanged with D20 and carried out petrol resupply to the same.

4 am 17th Tank repaired and returned to Assembly Point [Contalmaison]
18th Same track broken again.
19th ditto
Cause thought to be track badly splintered by shell on 15th

22 September

G W Mann
Capt Comdg No 4 Section
D Company Heavy Sect MGC

Male tank 751 – D24 – Lt W Stones – 50th Division

Undated typewritten account by Gnr William Foster entitled *The First Tanks* copied to The Great War Archive, University of Oxford by Helen Callister.[16]

In the third week of August, I went by train to Southampton and across the Channel to Yvrench. From there, the tanks were taken by train in the railway Loop near the River Somme. By September 13th we were just behind the front line near the ruined village of Bazentin Le Petit. This was where we went over the top at 5 a.m. on September 15th with the shattered High Wood to our left and Delville Wood to our right.

---

16   *Memoire as letter: 'The First Tanks' by William Ernest Foster*   <http://www.oucs.ox.ac.uk/ww1lit/gwa/item/3815> (accessed 1 May 2021).

As we got into the tank, we could hear bullets whistling by, and we felt safer inside, for at least a short while. Shells were bursting all around the tank as we pushed through to the second German line of trenches, One burst just in front of us, injuring our officer in the head and the driver in his eyes. Another hit the right hand track of the tank and blew it off, so we were now stuck.

I was firing the six pounder on the other side. We were ordered to bale [sic] out and we took what cover we could from shell holes whilst shells and bullets were raining all around. After about five hours, we reached the shelter of the trenches occupied by the Durham Light Infantry. This was about one o'clock; at three o'clock, we left to find one of our officers, By about 9 p.m. we were back in camp and our historic day was over.

Appendix XIV

XIV Corps Operation Order No 59

---

20 September 1916

Ref. Map Sheet 57c S.W. (Sheets 3 and 4) 1:10,000

1. Previous warning orders, operation order No58 and maps issued therewith are cancelled and should be destroyed.
2. The Fourth Army will renew the attack on September 25 in combination with the attacks of the French to the South, and of the Reserve Army to the North.
3. The objectives of the XIV Corps include the villages of Morval and Lesboeufs and those of the XV Corps Gueudecourt.
4. The attack will be carried out by 5th Division on the right, 6th Division in the centre and Guards Division on the left, the 56th Division forming a protective flank facing South.
5. The boundaries between Corps and between Divisions of the XIV Corps and the objectives to be captured are shown on the attached map. [1]
6. Headquarters will be established as follows: Guards Division present 20th Division; 6th Division present 5th Division present 56th Division; 56th Div Billon (sic) Copse. [2]
7. The attack will be made in three stages, details of which are shown on the attached map.
8. The task of 56th Division is to protect the flank of 5th Division which, in the first instance, may be accomplished by obtaining fire positions about the north-east corner of Bouleaux Wood from which the valley running north-east from Combles can be swept by fire, but junction with 5th Division must eventually be obtained at T16c 4½.7.
9. At Zero the infantry will advance to the attack of the first objective (the Green Line).
   At Zero plus 1 hour they will advance to the attack of the second objective (the Brown Line).
   At Zero plus 2 hours they will advance to the attack of the third objective (the Blue Line).
10. Once the Blue Line is reached. divisions will patrol forward and occupy any ground from which good observation can be obtained. Points which should be seized include Morval

---

1 Author's note: The map was not attached to the copy of the C Company War Diary held at the National Army Museum.
2 Author's note: The allocation of divisional headquarters to the particular sites was probably designed to ensure the continuity of communications.

Mill (T11b ½,9) and the spur in T11d. These points should be consolidated and eventually joined up with our line.

11. Touch [Liaison] will be obtained with the XIV Corps by the Guards Division at T3a 4,9½ on the Green Line; N33d 2,8 on the Brown Line and N34a 3,2 on the Blue Line

12. A steady bombardment of the hostile positions will be commenced at 7 am on the 24 September and will be continued till 6.30 pm. It will be recommenced at 6.30 am on 25 September. The ground in front and rear of the German trenches which are being bombarded will be searched occasionally with 18 pounder shrapnel and high-explosive shell.

There will be no intensive fire previous to the hour of zero.

Night firing will be carried out between the hours of 6.30 pm and 6.30 am.

The attack in each stage will be carried out under cover of both a creeping and a stationary barrage.

13. A smoke barrage will be placed as shown on the attached map. Arrangements will be made direct between 56th Division and OC "O" and "Q" Sections, 4th Special Coy R.E.

14. Two Tanks are at the disposal of 56th Division and three at the disposal of the Guards and 5th Divisions, respectively.

15. Divisions will readjust their fronts under arrangements made direct between Divisions so as to cover their fronts of attack.

16. Flares will be lit on obtaining each objective and also at 6 pm on September 25th.

17. A contact patrol will be in the air from zero till 6.30 pm

18. Acknowledge by wire.

(Sgd.)   F. G. Hardy

Issued at 3.15 p.m.   Brig Gen General Staff XIV Corps

Addenda to 0.0.59

Owing to the difficulty of bombarding the Blue Line in the immediate vicinity of our own positions in it, 6th Division will arrange to bring a heavy fire of trench mortars onto the Blue Line in both T9d and T3d on the day of attack, at hours which will be detailed later.

(Sgd.)   F.   G.   Hardy,   Brig.

General

20 Sept 1916   General Staff XIV Corps

Appendix 1 B   **S78/121**

1. The Army Commander has definitely laid down that Tanks should not be employed during the hours of daylight except under exceptional circumstances.
2. Tanks for the operations of 23 September will be allotted as follows: 2 to 56th Division; 2 (or 3, should 3 be available) to 5th Division and 3 to the Guards Division.
3. The Tanks allotted to 56th Division should be used to assist in the neutralisation of Bouleaux Wood and may be used in daylight but should not move from their assembly positions until after the hour of zero.
4. Those allotted to the 5th and Guards Divisions should be brought up into covered assembly positions previous to the day of attack and might be usefully employed at dusk in Morval and Lesboeufs, should these villages not by then have been cleared.

    Guards, 5th and 56th Divisions will reconnoitre assembly positions and lines of approach and will make all arrangements direct with the OC C Coy HMG Corps to have the Tanks allotted in the positions by daylight on the 23rd.

(Sgd.) F. G. Hardy, Brig. General
General Staff, XIV Corps

20th Sept 1916

Appendix XV

18th Division Orders for the Employment of Tanks dated 25 September 1916

---

18 Division G.121

1. One section of "Tanks" consisting of six tanks placed at the disposal of the II Corps for the forthcoming operations. Of the section, four tanks are placed at the disposal of 18th Division and two are the disposal of 11th Division.

2. Of the tanks allocated to 18th Division, two will operate with the left Brigade and will be known as the western couple and the two on the right Brigade will be known as the eastern couple.

3. **First Objective Western Couple**. The Western couple will have as their first objective the Chateau at Thiepval.

   Route. (a) They will move by day to about W11b 5,0 and by night to the Copse South of Thiepval Wood in Q30d.

   Hour of Start for Rendezvous.

   (b) At Zero these Tanks will move direct onto the Chateau.

4. **First Objective Eastern Couple**. The Eastern couple will have as their first objective the eastern end of Thiepval Village at about R26c 5,4.

   Route. By day. They will move to X7a 3,4. i.e., by the bend in the road.

   By night. By the south side of the road to the Quarry at X1b 5,1.

   Hour of start for Rendezvous

   (b) At Zero these Tanks will make for the East end of Thiepval Village (R38c 3,4.) moving up the valley which runs through R32a and R26c.

5. **Second Objectives**. The second objective for all four tanks will be Schwaben Redoubt. After reaching their first objective, they will remain assisting the Infantry in Thiepval village until the first wave of the Infantry moves forward at 1 hour 35 minutes from the line R25b 99,10 - R25b 7,2 - R25b 3.4. when they will move forward with the Infantry.

   Route. The western couple will move W [west] of the Cemetery onto point R19d 4,5. The eastern couple will move E [east] of the Cemetery onto point R19d 9,2.

6. The Brigade Commanders of 53rd and 54th Infantry Brigades will each detail an officer and one section of Infantry as escort to each tank. The chief duty of these escorts is to remove wounded men from the ground over which the tanks have to travel and so avoid delay.

7. The Officers Commanding the Tanks are to start their machines exactly at Z and all preparations for moving must, therefore, be made before Z. [1]

8. The Brigade Commander of 53rd Infantry Brigade will detail an officer to superintend the starting off of the Eastern couple. Divisional Headquarters will be responsible for starting off the Western Couple up to time.

9. During the morning, i.e., well before Z, the entire crew of each tank should examine the ground over which their advance is to take place and become acquainted with any landmarks available.

10. ACKNOWLEDGE.

(Signed) Wallace Wright
Lieutenant Colonel General Staff,
18th Division

September 25th, 1916.

---

1   Author's note: These orders would have made it impossible for the tanks to lead the infantry into action as their starting locations were well to the rear of the jumping-off trenches.

Appendix XVI

Reports by Maj H Knothe commanding 711 (Mechanical Transport) Company ASC and by Colonel H J Elles commanding the Corps of Heavy Armoured Cars

To OC HS MGC

Sir

I have the honour to respond to your request today for a report of the Tanks of C and D Companies, which were in action on the 15 and 16 instant.

1. On the 10, 11, 12, 13 and 14 instant, the available fitter personnel under my command worked continuously on the machines of these two companies, seeing that they were brought up to standard and that everything was adjusted. The tracks of every machine were adjusted before the machine left this camp [The Loop] on the 14 instant, I myself checking the adjustments. Every machine's guide rails were taken down and examined and new ones put in where necessary. I may add here that the officers, NCOs. and fitters worked continuously for five days and five nights, only snatching an hour's sleep whilst they were waiting for parts.

2. Several of the machines on the 15 instant ditched in going to their deployment positions chiefly owing to the extremely difficult land they had to traverse. In a few cases, it was owing to insufficient driving experience and to the fact that the ground was unlike anything the drivers had had an opportunity of driving over during their training.

    Note. It would be highly desirable if a moderately prepared road could be made to the deployment positions for the tanks going into action. This would obviate a great deal of strain and harsh usage of the tanks before action.

3. Mechanical troubles.

    a. The greatest has been track trouble. This has been due to two causes, one mud and the other lack of lubrication. The first is that the mud packs into the tracks so tightly and in such a solid manner, that it builds up and forms a hard film on the track links, bending the flanges of the links down. When the weight of the machine rolls over them, and beds so firmly into the bottom of the links that it causes the track to mount of the teeth of the idle wheel in the front of the machine, which eventually bursts or breaks the track. With regard to the bending over of the track lugs, caused by the mud, this eventually causes the track to come off its guides. There is I think no difficulty in curing these faults. It is essential that the tracks should be efficiently lubricated. In the design of the of the machine, there are tanks provided for the lubrication of oiling the tracks but unfortunately, they had not arrived in time to be fitted to the machines before they went into action. I only received on the 26 instant all the necessary parts to enable me to fit 14 machines with this necessary device. In my opinion these lubricators would have overcome 50% of the track trouble.

Note. Maj [Walter] Wilson has spent yesterday and today going over the ground the machines had to traverse and looking into these defects, and we have discussed together the cases of the tracks breaking and coming off their guides. Maj Wilson has now suggested a means of overcoming this trouble which I am trying on one of the machines and I have little or no doubt that it will effectively cure the above difficulty.

b. The tail has proved too weak, more especially the swivel axles, reference No 182 V 5. These have almost invariably broken before the tail frame has broken; the casting breaking where the steering arm is attached to it. This has caused the wheels to become out of control and they have been dragged sideways and caught in shell holes and debris thereby bending the axle and tail frame and often fracturing the tail frame. There have however been two cases in which the tail frames broke before the swivel axle and it is my opinion that the tail is too lightly constructed. Note. If these machines are to be used exclusively on soft ground and have not continuously to go over drops or rises with a sharp corner such as a 5 ft vertical rise or drop, it becomes a moot point as to whether the tail is necessary.

c. The track brakes are too weak and need increasing in power considerably with a very much less effort on the brake lever; as the brakes are now the work of taking them on and off is too hard for any man to do over an extended period.

d. Engine trouble has been very small and, in those cases, where is has occurred, it has entirely due to a lack of lubrication and lack of cleanliness. [1]

e. In some cases, the machines have given out a large number of sparks from the exhaust, caused by the carbon in the exhaust pipes becoming red hot and being shot out by the exhaust gases. This can be remedied by cleaning out the exhaust pipes before going to their deployment positions and again when they arrive at their deployment positions. The operation should not take more than 20 minutes.

f. **Transmission**. In one case the main worm reduction was stripped. Note. This machine I have not been able to get back to the workshops but I feel convinced this was due to insufficient lubrication which I gather occurred though the oil leaking from differential worm casing in the gearbox, from where it was drawn off and omitted to be refilled into the worm. This is not absolutely definite as there has not yet been an opportunity of thoroughly examining the machine.

g. Gear box coupling extension shaft reference no 446 V ^ for second change speed gear has, in seven cases, twisted in such a manner as to render it impossible to change the gears. This shaft I think should be made with a greater factor of safety.

---

1   Author's note: Insufficient emphasis had been paid to this during training at both Elveden and Yvrench. The issue of the manuscript orders for the Tank Crew Mechanical Duties on 14 September (Appendix XI) was too little too late.

4. In the case of some tanks, I think the mechanism did not get a fair chance owing to a lack of cleanliness and care, and further to insufficient training mechanically of both officers and crew.

5. **Repairs**. Considerable difficulty has been experienced owing to an insufficient of artificer personnel and to a considerable shortage of transport for conveying the above-mentioned personnel with their tools and heavy spare parts to the various tanks disabled at points widely separated. Further, it would be a great convenience if pack mules could be provided for taking up these heavy spares from the tank dump to where the machines are disabled or from where mechanical transport s unable to go further.

I have the honour to be, Sir, your obedient servant

28 September   (signed) Hugh Knothe
OC 711 MT Coy ASC   Maj HS MGC.

General Headquarters
Reference: O.B. 83 dated 27 September 1916.

1. The alterations and improvement in design desired in the existing type of tank are numerated in paragraph 2-13 below. I attach also a report by Maj Knothe, the Senior Workshop Officer, on the mechanical defects brought to light as a result of the operations of the 15 and 16 September, the first two days in which tanks were used in action. A summary of paragraphs 2-13 and Maj Knothe's report will be found in paragraph 14.

2. **Engines**. A more powerful engine would be a great advantage. More pace is necessary as the tactical employment of tanks under present conditions of relative speed with infantry is extremely difficult. It has been found that, in good going across country with occasional obstacles, tanks will go from 30 to 40 yards a minute, over very bad going about 15 yards a minute. Infantry can advance at a rate of 50 and 100 yards a minute. I am of the opinion that we should aim for 6 miles per hour for tanks across good ground without obstacles as against the present maximum speed of 4 miles per hour. In this connection, it has been suggested that a large number of high power (200 hp and upwards) marine petrol engines are produced in America to standard design and might be employed. The Sterling Company has, it is believed, supplied many such engines to the Admiralty.

3. **Armour**. The present armour is insufficient to keep out the German armour-piercing bullet if struck normally. It is possible that an armour piercing bullet from a heavy rifle of the hunting sort might soon be employed by the enemy so the armour needs strengthening.

4. **Shutters** [front hatches]. Some expedient should be fitted to prevent the splash of bullets getting in under the window shutters. A small steel rib fixed to the armour around the shutter would prevent this. All shutters and loopholes should have a catch on the inner side to prevent them being opened. The catches of the front window shutters are not strong enough. The design of the projecting front wall of the tank [glacis plate] induces very dangerous ricochets and splashing. [2]

5. Prisms are satisfactory but, if they were made of triplex glass, the danger of glass splinters would be lessened. It might be sufficient to cover the inner face of the prism with celluloid, provided always the view was not unduly obscured.

---

2   Author's note: A local modification was made and fitted to the female tank 554 *We're all in it*. See photograph 70.

6. Periscopes must be removable and replaceable. As at present fitted, they are liable to damage by fire and are greatly in the way,

7. **Protection against bombs**. Wire roofs appear to be satisfactory on the whole and the statement has been made by one officer that his roof was bombed through had not been verified. It would undoubtedly be an advantage to have a domed or pent-house roof off which all bombs would roll.

8. **Pigeons**. Communication by pigeon was successful. Accommodation for pigeons should be provided under the driver's seat.

9. **Sponsons.** Sponsons have been a fruitful source of trouble owing to the tanks becoming jammed on rough ground by sponsons failing to break their way though. It has been suggested that ploughs be fitted to the front edges of sponsons but the only remedy is, I believe, to have a small sponsor more in the nature of a bulge in the side of the tank. It is worthwhile to sacrifice the armament to get this. And I consider that, in the case of the female tank, we can dispose usefully of one of the machine guns on either side to obtain a less prominent sponson. As regards male tanks, we should either have a smaller gun and therefore a smaller sponson (see next paragraph) or abandon the male in favour of a female with two machine guns. In the female tank with two machine guns, one or two Hotchkiss rifles should be added and more emergency loopholes per provided, say one on each side and one in the rear.

10. **Armament**. The 6-pounder naval gun did good work, it is believed, but it has the disadvantage of the large sponsons. In addition, the muzzle is very liable to be choked with earth on very rough ground. A short gun capable of shooting a 6-pounder H.E. shell accurately, easier to load and with a point-blank range of 200 yards would meet the case. Both 6 pounder and machine guns should be mounted to allow greater depression.

11. **Bellying**. A number of failures occurred through bellying in soft ground. If any means of a belly track can be devised to overcome this, the utility of the machine could be increased by 50%.

12. **Tracks**. If possible, provision should be made for tightening the tracks from the inside of the tank. In any case, another 2" at least is required in the adjustment of the track tightening gear.

13. **Camouflage**. In future operations it will be very necessary to disguise tanks as lorries, buses, haystacks etc during the period of assembly, especially from observation by aeroplanes and balloons. The shape of the tank at present makes it very distinguishable from the air on account of the projection of the track from the body. Means should be provided for fixing brackets on the body to which wood and canvas superstructures can be attached.

14. To summarise the above notes and Maj Knothe's report. The important alternations required in order of urgency are.
    a. Overcome track problems.
    b. Overcome sponsons jamming and bellying.
    c. Move speed.
    d. Better Armour.

30 September 1916

(signed) H J Elles
Colonel commanding
Corps of Heavy Armoured Cars.

Appendix XVII

Notes on the Use of Tanks

1. In the present stage of their development they [tanks] must be regarded as entirely accessory to the ordinary methods of the attack i.e., to the advance of infantry in close cooperation with the artillery.
2. In cases where they have reached a hostile trench ahead of the infantry, they had undoubtedly done good service. Their morale effect on the enemy's infantry has been considerable. They have also not only drawn a good deal of hostile machine gun and rife fire on themselves, and therefore off the attacking infantry, but they have been able to cause considerable loss to the enemy in the trench, to knock out in many cases his machine guns, and, by the combined morale and material effect, to bring about the enemy surrender or retirement. In the event of his attempt to retire, they have been able to cause him further loss.
3. Cases have also occurred in which tanks, coming up after the infantry, have been able to deal with wire, machine guns and strong points which have been holding the infantry up.
4. On the whole the ideal seems to be that the tanks, or at any rate, the majority of them, should reach the enemy's trenches just ahead of the infantry, say 50 yards.
5. The ideal as described in the preceding paragraph is, however, undoubtedly difficult to attain. In the first place, the pace of the tanks varies much with the state of the ground and with the slopes. Downhill, over easy ground, they can move faster than the infantry, Uphill, or over difficult ground, they move slower. If they start originally any appreciable time in front of the infantry, they will bring down the enemy's barrage before the infantry have got away. If they do not start in sufficient time ahead of the infantry, the latter will soon pass them unless the ground is very favourable to the tanks. If they are moving any appreciable distance ahead of the infantry, there is an immediate complication as regards the barrage which it is so essential that the infantry should close up to. In the Fourth Army an attempt was made, and partially successful, to solve the latter difficulty by leaving lines in the barrage up which the tanks moved; so far as this attempt failed, the cause of failure seem to have been the breakdown of several tanks and there being lanes in the barrage up which no tanks were moving.
6. On the whole, it may be said that the most favourable conditions for the use of tanks in the present stage of development is where they and the infantry can move off to the assault from a starting line not more than 300 or 350 yards from the trench to be assaulted. If the ground is favourable, the tanks could start from this line simultaneously with the

infantry, with good prospects of reaching the enemy's trench a little before them. If the ground is less favourable, it will probably be possible to give the tanks a start of a minute of two without danger of the enemy's barrage catching the infantry before they leave their starting trenches. Nothing can be laid down on the subject except that it is advantageous if things can be arranged so that the tanks reach the hostile trench just in front of the infantry but, as they are merely accessory to the combined action of the infantry and the artillery, it would not be justifiable to take any risk of failure of an infantry attack through not affording our men the protection of our artillery barrage or by bringing down on them prematurely the enemy's barrage.

7. Tanks exposed when stationary to the enemy's artillery are likely to be knocked out. They are far less likely to be hit while in movement, and it is to be noted once that they have reached the enemy's positions, or are close to them, they are thereby protected from the hostile artillery. The number of tanks actually knocked out by the hostile artillery, or at any rate before having done very useful service, has so far been very small compared with the number which broke down owing to mechanical failure.

8. In bringing tanks up at night, to their starting positions, careful arrangements to find their way are necessary. Tapes laid out for the purpose were found to be effective in the Fourth Army.

9. Very careful instructions to the tank crews as to the route to be followed in the attack, and the best way to find it, are essential. Careful study beforehand of maps and photographs and sketches (in the manner of the old -fashioned Hasty Road Report) marking clearly recognised features by which they much pass – especially at points where they have to change direction – were found most useful.

Adv GHQ   (sgd) L E Kiggell
5 Oct 1916   Lt General Chief of the General Staff.

Appendix XVIII

C Company Heavy Section – Operation Order No 5

8th October 1916

Ref. 1/20,000 57D N.E. – S.E.

1. For the forthcoming operations "C" Company will be used as under: -
   To V Corps – 10 Tanks
       5 to No 2 Section – Capt Hiscocks
       5 to No 4 Section – Capt Cliveley
   To Army Reserve – 6 Tanks
       No 3 Section – Capt Walker

2. Position of Assembly will be at K27d 1,4 for all first line tanks and alternative must be reconnoitred at K33 8,2 for "E" Group (see para. [blank])

3. Tanks will be used in 5 groups of 2 tanks, each lettered A-E, from North to South. A, B and C groups will operate on III [3] Divisional area, D and E groups in II [2] Divisional area. Capt Clively will command tanks in III [3] Divisional area and Capt Hiscocks in II [2] Divisional area.

4. Movement

   Tanks will leave Acheux on night W/X and proceed to Beaussart to point P11 central where they will stay during X day.

   Tanks will leave Beaussart on night X/Y and move to position of assembly K27d 1.4 where they will stay Y day. All crews, with the exception of a small guard, will be withdrawn for Y day to a position in rear.

   No movement will be allowed at point of assembly during daylight.

   During night Y/Z tanks will leave Position of Assembly and move to Starting Points by their previously prepared and reconnoitred routes.

   Positions of Assembly, routes, starting points, point of crossing enemy front line and subsequent course are shown in attached map.

   Assistance in preparing routes by easing trenches by filling in or bridging will be given under Corps arrangements.

5. Company Headquarters will be at K28c 1,2.
       III [3] Div area Section Commander K28c 4½, 1.
       II [2] Div area Section Commander K34c 0,1.

6.   Rations
Company will leave Acheux carrying one day's rations, that is X day's. One day's rations, that is Y day's, will be delivered at Beaussart P.11 Central on evening of X day. One day's rations will be at Dump K27d1.4, that is Z day's and will be issued on evening of Y day (this will be carried in tank).
     Two days' rations, that is Z+1 and Z+2 days, will be at Dump available for issue. Rations will be procured and place in Dump etc. under arrangement with Quartermaster. Note - rations for Z day and Z+1 and Z+2 will be preserved meat.

7.   Tank Supplies
The following will be held in Company Dump for tanks:

Petrol A" Spirit	1,500 gals.
Oil Heavy Steam Cylinder	150 gals.
Oil, Engine	80 gals.
Grease	300 lbs.
Water	[blank]

Capt Walker will immediately detail an officer to find if water can be obtained at Signy Farm. Tanks' supplied will be procured and placed in Dump under Corps arrangements on night X/Y.

8.   Ammunition
The following will be held in the Dump:

6-pdr. ammo	400 rounds
.303 ammo	50,000 rounds
.45 ammo (pistol)	1,000 rounds

This will be at Dump on night X/Y

9.   Further orders re conduct of the attack will be issued at a later date.
                              Major, O.C. "C" Company, Machine Gun Corps.

Issued at _____ p.m.

Copy No 1 to OC No 2 Section
Copy No 2 to OC No 3 Section
Copy No 3 to OC No 4 Section
Copy No 4 to BG GS V Corps
Copy No 5 to HQ HS MGC
Copy No 6 to War Diary
Copy No 7 to Quartermaster C and D Company

Appendix XIX

Tank Action at St Pierre Division – 13 November 1916

39th Division's Orders dated 24 October 1916

Officer Commanding Tank Section

1. You will receive a copy of 39th Division Orders for the attack on ST PIERRE DIVION and the line of the ANCRE in due course.
2. Tanks will proceed by the routes shown on the attached map. [1]
3.

    a. Tank A will proceed down the STRASBURG LINE as shown on the map as far as R19a 1,8. It will then return to R19a 6,0 and proceed along SERB ROAD clearing it of the enemy and down HANSA LINE to R13b 3,5 where instructions will be sent to it though the Battalion HQ of the right attacking battalion either to clear up the situation at any point in the valley where the enemy may be holding out OR proceed to GRANDCOURT. The tank will not proceed North or East of R13b 3,5 without orders from 39 Division Headquarters.

    b. Tank B will proceed as shown down the German support line and, turning northeast on reaching Q24b 7,1 enter ST PIERRE DIVION from the East. After the capture of ST PIERRE DIVION, this tank will proceed to R13c 3, 8 and assist seizing the crossing over the ANCRE at Q18c 6,8. This tank will also deal with the group of buildings at Q18d 7,0.

    c. Tank C will move down the enemy's front line as shown, crushing the wire at Q24b 1,1 and destroy the machine gun emplacements at the point. The road from here to St PIERRE DIVION appears impassable, this tank will therefore come back to about Q24b 5,0 and, turning North, approach St PIERRE DIVION from the South. On the way special attention should be paid to the Strong Point (House) at S26b 5,4, and the trench Q24b 6,4 to Q24b 2,6. The SUMMER HOUSE (Q24d 2,6) and the valley. Further instructions for this tank will be sent to ST PIERRE DIVION church.

---

1   Author's note: This map was missing from the file.

4.   The road for tanks has been prepared up PAISLEY VALLEY (Q30d) and through NO MAN'S LAND. Tanks will follow each other in single file. Tank C will be the leading tank. It is hoped to prepare a route as shown on the past post R19a 4,5 and 4,7.

5.   A tank guard of a 1 x NCO and 2 men for each tank will be detailed to report at 110th Infantry Brigade headquarters at PAISLEY DUMP at 1800 hours on the day proceeding the attack. These men should travel inside the tank.

6.   In case of one tank breaking down or only two tanks being available, the two remaining tanks will carry out the tasks allocated to B and C tanks.

Battle History of Female tank no 544 commanded by Lt H W Hitchcock

Unit to which attached	……..	39th Division.
Hour the Tank Started for action	……..	5.45 am 13/11/16.
Hour of Zero …. …. ….		5.45 am
Extent and nature of hostile shell fire		Very heavy, HE and shrapnel.
Ammunition expended ….		About 2,000 rounds S.A.A.
Casualties ….		Killed 1 Officer 1 other rank.
		Wounded 2 other Ranks.
Position of Tank After action -		Q24b 8,1
Condition of Tank after action		Undamaged but very badly buried.

Orders Received.

To proceed at Zero from Starting Point (R25a 6,4) along No Man's Land to Q24b 1,1 and destroy machine gun emplacements at that point, then return to Q24b 5,0 and make for ST PIERRE DIVION, on the way special attention to be paid to Strong Point Q24b 5.4 and the trench Q24b 6,4. to Q24b 2,6. (SUMMER HOUSE). After the capture of ST PIERRE DIVION to proceed to R13c 3,8 assisting to seize the crossing over the ANCRE at Q18b 8,3.

Report of Action.

The following is the report made by 40429 Cpl Taffs A, and two men who returned with him, which is borne out by M2/106388 L/Cpl Bevan R the driver.

    At five minutes before Zero hour the engine was started and, at Zero, Car no 544 advanced and was directed by Lt Hitchcock on its course till about 7 am when it reached the German front line at Q24d 6,8. and was temporarily unable to proceed as tracks would not grip owing to the condition of the ground. This had already occurred once in No Man's Land. Up till now, none of our troops had been seen and the car was surrounded by the enemy. About this time, Lt H W Hitchcock was wounded in the head and gave orders to abandon the Car, and then handed the Command over to Cpl Taffs. Three men and Lt Hitchcock got out of the car; Lt Hitchcock was seen to fall at once, but no more was seen of two of the three men who had evacuated the tank. The third man was pulled back unto the Tank after he had been wounded in the fore-arm, and as the enemy were shooting through the open door, it was immediately closed. Fire was at once opened upon the enemy who retired to cover and opened on the Tank with machine guns and rifles.

Cpl Taffs decided not to abandon the Tank but decided with the help of the driver, L/Cpl Bevan, who had been previously wounded about the face by splinters from his prism, to carry on and try to get the tank forward to its objective. They managed to extricate the tank by using the reverse and then drove forward as far as the German second line where the tank crushed into a dugout at Q24b 8,1 and was hopelessly engulfed and lying at an angle of about 45 degrees thereby causing the two guns on the lower side to be useless and the two guns on the upper side only capable of firing at a high angle.

The tank was now attacked by the Germans with machine guns and also bombed from the sides, front and underneath. At about 8 a.m. as none of our troops had yet been seen, probably owing to the thick mist which prevailed during the whole action, Cpl Taffs sent a message by Carrier Pigeon asking for help. This message was received by 2nd Corps who passed it on to the 118th Infantry Brigade, who gave orders to the "Black Watch" to render all assistance possible. At about 9 a.m. the Tank was relieved by a party of the Notts & Derby Regt who were soon followed by the Black Watch. Cpl Taffs and the remainder of the crew left the tank when our line was established well in front of it and was safe from capture by the enemy.

The bodies of Lieut Hitchcock and 40066 Gnr W J Miles were found and identified today. 38166 Gnr Stanley W A was seen being conveyed to hospital after the action.[2]

The guns have been removed from the Tank by a salvage party today and brought back to Camp.

The crew of the Tank was as under: -

	Lt	H W Hitchcock.	(Killed).
40489	Cpl	Taffs A.	
M2/106388	L/Cpl	Bevan R (ASC Driver)	(Wounded).
32092	L/Cpl	Moss S A	
38166	Gnr	Stanley W A	(Wounded).
40066	Gnr	Miles W J	(Killed).
32175	Gnr	Ainley F	(Wounded).
38046	Gnr	Tolley A W	

Cpl Taffs and the men who remained in the Tank with him, undoubtedly did splendid work by remaining at their posts. I would specially bring to notice the names of 40429 Cpl Taffs A and M2/106388 L/Cpl Bevan R.

14/11/16.

Sd. C M Tippetts
Major Commanding
A Company Heavy Section MGC

---

2   Author's note: Gnr William Stanley died of his wounds on 17 November 1916.

Appendix XX

Report on Tank Action 15 November 1916

To: OC C Coy
Sir,
I have the honour to report that, in pursuance of your orders, I sent 2nd Lt R G Lambert and 2nd Lt J Rearden into action on the morning of the 15 November 1916. The two tanks concerned moved off from COLINCAMPS, SUCRERIE AVENUE at 2.00 am and proceeded along the tape already laid. Ground was good over the tape and the tanks reached 6th Brigade H.Q. VALLADE TRENCH at 5 am where Clively reported their arrival.

I asked the GOC to inform his Battalion COs that I had arrived and would like them to send any information of value to my Tank COs by Scout Orderly to the tanks lying just west of VALLADE TRENCH. By some accident, my tanks never got any information at all from the Battalions attacking.

I gave orders for the tanks to proceed at 6 am on a course slightly South of East as far as the enemy's front line, paying special attention to enemy machine gun at K35c 40.85, which had been giving a lot of trouble to our infantry. After crossing German front line to change course Northwards along Frontier Lane and assist the infantry in forming a defensive flank on the line K35a 9,2 and K35a 6,3. After consolidating they were to return by route followed in the advance.

At 6 am tanks proceeded and were lost in the mist. I received a message at 8.15 am that tank 744 (2nd Lt Reardon) was stuck at [illegible] per reference in his report and tank 523 (2nd Lt Lambert) was also stuck at K34d 9,8. Later in the morning, all ranks reported to me at 6th Brigade HQ, having salved their guns and placed the tanks out of action. I attribute the fact of the tanks failing to gain their objective to the extraordinarily bad ground they had to cross, which was worse than I had imagined possible.

The officers and men under my command did all humanly possible to get the tanks into a successful action and I would like to bring their efforts to your notice. As the tanks were under shellfire and machine gun fire from SERRE, I decided to withdraw their crews and brought them back without casualties to Point of Assembly. SUCERIE AVENUE, COLINCAMPS and SUCRERIE.

(Sgd) Richard Cliveley
Capt. Comd. Section

Appendix XXI

Fatalities, Honours and Awards

Fatalities

15 September 1916

Fred Bardsley of Oldham (D6) – Killed in Action (KIA) aged 24 near Gueudecourt
Edgar Barnsby of Edgbaston (D5) – KIA aged 25 near Flers
Horace Brotherwood of Woking (C1) – KIA aged 18 near Pozieres
Cyril Coles of Creekmoor (D15) – KIA aged 23 near Flers
George Goodwin-Cook of Westminster (D6) – KIA aged 28 near Gueudecourt
William Debenham of Coventry (D12) – KIA aged 24 near Flers
John Garner of Long Eaton (D6) – KIA aged 25 near Gueudecourt
Bernard "Bag" Giles of Colchester (C14) – KIA aged 18 at Bouleaux Wood
Leslie Gutsell of Shaftesbury (D5) – KIA aged 20 near Flers
Charles Hoban of Warwick (D15) – KIA aged 29 near Flers
George Macpherson of Huntly (C20) – Died of Wounds (DOW) aged 20 at Grovetown
Gerald Pattinson of Gosforth (C14) – KIA aged 30 at Bouleaux Wood

16 September 1916

Alfred Andrew of Eastbourne (D9) – KIA aged 29 near Flers
William Barber of Smethwick (D14) – KIA aged 35 near Gueudecourt
Ronald Chapple of Coventry (D9) – KIA aged 19 near Flers
Gordon Court of Herne Bay (D14) – KIA aged 23 near Gueudecourt
Thomas Cromack of Hackney(D14) – KIA aged 36 near Gueudecourt
Joseph Crowe of Towlaw (D14) – KIA aged 24 near Gueudecourt
Andrew Lawson of Highgate London (D14) – KIA aged 21 near Gueudecourt
Reginald Legge of Lindfield (D6) – DOW aged 24 at Gueudecourt
George Monro Mann of Avock (D14) – KIA aged 24 near Gueudecourt
Robert Pebody of Daventry (D14) – DOW aged 20 near Gueudecourt
Lawrence Upton of Barnby Dun (D14) – DOW aged 24 near Gueudecourt

22 September 1916

Tom "Tippo" Wilson of Grasmere (D15) – DOW aged 28 at Mericourt

25 September 1916

Fred Horrocks of Bacup (D Company) – KIA aged 34 at Delville Wood

28 September 1916

Frank Bull of Bridgnorth (C Company) – DOW aged 25 at Grovetown

24 October 1916

George Steven (A Company) of Glasgow – killed aged 23 near Aveluy

29 October 1916

Lawrence Maeers (A Company) of Camberwell – killed aged 18
Arthur Warner (A Company) of Wolverhampton – killed aged 22

2 November 1916

Meurig Jones of Cann (D Company) –died of dysentery aged 30 at Étaples

13 November 1916

Herbert Hitchcock (A13) of Teddington – KIA aged 22 at St Pierre Divion
William Miles (A13) of Birmingham – KIA aged 31 at St Pierre Divion

14 November 1916

Arthur Ritchie of Norland (C14) – DOW aged 21 at Abbeville

17 November 1916

William Stanley (A13) of Burnley – DOW aged 23 at Contay

Honours and Awards

Companion of the Order of the Bath			
Brevet Col Ernest Swinton DSO			
Distinguished Service Order			
Capt Elliott Hotblack MC	Maj Hugh Knothe MC	Capt Arthur Inglis	2Lt Charles Storey
Maj Frank Summers DSC			
Military Cross and equivalent foreign decorations			
2Lt John Allan	Lt Arthur Arnold	2Lt Frank Arnold	2Lt Arthur Blowers
Lt Leonard Bond	2Lt George Bown	2Lt Geordie Campbell	Lt Edward Colle
Lt Harold Darby	Lt Harry Drader	Lt Stuart Hastie	Maj Allen Holford-Walker
Lt Harold Head	2Lt Walter Partington	2Lt Herbert Pearsall	Lt Eric Purdy
Lt Eric Robinson	2Lt Billy Sampson	Lt Walter Stones	Lt Charles Weaver Price
Distinguished Conduct Medal			
Pte George Foot	Gnr Jake Glaister MM	A/Cpl George Shepherd	
Military Medal and equivalent foreign decorations			
Gnr Fred Ainley	Gnr Ernest Bax	Gnr Tom Bernard	LCpl Reginald Bevan
Cpl Wilfred Brooks	Gnr William Chandler	Sgt David Davies	LCpl William Fenton
Cpl Ted Foden	Gnr Jake Glaister	Gnr Ernie Hunt	Pte Cecil Howes
Cpl Ernest Keats	Cpl Jimmy Lindsay	LCpl Stanley Moss	LCpl Harry Nixon
Gnr Percy Raworth	Gnr Roy Reiffer	Gnr Fred Roberts	Gnr Alfred Simpson
Gnr Albert Smith	Gnr William Smith	Pte Frank Still	Cpl Albert Taffs
A/Sgt Herbert Thacker	Pte George Thomas	Gnr Harold Thomas	Gnr William Tolley
Cpl Frank Vyvyan	Gnr Billy Williams	Pte Bertie Young	
Meritorious Service Medal			
Sgt William Gibson			
Mentioned in Despatches			
Gnr Edwin Bailey	Lt Hugh Bell	Pte J Black	Maj WFR Bradley DSO
Lt Col John Brough CMG	Lt Cameron Bruce	Sgt David Davies	Gnr Wilfred Dyer
Capt Beresford Edkins	A/Col Hugh Elles	Gnr James Hawkins	A/Sgt Robert Hillhouse
Capt Percy Jackson MC	Pte William Jeffs	Pte Reginald Kerrison	Maj Hugh Knothe MC
Maj WFR Kyngdon	A/Maj George Mann	Capt Harold Mortimore	2Lt Walter Partington
Lt William Rendle	Gnr Hugh Russell	Gnr Charles Smith	Lt Col Bertie Stern
Sgt Walter Stickler	2Lt Charles Storey	Lt Henry Strange	Maj Frank Summers DSC
Col Ernest Swinton DSO	Capt Kenneth Symes	Capt Tom Tulloch	Capt Jean Paul Valon
CSM Thomas Walsh	Capt Richard Williams	Major Walter Wilson	Capt Graham Woods

Bibliography

War Diaries and Official Records

C Company HS MGC War Diary (TNA WO 95/96).
Central Workshops War Diary, (TNA WO 158/805).
D Company HS MGC War Diary (TNA WO 95/110).
8th KRRC War Diary (TNA WO 95/1895).
41st Division War Diary (TNA WO 95/110).
42nd Infantry Brigade War Diary (TNA WO 95/897).
NZ Division's 'Tanks' file (R25968529), National Archives Wellington.
Inspection Department Royal Arsenal [Information about] Tanks and Ancillary Vehicles 1915-1918, January 1925 (TNA WO 194/54).
War History 3rd Light Tank Battalion (TNA).

Books & Journals

Arnold, Arthur, Letter to Frank Summers dated 19 September 1916, *Tank Journal* No 529 (November 1963).

Arnold, Arthur, 'The First Tank Engagement', *Tank Journal* No 529 (November 1963).

Ashton, John & Duggan, L M, *History of 12th (Bermondsey) Battalion East Surrey Regiment* (London: The Union Press,1936).

Bond, Charles, Article on tank action on 15 September 1916 originally published in the 'Morganian', *Bridgwater Mercury,* 25 July 1917.

Bunch, Christopher, 'Bisley at War', *National Rifle Association Journal*, Vol XCIV No 2 (2015).

Campbell, Christy, *Band of Brigands* (London: Harper, 2007).

Campbell, David, 'A Forgotten Victory: Courcelette, 15 September 1916', *Canadian Military History* Vol 16, Issue 2, (2007), Article 4.

Dudley Ward, Charles, *History of the 56th Division* (Uckfield: N&MP facsimile, 2001).

van Emden, Richard and Humphries, Steve, *Veterans: The Last Survivors of the Great War* (Barnsley: Leo Cooper, 1998).

Fletcher David (ed), *Tanks and Trenches: First-hand accounts of Tank warfare in the First World War* (Gloucester: Sutton, 1996).

John Foley, The Boilerplate War (London: Star, 1981).

Fuller, JFC, *The Tanks in the Great War (*London: John Murray, 1920).

Gale, Tim, *French Tanks of the Great War* (Farnham: Ashgate Studies in Military History, 2013).

Glanfield, John, *The Devil's Chariots* (Stroud: Suttons, 2001).

Hare, Steuart, *The Annals of the King's Royal Rifle* Corps, Vol V, (Uckfield: N&MP facsimile, 2009).

Head, Harold, Interview on 16 September 1986; published in Fletcher, *Tanks and Trenches* – see above.

Henriques, Basil, *The Indiscretions of a Warden* (London: Methuen, 1937).

Huffam, Victor, 'Flers September 15 and 16, 1916' *Tank Journal* No 529 November 1963 pp. 89-90.

Liddell Hart, Basil, *The Tanks Volume One 1916-1939* (London: Cassell, 1959).

Loewe, Lionel, *Basil Henriques: A Portrait* (London: Routledge & Kegan Paul, 1976).

Maude, Alan, *History of the 47th Division* (London: Amalgamated Press, 1922).

McAdam, Lionel, 'The History of the Tank' *The Motor* (Toronto, August 1919).

Miles, Wilfred, *Official History of the Great War: Military Operations France and Belgium 1916, Vol 2*, (Uckfield: N&MP undated facsimile).

Maurice, R Fitz George (ed), *The Tank Corps Book of Honour* (Uckfield: N&MP undated facsimile).

McNorgon, Michael, *Great War Tanks in Canadian Service* (Service Publications: Ottawa, 2009).

Nichols, George, *The 18th Division in the Great War* (Uckfield: N&MP facsimile, 2012).

Norman, Terry, *The Hell They Called High Wood* (Wellingborough: Patrick Stephens, 1989).

Pidgeon, Trevor, *Flers and Gueudecourt* (Barnsley: Leo Cooper, 2000).

Pidgeon, Trevor, *The Tanks at Flers* (Cobham: Fairmile,1996).

Pidgeon, Trevor, *The Tanks on the Somme* (Barnsley: Leo Cooper, 2010).

Pope, Stephen, *The First Tank Crews: The Lives of the Tankmen who Fought at the Battle of Flers-Courcelette, 15 September 1916* (Solihull: Helion & Company, 2021).

Prior, Robin & Wilson, Trevor, *Command on the Western Front: The Military Career of Sir Henry Rawlinson 1914–1918* (Barnsley: Pen and Sword, 2004).

Pugh, Roger, *The Most Secret Place on Earth* (Dereham: Larks Press, 2014).

Reed, Paul, *Combles* (Barnsley: Pen & Sword, 2002).

Sheffield, Gary, *The Chief* (London: Aurum, 2011).

A Rifleman (Smith, Aubrey), *Four years on the Western Front* (London: Odhams, 1922).

Stern, Albert, *Tanks 1914-18 - the Logbook of a Pioneer* (Uckfield: N&MP facsimile, 2009).

Swinton, Ernest, *Eyewitness* (London: Hodder & Stoughton 1932).

Watson, William, *Adventures of a Despatch Rider* (London: Blackwood & Sons, 1915).

Williams-Ellis, Clough & Amabel, *The Tank Corps* (London: George Newes, 1919).

Winder, Teddy, 'A Subaltern on the Western Front', *The Springbok* December 1976 and March 1977.

Wyrall, Edward, *History of the 50th Division* (Uckfield: N&MP facsimile, 2012).

Young, Michael, *Army Service Corps 1902-1918*, (Barnsley: Leo Cooper, 2000).

Electronic Sources

Austin, William, *The Official History of the NZ Rifle Brigade* extracted from the NZ Electronic Text Collection website:
<http://nzetc.victoria.ac.nz//tm/scholarly/tei-WH1-NZRi-t1-body-d6-d2-d2.html>

Eyewitness to History 'The Battlefield Debut of the Tank 1916' (2005) <http://www.eyewitnesstohistory.com/tank.html>

Baker, Chris. *The Long Long Trail* – 63rd (RN) Division. <https://www.longlongtrail.co.uk/army/order-of-battle-of-divisions/63rd-royal-naval-division/>

Baker, Chris. *The Long Long Trail* – The Battle of Mons, <https://www.longlongtrail.co.uk/battles/battles-of-the-western-front-in-france-and-flanders/the-battle-of-mons/>

Bewsher, Frederick, *The History of 51st (Highland) Division 1914-1918* (London: Blackwood and Sons, 1921). <http://www.scotlandswar.co.uk/pdf_51st_Highland_Div_History_(Part%201).pdf>

Carbery, Andrew. *The NZ Medical Service in the Great War 1916 – 1918* (Auckland: Whitcomb and Tombs, 1924) <http://nzetc.victoria.ac.nz/tm/scholarly/tei-WH1-Medi.html>

Foley, Robert T, 'Baptism of Fire; the German Armies' Lost Victory' Presentation at the Western Front Association conference in Birmingham on 5 July 2014 <https://www.youtube.com/watch?v=-mudhjZe8X8>

Foster, William, *The First Tanks*, undated typewritten account copied to The Great War Archive, University of Oxford by Helen Callister
<http://www.oucs.ox.ac.uk/ww1lit/gwa/item/3815>

Haig, Douglas. *Second Despatch on the Battle of the Somme dated 23 December 1916,*
<https://www.longlongtrail.co.uk/battles/british-field-commanders-despatches/sir-douglas-haigs-second-despatch-battle-somme/>

Maude, Alan, *History of the 47th Division* (London: Amalgamated Press, 1922)
<https://archive.org/details/47thlondondivisi00maudrich>

Roberts, George, *Canada in Flanders The Official Story of the Canadian Expeditionary Force (CEF) Volume III,* (Hodder and Stoughton, 1918) <https://www.gutenberg.org/files/46114/46114-h/46114-h.htm>

Stewart, Hugh, *The New Zealand Division, 1916-1919: a popular history based on official records* (Auckland: Whitcombe and Tombs, 1921) extracted from NZ Electronic Text Centre <http://nzetc.victoria.ac.nz/tm/scholarly/tei-WH1-Fran.html>

Unpublished Sources

Archard, Victor, Diary and Letters, TMA.

Atkins, Walter, Letters to his mother from March to September 1916, Herbert Art Gallery and Museum, Coventry.

Bond, Charles, Undated report, D Company Correspondence Book, TMA.

Cutting, Frederick, Diary, TMA.

Dawson, William, *Reminiscences of my experience in the first tanks*, TMA.

Henriques, Basil, Presentation script given on 6 March 1917 at Bovington, TMA.

Holford-Walker, Allen, Letter to Sir John Edmonds 'General Remarks on preparations for action prior to 15 September 1916' dated 22 April 1935, National Army Museum Chelsea.

Mortimore, Harold, Undated report: D Company Correspondence Book, TMA.

Pearsall, Herbert, Undated report: D Company Correspondence Book, TMA.

Pidgeon, Trevor, 'The Secret Siding' typed manuscript dated 1998, Trevor Pidgeon papers.

Reiffer, Roy, 'Accounts written by AHR Reiffer MM 14-16 September 1916', TMA.

Reiffer, Roy, Letter to Stuart Hastie dated 8 November 1963, Trevor Pidgeon papers.

Steedman, Henry 'Historical account of 711 MT Company ASC attached to Tanks in France' dated 17 Jul 1917, Trevor Pidgeon papers.

Woods, Graham, Manuscript D Company Correspondence Book -18 September to 5 October 1916, facsimile copy held at TMA.

Woods, Graham, Manuscript Notebook 1916, TMA.

Woods, Graham, Manuscript Diary 1916, TMA.

Index

Places